CORPORATE ENTREPRENEURSHIP AND INNOVATION

Entrepreneurial Development within Organizations

Third Edition

Michael H. Morris, Ph.D.
N. Malone Mitchell Chair in Entrepreneurship
Spears School of Business
Oklahoma State University

Donald F. Kuratko, Ph.D.
The Jack M. Gill Chair of Entrepreneurship
The Kelley School of Business
Indiana University—Bloomington

Jeffrey G. Covin, Ph.D.
The Samuel & Pauline Glaubinger Professor of Entrepreneurship
The Kelley School of Business
Indiana University—Bloomington

 CENGAGE

Australia • Brazil • Mexico • Singapore • United Kingdom • United States

CENGAGE

Corporate Entrepreneurship and Innovation: Entrepreneurial Development within Organizations, **Third Edition**

Michael H. Morris, Donald F. Kuratko, and Jeffrey G. Covin

VP/Editorial Director: Jack Calhoun

Editor-in-Chief: Melissa S. Acuna

Sr. Acquisition Editor: Michele Rhoades

Developmental Editor: Erin Curtis

Sr. Editorial Assistant: Ruth Belanger

Marketing Manager: Clinton Kernen

Executive Marketing Manager: Keri Witman

Content Project Management: PreMediaGlobal

Media Editor: Danny Bolan

Manufacturing Coordinator: Miranda Klapper

Production House/Compositor: PreMediaGlobal

Senior Art Director: Tippy McIntosh

Permissions Acquisition Manager/Photo: Mardell Glinski Schultz

Permissions Acquisition Manager/Text: Mardell Glinski Schultz

Cover and Internal Designer: Tippy McIntosh

Cover Image: © Andrey Prokhorov

For product information and technology assistance, contact us as **Cengage Customer Sales Support, 1-800-354-9706 or support.cengage.com.**

For permission to use material from this text or product, submit all requests online at **www.cengage.com/permissions.**

Library of Congress Control Number: 2010936515

Student Edition:

ISBN-13: 978-0-538-47892-2

ISBN-10: 0-538-47892-6

Cengage
20 Channel Center Street
Boston, MA 02210
USA

Cengage is a leading provider of customized learning solutions with employees residing in nearly 40 different countries and sales in more than 125 countries around the world. Find your local representative at: **www.cengage.com.**

Cengage products are represented in Canada by Nelson Education, Ltd.

To learn more about Cengage platforms and services, register or access your online learning solution, or purchase materials for your course, visit **www.cengage.com.**

Printed in Mexico
Print Number: 04   Print Year: 2018

To the leading ladies in our lives:

Jennifer, Jessica, Julia, and Katie
—Michael H. Morris

Debbie, Christina, and Kellie
—Donald F. Kuratko

Tricia
—Jeffrey G. Covin

TABLE OF CONTENTS

PREFACE

Welcome to the "Innovation Revolution"

The nature of business has been transformed in the twenty-first century. Today, companies must survive in a fast-paced, highly threatening, and increasingly global environment. Dramatic and ongoing change forces executives to regularly reexamine the basic purpose of their organizations, and to become much more flexible in their approach to serving multiple stakeholders. Executives find themselves having to continually redefine markets, restructure operations, and modify the business models for their companies in the new competitive era. The strategy and structure that work today may be ineffective six months from today.

As the rules of the competitive game keep changing, companies begin to realize that sustainable competitive advantage is fleeting. And yet, in the midst of this turmoil, successful companies have made a fundamental discovery—the dynamic that drives real competitive advantage is entrepreneurship and innovation. The abilities to think and act entrepreneurially, to continually innovate, and to engage in an ongoing process of "creative destruction" have become the source of that competitive advantage.

It is one thing to recognize the need for innovation and quite another to make it happen. In recent years, major corporations floundered through a sagging economy with downsizing, rightsizing, budget cuts, and a depressed morale in their workforces. How could an organization develop innovations when its personnel were being pressured to do more with less? Leading edge companies found the answer in another sector of the economy—*the entrepreneurial sector*. They witnessed entrepreneurs like Steven Jobs of Apple Computer, Fred Smith of Federal Express, Jeff Bezos of Amazon.com, Larry Page and Sergey Brin of Google, and Bill Gates of Microsoft capture the economic spotlight by demonstrating that *people* create new ideas, not *institutions*. More importantly, these new ideas grew into major corporations, and in some cases, dominant competitors within the Fortune 500. Harsh lessons were learned and executives realized that the same entrepreneurial spirit that drove the people who developed these amazing new ventures could be found within their own corporate boundaries.

The critical importance of entrepreneurial thinking inside organizations was recognized by Peter Drucker, one of the most significant management scholars of the twentieth century. In his groundbreaking work entitled *Innovation and Entrepreneurship* (2006), Drucker states,

> Entrepreneurship is based upon the same principles, whether the entrepreneur is an existing large institution or an individual starting his or her new venture single-handed. It makes little or no difference whether the entrepreneur is a business or a non-business public-service organization, not even whether the entrepreneur is a governmental or non-governmental institution. The rules are pretty much the same, the things that work and those that don't are pretty much the same, and so are the kinds of innovation and where to look for them. In every case, there is a discipline we might call Entrepreneurial Management.

A quarter century ago, Gifford Pinchot released the popular book *Intrapreneuring* (1985) in which he coined the term "intra" (within) "preneurship" (derived from entrepreneurship). The gimmick word became a popular representation of corporate entrepreneurship. Pinchot's book outlined the guidelines and recommendations for people inside organizations to bring forth and develop new ideas into actual business ventures. Some experts argued that the two terms were mutually exclusive. You could not have entrepreneurship within a corporation. However, most executives began to pursue the possibility of bringing forth new ideas and new innovations from their employees. The success stories have been remarkable, yet they don't offer a simple strategy for duplication. Corporate entrepreneurship is a complex process because it challenges so many of the preexisting structures and processes of each organization. As Steven Brandt (1986) of Stanford University stated,

> The challenge is relatively straightforward. The United States must upgrade its innovative prowess. To do so, U.S. companies must tap into the creative power of their members. Ideas come from people. Innovation is a capability of the many. That capability is utilized when people give commitment to the mission and life of the enterprise and have the power to do something with their capabilities. Non-commitment is the price of obsolete managing practices, not the lack of talent or desire. Commitment is most freely given when the members of an enterprise play a part in defining the purposes and plans of the entity. Commitment carries with it a de facto approval of and support for the management. Managing by consent is a useful management philosophy if more entrepreneurial behavior is desired.

The message is that continuous innovation (in terms of products, processes, technologies, administrative routines, and structures) and an ability to compete proactively in global markets are the key skills that will determine corporate performance in this twenty-first century environment. Entrepreneurial attitudes and behaviors are necessary for companies of all sizes to prosper and flourish. The challenge to managers is one of creating an internal marketplace for innovation to flourish within their companies, and encouraging employees to implement creative ideas.

To establish a corporate entrepreneurship strategy, organizations need to allow the freedom and provide the capital that corporate entrepreneurs require to develop their innovative concepts. Unfortunately, it is no simple process to move a traditional hierarchical company to the point that entrepreneurship becomes a meaningful and important component of an organization's strategy. Traditional management practices that have focused upon doing tasks more efficiently are not sufficient solutions to new challenges. Companies need to become more flexible and creative as well as more tolerant of failure. In fact, failure needs to be seen as a learning process. An environment must be established where innovative pursuits are the norm and corporate entrepreneurs are stimulated, supported, and protected.

The pressing global economic problems have stripped away the security of traditional management practices and thrust organizational leaders into an innovation revolution. Today's leaders must create, ignite, and sustain innovation within their own organizations (Estrin, 2008). Once this is acknowledged, organizational leaders can begin the tasks of learning the "entrepreneurial" mindset and intensity required to navigate through the challenging years ahead (Lafley and Charan, 2008). Today, most executives of major companies would acknowledge the importance of innovation to their companies' survival. However, while the desire may exist, the knowledge of how to implement innovation throughout an organization still remains a challenge.

This book provides a framework for learning and understanding the critical elements driving the entrepreneurial revolution inside companies. Using a three-phased model, we explore how to introduce entrepreneurial behavior into all facets of company operations. Specifically, we examine (1) the building blocks needed to grasp the nature of entrepreneurship when it is applied to established organizations, (2) how to build work environments that support entrepreneurship, and (3) how to sustain entrepreneurial performance over time. Underlying this structure is the goal of helping the reader to appreciate the entrepreneurial mindset and what it means for organizational success. It is this mindset that will enable managers to transform their companies—making it possible for them not merely to face the revolution but actually to ignite it.

The words used to describe the new innovation regime of the twenty-first century are *Dream, Create, Explore, Invent, Pioneer,* and *Imagine!* As scholars and researchers dedicated to the field of corporate entrepreneurship, we believe this is a point in time when the gap between what can be imagined and what can be accomplished has never been smaller.

Tomorrow belongs to those who have vision today! It is an entrepreneurial age—a time requiring innovative vision, courage, calculated risk-taking, and strong leadership.

In paraphrasing Robert F. Kennedy in a speech made over 40 years ago, we share a message that is relevant for all managers and organizational leaders today. *"You are living in one of the rarest moments in business history—a time when all around us the old order of things is crumbling and a new world is painfully struggling to take shape. If you shrink from this struggle and the many difficulties it entails you will betray the trust which your own position forces upon you. You possess one of the most privileged positions; for you have been given the opportunity to innovate and to lead. You can use your enormous privilege and opportunity to seek purely your financial gains. But entrepreneurial history will judge you, and, as the years pass, you will ultimately judge yourself, on the extent to which you have used your abilities to pioneer and lead our organizations into a new horizon. In your hands ... is the future of your entrepreneurial world and the fulfillment of the best qualities of your own spirit."*

Organization of the Book

The chapter sequence of *Corporate Entrepreneurship and Innovation: Entrepreneurial Development within Organizations*, third edition, is systematically organized around the nature of entrepreneurship in established organizations. More than simply discussing the concept in general, this book pursues the details involved when implementing an entrepreneurial strategy inside existing organizations. Each of the three major sections of the book is designed around a summary model of the Sustainable Corporate Entrepreneurship process. This model was developed by the authors after years of research and consulting with numerous corporations seeking to establish corporate innovation programs. It is discussed in the opening chapter.

This first section of the book lays the foundation for understanding the nature of corporate entrepreneurship. Consisting of the first five chapters, Section I introduces basic concepts, tools, and frameworks that help explain how entrepreneurial behavior can occur within established organizations. Examining the evolution of corporations and the entrepreneurial imperative that is needed today, the unique nature of corporate entrepreneurship in established companies is investigated. A careful look at the concept of entrepreneurial intensity helps explain how different levels of entrepreneurship can be found in organizations. Finally, the different forms of corporate entrepreneurship and the differing contexts within which entrepreneurship occurs are explored.

Once the reader has a grasp of the basic building blocks of corporate entrepreneurship, we turn to the question "How do you actually make entrepreneurship happen in established organizations?" The five chapters in the second section explore major elements that must come together to create work environments that not only support, but actually encourage, entrepreneurial behavior from employees. Human resources, strategy, structure, and culture all form the critical aspects that must be addressed by any organization seeking to find the pathway to entrepreneurial activity.

The final section of the book outlines practical methods for achieving and sustaining high levels of entrepreneurial performance within organizations. Each of these five chapters is designed to examine a particular facet of entrepreneurial performance. These facets include the major constraints that entrepreneurial employees must regularly overcome, the roles that leaders must play when initiating and implementing entrepreneurial activity, the methods to assess entrepreneurial activity over time, and the critical ways in which organizational controls can hinder or facilitate entrepreneurial behavior.

Our goal is to help managers build the innovative organization of tomorrow. After all, tomorrow is where the entrepreneurial mindset already resides!

New to this Edition

- Fifteen updated or new examples of corporate entrepreneurship in practice featured in the Innovator's Notebooks with discussion questions now added.

- A case map of Harvard Business School cases with chapter correlations is included on the front sheets for an easy way to add business cases to a course.

- Updated material on the forms that corporate entrepreneurship can take, application of entrepreneurship at different levels of management, entrepreneurial strategy, entrepreneurship in nonprofit and public organizations, and much more.

- New findings are discussed regarding the reasons why companies engage in corporate venturing and the associations between various corporate venture founding motives and venture performance (Chapter 3).

- Inclusion of a discussion on how companies can better organize resources to support entrepreneurial initiatives. Expanded examination of the practices and results associated with corporate venture capital investments (Chapter 4).

- A new look at reward systems and the role they play in corporate innovation (Chapter 7).

- Greater emphasis is placed on the topic of technology strategy and how such strategy should be formulated within corporations (Chapter 8).

- New insights on how to understand and manage paradoxes surrounding entrepreneurship in established companies (Chapters 10 and 14).

- Updated findings on the "Best Practices" of innovative companies (Chapter 8).

- New material on how to deal with failed innovation projects in organizations (Chapter 10).

- Additional perspectives on the obstacles to entrepreneurial behavior in established organization and how they can be overcome (Chapter 11).

- Introduction of the entrepreneurial health audit as a tool for assessing the climate for entrepreneurship in an organization (Chapter 13).

- Streamlined treatment of how to measure and monitor levels of entrepreneurship in companies (Chapter 13).

- Updated approach to putting together a corporate venture plan (Chapter 13).

- The latest insights on how human resource management systems, organizational structure, culture and control systems must complement one another in fostering innovation (Chapter 15).

TEACHING AIDS

The inside front and back covers of the book include a case map of Harvard Business School Cases with chapter correlations. This easy-to-use guide provides a straightforward way to select cases to use in your course.

Additional resources, including PowerPoint's, sample syllabi, detailed descriptions of the Harvard Business School Case maps, and entrepreneurial audits are available on the product Web site at *http://www.cengage.com/management/morris*.

Acknowledgments

Many individuals played an important role in helping us develop and refine our book, and they deserve special recognition. We would like to express our appreciation to Michele Rhoades, Senior Acquisitions Editor at Cengage/South-Western Publishers who believed in this book and who worked to make this third edition a reality. We also are grateful to our professional editorial staff at Ohlinger Publishing, in particular Erin Curtis who worked diligently to help us produce an excellent edition.

We would also like to thank the following reviewers for their valuable suggestions and insights:

Ashwin Mehta, University of Massachusetts Lowell
Gad Selig, University of Bridgeport
Terry J. Schindler, Ph.D., University of Indianapolis
Yi Yang, University of Massachusetts Lowell

Finally, we would like to express a special appreciation to our schools of business and our universities (The Spears School of Business at Oklahoma State University and The Kelley School of Business at Indiana University—Bloomington) for always supporting our entrepreneurial efforts and for being world leaders in entrepreneurship research and education.

Michael H. Morris
Oklahoma State University

Donald F. Kuratko
Indiana University

Jeffrey G. Covin
Indiana University

Brandt, S. C. 1986. *Entrepreneuring in Established Companies* (Homewood, IL: Dow-Jones-Irwin): 54.

Drucker, P. F. 2006. *Innovation and Entrepreneurship* (New York: Harper Paperbacks): 143.

Estrin, J. 2008. *Closing the Innovation Gap: Reigniting the Spark of Creativity in a Global Economy* (New York: McGraw Hill).

Lafley, A. G. and Charan, R. 2008. *The Game Changer: How You Can Drive Revenue and Profit Growth with Innovation* (New York: Crown Business).

AUTHOR PROFILES

DR. MICHAEL H. MORRIS holds the N. Malone Mitchell Chair in Entrepreneurship at Oklahoma State University and is the Head of the School of Entrepreneurship at OSU. Formerly the Witting Chairholder at Syracuse University, his entrepreneurship programs have consistently been ranked among the top ten by *US News and World Report, Fortune Small Business, The Princeton Review,* and *Entrepreneur* magazine. A widely published author and researcher, Dr. Morris has written seven books and over 100 peer-reviewed academic articles in the *Journal of Business Venturing, Journal of Management, Entrepreneurship Theory and Practice, Journal of Business Ethics, Journal of International Business Studies,* and *Journal of the Academy of Marketing Science,* among others. He annually leads the Entrepreneurship Empowerment in South Africa (EESA) Program, working with historically disadvantaged entrepreneurs. He is the coeditor of the Entrepreneurship Series published by Prentice Hall, the Immediate Past President of the United States Association for Small Business & Entrepreneurship, and has chaired the American Marketing Association's Task Force on Marketing and Entrepreneurship. For six years he served as editor of the *Journal of Developmental Entrepreneurship.* In addition, he has been a principal in three entrepreneurial start-ups and has consulted widely to companies around the world. Twice honored by Pi Sigma Epsilon as national Faculty Advisor of the Year, Dr. Morris has received the Edwin M. and Gloria W. Appel Prize for contributions to the field of entrepreneurship, and is a recipient of the regional Ernst & Young Entrepreneur of the Year Award. He is a former Fulbright Scholar (South Africa, 1993), was selected as one of the top twenty entrepreneurship professors in the United States by *Fortune Small Business,* and has been inducted as a 21st Century Entrepreneurship Research Fellow by the Global Consortium of Entrepreneurship Centers.

DR. DONALD F. KURATKO is the Jack M. Gill Chair of Entrepreneurship and Professor of Entrepreneurship & Executive Director of the Johnson Center for Entrepreneurship & Innovation, The Kelley School of Business, Indiana University—Bloomington. Professor Kuratko is considered a prominent scholar and national leader in the field of entrepreneurship; publishing over 180 articles on aspects of entrepreneurship and corporate entrepreneurship. His work has been published in journals such as the *Journal of Business Venturing, Entrepreneurship Theory & Practice, Strategic Management Journal, Journal of Operations Management, Academy of Management Executive, Journal of Small Business Management, Family Business Review,* and the *Journal of Business Ethics.* Professor Kuratko has authored or coauthored 30 books, including one of the leading books in universities today, *Entrepreneurship: Theory, Process, Practice*, 8th ed. (2009), as well as *Corporate Entrepreneurship and Innovation* 3rd ed. (2011), and *New Venture Management* (2009). In addition, Dr. Kuratko has been consultant on Corporate Entrepreneurship and Innovation to a number of major Fortune 100 corporations as well as the Executive Director of the Global Consortium of Entrepreneurship Centers (GCEC), an organization comprised of over 250 top university entrepreneurship centers throughout the world. Dr. Kuratko's honors include earning the Entrepreneur of the Year for the state of Indiana and induction into the Institute of American Entrepreneurs Hall of Fame. He has been honored with The George Washington Medal of Honor; the Leavey Foundation Award for Excellence in Private Enterprise; the NFIB Entrepreneurship Excellence Award; and the National Model Innovative Pedagogy Award for Entrepreneurship. In addition, he was named the National Outstanding Entrepreneurship Educator by the U.S. Association for Small Business and Entrepreneurship and he was named a 21st Century Entrepreneurship Research Fellow by the Global Consortium of Entrepreneurship Centers. Dr. Kuratko was honored by his peers in *Entrepreneur* magazine as the #1 Entrepreneurship Program Director in the nation as well as being selected one of the Top Entrepreneurship Professors in the United States by *Fortune Small Business* magazine. Professor Kuratko was honored by the National Academy of Management with the highest award bestowed in entrepreneurship—the prestigious Entrepreneurship Advocate Award—for his contributions to the development and advancement of the discipline of entrepreneurship. Under Professor Kuratko's leadership and with one of the most prolific entrepreneurship faculties in the world, Indiana University's Kelley School of Business has been ranked the #1 Business School for Entrepreneurship Research by the *World Rankings for Entrepreneurship Productivity;* as well as the #1 Graduate and Undergraduate Business School for Entrepreneurship (Public Institutions) by *U.S. News & World Report* and *Fortune* magazine. In addition, Indiana University has earned the National Model MBA and National Model Ph.D. Programs in Entrepreneurship.

DR. JEFFREY G. COVIN is the Samuel and Pauline Glaubinger Professor of Entrepreneurship and Professor of Strategic Management at the Kelley School of Business, Indiana University—Bloomington. Dr. Covin is a leading scholar in the fields of entrepreneurship, strategic management, and technology management, with several dozen articles published in journals such as *Strategic Management Journal, Journal of Management, Journal of Business Venturing, Entrepreneurship Theory & Practice, Journal of Management Studies, Journal of Business Ethics, Sloan Management Review, Journal of Business Research, Journal of Operations Management,* and the *Journal of High Technology Management Research.* His research has been recognized nationally with awards including ET&P's Best Journal Article Award for the years 1991 and 1997 and the U.S.

Association of Small Business and Entrepreneurship (USASBE) Best Journal Article in Corporate Entrepreneurship Award for the years 1991 and 2000. Dr. Covin was identified as the second most published author of scholarly articles on the topic of entrepreneurship in a study published in the *Journal of Management* in 1997. Dr. Covin codeveloped the Ph.D. in Entrepreneurship Program at Indiana University, which received national acclaim by being named the National Model Ph.D. Program in Entrepreneurship by USASBE. Dr. Covin has been named a 21st Century Entrepreneurship Research Fellow by the National Consortium of Entrepreneurship Centers. In 2005, he was awarded the prestigious Entrepreneurship Mentor Award by the Academy of Management for his exemplary work in developing Ph.D. students and junior-level faculty in the entrepreneurship field. In 2008, Dr. Covin received the USASBE Award for Outstanding Research in Corporate Entrepreneurship and Strategy. Prior to joining the Kelley School of Business, Dr. Covin held the Hal and John Smith Chair of Entrepreneurship and Small Business Management at the Georgia Institute of Technology.

BUILDING BLOCKS FOR CORPORATE ENTREPRENEURSHIP

"Wealth in the new regime flows directly from innovation, not optimization; that is, wealth is not gained by perfecting the known, but by imperfectly seizing the unknown."
—KEVIN KELLY, "NEW RULES FOR THE NEW ECONOMY," *WIRED*

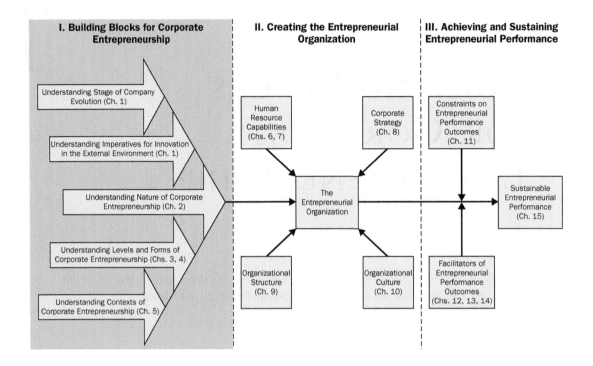

Section Introduction

How does entrepreneurship apply to established organizations? As illustrated in the model above, we begin to address this question by examining key building blocks for understanding the nature of corporate entrepreneurship. This first section of the book introduces basic concepts, tools, and frameworks that help explain how and why entrepreneurial behavior occurs in organizations, even as they become larger and more complex. It consists of the first five chapters. Building on this foundation, we will identify ways to encourage greater levels of entrepreneurship within existing organizations (Section 2 of the book), and then explore how it can be sustained over time (Section 3).

CHAPTER 1

THE NEW ENTREPRENEURIAL IMPERATIVE

Introduction

We are in the midst of a global entrepreneurial revolution. In virtually every nation, every industry, and every market, entrepreneurs are challenging existing assumptions and creating value in novel ways. Not only are for-profit and non-profit venture start-up rates at an all-time high but also the rate of new product and service introduction is at record levels in most industries. The same can be said for patents issued and the licensing of new products and processes. The development, application, and enhancement of new technologies are occurring at a breathtaking pace. New forms of business organization and business relationships are appearing almost daily. Entrepreneurial thinking and acting is changing the way business is conducted at every level. It does not matter if you are a chip manufacturer or a plastics company, or whether you are based in Los Angeles, Johannesburg, or Peking—entrepreneurship is redefining what you make, how you make it, where you sell it, and how you distribute it.

As the number of new ventures, new products, new technologies, and new patents literally explodes worldwide, established companies are faced with a fundamental choice. They can either become victims of this revolution as aggressive, upstart companies move quickly in undermining their positions in existing markets and in creating whole new markets—or, they can join the revolution.

Companies cannot be static—they must continually adjust, adapt, and redefine themselves. This is a fundamental principle in a free market economy. However, in this entrepreneurial age, the rate at which companies must transform themselves is accelerating. In fact, many of those who have been part of the evolution (and revolution) of corporations in recent years have an amazing story to tell. The past quarter century has produced immense transformation in the functions, patterns, and cycles of organizations. Many of the conventional rules of business no longer apply. Fundamental assumptions about employees, products, resources, technologies, and markets have been challenged and in some cases discarded altogether. For many companies, turbulence in their external environments has become a way of life.

In the midst of all of this comes the question of the relevance of the traditional theories and principles that guide managerial practice. On the one hand, the nature and relationships among variables that define how companies operate have changed to the point that different models and theories are required to address the practical needs of the contemporary executive. As a result, managers have been surfeited with a whole range of new concepts and tools ranging from total quality management and business process reengineering to right-sizing, strategic alliances, and self-directed work teams. We can call this the "new management thinking." On the other hand, many of the basic lessons and principles of good business practice still apply. It is important to remember the adage, "Those who do not learn from the past are destined to repeat it."

In this chapter, we explore the changing shape of the managerial challenge in companies. We build on the relevant lessons of conventional management theory, and identify a new paradigm for achieving sustainable competitive advantage. As we shall see, entrepreneurship represents a unifying framework for successful management practice in the twenty-first century. An overall model of corporate entrepreneurship will be introduced, and will serve as the foundation for the structure and flow of the chapters to come.

Turbulent Environments and the Embattled Corporation

To understand modern corporations, we must consider their "external" and "internal" environments. We use the term "external environment" to speak of everything outside the company, including the competitive, customer, technological, economic, regulatory, social, labor, and supplier environments. Each of these domains of the external environment has critical implications for how things are done inside the company (i.e., the internal environment). The internal environment, then, includes the structures, systems, processes, and culture that make up the climate within which people do the work of a company.

The external environment today is all about change. This is not a radical or new revelation. Heraclitus stated in 500 B.C. that, "nothing endures but change." However, the pace and magnitude of change are significantly greater than ever before. It is continuous change, with a never-ending stream of new challenges deriving from each domain of the external environment. It is complex change, as developments in technology combine with developments with suppliers to affect developments with customers. And it is the kind of change that threatens the very survival of the company on a month-to-month basis. Even the most dominant company can be out of business in a blink of an eye.

Consider just a sampling of recent developments in eight major domains of a company's external environment:

- Technological Environment   Accelerated development of new technologies; rapid product obsolescence; greater difficulty in protecting intellectual property

- Economic Environment

  Unpredictability of prices, costs, exchange rates, interest rates, tax incentives, business cycles

- Competitive Environment

  Aggressive "take no prisoners" competition; highly innovative competitors; competition from non-traditional sources with non-traditional tactics; threats from niche players; competitors who are also customers or partners

- Labor Environment

  Growing scarcity of skilled workers; employees more mobile and less loyal; higher employee benefit costs; reliance on contract labor

- Resource Environment

  Increasing resource scarcity; resources increasingly specialized; unknown sources of supply; more rapid resource obsolescence

- Customer Environment

  More demanding and complex customers; markets that are more fragmented and more narrowly segmented; emphasis on investing in and capturing a customer's life time value

- Legal and Regulatory

  More aggressive regulation; virtually unlimited product liability; Environmental regulatory compliance costs; growing emphasis on free and fair trade; increasing environmental regulation and associated compliance costs; mandated employee benefits costs

- Global Environment

  Real-time communication, production, and distribution virtually anywhere in the world; more sophisticated suppliers, customers, and competitors located around the world; competitive advantage achieved through global outsourcing and international strategic alliances

These dramatic changes have important implications for companies and how they are managed (Romero-Martinez, et al., 2010). Quite simply, the modern corporation finds itself embattled as it struggles to survive, much less to achieve sustained growth. Figure 1-1 illustrates how trends in some of these areas force companies to abandon conventional business practices. Managers face shortened decision windows and diminishing opportunity streams, meaning they must act much more quickly or find themselves missing out on opportunities. The constituencies (e.g., customers, suppliers,

FIGURE 1-1

How Environmental Turbulence Creates a Need for New Management Practices

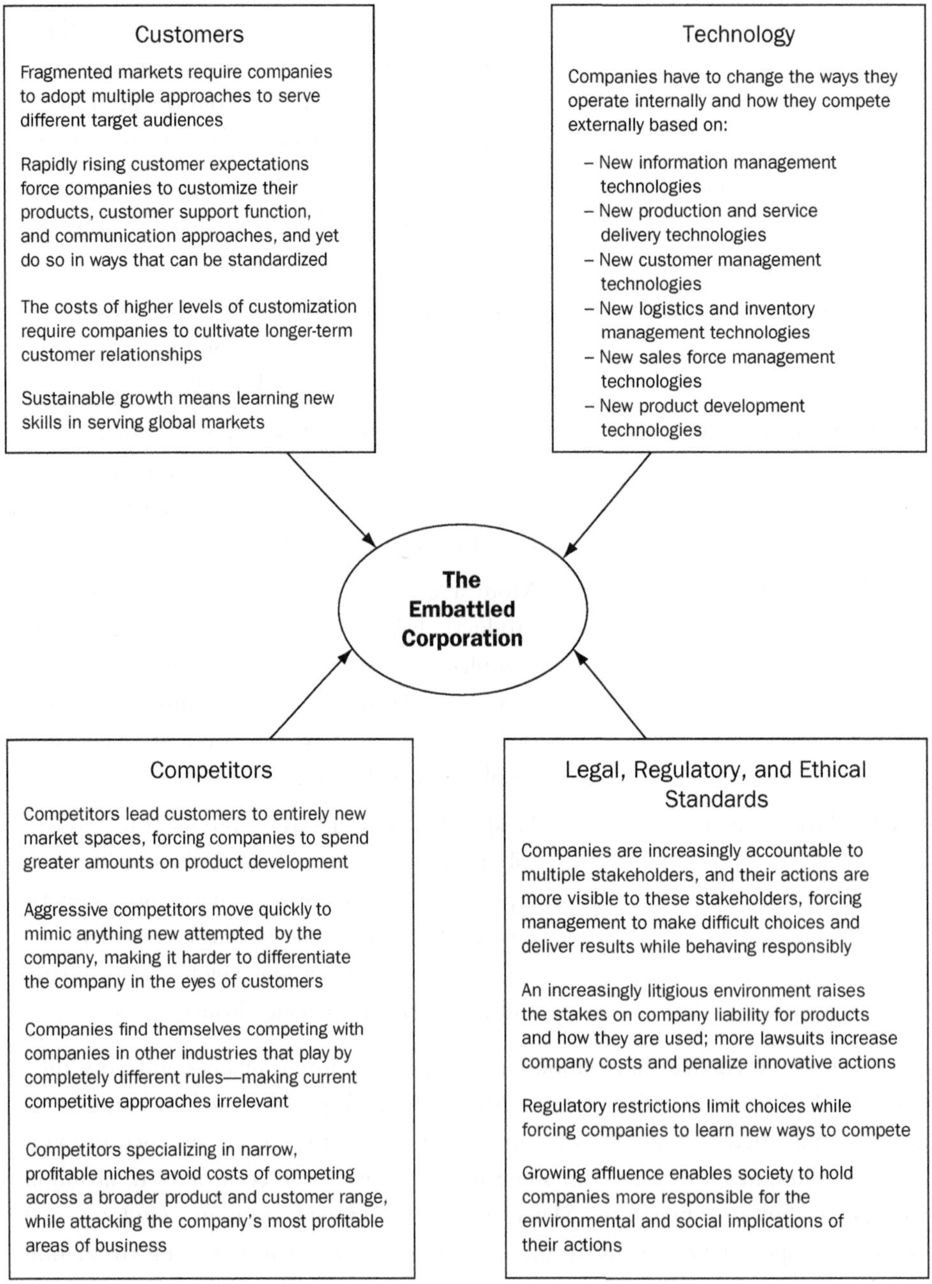

Customers

Fragmented markets require companies to adopt multiple approaches to serve different target audiences

Rapidly rising customer expectations force companies to customize their products, customer support function, and communication approaches, and yet do so in ways that can be standardized

The costs of higher levels of customization require companies to cultivate longer-term customer relationships

Sustainable growth means learning new skills in serving global markets

Technology

Companies have to change the ways they operate internally and how they compete externally based on:

– New information management technologies
– New production and service delivery technologies
– New customer management technologies
– New logistics and inventory management technologies
– New sales force management technologies
– New product development technologies

The Embattled Corporation

Competitors

Competitors lead customers to entirely new market spaces, forcing companies to spend greater amounts on product development

Aggressive competitors move quickly to mimic anything new attempted by the company, making it harder to differentiate the company in the eyes of customers

Companies find themselves competing with companies in other industries that play by completely different rules—making current competitive approaches irrelevant

Competitors specializing in narrow, profitable niches avoid costs of competing across a broader product and customer range, while attacking the company's most profitable areas of business

Legal, Regulatory, and Ethical Standards

Companies are increasingly accountable to multiple stakeholders, and their actions are more visible to these stakeholders, forcing management to make difficult choices and deliver results while behaving responsibly

An increasingly litigious environment raises the stakes on company liability for products and how they are used; more lawsuits increase company costs and penalize innovative actions

Regulatory restrictions limit choices while forcing companies to learn new ways to compete

Growing affluence enables society to hold companies more responsible for the environmental and social implications of their actions distributors, alliance partners, regulators) with whom they interact are continually changing, suggesting new performance standards and expectations must be met. As resources become increasingly specialized and resource needs become less predictable, companies tend to make shorter-term commitments to a given resource, and to rely more heavily on the outsourcing, leasing, and leveraging (rather than ownership) of resources. The dramatic pace of technological change combined with the fragmentation of markets forces companies to develop more new products and to do so much faster. The company's resources and its products become obsolete more quickly, changing the economic realities that surround decisions regarding which resources to employ, which products to develop, and which markets to enter.

In the final analysis, companies are experiencing a general lack of long-term control over their external environments. Never before have incumbency and past experiences been worth so little. No longer does company size matter, while being resource rich is hardly a guarantee of marketplace performance. And the riskiest strategy of all is simply to pursue business as usual.

The New Path to Sustainable Competitive Advantage

How are today's companies reacting to this challenge? The response has been dramatic. A veritable cornucopia of new strategic initiatives has preoccupied the time of executives over the past decade. These include rightsizing, unbundling, focusing on core businesses while divesting others, business process reengineering, total quality management, flattening structures and decentralizing decision-making, outsourcing, creating self-directed work teams, forming strategic alliances, and more. Meanwhile, major companies have found themselves eliminating millions of jobs, closing plants, moving operations to low-cost countries, and attempting to become "lean and mean." Yet they continue to struggle.

There are important lessons to be learned from all of this. Firstly, turbulence in the external environment is causing a fundamental transformation in the internal operations of companies. Or, more simply put, external change forces internal change. Secondly, there are no simple formulas for success in the new competitive environment. While it is clear that traditional models of bureaucracy, hierarchical management systems, and companies operating on a command-and-control philosophy do not work in the contemporary environment, it is less clear what does work. It is all about experimentation, as management looks for the right structure, right approach to control, right leadership style, and right way to reward employees. Thirdly, there is an important upside to external environments as they become more complex, dynamic, and hostile. Turbulence also means opportunity. That is, changes in markets, technologies, regulation, and other areas close some doors while opening others. Market fragmentation also means new market segments are appearing; new technologies create new company capabilities; a regulatory change results in some sort of new need; and so on. While some companies focus only on defending themselves against threats, others understand that there is a new opportunity to be found behind every threat.

But what is the ultimate "bottom line"? That is, what is the real quest as managers sort through the various theories, concepts, and new techniques and tools? The answer is and always will be *sustainable competitive advantage*. But the rules have changed here as well. Traditionally, competitive advantage was achieved by having lower costs than the competition, achieving higher quality or product performance, adding a new product feature, offering more selection or delivering better customer service. Unfortunately, this game of "one-upsmanship" can no longer produce sustainable advantage. Whatever one company does in these areas is quickly matched by other companies. Moreover, to be successful in any industry today, companies must continually reduce costs, improve quality, enhance customer service, and so forth. Such continuous improvement is a minimal criterion for remaining in the competitive game.

Remaining competitive is very different from achieving sustainable competitive advantage. The quest for competitive advantage requires that companies and the managers within them continually reinvent themselves. Specifically, we believe advantage derives from five key company capabilities. These include:

- *Adaptability*—the ability to adjust, on a timely basis, to new technologies, new customer needs, new regulatory rules, and other changes in conditions without losing focus or causing significant disruption of core operations and commitments;

- *Flexibility*—the ability to design company strategies, processes, and operational approaches that can simultaneously meet the diverse and evolving requirements of customers, distributors, suppliers, financiers, regulators, and other key stakeholders;

- *Speed*—the ability to act quickly on emerging opportunities, to develop new products and services more rapidly, and to make critical operational decisions without lengthy deliberations;

- *Aggressiveness*—an intense, focused, and proactive approach to eliminating competitors, delighting customers, and growing employees;

- *Innovativeness*—a continuous priority placed on developing and launching new products, services, processes, markets, and technologies, and on leading the marketplace.

Companies that are more adaptable, flexible, fast, aggressive, and innovative are better positioned not only to adjust to a dynamic, threatening, and complex external environment, but to create change in that environment (Heavey et al., 2009). That is, they do not take the external environment as a given, and instead define themselves as agents of change, leading customers instead of following them, creating markets, and rewriting the rules of the competitive game.

These five capabilities ultimately come down to one—entrepreneurship. Entrepreneurship is the core source of sustainable advantage in companies today. Advantage lies in finding ways to tap the spirit of Richard Branson, Mark Zuckerberg, Steven Jobs, Anita Roddick, and other great entrepreneurs within the mainstream of the company—on the production floor, inside the sales force, among the purchasing agents. Continuous innovation and an ability to continually redefine the competitive playing field are among the skills that define corporate performance in the global economy of the twenty-first century (Pitelis and Teece, 2009). As Steven Brandt (1986) noted in early work on corporate entrepreneurship: "The challenge is relatively straightforward ... companies must tap into the creative power of their members. Ideas come from people. Innovation is a capability of the many. That capability is utilized when people give commitment to the mission and life of the enterprise and have the power to do something with their capabilities."

What Is Entrepreneurship?

Although the term "entrepreneurship" has been in use for well over 200 years, there is considerable disagreement over its meaning. People hold disparate views regarding who is an entrepreneur, what an entrepreneurial venture looks like, and the nature of the activities that constitute entrepreneurial behavior. Although literally hundreds of perspectives have been presented over the years, seven of the most prevalent themes are summarized in Table 1-1. At the center of these themes is creation. Entrepreneurship is about creating organizations, change, innovation, and wealth. One study performed a content analysis of key words found in dozens of definitions of entrepreneurship (Morris et al., 1994). As can be seen in Table 1-2, the most common terms include starting or creating a new venture; innovating or putting together new combinations of resources; pursuing opportunity; acquiring necessary resources; risk-taking; profit-seeking; and creating value.

Of the available perspectives, one definition captures the essence of entrepreneurship by integrating its core elements. Entrepreneurship is "the process of creating value by bringing together a unique combination of resources to exploit an opportunity" (Stevenson & Jarillo-Mossi, 1986). This definition has four key elements. First, entrepreneurship involves a process. This means it is manageable, can be broken down into steps or stages, and is ongoing. Moreover, as a process, entrepreneurship can be applied in *any* organizational context. Second, entrepreneurs create value where there was none before. They create value within organizations and they create value in the marketplace. Thirdly,

TABLE 1-1

Seven Perspectives on the Nature of Entrepreneurship

Creation of Wealth	Entrepreneurship involves assuming the risks associated with the facilitation of production in exchange for profit.
Creation of Enterprise	Entrepreneurship entails the founding of a new business venture where none existed before.
Creation of Innovation	Entrepreneurship is concerned with unique combinations of resources that make existing methods or products obsolete.
Creation of Change	Entrepreneurship involves creating change by adjusting, adapting, and modifying one's personal repertoire, approaches, and skills to meet different opportunities available in the environment.
Creation of Jobs	Entrepreneurship is concerned with employing, managing, and developing the factors of production, including the labor force.
Creation of Value	Entrepreneurship is a process of creating value for customers by exploiting untapped opportunities.
Creation of Growth	Entrepreneurship is defined as a strong and positive orientation toward growth in sales, income, assets, and employment.

SOURCE: Michael H. Morris, *Entrepreneurial Intensity*, Westport, CT: Quorum Books, 1998: 14.

entrepreneurs put resources together in a unique way. Unique combinations of money, people, procedures, technologies, materials, facilities, packaging, distribution channels, and other resources represent the means by which entrepreneurs create value and differentiate their efforts. Fourthly, entrepreneurship involves opportunity-driven behavior. It is the pursuit of opportunity without regard to resources currently controlled (Stevenson et al., 2006). The abilities to recognize new opportunities in the external environment, evaluate and prioritize these opportunities, and then translate these opportunities into viable business concepts lie at the heart of the entrepreneurial process.

Timmons and Spinelli (2008) take us further, in elaborating on what entrepreneurs do. They view entrepreneurship as the ability to create and build a vision from practically nothing. Fundamentally, it is a human, creative act. It is the application of energy to initiate a novel concept or build an enterprise or venture, rather than just watching or analyzing. This vision requires a willingness to take calculated risks—and then to do everything possible to reduce the chances of failure. Entrepreneurship also includes the ability to build a team with complementary skills and talents. It is the knack for sensing opportunity where others see chaos, contradiction, and confusion. It is possessing

TABLE 1-2	

Key Terms Identified in Content Analysis of 75 Contemporary Definitions of Entrepreneurship*

	# of Mentions
1. Starting/founding/creating	41
2. New business/new venture	40
3. Innovation/new products/new market	39
4. Pursuit of opportunity	31
5. Risk-taking/risk management/uncertainty	25
6. Profit-seeking/personal benefit	25
7. New combinations of resources, means of production	22
8. Management	22
9. Marshalling resources	18
10. Value creation	13
11. Pursuit of growth	12
12. A process activity	12
13. Existing enterprise	12
14. Initiative-taking/getting things done/proactiveness	12
15. Create change	9
16. Ownership	9
17. Responsibility/source of authority	8
18. Strategy formulation	6

* Terms receiving five or more mentions.

the know-how to find, marshal, and employ resources—resources often controlled by others.

What Is Corporate Entrepreneurship?

The definition above makes it clear that entrepreneurship is a phenomenon that can occur in a variety of different organizational contexts. "Corporate entrepreneurship" is a term used to describe entrepreneurial behavior inside established mid-sized and large organizations. Other popular or related terms include "organizational entrepreneurship," "intrapreneurship," and "corporate venturing."

Definitions of corporate entrepreneurship have evolved over the past thirty years. At a basic level, it involves the generation, development, and implementation of new ideas and behaviors by a company (Damanpour, 1991). This perspective centers on innovation, which can include new products or services, processes, administrative systems, or programs pertaining to employees of the organization. In this context, corporate entrepreneurship centers on enhancing the company's ability to acquire and act upon innovative skills and capabilities. Other definitions are concerned with the ability of established companies to renew themselves. For instance, Salvato et al. (2009) emphasize the capability that allows managers to systematically overcome internal constraints so they can reinvent the company through novel business initiatives. Alternatively, some researchers focus on the ability of the company to create new ventures. Hence, Zahra et al. (2000) argue that corporate entrepreneurship can include formal or informal activities aimed at creating new businesses inside of established companies through product and process innovations and market developments. They suggest the activities that can take place at the corporate, division, functional, or project levels, with the unifying objective of improving a company's competitive position and financial performance.

Ling et al. (2008) bring these perspectives together by approaching corporate entrepreneurship as the sum of a company's innovation, renewal, and venturing efforts. Under this definition, innovation (which is concerned with introducing something new to the marketplace), strategic renewal (concerned with organizational renewal involving major strategic and/or structural changes), and corporate venturing (entrepreneurial efforts that lead to creation of new business organizations within the corporation) are all important and legitimate parts of the concept of corporate entrepreneurship. Building on this integrated approach, as we shall see in Chapter 4, entrepreneurship can manifest itself in many different ways inside an established company.

Management versus Entrepreneurship

Entrepreneurship differs from management. Management is the process of setting objectives and coordinating resources, including people, in order to attain those objectives. In essence, management involves getting things done through other people. The effective manager is a planner, organizer, communicator, coordinator, leader, motivator, and controller; and most of all, a facilitator. In a sense, management is a transformation process, where technical, human, and conceptual skills are used to transform inputs into outputs. Further, to carry out their responsibilities, managers must understand how the organization interacts with the external environments and how the different parts of the organization work together.

Management is both an art *and* a science. As an art, management requires the use of behavioral and judgmental skills that cannot be quantified or categorized the way scientific information in the fields of chemistry, biology, and physics can be. For example, management involves motivating people, communication, leading, and using qualitative judgment, intuition, gut feeling, and other non-quantifiable abilities. As a science, management requires the use of logic and analysis. The manager arrives at a solution by systematically observing, classifying, and studying facts in relation to the problem at hand.

The primary roles of the manager are contrasted with those of the entrepreneur in Figure 1-2. Managers are charged with the *efficient* and *effective* utilization of the resources under their control. They tend to be focused on optimizing current operations. Efficiency is improved when the amount of work being done (the output) remains the same while the cost of producing this output (the input) declines. Effectiveness pertains to the manager's ability to choose appropriate objectives and the means for achieving them. While efficiency means doing things right, effectiveness

---

FIGURE 1-2

Comparing and Combining Key Roles of Managers and Entrepreneurs

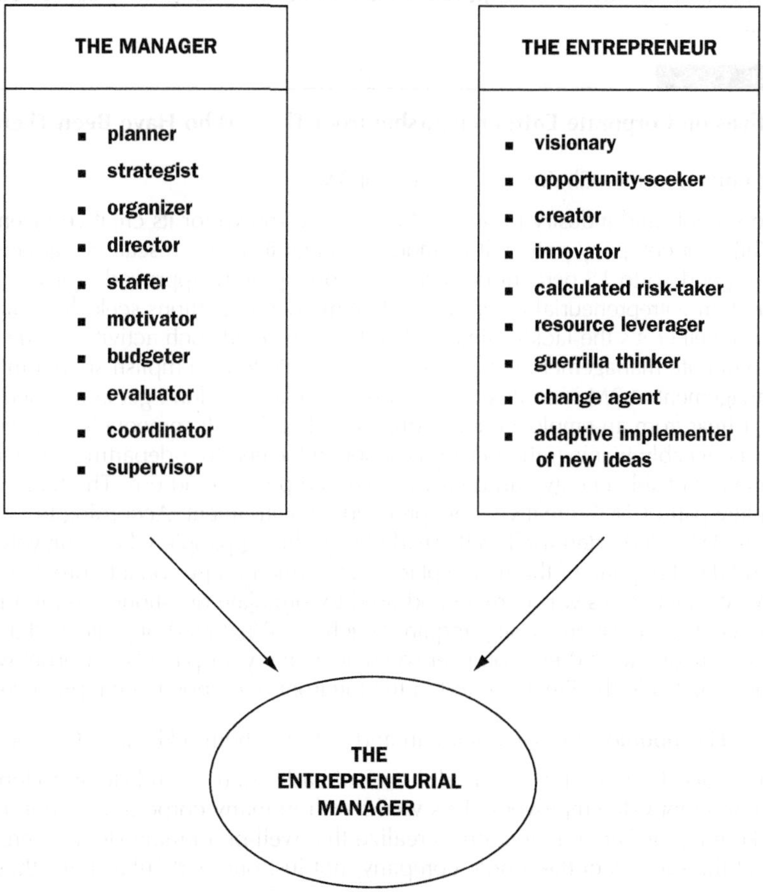

THE MANAGER	THE ENTREPRENEUR
■ planner	■ visionary
■ strategist	■ opportunity-seeker
■ organizer	■ creator
■ director	■ innovator
■ staffer	■ calculated risk-taker
■ motivator	■ resource leverager
■ budgeter	■ guerrilla thinker
■ evaluator	■ change agent
■ coordinator	■ adaptive implementer of new ideas
■ supervisor	

THE ENTREPRENEURIAL MANAGER

means doing the right things. The entrepreneur, alternatively, is preoccupied not with what is, but with what can be. They envision the future, recognize emerging patterns, identify untapped opportunities, and come up with innovations to exploit those opportunities. As we noted earlier, they pursue opportunity regardless of resources controlled. They do this by demonstrating creative capabilities in obtaining and leveraging resources, overcoming obstacles, mitigating risks, and persisting in implementing new ideas that represent change.

Within great organizations, a balance is achieved between disciplined management and entrepreneurship (Ireland et al., 2009). Disciplined management requires focus, attention to basic management principles and values, and a strong sense of accountability for results. Entrepreneurship requires vision, a willingness to take risks, and a focus on creating the future. Achieving this balance suggests that managers must become entrepreneurs. That is, managers must be able to optimize current operations while at the same time engaging in activities that make current operations obsolete. This is a difficult challenge, and companies have achieved mixed results in striking the balance. Table 1-3

TABLE 1-3

Perspectives on Corporate Entrepreneurship from Those Who Have Been There

L.D. DeSimone, former Chairman and CEO of 3M

Among b-schools and industry pundits, 3M is widely known for its creative inventions. While not company policy, it is understood that its 8,000 researches are expected to spend up to 15 percent of their time working on unapproved projects. It is this kind of an entrepreneurial environment that many corporations seek to emulate. However, whether it's the lack of financial ability to support such activity, or the lack of an appropriate management team, many still struggle to accomplish such a mission. Management at 3M is so flexible and trusting that they don't get concerned if they don't hear from an employee for a long period of time. If someone's creative energy is noticeably waning, the person is simply relocated to a department where their original, hireable energy can be revitalized and put to good use. The hiring process is a key part of 3M's creative, entrepreneurial environment. According to DeSimone, 3M rededicated itself in the early 90s to hiring people who intuitively understand the discipline of the marketplace. Furthermore, a personality profile with innovative characteristics was derived and used to formulate questions used in interviews for technical positions. Using inquiries such as "What kind of projects did you initiate as a child?" and "Were you ever so creative that your parents got upset with you?" has kept 3M in the limelight and in the forefront of corporate entrepreneurship.

George N. Hatsopoulos, former Chairman and CEO of Thermo Electron Corporation

For many years, Thermo Electron used the usual cash bonuses and stock options to maintain and motivate employees. This works well in many corporations, but it didn't take long for Thermo Electron to realize that well-performing stocks were indicative of the success of the whole company, not just one particular unit—thus no

(Continued)

real intrinsic motivation. The result: spin-outs. The publicly traded spin-outs, unlike many spin-offs, remain as part of the business family (Thermo Electron does keep a majority interest), and have the desired effect on employee attitude and work ethic. Over 12 years, the corporation supported 12 spin-outs by providing financial and legal services, employee benefits administrations, risk management, and investor relations for a simple 1 percent of revenues. In 1995, 80 percent of their 12,000 employees worked for spin-outs, many of which had stock options in spin-outs other than their own and had options valued at $1 million or more.

William F. O'Brien, *President and CEO of Starlight Telecommunications*

William O'Brien and his colleague, Pete Nielsen, experienced how tough it can be to "dance with an elephant." GTE has a new ventures group that supports creativity and idea-generation within the corporate walls. However, for O'Brien and Nielsen, after two years of working with senior management and refining their business plan on their own time, their project was denied. Unfortunately, protocol was that new ventures couldn't be funded unless the supervisors for whom you worked signed off on the initiative. Their main sponsor had retired, and the successor didn't want to lose their talent to another division. Both O'Brien and Nielsen ultimately resigned and started Starlight Telecommunications, which is now making waves in the African telecom industry. While reflecting on his experience with GTE, O'Brien developed three guidelines for true intrapreneurship: (1) Corporate goals relating to new ventures should be identified and disseminated, and managers should be encouraged to support spin-offs that advance these goals, (2) Employees who identify new business ideas should be protected and rewarded, and (3) Proposals should move quickly through the approval process.

Bill Harris, *Executive Vice President of Intuit, Former President and CEO of Chipsoft, acquired by Intuit*

For Intuit, acquiring the entrepreneurial edge wasn't the problem. It was maintaining it. The company grew fast, and it grew well—management easily recognized the fact that they were not going to be able to "maintain their entrepreneurial agility" as they went from a $50 million to a $500 million entity. Like Thermo Electron, Intuit's CEO decided to break up the organization into eight core-product units, each under the direction of a different general manager and customer mission. Suddenly, the only centralized issues were among that of MIS and compensation. Harris knew that to sustain cutting-edge innovation and be truly entrepreneurial, "we must encourage and allow our people—at all levels—to respond completely and immediately to our customers." Harris believes that continued entrepreneurial thinking in the unpredictable business will occur by encouraging employees to look to the customer for inspiration and instruction rather than the boss. While this action might not always have the best results, Intuit would rather reward intelligent failure than succumb to a diminishing quality of effort. Intuit fosters such creativity by investing one-third to one-half of its operating income in unproved and unprofitable new products. It took six years and multiple attempts before QuickBooks ever made a profit for the company.

SOURCE: Reprinted by permission of *Harvard Business Review*, Vol. 73, Issue 6. From *"How Can Big Companies Keep the Entrepreneurial Spirit Alive?"* by L.D. Simone, George Hatsopoulos, William F. O'Brien, Bill Harris, and Charles P. Holt, Nov/Dec 1995. Copyright © 1995 by the Harvard Business School Publishing Corporation; all rights reserved.

provides a number of real world examples of success and failure. These challenges and how they can be addressed is the focus of this book. A beginning point in understanding the nature of this challenge is to recognize the ways in which companies tend to evolve, or the organizational life cycle.

Why Companies Lose Their Entrepreneurial Way: The Organizational Life Cycle

To understand the entrepreneurial challenge in established companies, we must understand how companies evolve. While every organization is unique, patterns have been identified in the ways companies evolve. Organizations experience the natural patterns of life cycle stages. Various observers have described these stages in different terms. For example, Kuratko (2009) discusses stages that include initial venture conceptualization, start-up activities, venture growth, stabilization, diversification, strategic renewal, and/or decline. Adizes (1999) developed the analogy of life cycle passages from nature and applied the terms courtship, infancy, go-go, adolescence, prime, maturity, and death to the stages that companies go through. Greiner's (1972) classic article on evolution and revolution as companies evolve depicted the stages as creativity, direction, delegation, coordination, and collaboration. In short, authors may differ in terminology, but they generally agree that patterns emerge over time. As we will see, this evolutionary process has important implications for entrepreneurship within companies.

The evolutionary process can be demonstrated by considering the seminal work of Griener (1972). He suggests a process whereby companies enter a particular stage, during which they prosper until they reach a crisis point. How they deal with the crisis determines whether they move on to the next stage, or alternatively, whether they begin a process of decline, failure, or become a candidate for acquisition. Hence, each growth stage culminates in a crisis point where major and sometimes radical changes must be made in managerial assumptions and approaches to running the company.

- *Start Up and Early Growth:* This stage encompasses the launching of a venture and the initial penetration of the market. It is a highly creative stage. A venture is created where none existed, often based on innovative new products or services, creative methods of production or service delivery, imaginative approaches to marketing and distribution, and/or alternative methods of customer interaction and servicing. The work environment in the early stages is exciting, stressful, demanding, uncertain, experimental, and highly ambiguous. The organization is run somewhat informally, with everyone helping out with everything, and significant flexibility in what is being done and how it is being done. Employees feel they are part of something as the new venture begins to achieve meaningful results. However, a crisis eventually results because the demands of greater size require more professionalized management, and more formal structures, administrative systems, budgets, and controls.

- *Growth through Direction:* Companies fail because they will not formalize. Where management puts the necessary systems and structures in place, and augments the leadership team with functional area professionals, another period of sustained growth ensues. Over time, however, a crisis develops from demands for greater autonomy on the part of lower-level managers and employees. The solution adopted by many companies is to move toward greater delegation. Yet it is difficult for top managers that were previously successful at being fairly directive to give up responsibility and control.

- *Growth through Delegation:* Delegation takes the form of creating semi-autonomous product divisions and strategic business units. These operations are given targets to achieve and, so long as they perform satisfactorily, they have considerable room to grow their businesses as they see fit. Senior management focuses on major strategic moves and acquisitions. Sustained growth again results, but it ultimately produces the next crisis. Management begins to sense it is losing control over a highly diversified field operation. Autonomous managers prefer to run their own shows without coordinating plans, money, research, technology, and manpower with the rest of the organization. Freedom breeds a parochial attitude. Inefficiencies result as divisions duplicate one another's efforts, communication among divisions is not timely, customers receive mixed signals, and inconsistent strategic directions are pursued.

- *Growth through Coordination:* Companies respond to this loss of control by centralizing operations. Head office staff is developed to coordinate marketing, human resource management, production, research and development, information technology, and other operations across the various divisions and operating units. Consistency and synergies are brought to the efforts of the various divisions and units, resulting in the next period of sustained growth. However, centralization over time tends to breed bureaucracy, and a crisis of red tape eventually occurs. Organizational leaders will develop a myriad of procedures and systems during the fourth stage. However, the proliferation of systems and programs begins to exceed its utility. Procedures take precedence over problem solving, and innovation is dampened. Those in field operations find themselves to be increasingly constrained by head office staff, while central administrators are increasingly frustrated with noncooperating field personnel. In short, the organization has become too large and complex to be managed through formal programs and rigid systems.

- *Growth through Collaboration:* Many companies struggle to overcome the crisis of red tape, often finding it a losing battle. It is difficult to replace bureaucrats and administrators with innovators, and to transform a machine bureaucracy into an innovation factory. Hence, most companies never make it to this next growth stage. The very nature of the enterprise has to be reinvented. Companies must simplify structures and procedures, reduce head office staff, reassign staff experts to consulting teams assisting field operations, create matrix structures, encourage experimentation in all facets of the business, and emphasize innovative projects involving cross-functional teams. And while unsure of the next crisis, it will inevitably come. It is likely a crisis related to the challenge of achieving sustainable entrepreneurship.

The demands on management change over a company's life cycle, as the scope and nature of operations become more diverse and complex. Each stage poses different strategic challenges, and each requires a very different managerial approach. There is an ongoing need for changes in how a company is run, including how goals are set, decisions are made, resources are allocated, and performance is assessed. Table 1-4 provides a description of company practices as they tend to change through the five stages of development. Changes are identified in terms of management focus, organizational

---

TABLE 1-4

Changing Organizational Practices as Companies Evolve

	Stage 1 Creativity	Stage 2 Direction	Stage 3 Autonomy	Stage 4 Coordination	Stage 5 Collaboration
Managerial Focus	Make & sell	Efficiency of operations	Expansion of market	Consolidation of organization	Problem solving & innovation
Approach to Company Structure	Informal	Centralized & functional	Decentralized & geographical	Line-staff & product groups	Matrix of teams
Style of Top Managers	Individualistic & entrepreneurial	Directive	Delegative	Watchdog	Participative
Source of Controls	Market results	Standards & cost centers	Reports & profit centers	Plans & investment centers	Mutual goal setting
Types of Rewards Emphasized	Ownership	Salary & merit increases	Individual bonus	Profit sharing & stock options	Team bonus

SOURCE: Adapted from Larry E. Greiner, "Evolution and Revolution as Organizations Grow," *Harvard Business Review*, July–August, 1972, p. 45.

structure, management styles, control systems, and reward systems as the organization moves through its life cycle.

Understanding the stages of development and the changing organization practices that are needed for each stage allows managers to be in a position to *predict* future challenges, and thereby to prepare strategies before crises arise. Managers often fail to realize that organizational solutions that are not flexible and changing could create problems for the future. Organizational evolution is not an automatic affair; it is a contest for survival. To move ahead, companies must consciously introduce planned structures that not only are solutions to a current crisis, but also are fitted to the *next* phase of growth. This requires considerable self-awareness on the part of top management, as well as great interpersonal skill in persuading other managers that change is needed.

One of the great lessons of the organizational life cycle is that, in far too many companies, the entrepreneurial spirit tends to be systematically destroyed over time. That is, an organization that was highly entrepreneurial in the start-up stage becomes progressively bureaucratic over time. As each stage unfolds, new systems, structures, rules, controls, and procedures are added, while others are modified. Successful companies make changes based on situational contingencies that accumulate over time. These internal changes are made for logical reasons given the exigencies of company life at different moments in time. However, in the process, the company can become less adaptable, more inflexible, slower to act, and more reactive. Growing levels of specialization within the organization reinforce a commitment to maintaining the status quo. Innovation is approached conservatively, with new initiatives pursued only when they are virtually guaranteed to be successful. In critical moments, the company finds it is either not sufficiently entrepreneurial, or its innovative efforts are misdirected.

The Entrepreneurial Imperative: A Persistent Sense of Urgency

Over the stages of the life cycle, managers become increasingly adept at "producing," "administering," and "integrating." Otherwise, the company could not have achieved its size and level of success. All the while, managers fail to become adept at "entrepreneuring." They operate in a reactive mode, attempting to respond to the many entrepreneurial changes occurring in the external environment, but unaware of the need to rekindle, and the methods for rekindling, the entrepreneurial fires within the company itself. It is this entrepreneurial role of management that is most vital for addressing the exponential changes acting on organizations in the twenty-first century.

There are no rules regarding how to achieve sustainable competitive advantage in a complex, discontinuous, hyper-competitive, nano-speed world. It is a world that has stripped away the security of traditional management practices and thrust organizational leaders into a revolution. Gary Hamel, a leading strategic thinker, believes that leaders must find, ignite, and sustain the revolution rather than be victimized by it. Hamel (2007) points to the inevitable diminishing returns experienced by most organizations using traditional strategies, suggesting that conventional management practice has simply run its course, and that an entirely new model of management is needed in our companies. The following questions help to demonstrate why a new model is needed:

- How much more cost savings can the company wring out of its current business? Are managers within the company working harder and harder for smaller and small efficiency gains?

- How much more revenue growth can the company squeeze out of its current business? Is the company paying more and more for customer acquisition and market share gains?

- How much longer can the company keep propping up its share price through share buybacks, spin-offs, and other forms of financial engineering? Is top management reaching the limits of its ability to push up the share price without actually creating new wealth?

- How many more scale economies can the company gain from mergers and acquisitions? Are the costs of integration beginning to overwhelm the savings obtained from slashing shared overhead costs?

- How different are the strategies of the four or five largest competitors in the industry from the company's strategy? Is it getting harder and harder to differentiate the company from its competitors?

For too many companies, more than one of these questions will elicit answers of "not much" and "yes," suggesting the company may be reaching the point of diminishing returns. Once this is acknowledged, organizational leaders can begin the tasks of learning the "entrepreneurial" perspective and apply the radically different approaches required to navigate the challenging years ahead.

Corporate entrepreneurship represents a framework for facilitating ongoing change and innovation in established organizations. It provides a blueprint for coping effectively with the new competitive realities. As we shall see in the coming chapters, corporate entrepreneurship transcends the company's strategy, structure, culture, control systems, rewards, and human resource management approaches. It redefines the purpose of the enterprise, where the philosophy becomes one of "healthy dissatisfaction," of continually putting the company's own products and services out of business with better ones, with leading customers instead of following them, and with turning traditional assumptions about price and performance on their head.

Unfortunately, it is no simple process to move a traditional hierarchical company to the point that sustainable entrepreneurship becomes a meaningful and important component of the organization. Traditional management practices that have focused upon doing tasks more efficiently are not sufficient solutions to new challenges. Organizations need to allow the freedom and provide the resources that corporate entrepreneurs require to develop their ideas. Management needs to become more flexible and creative, and more tolerant of failure. In fact, failure needs to be seen as a vital learning process. Corporate entrepreneurs must be stimulated, supported, and protected. And ultimately, companies must create environments within which there is a constant sense of urgency—urgency to challenge assumptions, urgency to change, and urgency to innovate. Innovate or dissipate must become the mantra.

A Model of Corporate Entrepreneurship and Guide to Coming Chapters

What does it take to transform a non-entrepreneurial company into highly entrepreneurial company? The fundamental purpose of this book is to address this question. To guide the reader through this journey, the authors have developed an integrative model of corporate entrepreneurship. Presented in Figure 1-3, the model has three major components.

The beginning point is to develop an in-depth understanding of the nature of entrepreneurship and how it can be applied to established organizations. While entrepreneurship has certain defining aspects no matter where it is applied, there are also unique differences involved when attempting to apply it within an existing enterprise. Building on this foundation, company leaders must then build a work environment that encourages employees to recognize and act upon their own innate entrepreneurial potential. Four key elements of this work environment include the organization's strategy, structure, culture, and human resource management system. Finally, the ability to achieve entrepreneurial performance on a sustainable basis requires a clear understanding of the ongoing obstacles that constrain entrepreneurship, together with specific facilitators and measures of entrepreneurial outcomes.

This model can be applied in addressing the entrepreneurial challenges within any organization. It also provides the basic structure for the chapters to come. Thus, Section 1 of the book, consisting of Chapters 1 through 5, provides the building blocks for corporate entrepreneurship. We will examine the unique aspects of entrepreneurship

A Model of Corporate Entrepreneurship and Guide to the Book Structure

I. Building Blocks for Corporate Entrepreneurship	II. Creating the Entrepreneurial Organization	III. Achieving and Sustaining Entrepreneurial Performance

Understanding Stage of Company Evolution (Ch. 1)

Understanding Imperatives for Innovation in the External Environment (Ch. 1)

Understanding Nature of Corporate Entrepreneurship (Ch. 2)

Understanding Levels and Forms of Corporate Entrepreneurship (Chs. 3, 4)

Understanding Contexts of Corporate Entrepreneurship (Ch. 5)

Human Resource Capabilities (Chs. 6, 7)

Corporate Strategy (Ch. 8)

Constraints on Entrepreneurial Performance Outcomes (Ch. 11)

The Entrepreneurial Organization

Sustainable Entrepreneurial Performance (Ch. 15)

Organizational Structure (Ch. 9)

Organizational Culture (Ch. 10)

Facilitators of Entrepreneurial Performance Outcomes (Chs. 12, 13, 14)

when it is practiced in larger, established companies. The steps in the entrepreneurial process will be investigated. The concept of entrepreneurial intensity will be introduced to capture the different degrees and amounts of entrepreneurship that can occur in an organization. In addition, we will explore the different forms that entrepreneurship takes in companies. Further, attention will be devoted to ways in which entrepreneurship can be applied not only to corporations, but also to established non-profit and public sector organizations. Section 2 of the book, which includes Chapters 6 though 10, then examines the core elements that must come together in order to create an entrepreneurial organization. Specific chapters are devoted to examining how corporate strategy, structure, culture, and human resource management can each be designed in ways that foster entrepreneurial behavior. Section 3 of the book is concerned with achieving and sustaining entrepreneurial performance, and includes chapters 11 through 15. Individual chapters are devoted to obstacles to ongoing entrepreneurship, entrepreneurship at different levels of management, control systems and entrepreneurship, measuring entrepreneurial performance, and the challenges of sustainability.

Microsoft: Trailing in the Innovation Race?

It is hard to believe that the $60 billion powerhouse located in Redmond, Washington, and known as Microsoft could be actually losing ground in the innovation race. Yet success can breed complacency in large companies. Microsoft rode the wave of PCs into consumers' homes, and still sells a copy of its software with virtually every one of the millions of PCs sold every year. Office and Windows, its core products, have become standards for most consumers, and the popularity of Windows has led to both American and European courts declaring Microsoft's operating-system business an illegal monopoly. Microsoft's reputation as a monopolist has led to strong opposition from competitors as well as consumers. The company's movement into the markets for mobile phones, cable television, and home gaming consoles prompted the following action in each area: mobile phone companies formed a software consortium to slow Microsoft's progression; cable operators hesitated to install Microsoft's software on cable set-top boxes due to concerns that using the software would allow Microsoft to control their networks; and consumers and game development companies grew skeptical of Microsoft's intentions when the company insisted on maintaining control of the online-gaming service provided through the Xbox. In all three cases, Microsoft's dominance in the PC market led to players in other markets taking defensive measures to prevent the company from becoming a competitor. So, what's a company to do?

The answer is simple: innovate! As technology progresses, electronic devices are dominating the business and consumer landscapes today. This fact has not been lost on Microsoft, and it has been strategically positioning itself for innovation.

Microsoft has one of the largest laboratories in the world and three chief technology officers yet the company has been accused of frustrating the efforts of its innovators. This can easily happen when a company grows too large and bureaucratic. With over 90,000 employees it is understandable that bureaucratic layers begin to build in an organization. To combat this problem Microsoft has 800 computer scientists, sociologists, psychologists, mathematicians, physicists and engineers working across the globe in search of new ideas. During the economic downturn in 2009 the company invested over $9 billion in research and development.

In 2010, CEO Steven A. Ballmer outlined four areas of focus for long-term research aimed at pioneering the next generation of breakthrough technologies.

- **Cloud computing and software plus services:** Combining the power of desktop and server software with the reach of the Internet is creating important opportunities for growth. Microsoft is focused on delivering end-to-end experiences that connect users to information, communications, entertainment, and people in new and compelling ways across their lives at home, at work, and the broadest-possible range of mobile scenarios.

- **Natural user interfaces:** Dramatic changes in the way people interact with technology, as touch, gestures, handwriting, and speech recognition become a normal part of how devices are controlled create opportunities to reach new markets and deliver new kinds of computing experiences.

- **Natural language processing:** The increase in computing power will enable a new generation of software that has the knowledge and intelligence to respond to simple natural language input and quickly carry out complex tasks in a way that accurately reflects users' needs and preferences.

- **New scenario innovation:** Global issues including healthcare, environmental sustainability, and education can be opportunities for software that could enable people without specialized programming skills to quickly create models and simulations that could transform scientific research and have a dramatic impact on a wide range of industries, from financial services, to engineering, aerospace, and manufacturing.

Today at Microsoft's Redmond campus it becomes apparent that the future needs of consumers is the innovative focus. Microsoft envisions this future as a world of multiple sensors, where our plants tell homeowners when to water them and our doorbell automatically sends photos of visitors to our mobile phone. Inside the house the coffee table will have its own touch interface, connecting to 3D cloud applications all accessible on every surface of the home. Where surfaces are inaccessible, skin may be used as a display and input device. The basis of Microsoft's research is the transition from a graphical user interface (GUI) that we use today in computers and phones to natural user interaction (NUI).

Microsoft may also consider buying start ups whose technology is considered good by using a program called BizSpark, which gives startup companies free access to Microsoft tools, technologies, and services. The program is open to private companies that are less than three years old and have less than $1 million revenue. Thirty thousand companies have signed on to BizSpark.

The challenge comes down to size. The question for Microsoft is how to turn new innovations into success stories on a scale of Windows and Office, which continue to dominate their business by accounting for almost half annual revenues. Microsoft is aware that success is fleeting, and staying in place means getting left behind. The company is taking steps today that will surely payoff in the future.

Discussion Questions

1. Describe how the "new entrepreneurial imperative" has affected Microsoft.
2. How would you apply the organizational life cycle to Microsoft today?
3. What specific actions indicate that Microsoft is trying to exhibit corporate entrepreneurship?

SOURCES: Adapted from "Microsoft: Way beyond the PC," *The Economist,* November 30, 2005, pp. 83–85; and the Microsoft Web site, http://www. microsoft.com/msft/reports/ar09/index.html, accessed April 14, 2010.

Summary and Conclusions

A revolution is underway in modern organizations. Highly turbulent external environments are forcing managers to rethink literally every aspect of organizational life. As the nature of the competitive challenge continually redefines itself, larger companies find themselves becoming too slow, too reactive, and too complacent. To address these shortcomings, many companies are down-sizing, right-sizing, outsourcing, reengineering, restructuring, and generally attempting to reinvent themselves.

All of this represents a quest for sustainable competitive advantage; an elusive goal that can no longer be achieved based on conventional management practices. Sustainable advantage in the twenty-first century derives from being more adaptable and flexible, from being faster and more aggressive, and from generating higher rates of innovation compared to other companies. In short, the ultimate source of marketplace advantage is entrepreneurship.

In this chapter, entrepreneurship has been defined as an opportunity-driven process of value creation, where value is created through unique combinations of resources.

When this process is applied to established organizations, our focus becomes corporate entrepreneurship. The chapter draws a distinction between entrepreneurship and management, in the process arguing that today's managers must find ways to become entrepreneurs. The corporate imperative in twenty-first century organizations is to strike a balance between disciplined management and entrepreneurial behavior. Leading-edge companies find ways to optimize current operations while at the same time inventing the future. They serve existing stakeholders while also leading customers to new sources of value, creating new markets, and redefining the rules of the competitive game.

Although companies tend to be highly entrepreneurial in their early stages, they subsequently create bureaucracies and cultures that stifle the entrepreneurial spirit. This is the lesson of the organizational life cycle. The changing competitive landscape suggests that, as companies evolve, the need for entrepreneurial behavior does not dissipate. Yet, the abilities to think and act in an entrepreneurial fashion at every level of management, and within every area of the company, tend to decline in direct proportion to the size and age of the company.

The challenge thus becomes one of fostering entrepreneurial transformations within organizations. Toward this end, the chapter has introduced an integrative model of corporate entrepreneurship designed around three major components: building blocks for corporate entrepreneurship, the creation of an entrepreneurial work environment, and the achievement of sustainable entrepreneurial performance. This model provides the guiding structure for the layout of the book. Subsequent chapters will examine each of the key elements within the three components of the model. When combined, these elements provide a roadmap to entrepreneurial success.

References

Adizes, I. 1999, *Managing Corporate Lifecycles* (Englewood Cliffs, NJ: Prentice-Hall).

Brandt, S. C. 1986, *Entrepreneuring in Established Companies* (Homewood, IL: Dow-Jones-Irwin), 54.

Crandall, R. E. 1987, "Company Life Cycles: The Effects of Growth on Structure and Personnel," *Personnel* (September): 28–36.

Damanpour, F. 1991, "Organizational Innovation: A Meta-Analysis of Determinants and Moderators," *Academy of Management Journal*, 34: 355–390.

Greiner, L. E. 1972, "Evolution and Revolution as Organizations Grow," *Harvard Business Review* (July–August): 37–46.

Guth, W. D. and Ginsberg, A. 1990, "Corporate Entrepreneurship," *Strategic Management Journal*, Special Issue, 11: 5–15.

Hamel, G. 2007, *The End of Management* (Boston, MA: Harvard Business School Press).

Heavey, C., Simsek, Z., Roche, F. and Aidan, K. 2009. "Decision Comprehensiveness and Corporate Entrepreneurship: The Moderating Role of Managerial Uncertainty Preferences and Environmental Dynamism," *Journal of Management Studies*, 46(8): 1289–1306.

Ireland, R. D., Covin, J. G., and Kuratko, D. F. 2009. "Conceptualizing Corporate Entrepreneurship Strategy," *Entrepreneurship Theory and Practice*, 33(1), 19–46.

Kuratko, D. F. 2009, *Entrepreneurship: Theory, Process, & Practice*, 8th edition (Mason, OH: Cengage/SouthWestern Publishing).

Ling, Y., Simsek, Z., Lubatkin, M., and Veiga, J. 2008. "Transformational Leadership's Role in Promoting Entrepreneurship: Examining the CEO-TMT Interface." *Academy of Management Journal*, 51: 557–76.

Morris, M. H. 1998, *Entrepreneurial Intensity* (Westport, CT: Quorum Books).

Morris, M. H., Lewis, P. S., and Sexton, D. 1994, "Reconceptualizing Entrepreneurship: An Input-Output Perspective," *SAM Advanced Management Journal*, 59(1): 21–30.

Pitelis, C. and Teece, D. 2009. "The (New) Nature and Essence of the Firm," *European Management Review*, 6(1): 5–16.

Romero-Martinez, A., Fernandez-Rodriguez, Z., and Vazquez-Inchausti, E. 2010. "Exploring Corporate Entrepreneurship in Privatized Firms." *Journal of World Business*, 45(1): 2–19.

Salvato, C., Sciascia, S., and Alberti, F. 2009. "The Microfoundations of Corporate Entrepreneurship as an Organizational Capability," *International Journal of Entrepreneurship and Innovation*, 10(4): 279–298.

Sharma, P. and Chrisman, J. J. 1999. "Toward a Reconciliation of the Definitional Issues in the Field of Corporate Entrepreneurship," *Entrepreneurship Theory and Practice*, 23(3): 11–28.

Stevenson, H. H. and Jarillo-Mossi, J. C. 1986. "Preserving Entrepreneurship as Companies Grow," *Journal of Business Strategy* (Summer): 10.

Stevenson, H. H., Roberts, M. J., Sahlman, W., and Hammermesh, R. 2006. *New Business Ventures and the Entrepreneur* (Homewood, IL: McGraw-Hill Irwin Publishing).

Timmons, J. A. and Spinelli, S. 2008, *New Venture Creation* (Homewood, IL: Irwin Publishing).

Zahra, S., Neubaum, D., and Huse, M. 2000. "Entrepreneurship in Medium-Size Companies: Exploring the Effects of Ownership and Governance Systems," *Journal of Management*, 26(5): 947–966.

CHAPTER 2

THE UNIQUE NATURE OF CORPORATE ENTREPRENEURSHIP

Introduction

While many people associate entrepreneurship with the start-up of a new business, this is a very narrow view. Entrepreneurship happens in organizations of all sizes and types. Seeking and capitalizing on opportunity, taking risks beyond what is secure, and having the tenacity to push an innovative idea through to reality represent the essence of what entrepreneurs do. Further, entrepreneurship is not limited to a select set of people. An entrepreneurial perspective can be developed in any individual. It is a perspective that can be exhibited inside or outside an organization, in profit or not-for-profit enterprises, and in business or non-business activities (Kuratko, 2009b). The purpose is to turn innovative ideas into organizational realities. Entrepreneurs create the new, while replacing or destroying the old. They challenge assumptions and bend or break old rules while creating the future.

Entrepreneurs are ordinary people who do extraordinary things. They make change happen as a function of vision, hard work, and passion. They are not necessarily trying to change the world, even if that is sometimes the outcome. Dissatisfaction with the status quo, a desire to improve things, and a belief that there is a better way—these are the motives that drive entrepreneurs. For them, entrepreneurship is not a discrete event that happens at a point in time. Rather, it is a philosophy of business that continually governs how they approach problems and opportunities (Morris et al., 2001).

Entrepreneurship has both attitudinal and behavioral dimensions, meaning it is both a way of thinking and acting. As a mindset or way of thinking, the entrepreneurial manager focuses on recognizing opportunity, demonstrates healthy dissatisfaction with existing ways, has a sense of optimism, places emphasis on the future and how things can be, and embraces change. Behaviorally, the entrepreneur is an innovator, takes calculated risks, is adept at "bootstrapping" and leveraging resources, demonstrates "guerrilla" skills in overcoming obstacles and getting more done with less, and perseveres in pursuing a vision.

In this chapter, we will further explore the nature of entrepreneurship and how it applies within established companies. A number of myths exist regarding entrepreneurship, and these have led some to question the relevance of entrepreneurship in larger, established organizations. In the pages ahead, we will review and hopefully dispel some of these misconceptions. The nature of the entrepreneurial process will be investigated, and fundamental differences between corporate and start-up entrepreneurship will be established. Ways in which entrepreneurship is manifested in companies are then identified. Finally, we will introduce some integrative frameworks that are useful for conceptualizing corporate entrepreneurship and innovation in an established organization.

Dispelling the Myths and Sidestepping the Folklore

It is not unusual for executives to question the relevance of entrepreneurship for their organizations. Some are concerned with the difficulties and implications of applying entrepreneurship; others simply do not believe that it applies or has meaning in a big company. Such skepticism can often be traced to certain long-standing myths about entrepreneurship. These myths have developed through the years and reflect limited knowledge and research in the field of entrepreneurship. It is important to keep in mind that entrepreneurship is still emerging as a field of study, and "folklore" will prevail until it is dispelled with contemporary research findings. Listed below are ten of the most notable myths, together with an explanation regarding why each is inaccurate or incomplete (Kuratko, 2009a; Morris, 1998).

1. *"Entrepreneurs Are Born, Not Made"*
There is a long-prevailing notion that the characteristics of entrepreneurs cannot be taught or learned, and that they are traits with which one must be born. This is not true. Key traits associated with entrepreneurship include achievement motivation, aggressiveness, initiative, drive, willingness to take risks, tolerance of ambiguity, and self-confidence, among others. Today, however, it is recognized that such traits and characteristics are heavily influenced by environmental conditions (family, work, peer group, social), and that each of us has significant entrepreneurial potential. The challenge is to help people recognize and develop these characteristics within themselves.

2. *"Entrepreneurs Must Be Inventors"*
The idea that entrepreneurs are inventors is a result of misunderstanding and tunnel vision. While many inventors are also entrepreneurs, there are numerous entrepreneurs who pursue all sorts of innovative activity beyond formal inventions, and/or who capitalize on the creative ideas of others. For example, Ray Kroc did not invent the fast-food franchise, but his innovative ideas made McDonald's the largest fast-food enterprise in the world. Moreover, the innovativeness of many entrepreneurial concepts can be found in the operating processes, the pricing approach, the packaging, the distribution method, or some other means of value creation that does not entail inventing a new product. There is always some level of innovativeness in entrepreneurship, but innovative behavior takes many forms.

3. *"There Is a Standard Profile or Prototype of the Entrepreneur"*

Many books and articles have presented checklists of characteristics and skills of the successful entrepreneur. These lists were neither validated nor complete; they were based on case studies and on research findings among achievement-orientated people. Today we realize that a standard entrepreneurial profile is hard to compile. The environment, the venture itself, and the entrepreneur have interactive effects, which result in many different types of profiles. That is, there are different kinds of entrepreneurs. It is more likely that successful entrepreneurs may benefit from an "Entrepreneurial Perspective" within themselves rather than fit a particular profile.

4. *"All You Need Is Luck to Be an Entrepreneur"*

Being at "the right place at the right time" is always an advantage. But "luck happens when preparation meets opportunity" is an equally appropriate adage. Prepared entrepreneurs who seize the opportunity when it arises often appear to be "lucky." They are, in fact, simply better prepared to deal with situations and turn them into successes. What appears to be luck really is preparation, determination, desire, knowledge, and innovativeness.

5. *"Entrepreneurs Are Extreme Risk Takers (Gamblers)"*

The concept of risk is a major element in the entrepreneurship process. However, the public's perception of the risk assumed by most entrepreneurs is distorted. While it may appear that an entrepreneur is "gambling" on a wild chance, the fact is that the entrepreneur is usually working on a moderate or "calculated" risk. Most successful entrepreneurs work hard through planning and preparation to mitigate or minimize the risk involved. Few like risk. They seek to creatively manage risks in order to better control the destiny of their vision.

6. *"Entrepreneurial People Are Academic and Social Misfits"*

The belief that entrepreneurs are academically and socially ineffective is a result of some hard-headed business owners having started successful enterprises after dropping out of school or quitting a job. In many cases such an event has been blown out of proportion in an attempt to "profile" the typical entrepreneur. Historically, in fact, educational and social organizations did not recognize the entrepreneur. They abandoned him or her as a misfit in a world of corporate professionals. Business education, for example, was aimed primarily at the study of corporate activity. Today's entrepreneur wears two hats, that of visionary change agent and effective manager. He or she is typically adept socially, economically, and academically. No longer a misfit, the entrepreneur is now viewed as a professional.

7. *"All Entrepreneurs Need Is Money"*

It is true that an innovative idea needs capital to survive; it is also true that a large number of business failures occur because of a lack of adequate financing. However, many other resources are vital for entrepreneurial success, such as a skilled and balanced team, technical and selling capabilities, distribution channels, licenses, and more. Money is not always a guarantee that the right resources are put together in the right way at the right time. Also, entrepreneurs do not own all the resources that they use—they are adept at borrowing, sharing, leasing, renting, and networking resources. Further, having money is not a bulwark against failure. Failure due to a lack of proper financing often is an indicator of other problems: managerial incompetence, lack of financial understanding, poor investments, poor planning, and the like. To entrepreneurs, money is a resource but never an end in itself.

8. *"Ignorance Is Bliss for Entrepreneurs"*

The myth that too much planning and evaluation lead to constant problems—that overanalysis leads to paralysis—does not hold up in today's competitive markets which demand detailed planning and preparation. Identifying the strengths and weaknesses of a concept or venture, setting up clear timetables with contingencies for handling problems, and minimizing these problems through careful strategy formulation are all key factors for successful entrepreneurship. Thus careful planning—not ignorance of it—is the mark of an accomplished entrepreneur.

9. *"Most Entrepreneurial Initiatives Fail"*

It is true that many entrepreneurs suffer a number of failures before they are successful. They follow the adage "if at first you don't succeed, try, try again." In fact, failure can teach many lessons to those willing to learn and often leads to future successes. This is clearly shown by the "corridor principle," which states that with every venture launched, new and unintended opportunities often arise. The 3M Corporation invented Post-it notes using a glue that had not been strong enough for its intended use. Rather than throw away the glue, the company focused on finding another use for it and, in the process, developed a multimillion-dollar product. The statistics of entrepreneurial failure rates have been overstated. In fact, one researcher, Bruce Kirchoff, has reported that the "high failure rate" most commonly accepted may be misleading. Tracing 814,000 businesses started in 1977, Kirchoff found that more than 50 percent were still surviving under their original or new owners. Additionally, 28 percent voluntarily closed down, and only 18 percent actually "failed" in the sense of leaving behind outstanding liabilities. In a corporate context, success rates of projects and products also exceed 50 percent.

10. *"Entrepreneurship Is Unstructured and Chaotic"*

There is a tendency to think of entrepreneurs as gunslingers—as people who shoot from the hip and ask questions later. They are assumed by some to be disorganized and unstructured, leaving it to others to keep things on track. The reality is that entrepreneurs are heavily involved in all facets of their ventures, and they usually have a number of balls in the air at the same time. As a result, they are typically well-organized individuals.

They tend to have a system—perhaps elaborate, perhaps not—personally designed to keep things straight and maintain priorities. In fact, their system may seem strange to the casual observer, but it works.

When doing something entrepreneurial, one is dealing with the unknown, and there is a need to be tolerant of ambiguity. Unanticipated developments arise all the time. Success is often a function of how prepared one is for the unknown, and whether one is in position to capitalize on the unanticipated. The entrepreneur's ability to meet daily and weekly obligations, while also growing the venture and being able to move quickly when novel events occur, is strongly affected by his or her organizing capabilities. Plans, outlines, forecasts, checklists, timetables, budgets, databases, and PERT charts are examples of tools that the contemporary entrepreneur always keeps close at hand.

The conclusion is that entrepreneurship is a planned activity that can be managed as a process, involves risk and requires innovation, and can be applied in virtually any organizational context. In addition, it is an activity requiring significant dedication, perseverance, and adaptability. Virtually anyone is capable of being entrepreneurial, and many people manage to be entrepreneurial on a continuous basis.

Entrepreneurial Realities: Understanding the Process

Consistent with our definition in Chapter 1, the beginning point in understanding how entrepreneurship actually works is to recognize that a process is involved, and processes can be managed. It is a process that can occur in many different settings, including larger, established companies. Although the process has been described in various ways, it generally consists of the following six stages:

Identifying the Opportunity Entrepreneurship does not start with the creative concept for a new product, service, or process. It begins with an opportunity, which can be defined as a favorable set of circumstances creating a need or an opening for a new business concept or approach. The reality is that many new concepts fail because there was no opportunity. An example is the so-called better mousetrap that nobody wanted. Arguably the single largest category of new product failures, these are often highly innovative, state-of-the-art advances—innovations that the casual observer might find quite intriguing. And yet, when the test of the marketplace is applied, not enough customers are willing to buy, either because they are already satisfied, the concept is too complex or difficult to understand, the perceived switching costs from current solutions are too high, or they do not have a real need for the innovation.

Just because something is "better" does not mean it is needed. The adage "if you build it, they will come" is foolish when discussing entrepreneurial initiatives. All too often, new products, services and concepts are developed in isolation, where the sole focus is on overcoming technical, financial and human challenges. The underlying opportunity is simply assumed. Further, having a better product at a better price with better product availability and better customer service means nothing if the market does not exist, is too small, or is unwilling to change; if competitors are completely entrenched; or if any other components of the opportunity are inadequate.

Key questions confronting the manager include the source(s) of the opportunity, the size of the opportunity, and the sustainability of the opportunity. Just as important is the need to understand the "window of opportunity." Timing is everything when it comes to new ideas, and the concept of a window means there is an optimal time period during which a new concept can be implemented with a reasonable chance of success. One can introduce something too early (before the market exists) or too late (once the market is saturated or new technologies have begun to emerge).

Defining the Business Concept   With an opportunity clearly in mind, the entrepreneur specifies a business concept. Opportunities represent potential—and with most opportunities, this potential can be capitalized upon in multiple ways. Thus, a business concept is defined as an innovative approach for capitalizing on an opportunity. The concept could be a new product or service, or a new process or method for accomplishing a task. This latter category, process innovation, is especially relevant in larger corporations where there is a need for new administrative systems, new production methods, new marketing approaches, new methods for managing logistics, and so forth.

A well-conceptualized concept has certain characteristics. It provides an overt benefit to a user. It is unique, and not easy to imitate. It is comprehensive in the sense that it represents an entire value proposition. It is feasible, and there is reason to believe it can be implemented. And, of course, its returns significantly exceed its costs.

Assessing the Resource Requirements   The natural tendency is to assume that the principal resource required for any entrepreneurial venture is money. Financial resources certainly matter, and entrepreneurs are notorious for under- or overestimating their financial requirements, but entrepreneurial success or failure is often a function of other resources, some of which money cannot buy. Identifying critical nonfinancial needs requires insight, judgment, and patience. Examples of such resources include creative technical skills, a permit/license or patent, well-established customer contacts, a great location, a well-constructed and motivated team, excess production capacity, or a loyal distributor. And, in a corporate context, obtaining endorsement or sponsorship from a senior executive can be the most valuable resource of all.

Acquiring the Necessary Resources Some of the most entrepreneurial behaviors involve the ways in which resources are brought together. Entrepreneurs are great at "resource leveraging," meaning they know how to borrow or share resources, use other people's resources, stretch resources, apply resources in nonconventional ways, and use certain resources to acquire other resources. The entrepreneur often must be a trader, bargainer, negotiator, networker, and borrower. He or she may need to make currently controlled resources appear greater than they are. Further, not all resources have to be owned or directly controlled by the entrepreneur. The leveraging concept suggests resources might be rented, leased, shared, contracted for, outsourced, or employed temporarily. Leveraging allows the entrepreneur to move concepts along the development path without major financial commitments, in the process lessening risk and increasing the firm's flexibility.

Implementing and Managing the Concept The entrepreneur is involved in "creating the new." As a result, no matter how well planned, implementation of an innovative concept is typically hectic, uncertain, and ambiguous. Tremendous learning is taking place. The entrepreneur is faced with myriad decisions that must be quickly resolved, and often there is no precedent or history to guide such decisions. Problems and obstacles arise that were not anticipated, and a number of assumptions made when planning the concept prove to be wrong. Keys at this stage of the process are tolerance of ambiguity on the one hand, and adaptability on the other. Moreover, anything new and different is threatening to the status quo, so the entrepreneur must be adept at overcoming both resistance and deliberate obstruction.

Given the time it takes for an entrepreneurial concept to unfold, the entrepreneur must set intermediate targets to ensure steady progress is being made along an inherently vague path. Further, the significant number of internal crises that occur as the process unfolds often create a "fire-fighting" mentality, where the entrepreneur loses sight of critical developments both within the company and in the marketplace.

Because entrepreneurship often involves the creation of something from nothing, taking meaningful risks, and overcoming significant resistance, entrepreneurs can become insular and closed-minded during the implementation process. They sometimes feel such total ownership of a concept that they become micromanagers, unwilling to properly delegate. They can step on toes, and refuse to listen to sound advice when that advice is critical or warns of potential dangers.

Harvesting the Venture We live in an age when opportunity windows and product life cycles are getting shorter, resources are becoming more quickly obsolete, and customer loyalties are more fleeting. Moreover, the environmental turbulence discussed in Chapter 1 suggests that companies face more threats, but are also confronted with a lot more opportunities from which they must choose. These realities indicate that the entrepreneur must have an exit strategy for his or her concept. That is, there is a need for a model regarding how to implement a concept, but also for how to harvest the concept. Harvesting is concerned with how returns will be realized, over what time period, and the manner in which the concept will eventually be absorbed by some other business entity, spun off, replaced, eliminated, or allowed to die a natural death (Timmons and Spinelli, 2007)

How Corporate Entrepreneurship Differs

Successfully applying the entrepreneurial process within larger, established organizations requires that the manager appreciate the unique nature of corporate entrepreneurship (Covin and Miles, 1999). Entrepreneurship has long been associated with bold individuals who persevere against the odds in creating a new venture. The entrepreneur is often thought of as a type of hero, with celebrity status given to such luminaries as Mark Zuckerberg (Facebook), Steve Jobs (Apple), Jeff Bezos (Amazon.com), and Michael Dell (Dell Computer). Most start-up efforts are fairly opportunistic and highly individualistic endeavors that become all-consuming in terms of the demands on the entrepreneur.

Characteristics such as these raise problems when we start speaking of entrepreneurship within a larger, established company. For instance, do companies really want bold, aggressive, risk-taking individuals inside the corporate walls? Is opportunistic behavior consistent with the planned, controlled strategic direction of a company? Are corporate entrepreneurs really "starting up" anything when the company exists and has an established market presence? Are stockholders willing to let management "bet the farm" on entrepreneurial initiatives? Two consequences of questions such as these are (1) considerable confusion about the nature of corporate entrepreneurship, and (2) a certain skepticism about whether entrepreneurship is even possible within larger companies. To bring some clarity to these issues, let's consider the similarities and differences between corporate entrepreneurship and the start-up of a new business.

THE BASICS APPLY NO MATTER WHAT THE CONTEXT

The basic nature of entrepreneurship is universal. If we consider the definition of entrepreneurship provided in Chapter 1, the focus was on a process of value creation through unique resource combinations for the purpose of exploiting opportunity. This definition says nothing about starting a small business. In fact, the context within which entrepreneurship occurs is not part of the definition. This phenomenon can occur in start-up ventures, small firms, mid-sized companies, large conglomerates, non-profit organizations, and even public sector agencies.

The nature of the entrepreneurial process was previously described. Again, these six stages in the process describe how a new company might be started, but they just as readily apply to the application of entrepreneurship inside a large company. For instance, these same stages would be pursued by a manager attempting to introduce a new service concept within an operating division, or one trying to pursue entrepreneurship within a company sales force. In both instances, opportunities must be identified, innovative concepts developed, resources mustered, ideas implemented, and initiatives harvested. Similarly, the major objectives to be accomplished in each stage remain the same.

The reality is that all companies contain some amount of entrepreneurship. The question is how much. Some new start-ups are highly entrepreneurial, while others (e.g., many so-called mom and pop operations) are not very entrepreneurial at all. Similarly, many large firms tend to be fairly bureaucratic, and struggle to produce innovations. Yet there are others, such as 3-M and Google, that are able to maintain fairly high levels of entrepreneurship. This is a subject to which we shall return in Chapter 3.

Table 2-1 summarizes many of the similarities between start-up and corporate entrepreneurship. Understanding these similarities is important for at least three reasons. First, this understanding helps dispense the notion that corporate entrepreneurship is

---

TABLE 2-1

Similarities between Corporate and Start-Up Entrepreneurship

- Both involve opportunity recognition and definition.
- Both require a unique business concept that takes the form of a product, service, or process.
- Both are driven by an individual champion who works with a team to bring the concept to fruition.
- Both require that the entrepreneur be able to balance vision with managerial skill, passion with pragmatism, and proactiveness with patience.
- Both involve concepts that are most vulnerable in the formative stage, and that require adaptation over time.
- Both entail a window of opportunity within which the concept can be successfully capitalized upon.
- Both are predicated on value creation and accountability to a customer.
- Both find the entrepreneur encountering resistance and obstacles, necessitating both perseverance and an ability to formulate innovative solutions.
- Both entail risk and require risk management strategies.
- Both find the entrepreneur needing to develop creative strategies for leveraging resources.
- Both involve significant ambiguity.
- Both require harvesting strategies.

just a popular management fad, and that interest in it will fade once the consultants and popular business writers move on to the next new tool, concept, or perspective. By recognizing that entrepreneurship is a universal concept, we begin to understand that it lies at the heart of the corporation. Sustainable competitive advantage is impossible without it. Entrepreneurship is not a quick fix or an operational experiment in companies. In fact, the company that is not interested in developing and tapping into the entrepreneurial potential of its employees has effectively signed its own death warrant—the question is only one of whether it will be a quick demise or a slow, lingering decline. Second, it is vital that both the senior executives who commit the company to an entrepreneurial path, as well as the champions within organizations expected to carry out the entrepreneurial mission, understand the phenomenon with which they are dealing. Entrepreneurship is real; it entails risks; failure is likely; and the psychological, emotional, and financial costs can be significant. Employees in companies should think of themselves *as* entrepreneurs. They should not think of themselves as *somewhat like* entrepreneurs. The corollary, of course, is that senior executives must let them be entrepreneurs, with all that this encompasses. Third, virtually all of the research on entrepreneurship has emphasized the start-up context. The commonalities between start-up and corporate entrepreneurship suggest company executives can learn much from examining what we know about the start-up context, rather than discard those insights as irrelevant (Gartner, 1990; Covin and Slevin, 1991; Sharma and Chrisman, 1999).

It is for the reasons previously cited that words like "intrapreneurship," coined by Gifford Pinchot (1985) to describe entrepreneurship in established companies, can be misleading. They make corporate entrepreneurship sound like something completely unique, or as if it were the stepchild of entrepreneurship, borrowing some of the name but not really constituting the real thing. As a result, throughout this book we use the term "corporate entrepreneurship"—the fundamentals do not change, only the context.

There Are Some Important Differences

At the same time, entrepreneurship takes on some unique characteristics when pursued inside established companies. Table 2-2 provides a summary of the differences between corporate and start-up entrepreneurship. Entrepreneurship is often conceptualized in terms of risks and rewards, and both have distinct nuances in a corporate setting. While the types of risk (e.g., financial, market, supplier, competitive, career-related, etc.) are similar, at issue is the party that actually takes the risks. In a start-up context, all of the risk falls on the entrepreneur. Although start-up entrepreneurs are typically adroit at sharing or spreading risk, they are ultimately accountable for the risks

TABLE 2-2

Corporate and Start-Up Entrepreneurship: Major Differences

Start-Up Entrepreneurship	*Corporate Entrepreneurship*
• Entrepreneur takes the risk	• Company assumes the risks, other than career-related risk
• Entrepreneur "owns" the concept or innovative idea	• Company owns the concept, and typically the intellectual rights surrounding the concept
• Entrepreneur owns all or much of the business	• Entrepreneur may have no equity in the company, or a very small percentage
• Potential rewards for the entrepreneur are theoretically unlimited	• Clear limits are placed on the financial rewards entrepreneurs can receive
• One misstep can mean failure	• More room for errors; company can absorb failure
• Vulnerable to outside influence	• More insulated from outside influence
• Independence of the entrepreneur, although the successful entrepreneur is typically backed by a strong team	• Interdependence of the champion with many others; may have to share credit with any number of people
• Flexibility in changing course, experimenting, or trying new directions	• Rules, procedures, and bureaucracy hinder the entrepreneur's ability to maneuver
• Speed of decision making	• Longer approval cycles
• Little security	• Job security
• No safety net	• Dependable benefit package
• Few people to talk to	• Extensive network for bouncing around ideas
• Limited scale and scope initially	• Potential for sizeable scale and scope fairly quickly
• Severe resource limitations	• Access to finances, R&D, production facilities for trial runs, an established sales force, an existing brand, distribution channels that are in place, existing databases and market research resources, and an established customer base

incurred. They have a considerable amount on the line financially, professionally, and personally. The other side of the equation finds the start-up entrepreneur in a position to earn unlimited rewards. Most of them do not become millionaires, but the possibility exists. The reward picture is affected by another key aspect of the start-up context. The entrepreneur owns all or a considerable portion of the company. He or she can realize returns not simply though a salary, but through dividend payments, licensing fees, a range of perquisites, and through capital gains from selling shares of stock as the value of the company increases.

With corporate entrepreneurs, most of the risks are assumed by the company. In fact, the major risk taken by the entrepreneur is career-related. By pursuing new concepts rather than simply concentrating on normal job responsibilities, especially where concepts are highly innovative or encounter severe resistance within the company, the entrepreneur may jeopardize future pay increases, career advancement, and even his or her job. Correspondingly, the entrepreneur generally finds real limitations to the possible rewards he or she can realize if the concept is successfully implemented, and most of the returns go to the company. Further, because the entrepreneur generally owns little to none of the company, returns are limited to salary and perhaps a bonus, with some companies going so far as to offer a small share of the profits or cost savings that result from the entrepreneur's efforts. There are often concerns that the entrepreneur does not earn amounts that exceed the salaries of his or her superiors.

Start-up entrepreneurs own more than the company. They own their ideas, concepts, and intellectual contributions. A product that is invented or a new customer service approach that is implemented belongs to the entrepreneur. The entrepreneur personally identifies with the concept, and enjoys a sense of pride when it succeeds. In a corporation, ideas and concepts belong to the organization. There can still be a sense of pride, but the employee must be prepared for the ways in which the company will modify the concept, the extent to which it will support the concept, and the people who will take credit for the success of the concept. In this sense, the employee not only does not have legal ownership, but his or her sense of psychological ownership can be undermined.

Until the venture is well established, which can take many years, the start-up entrepreneur enjoys little security. He or she may take a deficient salary at the outset, while earnings may be tied to company performance. Failure of the company means loss of one's job and livelihood. The company may not be able to afford extensive benefits packages. Conversely, the corporate entrepreneur generally knows he or she has a job tomorrow, receives a dependable and often attractive salary, and is provided with excellent health and disability insurance, a pension fund, and associated benefits. In a sense, the corporate entrepreneur has much more of a safety net should things go wrong. As we shall see in subsequent chapters, the desire for security is a factor that distinguishes the corporate entrepreneur, and is an incentive to not leave the company and strike out on one's own.

Related to the distribution of risks and rewards is the vulnerability of the start-up entrepreneur. The venture can be dramatically affected by external developments such as a supplier that fails to deliver, a regulatory change, or an economic downturn. Further, regardless of how successful the start-up entrepreneur is from the start, or the levels of sales achieved, one major misstep (e.g., running out of cash, the addition of a new product that does not fit, hiring the wrong employee, expanding too quickly) can quickly put the entrepreneur out of business. The corporate entrepreneur is certainly affected by external developments, but is also more insulated from their impacts. For instance, the corporation's bargaining power with suppliers is typically greater, as is the ability to find and switch to a new supplier. The financial stability of the company, the well-developed infrastructure (operations, sales, R&D, logistics, etc.), and the established lines of products and services all combine to make the corporate entrepreneur less vulnerable. He or she has more time and ability to endure negative developments.

While external forces can be especially problematic for the start-up entrepreneur, the corporate entrepreneur deals with a number of unique internal challenges. In an established corporation, one does not enjoy the relative independence enjoyed by the start-up entrepreneur. Rather, the corporate entrepreneur's success is directly tied to the ability to win approval from various managers (or to get managers to "look the other way"), obtain resources and cooperation from key departments or units, and build coalitions or alliances. The entrepreneur's project can be terminated at any time, sometimes for arbitrary reasons. Alternatively, other corporate priorities can lead to the sidelining of what appear to be promising projects. Not only does the entrepreneur have less personal control over the destiny of the concept, but he or she is far more interdependent with others than independent. This characteristic also affects outcomes, as even if the concept or idea is successful, the corporate entrepreneur may or may not receive the credit, but almost certainly a number of other people will share the credit.

The internal corporate environment has two other distinguishing aspects. The size and scope of the established company are such that the company cannot operate without sophisticated administrative and control systems. These systems typically imply a level of bureaucracy and red tape. Approval cycles can be relatively slow as the entrepreneur attempts to move the idea or concept through numerous approval levels. Alternatively, the start-up entrepreneur has more flexibility, can change course relatively easily, and is able to move with greater speed.

Finally, and perhaps most significantly, comes the question of resources. The start-up entrepreneur operates under severe resource constraints, and these constraints often result in significant modifications of the core concept and the direction the business takes. The rate at which the venture is able to grow is often hindered by these constraints, and failure to grow can mean missed opportunities as well as greater vulnerability to competitor entreaties. The corporate entrepreneur is in a very different situation. While he or she does not usually control the needed resources, they are available in ample supply within the organization. Consider just a few of the preexisting resources available in many established companies. In addition to money, the company might have a known brand name, an established customer base, market research capabilities, market intelligence databases, distribution channels in place, relationships with suppliers, technical or research and development staff, production facilities, and more. The skilled entrepreneur finds creative ways to tap into these resources.

Let's assume that the corporate entrepreneur is successful. Because of the resources of the company, a new product or service can achieve global distribution fairly quickly. A new process can be implemented throughout the organization and affect the way thousands of employees do their jobs. It could take the start-up entrepreneur many years to get a venture to the same point in terms of its impact. Stated differently, the corporate entrepreneur can operate on a bigger scale and scope much more quickly.

A resource that corporate entrepreneurs often take for granted, but one that makes a considerable difference, is "people to talk with." In the early stages, start-up entrepreneurs are often extremely worried about others stealing the idea, moving faster, and taking the opportunity for themselves. They can develop a kind of paranoia, where they are hesitant to say too much to anyone about their concept. Corporate entrepreneurs are in a very different situation. There are experienced, knowledgeable people throughout the company with whom they can explore the idea, test it out, and make modifications and refinements. This internal network of expertise can also be a source of insights regarding how to effectively position the concept within the company (Covin and Kuratko, 2010; Zahra et al., 1999).

THE POLITICAL FACTOR

Of special note when considering factors that distinguish the corporate context is organizational politics. Organizations are nothing more than the people within them, and these people differ in terms of their needs, objectives, values, and capabilities. As a result, organizations are political, and politics will be instrumental in the success or failure of any entrepreneurial initiative within an established company.

The need for political skills is tied to three major challenges faced by the corporate entrepreneur: achieving credibility or legitimacy for the concept and the entrepreneurial team, obtaining resources, and overcoming inertia and resistance (Block and Macmillan, 1993). The entrepreneur is usually limited in terms of formal power within the organization. Further, the more innovative or different the concept, the more skeptical people are likely to be of its viability or value. The entrepreneur must achieve credibility by giving others within the organization a "reason to believe." Some of the ways legitimacy might be established include building and using an influence network, securing endorsements from senior executives or other significant players, making small advances and sharing the credit with others, sharing valuable information with key influencers, and demonstrating competence by helping others with their problems while also asking for help. When it comes to obtaining resources, corporate entrepreneurs are good bootstrappers. They identify underutilized resources within the company and use some of the tactics previously discussed to convince resource owners to share them. They are adroit at borrowing, begging, and scavenging for resources. The greatest challenge lies in overcoming inertia (e.g., the new idea represents change and people are comfortable with the status quo, see no need for change, or feel the new idea will create work for them) and overt resistance (e.g., the new idea threatens the positions of others or will take resources away from them). We will explore this challenge in greater detail in Chapter 11.

In reality, an unlimited number of political tactics are available to the corporate entrepreneur. These will also be examined in more depth in Chapter 11. Examples of tactics the entrepreneur might employ include creative use of existing rules, creative ways to evade existing rules, use of alliances and coalitions, negotiation ploys, reliance on the exchange of personal favors, and efforts to educate or provide information to others.

IMPLICATIONS OF THE DIFFERENCES

Sustainable entrepreneurship is more likely where managers recognize the implications of how entrepreneurship differs in a corporate context. Implications can be drawn for the motivation and attitudes, time horizons, accountability, risk orientation, skills, and operating styles of the corporate entrepreneur.

Corporate entrepreneurs do not have to do all the things involved in starting up one's own business. And they are not looking to get rich. Rather, their motivation has more to do with the desire to create something successful, to bring to fruition an idea that they really believe in, and to put their own mark on something that will make a substantive contribution to the company. They enjoy the security of the company and, while frustrated with the bureaucracy, they identify with the organization. They have a healthy cynicism about many of the systems within the company, but also appreciate the need to be politically savvy. Just as important is the motivation of an entrepreneur's sponsor. One observer has argued that the sponsor "is motivated not by personal ambition but by a desire to serve the corporation and an admiration for the maverick's way of operating" (Pinchot, 1985, p. 150).

The corporate context finds the entrepreneur with a number of conflicting pressures that must be balanced. One of the key conflicts concerns time. Corporate entrepreneurs are self-driven, with self-imposed timelines and performance benchmarks.

Yet the timeline for moving a project through to completion is almost always at odds with the normal monthly, quarterly, and annual performance review cycles of the corporation. The development cycle of an entrepreneurial project can be anywhere from two to ten or more years. The challenge becomes one of (a) performing satisfactorily on the normal performance measures, while (b) meeting one's own goals for project development and completion, and (c) ensuring that one's own goals exceed anything that senior management would ever have expected.

In a related vein, measures of the entrepreneur's performance may not be as clear-cut in a corporation. In a start-up context, there are numerous readily identifiable and visible performance measures. A business is established, jobs are created, sales levels and profits are achieved, and investors receive a rate of return. With the corporation, if the innovation is a product or service, although there are sales and profit measures to assess, many factors beyond the entrepreneur's control affect these measures. For instance, sales revenue may be influenced by the performance of other products in the company's line, and by levels of sales and marketing support. Profits are affected by the costs that are allocated to the product or service. When the innovation is a process, performance measures might relate to cost savings, shortened operating cycles, improved customer service levels, or some other indicator. The key for corporate entrepreneurs is to identify performance measures that they can influence, build these into their plans, and track performance along the way.

Start-up entrepreneurs like to think of themselves as their own boss. Technically, they are. However, they frequently have other stockholders or partners to whom they are accountable, and they may also be beholden to financiers, suppliers, and distributors. The corporate context finds entrepreneurs with a different set of masters. They report to a boss, but are also accountable to their sponsors and to any of the senior managers whose departments have lent support along the way. If part of a team in a matrix-type structure, entrepreneurs have to be concerned about the senior executives in all the areas represented on the team.

Because they stay in a company instead of going it alone, one might expect corporate entrepreneurs to be fairly risk averse. This is not the case. As the company is effectively assuming much of the risk that surrounds the concept, the entrepreneur might actually tend to take greater risks. It is the company's money to lose, but the entrepreneur's job that is at stake. However, few companies fire people because they try something entrepreneurial and fail. It is far more likely that they try something entrepreneurial, get frustrated because of the resistance and obstacles within the company, and leave on their own. The reality is that corporate entrepreneurs are moderate risk-takers. They tend to first look at a situation carefully and identify all the associated risk factors (customer, competitor, financial, political, job-related, etc.). They then develop strategies for managing or mitigating the risks. They also craft approaches for communicating the risks and their risk management strategy to key managers within the company. This is a critical element for success. The risks must be positioned in a way that fits the general risk profile of the company, and is politically acceptable.

One of the most daunting tasks confronting senior executives, based on the differences encountered in larger firms, involves creating a sense of autonomy and ownership in an environment where the employee may actually have relatively little of each. This is a theme to which we will return in the chapters to come. No one action or program will accomplish this task. It requires a well-crafted mix of decision variables, including company structure, planning approaches, control systems, reward and appraisal systems, internal communication styles, employee training programs, and aspects of the company culture.

In the end, the challenge of getting employees to act on their entrepreneurial potential may not be as difficult as retaining employees who have been entrepreneurial. In our work with successful corporate entrepreneurs, we frequently ask them why they do not quit and start their own ventures. Their responses are directly related to the differences we have previously noted. The three most common answers are:

- The resource base that I can tap into

- The potential to operate on a fairly significant scope and scale fairly quickly

- The security I enjoy when operating in an existing company

We also ask them why they would leave. This question produces a variety of responses, but organizational politics always features highly.

Thus, it becomes critical that senior management create environments where employees have a sense that resources can be accessed if an idea is sound and they are willing to fight for it. Further, management must find ways to reinforce the ability of anyone in the company to champion an idea and get it implemented corporate-wide in a reasonable time span. In addition, they must invest in the development of people. There is little sense of security if companies are less loyal to their employees and employees are less loyal to their companies. Table 2-3 provides some general guidelines for managers as they attempt to move a company in this direction. The lesson learned from entrepreneurial firms like Southwest Airlines is that traditional priorities must be turned upside down—that firms must invest in employees first, understand that value creation for customers then follows, and then recognize that productive employees and satisfied customers will create more wealth for stockholders.

TABLE 2-3

Rules for Fostering an Innovative Organization

Rule #1 – Unreasonable Expectations
- Only when people subscribe to unreasonable goals will they start searching for breakthrough ideas.
- There are no mature industries, only mature managers who unthinkingly accept someone else's definition of what is possible.

Rule #2 – Elastic Business Definition
- Too many companies define themselves by what they do rather than by what they know (core competencies) and what they own (strategic assets).

Rule #3 – A Cause, Not a Business
- Revolutionaries draw much of their strength from their allegiance to a cause that goes beyond growth, profits, or even personal wealth accumulation.
- The courage to leave some of oneself behind and strike out for parts unknown comes not from some assurance that "change is good" but from a devotion to a wholly worthwhile cause.

Rule #4 – New Voices
- Let the youth be heard.
- Listen to the periphery.
- Let newcomers have their say.

Rule #5 – An Open Market for Ideas
- Create a market for entrepreneurial ideas inside your company.
- New ideas are the currency of the realm.

Rule #6 – Create an Open Market for Capital
- Within a corporation, why set the hurdle for accessing a small investment for the purpose of funding an unconventional idea, building a prototype, or designing a market trial at the same difficulty as obtaining a large investment in an irreversible, existing business?

Rule #7 – Open a Market for Talent
- "A" people work on "A" opportunities.
- Provide incentives for employees who are willing to take a "risk" on something out of the ordinary.

Rule #8 – Low-Risk Experimentation
- Being revolutionary does not mean being a high-risk taker.
- False dichotomy: Cautious follower vs. high-risk taker. Neither is likely to pay off in the age of revolution.

SOURCE: Adapted from Gary Hamel, *Leading the Revolution*, Boston, MA: Harvard Business School Press, 2000.

Where to Find Entrepreneurship within a Company

Entrepreneurship can be manifested in many ways in an established company. For instance, it can come from above, from below, or from separate units. Thus, senior management could chart a bold new strategic direction for the company, such as the decision by Target, a major discount retailer, to move into designer fashions, or the decision by Walt Disney Company to purchase Pixar and the development of Disney Animation Studios to innovate in the digital media market. Alternatively, entrepreneurship can be the result of initiatives from below. An employee has an idea for a radically improved approach to getting products to distribution points on time, a way to make money selling add-on services to customers, or an idea for a product line extension. Then again, the source of the entrepreneurship could be a separate department or unit that has been set up for the explicit purpose of innovating. The creation of the New Ventures Division at Procter & Gamble would be a case in point.

Taken a step further, and building on the early work of Schollhammer (1982), we can identify seven major ways in which entrepreneurship is fostered in established firms (see Table 2-4). The first of these can be termed **traditional R&D**. Many companies have a department staffed by people who are technically qualified that works on improving existing products and developing new ones. It is not always called Research & Development, but the focus is usually on technical advancements and overcoming technical obstacles. The work is research-based and any number of projects are underway at a given

---

TABLE 2-4

Seven Ways in Which Entrepreneurship Is Manifested in Established Companies

Traditional R&D
"Leave it to the technical guys"

Ad Hoc Venture Teams
"Here's the concept, the budget, and a deadline—go to it"

New Venture Divisions or Groups
"We want a factory for breakthrough concepts"

Champions and the Mainstream
"It's up to everyone, including you"

Acquisitions
"We can buy growth and obtain the products, markets, and technologies of others"

Outsourcing
"Let's have someone else develop it for us, and then we'll make the money"

Hybrid Forms
"Mix and match the other approaches to fit our context"

time. These projects are usually closely tied to the current strategic direction of the company. Some may represent bold new concepts, while others are replications of achievements by other firms. In essence, it becomes the job of this department to produce the new products, making it easy for everyone else in the company to escape responsibility for innovation.

A second approach is the **ad hoc venture team**. Senior management commits to an opportunity, or finds itself needing to respond to an impending competitive threat. They put together a team of employees, charge them with coming up with a specific innovation, and set them up autonomously, out of the corporate mainstream. Team members often come from diverse parts of the company, and some may come from outside. The venture team usually has more freedom and flexibility, and does not have to operate within many of the standard systems and procedures that govern the rest of the company. They may be given ample financial resources, but a demanding timeline for project completion. A case in point is the venture team that developed Apple's original Macintosh computer. Trying to quickly change the way computers were viewed, Apple's CEO Steve Jobs located the team away from the corporate headquarters and gave them a very clear mission and a very tight deadline. The Macintosh team even flew a pirate flag (skull and crossbones) to signify their maverick approach. Such teams tend to be good at accomplishing the specific mission, but not at producing sustained entrepreneurship.

A number of firms have taken the venture team concept a step further, and created **new venture divisions**. Here, a permanent unit is established where the objective is breakthrough innovation and the creation of entirely new markets. In a sense, the division or group is a kind of incubator where bold new ventures can be formulated and brought to life. By separating this division from the rest of the company, the theory is that traditional assumptions relied on within the firm's normal operations will be abandoned, including assumptions about customers, products, distribution, costs, technology, and competitors. While the types of innovations produced will typically reflect the core capabilities of the company, the focus is on innovations that move the company in major new strategic directions. The new market opportunities must have huge market potential to be considered. One of the great challenges of these divisions lies in producing new products and services that will be supported by mainstream operating units once they are launched. That is, it can be quite difficult to get an operating division to adopt or take ownership of an initiative that they played no role in creating.

A major focus of this book is entrepreneurship that derives from **champions and the mainstream**. Here, it is recognized that entrepreneurship can originate from any person, level, or department in the organization. Employees recognize opportunity, develop innovative concepts, and then attempt to sell them to senior management.

They become "champions" and seek out higher level "sponsors." They beg and borrow resources, often relying on informal networks, exchanging favors, and doing considerable development work in secret, or at least prior to formal approval and support for the concept. In fact, many of these concepts are rejected multiple times by management, but the champion perseveres in keeping the idea alive and adapting it into a form management will accept.

Some companies prefer to achieve entrepreneurial growth through **acquisitions**, or purchasing other companies. A classic example is Cintas Corporation, a highly innovative supplier of uniforms in the workplace. They have become the dominant player in the industry through an aggressive acquisitions strategy. The key here is strategic fit, on making acquisitions that are related to the core competencies of the company, or on acquiring skills, technologies, and customers that complement the strategic direction of the company. The challenge for Cintas, an inherently entrepreneurial company, is to instill its values and culture in each new acquisition.

Rather than acquiring another firm, an increasing number of companies are buying some of the intellectual capital of other companies and individuals. In effect, they are **outsourcing innovation**. For some, this is a realistic path simply because of the significant infrastructure and personnel cost associated with having the necessary in-house capabilities. For others, it is more about timing and speed. The rapid pace of technological change, the parallel and complementary technological advances that are happening in many fields, and the difficulty in making substantive progress on a whole array of projects at the same time, find the company relying on others. They either acquire the rights to the invention, or effectively pay someone else to develop it while retaining ownership.

Lastly, any number of **hybrid approaches** are possible. The reality is that organizations are experimenting today in attempts to spur entrepreneurial performance. Even within the six approaches we have described, one will find considerable variance across firms. An example of a hybrid approach would be the company that tries the new venture division approach, but instead of having just one corporate-level new venture division, it attaches new venture divisions to each of the major units within the company. Alternatively, one might find champions within the mainstream who are empowered to outsource some of the new product development work as they move a project through to completion.

These various approaches to corporate entrepreneurship are likely to produce different kinds of outcomes. While there is no clear empirical evidence, we can make some general propositions. For example, the traditional R&D approach will often have a strong technology-push orientation (see Chapter 8 for further discussion of this concept), suggesting projects are undertaken that result in technically superior products for which the market may not have sufficient need, at least at the present time. Many R&D departments are better at invention than at entrepreneuring, suggesting they too often produce inventions that are "commercially challenged." The degree of innovativeness is also likely to vary across these approaches. Bolder breakthroughs would seem more likely from new venture groups and traditional R&D, while the mainstream might produce more incremental innovation, with ad hoc teams and outsourcing somewhere in between. Speed of innovation is an especially interesting issue. The performance record of many R&D departments and new venture groups suggests they are not all that timely in terms of getting projects completed and ready for launch. Alternatively, ad hoc venture teams, outsourcing, and champions in the mainstream are likely to produce faster results. While this is just conjecture, it suggests that senior management have a realistic set of goals and performance expectations as it decides to implement a given approach. There is also no reason that all of the approaches listed could not be operating in a given company, with differing roles and performance standards established for each.

General Frameworks for Understanding Corporate Entrepreneurship

This chapter has emphasized the unique nature of corporate entrepreneurship. Yet to be a meaningful concept in an established company, entrepreneurship must be woven into the basic fabric of the firm. Toward this end, a variety of integrative frameworks or models have been developed to aid our understanding of entrepreneurship as an organization-wide phenomenon. Together they help paint a picture of the kinds of factors that must come together for entrepreneurship to happen.

A DOMAIN FRAMEWORK

Guth and Ginsberg (1990) provided one of the first frameworks for integrating corporate entrepreneurship into the strategic management of a company (see Figure 2-1). They argue that the domain of corporate entrepreneurship encompasses two types of processes: **internal innovation**, or venturing through the creation of new businesses within existing organizations, and **strategic renewal**, or the design of corporate initiatives that transform organizations. Further, the extent to which corporate entrepreneurship occurs and the ways in which it is manifested are driven by factors that can be organized into four domains. First is the external environment, as discussed in Chapter 1. Turbulence in external environments is a major driver of higher levels of entrepreneurship. Second is leadership within the company, and the extent to which leaders demonstrate certain characteristics (e.g., opportunity orientation, comfort with

FIGURE 2-1

Fitting Corporate Entrepreneurship into Strategic Management

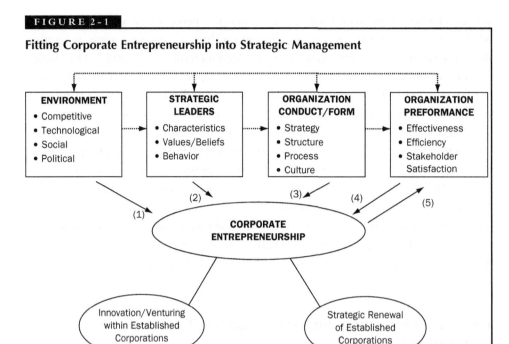

SOURCE: W. D. Guth and A. Ginsburg, "Corporate Entrepreneurship," *Strategic Management Journal,* 11 (Summer 1990): 5–15. Copyright John Wiley & Sons Limited. Reproduced with permission.

change), values (e.g., desire for achievement, competitiveness), and behaviors (e.g., risk taking and innovation). Third is aspects of the work environment inside the company, including company strategies, structures, processes, and cultures. And the final factor is company performance, and the extent to which performance drives and is driven by innovative behaviors.

A Sustaining Framework

An alternative framework can be found in the work of Kuratko et al. (2004). These researchers focus on an organization's ability to sustain entrepreneurship on an ongoing basis. They demonstrate that sustainability is contingent upon individual members of the organization continuing to undertake innovative activities and positive perceptions of these activities by the executive management, which will in turn lead to further allocation of necessary organizational support and resources. Figure 2-2 illustrates the key relationships that combine to produce ongoing entrepreneurship. The model demonstrates that a transformational trigger (something external or internal to the company that creates a threat or opportunity) initiates the need for strategic change.

FIGURE 2-2

A Model of Sustained Corporate Entrepreneurship

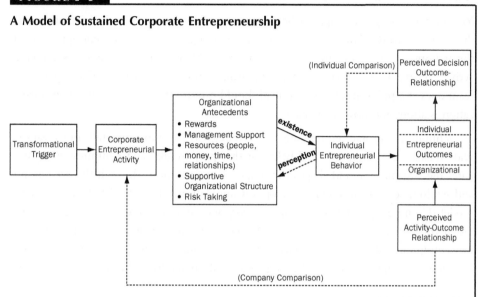

SOURCE: D. F. Kuratko, J. S. Hornsby, and M. G. Goldsby, "Sustaining Corporate Entrepreneurship: A Proposed Model of Perceived Implementation/Outcome Comparisons at the Organizational and Individual Levels," *International Journal of Entrepreneurship and Innovation*, 5(2) (May 2004): 77–79.

One way to accomplish this change is through entrepreneurial activity. This entrepreneurial activity (e.g., a new product or service or process) is driven by individuals within the company. Hence, the proposed model centers around the individual employee's decision to behave entrepreneurially. Sustained entrepreneurial activity is the result of the perception by the individual that several organizational antecedents are present, such as top management support, autonomy, rewards, resources, and flexible organizational boundaries. The outcomes realized from this entrepreneurial activity are then compared at both the individual and organizational level to previous expectations. Thus, entrepreneurial behavior will result when both the individual employee and the leadership of the company perceive that the outcomes are equitable, or that they meet or exceed expectations. Both parties must be satisfied with the outcomes or the amount of entrepreneurial activity will decline. Satisfaction with performance outcomes serves as a feedback mechanism for either sustaining the current strategy or selecting an alternative one. Individuals, as agents of strategic change, must also be satisfied with the intrinsic and extrinsic outcomes they receive for their entrepreneurial behavior. While it may be a "chicken-and-egg" question as to whether individual behavior or organizational strategy should change first, the model suggests that with any major strategic change, both are instrumental in making the change successful.

A STRATEGIC INTEGRATION FRAMEWORK

Yet another perspective approaches entrepreneurship as an overall orientation that drives a company. The focus here is the ongoing integration of entrepreneurship throughout the entire organization, which is very different than viewing it as a discrete activity or event or behavior. Entrepreneurship is not just something that a person or team does at a point in time, but instead should capture the essence of what an organization is about and how it operates.

Defining a corporate entrepreneurship strategy as "a vision-directed, organization-wide reliance on entrepreneurial behavior that purposefully and continuously rejuvenates the organization and shapes the scope of its operations through the recognition and exploitation of entrepreneurial opportunity," Ireland et al. (2009), developed a model (Figure 2-3) that illustrates how a corporate entrepreneurship strategy is manifested through the presence of three elements: an entrepreneurial strategic vision, a pro-entrepreneurship organizational architecture, and entrepreneurial processes and behavior as exhibited across the organizational hierarchy. This model has several

FIGURE 2-3

Strategic Integration of Entrepreneurship throughout the Organization

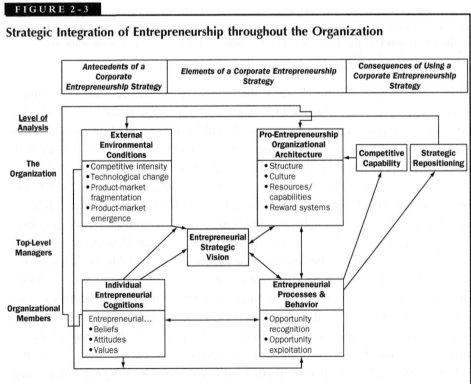

SOURCE: Adapted from R. D. Ireland, J. G. Covin, and D. F. Kuratko (2009), "Conceptualizing Corporate Entrepreneurship Strategy," *Entrepreneurship Theory and Practice*, 33(1): 19–46.

linkages, which include: (1) individual entrepreneurial cognitions of the organization's members, (2) external environmental conditions that invite entrepreneurial activity, (3) top management's entrepreneurial strategic vision for the company, (4) organizational architectures that encourage entrepreneurial processes and behavior, (5) the entrepreneurial processes that are reflected in entrepreneurial behavior, and (6) organizational outcomes that result from entrepreneurial actions.

The major thrust behind all of these frameworks is a revitalization of personal creativity, product and process innovation, and ongoing managerial development in companies. The strategies and insights presented in the models here can serve as a foundation for understanding the current increase in entrepreneurial action inside organizations. Further, they can guide the efforts of managers striving to create work environments that are supportive of the entrepreneurial spirit. In the chapters ahead, we will further investigate how to create such environments, while identifying specific ways in which corporate entrepreneurship can serve as the source of competitive advantage in companies.

THE INNOVATOR'S NOTEBOOK

The Challenge of Entrepreneurial Growth

For some companies, growth is about acquiring other firms. After all, if you can just buy a new business rather than developing it from the ground up, isn't that preferable? Not necessarily. Stories of failed acquisitions abound with causes ranging from mismatched cultures to misunderstood markets. Other firms prefer to achieve growth organically. This is growth achieved by applying entrepreneurship to the firm's core business. They grow new products internally, and their employees become intimately involved with products as they are developed. Even though R&D costs are incurred with entrepreneurial growth, companies gain a greater understanding of the processes involved with new product development, leading to greater innovation in the future.

Following are four examples of entrepreneurial companies that have achieved tremendous growth by pursuing the organic route.

Walmart

Walmart serves customers and members more than 200 million times per week at more than 8,400 retail units under 53 different banners in 15 countries. With fiscal year 2010 sales of $405 billion, Walmart employs more than 2.1 million employees worldwide. A leader in sustainability, corporate philanthropy, and employment opportunity, Walmart ranked first among retailers in Fortune Magazine's 2009 Most Admired Companies survey. When a company's annual revenue reaches $405 billion, growth becomes quite an accomplishment. To achieve growth entrepreneurially is downright amazing. So, how did Walmart manage to grow its sales to $405 billion in 2010? The answer is by diversifying. Walmart began to apply its mastery of supply chain, everyday low pricing, and strategic sourcing to other items such as groceries and home design décor and accessories. The company added 50 million square feet of space for the sale of food from 2000 to 2004, leading to food becoming its largest and fastest-growing category, representing a quarter of its total sales at super centers and almost a third at Sam's Clubs. In 2010, recognizing the need for families to upgrade their homes in the midst of a struggling economy, Walmart added a complete hometrends line of bedding, bath, dining, furniture, home décor, and accessories.

Best Buy

The Best Buy family of brands and partnerships collectively generates more than $45 billion in annual revenue. In an effort to thwart the advance of Walmart and other retailers, Best Buy has introduced new designs and brands that include Best Buy, Audiovisions, The Carphone Warehouse, Future Shop, Geek Squad, Jiangsu Five Star, Magnolia Audio Video, Napster, Pacific Sales, The Phone House, and Speakeasy. Approximately 155,000 employees bring these brands to customers through retail locations, multiple call centers and Web sites, in-home solutions, product delivery, and activities in its communities. The creation of the "Geek Squad," a group of repair and installation specialists that sets up new products for customers, has been heralded as a major success.

Sysco

With 2009 record sales of $37.5 billion, a 7.1 percent increase and record net earnings on $1.1 billion, a 13.1 percent increase (FY08), Sysco continues to be the global leader in the foodservice industry. Maintaining its customer service with its 51,000-person sales force, and developing private-label foods, Sysco focuses on the distribution of food and related products and services to restaurants, nursing homes, hospitals, hotels, motels, schools, colleges, cruise ships, sports parks, and summer camps—wherever a meal is prepared away from home.

Sysco provides a full spectrum of foodservice supplies and equipment to complement its broad food product offerings. Customers can receive everything they need for their operations, from sparkling front-of-the-house service ware to heavy-duty, back-of-the-house janitorial supplies and everything in between.

Walgreens

With 6,700 stores in 48 states, Walgreens took a major step in the healthcare sector by opening more than 715 convenient care clinics as well as 24-hour and drive-through pharmacies in order to have customers rely on Walgreens for their emergency pharmaceutical needs, which in turn has led to loyal customers. By strategically selecting sites for new locations and striving to make the shopping experience as convenient as possible, the company grew sales to $63.3 billion. Walgreens has realized that with managed care desensitizing customers to prescription price differences, the remedy for slowing growth is not lower prices, but improved service.

Discussion Questions

1. What entrepreneurial processes are evident with these four companies?

2. Can any of the "rules for fostering an innovative environment" (Table 2-3) be applied to any of these companies?

3. Describe clearly what form of entrepreneurship is being manifested in these companies. (Use Table 2-4.)

SOURCE: Adapted from "Big Firms, Big Growth," *Fortune Online*, May 31, 2004; and updated March 15, 2010 with each company's Web site: http://walmartstores.com/pressroom/news/9700.aspx; http://www.bby.com/2010/01/08/best-buys-december-revenue-grows-13-to-8-5-billion/; http://www.sysco.com/aboutus/aboutus.html; http://news.walgreens.com/article_display.cfm?article_id=1047

Summary and Conclusions

In this chapter, we have attempted to expand on the nature of entrepreneurship and how it applies in established organizations. The ability to apply entrepreneurship to mid-sized and large firms requires that we dispense with many of the myths and misconceptions that surround this phenomenon. A number of these misconceptions were discussed. The underlying need is to remove the mystique from both the entrepreneur as a person and the phenomenon of entrepreneurship as it occurs in practice. Entrepreneurship is not only about vision and insight, but also hard work, perseverance, and adaptability. Entrepreneurs themselves are ordinary people who, working through teams, create the new. Importantly, entrepreneurial potential is something that resides in each and every employee in a company. It has been argued that entrepreneurship is not limited to starting one's own business. It is about putting resources together in a unique way to exploit an opportunity. As such, entrepreneurship is a universal concept that can be applied in any organizational context. In fact, the business world is filled with start-up firms that are not especially entrepreneurial, and any number of large firms that are highly entrepreneurial.

The chapter explored the commonalities and differences between the start-up context and the larger, established corporate context. Large companies can learn a great deal from the experiences of start-up entrepreneurs. Sadly, too many corporate executives see their situation as far more sophisticated and complex than that of the start-up. Thus they close their minds to potential lessons regarding the ways in which small companies acquire and leverage resources, their guerrilla approaches to marketing and finance, the ways in which they structure themselves, their decision-making styles, their approaches to budgeting, and so forth.

At the same time, corporate entrepreneurs must operate in an environment filled with nuances and obstacles to which a start-up entrepreneur could not relate. Risks, rewards, ownership, security, vulnerability, bureaucracy, politics, and resources are all very different in a corporate context. Moreover, entrepreneurship takes a variety of unique forms in the corporation, and each of these forms poses its own distinct set of problems and opportunities for both the entrepreneur and the senior management of the company. In the final analysis, we can conclude that entrepreneurship in a company is like entrepreneurship in a start-up, only different.

It has also been emphasized that entrepreneurship occurs as a function of the interactions among a number of key variables. Three frameworks were provided for understanding the unique nature of entrepreneurship when it happens inside an established organization. The reality is that entrepreneurship in corporations takes many forms and manifests itself in many ways. Moreover, companies can differ significantly in terms of how entrepreneurial they are. This last point, which is concerned with the variable nature of entrepreneurship, will be the subject of our attention in the next chapter.

References

Block, Z., and Macmillan, I. C. 1993. *Corporate Venturing: Creating New Businesses within the Firm* (Boston: Harvard Business School Press).

Covin, J. G., and Kuratko, D. F., 2010. "The Concept of Corporate Entrepreneurship," in Vadake K. Narayanan and Gina C. O'Connor (eds.) *The Blackwell Encyclopedia of Technology and Innovation Management* (UK: West Sussex, Wiley Publishers), 207–213.

Covin, J. G., and Miles, M. P. 1999. "Corporate Entrepreneurship and the Pursuit of Competitive Advantage," *Entrepreneurship Theory and Practice*, 23(3): 47–64.

Covin, J. G., and Slevin, D. P. 1991. "A Conceptual Model of Entrepreneurship as Firm Behavior," *Entrepreneurship Theory and Practice*, 16(1): 7–26.

Gartner, W. B. 1990. "What Are We Talking About When We Talk About Entrepreneurship?" *Journal of Business Venturing*, 5: 15–28.

Guth, W. D., and Ginsberg, A. 1990. "Corporate Entrepreneurship," *Strategic Management Journal* (special issue) 11: 5–15.

Hamel, G. 2000. *Leading the Revolution* (Boston: Harvard Business School Press).

Ireland, R. D., Covin, J. G., and Kuratko, D. F. 2009. "Conceptualizing Corporate Entrepreneurship Strategy," *Entrepreneurship Theory and Practice*, 33(1): 19–46.

Kuratko, D. F. 2009a. *Entrepreneurship: Theory, Process and Practice*, 8th ed. (Mason, OH: Cengage/South-Western Publishers): 30–33.

Kuratko, D. F. 2009b. "The Entrepreneurial Imperative of the 21st Century," *Business Horizons*, 52(5): 421–428.

Kuratko, D. F., Hornsby, J. S., and Goldsby, M. G. 2004. "Sustaining Corporate Entrepreneurship: A Proposed Model of Perceived Implementation/Outcome Comparisons at the Organizational and Individual Levels," *International Journal of Entrepreneurship and Innovation*, 5(2): 77–89.

Morris, M. H. 1998. *Entrepreneurial Intensity* (Westport, CT: Quorum Book).

Morris, M.H., Kuratko, D.F., and Schindehutte, M. 2001. "Understanding Entrepreneurship Through Frameworks," *International Journal of Entrepreneurship and Innovation*, 2(1): 35–49.

Pinchot, III, G. 1985. *Intrapreneuring* (New York: Harper and Row).

Schollhammer, H. 1982. "Internal Corporate Entrepreneurship," in Kent, C. A., Sexton, D. L., and Vesper, K. H. (eds.) *Encyclopedia of Entrepreneurship*. (Englewood Cliffs, NJ: Prentice-Hall), 209–229.

Sharma, P., and Chrisman, J. J. 1999. "Toward a Reconciliation of the Definitional Issues in the Field of Corporate Entrepreneurship," *Entrepreneurship Theory and Practice*, 23(3): 11–28.

Timmons, J. A., and Spinelli, S. 2007. *New Venture Creation: Entrepreneurship for the 21st Century*, 7th ed. (New York: McGraw Hill Irwin).

Zahra, S. A., Jennings, D. F., and Kuratko, D. F., 1999. "Corporate Entrepreneurship in a Global Economy," *Entrepreneurship Theory and Practice*, 24(1): 5–8.

CHAPTER 3

LEVELS OF ENTREPRENEURSHIP IN ORGANIZATIONS: ENTREPRENEURIAL INTENSITY

Introduction

What does it mean to characterize an organization as "entrepreneurial"? We make the mistake of thinking in either–or terms, as in "that's an entrepreneurial firm, while that one is not." However, entrepreneurship is not something an organization either has or does not have; it is a variable. There is some level of entrepreneurship in every organization. Even in the largest, most staid and conservative companies, elements of entrepreneurial behavior can be found somewhere in the firm. Within the most bureaucratic government organizations, one can find highly entrepreneurial people. The question becomes one of determining how entrepreneurial a given organization is. The answer to this question lies in the three underlying dimensions of entrepreneurship: *innovativeness*, *risk-taking*, and *proactiveness*. Let us explore each of these dimensions in greater detail.

Exploring the Dimensions of Entrepreneurship

INNOVATIVENESS

The first dimension that characterizes an entrepreneurial organization is innovativeness. Here, the concern is with the relative emphasis on concepts or activities that represent a departure from what is currently available. Simply stated, to what extent is the company doing things that are novel, unique, or different?

A range, or continuum, of possibilities exists (see Figure 3-1). Does the concept address a need that has not previously been addressed, as the first laser surgical tool did? Does it change the way one goes about addressing a need, as the original fax machine or the microwave oven did? Is it a dramatic improvement over conventional solutions, as the cellular telephone or the electric automobile were? Does it represent a minor modification or improvement to an existing product, as a longer lasting light bulb or less fattening dessert product do? Is it just the geographic transfer of a proven product, such as the sale of frozen yogurt in a country where the product is unknown?

In addition to these product examples, innovation can take the form of new or improved services. The tremendous growth of the service sector is a testimonial to the

FIGURE 3-1

A Range of Options: Innovativeness as it Applies to Products and Services

New to the World Products/Services

⇑

New to the Market Products/Services

⇑

New Product/Service Lines in a Company

⇑

Additions to Product/Service Lines

⇑

Product Improvements/Revisions

⇑

New Applications for Existing Products/Services

⇑

Repositioning of Existing Products/Services

⇑

Cost Reductions for Existing Products/Services

entrepreneurial spirit at work. Google, Facebook, Jet Blue, MSNBC, 3-Com, E★Trade, Jani-King, and Servpro represent just a few of the thousands of successful entrepreneurial service concepts. In fact, given their intangible nature and the ease with which they can be replicated, services lend themselves to continuous innovation and improvement. American Express is an excellent example of a company that is continually looking for service line extensions, modifications, and enhancements.

The third innovation frontier is in processes, or finding new and better ways to accomplish a task or function (see Table 3-1). Many entrepreneurial ventures offer products that are fairly standard and certainly not unique. However, they have come up with highly innovative process innovations that are a major source of competitive advantage (i.e., they result in lower costs, faster operations, more rapid delivery, improved quality, or better customer service). Examples include innovative production techniques, distribution approaches, selling methods, purchasing programs, and administrative systems. Consider the novel hub-and-spoke transport system used by Federal Express to provide quick and dependable overnight parcel delivery service, or the highly inventive production techniques mastered by Nucor that result in high quality and affordable specialty-grade steel produced in a minimill.

Companies today find that they must innovate more than in times past. Much of the pressure to innovate is due to external forces, including the emergence of new and improved technologies, the globalization of markets (resulting in intensified

---

TABLE 3-1

A Range of Options: Innovativeness as It Applies to Processes

Degree of Innovation	Type of Process
Major new process	Administrative systems
	Service delivery systems
Minor new process	Production methods
	Financing methods
Significant revision of existing process	Marketing or sales approaches
	Procurement techniques
Modest improvement to existing process	Compensation methods
	Supply chain management techniques
	Distribution methods
	Employee training programs
	Pricing approaches
	Information management systems
	Customer support programs
	Logistical approaches
	Hiring methods

---

competitive pressures), the fragmentation of markets (resulting in intensified customer pressures), government deregulation, and dramatic social change. Financial markets are actually penalizing companies who fail to demonstrate an effective innovation strategy. However, internal pressures exist as well, including pressures to cut costs and develop new capabilities. One of the great internal challenges facing companies in the twenty-first century concerns the ability to attract and retain high-quality employees. Employees are attracted to companies that are experimenting, trying new things, and continually learning.

The push for more innovation manifests itself in a variety ways. The most obvious manifestation is an increase in the number of innovation projects underway within a company at a given point in time. We will expand on this pattern in Chapter 8 when the concept of the innovation portfolio is introduced. Companies are also finding they must become faster, with pressure to significantly reduce the time from idea generation to innovation launch. The ability to innovate more extensively and at a faster rate increasingly requires that more departments and functional areas within the firm become heavily involved in the innovation process. All of this suggests the need for greater innovation-relevant resource commitments, including people, money, time, facilities, and equipment.

Less clear is the impact of heightened innovation activity on success rates. On the one hand, companies might expect that the more they innovate, the better they will get at it. On the other hand, if the innovative activity is performed in product, market, or technology domains that are not well understood by the firm, there may be no reason to expect that future innovative initiatives will be any more successful than past ones. Still, maximizing innovation success rates may be less important to the long-term competitiveness of companies than minimizing the costs of innovation failures. Managing the downside risks of innovative initiatives is, thus, an innovation management imperative—one that is often met, for example, by making resource commitments in stages rather than all at once and by establishing milestones in conjunction with project termination policies that are invoked if interim targets are not reached during the initiative's development.

If innovation were simple or cheap, companies would do a lot more of it. The irony is that companies actually resist something that is so vital to their futures. For too many firms, the tendency is to innovate only when in trouble or in response to a competitor move. Some of this tendency can be traced to the adage "If it ain't broke, don't fix it," so managers focus their efforts on maximizing the success of proven products, services, or processes in the face of immediate competitive threats. Innovation is about tomorrow while managers are concerned with the here and now. But at a deeper level, innovation is an activity that challenges many of the basic principles of management.

Consider the expression "management of innovation." It might be construed as an oxymoron, or contradiction in terms. Management implies control, while innovation is about the unknown and is often unpredictable. How does a manager control the unknown? Quite simply, he or she does not. While this is not to say that innovation cannot be managed, it does suggest that traditional approaches to management may not apply. In fact, innovations represent departures from the past, meaning they often break with established rules and challenge traditional ways of thinking and doing. The reality is that a corporate entrepreneur must break rules to accomplish innovation in many firms. This creates a dilemma, in that employees who regularly break rules typically do not last long in most companies.

In fact, innovation poses a large number of dilemmas for corporate managers, as illustrated in Table 3-2. For example, innovations can make existing products obsolete, including possibly some of the company's own successful products. Because of this, and the tendency for new products to receive a greater share of production, marketing, and distribution resources, many inside the firm have an incentive to resist innovation. Another dilemma considers the extent to which the firm is first to market. There is a

---

TABLE 3-2

Sixteen Dilemmas of Innovation

1. Not all entrepreneurs are innovators, and not all innovators are entrepreneurs, but successful entrepreneurship tends to involve continued innovation (in products, services, and processes/methods).

2. Innovation is about the unknown. Management is about control. How do you control the unknown?

3. Innovation is often about breaking the rules. People who break rules don't last long in organizations.

4. Successful innovation tends to occur when there are constraints, routines, and deadlines. There is a need for both freedom and discipline, and the issue is one of balance.

5. Failure is likely if the firm does not innovate. But the more the firm innovates, the more it fails.

6. An innovation succeeds because it addresses customer needs. Yet when you ask customers about their needs, many do not know or cannot describe them to you except in very general terms.

7. Innovating can be risky. Not innovating can be more risky.

8. Innovation can be revolutionary or evolutionary. The costs, risks, and returns of both types differ, and both require different structures and management styles.

9. A company that innovates is frequently making its own products obsolete when there was still profit potential in those products.

10. Innovation requires supporting infrastructure to be successful, and the existing infrastructure is often inadequate. However, these infrastructure needs may not become apparent until after the innovation is developed.

11. While innovation is more technically complex and costly today, many break-through innovations do not come from large companies or corporate R&D labs with sizeable budgets, but from individual inventors and entrepreneurs.

12. People who design innovations typically seek to perfect their new product or service, making it the best possible. But the marketplace often wants it to be "good enough," not perfect. The additional time and money necessary to make the innovation the "best possible" drive up prices beyond what the customer will pay, and result in missed opportunity.

13. Technology-driven innovation often leads to dramatic new products that prove to be "better mousetraps" nobody wants. Customer-driven innovation often leads to minor modifications to existing products or "me-too" products meeting a competitive brick wall.

14. While frequently assumed to be associated with genius or brilliance, innovation is more often a function of persistence.

15. While innovation is sometimes associated with breaking the rules of the game (e.g., 3M), it frequently entails playing an entirely different game (e.g., Starbucks, Dell).

16. Being first to market is not consistently associated with success, while being second or third is not consistently associated with failure.

first-mover advantage in many markets, but the first mover also frequently makes the most critical mistakes. The firm that is reasonably quick, but a second- or third-mover firm, has a chance of ultimately being the winner. The evidence is quite mixed with regard to which firms will ultimately succeed or fail in a new product category.

There is also the dilemma of control. Innovation works because employees are given a level of freedom, autonomy, and discretion. That is, there is a degree of flexibility in terms of rules, budgets, controls, and processes. At the same time, successful innovation often occurs where there is pressure, deadlines, routines, and operating constraints. In fact, breakthroughs often do not come from large research laboratories with sizeable budgets, but from individuals and smaller entrepreneurial units operating under much tougher limitations.

A number of researchers have attempted to characterize the "best practices" of companies that seem to be especially good at innovation. That is, what are the things that these firms do that seem to make a difference? Let us consider the results of two major studies of the determinants of innovation success.

Synectics, a leading international firm specializing in innovation consulting, studied the innovation practices and performance of 150 major U.S. companies (Synectics, 1993). The analysis produced three categories of firms: Stars, Seekers, and Spectators. Stars were high-performing companies that had successfully integrated innovation and creativity into their daily business practices. Seekers were companies that displayed a number of appropriate innovation practices, but came up short in terms of innovation performance and company-wide commitment to innovation. Spectators tended to acknowledge the importance of innovation but provided little support for it. They shunned formal programs for innovation and were reluctant to seek outside ideas and perspectives.

Stars had a number of characteristics that distinguished them from the other two groups, and Synectics concluded that a number of them were critical for sustained innovation. These characteristics included the following:

- Having CEOs who were heavily involved in fostering innovation
- Defining innovation as critical to long-term company success
- Attaching great importance to the concept of managing change
- Having the words *innovation* and *creativity* in the mission statement
- Demonstrating an openness to outside ideas
- Having formal programs for idea generation and problem solving
- Placing strong emphasis on cross-functional communications
- Implementing programs to encourage employees to talk to customers

- Increasing levels of investment in R&D and a strong focus on product development
- Creating budgets allocated exclusively to innovation
- Providing rewards for individual creativity and innovation
- Spending time in meetings that were highly productive

The companies that were Stars also tended to outperform the other firms not only in terms of sales and profit growth, but in such areas as employee satisfaction, employee retention, and product/service quality.

A separate study was conducted under the auspices of the Product Development and Management Association (Page, 1993). Their "Best Practices Survey" attempted to establish norms across companies in the new product development area. Table 3-3 highlights some of the key findings. Among other insights, the results indicated a tendency to have a formal innovation strategy, rely heavily on cross-functional teams, and use formal criteria to measure new product performance. Additional noteworthy findings included the fact that firms anticipated on average that they would introduce 20 new products over the next five years, while the new product success rate approximated 58 percent. For every 11 ideas that entered the new product development process, one product was successfully launched. Just over half the budget spent on new product development was spent on products that proved to be successful.

The Product Development and Management Association's "Best Practices Survey" has been updated several times since the original data collection effort, with the most recent results reported in 2009 (Barczak, Griffin, and Kahn, 2009). A particularly informative aspect of the most recent survey is the presentation of comparative results that differentiate *"The Best"* innovators from *"The Rest."* In this survey, the *Best* firms were identified as those (1) most successful or in the top third of their industry's success rate for new product development initiatives and above the mean for the overall sample in terms of (2) reported innovation program, success rates and (3) percentage of sales and profits generated from recently introduced products. The *Rest* firms were those that failed to meet these three criteria.

Results of the comparative analysis yielded several striking distinctions. In particular, the *Best* firms were significantly more likely than the *Rest* firms to have their new product development efforts guided by a formal new product strategy. This result suggests the importance of treating innovation as a rules- and discipline-based activity, as opposed to a random, chaotic, or unknowable process. A second distinction is that the *Best* firms were almost twice as likely as the *Rest* firms to pursue a "first-to-market" innovation strategy (49.5 percent of the *Best* firms versus 26.3 percent of the *Rest* firms). Thus, despite the inherent risks and uncertainties associated with product-market pioneering

TABLE 3-3

Findings of the PDMA Best Innovation Practices Study

In one of the major benchmarking studies of corporate innovation in American companies, the Product Development Management Association (PDMA) surveyed 189 large
companies that are active product innovators. Below are some of their more notable
findings.

1. Over 76 percent of the responding companies now use multidisciplinary teams to
   develop new products.
2. Only 56.4 percent of the companies had a specific new product strategy; only
   54.5 percent had a well-defined new product development process; 32.8 percent
   had neither.
3. It takes the average company in the study 2.95 years to develop innovative types
   of new products.
4. Formal financial criteria to measure the performance of new products are developed by 76 percent of the companies.
5. Having insufficient resources is the most frequently mentioned obstacle to successful product development.
6. Companies are developing one successful new product for every 11 new product
   ideas or concepts they consider.
7. Over a recent five-year period, the companies introduced an average of 37.5 new
   products, whereas the median was 12.
8. The companies achieved a success rate of 58 percent of the products they introduced during the recent five-year period.
9. The companies spent 52 percent of their new product expenditures on new
   products that were financially successful.
10. Thirty-two percent of company sales came from new products introduced during
    the previous five years.

SOURCE: A. L. Page, "Assessing New Product Development Practices and Performance:
Establishing Crucial Norms," *Journal of Product Innovation Management*, 10 (1993): 273–290.
Reprinted with permission of John Wiley and Sons.

efforts, nearly half the innovation leaders across a wide variety of industries embraced an
early-mover approach to innovation. A final noteworthy distinction between the *Best*
and the *Rest* is that the former firms were significantly more likely than the latter to
have a higher percentage of radical and next-generation innovation projects (versus
incremental and line-extension projects) in their overall project portfolios. Collectively,
these results suggest that innovation leaders—at least those focused on new product efforts—manifest a bold yet structured approach to innovation activity. Their innovation
efforts are strategy-driven, targeted, purposeful, and, in general, formalized to an extent
not observed in their less-successful counterparts.

Further insights on innovation success can be found in the anecdotal observations of such respected commentators as Gary Hamel (2000), Tom Peters (1997), and Thomas Kuczmarski et al. (2001). Based on their consulting interactions with large cross-sections of companies, these authors reinforce many of the findings previously cited. They also note a tendency for highly innovative companies to manage a portfolio of innovations and to have a systematic and well-defined new product development process. These authors emphasize that highly innovative companies are customer-centered as well as employee-centered. Additionally, the most innovative companies take the entire business concept (or value-creating package) as the starting point for innovation, rather than just a product or service. Employees in these firms demonstrate a passion for innovation and exhibit a clear focus on well-defined innovation objectives.

As a final comment on the matter of innovation success, it should be noted that the type of innovation being performed has great implications for the likely success rate. For example, the PDMA studies cited above have consistently reported innovation success rate figures for new products of about 60 percent. However, most new products commercialized by firms are not radically different from those firms' existing products. One might expect that the less related a new product is to the firm's existing products, the less likely the new product innovation will be successful. Data tend to confirm this possibility. In a recent study of 145 internal corporate ventures, Kuratko, Covin, and Garrett (2009) reported that corporate managers rated 36.6 percent of their venturing initiatives as successful, 18.2 percent as marginal, 16.1 percent as unsuccessful, and 29.4 percent as impossible to evaluate (due to the venture being too young to judge, the presence of "mixed" results data, etc.). While internal corporate ventures may be established to commercialize new products for a corporation, they also represent new *businesses* for the corporation and, as such, are diversifying the corporation into arenas where the firm's prior knowledge and competencies may not be highly transferable. The novelty inherent to managing truly new businesses may account for internal corporate ventures having lower success rates than those typically associated with new product innovations.

RISK-TAKING

Our second dimension of an entrepreneurial orientation is risk-taking. Anything new involves risk, or some likelihood that actual results will differ from expectations. Risk-taking involves a willingness to pursue opportunities that have a reasonable likelihood of producing losses or significant performance discrepancies. Approached in terms of loss, a given course of action is riskier depending upon both the probability of loss and magnitude of loss. So the launch of a new product or entry into a new market might be only moderately risky if the probability of loss is small, but the magnitude of loss is large.

The emphasis in corporate entrepreneurship is not on extreme, uncontrollable risks, but instead on the risks that are moderate and calculated. Entrepreneurship does not entail reckless decision making. It involves a reasonable awareness of the risks involved—including financial, technical, market, and personal—and an attempt to manage these risks. These risks are reflected in the various resource allocation decisions made by an individual or organization, as well as in the choice of products, services, and markets to be emphasized. Risk-taking can thus be viewed as both an individual-level trait, as well as an organization-level concept.

An interesting perspective on calculated risk-taking is provided by Hamel and Prahalad (1994). They use the analogy of the baseball player who comes to bat, concentrating intently on perfecting his or her swing, and strives to hit a home run. Further, the batter is preoccupied with his or her batting average. Obviously, if he or she comes to bat only twice and gets a hit on one of those occasions, the result is a .500 batting average. Unfortunately, companies often approach the development of new products, services, and technologies as does our baseball player. They pursue few projects, rely on cautious, "go-slow" strategies that aim to perfect the concept, and hold off on introduction until they are certain they have a major winner. Meanwhile, scrappier competitors move quickly and beat them to the punch.

Successful hits are a function of both one's batting average and the number of times one comes to bat. The message is that entrepreneurs and entrepreneurial companies need to come to bat more often. Risks are better managed by focusing on frequent, lower-risk market incursions with a variety of new product and service options or by pursuing higher-risk (with commensurately higher reward potential) product and service initiatives that are terminated quickly if favorable intermediate results are not realized. By engaging in lots of experiments, test markets, and trial runs, the entrepreneur is better able to determine what works and what does not. Such quickened learning may come at the expense of minor failures, but it is also likely to ensure more sustainable long-term success.

One might be tempted to assume that innovativeness and risk-taking are directly correlated, that doing more innovative things means taking higher risks and vice versa. In reality, the relationship may be more complex, as shown in Figure 3-2. Here the relationship is shown as a curvilinear function. As can be seen, risk is high when the company ignores new product and service opportunities, and engages in little to no innovation. Companies that do not innovate are faced with higher risk of market and technology shifts that are capitalized on by competitors. But risk is also high when companies take the opposite track, and attempt to come up with breakthrough innovations that create new markets and redefine industries. In Figure 3-2 this is referred to as a "home run" strategy. In between these two endpoints is the Hamel and

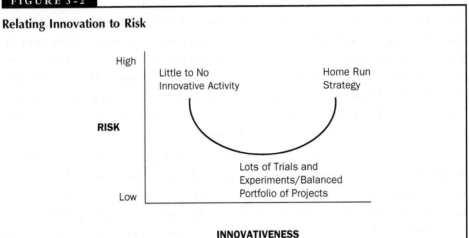

FIGURE 3-2

Relating Innovation to Risk

Prahalad strategy previously discussed. Risk is lower and more manageable when lots of trials and experiments are regularly pursued; in effect, a balanced portfolio of innovation projects is being managed. We shall further investigate the concept of an "innovation portfolio" in Chapter 8.

Moreover, the level of risk being assumed by a company will vary greatly with the type of innovation being considered. With respect to product innovation, for example, a distinction can be drawn among four innovation types, as follows:

Discontinuous innovation—a breakthrough innovation. It usually results in products or services that address a need that has not been addressed before or that change the way customers go about addressing a need. The integrated circuit, cellular telephone, and microwave oven were discontinuous innovations when first introduced.

Dynamically continuous innovation—a dramatic improvement over the existing state-of-the-art solution. It is not as disruptive to buyer behavior as discontinuous innovation. The first electric toothbrush and laptop computer are examples.

Continuous innovation—incremental or step-at-a-time innovation. With this type of innovation, performance of an existing product is enhanced, new features or options are added, and/or new applications are developed. Making a light bulb burn for an extra 100 hours, adding a new flavor to a line of soft drinks, or adding a safety feature to a machine tool represents continuous innovation.

Imitation—copying, adapting, or mimicking the innovations of other firms. If Lexmark successfully introduces a new type of printer/copier for use in laptop computers, it is likely that Hewlett-Packard will be forced to introduce its version of the same thing.

Companies tend to devote most of their resources toward continuous innovation and imitation. On the surface, this would seem to be a prudent risk-management strategy. That is, it might be postulated that risk is highest with discontinuous innovation and steadily declines as a company moves down the list toward imitation. However, this is not the case. As Figure 3-3 suggests, the risk equation is U-shaped, with high levels of risk both at the imitation and discontinuous innovation ends of the continuum.

The company that innovates only in response to the moves of other firms and pursues an imitation strategy incurs high risk principally because of the nature of the contemporary business environment. With the pace of technological and marketplace change, the imitative company is apt to miss out on entire market opportunities by the time it is able to respond to an innovative new product or service. When the firm does move, it finds its role to be that of a niche player in the marketplace. It also becomes harder and harder to catch up as innovative competitors move from incremental advances in a current technology to a major advance using a new technology. Meanwhile, new competitors emerge from other industries to attack the firm's most profitable lines of business with innovative marketing, distribution, and customer service approaches.

At the same time, firms that engage in breakthrough innovation are often moving into uncharted waters where no one has been before. Consequently, there is high risk of market failure through improper market analysis, mismatch of technology to

FIGURE 3-3

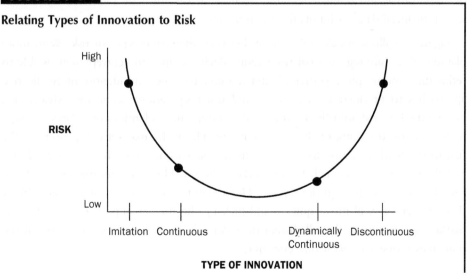

Relating Types of Innovation to Risk

High

RISK

Low

Imitation   Continuous   Dynamically   Discontinuous
                                          Continuous

TYPE OF INNOVATION

customer needs, or inadequate design of marketing programs. In many instances, the window of opportunity has yet to open, and the firm is too early. Sometimes the requisite infrastructure to support the innovation, including logistical systems and service networks, is inadequate. In still other cases, the firm is unable to penetrate the market beyond the so-called innovators and early adopters because the value package represented by a new product or service fails to have general market appeal.

In the middle of the continuum, risks are more moderate. The firm is continually improving existing products and discovering new market applications, while also adding new products to its product mix that represent significant advances in the current state of the art. Fundamental to a moderate or calculated risk posture is the recognition that risks become more manageable not by pursuing less innovation, but by innovating more and by innovating more intelligently.

It is also critical to note that, from an entrepreneurial standpoint, there are actually two sides to the risk equation. Discussions of risk generally focus on what happens if the entrepreneur pursues a concept and it does not work out. This side of the equation has been labeled "sinking the boat" risk by Dickson and Giglierano (1986). It is reflected in such factors as a poorly thought-out concept, bad timing, an already well-satisfied market, inadequate marketing and distribution approaches, and inappropriate price levels. The other side of the equation is called "missing the boat" risk, or the risk in not pursuing a course of action that would have proven profitable. It occurs when the entrepreneur delays acting on a concept for too long and is preempted by competitors or changing market requirements. Here, the entrepreneur is being too cautious or conservative and often seeks more security in the form of additional market research, financial data, or inputs from consultants.

Figure 3-4 illustrates the relationship between these two types of risk. With more planning time, sinking the boat risk steadily declines, since the entrepreneur is able to refine the concept; put together a better resource package; and identify more effective approaches to production, marketing, and other operational concerns. Meanwhile, missing the boat risk initially declines, as the entrepreneur identifies fatal flaws that represent reasons to rethink or shelve the concept. He or she may let competitors be the first to the market, letting them make the mistakes from which he or she can learn, and then enter with a much better market solution. However, missing the boat risk soon begins to rise and can rise rapidly. The longer the delay in action, the more likely that competitors will move quickly and lock up the market opportunity, or that the market opportunity itself will disappear. Total risk, then, becomes a function of the outcomes if one acts *and* if one does not.

FIGURE 3-4

"Missing the Boat" and "Sinking the Boat" Risk

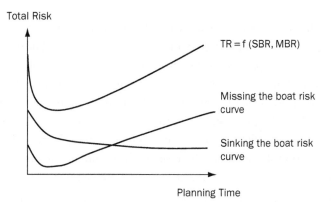

SOURCE: Dickson, P. R. and J. J. Giglierano, "Missing the Boat" and "Sinking the Boat" Risk, from "Missing the Boat and Sinking the Boat: A Conceptual Model of Entrepreneurial Risk," *Journal of Marketing*, 50, 1986, pp. 43–51. Reprinted by Permission of the American Marketing Association.

PROACTIVENESS

The third dimension of entrepreneurship, proactiveness, is less easy to define. The opposite of reactiveness, it has come into popular usage as a term to describe an action orientation. The essence of proactiveness is captured in the well-known Nike slogan "Just do it." At a company level, Miller (1987) associates proactiveness with assertiveness, which he in turn views as a dimension of strategy making. He sees entrepreneurial firms as *acting on* rather than *reacting to* their environments. His short scale to measure proactiveness includes three items: following versus leading competitors in innovation; favoring the tried and true versus emphasizing growth, innovation, and development; and trying to cooperate with competitors versus trying to undo them.

Proactiveness is concerned with implementation, with taking responsibility and doing whatever is necessary to bring an entrepreneurial concept to fruition. It usually involves considerable perseverance, adaptability, and a willingness to assume responsibility for failure. In his study of the strategic orientation of business enterprises, Venkatraman (1989) uses the term to refer to a continuous search for market opportunities and experimentation with potential responses to changing environmental trends. He suggests it is manifested in three key ways:

1. Seeking new opportunities that may or may not be related to the present line of operations;

2. Introducing new products and brands ahead of competition; and

3. Strategically eliminating operations that are in the mature or declining stages of the life cycle.

Proactive behavior has also been approached as a person's disposition to take action to influence his or her environment (Bateman and Grant, 1993). This perspective holds that the behavior of people is both internally and externally controlled, and that situations are as much a function of individuals as individuals are themselves functions of their environments. As Buss (1987) has put it, people are not "passive recipients of environmental pressures." Rather, they influence their own environments. This perspective on proactiveness is one that fits with corporate entrepreneurship very well—namely, that people can intentionally and directly change their current circumstances, including aspects of their work environment and the external marketplace.

It should be noted that the exhibition of proactiveness does not and should not preclude firms from reacting as necessary to the circumstances in which they find themselves. Indeed, recent research by Green, Covin, and Slevin (2008) reported that the highest performing firms in their sample of 110 manufacturers were concurrently highly proactive and able to strategically adapt as new opportunities arose or the superior effectiveness of alternative competitive approaches became apparent. Having said this, the exhibition of strategic adaptiveness alone would typically not be associated with corporate entrepreneurship.

To illustrate the proactiveness dimension, consider the engineer from a large telecommunications company whose job involves delivering engineering services to customer sites, many of which are in remote locations. Routinely, crews must drive company trucks loaded with sensitive technical equipment to these customer sites. Traveling along bumpy, rural, and sometimes unpaved roads, the equipment is often damaged or knocked out of calibration. The field crews may have to wait at a site while more equipment is sent out from the head office, or they must return another day. Our engineer takes it upon himself to fix the problem in his free time. He obtains resources by "begging, borrowing, and stealing" from the organization. Lo and behold, he comes up with a design for the truck bed that would allow the truck to be driven through a veritable hurricane without the equipment losing calibration or otherwise being damaged.

Is this proactive? Yes and no. Our engineer certainly has done much more than analyze a problem; he has produced a solution. But proactiveness is more than this. The engineer must sell the solution to his boss, who likely will not have the time or money to support the engineer. He then has to persist in selling it to the organization, which will entail building a coalition of supporters, overcoming large numbers of obstacles, and demonstrating adroit political skills. This is where the real proactiveness comes into the picture. If, in the end, the company's truck fleet is converted to his design, successful entrepreneurship has occurred. Even better than this would be the subsequent licensing of the design to other companies.

The distinction drawn here is similar to the distinction between the inventor and the (corporate) entrepreneur. Inventors are more than dreamers, in that they translate an idea into a product. But entrepreneurs go further, and this is the essence of proactiveness. Entrepreneurs may invent a product or process, or rely on someone else's invention. Their real contribution lies in recognizing, properly defining, and effectively communicating the potential of the invention and then in achieving acceptance for the invention within the company, getting it implemented (if it is a process), launching it (if it is a product), and achieving commercial success or failure.

COMBINATIONS OF THE DIMENSIONS: THE CONCEPT OF DEGREE

Different combinations of these three dimensions are possible. A given entrepreneurial event (e.g., a new product, service, or process) might be highly or only nominally innovative, entail significant or limited risk, and require considerable or relatively little proactiveness. Accordingly, the "degree of entrepreneurship" refers to the extent to which events are innovative, risky, and proactive.

Of course, the three dimensions of entrepreneurship do not always vary positively and in close unison. Some entrepreneurial events might reflect, for example, high innovativeness, high risk-taking, and low proactiveness. An example is when a manufacturing firm adopts a radically different (high innovativeness) and unproven (high risk-taking) production technology, yet lags behind the industry leaders (low proactiveness) in doing so.

A relevant question pertaining to cases such as this, for which not all the entrepreneurial dimensions (i.e., innovativeness, risk-taking, and proactiveness) exhibit "high" values, is to what extent should that event be considered entrepreneurial? A restrictive definition of entrepreneurship, such as that suggested by Miller (1983), would delimit the label of "entrepreneurial" to events or organizations that are concurrently high on the innovativeness, risk-taking, and proactiveness dimensions. Stated differently, in the most restrictive conceptualization of an entrepreneurial event, degree of entrepreneurship exists as a multiplicative function of the degree of innovativeness × the degree of risk-taking × the degree of proactiveness. In such a multiplicative function, an event's score on each of the dimensions weights that event's scores on the others. By contrast, in a less restrictive conceptualization of an entrepreneurial event, degree of entrepreneurship can be thought of as an additive function of the event's scores on the three entrepreneurial dimensions; that is, degree of entrepreneurship = the degree of innovativeness + the degree of risk-taking + the degree of proactiveness.

In general, this additive conceptualization of degree of entrepreneurship corresponds more closely than the multiplicative conceptualization to how individuals generally think of entrepreneurial events. Consider again the example offered of the manufacturing firm that adopts a radically new and unproven technology, but does so only after industry leaders have made this move. If this event rates, on a 1-to-5 scale, an innovativeness score of 5, a risk-taking score of 5, and a proactiveness score of 2, a multiplicative conceptualization of degree of entrepreneurship would result in the computation of an total score of 50 (5 × 5 × 2) on a 1- (1 × 1 × 1) to-125 (5 × 5 × 5) possible range, in other words, a relatively low entrepreneurship score. An additive conceptualization of degree of entrepreneurship, by contrast, would result in the computation of an entrepreneurship score of 12 (5 + 5 + 2) on a 3- (1 + 1 + 1) to-15 (5 + 5 + 5) possible range, in other words, a moderately high entrepreneurship score. Inasmuch as two of the three entrepreneurship dimensions are strongly exhibited through this technology adoption event, a characterization of the event as reflecting relatively high entrepreneurship seems appropriate. This additive conceptualization of degree of entrepreneurship is the one we adopt in this book.

Entrepreneurial Intensity: Combining Degree and Frequency of Entrepreneurship

We began the chapter by noting that entrepreneurship is a variable. An entrepreneurial event varies in terms of the degree of entrepreneurship, or how much innovativeness, risk-taking, and proactiveness is involved. Just as important is the question of how many entrepreneurial events take place within a company over a given period of time. We will refer to this as the "frequency of entrepreneurship." Some companies produce a steady stream of new products, services, and processes over time, while others very rarely introduce something new or different.

This brings us to the concept of "entrepreneurial intensity." To assess the overall level of entrepreneurship in a company, the concepts of degree and frequency must be considered together. Any number of combinations can result. Thus, a firm may be engaging in lots of entrepreneurial initiatives (high on frequency), but none of them are all that innovative, risky, or proactive (low on degree). Another company may pursue a path that emphasizes breakthrough developments (high degree) that are done every four or five years (low frequency).

To better understand the entrepreneurial intensity (EI) concept, consider Figure 3-5. A two-dimensional matrix has been created with the number, or frequency, of

FIGURE 3-5

The Entrepreneurial Grid

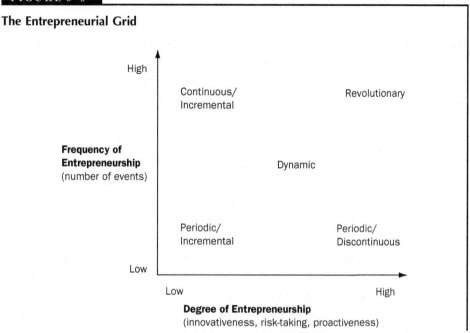

entrepreneurial events on the vertical axis, and the extent or degree to which these events are innovative, risky, and proactive on the horizontal axis. We refer to this matrix as the "entrepreneurial grid." For purposes of illustration, five sample scenarios have been identified in Figure 3-5, and these have been labeled Periodic/Incremental, Continuous/ Incremental, Periodic/Discontinuous, Dynamic, and Revolutionary.

Each of these reflects the variable nature of entrepreneurial intensity. For example, where few entrepreneurial events are produced, and these events are only nominally innovative, risky, and proactive, the organization can be described as Periodic/Incremental in terms of its (modest) level of EI. Similarly, an organization that is responsible for numerous entrepreneurial events that are highly innovative, risky, or proactive will fit into the Revolutionary segment of the entrepreneurial matrix and will exhibit the highest levels of EI.

While Figure 3-5 depicts five discrete segments, it is important to note that these segments have been arbitrarily defined to illustrate how EI can vary. Amounts and degrees of entrepreneurship are relative; absolute standards do not exist. Further, any given organization could be highly entrepreneurial at some times and not very entrepreneurial at others. Consequently, they could occupy different points on the grid or matrix at different periods in time.

Applying the Entrepreneurial Grid to Organizations

The entrepreneurial grid is a useful tool for managers attempting to define the role of entrepreneurship within their organizations. By identifying where the company falls on the grid, management is effectively defining the firm's entrepreneurial strategy. Consider an application of the grid to five successful companies (Figure 3-6). These are firms that exhibit varying degrees of EI and, as a consequence, are representative of different spaces or scenarios. They include:

- *Wendy's.* Started in 1969, this highly successful fast-food chain rapidly captured third place in the industry by developing an innovative product/service delivery system and by targeting a relatively untapped market consisting of young adults with a desire for higher-quality food. Throughout the years, it has maintained a competitive advantage by responding to environmental trends. For example, an increasing demand for convenience led Wendy's to pioneer drive-up window service, and shifting consumer preferences for lighter, low-calorie meals were met through the introduction of salads and baked potatoes. Responding to saturated demand and heightened competitive intensity, a "value menu" was added. While none of these activities can be considered highly innovative, Wendy's can be credited with introducing a few creative changes to the fast-food industry. As such, Wendy's is representative of the Periodic/Incremental segment of the entrepreneurial grid.

FIGURE 3-6

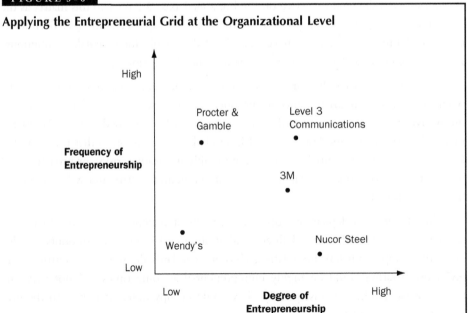

Applying the Entrepreneurial Grid at the Organizational Level

- *Procter & Gamble* (P&G). With the leading brand in approximately half of all product categories in which it competes, P&G has remained on top in the highly competitive consumer packaged goods industry by placing priority on research and development. The result has been a continuous stream of product improvements, with an occasional new product entry. P&G excels at evolutionary adaptations to, and improvements in, existing product concepts. Therefore, this company is representative of the Continuous/Incremental segment of the grid.

- *Nucor.* Founded in 1968 as a minimill that produced steel construction joints, Nucor introduced a radically new technical process for producing sheet metal in small electric arc furnaces. It mastered the ability to produce a ton of sheet steel in three-quarters of a man-hour versus the conventional three man-hours. In addition to transforming the competitive and economic structure of the steel industry, this innovation has affected the cost structure of firms in many other industries (e.g., automobile, construction). Therefore, while Nucor has been responsible for a few entrepreneurial initiatives, its efforts have had a relatively dramatic effect on several industries. As such, Nucor represents Periodic/Discontinuous entrepreneurship.

- *Minnesota Mining and Manufacturing Company (3M).* The 3M Company's unique talent is finding commercial uses for new product technology, developing that technology into dozens of marketable forms, and finding novel applications for these products. An example is Scotch cellophane tape, from which many successful products were derived. 3M sets a goal of achieving 25 percent of annual sales from products that have been developed in the last five years. The series of innovative products that come from this firm suggests that it is representative of the Dynamic segment of the entrepreneurial grid.

- *Level 3 Communications.* Capitalizing on fundamental changes in communication technology, Level 3 is the first company to build an end-to-end Internet Protocol (IP) international communications network from the ground up. Characterized as the very model of a modern major bandwidth merchant, the company has built more than 20,000 miles of fiber-optic networks in the United States and Europe. Level 3's IP-based network also includes undersea capacity across the Atlantic and Pacific. Packing its network with fiber and spare conduits for future upgrades, Level 3 serves such data-intensive customers as ISPs and telecom carriers. Services include dedicated circuits, Internet access, server and network equipment collocation, and dark fiber leasing. The speed and aggressiveness of Level 3, its high-risk profile, and its visionary approach to the future suggest the company is in the Revolutionary sector of the grid.

These companies represent a study in contrasts. Consider a comparison of Nucor's major technological advancement in the production of steel to the constant flow of new products and processes that come from cross-functional ranks of 3M or the development of the drive-up window concept to the development of laser technology. Yet each firm has an effective strategy for EI that has proven to fit with its internal and external environments and to be profitable.

Where a company falls on the entrepreneurial grid will vary depending on a number of internal and external factors. Internally, entrepreneurship is more evidenced where company structures are flat, control systems contain a measure of slack, appraisal systems include innovation and risk-taking criteria, jobs are broad in scope, and reward systems encourage a balance of individualism and group orientation. Externally, industries that are highly concentrated and have little direct competition, demand that is captive, technologies that rarely change, and margins that are comfortable will likely contain companies with low EI scores. Frequency of entrepreneurship may be directly related to the intensity of competition and amount of market heterogeneity, while degree of entrepreneurship is likely to be related to the rate of technological change in an industry and amount of product heterogeneity.

Applying the Grid at the Level of the Individual Manager

There are many types of corporate entrepreneurs. Some are technically oriented, some are aggressive promoters of a concept, and others are good managers. In Chapter 6, we will explore some of their characteristics in more depth. However, it is also important to focus on the ways in which a manager is entrepreneurial. Managers differ significantly in terms of their own entrepreneurial profiles, and the entrepreneurial grid can also serve as a useful means for diagnosing these profiles.

In essence, the concepts of degree and frequency previously discussed apply equally well at the individual level as they do at the organizational level. Thus, someone such as Ted Turner not only does things that are fairly innovative, risky, and proactive (e.g., the initial launch of Cable News Network), but also demonstrates a high frequency of entrepreneurship. In a relatively short period of time, Turner rolled out Headline News, CNN International, CNN Airport, CNN en Espanol, CNNfn.com, TNT, TBS Superstation, Turner Classic Movies, Cartoon Network, and more.

Entrepreneurs can fall into different areas on the entrepreneurial grid. Figure 3-7 provides some hypothetical examples. Someone like Richard DeVos, founder of Amway Products, probably falls into the Continuous/Incremental segment, as his orientation has been a steady stream of complementary lines and product improvements. Bill Gates of Microsoft might be characterized as a Dynamic entrepreneur, since he has championed a substantial number of significant software innovations. Howard Head, who personally drove the development of the metal ski in the 1950s and the oversize

FIGURE 3-7

Applying the Entrepreneurial Grid to Individual Managers

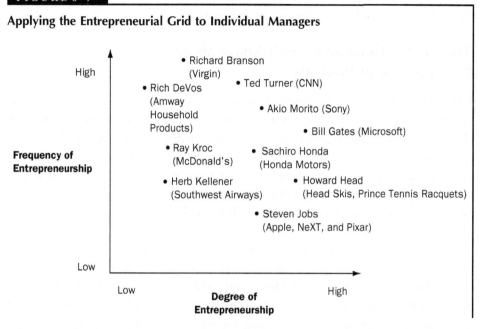

Prince tennis racket in the 1970s, most likely falls into the Periodic/Discontinuous area of the grid. Finally, someone like Herb Kelleher, of Southwest Airlines fame, has built his very service-oriented company around a clearly defined strategy and a people-oriented management style. He probably would fall more in the Periodic/Incremental section of the grid.

Another way in which the grid might be applied to individuals would involve characterizing how the entrepreneur approaches external change. Many individuals achieve success by quickly adapting to environmental change. Others base their efforts on actually creating major change in the environment. Ray Kroc was a great adapter, while Steven Jobs is more of a change agent. If we drew a vertical line at the midpoint of the horizontal, or degree axis, the former group (change adapters) would fall on the left-hand side of the grid, while the latter group (change creators) would fall on the right-hand side.

Environmental circumstances are apt to influence the personal strategy one pursues in terms of where one falls on the grid. Not only might the industry and market conditions influence one's personal strategy, but so too might such factors as the perceived cost of failure at different times, developments in one's personal life, one's past record of entrepreneurial success or failure, and the extent to which one is working alone or as part of a sanctioned company team. In addition, positioning in the grid is probably influenced by other psychological traits, such as need for achievement, locus of control, risk-taking profile, and tolerance of ambiguity.

Things We Know and Don't Know about Entrepreneurial Intensity

Our understanding of entrepreneurial intensity in organizations has significantly increased over the past few decades. Of the studies that have been done to date, perhaps the most significant finding concerns a very basic question: Does it matter? That is, do companies with stronger entrepreneurial orientations perform better? The results of a recent meta-analysis of empirical studies on this topic suggest that the answer is an unequivocal "yes" (Rauch et al., 2009). Researchers have demonstrated statistically significant relationships between EI and a number of indicators of company performance. Examples of such indicators include profits, the income-to-sales ratio, the rate of growth in revenue, the rate of growth in assets, the rate of growth in employment, and a composite measure of 12 financial and nonfinancial criteria (e.g., Covin and Slevin, 1989; Davis, Morris, and Allen, 1991; Miller and Friesen, 1982; Morris and Sexton, 1996; Wiklund and Shepherd, 2005; Zahra, 1986). The linkage between EI and performance appears especially strong for companies that operate in increasingly turbulent environments (Miles, Covin, and Heeley, 2000). Recent evidence suggests that EI may also benefit companies by contributing to their strategic learning capabilities—that is, the firm's ability to derive knowledge from past strategic actions and subsequently leverage that knowledge to adjust firm strategy (Anderson, Covin, and Slevin, 2009). Overall, there is growing evidence that the exhibition of EI generally improves firm functioning and performance.

This does not mean that more entrepreneurship is always better. The likelihood is that there are norms for entrepreneurial intensity in every industry. Such norms suggest there is no best place to be in the entrepreneurial grid—the ideal point is industry and market specific. Further, as noted below, it is also time specific. The better-performing firms are often those that demonstrate a stronger entrepreneurial orientation than their counterparts in the same industry. But norms for industries vary widely. One might expect a grocery retail chain to be higher on frequency, lower on degree, and have a heavier emphasis on process innovation over product innovation. Alternatively, leading pharmaceutical companies will likely occupy the dynamic sector of the grid, with high frequency of new products and a portfolio of innovations that includes both incremental advances and breakthrough products.

Within companies, entrepreneurial orientations can be expected to differ significantly among various divisions, units, departments, and areas. In addition, there is no pattern such that marketing departments in companies are predictably more entrepreneurial or procurement departments are always less entrepreneurial. Not only will entrepreneurial activity differ by company, but an entrepreneurial manager can guide a staid, conservative unit of any kind towards a more entrepreneurial profile. At the same time, the more a given unit or department must operate under conditions of turbulence, financial uncertainty, and other threats, the more one would expect a higher entrepreneurial profile in that unit or department.

There is also much we do not know about entrepreneurship's exhibition in established companies. For example, to what extent does the relative importance of degree versus frequency vary depending on such strategic factors as the pace of technological change in an industry, the levels of competitive intensity, or the heterogeneity of market demand? Under what conditions is degree versus frequency the strongest contributor to company performance? It is also necessary to determine if frequency and degree contribute equally to short-term as opposed to long-term performance. It may be that frequency has more of a short-term impact, whereas degree has a stronger impact on long-term outcomes. Although hypothetical, such a possibility is implicit in the seminal work of Hamel and Prahalad (1991). Using a baseball analogy of hitting many singles versus attempting to hit a home run, they emphasize the value of companies pursuing multiple smaller projects at a time as opposed to pursuing one potentially breakthrough project. A risk–reward trade-off is involved in which the former are thought to generate short- and medium-term profits, whereas the latter significantly impacts long-term profitability.

Another critical question concerns the types and amounts of costs associated with EI. Resource requirements are likely to vary considerably at different levels of EI within a given industry, and the shape of the cost curve should be estimated. A related question concerns the failures that result from EI. Product and service failure rates are likely to be positively associated with both the frequency and degree components of EI, and research is needed to determine which is greater and why.

Entrepreneurial intensity also is likely to play a role in determining relationships between the nature of the external environment facing a company, the strategy of the company, and the internal structure of the company. It would seem that EI serves a potentially critical role in integrating these three variables. As a case in point, firms experiencing higher levels of environmental turbulence may require higher levels of EI to survive and grow, which in turn generates corporate strategies that are more aggressive (e.g., focusing on new product and market development) as well as structures that are more flexible, decentralized, and open.

Finally, it is not clear that high levels of entrepreneurial intensity are sustainable. It may be that there are patterns to a company's entrepreneurial performance over time.

One theory is that companies alternate, or "cycle," between fairly dynamic periods of higher entrepreneurial intensity, and periods where innovations are more incremental and intensity is lower (e.g., Slevin and Covin, 1990). During these less intense periods, the focus is more on consolidation and administrative control. Yet there are companies such as 3M, who sustain a given level of entrepreneurship for extended periods.

THE INNOVATOR'S NOTEBOOK

Keeping Innovation Alive at Proctor & Gamble

Proctor & Gamble is far from being a start-up; yet, former CEO A. G. Lafley (author of *The Game Changer*) had taken measures to insure that entrepreneurship was alive and well in the company. He made the following eight recommendations for keeping established firms nimble:

Increase one-on-one consumer research. Given that most of the obvious needs of consumers have already been met, the opportunities now lie in meeting the less evident consumer needs. What this translates into is fewer focus groups and more nontraditional market research tools, such as observing consumers in their homes. Lafley encouraged his employees to look at products from the consumer's perspective rather than as scientists, leading one employee to launch a diaper-testing facility down the hall from her office where mothers bring in their children to test new product offerings.

Consider brand expansions. Vision statements for a company as well as for divisions can be useful tools in helping employees work towards a common goal; they also can pigeon-hole the thinking of those employees. Changing statements like "we want the driest diapers" to "helping moms with baby's development" for Pampers has led to product innovations like Kandoo baby wipes and Easy Ups training pants. Broadening Crest Toothpaste's mission to "a beautiful smile for life" has led to the development of the SpinBrush toothbrush and Crest Night Effects whitening gel.

Encourage cross-division exchange of ideas. By crediting employees for giving ideas rather than for just receiving them, collaboration across the company was fostered. Given the development of new toothpaste flavors with assistance from employees working on coffee and shampoo as well as new car wash technology based on insights gained from purifying water and cleaning dishes, the infrastructure that Lafley helped to build is still producing interesting outcomes.

Mechanisms that have been put in place to facilitate this cross-division interaction include "poster shows," internal trade shows where divisions display recent successes and new ideas; "innovation reviews," annual half-day reviews in each unit that are conducted by the CEO; an internal Web site where employees can post questions; and "communities of practice," consortiums of employees interested in specific topics.

Be willing to consider ideas from outside sources. In the past, P&G has been introverted in its R&D, but Lafley set a goal to derive 50 percent of P&G's inventions externally. Based on P&G's estimates that the pace of innovation was twice as great as a decade ago, Lafley argued that companies should take advantage of the full pool of resources at their disposal, which are not confined to the organization. One way P&G utilized outside innovation was through acquiring technologies, as it did when it bought the SpinBrush from an inventor in 2001. Another is by partnering with its competitors, as seen when it partnered with Clorox to use P&G's patented adhesive-film technology to produce Glad Press & Seal, an adhesive food wrap. Finally, P&G's employees look for product offerings of which P&G could mimic functionality, as was done with the development of the Mr. Clean Magic Eraser that was based on an eraser sold in Japan for removing marks on walls.

Know when you've tested enough. Although counter-intuitive to most employees, perfecting products can lead to lost sales. By reducing test-marketing, Lafley was able to shorten from three years to eighteen months the launch time from lab to roll-out across the company. Making the "best" product can come at the cost of being late to market or missing a market opportunity altogether. When Botox became popular with baby-boomers, P&G soon thereafter launched Olay Regenerist, a premium skincare product that utilizes wound-healing technology, leading to the product taking the number one spot in the U.S. anti-aging category.

Get designers more involved. Based on his emphasis on the consumer's experience of the product, which includes how it looks, feels, and smells, Lafley took designers that were solely focused on the logos and packaging and brought them into other aspects of product development. For example, designers assisted in the formulation and fragrance of Olay Regenerist. Designers are also working on the displays for SK-II, P&G's new line of prestige cosmetics, which will be offered exclusively at Saks. An indication of Lafley's commitment to the consumer experience is that he created a head of design who reports directly to the CEO.

Discussion Questions

1. Describe the "dimensions of entrepreneurship" as they apply to P&G.

2. How would "entrepreneurial intensity" be viewed at P&G?

3. Plot P&G on the entrepreneurial grid (Figure 3-5) and explain your position.

SOURCE: Adapted from "P&G: Teaching an Old Dog New Tricks," from the May 31, 2004 Issue *Fortune Online* by Patricia Sellers. Updated, April 8, 2010.

Summary and Conclusions

With today's competitive conditions, many senior executives recognize the need for more entrepreneurship in their companies. However, they often struggle when attempting to define what it really means to be entrepreneurial, and how entrepreneurship should manifest itself within their individual businesses. In this chapter, we have provided a beginning point. Management must first determine where the firm falls in the entrepreneurial grid, the relative importance of frequency and degree, and the specific types of innovation, risk-taking; and proactive behaviors that are consistent with the firm's strategic direction.

We have also introduced the concept of entrepreneurial intensity. There is nothing special about this particular term, but much support exists for it as a managerial concept. Researchers and consultants have used other terms as entrepreneurial posture, entrepreneurial orientation, organic emphasis, entrepreneurship level, and entrepreneurial aggressiveness to talk about what, in essence, is the same thing (Cheah, 1990; Covin and Slevin, 1989; Jennings and Seaman, 1990; Keats and Bracker, 1988; Schaefer, 1990; Stuart and Abetti, 1987; Morris et al., 1994). The key for managers is to specify the dominant logic of the firm, and the extent to which entrepreneurial intensity is part of that dominant logic. In subsequent chapters, we will further examine the interplay between dominant logic, entrepreneurial intensity, and corporate strategy.

Entrepreneurial intensity must become a key activity ratio that is monitored on an on-going basis within organizations. Assessment at the level of the organization can be used to benchmark and track levels of entrepreneurship, establish norms and draw industry comparisons, establish entrepreneurship goals, develop strategies, and assess relationships between EI and company performance variables over time. At the individual manager level, assessments can be useful in helping managers and others to examine and refine their own leadership styles, as well as in characterizing employee behavior over time.

References

Anderson, B. S, Covin, J. G., and Slevin, D. P. 2009. "Understanding the Relationship between Entrepreneurial Orientation and Strategic Learning: An Empirical Investigation," *Strategic Entrepreneurship Journal*, 3(2): 218–240

Barczak, G., Griffin, A., and Kahn, K. B. 2009. "Perspectives: Trends and Drivers of Success in NPD Practices: Results of the 2003 PDMA Best Practices Study," *Journal of Product Innovation Management*, 26(1): 3–23.

Bateman, T. S., and Grant, J. M. 1993. "The Proactive Component of Organizational Behavior: A Measure and Correlates," *Journal of Organizational Behavior*, 14 (March): 103–118.

Buss, D. M. 1987. "Selection, Evocation and Manipulation," *Journal of Personality and Social Psychology*, 53(4): 1214–1221.

Cheah, H. B. 1990. "Schumpeterian and Austrian Entrepreneurship: Unity within Duality," *Journal of Business Venturing*, 5 (December): 341–347.

Covin, J. G., and D. P. Slevin. 1989. "Strategic Management of Small Firms in Hostile Environments," *Strategic Management Journal*, 10(1): 75–87.

Davis, D., Morris, M., and Allen, J. 1991. "Perceived Environmental Turbulence and Its Effect on Selected Entrepreneurship, Marketing and Organizational Characteristics in Industrial Firms," *Journal of the Academy of Marketing Science* 19 (Spring): 43–51.

Dickson, P. R., and Giglierano, J. J. 1986. "Missing the Boat and Sinking the Boat: A Conceptual Model of Entrepreneurial Risk," *Journal of Marketing*, 50: 43–51.

Green, K. M., Covin, J. G., and Slevin, D. P. 2008. "Exploring the Relationship between Strategic Reactiveness and Entrepreneurial Orientation: The Role of Structure-Style Fit," *Journal of Business Venturing*, 23(3): 356–383.

Hamel, G. 2000. *Leading the Revolution* (Boston: Harvard Business School Press).

Hamel, G., and Prahalad, C. K. 1994. *Competing for the Future* (Boston: Harvard Business School Press).

Hamel, G., and Prahalad, C. K. 1991. "Corporate Imagination and Expeditionary Marketing," *Harvard Business Review*, 69 (July–August): 31–39.

Jennings, D. F., and Seaman, S. L. 1990. "Aggressiveness of Response to New Business Opportunities Following Deregulation: An Empirical Study of Established Financial Firms," *Journal of Business Venturing*, 5 (October): 177–189.

Keats, B. W., and Bracker, J. S. 1988. "Toward a Theory of Small Business Performance: A Conceptual Model," *American Journal of Small Business*, 13 (Spring): 14–58.

Kuczmarski, T., Middlebrooks, A., and Swaddling, J. 2001. *Innovating the Corporation* (Chicago: NTC Publishing Group).

Kuratko, D. F, Covin, J. G., and Garrett, R. P., Jr. 2009. "Internal Corporate Venturing: Insights from Corporate Level and Venture Level Managers," *Business Horizons*, 52(5): 459–467.

Miles, M. P., Covin, J. G., and Heeley, M. B. 2000. "The Relationship between Environmental Dynamism and Small Firm Structure, Strategy, and Performance," *Journal of Marketing Theory and Practice*, 8(2): 63–78.

Miller, D. 1983. "The Correlates of Entrepreneurship in Three Types of Firms," *Management Science*, 29: 770–791.

Miller, D. 1987. "Strategy Making and Structure: Analysis and Implications for Performance," *Academy of Management Journal*, 30(1): 7–32.

Miller, D., and Friesen, P. H. 1982. "Innovation in Conservative and Entrepreneurial Firms: Two Models of Strategic Momentum," *Strategic Management Journal*, 3(1): 1–25.

Morris, M. H., and Sexton, D. L. 1996. "The Concept of Entrepreneurial Intensity," *Journal of Business Research*, 36(1): 5–14.

Morris, M. H., Sexton, D., and Lewis, P. 1994. "Reconceptualizing Entrepreneurship: An Input-Output Perspective," *SAM Advanced Management Journal*, 59(1): 21–31.

Page, A. L. 1993. "Assessing New Product Development Practices and Performance: Establishing Crucial Norms," *Journal of Product Innovation Management*, 10: 273–290.

Peters, T. 1997. *The Circle of Innovation* (New York: Alfred A. Knopf).

Rauch, A., Wiklund, J., Lumpkin, G. T., and Frese, M. 2009. "Entrepreneurial Orientation and Business Performance: An Assessment of Past Research and Suggestions for the Future," *Entrepreneurship Theory and Practice*, 33(3): 761–787.

Schaefer, D. S. 1990. "Level of Entrepreneurship and Scanning Source Usage in Very Small Businesses," *Entrepreneurship Theory and Practice*, 15(1): 19–31.

Slevin, D. P., and Covin, J. G. 1990. "Juggling Entrepreneurial Style and Organization Structure—How to Get Your Act Together," *Sloan Management Review*, 31 (Winter): 43–53.

Stuart, R., and Abetti, P. A. 1987. "Start-Up Ventures: Towards the Prediction of Initial Success," *Journal of Business Venturing*, 2(3): 215–230.

Synectics. 1993. *Succeeding at Innovation: Report on Creativity and Innovation in U.S. Corporations* (Boston: Synectics Corporation).

Venkatraman, N. 1989. "Strategic Orientation of Business Enterprises: The Construct, Dimensionality, and Measurement," *Management Science*, 35: 942–962.

Wiklund, J., and Shepherd, D. 2005. "Entrepreneurial Orientation and Small Business Performance: A Configurational Approach," *Journal of Business Venturing*, 20(1): 71–91.

Zahra, S. A. 1986. "A Canonical Analysis of Corporate Entrepreneurship Antecedents and Impact on Performance," in *Academy of Management Best Paper Proceedings*, J. Pearce and R. Robinson (eds.): 71–75.

Chapter 4

The Forms of Corporate Entrepreneurship

Introduction

Chapter 3 introduced the concept of entrepreneurial intensity. Entrepreneurial intensity represents the overall level of entrepreneurship exhibited by an organization and is reflected in the frequency of entrepreneurial events and the degree to which that overall set of events is innovative, risk-taking, and proactive. In essence, entrepreneurial intensity represents a quality of the organization. It can enable firms to achieve and sustain success in the face of ever-changing market and competitive demands. Thus, entrepreneurial intensity is an organizational quality that should serve firms well over the long term.

However, there are different paths to achieving a given level of entrepreneurship within an organization. Two companies that exhibit the same overall level of entrepreneurial intensity can differ significantly in how entrepreneurship is manifested. This chapter delineates the major forms assumed by entrepreneurship in organizations and then briefly reviews the open model of innovation within which corporate entrepreneurship forms are increasingly pursued.

Entrepreneurship is manifested in companies either through corporate venturing or strategic entrepreneurship (see Figure 4-1). *Corporate venturing* approaches (or forms) have as their commonality the adding of new businesses (or portions of new businesses via equity investments) to the corporation. This can be accomplished through three implementation modes—internal corporate venturing, cooperative corporate venturing, and external corporate venturing. By contrast, *strategic entrepreneurship* approaches (or forms) have as their commonality the exhibition of large-scale or otherwise highly consequential innovations that are adopted in the firm's pursuit of competitive advantage. These innovations may or may not result in new businesses for the corporation. With strategic entrepreneurship approaches, innovation can be in any of five areas—the firm's strategy, product offerings, served markets, internal organization (i.e., structure, processes, and capabilities), or business model. We now discuss each of these categories of corporate entrepreneurship phenomena in greater detail.

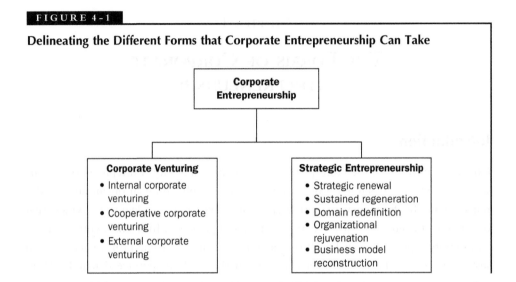

FIGURE 4-1

Delineating the Different Forms that Corporate Entrepreneurship Can Take

Corporate Venturing: Bringing New Businesses to the Corporation

THE CONCEPT OF CORPORATE VENTURING AND ITS MODES

Corporate venturing includes various methods for creating, adding to, or investing in new businesses. With *internal corporate venturing*, new businesses are created and owned by the corporation. These businesses typically reside within the corporate structure but, occasionally, may be located outside the firm and operate as semiautonomous entities. Among internal corporate ventures that reside within the firm's organizational boundaries, some may be formed and exist as part of a preexisting internal organization structure and others may be housed in newly formed organizational entities within the corporate structure. *Cooperative corporate venturing* (also known as joint corporate venturing and collaborative corporate venturing) refers to entrepreneurial activity in which new businesses are created and owned by the corporation together with one or more external development partners. Cooperative ventures typically exist as external entities that operate beyond the organizational boundaries of the founding partners. *External corporate venturing* refers to entrepreneurial activity in which new businesses are created by parties outside the corporation and subsequently invested in (via the assumption of equity positions) or acquired by the corporation. These external businesses are typically very young ventures or early growth-stage firms. In practice, new businesses might be developed through a single venturing mode, any two venturing modes, or all three venturing modes. A firm's total venturing activity is equal to the sum of the ventures enacted through the internal, cooperative, and external modes.

WHAT IS A NEW BUSINESS?

With corporate venturing, the corporation is creating an entirely new business. Unfortunately, there is no generally agreed-upon definition of a "new business" within an existing company. One approach to determining what constitutes a new business involves the four strategies found in the product/market growth matrix shown in Figure 4-2. Firms that seek growth in current markets with current products are pursuing market penetration strategies. Firms that seek growth in new markets with current products are pursuing market development strategies. Firms that seek growth in current markets with new products are pursuing product development strategies. Finally, firms that seek growth in new markets with new products are pursuing diversification strategies. Considering these four types of growth strategy, the most restrictive operational definition of new business would be that which results from diversification. When a company finds itself dealing with new categories of customers and selling them products or services that are new to the firm, we can assume the firm is pursuing a new business.

However, there is a less restrictive way to define a new business that is more consistent with the conventional usage of the term. In Figure 4-3, the original matrix has been modified to include intermediate-level variations in market and product novelty. Hence, extensions of current markets and products are considered, so that more degrees of "newness" are allowed for. Figure 4-3 recognizes that a market can be new to the firm or new to the world (market creation) and that new products can be introduced to a firm's current industry or move the firm into a new industry that is pre-existing or newly created by the firm's new product offering. (An industry can be defined as the entire group of firms selling identical or highly similar products.) With

---

FIGURE 4-2

Corporate Growth Strategy Matrix

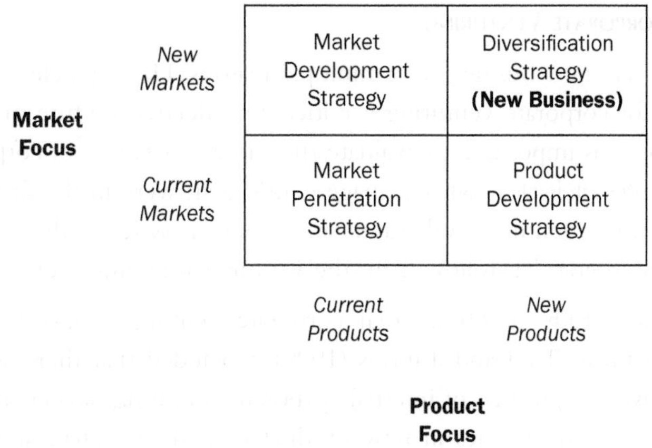

		Current Products	New Products
Market Focus	New Markets	Market Development Strategy	Diversification Strategy **(New Business)**
	Current Markets	Market Penetration Strategy	Product Development Strategy

Product Focus

FIGURE 4-3

The Domain of a New Business

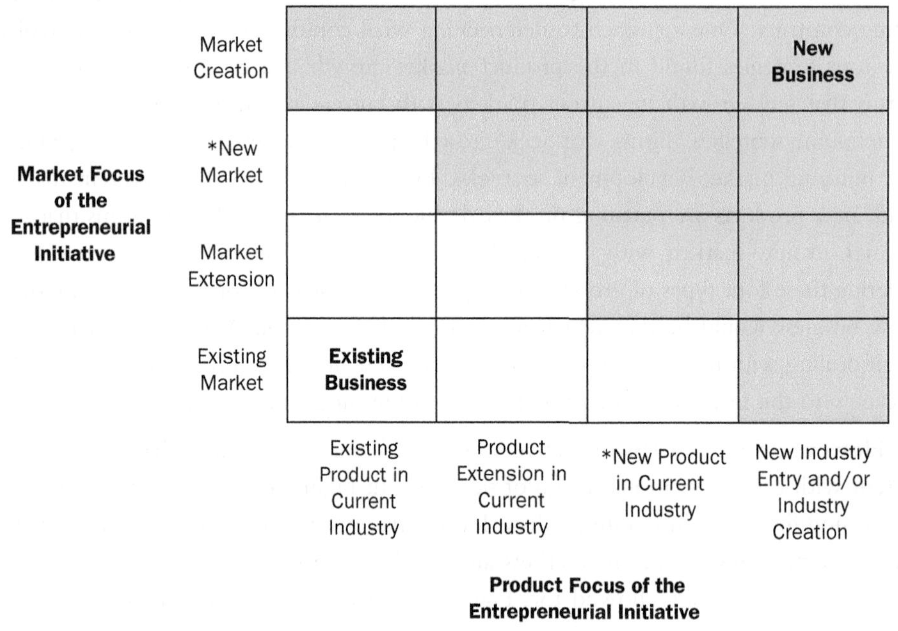

Figure showing a grid with "Market Focus of the Entrepreneurial Initiative" on the vertical axis (from bottom to top: Existing Market, Market Extension, *New Market, Market Creation) and "Product Focus of the Entrepreneurial Initiative" on the horizontal axis (from left to right: Existing Product in Current Industry, Product Extension in Current Industry, *New Product in Current Industry, New Industry Entry and/or Industry Creation). The bottom-left cell is labeled "Existing Business" and the top-right region is labeled "New Business."

* The point of reference for *new* is *new to the firm.*

these elaborations, Figure 4-3 suggests that firms need not move from their current positions on both the market and product dimensions in order to enter new businesses, and that some variants of pure market development activity and pure product development activity can be considered new businesses.

MOTIVES FOR CORPORATE VENTURING

Corporations create new businesses for multiple reasons. Having a clear understanding of the motives for corporate venturing is critical for effective venture management. In the final analysis, it is impossible to evaluate the success or failure of corporate venturing initiatives unless it is clear what management's goals were in the first place. Companies must create venture evaluation and control systems that assess venture performance on criteria that follow from the venture's founding motive.

Based on their study of 60 internal corporate ventures founded in 15 United Kingdom-based firms, Tidd and Taurins (1999) concluded that there are two sets of motives that drive the practice of internal corporate venturing: leveraging—to exploit existing corporate competencies in new product or market arenas, and learning—to acquire new knowledge and skills that may be useful in existing product or market arenas. When the overall motive is leveraging, some of the specific reasons that firms engage in corporate venturing include:

- To exploit underutilized resources—build a new business around internal capabilities that remain idle for prolonged periods; the new business becomes the vehicle for outsourcing those capabilities to others.

- To extract further value from existing resources—build a new business around corporate knowledge, capabilities, or other resources that have value in product-market arenas not currently being served by the firm.

- To apply competitive pressure on internal suppliers—build a new business that becomes an alternative supplier to existing internal supply sources.

- To spread the risk and cost of product development—build a new business whose target market promises to be larger than that for which the core product to be offered by the business was initially developed.

- To divest noncore activities—build a new business to pursue business opportunities that the firm is in a favorable position to exploit and that the firm has no strategic interest in.

The learning motives can be broken down further as well. Three major types of organizational learning tend to receive the greatest emphasis:

- To learn about the process of venturing—build a new business as a laboratory in which the innovation process can be studied.

- To develop new competencies—build a new business as a basis for acquiring new knowledge and skills pertaining to technologies, products, or markets of potential strategic importance.

- To develop managers—build a new business as a training ground for the development of individuals with general management potential.

In another study of corporate venturing practice—this one including firms engaged in both internal and external corporate venturing—Miles and Covin (2002) reported that the firms pursued venturing for three primary reasons: (1) to build an innovative capability as the basis for making the overall firm more entrepreneurial and accepting of change, (2) to appropriate greater value from current organizational competencies or to expand the firm's scope of operations and knowledge into areas of possible strategic importance, and (3) to generate quick financial returns. Both of these studies reinforce the importance placed by companies on learning about the process of venturing—something not well understood in most organizations.

Another study of the motives for corporate venturing was recently completed by researchers at Indiana University (see Kuratko et al., 2009). In this study, only internal corporate ventures were examined. Data were collected on the motives for corporate venturing from 145 ventures operating in 72 corporations. A unique aspect of the Indiana study is that data on venture founding motives were collected from both corporate-level managers who oversaw the overall venturing activity within their corporations as well as from venture managers who administered the day-to-day operations of the ventures. The results of this study are summarized in Table 4-1.

TABLE 4-1

The Founding Motives of Internal Corporate Ventures

For the 145 internal corporate ventures in the Indiana University study, venture founding motive was assessed from the perspectives of (a) the corporate managers who had detailed knowledge of those ventures and (b) the venture managers who administered those ventures' day-to-day operations. The mean scores of these two levels of managers in response to the various venture founding motives are shown below. Correlations between the individual venture founding motive scores and the managers' perceptions of the venture's performance are also shown.

Using the following scale, please indicate (by circling the appropriate number) the extent to which the following motives prompted the initiation of the venture.

Not at all a founding motive			A moderately strong founding motive		A very strong founding motive of the venture	
1	2	3	4	5	6	7

Possible Venture Founding Motive	Mean (s.d.)[a] Score as Reported by Corporate Manager	Corr. with Performance as Reported by Corporate Manager	Mean (s.d.) Score as Reported by Venture Manager	Corr. with Performance as Reported by Venture Manager
To realize greater value from the corporation's pre-existing resources (e.g., knowledge, technologies, competencies) through leveraging these in the venture's business.	5.88 (1.23)	.18*	5.72 (1.38)	.21*
To enable the corporate parent to learn about new products or technologies.	4.37 (1.91)	−13	4.10 (1.95)	−.11

(Continued)

To enable the corporate parent to learn about new markets.	4.46 (1.86)	−.12	4.29 (1.88)	−.08
To develop new capabilities within the corporation.	5.24 (1.73)	.10	5.10 (1.73)	.04
To enable the corporate parent to move quickly into a new business arena when and if such movement is desired.	4.13 (1.89)	.10	4.27 (1.98)	−.02
To generate quick and predictable financial returns for the corporate parent.	4.59 (1.72)	.18*	4.64 (1.69)	.23*
To create a business that would be spun off from the corporation.	2.06 (1.60)	−.13	2.25 (1.74)	−.05
To provide "insurance" for the corporate parent in the event that its core businesses fail to yield desired results.	3.25 (1.96)	.02	3.35 (1.95)	.13
To diversify the corporate parent for overall risk management purposes.	4.34 (2.05)	.12	4.12 (1.99)	.13

[a] Standard deviations are shown in parentheses.
* Statistically significant at the p<.05 level.
SOURCE: Adapted from Kuratko, D. F., Covin, J. G., and Garrett, R. P. Jr., 2009. "Internal Corporate Venturing: Insights from Actual Performance," *Business Horizons*, 52(5): 459–467.

Several noteworthy observations emerge from the results shown in Table 4-1. First, consistent with the aforementioned Miles and Covin (2002) study, internal corporate ventures are shown to be most strongly motivated by desires to (1) leverage the parent corporation's resources in new business arenas, (2) develop new capabilities, and (3) generate quick and predictable financial returns for the corporation. Second, of the venture founding motives assessed in the research, only two are significantly correlated with venture performance: the desire "to realize greater value from the corporation's preexisting resources (e.g., knowledge, technologies, competencies) through leveraging these in the venture's business" and the desire "to generate quick and predictable financial returns for the corporate parent." Regarding this second founding motive, it should be kept in mind that the desire for quick and predictable financial returns likely did not lead to higher venture performance. More plausibly, the ventures to which this motive was attributed were recognized as "good bets" based on available information, and this assumption appears to be true as evidenced through the reported significant correlation between this founding motive and venture performance.

A third noteworthy observation pertaining to the results shown in Table 4-1 is that corporate managers who oversee their firms' corporate venturing initiatives and venture managers who administer the day-to-day operations of those ventures tend to agree on the reasons why particular ventures were said to have been founded. This result is encouraging inasmuch as prior research suggests that lack of consensus on founding motives among the managers involved in a corporation's venturing efforts may be a root cause of venture failure (Tidd and Taurins, 1999). Lastly, the finding that the surveyed internal corporate ventures were not, in general, strongly motivated by a desire "to provide 'insurance' for the corporate parent in the event that its core businesses fail to yield desired results" suggests that the role of internal corporate venturing may be changing. Prior research on the phenomenon suggested that internal corporate venturing was often viewed as a form of "business insurance"; that is, a possible source of revenue that may be useful to have if prospects in the corporation's core businesses deteriorate (Burgelman, 1983; Peterson and Berger, 1971). The current results suggest that internal corporate venturing may play a much more strategic role in firms' operations than that previously observed in research on the topic.

Corporate Venture Capital

The term *corporate venturing* is sometimes interpreted to mean corporate venture capital investment activity. Many corporations have internal venture capital funds that are used to invest in external new ventures deemed strategically important or financially attractive to the corporation. Corporations also sometimes operate as investment partners in external venture funds that are owned and controlled by multiple parties. The external venture funds in which corporations invest often target new businesses in specific technology or product-market arenas of interest to the fund owners and in which those owners have, ideally, developed some investment competence.

Over the past few decades, the popularity of directly investing corporate funds into external business start-ups has varied with the strength of the market for initial public offerings (IPOs). In general, when the stock market has been strong, corporate venture capital investments have been popular. In times when the stock market has dropped, investment in external start-ups has fallen off. Historically, corporate venture capital investments have occurred in three waves or boom-and-bust cycles (see Gompers, 2002). The first wave happened during the late 1960s and early 1970s when more than 25 percent of the Fortune 500 firms established venture capital programs. The economic recession of 1973 led to the collapse and termination of the majority of these programs. A second wave followed in the late 1970s and early 1980s, spurred on by regulatory changes (e.g., capital gains tax cuts) and technological advancements (e.g., software, personal computers) that made many new businesses—particularly high-tech start-ups—attractive investment targets. When the stock market crashed in 1987, corporate venture capital investments again dropped off precipitously. By 1992 corporate venture capital funds were estimated to represent only 5 percent of all venture capital under management, which was itself diminished considerably from prior years. The telecommunications and Internet/dot-com boom of the late 1990s spurred the third wave of corporate venture capital investing. Corporate venture investments grew 158 percent from 1996 to 2000. However, during the first three months of 2001, following the bursting of the dot-com bubble, corporate venture capital investments fell by 81 percent and, by late 2001, approximately 45 percent of the corporate venture fund programs that existed in 2000 had been closed (Garvin, 2002).

A survey of global corporate venture capital practices was conducted by Ernst & Young's Venture Capital Advisory Group in 2008. Data on corporate venture capital investments were obtained from 37 corporate venture capital units operating in 17 industries and 8 countries. The focus of the study and associated results were wide ranging. Some of the key results are summarized in Table 4-2.

One noteworthy finding from the Ernst & Young survey relates to the degree to which corporate venture capital investments are strategically used as a basis for learning about new technological developments, product innovations, and market opportunities. In particular, a comparison of Tables 4-1 and 4-2 suggests that corporate venture capital may take precedence over internal corporate venturing when the parent corporation's strategic objectives principally relate to *learning* about new technologies, products, or markets (versus *leveraging* the parent corporation's resources and competencies). Also noteworthy is the finding that managers are once again optimistic about the future of corporate venture capital investments. This optimism exists despite the fact that the number of CVC investment deals continued to fall by about 3 percent per year between 2000 and 2008, with the number of corporations participating in venture capital investments contracting into a relative small group of long-term players—approximately 100 corporations globally by the late 2000s according to *Dow Jones VentureSource*.

A useful framework for linking corporate venture capital investments with a company's larger strategic agenda has been proposed by Chesbrough (2002). He observes

---

TABLE 4-2

Key Findings of Ernst & Young's 2008 Corporate Venture Capital Survey

- The top operational challenge as identified by respondents from the 37 corporate venture capital (CVC) units surveyed was "securing business unit sponsorship for investments." In general, CVC units struggled with gaining the parent corporation's support for corporate venturing as a concept. Obtaining parent support on individual external venture investment "deals" was also identified as a major challenge.

- Eighty percent of the respondents said their external venture investment programs were aimed at a blend of strategic and financial objectives; 17% said their programs were focused solely on strategic objectives; 3% said their programs were focused solely on financial objectives.

- The CVC strategic objectives identified as most important by the respondents included "map emerging innovations and technical developments" [mean of 4.7 on a 5-point scale] and "window on new market opportunities" [mean of 4.6 on a 5-point scale].

- The vast majority of the CVC units surveyed were either internal business units of their parent corporations or subsidiaries or LLPs of their parent corporations. This close alignment between CVC units and their parent corporations was identified as essential to enabling those units to strategically support and fulfill the needs of the parents' core businesses.

- Ninety percent of the respondents assessed the success of their corporations' CVC programs by looking at "overall financial results"; 55% considered "performance of individual investments"; 53% considered "value-added contribution to business units"; 50% considered CVC activity (deals screened); 50% considered CVC output (deals made).

- Eighty percent of the CVC units had fewer than 10 full-time investment professionals.

- Seventy-five percent of CVC investment professionals are rewarded using flat-rate salaries.

- The CVC fund size of the surveyed corporations ranged from less than $50 million to more than $750 million, with the majority of funds within the $50 to $249 million range.

- The external ventures in which CVC investments are made—i.e., the venture portfolio companies—realize benefit from such investments by taking advantage of the parent corporations' resources. Resource bases identified as most valuable to portfolio companies include those involving logistical networks (e.g., national/international delivery networks) and market access/contacts (i.e., the parent facilitates contact with potential customers and alliance partners).

- The majority of the 37 CVC units surveyed made from one to five investments in the prior year, with Intel Capital making, by far, the largest number of CVC investments at 66.

- As of 2008, CVC investing was projected in the short-to-medium term (2-year horizon) to remain most active in the United States (79% of respondents rated the U.S. market as "very important" for CVC activity), distantly followed by the

(Continued)

European Union (25% rated as "very important"), India (24% rated as "very important"), and China (21% rated as "very important"). Overall, the respondents expressed optimism with regard to the likelihood of increased CVC activity, the global expansion of CVC activity, and the ability of corporations to access new sources of innovation via CVC investments.

- "Cleantech" investments accounted for an average of 41% of the capital investments of the surveyed CVC units. As described in the E&Y white paper, "Cleantech is the enabler of the world's response to climate change. It encompasses a diverse range of innovative products and services that optimize the efficiency of natural resource consumption, minimize the environmental impact of their use and provide value by lowering costs or providing superior performance."

- Information technology is the leading sector for CVC investments, followed by healthcare.

- The number of CVC investment deals fell by about 3% per year between 2000 and 2008.

- In 2001, an average of 269 CVC units from around the globe were active investors (i.e., made investments every quarter). By 2007, this figure had fallen to 108 units.

- CVC investing is increasingly dominated by a small group of long-term participants, including such corporations as Intel, Siemens, and Motorola.

SOURCE: Adapted from *Global Corporate Venture Capital Survey 2008–09*. White paper published by Ernst & Young. Available in the Ernst & Young Library at www.ey.com.

that corporate venture capital investments can be sorted into categories according to (1) their objectives (strategic or financial) and (2) the degree to which the new business being invested in (typically a start-up) has operational capabilities (i.e., resources and processes) that are linked to those of the investing corporation (tight or loose linkages). Firms with strategic investment objectives invest in external start-ups whose success promises to increase the sales and profits of the firm's existing businesses. Firms with financial investment objectives, by contrast, are principally seeking attractive financial returns through their investments. Tight operational linkages portend the possibility of leveraging the corporation's competencies in ways that contribute to the success of the venture (e.g., the venture might use the existing distribution channels of another business of the corporation); loose operational linkages imply that the corporation and the start-up have minimal resource or process overlap and that the start-up operates in a partially or wholly autonomous manner vis-à-vis the investing corporation.

Based on these two considerations, Chesbrough (2002) discusses four pure types of corporate venture capital investment:

- *Driving investments* (strategic rationale for investment and tight operational links between the start-up and the investing company)—These investments extend the corporation's presence in product–market or technological arenas regarded as strategic to the corporation. An example is Microsoft's investments in Internet services start-ups that rely on and help advance the corporation's Internet architecture.

- *Enabling investments* (strategic rationale for investment and loose operational links between the start-up and the investing company)—These investments complement the strategy of the corporation by stimulating demand for the corporation's current products through the development of the larger ecosystem within which the corporation or its businesses operate. An example is Intel's investments in computer-related start-ups whose success would guarantee a continuing demand for Intel's microprocessors.

- *Emergent investments* (financial rationale for investment and tight operational links between the start-up and the investing company)—These investments are targeted toward start-ups whose success may be of strategic relevance to the corporation (i.e., these start-ups have strategic option value to the corporation) or toward start-ups for whom the corporation's resources or processes provide needed and critical value within the start-up's overall business model. An example is Lucent's investments in start-ups that rely on telecommunications technology developed by, but not strategically valuable to, Lucent.

- *Passive investments* (financial rationale for investment and loose operational links between the start-up and the investing company)—These investments are diversification actions in which the corporation operates as a money manager or investment intermediary for its shareholders. An example is Dell's investments in high-tech information technology start-ups whose industries have been more lucrative, on average, than that those of Dell's core businesses.

According to Chesbrough (2002), passive investments are seldom if ever justifiable inasmuch as the corporate shareholders can diversify their own portfolios—they do not need the corporation to do this for them. Driving, enabling, and emergent investments, on the other hand, can foster growth in the corporation's current business or lead the firm into desirable new business arenas. Perhaps most significantly, poor short-term financial returns should not discourage corporations from making investments in external start-ups deemed to be of strategic importance within the scope of the corporation's current or planned business operations.

Satisfaction with Corporate Venturing

Bain & Company's 2003 Management Tools survey of 708 major companies from around the world revealed a low level of managerial satisfaction with corporate venturing practice, which includes the use of corporate venture capital investments

(Rigby, 2003).These survey results can be partially explained by the possibility that many of the firms responding to the survey were venturing for purely financial purposes, using corporate venture capital investments in external ventures to augment returns from the firms' core businesses. When the dot-com bubble burst in the early 2000s, external corporate venturing often failed to yield the level of returns seen in prior years and the entire practice of corporate venturing seemed to have gotten a black eye.

Still, disappointment in corporate venturing results cannot be attributed solely to the failings of financial venturing. A 2001 Accenture study of corporate venturing practice in Fortune 1000 firms revealed that 30 percent of the firms were venturing primarily for financial purposes, but nearly twice that number were venturing for strategic purposes (Dickman et al., 2002). The disappointment indicated in managers' responses to the Bain & Company survey probably reflects the fact that many companies are not very good at corporate venturing, or creating new businesses within their existing business. Yet this is to be expected, as managers know their current business, while there is a significant learning curve involved in creating and then running new businesses. Just as challenging is the need to integrate a new business into the company's overall strategic direction. As argued by Covin and Miles (2007), "Firms have historically struggled with the successful employment of corporate venturing for long-term growth and corporate renewal purposes, and much of this struggle relates to managerial uncertainty over how corporate venturing might be operationally linked to the firm's overall strategic process and agenda."

Strategic Entrepreneurship: Innovating in Pursuit of Competitive Advantage

THE CONCEPT OF STRATEGIC ENTREPRENEURSHIP

Strategic entrepreneurship constitutes a second major category of approaches to corporate entrepreneurship (see Figure 4-1). While corporate venturing entails company involvement in the creation of new businesses, strategic entrepreneurship corresponds to a broader array of entrepreneurial initiatives that do not necessarily involve new businesses being added to the firm. All forms of strategic entrepreneurship have one thing in common: They all involve organizationally consequential innovations that are adopted in the pursuit of competitive advantage.

Strategic entrepreneurship involves simultaneous opportunity-seeking and advantage-seeking behaviors (Ireland et al., 2003). The innovations that are the focal points of strategic entrepreneurship initiatives represent the means through which opportunity is capitalized upon. These are innovations that can happen anywhere and everywhere in the company. By emphasizing an opportunity-driven mindset, management seeks to achieve and maintain a competitively advantageous position for the firm.

These innovations can represent fundamental *changes from the firms' past* strategies, products, markets, organization structures, processes, capabilities, or business models. Or, these innovations can represent bases on which the firm is fundamentally *differentiated from its industry rivals*. Hence, there are two possible reference points that can be considered when a firm exhibits strategic entrepreneurship: (1) how much the firm is transforming itself relative to where it was before (e.g., transforming its products, markets, internal processes, etc.) and (2) how much the firm is transforming itself relative to industry conventions or standards (again, in terms of product offerings, market definitions, internal processes, and so forth).

With regard to differentiation relative to one's industry, some firms consistently exhibit high levels of innovativeness from the time of their founding and, as such, they have always been tagged with the label of *entrepreneurial firm* (e.g., Dell, Intel). Moreover, as discussed in Chapters 1 and 2, some industries invite continuous entrepreneurial behavior (e.g., fashion-related and technology-based industries). Therefore, innovativeness per se may not be a basis on which firms in those industries are differentiated from their industry rivals. Rather, it is the products, services, and processes that result from this innovativeness that determine how well they are differentiated.

Strategic entrepreneurship can take one of five forms—*strategic renewal, sustained regeneration, domain redefinition, organizational rejuvenation,* and *business model reconstruction* (Covin and Miles, 1999). Some defining attributes of these different forms or approaches are presented in Table 4–3. These forms are discussed in greater detail below.

THE FORMS OF STRATEGIC ENTREPRENEURSHIP

Strategic renewal is a type of entrepreneurship in which the firm "seeks to redefine its relationship with its markets or industry competitors by fundamentally altering how it competes" (Covin and Miles, 1999, p. 52). As originally defined by Guth and Ginsberg (1990, p. 5), the label *strategic renewal* referred to "the transformation of organizations through renewal of the key ideas on which they are built." Yet strategic renewal has a more specific meaning and focus. As shown in Table 4–3, with strategic renewal the focus of the entrepreneurial initiative is the firm's strategy. However, not all firms that adopt new strategies are pursuing strategic renewal. Rather, new strategies constitute strategic renewal when they represent fundamental repositioning efforts by the firm within its competitive space. An example is Sears' attempt to reposition itself within the retail merchandising industry by moving "up-market" from a mass merchandiser position to a more high-end, branded position. Additionally, companies that are founded based on unique value propositions that deviate from accepted

TABLE 4-3

Forms of Strategic Entrepreneurship

Form of Strategic Entrepreneurship	Focus of the Entrepreneurial Initiative*	The Entrepreneurial Event	Typical Frequency of the Entrepreneurial Event
Strategic Renewal	*Strategy* of the firm	Adoption of a new strategy	Low
Sustained Regeneration	*Products* offered by the firm or *markets* served by the firm	Introduction of a new product into a preexisting product category or introduction of an existing product into a new (to the firm) but preexisting market	High
Domain Redefinition	*New competitive space*	Creation of new or re-configuration of existing product categories or market space	Low
Organizational Rejuvenation	*Organization structure, processes, and/or capabilities* of the firm	Enactment of a major, internally focused innovation aimed at improving strategy implementation	Low to moderate
Business Model Reconstruction	*Business model* of the firm	Design of a new or re-design of an existing business model	Low

* The focus of the entrepreneurial event can be the entire firm or, in the case of multi-business firms, one or more of its businesses.

industry strategic recipes are practicing the strategic renewal form of strategic entrepreneurship. They are playing new strategic games designed to place themselves in more favorable industry positions. Formule 1, a French hotel chain, is an example of a firm that has been successful in such an effort. This company deviated from conventional practice in the price-competitive end of the hotel industry by greatly reducing emphasis on hotel attributes and amenities not particularly valued by budget hotel customers (e.g., architectural aesthetics, eating facilities, lounges) and greatly increasing emphasis on hotel attributes and amenities valued by these customers, but on which they were being underserved (e.g., bed quality, hygiene, room quietness) (see Kim and Mauborgne, 1997). Within the popular business press and practitioner-oriented journals, strategic renewal has also been called strategic innovation (e.g., Hamel and Prahalad, 1995) and value innovation (e.g., Kim and Mauborgne, 1997, 1999).

Sustained regeneration refers to the entrepreneurial phenomenon whereby the firm "regularly and continuously introduces new products and services or enters new markets" (Covin and Miles, 1999, p. 51). With this form of strategic entrepreneurship the firm is in constant pursuit of entrepreneurial opportunities. Most of these opportunities will result in incremental innovations as represented by the offering of product extensions or movement into adjacent market arenas. On occasion, employment of the sustained regeneration form of strategic entrepreneurship will result in new business creation—3M's Post-it notes is an example. Sustained regeneration is most commonly employed as a basis for attaining or sustaining competitive advantage under conditions of short product-life cycles, changing technological standards, or segmenting product categories and market arenas. In the household consumer products industry, Procter & Gamble is an example of a firm whose actions reflect the sustained regeneration form of strategic entrepreneurship. In the telecommunications industry, Motorola is an example. Arguably, sustained regeneration is the most recognized and common form of strategic entrepreneurship. Firms that successfully practice sustained regeneration have reputations as "innovation machines." Unlike the other forms of strategic entrepreneurship, sustained innovation cannot be represented by a single, discrete event. Rather, sustained regeneration exists when firms exhibit an ongoing pattern of new product introductions and/or new market entries.

Domain redefinition refers to the entrepreneurial phenomenon whereby the firm "proactively creates a new product-market arena that others have not recognized or actively sought to exploit" (Covin and Miles, 1999, p. 54). Through domain redefinition, firms move into uncontested markets, or what Kim and Mauborgne (2005) have called "blue oceans." These are product-market arenas in which new product categories are represented. A product category refers to a group of products that consumers view as substitutable for one another yet distinct from those in another product category. These new product categories can either give rise to completely new industries or redefine the boundaries of existing industries. An example of the former is eBay, the first-mover or market pioneer of the online auction industry. An example of the latter is Cirque du Soleil, a Canadian firm that has, to use their expression, "reinvented the circus" by combining elements of the circus industry with elements of the theater industry. Domain redefinition renders a firm's current competition moot, at least temporarily, inasmuch as this entrepreneurial activity takes place in unoccupied competitive space. The entrepreneurial firm's hope is that its first-mover status will create a basis for sustainable competitive advantage when and if competitors follow. The domain redefinition phenomenon is discussed within the business literature under a variety of labels including bypass strategy (Fahey, 1989), market pioneering (Golder and Tellis, 1993), whitespace marketing (Maletz and Nohria, 2001), and blue ocean strategy (Kim and Mauborgne, 2004, 2005). Unlike the other forms of strategic entrepreneurship, domain definition necessarily results in new business creation.

Organizational rejuvenation refers to the entrepreneurial phenomenon whereby the firm "seeks to sustain or improve its competitive standing by altering its internal processes, structures, and/or capabilities" (Covin and Miles, 1999, p. 52). With organizational rejuvenation, the focus of the innovation effort is a core attribute or set of attributes associated with the firm's internal operations. The objective of these efforts is to create a superior organizational vehicle through which the firm's strategy can be implemented. When pursued successfully, organizational rejuvenation enables a firm to achieve a competitive advantage without changing its strategy, product offerings, or served markets. Sometimes organizational rejuvenation will entail a fundamental redesign of the entire organization, such as might result from major business process reengineering projects that reconfigure the company's internal value chain. Organizational rejuvenation can also involve single innovations that have sweeping implications for the firm (e.g., major restructuring efforts) or multiple smaller innovations that collectively contribute to significantly increased organizational efficiency or effectiveness at strategy implementation (e.g., administrative innovations designed to facilitate inter-unit communications or the transference of core competencies). In order to constitute organizational rejuvenation, the innovation(s) in question cannot simply imitate initiatives that are common to the firm's industry. Rather, the innovation(s) must, at least temporarily, distinguish the firm from its industry rivals.

Springfield Remanufacturing Corporation (SRC) is a firm whose entrepreneurial behavior reflects the organizational rejuvenation form of strategic entrepreneurship. SRC's core business is rebuilding diesel engines for the truck market. This company's deteriorating business situation was turned around through instituting a set of managerial practices known internally as open-book management. By sharing important competitive and financial information with the SRC workforce and actively soliciting their involvement in matters regarding job design and process innovation, management was able to build a high-performing organization to which the workforce feel great commitment and in which they take great pride. In short, SRC has achieved competitive success by rebuilding their organization, focusing on entrepreneurial initiatives pertaining to internal structure-, culture-, and process-related matters.

Business model reconstruction finds the firm applying entrepreneurial thinking to the design or redesign of its core business model(s) in order to improve operational efficiencies or otherwise differentiate itself from industry competitors in ways valued by the market. Business models have been described as "stories that explain how enterprises work" (Magretta, 2002, p. 87). Well-known examples of business model reconstruction pioneers include Dell Computer with its direct sales model and eBay with its online auction model. Dell employed a new business model within an established industry; eBay created a new industry with its business model. Other firms are not founded on the basis of novel business models, but instead adopt new business models in their pursuit of competitive advantage. Common forms of such business model reconstruction include outsourcing (i.e., relying on external suppliers for activities previously performed internal to the firm) and, to a lesser extent, vertical integration (i.e., bringing elements of the supplier or distributor functions within the ownership or control of the firm).

An example of an established firm that has employed business model reconstruction in an entrepreneurial fashion is 7-Eleven. This firm began its operations as a traditional, vertically integrated company within the convenience store industry—it even owned the cows that produced the milk it sold. Soon after 7-Eleven's former CEO, Jim Keyes, assumed responsibility for planning and operations in the early 1990s he decided to "outsource everything not mission critical" (see Gottfredson et al., 2005, for a detailed discussion of the 7-Eleven example). As of 2005, 7-Eleven employed a business model unlike any other in the convenience store industry. 7-Eleven has kept in-house functional activities over which the firm wants to maintain proprietary knowledge as well as functional activities that can be performed in the most effective or efficient manner within the corporate structure. These activities include in-store merchandising, pricing, ordering, and customer data analysis. Virtually all other business-related functional activities are outsourced. The result is a much more streamlined business model than that employed throughout the convenience store industry, albeit one in which more control over mission-critical activities is achieved relative to that typically afforded by rivals' business models. For example, whereas other firms in the convenience store industry allow one of the industry's key suppliers, Frito-Lay, to determine the order quantities and shelf placement for its snack food products, 7-Eleven maintains in-house control over these decision areas.

Because of its importance in the contemporary competitive environment, we will next explore the concept of a business model in greater detail.

The Business Model as a Vehicle for Corporate Entrepreneurship

A firm's business model can be defined as "a concise representation of how an interrelated set of decision variables in the areas of venture strategy, architecture, and economics will be addressed to create sustainable competitive advantage in defined markets." According to Morris et al. (2005), a business model should address six basic questions:

1. How does the firm create value?

2. For whom does the firm create value?

3. What is our source of internal advantage or core competency?

4. How does the firm externally differentiate itself in the marketplace?

5. What is the firm's model for making money?

6. What is management's growth ambition and over what time period?

These authors further suggest that decisions in these six areas can be made at three levels, which they term the foundation, proprietary, and rules levels. At the *foundation level*, management makes generic decisions regarding what the business is and is not, and ensures such decisions are internally consistent. The foundation level addresses basic decisions in each of the six areas.

While the foundation level is adequate to capture the essence of many firms' business models, sustainable advantage is ultimately dependent on the ability of the firm to apply unique approaches to one or more of the foundation components. Having determined the firm will sell some combination of goods directly to businesses, or that it will sell in consumer markets at high margins and low volumes, the corporate entrepreneur identifies ways to implement such decisions in a novel manner. This is referred to as the *proprietary level* of the model, as it entails innovation that is unique to a particular entrepreneur and venture. Where the foundation level is more generic, the proprietary level becomes strategy specific. The foundation level model is fairly easy for competitors to replicate, whereas the proprietary level is not. Replication is especially difficult because of the interactions *among* the proprietary-level components of the model. Consider the example of Dell Computer. At the foundation level, the company sells a mix of products and services; with a heavier product focus, the offering is customizable and sold directly to business and consumer markets. However, competitive advantage derives from unique approaches applied to two model components. The "Dell Direct Method" is the result of proprietary approaches both to defining the value proposition and organizing internal logistical flows. Interactions among these proprietary concepts enable the firm to consistently deliver speed and customization at a moderate price.

The usefulness of any model is limited, however, unless it provides specific guidance and discipline to the operations of a business. The need to consider operational issues necessitates a third level of decision making. The *rules level* of the business model delineates guiding principles (e.g., a set of rules) that govern execution of the decisions made at levels one and two. These guidelines help ensure the model's foundation and proprietary elements are reflected in ongoing strategic actions of the firm. Further examples can be found by considering a study of Excite and Yahoo! performed by Girotto and Rivkin (2000). They observe that Yahoo! adheres to a set of guiding rules in the formation of partnerships, a critical part of the firm's business model, including: "Put the product first. Do a deal only if it enhances the customer experience. And enter no joint venture that limits Yahoo!'s evolvability." In the previous Dell Computer example, examples of rules might include turning inventory in four days or less, or delivering replacement parts to the customer by the next business day. Rules are important at the level of execution of the business model. Consistent adherence to basic principles can make the difference between two companies that otherwise have identical models.

Table 4-4 illustrates the highly entrepreneurial business model of Southwest Airlines. This powerful model has sustained the company's growth for over 30 years. Not only has the company achieved profitability every year since 1972, but it is consistently ranked among the top ten most desired companies to work for by *Fortune* magazine, and has won a number of industry awards for efficiency and service. The robustness of the firm's model is evidenced in the firm's sustained levels of performance in the aftermath of the 9/11 terrorist tragedy that devastated the industry. Not surprisingly, the Southwest model has been copied in whole or in part by others (e.g., JetBlue, AirTran, Continental "Light"). While there are notable success stories among them, none of these firms has achieved the level of success as Southwest, and none has competed successfully on a head-to-head basis with Southwest. The superiority of Southwest in exploiting this model makes it clear that a well-conceived and well-implemented business model both affects and is affected by such organizational variables as culture and quality leadership.

The Southwest model is first captured at the foundation level. Here, the focus is on *what* the firm is doing, as opposed to *how*. This level gets at the basics of the firm's approach, and represents a standardized set of questions that can be easily quantified. At the proprietary level, Southwest has innovated in a manner that has changed the ways in which other airlines operate, and yet in a manner that others have been unable to replicate. From Table 4-4 it can be seen how each of the basic components of the model is tailored, and how each element is intertwined and internally consistent with the others. Arguably, the model centers on the firm's core competency, its production/operating system. This unique operating system (e.g., employee policies, airport and route selection, no code sharing, independent baggage handling, standardization of aircraft) makes possible a unique value proposition (short haul, low-fare, direct service that is on-time, and "fun"). Finally, it would be easy to deviate from this model,

TABLE 4-4

Characterizing the Business Model of Southwest Airlines

	Foundation Level	Proprietary Level	Rules Level
Component 1 (factors related to offering)	• Sell services only • Standardized offering • Narrow breadth • Shallow lines • Sell the service by itself • Internal service delivery • Direct distribution	• Short haul, low-fare, high-frequency, point-to-point service • Deliver fun • Serve only drinks/snacks • Assign no seats/no first class • Do not use travel agents/intermediaries • Fully refundable fares, no advance purchase requirement	• Maximum one-way fare should not exceed $___ • Maximum food cost per person should be less than $___
Component 2 (market factors)	• B2C and B2B (sell to individual travelers and corporate travel depts.) • National • Retail • Broad market • Transactional	• Managed evolution from regional airline to providing service to 59 airports in 30 states • Careful selection of cities based on fit with underlying operating model	• Specific guidelines for selecting cities to be serviced • 85% Penetration of local markets
Component 3 (internal capability factors)	• Production /operating systems	• Highly selective hiring of employees that fit profile; intense focus on frontline employees • Do not operate a hub-and-spoke route system • Fly into uncongested airports of small cities, less congested airports of large cities • Innovative ground operations approach	• At least 20 departures per day from airport • Maximum flight distance should be less than___ miles • Maximum flight time should be less than___ minutes • Turnaround of flights should be 20 minutes or fewer

(Continued)

	Foundation Level	Proprietary Level	Rules Level
TABLE 4-4 (Continued) **Characterizing the Business Model of Southwest Airlines**			
		• Independent baggage handling system • Use of Boeing 737 aircraft • No code sharing with other airlines	
Component 4 (competitive strategy factors)	• Image of operational excellence/consistency/dependability	• Differentiation is achieved by stressing on-time arrival, lowest possible fares, and passengers having a good time (a spirit of fun) • Airline that love built	• Achieve best on-time record in industry
Component 5 (economic factors)	• Fixed revenue source • High operating leverage • High volumes • Low margins annual profitability	• Short-haul routes and high frequency of flights combined with consistently low prices and internal efficiencies result in regardless of industry trends	• Maintain cost per passenger mile below $___
Component 6 (personal/ investor factors)	• Growth model	• Emphasis on growth opportunities that are consistent with business model	• Managed rate of growth

SOURCE: Reprinted from *Journal of Business Research*, Vol. 58, Morris, et al., Characterizing the Business Model of Southwest Airlines, from "The Entrepreneur's Business Model: Toward a Unified Perspective," pp. 726–735, © 2005, with permission from Elsevier.

especially given competitive and regulatory pressures. However, a number of rules help ensure that strategic or tactical moves that are inconsistent with the business model are not made. Rules regarding maximum fares, flight turnaround times, or on-time performance effectively delimit courses of action management might consider, while also reinforcing in the minds of operating personnel the strategic intent of the firm.

One of the most noteworthy examples of the power of business model reconstruction as a mechanism for facilitating the achievement of competitive advantage is the case of Apple Computer. Apple's traditional emphasis on the proprietary design of its products and software relegated the firm to a niche player within the computer industry and precluded the firm from competing on the basis of price. By the late 1990s, Apple's growth prospects had become severely limited. However, in the early 2000s Apple began introducing a series of new products and services including the iPod and the iTunes online music service. The success of these new market offerings has helped to propel Apple to a leading position within its industry segments. Notably, the success realized by Apple throughout the 2000s has not been spawned simply and solely from product innovations. Rather, Apple has succeeded by being the first firm to develop a workable business model for downloading music and by developing new product (iPod) and service (iTunes) categories that support that model. The challenge of developing such a business model had eluded firms in the music industry for years. The popularity of the iPod is credited with leading customers to reconsider Apple computers and embrace the firm's newer product offerings, including the iPhone and iPad. In short, it might be argued that business model reconstruction has revitalized Apple Computer in the twenty-first century.

The Open Innovation Revolution

As companies respond to the innovation imperative, they are increasingly relying on a model of innovation variously known as open-source innovation (Grand et al., 2004), open-market innovation (Rigby and Zook, 2002), or, more simply, open innovation (Chesbrough, 2003). Open innovation refers to *a general approach to innovation*, not a specific form of corporate entrepreneurship. Open innovation implies that the firm is not solely reliant upon its own innovative resources for new technology, product, or business development purposes. Rather, the firm acquires critical inputs to innovation from outside sources. Additionally, the firm may choose to commercialize its innovative ideas through external pathways that operate beyond the bounds of the firm's current business(es).

Through open innovation firms move from a traditional closed system model of innovation, where they generate, develop, and commercialize their own innovative ideas, to one in which the organizational boundaries to innovation are porous and innovative ideas flow into and out of the organization with ease. The open innovation model encourages firms to exploit creative ideas through different innovation modes. Open innovation can entail, for example, licensing agreements in which the firm sells its technology and/or acquires technology from others, joint ventures, corporate spin-offs of new businesses that are enabled by the firm's resources but not central to the firm's strategy, venture capital investments, and participation in external R&D consortia/ alliances. In short, open innovation enables others' innovative ideas to enter the firm's innovation process and the firm's innovative ideas to be exploited outside the firm's organizational boundaries by the firm itself or by others, to the firm's benefit. Firms currently pursuing innovation through an open model include Intel, Eli Lilly, Phillips, Merck, and IBM. According to a survey conducted by NineSigma (2009), a service provider in the innovation solutions industry, the practice of open innovation is expanding rapidly on a global basis. Some of the benefits of open innovation identified by the companies surveyed by NineSigma include an increase in the richness of their technology portfolios (77 percent of respondents), the ability to find noncore competencies through external partners (66.7 percent of respondents), increased R&D productivity (58.3 percent of respondents), and an increase in the speed to use of innovation (51.6 percent of respondents). Additionally, more than half of the surveyed firms reported that their reputations had strengthened as a result of adopting open innovation programs. Why are companies increasingly choosing to pursue an open innovation model? Rigby and Zook (2002) offer four reasons:

1. *Importing new ideas is a good way to multiply the building blocks of innovation.* That is, by accessing external inputs to innovation (e.g., others' technology that is available through licensing) firms can potentially offer more and better innovative outputs (e.g., new products).

2. *Exporting ideas is a good way to raise cash and keep talent.* A company's innovative ideas, such as its proprietary technology, can have market value that is exploitable through its sale to outside customers. Additionally, by selling internally developed but unexploited innovative ideas to outside parties, firms can avoid discouraging the people who generated those ideas.

3. *Exporting ideas gives companies a way to measure an innovation's real value and to ascertain whether further investment is warranted.* Offers to sell internally developed innovative ideas to external markets can be litmus tests for the true value of those ideas (which are often undervalued or overvalued when viewed through purely internal lenses).

4. *Exporting and importing ideas helps companies clarify what they do best.* Collaborative efforts, the purchase of innovations or inputs to innovations from others, and offers to sell the firm's innovations or inputs to innovations to others can reveal where a firm's real bases for competitive advantage lie and, accordingly, how it should define its business.

The open innovation model has great promise as a new paradigm within which the challenges of innovation can be addressed. However, to quote Denning (2005, p. 8), open innovation "is a supplement to the steps that are needed to resolve the basic problem of innovation, not a solution in itself. The fundamental problem in innovation isn't one of finding more ideas: it's a matter of establishing a way of running the organization that is open to exploring new ideas and willing to back the most promising of them with resources and talent." These issues are explored in detail in later chapters.

THE INNOVATOR'S NOTEBOOK

The World's Best Companies for Innovation

Every year business magazines are ranking the most innovative companies. Some of the top ranked names would not surprise you but it is indeed interesting to see the different industries that these innovative leaders represent. Here is a sampling of those companies that seem to be on everyone's list these days.

Facebook is by some measurements the most popular social network with more than 200 million active users worldwide. It is one of the fastest-growing and best-known sites on the Internet today. In May 2009, a Russian investment firm, Digital Sky Technologies, invested $200 million in Facebook in return for a 1.96 percent stake. That investment valued Facebook at $10 billion, a $5 billion drop from October 2007 when Microsoft paid $240 million for a 1.6 percent stake. With the latest round of financing, Facebook has raised about $600 million since it was founded in 2004.

Amazon is an American-based multinational electronic commerce company. Headquartered in Seattle, Washington, with sales of over $24 billion it is America's largest online retailer, with nearly three times the Internet sales revenue of the runner-up, Staples, as of January 2010. Amazon.com opened on the World Wide Web in July 1995 and today seeks to be a customer-centric company, where customers can find and discover anything they might want to buy online, and endeavors to offer its customers the lowest possible prices. Amazon.com and other sellers offer millions of unique new, refurbished, and used items in categories such as Books; Movies, Music & Games; Digital Downloads; Computers & Office; Electronics; Home, Garden & Pets; Grocery, Health & Beauty; Toys, Kids & Baby; Clothing, Shoes & Jewelry; Sports & Outdoors; Tools & Home Improvement; and Automotive & Industrial.

Apple is an American multinational corporation that designs and manufactures consumer electronics, computer software, and personal computers. The company's best-known hardware products include Macintosh computers, the iPod, the iPhone, and the iPad. Apple software includes the iTunes media browser; the iLife suite of multimedia and creativity software; the iWork suite of productivity software; and Aperture, a professional photography package. As of January 2010 the company had revenues exceeding $50 billion and operated 284 retail stores in ten countries, and an online store where hardware and software products are sold. Now the tenth largest company in the world, *Fortune* magazine named Apple the most admired company in the world in 2008, 2009, and 2010.

Google is considered the world's leading search engine with over 19,000 employees and over $24 billion in revenue. Founders Larry Page and Sergey Brin named the search engine they built "Google," a play on the word "googol," the mathematical term for a 1 followed by 100 zeros. The name reflects the immense volume of information that exists, and the scope of Google's mission, which is to organize the world's information and make it universally accessible and useful. Google primarily generates revenue by delivering relevant, cost-effective online advertising. Businesses use Google's AdWords program to promote products and services with targeted advertising. In addition, the thousands of third-party Web sites that comprise the Google network use the Google AdSense program to deliver relevant AdWords ads that generate revenue and enhance the user experience.

Novartis is one of the world's largest pharmaceutical companies, created in 1996 through the merger of Ciba-Geigy and Sandoz. Throughout the years, Novartis and its predecessor companies have discovered and developed many innovative products for patients and consumers worldwide. Today Novartis is a $45 billion company organized into four divisions: Pharmaceuticals: Innovative patent-protected medicines; Vaccines and Diagnostics: Human vaccines and diagnostic tools to protect against life-threatening diseases; Sandoz: Generic pharmaceuticals that replace branded medicines after patent expiry and free up funds for innovative medicines; and Consumer Health: Readily available products that enable healthy lifestyle choices: OTC (over-the-counter), Animal Health and CIBA Vision. The company's mission is to discover, develop, and successfully market innovative products to prevent and cure diseases, to ease suffering, and to enhance the quality of life.

Walmart is the world's largest discount department store chain and the world's largest public corporation by revenue, according to the Fortune Global 500. Founded by Sam Walton in 1962, Walmart is the largest private employer and the largest grocery retailer in the United States. It also owns and operates the Sam's Club retail warehouses in North America. In 2009, Walmart paid a combined $933.6 million in bonuses to every full- and part-time hourly worker of the company. An additional $788.8 million in profit sharing, 401(k) contributions, and hundreds of millions of dollars in merchandise discounts and contributions to the employees' stock purchase plan was also included. While the economy at large was in an ongoing recession, Walmart reported solid financial figures for the most recent fiscal year (2009), with $401.2 billion in net sales.

Nike is the world's leading supplier of athletic shoes and apparel, and a major manufacturer of sports equipment with revenue in excess of $19 billion and a workforce of more than 30,000 people worldwide. The company was founded in 1964 as Blue Ribbon Sports and officially became Nike, Inc. in 1978. The company takes its name from the Greek goddess of victory. Nike has contracted with more than 700 shops around the world and has offices located in 45 countries outside the United States. In 2010, Nike CEO Mark Parker outlined the goals for the company as: deliver compelling product; maintain the integrity of brands while building even stronger relationships with consumers; strengthen and leverage operational capability; and create compelling retail experiences—both in owned retail and with wholesale partners. Nike sees the highest potential opportunities in Brazil, China, India, Japan, Russia, U.K., and the United States, with seven key performance and lifestyle categories—action sports, basketball, football, men's training, running, sportswear, and women's training.

Disney is the largest media and entertainment conglomerate in the world. Founded in 1923 by brothers Walt and Roy Disney, the company was reincorporated as Walt Disney Productions in 1929. Walt Disney Productions established itself as a leader in the American animation industry before diversifying into live-action film production, television, and travel. Taking on its current name in 1986, the Walt Disney Company expanded its existing operations and also started divisions focused upon theatre, radio, publishing, and online media. In addition, it has created new divisions of the company in order to market more mature content than it typically associates with its flagship family-oriented brands. The company is best known for the products of its film studio—the Walt Disney Motion Picture Group today is one of the largest studios. Disney also owns and operates the ABC television network; cable television networks such as Disney Channel and ESPN; and 11 theme parks around the world.

Discussion Questions

1. What specific motives might these companies have for pursuing corporate innovative activities? Be specific in your examples.

2. How would "Strategic Entrepreneurship" apply to each of these companies?

3. Describe the "Business Model" for each of these innovative companies. You may need to research each company further to establish a sound answer.

SOURCES: Adapted from: "The World's 50 Most Innovative Companies," *Fast Company,* March 2010; and company Web sites accessed April 14, 2010.

Summary and Conclusions

This chapter has reviewed the two categories of phenomena that represent the major forms of corporate entrepreneurship. These categories are corporate venturing and strategic entrepreneurship. Corporate venturing refers to a set of entrepreneurial phenomena where new businesses are created by, added to, or invested in by an existing corporation. Corporate venturing occurs in three modes: internal corporate venturing (new businesses are created and owned by the corporation), cooperative corporate venturing (new businesses are created and owned by the corporation and one or more external development partners), and external corporate venturing (new businesses are created by parties outside the corporation and subsequently invested in through the assumption of equity positions or acquired by the corporation). External corporate venturing is often pursued through corporate venture capital investments. Strategic entrepreneurship refers to a broad array of entrepreneurial phenomena, which may or may not result in new businesses being added to the corporation, in which large-scale or otherwise organizationally consequential innovations are adopted in the firm's pursuit of competitive advantage. The forms of strategic entrepreneurship include strategic renewal, sustained regeneration, domain redefinition, organizational rejuvenation, and business model reconstruction. In their approaches to corporate entrepreneurship, firms are increasingly relying on an approach to innovation known as open innovation. Under an open innovation paradigm, firms use internally generated and externally sourced innovations (and inputs to innovations) to advance their business interests. External channels are also used as pathways through which firms leverage the value of their innovative ideas.

References

Burgelman, R. A. 1983. "Corporate Entrepreneurship and Strategic Management: Insights from a Process Study," *Management Science*, 29(12): 1349–1364.

Chesbrough, H. W. 2002. "Making Sense of Corporate Venture Capital," *Harvard Business Review*, 80(3): 90–99.

Chesbrough, H. W. 2003. "The Era of Open Innovation," *MIT Sloan Management Review*, 44(3): 35–41.

Covin, J. G., and Miles, M. P. 1999. "Corporate Entrepreneurship and the Pursuit of Competitive Advantage," *Entrepreneurship Theory and Practice*, 23(3): 47–63.

Covin, J. G., and Miles, M. P. 2007. "Strategic Use of Corporate Venturing," *Entrepreneurship Theory and Practice*, 31(2): 183–208.

Denning, S. 2005. "Why the Best and Brightest Approaches Don't Solve the Innovation Dilemma," *Strategy & Leadership*, 33(1): 4–11.

Dickman, K., Kambil, A., and Wilson, J. 2002. "Hidden Value in Corporate Venturing," *Strategy & Leadership*, 30(2): 47–38.

Fahey, L. 1989. "Bypass Strategy: Attacking by Surpassing Competitors," in L. Fahey (ed.), *The Strategic Planning Management Reader* (Englewood Cliffs, NJ: Prentice-Hall): 189–193.

Garvin, D. A. 2002. "A Note on Corporate Venturing and New Business Creation," *Harvard Business School Note*, 9-302-091.

Girotto, J., and Rivkin, J. 2000. "Yahoo! Business on Internet Time," *Harvard Business School Case*, 9-700-013 (Boston: Harvard Business School Press).

Global Corporate Venture Capital Survey 2008–09. White paper published by Ernst & Young. Available in the Ernst & Young Library at www.ey.com.

Golder, P. N., and Tellis, G. J. 1993. "Pioneer Advantage: Marketing Logic or Marketing Legend," *Journal of Marketing Research*, 30: 158–170.

Gompers, P. A. 2002. "Corporations and the Financing of Innovation: The Corporate Venturing Experience," *Federal Reserve Bank of Atlanta Economic Review*, Fourth Quarter: 1–17.

Gottfredson, M., Puryear, R., and Phillips, S. 2005. "Strategic Sourcing: From Periphery to the Core," *Harvard Business Review*, 83(2): 132–139.

Grand, S., von Krogh, G., Leonard, D., and Swap, W. 2004. "Resource Allocation Beyond Firm Boundaries: A Multi-Level Model for Open Source Innovation," *Long Range Planning*, 37(6): 591–610.

Guth, W. D., and Ginsberg, A. 1990. "Guest Editors' Introduction: Corporate Entrepreneurship," *Strategic Management Journal*, 11 (Summer Special Issue): 5–16.

Hamel, G., and Prahalad, C. K. 1995. "Thinking Differently," *Business Quarterly*, 59(4): 22–35.

Ireland, R. D., Hitt, M. A., and Sirmon, D. G. 2003. "A Model of Strategic Entrepreneurship: The Construct and Its Dimensions," *Journal of Management*, 29(6): 963–989.

Kim, W. C., and Mauborgne, R. 1997. "Value Innovation: The Strategic Logic of High Growth," *Harvard Business Review*, 75(1): 103–112.

Kim, W. C., and Mauborgne, R. 1999. "Creating New Market Space," *Harvard Business Review*, 77(1): 83–93.

Kim, W. C., and Mauborgne, R. 2004. "Blue Ocean Strategy," *Harvard Business Review*, 82(10): 76–84.

Kim, W. C., and Mauborgne, R. 2005. "Blue Ocean Strategy: From Theory to Practice," *California Management Review*, 47(3): 105–121.

Kuratko, D. F., Covin, J. G., and Garrett, R. P., Jr. 2009. "Internal Corporate Venturing: Insights from Actual Performance," *Business Horizons*, 52(5): 459–467.

Magretta, J. 2002. "Why Business Models Matter," *Harvard Business Review*, 80(5): 86–92.

Maletz, M. C., and Nohria, N. 2001. "Managing in the Whitespace," *Harvard Business Review*, 79(1): 102–111.

Miles, M. P., and Covin, J. G. 2002. "Exploring the Practice of Corporate Venturing: Some Common Forms and Their Organizational Implications," *Entrepreneurship Theory and Practice*, 26(3): 21–40.

Morris, M. H., Schindehutte, M., and Allen, J. 2005. "The Entrepreneur's Business Model: Toward a Unified Perspective," *Journal of Business Research*, 58(6): 726–735.

NineSigma. 2009. *Open Innovation Practices and Outcomes 2009 Benchmark Survey Report*. NineSigma, Inc. (www.ninesigma.com).

Peterson, R. A., and Berger, D. G. 1971. "Entrepreneurship in Organizations: Evidence from the Popular Music Industry," *Administrative Science Quarterly*, 16(1): 97–106.

Rigby, D. 2003. "Management Tools Survey 2003," *Strategy & Leadership*, 31(5): 4–11.

Rigby, D., and Zook, C. 2002. "Open-Market Innovation," *Harvard Business Review*, 80(10): 80–89.

Tidd, J., and Taurins, S. 1999. "Learn or Leverage? Strategic Diversification and Organizational Learning through Corporate Ventures," *Creativity and Innovation Management*, 8(2): 122–129.

CHAPTER 5

ENTREPRENEURSHIP IN OTHER CONTEXTS: NONPROFIT AND GOVERNMENT ORGANIZATIONS

Introduction

If major corporations can be entrepreneurial, what about organizations which are outside of the private sector? Does it make sense to talk about entrepreneurship in nonprofit organizations (NPOs) such as a major hospital, a university, or Habitat for Humanity? Is there a role for entrepreneurship in government organizations such as a highway department, a bureau of prisons, or a branch of the military? While evidence exists to suggest that entrepreneurship can enhance the ability of a private company to generate profits, some may question whether entrepreneurial behavior is consistent with the purpose and goals of organizations in these other sectors.

Consider nonprofit organizations, which are frequently associated with a social mission, such as feeding the homeless, saving the environment, or assisting the elderly. Funding is often driven by grants and donations, and success is not always easy to measure. One might not expect such organizations to take risks, invest in innovation, or to engage in a process of creative destruction where current methods are made obsolete. Similarly, with public sector organizations, one might assume we are dealing with monopolistic entities facing captive demand, enjoying guaranteed sources and levels of financing, and being relatively immune from the influences of voters, stakeholders, and political institutions such as legislatures and courts. Can we really expect to find entrepreneurs inside of bureaucracies where process often matters more than results?

In this chapter, we examine these questions and challenge some of the conventional stereotypes regarding nonprofit and public sector organizations. We will see that these organizations face unprecedented demands from a society that grows more complex and interdependent every day. As a result, entrepreneurship has become not only relevant, but often critical, for these organizations to accomplish their missions. The chapter will demonstrate how core concepts from entrepreneurship can be applied in nonprofit and public sector contexts. Unique obstacles to entrepreneurial behavior in both sectors will be highlighted, together with approaches for addressing these challenges.

Applying Entrepreneurial Concepts to the Nonprofit and Public Sectors

How do the basic concepts introduced so far in this book apply to nonprofit and public sector organizations? As noted in Chapter 1, the term "entrepreneurship" has historically referred to the efforts of an individual who takes on the odds in translating a vision into a successful business enterprise. More recently, however, entrepreneurship has been conceptualized as a *process* that can occur in organizations of all sizes and types. This process requires both an entrepreneurial event and an entrepreneurial agent. The event refers to the creation of a new product, service, process or entity. The agent is an individual or group who assumes personal responsibility for bringing the event to fruition.

In Chapter 2, we examined how the entrepreneurial process has attitudinal and behavioral requirements. Attitudinally, it refers to the willingness of an individual or organization to embrace new opportunities and take responsibility for effecting creative change. Behaviorally, the process includes the set of activities required to (a) identify and evaluate an opportunity, (b) define a business concept, (c) identify the needed resources, (d) acquire the necessary resources, and (e) implement, operate, and harvest the venture.

The basic six steps in this process (see Chapter 2) should be no different in a nonprofit or public sector context. Figure 5-1 provides an example of the application of these steps to a college or university. Some of the tools and concepts from the private sector that are useful when trying to understand or facilitate developments in each stage of the process are equally applicable in the nonprofit or public sectors (e.g., window of opportunity, leveraging of resources), while others must be adapted (e.g., criteria for evaluating an opportunity, sources of entrepreneurial concepts, harvesting strategies), and still others may not apply (e.g., competitive entry wedge, criteria for selecting financing sources).

Underlying entrepreneurial attitudes and behaviors are the three key dimensions of innovativeness, risk-taking, and proactiveness (see Chapter 3). To the extent that an undertaking demonstrates some amount of these three dimensions, it can be considered an entrepreneurial event, and the person behind it an entrepreneur. Further, any number of entrepreneurial events can be produced in a given time period. Accordingly, entrepreneurship is a question of "degree" and "frequency." Organizations can be characterized, then, in terms of their entrepreneurial orientation or "intensity," which is a reflection both of how many entrepreneurial things they are doing, and how innovative, risky, and proactive those things tend to be.

Entrepreneurship also has the same underlying dimensions when applied in nonprofit and public sector contexts. Innovativeness may tend to be more concerned with novel methods or processes, new services, and new organizational forms. Examples might include voter registration from one's automobile, day-care service for a welfare mother in

FIGURE 5-1

The Entrepreneurial Process Applied to a College or University

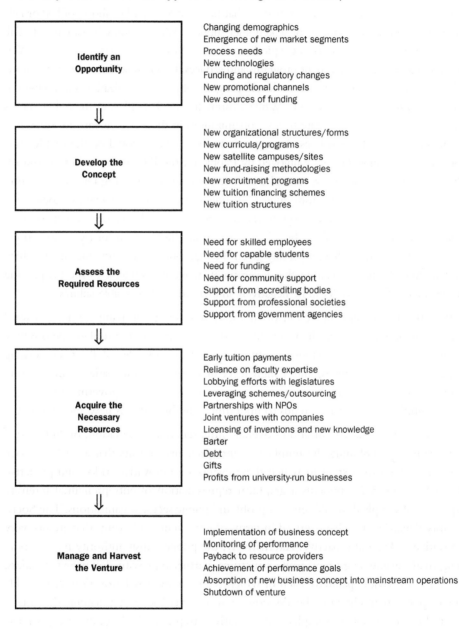

Identify an Opportunity

Changing demographics
Emergence of new market segments
Process needs
New technologies
Funding and regulatory changes
New promotional channels
New sources of funding

Develop the Concept

New organizational structures/forms
New curricula/programs
New satellite campuses/sites
New fund-raising methodologies
New recruitment programs
New tuition financing schemes
New tuition structures

Assess the Required Resources

Need for skilled employees
Need for capable students
Need for funding
Need for community support
Support from accrediting bodies
Support from professional societies
Support from government agencies

Acquire the Necessary Resources

Early tuition payments
Reliance on faculty expertise
Lobbying efforts with legislatures
Leveraging schemes/outsourcing
Partnerships with NPOs
Joint ventures with companies
Licensing of inventions and new knowledge
Barter
Debt
Gifts
Profits from university-run businesses

Manage and Harvest the Venture

Implementation of business concept
Monitoring of performance
Payback to resource providers
Achievement of performance goals
Absorption of new business concept into mainstream operations
Shutdown of venture

a job training program, or an agency that uses a guerrilla strategy for raising awareness of AIDS and its treatment.

Risk-taking involves pursuing initiatives that have a calculated likelihood of loss or failure either of financial resources or stakeholder support. While nonprofits can and do fail, public sector organizations do not typically go out of business or incur bankruptcy. Yet, failure still applies to government programs and services. Program failure can result in non-delivered services, cutbacks in service levels, program office or organizational unit closures, staff reassignments, and budget cuts. While scrutiny from stakeholders or the public means risk-taking tends to be moderate to low, organizations in these two sectors do sometimes undertake highly risky initiatives. A nonprofit sector example would be the highly confrontational educational tactics employed by People for the Ethical Treatment of Animals (PETA). For the public sector, examples include the controversial "Big Dig" construction project in Boston or the expensive luggage-handling system at the Denver, Colorado airport. There is also career-related risk in the nonprofit and public sectors. Leaders of nonprofits are highly accountable to boards that can easily dismiss them for trying something new and different and failing, especially given the tight budgetary constraints under which most nonprofits operate. Within the government, while it is difficult to fire people, the advancement of employees can be negatively influenced by their visible failures.

Proactiveness entails an action-orientation, tenacity in moving an idea toward implementation, and an emphasis on anticipating and preventing problems before they occur. Proactiveness also includes creative interpretation of rules, skills at networking and leveraging of resources, and a high level of persistence and patience in affecting change. This latter set of characteristics is especially critical in a government context, where significant bureaucracy tends to undermine anything that is new and different.

As noted above, an organization's overall entrepreneurial orientation, or "intensity," is the result of combining the number of entrepreneurial events that are taking place (frequency) with the extent to which these events are innovative, risky, and proactive (degree). Figure 5-2 represents a graphical representation of entrepreneurial intensity hypothetically applied to different nonprofit and public sector organizations. The Social Security department is characterized in terms of few events and events that are not very innovative, risky, and proactive. Alternatively, the public transit authority may be pursuing many events (e.g., new route structures, partnerships with downtown retailers, buses that are vividly painted), each of which is a fairly modest innovation. A very different approach might find the division of motor vehicles not pursuing that many events, but the ones it does implement are fairly entrepreneurial (e.g., driving examinations in simulators, automobile registration using the Internet). The nonprofit church is pursuing moderate levels of both degree and frequency, suggesting it is periodically introducing new products or methods (e.g., a new type of youth camp or new fundraising

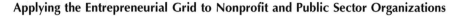

Applying the Entrepreneurial Grid to Nonprofit and Public Sector Organizations

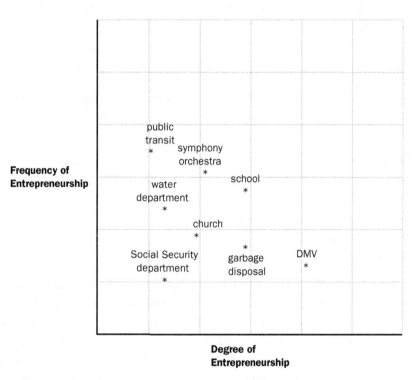

method), that reflect an intermediate level of innovativeness, risk, and proactiveness. The implication is that different levels of entrepreneurial intensity are appropriate for different types of nonprofit and public sector organizations, and organizations will design strategies that reflect their relative emphasis on frequency versus degree.

Exploring Entrepreneurship in Nonprofit Organizations

Let us first consider the nonprofit sector. In most societies, this is a rapidly growing sector that consists of a wide range of organizations serving many different purposes. As we shall see, these organizations have a number of distinct characteristics that pose a unique challenge to the concept of entrepreneurship.

THE UNIQUE NATURE OF NONPROFITS

The nonprofit sector consists of organizations of all sizes that typically serve a charitable or social purpose and do not distribute profits to shareholders. In the creation of a nonprofit, often the basis, or outcome, is the creation of some sort of public benefit. Some refer to this as "social capital" (Thompson, 2002). Social capital has multiple definitions, as well as different emphases. Social capital creates specific tangible and intangible assets within communities.

There is tremendous diversity among the many types of NPOs. From an overall standpoint, NPOs can also be categorized into three general groups:

- *Philanthropic Organizations*: Donating resources (tangible and intangible) for the betterment of those in need, motivated by humanitarian purposes (e.g., a foundation that funds scholarships for inner-city children);

- *Advocacy Organizations*: Supporters of causes or initiatives (e.g., agencies that seek to protect the environment, end spousal abuse, protect animals, or champion a political case); and

- *Mutual Benefit Organizations*: Agencies that provide services to constituencies, sometimes for a fee, often below actual cost (e.g., a community orchestra, health clinic, or school for the deaf).

Nonprofit or social enterprises differ in fundamental ways from their commercial counterparts (see Table 5-1 for a detailed list of differences). For example, the final recipients of NPO services are not always paying customers—they are often beneficiaries who pay little if any money. As such, NPOs are accountable to a greater number of stakeholders, ranging from those who receive their services to board members, donors, volunteers, the community, and government agencies. These stakeholders can have divergent interests. While for-profits are accountable for increasing the wealth of their shareholders, nonprofit goals are aimed at increasing social value to multiple stakeholders. Yet the accomplishment of nonprofit goals is often much harder to measure. How does the United Way know how much of a difference it is really making in a given community?

Conflicts can sometimes arise within NPOs between a focused dedication to the social mission and an emphasis on professional management practices. Professional management involves the setting of priorities that ensure the sustainability of the enterprise, the creation of processes and systems, strict fiscal discipline, and the need to make pragmatic trade-off decisions. Resistance may come from leaders whose priorities center on the immediate altruistic purpose, such as how to save souls, feed the homeless, or organize an arts function. Passion for the mission, and a preoccupation with immediate requirements of key constituencies, can lead to decisions that compromise the long-term viability of the social enterprise.

TABLE 5-1

What's Different about a Nonprofit Organization

While there is considerable diversity among nonprofits, they differ as a group from for-profit businesses in six key ways. These include:

Social Purpose: Rather than enhance owner wealth, the nonprofit exists to serve a social purpose. This purpose is central to everything the nonprofit does. Progress in accomplishing this purpose can be difficult to quantify (e.g., a cleaner environment, cultural enrichment of a community, reduction in spousal abuse).

Multiple Stakeholders: While all organizations have multiple stakeholders, the typical nonprofit faces a more complex set of linkages. Nonprofits must balance the interests of donors, users of their services, those who serve on their boards, the local community, regulatory authorities, members, volunteers, and others. These interests can be disparate and conflicting.

The Role of a Changing Product Portfolio Sold to Customers: While there are many examples of nonprofits that have set up revenue-generating operations (e.g., concerts, t-shirts, gift shops), the business of selling products is secondary to the nonprofit's primary focus on serving their social purpose. The selling of products, such as with Girl Scout cookies, is supplementary to or augments the social mission.

Dynamics of Competition: The existence of two or more environmental organizations operating in the same "market" may find them competing for funds and volunteers. However, the dynamics of competition do not generally find them attempting to capture market share from one another or put each other out of business. Rather, there tends to be a more collaborative spirit tied to a shared social purpose.

Lack of a Profit Motive and Different Personal Motives: Where private companies are focused on shareholder value driven by profits, nonprofits are driven by progress in achieving the social purpose, a need to provide value to multiple stakeholders, and the necessity to generate sufficient revenues to maintain or enhance operations. Individual employees and volunteers identify strongly with the social mission, motivating their behaviors. Moreover, when a nonprofit performs better financially, non-distribution constraints prevent founders, those in management, or board members from personally sharing in the excess of revenues over expenses. While a potential exists to increase the salaries of paid employees when financial performance is strong, compensation in nonprofits lags that received for equivalent private sector jobs.

Performance Measurement: The performance metrics employed by nonprofits can include both social (e.g., individuals counseled, pints of blood collected, souls saved) and financial indicators (e.g., revenues from operations, financial contributions, grants, volunteer hours). Improved social performance does not necessarily lead to better financial performance, nor is the converse always true.

It should also be noted that many NPOs blend both philanthropic and commercial interests. A museum can have a gift shop, while a women's rights organization might charge admission for the seminars that it sponsors. Yet, even when taking part in commercial activities that generate revenue, nonprofits will not do so at the expense of their missions. Further, pressures from stakeholders combined with a strong sense of stewardship regarding the nonprofit's core mission can find NPO managers less willing to pursue strategies that involve risk.

THE SOCIAL ENTREPRENEURSHIP CONCEPT

Nonprofits face serious challenges to their very existence. These organizations are dependent on funding from grants, endowments, donations, and fees, and many of them rely heavily on volunteers to staff their operations. The competition both for donor funds and volunteer time has intensified dramatically in recent years. Meanwhile, NPOs must address increasingly complex demands from their stakeholders, a growing maze of regulatory constraints, and tougher competition for high quality employees given the differential between what they can pay and what one can earn in the private sector.

These realities suggest fundamental changes to ways in which nonprofits are governed and managed. Meanwhile, the social needs and problems of communities only continue to multiply, creating a growing demand for new nonprofits and new services from existing nonprofits. The result of these trends is a significant emphasis on the concept of "social entrepreneurship." As Bryson et al. (2001) note, "to become self-sustaining, NPOs must generate resources that can produce valuable outputs that then activate additional, sustainable resource flows."

Social entrepreneurship can be defined as "new and novel mixes of opportunities, challenges, ideas, and resources in pursuit of potentially explosive (nonfinancial) rewards" (Brooks, 2009). It is based on furthering social good and meeting social needs through innovations that entail risks. In a broad sense, social entrepreneurship can be viewed as the creation of new NPOs as well as implementing innovative changes in established nonprofits (Short et al., 2009). Entrepreneurial behavior can take many forms inside of NPOs. Examples include:

- implementation of fees for services;
- development of new revenue-generating programs and related commercialization activities;
- launch of new enterprises;
- creative expansion of services and networks;

- diversification of funding sources to include unique types of sponsorships, advertising revenues, and rental of assets;

- resource sharing and blended funding streams;

- pursuit of consortia, mergers, and novel partnerships to maintain or generate additional resources;

- implementation of creative approaches to achieving greater staff efficiencies, operational improvements, and redesign of service delivery systems;

- incorporating new technologies into operations; and

- developing new performance metrics to capture social return on investment.

While some of the emphasis is on creating initiatives to generate additional revenues for the NPO, just as important is the development of bold new approaches to solving social problems. Toward this end, nonprofits are increasingly willing to adopt for-profit practices and models, and to partner with other organizations (profit, governmental, and other nonprofit entities) to accomplish their goals. Table 5-2 highlights 12 nonprofits that have demonstrated higher levels of entrepreneurial intensity.

Consider a major "soup kitchen" that feeds the homeless and poor in Washington, D.C. Beyond creative approaches to obtaining food donations from restaurants, food service companies, and corporations, the CEO used the kitchen to develop a successful catering service, which features ex-convicts as waiters. The venture is generating a healthy cash flow to support the basic soup kitchen operation. Going further, an innovative program was developed to tap into local public schools, using their kitchens during the many hours they are not operating, and teaching culinary skills to students—in the process producing more meals that enabled the food bank to reach a greater number of the disadvantaged members of the community.

Similar to commercial ventures, entrepreneurship in nonprofits is based on degree and frequency of entrepreneurial occurrences. The process of social entrepreneurship also mimics that seen in for profits: namely that opportunity is identified, a concept developed, necessary resources are determined and acquired, the organization is managed and finally harvested. Social entrepreneurship has as much to do with its leaders as with its processes and approaches. Social entrepreneurs are similar to their for-profit counterparts in their constant search for opportunities, greater tolerance for risk-taking, and proactiveness (Zahra et al., 2009). These individuals seek to further the development of civil society and contribute to the welfare of the needy. Social entrepreneurs seek opportunities that will allow them to attack the primary causes of needs, rather than merely remedying symptoms (Sullivan-Mort et al., 2003). They are able to combine business and entrepreneurial skills, while maintaining sight of their original social vision in order

---

TABLE 5-2

Examples of Entrepreneurial Nonprofit Organizations (NPOs)

Organization	Effects/Accomplishments
Nature Conservancy (United States)	Species/land conservation and preservation worldwide; developed more innovative/effective/accurate methods and measures to evaluate performance.
Defenders of Wildlife (United States)	Safeguards environmental/conservation/wildlife policies and laws worldwide; stimulates public awareness and education; lobbies for sustainability and protection of habitats; recognized as one of America's top 100 charities.
American Cancer Society (United States)	Cancer research; changed from a campaign of treatment to one of knowledge/prevention/treatment.
Central Kitchen (United States)	Cultivates restaurant industry skills to homeless and impoverished; established catering business that employs these beneficiaries, to generate sustainable revenue.
Soul City (South Africa)	Uses highly ranked prime-time television, radio, and literature to educate, interact with, and affect 79% of the South African population regarding health and development issues.
The Way Home (Ukraine)	Affects long-term change on homelessness and AIDS/HIV issues by educating beneficiaries on how to exercise their rights to government assistance.
The Population and Community Development Association (Thailand)	Addresses unsustainable overpopulation by educating about family planning, achieving rapid fertility declines; expanded activities to include poverty reduction, HIV/AIDS awareness, micro-credit, environmental restoration.
Human Rights (United States)	Utilizes visual media and technology to advocate for human rights in over 50 countries.
Grupo Ecologico Sierra Gorda (Mexico)	Focuses on rural development, the environment, and education by engaging the local population in resource management; resulted in the area being designated as a federally protected reserve.
Duck Revolution (Japan)	Developed a sustainable, integration of rice and duck farming systems, resulting in organic methods of reducing pollution, and increasing rice yield, food security, and rural farmer income.
Kashf Foundation (Pakistan)	Established the first and currently fastest-growing microfinance institution in its country, providing loans to women for enterprise development; attained a 100% recovery rate of loans.
Novica (United States)	Represents 50,000 people worldwide (artisans and their families) by marketing/distributing handmade crafts; takes advantage of technology for distribution, as well as global concerns over knowledge and quality of products.

to foster social change and create self-sufficiency. In doing so, they generate both economic and social benefits that all stakeholders find valuable.

OVERCOMING CHALLENGES TO SOCIAL OR NONPROFIT ENTREPRENEURSHIP

Is entrepreneurship really a relevant and valuable concept in a nonprofit context? Some might be concerned that an emphasis on entrepreneurship can compromise the basic values, missions, and services of the NPO (Pearce et al., 2010). For example, forming alliances may compromise the social missions and integrity of nonprofits. Further, nonprofit managers sometimes have less business-specific skills—therefore the amount of time, resources, and effort involved with establishment and upkeep of new innovations can distract them from their core social missions (Foster and Bradach, 2005). Conversely, since nonprofit leaders are heavily focused on their current missions, their ability to recognize new opportunities may be reduced (Dees et al., 2001).

Additionally, donors can also become alienated when the nonprofit attempts to engage in entrepreneurial actions, believing that their contributions should be directed toward the nonprofit's traditional needs, not toward new and potential risky undertakings. Other stakeholders can also prefer the status quo. NPO managers often find the need to serve the conflicting demands of multiple stakeholders limits their room to try new approaches. Finally, establishing for-profit initiatives may adversely affect the traditional tax-exempt status that benefits this sector, forcing them to compete on for-profit terms.

In spite of these challenges, the achievement of a specific social mission can be compatible with, and complementary to, entrepreneurial behavior. These are not opposing concepts. Those who are entrepreneurial stimulate social and economic improvement by embracing change and innovation, pursuing and recognizing opportunities that are mission-serving, using their resources imaginatively, and remaining accountable to their stakeholders. In fact, recent research has demonstrated that entrepreneurship has a direct, positive impact on the performance of nonprofits (Morris et al., 2007). Specifically, where NPOs adopted a strong entrepreneurial orientation in their management approaches, they tended to have higher net revenues (total revenues minus total expenses), and to generate more funds to support their operations (donations, grants, fees). Thus, it would appear that entrepreneurship contributes to the ability of the nonprofit to creatively advance their social cause.

Exploring Entrepreneurship in Government Organizations

Let us now turn to the public sector. Government organizations also have a number of unique characteristics that distinguish them from other work environments. However, the nature of these differences creates an even greater challenge for entrepreneurship than was the case with nonprofit organizations.

UNIQUE CHARACTERISTICS OF PUBLIC SECTOR ORGANIZATIONS

On the surface, public sector entrepreneurship would seem to have much in common with entrepreneurship in a large corporation. Both types of organizations typically have formalized hierarchies, established stakeholder groups with competing demands, deeply entrenched cultures, detailed rules and procedures to guide operations, a desire on the part of managers for power and security, and fairly rigid systems governing financial controls, cost allocations, budgeting, and employee rewards. Managers in both types of organizations are often more concerned with internal than external developments, and tend to focus more on considerations of process than on outcomes. Further, they are not independent, do not "own" the innovations they develop, and confront very finite limits on the rewards that they can receive. They have more job security, are not personally assuming the financial risks associated with a given innovative project, and have access to an established pool of resources.

Alternatively, a number of characteristics distinguish public sector organizations from private companies. With such comparisons, one must keep in mind the considerable diversity that exists among organizations in both sectors, particularly among those in the public sector. Some key differences (see Table 5-3 for a more comprehensive list) include the fact that public sector organizations

- do not have a profit motive, and instead are guided by social and political objectives; they typically seek to achieve a multiplicity and diversity of objectives; these objectives and performance toward them are harder to measure;

- have less exposure to the market and its incentives for cost reductions, operating economies, and efficient resource allocation; resources tend to be allocated based on equity considerations and political pressures;

- receive funds indirectly from an involuntary taxpayer rather than directly from a satisfied and voluntary customer;

- have difficulties in identifying the organization's "customer," as there typically are a number of different publics being served by a given agency, department, or unit;

- produce services that have consequences for others beyond those immediately involved; managers have greater accountability for the indirect consequences of their actions;

- are subject to public scrutiny, such that major decisions have to be made with transparency; decisions must involve consensus among and consultation with a variety of interest groups and constituencies; and

- face risk/reward trade-offs that strongly favor avoiding mistakes.

These differences raise fundamental questions regarding not simply whether entrepreneurship *can* be applied in public enterprises, but whether it *should* be applied.

TABLE 5-3

Fourteen Characteristics of Government and Bureaucracy

Pluralism. Administrative agencies are boxed in by intricately related and often strongly opposing interests. To survive, they must take into account, and be responsive to, all politically effective groups, any number of which may have problems with the change brought by an entrepreneurial enterprise. The bureaucracy becomes a contending and offsetting collection of fiefdoms.

Overload. The revolution in entitlements over the past 50 years has produced an expectation by dependent groups that the government is the first resort for their well-being. Increasing demands have made the government increasingly unable to cope. The more decisions it must handle, the more it becomes hostage to political and governmental influences.

Rational Limited Search. Bureaucracies fail to seek the most effective solutions and concentrate on precedent and standard operating procedures. Unlike entrepreneurs, they do not seek the greatest level of performance for the least cost. Similarly, faced with uncertainty, they do not estimate the relevant probability distribution of various outcomes and apply the appropriate discount rates to maximize rates of return to society.

Multiple Objectives and Constituencies. Bureaucrats rarely ask, "Who is our market?" Enabling legislation for the programs they administer often contains vague and conflicting objectives because of the necessity to achieve consensus.

Uncertain Production Functions. It is very difficult to measure the efficiency or effectiveness of bureaucratic performance. The production function is only partially known. A bureaucracy rarely knows what would happen if it employed alternative combinations of inputs. There is little incentive to experiment to see if the organizational design, the staff, and the technology used can be varied to increase, let alone maximize, output.

Input-Output Measures. Because performance tends to be measured by the amount of inputs from sponsors or publics, not by indicators of output or government impact, bureaucracies design programs, and conspire with clients and constituents, to achieve more staff and budget. Should the bureaucracy request fewer inputs, its client groups are apt to accuse it of dishonoring its mandate, while lower budget requests (e.g., due to productivity gains or problem resolution) invite even greater cuts the next time around.

Need for Symbols. In addition to their stated objectives, bureaucracies have symbolic and "signaling" objectives. Since a bureaucracy's sponsor faces conflicting claims and limited resources, bureaucracies will seek the most visible programs to justify their budget requests. Even though effectiveness may depend on concentrating resource expenditures, political pressures may dilute how expenditures are actually allocated.

Equity versus Effectiveness. Bureaucracies must make program trade-offs between effectiveness and equity. They tend to start a new program or initiative with an ostensibly effective design and rational criteria, but soon pressure is exerted to expand eligibility or entitlement. Unlike in the marketplace, those excluded from benefits find that bureaucracy itself becomes the vehicle for redress. So perverse is the syndrome that equity per se becomes the objective of most government programs.

(Continued)

TABLE 5-3   (Continued)

Fourteen Characteristics of Government and Bureaucracy

Budget Cycles and Floors. Bureaucracies operate with one- or two-year budget cycles that compress the need to justify the level of resources they receive and amplify the need to expand those resources. There is a built-in incentive to allocate resources to marginal projects. Unspent funds cannot be rationalized. Attempts to cut budgets will only make bureaucracies seek new constituencies that must be served. Staff reductions will result in potentially more money being spent on temporary personnel or outsourcing.

Tenure of Senior Decision-Makers. High-level managers, especially political appointees, have short tenure and no ownership claims on the organization. Perceived short-term success (e.g., expanding the budget) is often more important than long-term success (solving the problem).

Sunk Costs. In the private sector, sunk costs are not allocated to current operations but are recovered over a product's life cycle. In a bureaucracy, when sunk costs do not generate positive outcomes over time, the problem is explained not as too much money expended, but as too little.

Random Agenda Solution. Bureaucrats are driven by a combination of publicity concerns, pressure from and reporting requirements of funding bodies, agitation by public-interest organizations, and random developments. The agenda emphasized at a given time will vary depending upon the overriding source of influence.

Tunnel Vision. Bureaucracies bring an extreme perspective to risk-taking. Unable to see how any particular risk fits into the overall range of risks in the world, they fail to consider trade-off possibilities. Instead, they are obsessed with the last 10%. They insist not on reasonableness but on complete solutions to a given societal problem.

Inconsistency. Regulations do not deal with risks of similar magnitude in similar ways. At one extreme, the EPA's ban on asbestos might cost $250 million to save eight lives over 13 years. At the other extreme, disease screening and vaccination programs may save many thousands of lives at a cost of $50,000 to $70,000 each. Bureaucratic rules allow little leeway to adjust procedures to specific cases.

ENTREPRENEURSHIP IN THE PUBLIC SECTOR

The term "entrepreneurship" has appeared in the public administration literature with increasing frequency in recent years. It is a term that is applied in a number of diverse ways. For instance, one stream of research seeks to identify pioneers who have affected dramatic change in public sector organizations (e.g., Cooper and Wright, 1992). Mitchell and Scott (1987) suggest that being entrepreneurial is one of three criteria upon which the legitimacy of real administrative authority rests. These research efforts are grounded in a type of "great man" model, which presupposes that only a select few have the vision and skill necessary to provide substantive leadership in public sector organizations. Thus, Lewis (1980, p. 233) notes that "the outstanding fact that differentiates public entrepreneurs from ordinary managers and politicians is their ability to alter the existing allocation of scarce public resources in fundamental ways."

Entrepreneurship has alternatively been conceptualized in terms of the initiation of political movements or the creation of new public organizations that serve to produce meaningful social, political, or economic change (Drucker, 1995). Two related contemporary examples might be the impact of the Afrikaner movement through the National Party to introduce statutory "innovations" that served to facilitate apartheid or racial discrimination in South Africa over a 40-year period (Adam and Moodley, 1986), and the more recent efforts of the African National Congress in facilitating the peaceful move to democracy, majority rule, and a significant reallocation of societal resources. Such movements are less a function of any one person, and more linked to the efforts of groups of dedicated individuals.

A third point of view suggests that entrepreneurship may be a by-product of the application of strategic management and leadership principles to public enterprises (e.g., Zerbinati and Souitaris, 2005). To the extent that strategic management and leadership produce a directed, longer-term, external focus coupled with open communication and participative decision-making, public sector organizations are thought to be more likely to identify new opportunities and generate new process and service innovations, thereby affecting organizational transformation (Nutt and Backoff, 1993).

A fourth approach can be found in the "reinventing government" literature. Popularized by Osborne and Gaebler (1992), the notion of reinventing centers around three major initiatives. These include *downsizing*, or reducing the size of government; *reengineering*, or significantly redesigning the processes by which the work of government gets accomplished; and *continuous improvement*, or raising quality standards for service through participative management, bottom-up reform, and intrinsic motivation. Reinvention implies empowered employees who are able to effect innovative solutions to "customer" problems and needs, and the ability to do so is believed by advocates to be facilitated by each of these initiatives. Accordingly, employees at the lowest levels are encouraged to act entrepreneurially.

Yet another pertinent focus concerns privatization (Savas, 2000). Privatization entails reducing public sector involvement in service provision by effectively outsourcing certain responsibilities to the private sector. Thus, the public sector is leveraging resources by encouraging entrepreneurship in private companies.

These differing approaches suggest an acknowledgment of the potential applicability of entrepreneurship to public sector management, but little consensus as to what this means. Below are three perspectives that address key aspects of public sector entrepreneurship:

- an active approach to administrative responsibility that includes generating new sources of revenue, providing enhanced services, and helping to facilitate increased citizen education and involvement (Bellone and Goerl, 1992);

- a continuous attempt to apply resources in new ways so as to heighten the efficiency and effectiveness of public institutions (Osborne and Gaebler, 1992); and

- the ability of public officials to spot market opportunities and, through follower "manipulation," act upon them. (Boyett, 1997);

Themes that emerge from these definitions include the notion that a process is involved, that entrepreneurship is ongoing, and that the end result is innovative, proactive behavior. Each of these notions is consistent with the mainstream entrepreneurship literature, as discussed above. Building on that literature and these themes, we can make modifications to the efforts of Wei-Skillern et al. (2007) to produce the following working definition: *Public sector entrepreneurship is the process of creating value for citizens by bringing together unique combinations of public and/or private resources to exploit social opportunities.*

CHALLENGES AND REALITIES FOR ENTREPRENEURSHIP IN THE PUBLIC SECTOR

The external environment of today's public sector organizations can be characterized as increasingly turbulent, which implies a dynamic, hostile, and complex set of environmental conditions. One has only to consider the typical public medical facility. There are more beds than patients, competition is arising from entirely new sources, technological change is continuous, medical liability pressures are intense, costs are rising faster than the general rate of inflation, those who cannot pay must be served, and skilled labor is in short supply. Or, consider the challenges confronting the Federal Emergency Management Agency (FEMA). Often facing seemingly impossible challenges in attempting to respond to natural disasters, and more recently to terrorist acts, the public demands results at an acceptable cost. In fact, for public services in general, the public wants to pay lower taxes while expecting higher service levels.

Entrepreneurship represents an effective strategic response to environmental turbulence (see Chapter 1). Discontinuities in the environment threaten existing modes of operating public agencies, while also creating numerous opportunities for innovative behavior. The complex nature of twenty-first century society requires alternative frameworks to guide the management of public sector organizations. Various observers have emphasized a need to "reinvent" and "streamline" government, and to introduce to the public sector such market-related mechanisms as competition, market segmentation, user fees, and a customer focus (Bartlett and Dibben, 2002). Others have argued for the development of creative, risk-taking cultures inside of public organizations (Bellone and Goerl, 1992; Goldsmith et al., 2010).

Yet, public employees are not in a position to put taxpayer monies at significant risk, and this, combined with the difficulties in measuring risk/return trade-offs in the public sector, typically makes high-risk pursuits inappropriate. In addition, the high visibility of public officials and a need for consensus in decision-making suggest that incremental change is more realistic than bold innovation. Also, the lengthy periods of time required for an entrepreneurial event to unfold are inconsistent with public sector budgeting and reelection cycles. Moreover, bureaucracy and the civil service system serve to protect the status quo, ostensibly from the arbitrary or politically influenced behavior of political leaders and public executives. Because entrepreneurship often involves disrupting the status quo and effecting organizational change, again there would seem to be a potential inconsistency.

At a more fundamental level, some might argue that entrepreneurship can undermine basic democratic principles, especially when it results in innovative approaches (e.g., user fees, redevelopment agencies, off-budget enterprises, investment revenues, tax-increment financing, and development fees) for circumventing voter approval and increasing the autonomy of public officials and public administrators. Further, entrepreneurship entails the pursuit of opportunity regardless of resources currently controlled, while public sector managers are limited often by legislative or regulatory statute to using only those resources formally assigned to their organizations. Finally, the mission, structure, and major initiatives of the public organization are dictated from outside sources (legislative bodies, councils, authorities). Public managers are expected to implement these dictates in a reasonably effective and efficient manner. Entrepreneurship, alternatively, represents an internal dynamic that can serve to redirect the strategic course of an organization, potentially putting it in conflict with its stated mission or mandate. Similarly, entrepreneurial efforts can lead public enterprises to generate new services or fund-raising schemes that effectively put them in competition with private sector enterprises, which the private sector might argue is a form of unfair competition.

The counter argument is that there have always been elements of innovation and entrepreneurship in public sector organizations (e.g., Zerbinati and Souitaris, 2005), and that the issue is more one of formally defining the entrepreneurial role and then determining appropriate degrees and frequencies of entrepreneurship for a given organization or unit. Returning to our definition, creating value for customers, putting resources together in unique ways, and being opportunity-driven are not inherently in conflict with the purpose of public agencies.

Consider an example from state-level government in the United States (Harvard University, 2006). Since 2003, the State of Iowa has experimented with the Charter Agency Program, a unique model aimed at improving government. In effect, government agencies commit to delivering improved results in exchange for increased autonomy. That is, in exchange for their commitment to produce measurable benefits and to help save money—either by reducing expenditure or by increasing revenues—agencies are given greater authority and flexibility. For example, the director of a Charter Agency can "stand in the shoes" of the directors at the Department of Administrative Services, which allocates general services, personnel, and information technology to the state agencies. Charter Agencies are also exempt from statutory across-the-board budget cuts and can retain proceeds from asset sales and 80 percent of the revenues they generate, as well as half of their year-end general fund balances. They are exempt from several bureaucratic procedures such as full-time-equivalent employee caps and approval of the Executive Council for out-of-state travel, conference attendance, and professional membership. They also have access to a $3 million Charter Agency grant fund to foster innovation. In the first two years of the program, Charter Agencies produced a myriad of concrete results that have improved the life of the citizens of Iowa. Notable results include: improved rates of income tax returns filed electronically; reduced rate of failure of probationers; increased inmate work opportunities; and increased number of veterans served at the Iowa Veterans Home. Charter Agencies have successfully reached their target of producing $15 million in expenditure savings or additional revenues.

There is, one could further suggest, a growing need for these types of entrepreneurial approaches in public administration. The contemporary environment confronting public sector managers is far more complex, threatening, and dynamic than in years past. The ability of organizations to recognize and adequately respond to their changing circumstances is severely limited not only by resources, but by the management philosophies and structures that characterize public enterprises.

Bureaucracy has many advantages, and can be quite effective when operating in a relatively stable and predictable environment. However, when faced with circumstances where funding is not dependable, client demographics and needs are in flux, technology is rapidly changing, social and environmental pressures are increasing, skilled labor shortages are the norm, citizens are calling for privatization, litigation is rampant, and a host of other discontinuities continue to present themselves, the bureaucratic framework fails to provide the flexibility, adaptability, speed, or incentives for innovation that are critical for effectively carrying out the mission of the public enterprise. There are, of course, different degrees of bureaucratization, and the higher the degree, the greater the potential conflict with entrepreneurship.

Bellone and Goerl (1992) agree that potential conflicts do exist between public entrepreneurship and democracy, but suggest that these can be bridged with what they refer to as a "civic-regarding entrepreneurship." This concept emphasizes accountability, in that the principles of democratic theory are incorporated into the design of any entrepreneurial initiatives. In noting that "a strong theory of public entrepreneurship requires a strong theory of citizenship" (p.133), they argue that such initiatives should be developed in ways that facilitate citizen education and participation. They cite citizen budget committees, advisory boards, vehicles for elevating citizen choice (e.g., voucher programs), and volunteerism as examples of ways to accomplish such participation.

In practice, the public sector entrepreneur confronts unique obstacles. Ramamurti (1986) discusses multiplicity and ambiguity of goals, limited managerial autonomy and high political interference, high visibility, skewed reward systems, a short-term orientation (reinforced by budget and election cycles), and restrictive personnel policies. To these we would add lack of competitive incentives for improved performance, difficulties in segmenting or discriminating among users, and lack of accountability among managers for innovation and change. Approached differently, however, obstacles such as these can be used to facilitate entrepreneurial behavior. For instance, Ramamurti (1986) proposes that goal ambiguity is a potential source of discretion to the entrepreneurial manager, and that the media can be used as a source of power, while outsiders can be co-opted to enable one to take organizational risks without taking personal risks.

This brings us to a core question: "Who is the public entrepreneur?" Perhaps the most researched issue in the entrepreneurship literature has involved identifying the psychological and sociological traits associated with the entrepreneurial personality. Pinchot (1985) has taken this work further in attempting to characterize the corporate entrepreneur and contrast him/her with the start-up entrepreneur. In Table 5-4, we have attempted to extend Pinchot's efforts to incorporate findings on the public sector entrepreneur. The key characteristics being proposed include: a mix of power and achievement motivation; an ability to work strategically, beginning with small steps; strong political and external networking skills; calculated risk-taking; self-confidence; and an ability to tolerate and use ambiguity as a source of discretion. Further, and in spite of the inherent obstacles, the work environment in government organizations can contain a level of ambiguity, flex, and contradiction in values such that there is room for the entrepreneur to develop and act on such characteristics.

While an integration of concepts from the field of entrepreneurship with those from public administration provides a conceptual foundation from which to approach public sector entrepreneurship, it is also helpful to consider the perspectives of those who actually work in the public sector.

TABLE 5-4

Comparing Independent, Corporate, and Public Sector Entrepreneurs

	Independent Entrepreneur	Corporate Entrepreneur	Public Sector Entrepreneur
Primary Motive	Wants freedom; goal oriented and self-reliant; achievement-motivated	Wants freedom and access to corporate resources; goal orientated and self-motivated, but also responds to corporate rewards and recognition	Power motivated and achievement motivated; may think in grandiose terms; not constrained by profit motive
Time Orientation	End goals of 5–10 years growth of the business	End goals of 3–15 years depending on type of venture	End goals of 10–15 years; begins with impressive short-term success, then implements long-term plan as series of short-term programs
Skills	Knows business intimately; more business acumen than managerial or political skills	Strong technical skills or product knowledge; good managerial skills; weak political skills	Strong political skills; able to develop power sources beyond those formally assigned; adept at using public relations and the media to advantage
Attitude toward System	Frustrated by system so rejects it and starts his/her own	Dislikes system but learns to work within it and manipulate it	Tends to redesign or restructure the system to accomplish his/her own ends

(Continued)

Focus	External; markets and technology	Internal and external; builds internal networks and finds mentors or sponsors	Learns to co-opt or use external forces to accomplish internal change; builds constituencies of support among politicians, unions, the private sector, the media and the community
Risks and Failure	Assumes considerable financial and personal risk; clearly identifies key risk factors and tries to minimize them; sees failure as learning experience	Likes moderate risks; principal risks are career related; sensitive to need to appear orderly within corporation; hides risky projects so can learn from mistakes without political cost of public failure	Calculated risk-taker; takes big organizational risks without taking big personal risks by managing the process by which risky decisions are made; tends to deviate from rules only slightly at first, then progressively more, since failure is harder to define, will manage events to promote positive outcomes
Courage and Destiny	Self-confident, optimistic, bold	Self-confident, optimistic, bold; cynical about the system but believes he/she can manipulate it	Self-confident, optimistic, bold; high tolerance for ambiguity; uses ambiguity as a source of managerial discretion

How Public Sector Managers View Entrepreneurship

Morris and Jones (1999) surveyed a large cross-section of public sector managers to determine how they perceived the relevance of entrepreneurship within their organizations. These managers were asked to identify the individual and organizational characteristics they most associated with entrepreneurship in the public sector. Findings are summarized in Table 5-5. At the level of the individual, entrepreneurship was most associated with: self-confidence, strong drive, strong leadership abilities, good organizational skills, vision, and self-discipline. Least associated with the entrepreneurial individual were luck and good political connections. When asked if people with entrepreneurial characteristics are born that way, just under 40 percent expressed agreement.

TABLE 5-5

Public Sector Manager Perceptions of Characteristics Associated with Entrepreneurship

	Mean	Standard Deviation
*The Entrepreneurial Person**		
Self-confident	1.62	.77
Strong drive	1.70	.76
Strong leadership abilities	1.74	.79
Good organizer	1.79	.77
Self-disciplined	1.81	.78
Vision	1.81	.93
Action-oriented	1.84	.92
Persistent	1.87	.80
Good analytical skills	1.95	.84
Independent	1.99	.92
Resourceful	2.04	.93
Bold	2.05	.92
Concerned for public good	2.25	1.08
Strong moral values	2.29	1.02
Risk-taker	2.42	1.09
Good political skills	3.22	1.20
Good political connections	3.38	1.13
Lucky	3.62	1.12

(*Continued*)

TABLE 5-5	(Continued)

Public Sector Manager Perceptions of Characteristics Associated with Entrepreneurship

	Mean	Standard Deviation
*The Entrepreneurial Organization**		
Strong leader at the top	1.86	.96
Good planning system	1.95	.95
Customer driven	2.00	.93
Efficient operations	2.01	.87
Hands-on management	2.02	.97
Leader in the development of new program/services	2.05	.99
Better informed about regulatory policies	2.10	.91
Few layers of management	2.12	1.03
Long-term orientation	2.20	.89
Competitive orientation	2.20	1.03
Willing to pursue risks	2.41	1.03
Long-term funding stability	2.47	1.08
Recruit outside experts	2.61	1.14
Creative system for rewarding employees	2.63	1.32
Tolerant of failure	2.66	1.07
Face pressure to privatize	2.68	1.19
Small in size	2.68	1.28
Protected from political influence	2.93	1.38

*4-point scale, where 1 = definitely applies, 4 = does not apply
SOURCE: Morris, M. H. and F. Jones (1999), "Entrepreneurship in Established Organizations: The Case of the Public Sector," *Entrepreneurship Theory and Practice*, 24(1), p. 82.

Alternatively, when it comes to the entrepreneurial organization, a strong leader at the top, good planning systems, a customer-driven orientation, efficient operations, and hands-on management were the leading characteristics. Nearly half (48.6 percent) of respondents associated the term entrepreneurship more with a type of person, while 8 percent saw it predominantly as an organizational characteristic, and 43.5 percent indicated that it applies equally to both.

In general, the public sector managers saw a role for entrepreneurship in their organizations. When asked to respond to the statement "entrepreneurship does not really apply to organizations such as mine," 58.6 percent either disagreed or strongly disagreed. This does, however, suggest that a sizable minority do question the role of entrepreneurship. In a similar vein, ratings of the applicability of entrepreneurship on a 5-point scale from very relevant (=1) to not at all relevant (=5) produced a mean response of 2.32 (standard deviation = 1.04). At the same time, 86.4 percent perceived that fostering entrepreneurship would have a somewhat positive or significantly positive impact on organizational performance. The leading payoffs from higher levels of entrepreneurship were increased efficiency, productivity (mentioned by 39.9 percent of respondents), improved service delivery (mentioned by 28.2 percent), cost reductions (mentioned by 21.3 percent), improved employee morale (mentioned by 19.1 percent), and reduced dependency on tax revenue (mentioned by 9 percent).

Respondents also supported the notion that the environment in public sector organizations can be designed in ways that help employees develop their entrepreneurial tendencies (88.5 percent agreed or strongly agreed). When responding to the statement "no matter how entrepreneurial an individual employee might be, it is virtually impossible for an organization to act entrepreneurial," 62.2 percent disagreed or strongly disagreed.

As summarized in Table 5-6, respondents generally perceived that the most entrepreneurial individuals could be found in middle management (23.2 percent) and in mainstream functional areas (16.8 percent), both of which overlap with one another, as well as at an executive or senior management level (19.4 percent). The greatest opportunities for entrepreneurship were perceived to exist at the top management level (41.5 percent of responses), in a variety of functional areas throughout the organization (29.2 percent), at a middle management level (12.3 percent), and in service delivery/ direct customer contact areas (8.5 percent). The areas in which entrepreneurship is seen as most critical were planning/organizing/budgeting (33.1 percent), service delivery (28.7 percent), operations (21.9 percent), and human resources (9.5 percent).

In spite of the above, the public sector environment was not seen as being supportive of entrepreneurship. A large majority of respondents either strongly agreed (23 percent) or agreed (54 percent) with the statement "the civil service environment discourages the entrepreneurial individual," with 7.2 percent disagreeing or strongly disagreeing. Most of the managers (74.1 percent) also indicated agreement with the notion that public sector organizations naturally become less entrepreneurial as they get larger. The leading obstacles to entrepreneurship, as rated by these managers, were as follows:

1. Policies/procedures/red tape

2. Restrictions on personnel policies (hiring and firing)

3. Limited size of rewards

4. Limited managerial autonomy

5. Lack of a profit motive

6. Interference from politicians

TABLE 5-6

The Importance of Entrepreneurship within Specific Functional Areas of the Company

The Most Entrepreneurial People	Percentage
Middle management	23.2
Top management	11.4
In a variety of functional areas	16.8
Lower management	10.1
All management levels	9.2
Among professionals	7.6
Nonmanagerial levels	5.9
Other	7.8
The Greatest Opportunities for Entrepreneurship	
At top management level	41.5
In a variety of major functional areas/throughout the organization	29.2
At middle management level	12.3
In areas of direct contact with customers	8.5
In small autonomous departments	6.2
Nowhere in the organization	1.5
Other	0.8
Where Entrepreneurship Is Most Critical	
Planning/organizing/budgeting	33.1
Service delivery	28.7
Operations	21.9
Human resources	9.5
Marketing and communications	3.2
Everywhere in organization	2.4
Nowhere in organization	2.4
Other	0.8

SOURCE: Morris, M. H. and F. Jones (1999), "Entrepreneurship in Established Organizations: The Case of the Public Sector," *Entrepreneurship Theory and Practice*, 24(1), p. 83.

7. Pressure to emphasize equity over efficiency

8. Ambiguity of goals

9. Lack of competition among organizations

10. Public sector unions

These are quite similar to obstacles identified in the corporate entrepreneurship literature. In fact, distinct public sector characteristics such as multiplicity of goals, high visibility, and difficulties in defining one's customer were not rated all that highly as obstacles. In a separate, open-ended question, respondents suggested that the leading obstacles were inadequate rewards and incentives (27.3 percent), bureaucracy and red tape (19.5 percent), and autocratic management (13.6 percent).

Finally, respondents made suggestions for the most important thing that their organizations could do to encourage entrepreneurship. The priorities included improved rewards and recognition for innovation and risk-taking (29.1 percent of the responses), active promotion of employee participation, empowerment, accountability (27.4 percent), and elimination of red tape (7.7 percent).

Toward Entrepreneurial Government

A number of suggestions can be made regarding how government organizations must be transformed into entrepreneurial organizations. A beginning point is the introduction of market mechanisms, which is the core theme of Osborne and Gaebler (1992) in *Reinventing Government*. They discuss ten areas in which to focus:

- *Competition:* finding creative ways to introduce competition and the corresponding incentives for greater efficiency, more resource productivity, greater responsiveness to customers, encouragement of innovation and enhanced employee morale. Competition can be public versus private, private versus private (e.g., outsourcing to private bidders), or public versus public (e.g., school vouchers).

- *Citizen Empowerment:* involving citizens in ownership and control of services, where people feel they own the streets, schools, and other public assets.

- *Focus on Outcomes:* measuring results or outcomes of programs, not inputs, such as through the creation of revenue centers.

- *Mission over Rules and Regulations:* focusing decisions and resource allocations not on rules, but on the fundamental purpose of the public agency, and defining this fundamental purpose in terms of citizen needs instead of particular services or programs.

- *Customer-Orientation:* developing an obsession with customer service and satisfaction, where the focus is on value creation, customization to diverse groups, management of points of customer contact or interface, service quality, and continuous customer feedback.

- *Proactiveness:* instilling a focus on the future combined with an emphasis on anticipation and prevention of problems before they occur.

- *Earning over Spending:* searching for non-tax revenues, developing creative user-fee structures, charging impact fees, renting out unused or underutilized resources, selling or generating revenue from assets.

- *Decentralization:* focusing on participatory management, flattened organizational structures, decision-making that is pushed down in the organization, empowerment and rewards for champions, more broadly defined jobs and more autonomy, and an expectation of innovation from the bottom up.

- *Partnerships over Adversarial Relationships:* working with private sector employers and nonprofit organizations to develop creative solutions to problems and share resources.

- *Other Market Mechanisms:* finding creative ways to manage both supply and demand for services, such as with impact fees, emissions trading, tax credits, vouchers, incentives to private sector suppliers, and shared risk-taking with private sector and nonprofit organizations.

At the root of Osborne and Gaebler's suggestions is the need to move away from arguments regarding whether there should be less government or more government, and instead concentrate on the kind of governance that society wants. Entrepreneurial governance brings a flexible, dynamic, and innovative approach to the process by which problems are collectively solved and society's needs are met. Government must define itself less in terms of rowing, and more in terms of steering. The challenge is not to create bureaucracies that "do," but instead to design nimble units that "lead" and capitalize on opportunity by putting together unique resource combinations involving role players from all sectors.

Useful direction is also provided by Cullen and Cashman (2000), who discuss the "transition to competitive government." Table 5-7 summarizes this concept as it relates to government effectiveness, business/government roles, approach to resources, cycle time management, and communication. These authors argue for a strategic approach to affecting this transition. While their focus is on national government, the approach is applicable to government bodies at all levels. In essence, critical strategic questions are first raised about the three core missions of government: enhanced competitiveness, creation of social value, and governability. Based on the responses to these questions, objectives are established and elements of a transition strategy are proposed, together with performance benchmarks and verifiable outcomes. Support objectives and strategies are then established for government functions and services, and then for five key elements of general management reform: strategic leadership, cycle time management, performance management, comfort zone management, and results-based financial management.

Finally, a more operational perspective is provided by Linden (1990), who proposes an action agenda for public sector managers. His agenda begins with *Strategic Thinking and Acting*. Here, public managers move away from planning for planning sake and a preoccupation with the plan document itself. Instead, the focus is on a vision of what can be, on thinking strategically, and on determining the elements that need to be in

TABLE 5-7

Transition from Traditional Government to Competitive Government

Traditional (Function-Driven) Government	*Competitive (Performance-Driven) Government*
Effective Government	
• Government's role is to supply services and infrastructure, fund these operations from users and taxpayers, and provide an environment where persons are treated equitably and business can develop.	• Effective government is government that adds value by delivering improvements in competitiveness, social value, and governability.
• Unless government is failing, it is presumed to be working.	• Performance focuses on desired products.
• Evaluation cycle dominated by government budget and election cycles	• Innovation is a common activity.
	• Evaluation focuses on short-term impacts and relative performance.
Business/Government Roles	
• Government sets the business environment. The business role is to generate national competitiveness.	• Recognition that government and business need to work together to improve societal competitiveness.
Resources	
• Government budgets and legislative mandates are used to control allocations and drive priorities.	• Resources are a management variable.
• Performance is seen as a function of spending allocated resources.	• Resources are leveraged to accomplish results.
	• Performance is a function of delivering results on time and within budget.
Cycle Time Management	
• The management task is to fit management needs into preset cycles. The emphasis is on queuing customers to fit these preset cycles, reducing risks and increasing efficiency.	• Cycle time management is a key variable to managing the impacts of change and reducing the comfort zone tensions created by change.
Communication	
• The key communication task is to take the credit for national progress and to respond to failure by either denying or obscuring it. Where problems must be recognized, the communications task shifts to simple dramatic solutions which defer evaluation.	• Cycle-based and proactive communication.
	• Impacts are managed as part of a delivery and communication strategy. Expectations and benefits are managed throughout the government planning and implementation cycle.

SOURCE: Adapted from R. B. Cullen and D. P. Cushman (2000), *Transitions to Competitive Government*, Albany, N.Y.: State University of New York Press, p. 49.

place to have a maximum chance for success with minimal resistance. Next comes *Holding on and Letting Go*, where the manager let's others interpret and implement the vision, gives some autonomy, and, in a sense, gives up control to gain control. This step is followed by *Creating a Felt Need for Change*, where the manager sells the importance of change, defines change in terms of opportunities for employees, empathizes with fear and resistance to change, and presents disconfirming data regarding assumptions. It is important to *Start with Small Steps*, where the priority is action, not pronouncements, task forces, or the "paralysis of analysis." The manager attempts to move quickly on an innovation agenda, but one step at a time. Experimentation is stressed, and the manager reinforces those who pick up the banner. The manager also strives to *Use Structural Changes* to reinforce and validate new approaches, and on the assumption that attitudinal change will follow structural change. Examples include the use of boards of advisors, rotation of department heads, flattening of the structure, and formal roles for citizen participation. Along the way, the manager has mechanisms to *Deal with Risk*, including efforts to minimize exposure. Risk can be managed by starting new initiatives with volunteers, through the use of pilot projects, and by keeping initial expectations low. The manager does not focus on failures, instead highlighting and rewarding accomplishments, while stressing what is being learned. Lastly, the manager's ability to *Use Political Skills* is especially important. The manager respects the culture of the organization even while attempting to change it. He/she builds coalitions, understands and uses informal networks, seeks common areas of consensus, and develops talents for persuasion.

THE INNOVATORS NOTEBOOK

Innovative Code Enforcement by the City of Los Angeles

The recession of the early 1990s deeply impacted the City of Los Angeles. The phenomenon of abandoned buildings and problem properties with drugs and gangs increased, as did slum housing and city budget cutbacks for programs such as code enforcement. In a city where 60 percent of the residents rent and nearly 25 percent of these tenants pay half of their income for rent, the need to focus on maintaining an affordable rental housing stock was evident. Rather than constructing new affordable housing developments, the city decided to shift its focus to improving the existing housing stock.

In response to mounting concerns over slum housing, Los Angeles residents formed the Blue Ribbon Citizens Committee, which criticized the city's process for receiving code complaints and conducting inspection in multifamily rental housing. Spurred by these findings of the committee, the city established the Systematic Code Enforcement Program (SCEP) in 1998. The goals of SCEP are to achieve code compliance; to ensure that state health and safety codes are enforced so that all residents, including the city's poorest, live in decent, safe housing; and that the city's housing stock does not slide into irreversible disrepair.

Prior to the implementation of this program, the cost of complaint resolution was borne by the general public, but now, housing provision is a business with consumers and providers. The program is funded by an annual per-unit fee, which is charged to and paid by the property owner, who can then pass it on to the tenants. SCEP makes a concerted effort to work closely with both the tenants and the landlords, fostering trust among all parties involved. Moreover, SCEP is constantly educating its inspectors so that they are qualified to properly enforce the regulations. Inspectors are also required to complete sensitivity training so that they are able to best relate to the tenants and the landlords, bridging any cultural divides.

Since the establishment of the SCEP, more than 90 percent of the city's multifamily housing stock has been inspected and more than one and a half million habitability violations have been corrected. The result has been an estimated $1.3 billion reinvestment by owners in the city's existing housing stock. Furthermore, Los Angeles tenants and owners are better educated on their rights and the remedies available to them and possess greater confidence in the Housing Department's ability to provide these services effectively.

Discussion Questions

1. What underlying dimensions of entrepreneurship are apparent in this public initiative?

2. From the chapter, what characteristics of the public sector make the Los Angeles initiative especially noteworthy.

3. How does this story reflect the aspects of "entrepreneurial government" that are outlined in the chapter? Relate this example to Gaebler and Osborne's concepts for reinventing government.

SOURCE: Adapted from: Government Innovators Network, John F. Kennedy School of Government, Harvard University, http://www.innovations.harvard.edu/.

Summary and Conclusions

This chapter has argued that entrepreneurship is a universal construct and can be applied not only in large corporations, but also in both nonprofit and public sector organizations. The definition, process nature, and underlying dimensions of entrepreneurship are fundamentally the same regardless of the context. There are, however, fundamental differences in organizational realities, suggesting that the goals, constraints, approaches, and outcomes related to successful entrepreneurial efforts are unique both in nonprofits and in public sector organizations.

The early part of the twenty-first century is a time when nonprofits confront increasingly complex demands from their constituencies, rising costs, growing regulatory constraints, and intensified competition for funding, volunteers, and other resources. For their part, public sector organizations must deal with an erosion of the tax base, significant expansion of the audiences they serve, heightened public visibility and accountability, and strong pressures to reflect diversity requirements. These realities are forcing NPOs and government organizations to seek out new models of management. Entrepreneurship holds the key.

Leaders of nonprofits and public sector organizations must view themselves as entrepreneurs, and the process of pursuing their social or public mission as an entrepreneurial undertaking. For these organizations, an entrepreneurial model of governance emphasizes flexibility, adaptability, and innovativeness. Entrepreneurship represents a salient concept for identifying new sources of funding, promoting efficiency, improving productivity, and delivering novel solutions to stakeholders. It is a concept that should be woven into the very culture of schools, hospitals, arts organizations, advocacy agencies, welfare departments, economic development units, postal services, and every other type of nonprofit or public entity.

Yet, strong leadership is clearly necessary to overcome environments that are often in conflict with entrepreneurial behavior. Senior management must first establish goals and strategies for entrepreneurship. An important component here is the need to determine where within their organizations to place the entrepreneurial priorities. Different degrees and amounts of entrepreneurial behavior would seem appropriate depending on the activity or functional area, and managerial expectations should reflect such differences.

It is also imperative that senior managers of these organizations perform the symbolic behaviors that reinforce the priority given to innovative thinking. Employee values and attitudes must be the focal point—especially the tendencies to resist change and to avoid failure at all costs. The facilitation of entrepreneurship comes down to people, individuals who will champion innovation and change. In the nonprofit sector, entrepreneurial passion coupled with a passion for the social mission of the organization can produce bold solutions to community needs. This sort of passion is also vital in the public sector. As Mintzberg (1996, p.82), notes, "government desperately needs a life force … there is no substitute for human dedication."

Reward and measurement systems would appear to represent especially useful tools for accomplishing some of this required attitudinal change, yet in practice they appear to serve as a leading obstacle. Training is also important. While it is debatable as to whether or not one can be taught to be an entrepreneur, nonprofit and public sector employees would benefit from a better appreciation for the process nature of entrepreneurship, including such issues as opportunity identification and assessment, formulation of plans for new concepts, capitalizing on goal conflict and ambiguity, risk management strategies, and networking to obtain resources, among others.

In the final analysis, we believe that entrepreneurship must be an integral component in whatever models or frameworks that are adopted for managing nonprofit and public sector organizations in the twenty-first century. Entrepreneurship implies an innovative, proactive role for nonprofits and government in moving society toward improved quality of life. There is no formal blueprint or model regarding how entrepreneurship can be accomplished in the nonprofit or public sectors. The key appears to be experimentation. This includes generating alternative revenues, improving internal processes, and developing novel solutions to society's needs.

References

Adam, H., and Moodley, K. (1986). *South Africa without Apartheid: Dismantling Racial Domination* (Berkeley: University of California Press).

Bartlett, D., and Dibben, P. (2002). "Public Sector Innovation and Entrepreneurship: Case Studies from Local Government," *Local Government Studies*, 28(4), 107–121.

Bellone, C. J., and Goerle, G. F. (1992). "Reconciling Public Entrepreneurship and Democracy," *Public Administration Review*, 52(2), 130–134.

Boyett, I. (1997). "The Public Sector Entrepreneur—Definition," *International Journal of Entrepreneurial Behavior*, 3(2), 77–92.

Brooks, A. C. (2009). *Social Entrepreneurship: A Modern Approach to Social Value Creation* (Upper Saddle River, NJ: Pearson Prentice-Hall).

Bryson, J. M., Gibbons, M. J., and Shaye, G. (2001). "Enterprise Schemes for Nonprofit Survival, Growth, and Effectiveness," *Non-profit Management and Leadership*, 11(3), 271–288.

Cooper, T. L., and Wright, N. D. (Eds.) (1992). *Exemplary Public Administrators: Character and Leadership in Government* (Baltimore, MD: Johns Hopkins University Press).

Cullen, R. B., and Cushman, D. P. (2000). *Transitions to Competitive Government: Speed, Consensus and Performance* (Albany, NY: State University of New York Press).

Dees, J. G., Emerson, J., and Economy, P. (2001). *Enterprising Nonprofits* (New York: Wiley Publishing).

Drucker, P. F. (1995). "Really Reinventing Government," *The Atlantic Monthly*, February, 49–61.

Foster, W., and Bradach, J. (2005). "Should Nonprofits Seek Profits?" *Harvard Business Review*, 83(1), 92–100.

Goldsmith, S., Georges, G., and Burke, T. (2010). *The Power of Social Innovation: How Civic Entrepreneurs Ignite Community Networks for Good* (San Francisco: Jossey-Bass).

Harvard University (2006). "Charter Agencies: State of Iowa," *Government Innovators Network*, John F. Kennedy School of Government, http://www.innovations.harvard.edu/awards.

Lewis, E. (1980). *Public Entrepreneurship: Toward a Theory of Bureaucratic Power* (Bloomington: Indiana University Press).

Linden, R. (1990). *From Vision to Reality: Strategies of Successful Innovators in Government* (Charlottesville, VA: LEL Enterprises).

Mintzberg, H. (1996), "Managing Government, Governing Management," *Harvard Business Review*, 74(3), 75–83.

Mitchell, T., and Scott, W. G. (1987). "Leadership Failures, the Distrusting Public, and Prospects of the Administrative State," *Public Administrative Review*, 47(2), 445–452.

Morris, M. H., Coombes, S., Schindehutte, M., and Allen, J. (2007). "Antecedents and Outcomes of Entrepreneurial and Market Orientations in a Nonprofit Context: Theoretical and Empirical insights," *Journal of Leadership and Organizational Studies*, 13(4), 12–39.

Morris, M. H., and F. Jones (1999). "Entrepreneurship in Established Organizations: The Case of the Public Sector," *Entrepreneurship Theory and Practice*, 24(1), 71–91.

Nutt, P. C., and Backoff, R. W. (1993). "Transforming Public Organizations with Strategic Management and Strategic Leadership," *Journal of Management*, 19(2), 299–349.

Osborne, D., and Gaebler, T. A. (1992). *Reinventing Government: How the Entrepreneurial Spirit Is Transforming the Public Sector* (Reading, MA: Addison-Wesley).

Pearce, J. A., II, Fritz, D. A., and Davis, P.S. (2010). "Entrepreneurial Orientation and the Performance of Religious Congregations as Predicted by Rational Choice Theory," *Entrepreneurship Theory and Practice*, 34(1), 219–248.

Pinchot, G. (1985). *Intrapreneuring* (New York: Harper and Row).

Ramamurti, R. (1986). "Public Entrepreneurs: Who They Are and How They Operate," *California Management Review*, 28(3), 142–158.

Savas, E. (2000). *Privatization and Public–Private Partnerships* (New York: Chatham House Publishers).

Short, J.C., Moss, T.W., and Lumpkin, G.T. (2009). "Research in Social Entrepreneurship: Past Contributions and Future Opportunities," *Strategic Entrepreneurship Journal*, 3(2), 161–194.

Sullivan-Mort, G., Weerwardena, J., and Carnegie, K. (2003). "Social Entrepreneurship: Towards Conceptualization," *International Journal of Nonprofit and Voluntary Sector Marketing*, 8(1), 76–88.

Thompson, J.L. (2002). "The World of the Social Entrepreneur," *The International Journal of Public Sector Management*, 15(4/5), 412–430.

Wei-Skillern, J, Austin, J., Leonard, H., and Stevenson, H. (2007). *Entrepreneurship in the Social Sector* (Thousand Oaks, CA: Sage Publications).

Zerbinati, S., and Souitaris, V. (2005). "Entrepreneurship in the Public Sector: A Framework of Analysis in European Local Governments," *Entrepreneurship and Regional Development*, 17(1), 43–64.

CREATING THE ENTREPRENEURIAL ORGANIZATION

"To be able to innovate, the enterprise needs to put—every three years or so—every single product, process, technology, market, distributive channel, and internal staff activity on trial for life."
—PETER F. DRUCKER

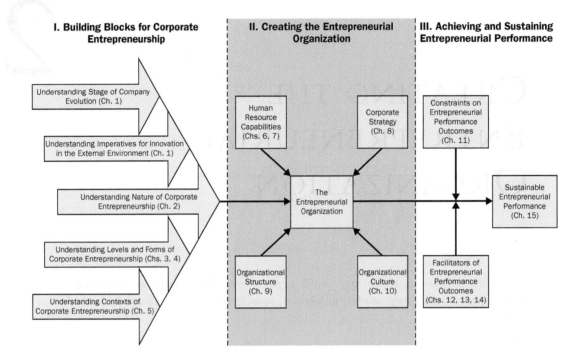

Section Introduction

In the first section of the book, we established the basic building blocks of corporate entrepreneurship, including how it is defined and conceptualized, why it is needed, the concept of entrepreneurial intensity, and the forms it takes. In Section II, we turn to what is arguably the core question of the book, namely, "how can companies become more entrepreneurial?" This is a vexing challenge, as a number of forces inside organizations work against entrepreneurship. It is a challenge filled with paradoxes, as companies strive to manage existing operations while creating the future. As illustrated in the model above, Section II consists of five chapters. We will examine how human resources (people and practices), strategy, structure, and culture together form the critical aspects that must be addressed by any organization seeking the pathway to entrepreneurial success.

Chapter 6

Human Resources in the Entrepreneurial Organization: The Creative Individual

Introduction

Of all the elements necessary for successful corporate entrepreneurship, the individual "champion" or "corporate entrepreneur" is the most critical. Without the visionary leadership and persistence demonstrated by this individual, little would be accomplished. Someone must come up with a concept, vision, or dream. They must translate this dream into products and processes within an organizational context. They must champion the concept to a wide range of individuals and stakeholder groups. They must adapt the concept to reflect the realities encountered within the internal and external environments. And they must persevere in overcoming the normal and the arbitrary obstacles that are thrown into their paths.

This chapter will examine ways in which people can develop breakthrough ideas on the job. Specifically, we will explore the nature of individual and group creativity in organizations. Our interest is both in identifying ways for employees to think about their own creativity and ways for managers to facilitate employee creativity. Also in this chapter we examine what is known about entrepreneurial individuals. Their personality characteristics will be explored from both a positive and negative perspective. Types of entrepreneurs will be identified. A model will be presented that captures the set of variables that lead an individual to pursue an opportunity. While most of the research on individual characteristics and behaviors has been done on start-up or independent entrepreneurs, many parallels can be drawn for corporate entrepreneurship. Unique differences of individuals who do entrepreneurial things in larger companies will also be explored.

The Creative Individual in a Company

Creativity is the soul of entrepreneurship. It is vital for spotting the patterns and trends that define an opportunity. It is needed to develop innovative business concepts. Most importantly, the corporate entrepreneur has to be highly creative in getting a sponsor, building and using a network, obtaining management buy-in for the concept, forming a team, coming up with resources, and overcoming the obstacles that will be thrown into his or her path.

While many perspectives exist, creativity can be defined as the application of a person's mental ability and curiosity to discover something new. It is the act of relating previously unrelated things. In fact, much of the work on creativity tends to focus on the ability to relate and connect, to put things together in novel ways (e.g., Jeffrey, 2008). Thus, while entrepreneurship is about making things happen, and deals with practical implementation, creativity is the capacity to develop new ideas, concepts, and processes.

People are inherently creative. Some act on that creativity all the time, others stifle it, and most of us are somewhere in between. The reality is that employees often do not realize when or how they are being creative. Further, they fail to recognize the large number of opportunities for creativity that arise within their jobs on a daily basis. The beginning point in fostering more creativity within a company is to realize that we are all creative in different ways. Table 6-1 summarizes seven general ways in which people are creative.

In a business context, creativity is more than originality. There is a pragmatic dimension, in that creative approaches or solutions must also be useful and actionable in the context of the company and its competitive situation. Amabile and Mueller (2008) suggest that there are three components of successful creativity in organizations: expertise, motivation, and creative thinking skills. *Expertise* encompasses what a person knows and can do. It defines the intellectual space that he or she uses to explore and solve problems. *Motivation* can be extrinsic (desire to achieve company rewards) or intrinsic (driven by more internal, intangible factors), with the latter being the most critical. Intrinsic motivation refers primarily to passion and interest, or the person's internal desire to do something. Hence, the employee may be driven by the challenge and joy of accomplishment and the sense of self-fulfillment. *Creative thinking skills* refer to the particular ways individuals approach problems and solutions, and the techniques they use for looking at a problem differently, seeking insights from other fields of endeavor, challenging assumptions, and so forth. One of the most important conclusions drawn from this work is that managers can influence all three of these components of creativity. The organization must emphasize managerial practices that result in employees being challenged, that provide them with freedom, and that give them access to resources. Similarly, practices that result in well-designed, mutually supportive, and diverse work teams are likely to spur creativity. Also valuable is encouragement from supervisors for creative outputs, and reinforcement in terms of the values, systems, and structures of the organization.

The Creative Process

Individual creativity is too often associated with brainstorming. That is, people must simply open up their minds, let everything go, apply no constraints, be positive, and

---

TABLE 6-1

The Arenas in which People Are Creative at Work

People frequently fail to recognize when they are being creative, and they often overlook opportunities to be creative. A good beginning point on the path to creativity is to first recognize all of the ways in which we can be creative. People at work can channel their creativity into seven different arenas:

- **Idea Creativity**—thinking up a new idea or concept, such as an idea for a new product or service or a way to solve a problem.

- **Material Creativity**—inventing and building a tangible object, such as a product, an advertisement, a report, or a photograph.

- **Organization Creativity**—organizing people or projects, and coming up with a new organization form or approach to structuring things. Examples could include organizing a project, starting a new type of venture, putting together or reorganizing a work group, and changing the policies and rules of a group.

- **Relationship Creativity**—innovative approaches to achieving collaboration, cooperation, and win-win relationships with others. The person who handles a difficult situation well or deals with a particular person in an especially effective manner is being creative in a relationship or one-on-one context.

- **Event Creativity**—producing an event or occasion, such as an awards ceremony, team outing, or annual meeting. Finding a way to bring two opponents together. The creativity here also encompasses décor, ways in which people are involved, sequence of happenings, background, and so forth.

- **Inner Creativity**—changing one's inner self. Being open to new approaches to how we do things and thinking about ourselves in different ways. Achieving a change of heart, or finding a new perspective or way to look at things that is a significant departure to how one has traditionally looked at them.

- **Spontaneous Creativity**—acting in a spontaneous or spur-of-the moment manner, such as coming up with a witty response in a meeting, an off-the-cuff speech, a quick and simple way to settle a dispute, or an innovative appeal when trying to close a sale.

SOURCE: Adapted from W. C. Miller (1999), *Flash of Brilliance*, Reading, Massachusetts: Perseus Books.

---

generate as many ideas as possible. Out of this activity will come a creative solution. However, it is important to recognize that creativity is much more than brainstorming. In fact, brainstorming is but one of many tools or techniques that can be useful in creative problem-solving.

On one level, creativity is messy, random, and unscientific. On another level, structure plays a role in creativity, and those who approach creativity from a more systematic perspective tend to come up with a lot more great ideas. The key to this distinction is to recognize that creativity involves heuristics, not algorithms. Algorithms are complete mechanical rules or formulas for solving a problem or dealing with a situation. Heuristics are incomplete guidelines or rules of thumb that can lead to learning or discovery. Thus, there is no clear path, the employee must create one.

Finding the appropriate path to a creative solution is much easier if the employee first approaches creativity as a logical process, and then utilizes some of the available creative problem-solving techniques as he or she moves through the process. While it is generally accepted among researchers and consultants that a process is involved, there are different opinions regarding the nature of that process. Table 6-2 summarizes seven views regarding the steps of stages involved in successful creativity.

On further examination, these perspectives have much in common. Accordingly, we believe the following five-stage approach captures the essence of all of them. The process begins with a problem or question or challenge. What is labeled "preparation" is a stage where the individual attempts to define the problem, gather information, and look for the right answer. Too often, people jump in looking for the solution without really understanding the real problem or question. In many instances, the different individuals in a work group think they are all solving the same problem, but because of their differing interpretations and assumptions, they are effectively solving different problems. This is why Hirshberg (1998) suggests one must first ask creative questions before coming up with creative answers. He encourages questions that are surprising, provocative, and destabilizing, that emanate from skewed vantage points, and that open new routes to a subject. The simplest questions can serve to get around constraining assumptions and help the employee get to the root of the true problem.

As a rule, the creative solution does not simply come. In fact, the path one pursues in trying to come up with the solution gets circuitous, confusing, and off the track. It leads to a series of dead ends that seem further and further removed from a viable solution, and the "frustration" stage sets in. This frustration is caused by and magnified by a set of creative blocks, a subject to which we will shortly return. It is at the frustration stage that most people arrive and then give up, or settle for a solution that is rather uncreative and closer to the status quo.

If one consciously steps away from the problem and puts it on the back burner, he or she is in the "incubation" stage. The individual is, in effect, non-intentionally working on the problem. Further, he or she is either consciously or unconsciously removing some of the key blocks. There may also be more data gathering in this stage, although it may also not be intentional. Insights can be found in areas, pursuits, or activities that are far afield of the actual problem, and may be quite removed from one's own background or field of expertise.

One next sees a ray of light, a thread, or piece of a possible solution. There may be an "aha" moment. This stage, called "illumination," involves the employee coming up

TABLE 6-2

Different Views of the Creative Process

(Van Oech)	(Strickland and Carlson)	(Ray and Myers)	(Kuhn)	(Rickards)	(Kao)	(Miller)
preparation	exploring what you have and what you need	information gathering	problem recognition	preparation	interest	be aware of your complete current situation
→	→	→	→	→	→	→
frustration	inventing ideas while roaming beyond the obvious	digestion of material	"naive" incubation/ gestation	incubation	preparation	be persistent in your vision
→	→	→	→	→	→	→
incubation	choosing the idea or combination that holds the most promise in terms of strengths and weaknesses	incubation or forgetting the problem	information search and preparation	insight/ inspiration	incubation	perceive all your alternatives
→	→	→	→	→	→	→
illumination	implementing, trying, evaluating	inspiration	"knowledgeable" incubation/ gestation	validation	illumination	entertain your intuitive guidance
→		→	→		→	→
elaboration		implementation	alternative solution formation		verification	assess and select among your alternatives
			→		→	→
			alternative solution evaluation		exploitation	be realistic in your actions
			→			→
			chosen solution implementation			evaluate your results
			→			
			feedback and evaluation			

with the outline or core of an answer. The answer often needs to be refined, adapted, expanded upon, tested, and further revised. Not only are there likely to be pragmatic problems in actually applying the solution, but the employee has to make changes as he or she tries to sell the idea to management. This period of refinement and adaptation is the stage of "elaboration."

Of course, the process is usually not as linear as it might sound. There could be points of incubation throughout, with some of them lasting quite long and some being very short. There may be feedback loops, where an insight at one point leads one to discard a principle or assumption made at an earlier point, suggesting a need to go back and move in a direction that was earlier rejected. There may also be little "eureka moments" along the way, and these come together to form an overall solution, rather than a single big eureka in the illumination stage.

As one moves through the creative process, it is also helpful to think of the stages in terms of divergence and convergence (Buis et al., 2009). Divergence is breaking from familiar, established ways of seeing and doing. It is a concern with generating lots of options and truly novel ideas, regardless of their practicality. Convergence is the achievement of some agreement regarding the merits of a given idea and the value in pursuing that idea. It is a reality check in terms of the implementation issues. An individual or group goes back and forth from divergence to convergence when successfully managing their creativity. Effective creativity requires balance, or equal time for casting one's net widely through divergence and narrowing one's focus through convergence. In fact, the failure to produce highly creative answers may be linked to groups that either spend too much time generating and discussing options, or, alternatively, devote most of their effort to taking an idea to task and arguing the nuances of detailed implementation issues.

The Creative Blocks

People do not need to be creative for most of what they do in a given day. In fact, they develop patterns and routines without which their lives would be in chaos. They then adopt attitudes that are consistent with maintaining the status quo. However, the same type of thinking that allows a person to function efficiently on a day-to-day basis becomes a major constraint when trying to be creative (Amabile, 1998). That is, the guidelines and rules people find so valuable in everyday life become the blocks limiting their own creative potential. The ability to master the creative process on an ongoing basis is very much linked to removing the blocks.

Roger von Oech (2008) argues that there are ten critical blocks. These are summarized in Table 6-3. In essence, he is arguing that employees are more likely to come

TABLE 6-3	

The Creative Blocks

"The Right Answer"	The fallacy that there is only one correct solution to a problem
"That's not logical"	The belief that logic is fine for the development of ideas but stifles creativity
"Be practical"	The tendency to allow practical considerations to kill concepts, halt the search for ideas, and deter one from considering alternatives
"Follow the rules"	Ignoring the fact that most revolutionary ideas are disruptive violations of existing systems and beliefs
"Avoid ambiguity"	Strict adherence to one fixed perspective on a situation
"To err is wrong"	Failure to see the connection between error and innovation: when you fail, you learn what doesn't work and can adjust
"Play is frivolous"	Unwillingness to acknowledge the creative power of play
"That's not my area"	Restriction of creativity through thinking that is overly narrow and focused
"Don't be foolish"	Unwillingness to think unconventionally out of fear of appearing foolish
"I'm not creative"	The worst of the blocks: self-condemnation that trumps talent, opportunity, and intelligence

SOURCE: Adapted from Roger von Oech, *A Whack on the Side of the Head*, New York: Warner Books, 2008, p.9.

up with breakthrough ideas if they look for multiple solutions, are illogical and impractical, break existing rules, are playful and not worried about looking foolish, embrace ambiguity, and recognize that failure is a sign of progress. Two additional blocks are especially relevant for corporate entrepreneurship. People miss creative opportunities because they are too narrow and focused in their jobs. By stating "that's not my area," possibilities are ignored because they do not fit a person's job description, or are outside of a person's education, experiences, and professional field. As von Oech (2008, p. 106) notes, "it's hard to see the dynamite idea behind you by looking twice as hard in front of you." The key lies in a willingness to look beyond one's field or job responsibilities, to explore how other disciplines approach similar problems, and to adopt different frames of references, languages, and assumptions. Creative individuals are explorers, looking in other areas for ideas. They find history in a hardware store, or fashion in a steel factory. They indulge hobbies, and read publications in diverse fields, and then bring all of this to bear on job-related challenges. Lastly, the worst of the blocks is "I'm not creative." A difference between people who are consistently creative and those who are not is that the former think of themselves as creative, while the latter assume they are not. The latter come to depend on the for-mer anytime a creative solution is needed. The objective evidence suggests that every-one is rich in creative potential, regardless of what we believe about ourselves.

From where do these blocks originate? Consider three sources. As the discussion above makes clear, employees impose the blocks on themselves based on their own perceptions. Second, fellow employees impose them on their coworkers. Refrains such as "that's not your job," "don't be foolish," and "that's not logical" are com-monly heard in team meetings, planning sessions, and hallway conversations. Even where the employee does not actually hear such phrases, he or she often perceives a need to not look foolish or step beyond their job responsibilities in front of coworkers. Finally, the workplace itself is a source of blocks. Certain companies may not tolerate failure, may penalize rule-bending or breaking, or may assign people to jobs with extremely narrow job descriptions.

Creativity Techniques and Creative Quality

A treasure trove of techniques and methods are available for use at different stages in the creative process. Techniques exist for generating creative concepts and ideas (e.g., brainstorming, role playing, mind mapping), for overcoming negativity (the "yes and" rather than "yes but" rule, which states that concerns about new ideas must be phrased in ways that find the positive in them), and for reaching convergence (e.g., backcast-ing, or imagining future scenarios and backing up to the present). The list is virtually endless, as can be seen in such books as Michalko's *Thinkertoys* (2006), Imber's *The Creativity Formula* (2009), or Hall's *Jump Start Your Brain* (1995). Table 6-4 provides a few examples.

The value of these techniques and exercises is likely to vary based on an employee's thinking or problem-solving style. People with a particular thinking style may respond more to certain techniques or stimuli than will those who have a different thinking style. Moving beyond the simple "left-brain" and "right brain" distinction, Leonard and Straus (1997) draw a distinction between those who are (a) logical, fact-based, and bottom-line oriented, (b) intuitive, rule breaking, and imaginative, (c) interpersonal, emotional, and people-focused, and (d) organized, planned, and detailed.

The purpose of the various exercises and techniques, and ultimately of approaching creativity in a more systematic manner, is to improve the quality of the creative out-put. In fact, producing a higher *quantity* of creative ideas is not of much value unless the end result is higher *quality* in terms of the ultimate concept or solution. This is an important point. While creativity itself is not something one can see or feel or touch, the quality of an individual's or group's creativity can be judged. While many criteria

TABLE 6-4

Linking Stages in the Process to Problem-Solving Approaches

Creativity Stage	*Activity*	*Cognitive Processes*
Interest	Environmental scanning	Intuition/emotion
Preparation	Preparing the expedition	Details/planning
Incubation	"Mulling things over"	Intuition
Illumination	The "eureka" experience	Intuition
Elaboration/Verification	Market research	Details/rationality
Exploitation	Implement and compete	Details/rationality

SOURCE: Adapted from Kao, J. J., *Entrepreneurship, Creativity and Organization*, Englewood Cliffs: Prentice-Hall, 1989, p.17.

are available for judging a creative concept or approach, a good beginning point is to consider the following three standards:

- **Overt benefit**—To what extent does the idea or concept convey a clear benefit or advantage to a user or customer? In what ways does it create value, and how much value is being created?

- **Reason to believe**—What supporting evidence are you able to provide, and is a user or customer likely to accept, that the concept or idea will deliver the same level of benefits that you claim?

- **Dramatic difference**—How unique or different is your concept or idea from current or conventional solutions? Is it an incremental or breakthrough advance? Can it be meaningfully differentiated from existing solutions on a sustainable basis?

Although creativity will always be an art, organizations need not view it as unmanageable. There is a role for structure, standards, expectations, and measures of performance. Clearly, creativity often happens inadvertently, and employees are frequently not conscious of the fact that they are being creative. Even so, their creative productivity is apt to be enhanced where they recognize the many ways in which they are currently creative, understand their immense creative potential, and adopt systematic approaches for tapping that potential.

The Entrepreneurial Personality

It is not enough, however, for employees to be creative. They must be able to think and act as entrepreneurs (Gartner, 1989; Shaver and Scott, 1991). Entrepreneurship requires that the employee take ownership of the creative idea, and assume responsibility for its implementation. The process of implementation requires further creativity in overcoming obstacles and finding critical resources.

To understand the challenge of being a corporate entrepreneur, let us review what is known about entrepreneurial individuals. The single most researched question within the field of entrepreneurship is "Who is the entrepreneur?". A variety of somewhat conflicting findings have been produced regarding the psychological and sociological makeup of entrepreneurs. Many of these studies suffer from significant methodological problems. Nonetheless, there do appear to be a few characteristics around which a consensus has emerged. On the psychological side, there is some agreement on at least six characteristics (see Table 6-5 for a more comprehensive list of psychological traits associated with the entrepreneurial personality). The first of these concerns motivation. The available evidence identifies entrepreneurs as being more achievement-motivated than driven by other factors such as the needs for

---

TABLE 6-5

Common Traits and Characteristics Associated with the Entrepreneurial Individual

Achievement motivation

Internal locus of control

Calculated risk-taking

Tolerance of ambiguity

Commitment/perseverance/determination

Independence

Self-confidence and optimism

Tolerance for failure

Persistent problem solving

Opportunity orientation

Integrity and reliability

High energy level/work ethic

Resourcefulness

Creativity and innovativeness

Vision

Team building

SOURCE: Adapted from Donald F. Kuratko and Richard M. Hodgetts, *Entrepreneurship (with InfoTrac)*, 7th ed. Copyright © 2007 South-Western, a part of Cengage Learning, Inc. Reproduced by permission. www.cengage.com/permissions.

power, money, status, or acceptance. They are driven by the task, the challenge; the opportunity to accomplish what others said could not, would not, or should not be done. Money certainly counts, but it is a by-product. Financial rewards serve as a scorecard, telling the entrepreneur that he or she is making progress.

Entrepreneurs also demonstrate a strong internal locus of control. Unlike those who believe that external events control their lives and dictate what happens around them, entrepreneurs are change agents. They fundamentally believe that, with enough time and effort and their own involvement, they can change their workplace, their markets, and their industries—in short, their environments.

Entrepreneurial individuals are calculated risk-takers. The entrepreneur tends to be about a 5.5 on a 10-point scale, where 1 = "risk avoidant" and 10 = "bold gambler." Calculated risk-taking can be defined as pursuit of a course of action that has a reasonable chance of costly failure, where failure is a significant negative difference between anticipated and actual results. It is calculated in the sense that (a) the individual has considered and attempted to estimate (at least conceptually) the likelihood and magnitude of the key risk factors; and (b) he or she has attempted to manage or mitigate the key risk factors through good planning and managerial decision-making.

The very nature of the entrepreneurial process demands that the entrepreneur demonstrate a high "tolerance of ambiguity." Things do not have to fit a precast mold or follow an exact pattern. In fact, they are often messy and imprecise, and there is tremendous uncertainty regarding whether one is on the right path, and what unanticipated obstacles lie around the next bend. The entrepreneurial process will inherently move in new and unanticipated directions. Most successful entrepreneurs find that, if their concept gets implemented and achieves success, it will look quite different than the concept they first started with. This is not because of poor conceptualizing or planning; it is the fundamental nature of the game.

Entrepreneurs are self-motivated, self-reliant, and prefer a degree of autonomy when accomplishing a task. The perception that they have room to maneuver in affecting their own destiny is highly valued. Finally, it is generally agreed that entrepreneurs are tenacious and demonstrate significant perseverance. Other common findings, about which there is less consensus, suggest that entrepreneurs are versatile, persuasive, creative, well-organized, extremely hard-working, and competitive (Morris, 1998).

Perhaps the two most significant conclusions that can be drawn from attempts to understand the traits and characteristics of the entrepreneur are that entrepreneurs are not born and that no single prototype of the entrepreneur exists. Although filled with controversy, the research makes it clear that traits associated with entrepreneurial behavior are strongly influenced by the environment and are developed over time. The list of traits and characteristics in Table 6-5 does not contain items that are clearly genetic, such as intelligence, physical prowess, or artistic talent. The tendencies to be self-confident, to have an internal locus of control, to be achievement-motivated, and similar attributes are the result of family, educational, social, and work experiences. They are also learned from the entrepreneurial experience itself. The message is that there is entrepreneurial potential in everyone, and companies can play a role in developing that potential. Our second conclusion concerns the tendency to look for a single profile of the entrepreneur. In reality, entrepreneurs differ significantly in terms of their risk profiles, need for independence, locus of control, and other characteristics. It would seem, instead, that there are different types of entrepreneurs. We shall discuss some of the major types that have been identified later in the chapter.

Characteristics such as the ones discussed above have important implications for corporate entrepreneurship. While entrepreneurs will differ markedly on a given characteristic, recognizing the key characteristics helps managers and employees know where to focus in developing a given individual's entrepreneurial potential. While it may not be possible to teach someone to be an entrepreneur, it is certainly possible to help them develop their achievement motivation, tolerance of ambiguity, or appreciation for calculated risk-taking. In addition, implications can be drawn for the design of the work environment. As managers make decisions about company structure, controls, rewards, policies, and other areas that define the workplace, these decisions must be made in a manner that is compatible with the types of characteristics associated with entrepreneurship. A work environment that does not allow a degree of autonomy, penalizes risk-taking, and discourages individual action is not one in which employees are likely to discover and act on their entrepreneurial potential.

Motivating Entrepreneurial Behavior

The willingness of an employee to identify entrepreneurial concepts and to devote oneself to pursuing a concept over time is directly related to an entrepreneur's personal makeup. In an interesting attempt to explain the motivational process that drives entrepreneurial behavior, Naffziger et al. (1994) propose the dynamic model that appears in Figure 6-1. Let's apply this model in a corporate context.

The decision to behave entrepreneurially results from the interaction of several factors. An individual has an idea or recognizes an opportunity. The tendency to act on it (as well as the manner in which he or she acts) is the result of the interplay between his or her personal characteristics, the individual's personal goal set, his or her personal environment, the current business environment, and the nature of the innovative idea (Reuber and Fischer, 1999).

FIGURE 6-1

A Model of Entrepreneurial Motivation

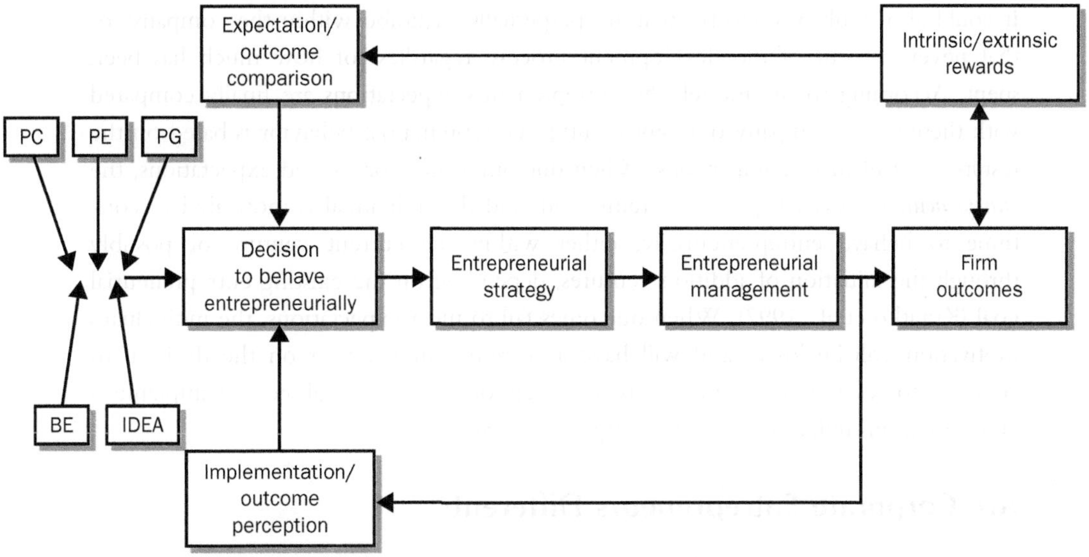

KEY; PC: Personal Characteristics of the Entrepreneur

PE: Personal Environment of the Entrepreneur

PG: Personal Goals of the Entrepreneur

BE: Business Environment for the Entrepreneurial Idea

IDEA: The Entrepreneurial Idea

SOURCE: Naffziger, D. W., Hornsby, J. S., and Kuratko, D. F. (1994), "A Proposed Research Model of Entrepreneurial Motivation," *Entrepreneurship Theory and Practice*, 18(3), p. 33.

However, before he or she actually acts on the idea, the individual takes into account two additional considerations. The first of these involves a comparison of his or her perceptions of the probable outcomes were the idea to be successfully implemented with the personal outcomes he or she has in mind. In a corporate setting, this comparison is influenced by the past experiences of the individual within the company, and the experiences of others with whom the individual is familiar. Next, an individual looks at the relationship between the implementation approach that would be required and likely outcomes from that approach. Here, the potential entrepreneur is concerned with what it will take to garner resources and support, overcome obstacles, and ensure the final concept meets market requirements. Again, the comparison is influenced by past experiences. Further, the more times the individual has attempted to pursue new ideas in the company, the more they have likely developed implementation approaches that work.

Assuming the concept is pursued, the strategy and managerial approaches of the corporate entrepreneur result in some sort of outcome within the company. This could range from a hugely successful new product or market to a glorious failure. It could also result in concepts that are perpetually in limbo within the company, or that never get out of the development process, regardless of how much has been spent. According to the model, the entrepreneur's expectations are finally compared with these actual company outcomes. Future entrepreneurial behavior is based on the results of all of these comparisons. When outcomes meet or exceed expectations, the *entrepreneurial behavior* is positively reinforced, and the individual is motivated to continue to behave entrepreneurially, either within the current venture or possibly through the initiation of addition ventures, depending on the existing entrepreneurial goal (Kuratko et al., 1997). When outcomes fail to meet expectations, the individual's motivation will be lower and will have a corresponding impact on the decision to continue to act entrepreneurially. These perceptions also affect subsequent implementation methods relied upon by the corporate entrepreneur.

Are Corporate Entrepreneurs Different?

The discussion up to this point has concentrated on what is known about entrepreneurs in general, and how this knowledge might apply in a corporate context. However, just as the corporate setting is very different from the start-up setting, the corporate entrepreneur (or "intrapreneur") is also a different kind of person (Busenitz and Barney, 1997; Stewart et al., 1999). Corporate entrepreneurs are not necessarily the inventors of new products, services, or processes (although they often are), but they turn ideas or prototypes into profitable realities. They are the drivers behind the implementation of innovative concepts. They are team builders with a commitment and the necessary drive to see ideas become realities. Importantly, they are very ordinary people who tend to do extraordinary things.

Entrepreneurial action can be thought of in terms of *conceptualization* and then *implementation*. From the employee's perspective, we can think of these as the stages of "dreaming" and "doing." There are many people in an organization that dream, or come up with new ideas. The issue from an entrepreneurial perspective concerns how much responsibility they take not only for refining their ideas into a workable or viable form, but for selling ideas, overcoming resistance, and following through on implementation (Herron and Sapienza, 1992). The shortage in most companies is not of dreamers, but of doers. Figure 6-2 characterizes different types of people in organizations on the extent to which they focus on the conceptualization part of things, or on making it happen. Thus, inventors and planners identify possibilities, while conventional managers focus on an action agenda. Corporate entrepreneurs represent a strong mix of strong vision and depth of action. They are the dreamers who do.

FIGURE 6-2

The Corporate Entrepreneurial Framework

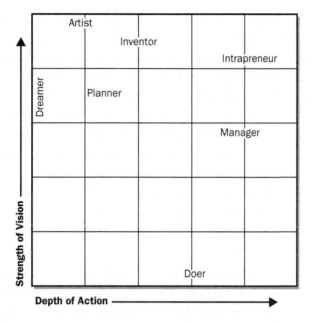

SOURCE: Pinchot, III, G. (1985), *Intrapreneuring*, New York: Harper & Row, p. 44

The corporate entrepreneur begins with a creative idea. This idea typically starts as a vision, which might be fairly loosely defined. In a sense, he or she goes through a "daydreaming phase." Here, the individual mentally envisions the process he or she will have to enact to take the idea from concept to successful implementation. Different pathways are thought through, and potential obstacles and barriers are mentally examined. The entrepreneur behind the innovative Fiero automobile, made by Pontiac some years ago, provides an example. When Hulki Aldikacti first came up with the idea for the Fiero, he was unsure of what the car should look like. So he built a wooden mock-up of the passenger compartment. He then sat in the model and imagined what it would feel like to drive the finished car. This helped him develop and perfect the final project.

Corporate entrepreneurs can move quickly to get things done. They are goal-oriented, willing to do whatever it takes to achieve their objectives. They are also a combination of thinker, doer, planner, and worker. Dedication to the new idea is paramount, as their action-orientation must be balanced against perseverance and tenacity. They must struggle to keep an idea alive, often after higher-level managers, committees, and others have "killed" it two or three times. Corporate entrepreneurs often expect the impossible from themselves and consider no setback too great to make their venture successful. They are self-determined pursuers of a vision who go beyond the call of duty in achieving their goals.

When faced with failure or setback, corporate entrepreneurs employ an optimistic approach. First, they do not admit they are beaten; they view failure as a temporary setback to be learned from and dealt with. It is not seen as a reason to quit. Second, they view themselves as responsible for their own destiny. They do not blame their failure on others but instead focus on learning how they might have done better. By objectively dealing with their own mistakes and failures, corporate entrepreneurs learn to avoid making the same mistakes again, and this, in turn, is part of what helps make them successful.

It could be argued that the discussion above could be equally applied to those who start new independent ventures and those who champion innovation in larger companies. And yet, there are important differences between these two individuals. Table 6-6 draws a fairly detailed comparison between the characteristics and skills of the corporate entrepreneur, those of the start-up or independent entrepreneur, and those of traditional managers.

An examination of the items in Table 6-6 reveals some important insights into the nature of the corporate entrepreneur. These individuals are closer to the traditional start-up entrepreneur than to the traditional corporate manager, but they have certain things in common with both. They desire a degree of autonomy, but also want access to corporate resources. Security matters to them, and they respond to corporate rewards and recognition. At the same time, they are cynical about many of the processes and systems within the company, but also optimistic that they can find ways around the rules and bureaucracy. They are more politically adept than the typical start-up entrepreneur, but more willing than the typical manager to get their hands dirty and do whatever task needs to be done.

Categories of Entrepreneurs

Earlier, we noted that there is no single prototype of the entrepreneur. The same is true of the corporate entrepreneur. There may actually be a number of different types. Early research examined a continuum of entrepreneurs ranging from the "craftsman" to the "opportunist" (Smith and Miner, 1983). The latter tend to do something that is more innovative, have a higher risk profile, and are more growth-oriented than the former.

Alternatively, Miner (1996) concludes that four different types of entrepreneurs exist, each of which achieves success by approaching entrepreneurship from a different route.

TABLE 6-6

Who Is the Corporate Entrepreneur?

Characteristic	Traditional Manager	Entrepreneur	Corporate Entrepreneur
Primary motives	Wants promotion and other traditional corporate rewards; power motivated	Wants freedom; goal-oriented, self-reliant, and self-motivated	Wants freedom, access to corporate resources; goal-oriented and self-motivated, but also responds to corporate rewards and recognition
Time orientation	Responds to quotes and budgets; to weekly, monthly, quarterly, and annual planning horizons; and to the next promotion or transfer	Uses end goals of 5- to 10-year growth of the business as guides; takes action now to move to next step along the way	End goal of 3 to 15 years, depending on the type of venture; urgency to meet self-imposed and corporate timetables
Tendency to action	Delegates action; supervising and reporting take most energy	Get hands dirty; may upset employees by suddenly doing their work	Gets hands dirty; may know how to delegate but, when necessary, does what needs to be done
Skills	Professional management; often business-school trained; uses abstract analytical, people-management, and political skills	Knows business intimately; more business acumen than managerial or political skill; often technically trained if in technical business; may have had formal profit-and-loss responsibility in the company	Very much like the entrepreneur, but usually professional or business-school trained. Ability to prosper within the corporation is always a challenge.
Attitude toward courage and destiny	Sees others being in charge of his or her destiny; can be forceful and ambitious but may be fearful of others' ability to do him or her in	Self-confident, optimistic, and courageous	Self-confident and courageous; many are cynical about the system but optimistic about their ability to outwit it

(Continued)

| TABLE 6-6 | (Continued) |

Who Is the Corporate Entrepreneur?

Characteristic	Traditional Manager	Entrepreneur	Corporate Entrepreneur
Focus of Attention	Primarily on events inside corporation	Primarily on technology and marketplace	Both inside and outside; sells insiders on needs of venture and marketplace but also focuses on customers
Attitude toward risk	Cautious	Likes moderate risk; invests heavily but expects to succeed	Likes moderate risk; generally not afraid of being fired, so sees little personal risk
Use of market research	Has market studies done to discover needs and guide product conceptualization	Creates needs; creates products that often cannot be tested with market research; potential customers do not yet understand them; talks to customers and forms own opinions	Does own market research and intuitive market evaluation, like the entrepreneur
Attitude toward status	Cares about status symbols (corner office, and so on)	Happy sitting on an orange crate if job is getting done	Considers traditional status symbols a joke; treasures symbols of freedom
Attitude toward failure and mistakes	Strives to avoid mistakes and surprises; postpones recognizing failure	Deals with mistakes and failures as learning experiences	Sensitive to need to appear orderly; attempts to hide risky projects from view so as to learn from mistakes without political cost of public failure
Decision-Making style	Agrees with those in power; delays making decisions until a feel of what bosses want is obtained	Follows private vision; decisive, action-oriented	Adept at getting others to agree with private vision; somewhat more patient and willing to compromise than the entrepreneur but still a doer
Who serves	Pleases others	Pleases self and customers	Pleases self, customers, and sponsors

Attitude toward the system	Sees system as nurturing and protective; seeks position within it	May rapidly advance in a system; then, when frustrated, may reject the system and form own company	Dislikes the system but learns to manipulate it
Problem-solving style	Works out problems within the system	Escapes problems in large and formal structures by leaving and starting over alone	Works out problems within the system or bypasses them without leaving
Socioeconomic background	Middle class	Lower class in some early studies; middle class in more recent ones	Middle class
Educational level	Highly educated	Less well educated in earlier studies; some graduate work but not Ph.D. in later ones	Often highly educated, particular in technical fields, but sometimes not
Relationship with others	Perceives hierarchy as basic relationship	Perceives transactions and deal making as basic relationship	Perceives transactions within hierarchy as basic relationship

SOURCE: Adapted from Gifford Pinchot III, *Intrapreneuring*, 1985: 54–56. Copyright ©1985 by Gifford Pinchot III. Adapted by permission of Harper Collins Publisher.

These include:

The Personal Achiever (the classic entrepreneur):

- high need for achievement
- need for performance feedback
- desire to plan and set goals
- strong individual initiative
- strong personal commitment and identification with their organization
- internal locus of control
- belief that work should be guided by personal goals, not those of others

The Super-Salesperson (achieves success through networking, selling, and people skills):

- capacity to understand and feel with another, to empathize

- desire to help others

- belief that social processes, interaction, and relationships are important

- need to have strong positive relationships with others

- belief that the salesforce is crucial to carrying out company strategy

- background often includes selling experience

The Real Manager (strong managerial skills combined with aggressive growth orientation):

- desire to be a corporate leader

- desire to compete

- decisiveness

- desire for power

- positive attitudes to authority

- desire to stand out from the crowd

The Expert Idea Generator (expertise combined with creativity):

- desire to innovate

- love of ideas, curious, open-minded

- belief that new product development is crucial component of company strategy

- good intelligence; thinking is at center of their entrepreneurial approach;

- intelligence as a source of competitive advantage

- desire to avoid taking risks

If we apply his scheme to the corporate context, personal achievers would be the type of bold, visionary, risk-takers that are typically associated with the classic entrepreneur. Super-salespeople would be entrepreneurial employees who successfully push concepts as a function of their networking and people skills. Real managers are more power-oriented, and tend to systematically and aggressively grow an internal venture. Expert idea generators, or technopreneurs, are inventors or creators, typically with a strong technical background. While they will champion a new idea within the organization and through implementation, they most enjoy the opportunity to go back and invent more new things. They are somewhat more risk-averse.

There may be many kinds of entrepreneurs in companies. However, this framework provides a beginning point for recognizing some of them. The critical point here is that corporate entrepreneurs take on various forms and exhibit different styles.

They can differ in terms of their relative risk profiles, sources of motivation, managerial capabilities, and other characteristics.

Critical Roles in Corporate Entrepreneurship

Entrepreneurship can happen anytime and anywhere in a company. The managerial challenge concerns how to make it sustainable—how to maintain the desired frequency and degree of entrepreneurship on an ongoing basis. Achieving continuous innovation requires that entrepreneurship be approached as a team sport, and that a number of key players get involved for an entrepreneurial event to successfully occur. Further, an environment must be created where various employees are willing to serve in different capacities on a regular basis. The key players are defined as follows:

Initiator—triggers a new entrepreneurial event, either by recognizing some external threat or opportunity, identifying some internal need, or pursuing some ongoing innovation initiative. This role is often, but not always, filled by the champion.

Sponsor/Facilitator—the leader or a major sponsor of the initiative, pushing for its acceptance and completion, playing a major advising or mentoring role as it unfolds and protecting it. This high-level person in the company acts as buffer, protector, and modifier of rules and policies and helps the venture obtain the needed resources.

Champion—takes the lead in driving and directing the project, overseeing the implementation process, adapting key aspects of the concept along the way, sustaining the project as obstacles and opposition arise, and bringing it through to completion.

Innovation Midwife—serves as a translator between the language, culture, and needs of the sponsor's world and the language, culture and needs of the champion's world. The midwife, as identified by Vincent (2005), nurtures, develops, and integrates innovations that might be rejected by the organization's core.

Supporter—augments the team, playing a secondary or more minor role, and providing expertise, intelligence, analysis, and marketing plans/programs on behalf of the initiative.

Reactor—plays more of a devil's advocate role, providing market intelligence and insight that serve to either pinpoint weaknesses in the entrepreneurial idea, possible ways in which it should be revised or refined, or reasons it should or should not be pursued.

Of all these players, the two most critical ones are arguably the champion and the sponsor. The focal point of any entrepreneurial initiative is the champion. The unique demands of the corporate environment require that the individual serving as champion must be able to wear many hats at the same time. However, he or she cannot be expected to wear all the necessary hats, and this is why a well-constructed team and strong network are important. Fifteen specific responsibility areas that must be filled in order to bring an entrepreneurial concept to fruition include:

- *Researcher/analyzer:* gather intelligence, assess potential, evaluate key factors in the market;

- *Interpreter/strategist:* identify patterns, trends, future development and draw implications for project development;

- *Visionary/inventory:* provide creativity, intuition, and judgment in recognizing opportunities and ways to capitalize upon them;

- *Catalyst or leader:* provide motivation and impetus to getting project off the ground;

- *Endorser:* endorse the entrepreneurial concept and lend the credibility to the pursuit of the concept by the project champion;

- *Team player:* play a collaborative role with people from other specialty areas;

- *Resource provider:* assist with informational, human, financial, and other inputs to exploit opportunity;

- *Problem-solver:* respond to a particular question or challenge that the innovation team encounters along the way;

- *Coordinator:* help to bring together and integrate key inputs and resources over time;

- *Negotiator:* help bridge differences among various involved parties regarding what the project or concept should consist of, its scope, its resource commitment levels, and its timetable;

- *Politician:* help overcome internal resistance and gain top management support;

- *Change manager:* oversee any strategic redirection, modification of infrastructure, and employee training or reorientation necessary to implement a new initiative;

- *Missionary:* motivate and inspire management and all relevant interest groups regarding ongoing need for innovation;

- *Opportunist:* react quickly to emerging developments, provide new direction if necessary;

- *Critic/judge:* identify key flaws, downside risks, and likely impact on other parts of the business.

In terms of their skill sets, at the beginning of their first innovative project corporate entrepreneurs start out as specialists. That is, the individual may specialize in one area of expertise, such as marketing or research and development. But once the entrepreneurial initiative gets underway, he or she is forced to learn all the facets of the venture. The corporate entrepreneur soon becomes a generalist with many skills.

With all we have now covered about corporate entrepreneurs, there still exist numerous myths about these individuals in organizations. Let's examine a few of the more popular ones.

Myths about Corporate Entrepreneurs

Just as a number of myths have been popularized about entrepreneurship in general (see Chapter 2), the entrepreneur inside of a company is often subject to misconceptions and false assumptions. That is, supervisors and peers in an organization have a tendency to stereotype employees that demonstrate strong entrepreneurial proclivities. Consider the following six myths, together with the countervailing reality:

- **Myth:** The primary motivation of corporate entrepreneurs is a desire for wealth; hence, money is the prime objective.

- **Fact:** The primary motivation of corporate entrepreneurs is the process of innovation: The freedom and ability to innovate are *the* prime motivators. Money is only a tool and a symbol of success.

- **Myth:** Corporate entrepreneurs are high risk-takers—they are gamblers who play for high stakes.

- **Fact:** Moderate risk-taking is a more realistic description of the corporate entrepreneur's actions. Because of their insatiable desire to achieve, smaller, calculated, and analyzed risks are the preferred stepping-stones of these individuals.

- **Myth:** Because corporate entrepreneurs lack analytical skills, they "shoot from the hip." This has led to a philosophy of "luck is all you need."

- **Fact:** Corporate entrepreneurs are fairly analytical. Although it may appear they are lucky and shoot from the hip, in truth, they are well prepared, understand innovation, and perceive market needs very well.

- **Myth:** Corporate entrepreneurs do not appreciate the importance of being a team player within the company, and often act as the proverbial "bull in a china shop."

- **Fact:** Corporate entrepreneurs often demonstrate strong political skills and are adept at working around rules, procedures, and constraints imposed by the company hierarchy without stepping on toes; they develop their innovative concepts "below the radar screen."

- **Myth:** Corporate entrepreneurs lack morals or ethics due to their strong desire to succeed. They do not care how they succeed, just as long as they do succeed.

- **Fact:** In today's demanding, educated, and critical society, where companies and their actions tend to be visible to the public, corporate entrepreneurs tend to be highly ethical and have moral convictions consistent with society's expectations. If they do not have these convictions, they do *not* survive.

- **Myth:** Corporate entrepreneurs have a power-hungry attitude and are most interested in building an empire. They want the venture to grow as big and as fast as it can.

- **Fact:** Most entrepreneurial initiatives are small and relatively conservative. The individual is more interested in the profit and growth of the concept or venture than in empire building. The focus is on doing things right rather than doing them big.

Many inside the organization view entrepreneurial individuals as threatening. They disturb comfort zones and create change. As a result, there is a tendency to cling to such stereotypes, or otherwise negatively portray the motives and actions of the entrepreneurial employee. For this reason, it is vital that senior executives clearly define the nature and role of the internal champion, communicate to everyone in the company the importance of this role, and publicly reinforce those who fill this role with recognition and rewards.

A Final Thought: Are You a Corporate Entrepreneur?

Before we leave this discussion regarding the nature of entrepreneurial individuals, it may be helpful for the reader to assess his or her own entrepreneurial profile. Gifford Pinchot (1985) proposes the following short set of items as a quick test (answer yes or no to the each question):

1. Does your desire to make things work better occupy as much of your time as fulfilling your duty to maintain them the way they are?

2. Do you get excited about what you are doing at work?

3. Do you think about new business ideas while driving to work or taking a shower?

4. Can you visualize concrete steps for action when you consider ways to make a new idea happen?

5. Do you get in trouble from time to time for doing things that exceed your authority?

6. Are you able to keep your ideas under cover, suppressing your urge to tell everyone about them until you have tested them and developed a plan for implementation?

7. Have you successfully pushed through bleak times when something you were working on looked as if it might fail?

8. Do you have a network of friends at work that you can count on for help?

9. Do you get easily annoyed by other's incompetent attempts to execute parts of your ideas?

10. Can you consider trying to overcome a natural perfectionist tendency to do all the work yourself and share the responsibility for your ideas with a team?

11. Would you be willing to give up some salary in exchange for the chance to try out your business idea if the rewards for success were adequate?

Pinchot suggests that, if an employee answers "yes" more times than "no," the chances are he or she is already behaving like an entrepreneur.

THE INNOVATOR'S NOTEBOOK

The Corporate Entrepreneur Personas

Ideo, the global design consultancy company, has more than 500 employees in eight offices on three continents. Over the past 30 years, the company has successfully handled projects such as building a better Pringle for Procter & Gamble; revitalizing the bicycle for Shimano; and rethinking airport-security checkpoints for the TSA. Ideo reports more than 1,000 patents since 1978 and it has won 346 design awards since 1991, more than any other company. With almost $100 million in annual revenue, Ideo's clients include giant companies such as Anheuser-Busch, Gap, HBO, Kodak, Marriott, Pepsi, and PNC. Ideo is the premier innovation consulting company for both American and foreign companies.

Given that innovation is the lifeblood of any business, the corporate entrepreneur is the heart that keeps pumping innovation into the business. At Ideo, the management has developed ten personas for innovation that employees are encouraged to play in order to spur innovative solutions. The goal at Ideo is to discourage those employees that often take the contrarian position when new ideas are presented, better known as "devil's advocates." Following are the ten personas grouped into three categories: learning—personas focused on challenging their perspectives as well as those of the organization; organizing—personas focused on the time-, resource-, and attention-limitations caused by introducing a new concept and how to effectively maneuver around them; and building—personas focused on leveraging the insights provided by the learning personas and the strategy provided by the organizing personas.

The Learning Personas

The *Cross-Pollinator* searches for new learning that can fit the unique needs of an organization by exploring other industries and cultures. An example of a cross-pollinator in action can be seen in the development of the Mujirushi Ryohin chain, a 300-store, billion-dollar retail empire. The business was based on a Japanese businesswoman finding a generic beer in a U.S. supermarket that she liked, which led to her building a retail chain based on offering only "no brand" products.

The *Anthropologist* observes human behavior in order to gain an understanding of how people interact physically and emotionally with products, services, and spaces and then introduces that learning into the organization. Employees at Ideo, known as human-factors people, act as anthropologists when they observe customers outside of the office—for instance, one employee stayed for 48 hours in the hospital room of an elderly patient undergoing surgery.

The *Experimenter* continuously prototypes new ideas in order to learn through trial-and-error and, in turn, to improve his or her success rate by taking calculated risks based on those lessons. Experimentation was clearly at work when BMW opted to develop short films for bmwfilms.com rather than using traditional advertising channels. The success of the initiative highlights the rewards that can be recognized by experimenters.

The Organizing Personas

The *Hurdler* is not only aware of the roadblocks that line the path to innovation, but he also possesses the agility required to circumvent those obstacles. When it came to the invention of masking tape at 3M, the employee responsible for its development was hindered by his $100 authorization limit. By submitting a series of $99 purchase orders to avoid attracting attention so that he could complete his project, this hurdler was able to bend the rules and provide 3M one of its signature products, which has generated billions of dollars in profits for the company.

The *Director* is both adept at casting teams and in directing the members of those teams to bring their talents to light. A Mattel executive assembling a team of designers and project leaders, sequestering them for three months and producing a new $100 million toy platform, epitomizes a director in action.

The *Collaborator* serves to bring diverse groups together by usually leading from within the team in order to facilitate the creation of new combinations and solutions. Collaborators were at work when Kraft Foods and Safeway set out to eliminate the traditional barriers between suppliers and retailers. One strategy, which on the surface was merely a method to streamline the transfer of goods between the companies, not only saved labor and carrying costs but led to the sales of Capri Sun juice drinks increasing by 167 percent.

The Building Personas

The *Storyteller* specializes at building internal morale and external awareness through the use of narratives that impart a basic human value or reinforce an element of the company's culture. Medtronic's culture is defined by its most effective storytellers, patients that have had their lives changed or even saved by the company's products and that provide firsthand narratives to the employees.

The *Caregiver* strives to move the company beyond customer service into a more intimate customer relationship known as "customer care." Best Cellars, a profitable wine retailer, has demonstrated the Caregiver role by removing the mystery and snobbery from wine in order to make the experience fun for its customers.

The *Set Designer* builds a stage that will allow innovation team members to do their best work. For the Cleveland Indians, building a new stadium led to a renewed winning ability for the team.

The *Experience Architect* goes beyond the obvious needs of customers in order to uncover their unexpressed needs. By turning the preparation of a frozen dessert into a fun experience with which the customer could get involved, Cold Stone Creamery developed a successful new customer experience, which has allowed it to enjoy premium prices.

Discussion Questions

1. How do these "personas" relate to the creative individual in an organization?

2. Using Table 6-5, discuss how the entrepreneurial personality fits into these personas.

3. From the chapter's critical roles in corporate entrepreneurship, which of these "personas" may be the most beneficial for an organization?

SOURCES: Adapted from Kelley, T. "The 10 Faces of Innovation," *Fast Company*, Issue 99, October 2005; Linda Tischler, "Ideo's David Kelley on 'Design Thinking,'" *Fast Company* online February 1, 2009, accessed April 17, 2010; and company Web site accessed April 17, 2010.

Summary and Conclusions

Creativity is the foundation upon which entrepreneurship is built. The corporate entrepreneur requires creative solutions to an array of challenges and obstacles as a concept goes from conceptualization to implementation. In the end, entrepreneurship in larger organizations cannot happen without technical creativity, political creativity, resource creativity, marketing creativity, and more.

Creativity brings with it a fresh start, a new way, a freedom from the constraints of what was, and a path to what can be. It is a manifestation of the human spirit, such that the act of successful creativity is by itself a tremendous source of employee motivation and pride. To create is to matter, to count, to make a difference, to have an impact, and to be a source of value.

The entrepreneurial personality takes on many forms. While there are some characteristics common to most entrepreneurial individuals, such as achievement motivation, internal locus of control, calculated risk-taking, and tolerance for ambiguity, there is no single profile or prototype. Further, entrepreneurs are not born. The entrepreneurial potential is rich in every employee in a company, no matter what their background or position is.

In this chapter, we also explored the concept of entrepreneurial motivation. Characteristics that distinguish corporate entrepreneurs from independent or start-up entrepreneurs, as well as from conventional managers, were identified. While there are also similarities among these three types, the corporate entrepreneur is closer in nature to the start-up entrepreneur than to the conventional manager. Just as important is the need to recognize the different kinds of entrepreneurs that can be found in a corporate setting, and an attempt was made to describe at least four different types.

Sustainable entrepreneurship is dependent on the ongoing ability of companies to fill a set of key roles, the two most important of which were the champion and the sponsor. Champions must wear many hats, and a number of their responsibilities were identified. The nature and scope of these responsibilities makes it clear that corporate entrepreneurship does not happen without teams, where other individuals can wear some of the required hats. When seeking someone to serve as sponsor, one must strive to achieve a fit not only between the champion and the targeted person, but also between the entrepreneurial concept and the type of sponsor selected.

References

Amabile, T. (1998). "How to Kill Creativity," *Harvard Business Review*, 76, (September–October): 77–87.

Amabile, T., and Mueller, J. S. (2008). "Studying Creativity, Its Processes, and Its Antecedents: An Exploration of the Componential Theory of Creativity," in J. Zhou and C. E. Shalley (eds.) *Handbook of Organizational Creativity* (New York: Lawrence Erlbaum Associates).

Busenitz, L., and Barney, J. B. (1997). "Differences between Entrepreneurs and Managers in Large Organizations: Biases and Heuristics in Strategic Decision-Making," *Journal of Business Venturing*, 12(1): 9–30.

Gartner, W. B. (1989). "Some Suggestions for Research on Entrepreneurial Traits and Characteristics," *Entrepreneurship Theory and Practice*, 13(1): 27–38.

Hall, D. (1995). *Jump Start Your Brain* (New York: Warner Books).

Herron, L., and Sapienza, H. J. (1992). "The Entrepreneur and the Initiation of New Venture: Launch Activities," *Entrepreneurship Theory and Practice*, 16(1): 49–55.

Hirshberg, J. (1998). *The Creative Priority* (New York: Harper Books).

Imber, A. (2009). *The Creativity Formula* (Alexandria, VA: Liminal Press).

Jeffrey, S. (2008). *Creativty Revealed: Discovering the Source of Inspiration* (Kingston, NY: Creative Crayon Publishers).

Kao, J. J. (1989). *Entrepreneurship, Creativity and Organization* (Englewood Cliffs: Prentice-Hall).

Kuratko, D. F., Hornsby, J. S., and Naffziger, D. W. (1997). "An Examination of Owner's Goals in Sustaining Entrepreneurship," *Journal of Small Business Management*, 35(1): 24–33.

Leonard, D., and S. Straus (1997). "Putting the Company's Whole Brain to Work," *Harvard Business Review*, 75 (July-August): 111–121.

Miller, W. C. (1999). *Flash of Brilliance* (Reading, MA: Perseus Books).

Michalko, M. (2006). *Tinkertoys*, 2nd ed. (Berkeley CA: Ten Speed Press).

Miner, J. B. (1996). *Four Routes to Entrepreneurial Success* (San Francisco: Berrett-Koehler).

Morris, M. H. (1998). *Entrepreneurial Intensity* (Westport, CT: Quorum Books).

Naffziger, D. W., Hornsby, J. S., and Kuratko, D. F. (1994). "A Proposed Research Model of Entrepreneurial Motivation," *Entrepreneurship Theory and Practice*, 18(3): 29–42.

Pinchott, III, G. (1985). *Intrapreneuring* (New York: Harper & Row).

Reuber, A. R., and Fischer, E. (1999). "Understanding the Consequences of Founder's Experience," *Journal of Small Business Management*, 37(2): 30–45.

Shaver, K. G., and Scott, L. R. (1991). "Person, Process, Choice: The Psychology of New Venture Creation," *Entrepreneurship Theory and Practice*, 16(2): 23–45.

Smith, N., and Miner, J. (1983). "Type of Entrepreneur, Types of Firm, and Managerial Motivation: Implications for Organizational Life Cycle Theory," *Strategic Management Journal*, 4(3): 325–340.

Stewart, W. H., Watson, W. E., Carland, J. C., and Carland, J. W. (1999). "A Proclivity for Entrepreneurship: A Comparison of Entrepreneurs, Small Business Owners, and Corporate Managers," *Journal of Business Venturing*, 14(2): 189–214.

Vincent, L. (2005). "Innovation Midwives: Sustaining Innovation Streams in Established Companies," *Research Technology Management*, 48(1): 41–49.

Buis, J. Smulders, F., and van der Meer, H. (2009). "Towards a More Realistic Creative Problem Solving Approach," *Creativity and Innovation Management*, 18(4): 286–298.

von Oech, R. (2008). *A Whack on the Side of the Head*, revised edition (New York: Warner Books).

Chapter 7

Human Resources and the Entrepreneurial Organization: The Organizational Perspective

Introduction

Entrepreneurship begins with people—they are the heart and soul of any enterprise. There are no entrepreneurial organizations without entrepreneurial employees. In other chapters, we have described how entrepreneurship, when applied to established companies, takes on unique characteristics and becomes subject to a number of constraints not found in most independent start-ups. The magnitude of these constraints suggests that very different approaches to company design and management are necessary if entrepreneurship is to be facilitated on an ongoing basis. As managers struggle with these issues, the most vexing question they face can be stated succinctly: "How do we create a work environment that supports entrepreneurial employees?"

Of all the decision areas that can affect the work environment, human resource management (HRM) is perhaps the most vital. The past few decades have witnessed a fundamental transformation of the HRM function in companies. Historically, those in the HRM area were principally concerned with administering employee benefits and imposing rules and procedures on employee hiring, promotions, and firing. Today, many companies understand that the HRM function must play a strategic role in developing core competencies and achieving sustainable competitive advantage through people.

Consistent with this more strategic role is the recognition that HRM practices might be associated with entrepreneurship. A case in point is the finding that poorly designed compensation and performance appraisal systems constrain entrepreneurial behavior (Balkin and Logan, 1988). Similarly, a number of other observers have suggested that various HRM-related policies can produce higher or lower levels of entrepreneurship in a company (e.g., Baden-Fuller, 1997; Hornsby and Kuratko, 2003; Hornsby and Kuratko, 2005; Jimenez-Jimenez and Sanz-Valle, 2008; Morris and Jones, 1993; Shane, 1996).

In this chapter, we explore the nature of the HRM function in organizations. A simple way to organize the multitude of HRM practices within a company is presented. Based on this organizing approach, an assessment is made of practices that facilitate rather than constrain entrepreneurial behavior. Evidence to support these relationships is summarized. Special attention is devoted to understanding how reward systems influence employee motivation to behave entrepreneurially.

Understanding the HRM Function

Human resource management is a broad concept that captures the set of tasks associated with acquiring, training, developing, motivating, organizing, and maintaining the employees of a company. While some companies still call it "personnel," "human resources" is the more prevalent term today, in part because it reflects a more comprehensive and strategic perspective. Specifically, the term reflects the idea that organizational goals and employee needs are mutually compatible if managed properly, and that employees represent continued investments on the part of the company, with continued returns. Some companies take this concept further, demonstrating a real passion for their people, and referring to the human resource management area as the "People and Leadership Development Department" (Southwest Airlines) or even "Central Casting" (the Walt Disney Company).

A wide array of activities can be included under the general human resource management heading, with differences among companies in terms of what they do or do not consider as part of HRM. Table 7-1 provides a summary list of these activities.

TABLE 7-1

The Major Human Resource Management Functions

Internal Challenges: Core HR Responsibilities

Job Analysis and Design

Human Resource Planning

Employee Recruitment

Performance Appraisals

Training and Development

Discipline

Compensation

Administration of Benefits

Employee Health and Safety

Employee Dismissal

Human Resource Information Systems

(Continued)

TABLE 7-1	(Continued)

The Major Human Resource Management Functions

External Challenges: Influences on Core HR Functions

Characteristics of the Changing Work Force

Increasing Legal Requirements

Complex Ethical Issues

Outsourcing and Other Global Challenges

Labor Relations and Union Pressures

Changing Technology Affecting the Workplace

SOURCE: Adapted from J. S. Hornsby and D. F. Kuratko, *Frontline HR*, 1st ed. Copyright © 2005 South-Western, a part of Cengage Learning, Inc. Reproduced by permission. www.cengage.com/permissions.

For simplicity, we can organize most of these into five general categories, which we will explore in further detail. These include job planning and design, recruitment and selection, training and development, employee performance evaluation, and compensation and rewards (see Figure 7-1). These categories are not all-inclusive, but represent core HRM areas having important strategic implications.

As we have noted, a traditional personnel function differs from a human resource management approach in that the latter is more strategic. This means that all of the

FIGURE 7-1	

Using Key Elements of the HRM System to Create an Entrepreneurial Environment

Job Planning and Design
What are employees asked to do and how do we allow them room to show initiative?

Recruitment and Selection
Who do we hire to be entrepreneurial and how do we hire them?

Creating an Entrepreneurial Work Environment

Performance Appraisals
How do we guide, reinforce, and help employees identify with entrepreneurial performance?

Compensation and Rewards
How do we incentivize employees to be entrepreneurial, take ownership, and stay with the company?

Training and Development
How do we help employees recognize their entrepreneurial potential and develop the skills to best capitalize on that potential?

company's HR practices are coordinated in a way that reflects (1) what is happening in the external competitive environment, (2) a longer-term focus, and (3) ways in which the skills and behaviors of all employees can be affected in a manner that supports and helps accomplish the overall strategies of the company. Simply put, *human resource management becomes a means for achieving the company's strategic direction* (Hornsby and Kuratko, 2005). Thus, human resource programs associated with recruitment, selection, and training are designed to ensure that employees possess characteristics that are critical for superior company performance over time. Performance appraisal, compensation, and discipline programs are designed to provide the behavioral cues and reinforcements that guide and motivate behaviors associated with key company strategies. Further, different corporate strategies or organizational initiatives require different employee characteristics (knowledge, skills, and abilities) and behaviors. In addition, for each human resource practice there exist design options that are, in fact, options to promote and reinforce particular employee characteristics and behaviors. For example, it has been demonstrated that the most appropriate way to approach employee recruitment and selection decisions depends upon whether organizations are pursuing an entrepreneurial-based strategy or an efficiency-based strategy (Olian and Rynes, 1984; Schuler and Jackson, 2007).

HRM is an area in transition. Targeted legislation and the changing dynamics of the workforce have put pressure on companies to increase their human resource emphasis. Among managers, some of the major issues of concern include attraction and retention of quality employees, design of benefit and wage packages that motivate sustainable employee performance, and the need to meet regulatory requirements (e.g., fair labor practices). This latter area is especially important, as these regulations can affect a company's ability to hire, fire, reward, promote, demote, or transfer an employee. The removal of flexibility in these areas tends to undermine entrepreneurship in companies, as the company is less able to move quickly, put the right people in the right place, or provide incentives that are effective in encouraging innovation and risk-taking. Companies are also struggling with trade-offs between the flexibility that results from a reliance on contract labor and outsourced services versus the loyalty and control possible from making longer-term commitments to employees.

Creating the Work Environment

While the entrepreneurial process always involves teams, it typically begins with an individual and is kept alive and nurtured by individuals. The dedicated employee who champions a concept, persists in overcoming internal and external obstacles, accepts responsibility for failure and, in effect, risks his or her job on the outcome of a venture, is the single most important ingredient for entrepreneurship to occur. As de Chambeau and Shays (1984, p. 132) concluded many year ago, "corporate entre-preneurs cannot be assigned or appointed; they must be volunteers who bring a clear vision of what they want to create."

It is our belief that each and every employee within an organization is rich in entrepreneurial potential. Yet most of them fail to capitalize on that potential. Some employees do not recognize their potential, while others believe the costs of acting on that potential are greater than the potential benefits. In either case, the challenge to management becomes one of creating a work environment that helps employees understand (1) the kinds of entrepreneurial behaviors sought by the organization, (2) their own innate ability to act in entrepreneurial ways, and (3) the incentives for acting in an entrepreneurial fashion and the disincentives for failing to do so.

Work environment refers to the context or surroundings in which employees find themselves when they come to the job each day. It is defined by the set of conditions under which employees must operate as they attempt to accomplish company tasks and personal goals. Employees develop perceptions about the environment based on experience and interactions over time. Included among these perceptions are the extent to which the work environment expects or permits employees to demonstrate individual initiative, experiment, try new things, persevere in the face of rejection, use resources that have not been formally allocated to them, and engage in related entrepreneurial behaviors.

The work environment is influenced by a host of factors, ranging from current business conditions and the pressure to perform, to the rules and procedures an employee must navigate to get anything done, and to the management style of the employee's supervisor. While some of these factors are not controllable by senior man-agement, many can be controlled or influenced. One of the most impactful tools for not only influencing the work environment but for actually defining it is the company's human resource management system.

HRM and the Paradox of Creative Abrasion

The focus of HRM policies should not be to create work environments where people look, think, and act alike. Too often, companies seem preoccupied with making new hires that "fit" with the current mix of employees and the prevailing norms and atti-tudes within the company. While harmony is important, and employees must always respect one another, diversity is an important component of an entrepreneurial work environment.

This brings us to a fundamental paradox. In an era where considerable attention is devoted to the need in organizations for teamwork, cooperation, consensus, and conflict avoidance, it may be that companies also need to highlight differences. On the one hand, creative organizations demonstrate great teamwork, collaboration, and collegiality. On the other hand, they feature diversity, debate, argument, and friction. The message is that such friction can be good. Collisions are a vibrant source of energy in a company.

The fostering of entrepreneurship requires that managers figure out how to get different approaches and perspectives to grate against one another in a productive process that can be termed "creative abrasion." The point is not to create a scenario where colliding ideas or viewpoints or priorities battle one another, with one winning out or dominating, and the other losing and being discarded. Nor is the objective to encourage compromise, alignment of positions, or watering down of one or both positions so as to achieve unity of direction. Hirshberg (1998, p. 33) notes:

> "Creative abrasion calls for the development of leadership styles that focus on first identifying and then incorporating polarized viewpoints. In doing so, the probabilities for unexpected juxtapositions are sharply increased, as are the levels of mutual understanding. The irony is that out of a process keyed on abrasiveness, a corporate culture of heightened sensitivity and harmony is achieved."

Creative abrasion serves to facilitate divergence, and it must be complemented by leadership styles and structures that ultimately produce convergence. This discussion is not about clashes that are arbitrary or based on personalities and egos. It is about highlighting differences that are natural, and that increase the level of stimulation and variety in the organization. Further, there are different degrees of creative abrasion. Examples of efforts to take advantage of abrasion could include hiring people who are not like current staff; putting together inter-functional teams with members who have very different backgrounds and orientations; challenging a team with two seemingly incompatible goals; introducing a perspective that threatens the positions and assumptions of those in the group; blurring responsibilities between departments or functions; and bringing in consultants, temporary staff, or speakers who hold very different points of view. Management of abrasion is an art. It requires patience and a sense of when to let the friction run its course, and when to interfere so as to avoid permanent dead ends.

HRM Policies and Entrepreneurship

Entrepreneurial activities require employees to act and think in ways not normally associated with highly structured or bureaucratic organizations. Thus, one would expect to observe differences in human resource practices based on differences in the levels of entrepreneurship observed across organizations.

Randall Schuler, a leading scholar in the HRM area, has suggested (1989) the following employee characteristics are associated with successful entrepreneurial efforts: creative and innovative behavior, risk-taking, a long-term orientation, a focus on results, flexibility to change, cooperation, independent behavior, tolerance of ambiguity, and a preference to assume responsibility. He also notes that HRM practices are a reflection of a company's culture, and others (Hamel, 2000; Sathe, 2006) have suggested corporate entrepreneurship requires a culture built around emotional commitment, autonomy, empowerment, earned respect, and a strong work ethic. Using these desired employee and cultural characteristics, it becomes possible to identify the HRM policy combinations most conducive to fostering entrepreneurial behavior.

The categories of HRM practices presented in Table 7-2 and in Figure 7-1 provide a useful framework for establishing specific linkages between HRM and entrepreneurship. The following discussion also draws extensively on works of Schuler (1989) and Morris and Jones (1993). Beginning with planning choices, innovation and risk-taking behaviors would seem more consistent with a long-term orientation and an emphasis on formal planning with high employee involvement in job design. Job-related tasks need to be defined more broadly, with some discretion given to the employee in determining how the job gets done. Also, greater emphasis should be placed on achieving results over a preoccupation with ensuring processes or procedures are strictly followed. Jobs are likely to be less structured or constrained by rigid organizational policies. Detailed and overlapping policies and procedures, along with centralized decision-making, tend to constrain action alternatives and inhibit the proactive decision-making necessary for successful entrepreneurial action.

TABLE 7-2	
HRM Policies Consistent with Entrepreneurial Behavior	
General Area	*Practices Encouraging Entrepreneurship*
Planning/Overall Job Design	Reliance on formal planning
	Long-term orientation in planning and job design
	Implicit job analysis
	Jobs that are broad in scope
	Jobs with significant discretion
	Jobs that are less structured
	Integrative job design
	Results-oriented job design
	High employee involvement in designing jobs

(Continued)

TABLE 7-2	(Continued)

HRM Policies Consistent with Entrepreneurial Behavior

General Area	*Practices Encouraging Entrepreneurship*
Recruitment and Selection	Reliance on external and internal candidates when hiring
	Innovative approaches to finding employees
	Broad career paths
	Multiple career ladders
	General, implicit, less formalized selection criteria
	Extensive job socialization
	Open recruitment and selection procedures
Training and Development	Long-term, career-oriented training
	Training with broad applications
	Individualized training
	High employee participation
	Unsystematic training
	Emphasis on entrepreneurial skills
	Continuous/ongoing training
Performance Appraisal	High employee involvement
	Balanced individual–group orientation
	Emphasis on effectiveness over efficiency
	Result-oriented (vs. process)
	Based on subjective criteria
	Emphasis on long-term performance
	Includes innovation and risk criteria
	Reflects tolerance of failure
	Appraisals done based on project life cycle
Compensation/ Rewards	Emphasizes long-term performance
	Decentralized/customized at division or department levels
	Tailored to individuals
	Emphasizes individual performance with incentives for group efforts
	Merit- and incentive-based
	Significant financial reward
	Based on external equity

Turning to the staffing choices of the company, entrepreneurial behavior implies unpredictable external environments and internal requirements. The fit between company direction and available internal resources may be poor. As such, companies may be forced to rely on a balance of external and internal sources for job candidates. The need to create and maintain an entrepreneurial culture combined with a reliance on external sources for employees would, in turn, increase the need for extensive orientation and socialization programs when people come into the company. Further, rapid environmental change and continuous product/market innovation can be expected to produce time pressures as well as variable job demands and requirements. The result in entrepreneurial organizations is likely to be a reliance on more general, implicit, and less formalized criteria for selecting new employees.

Once a person is hired into the organization, staffing practices should be designed around broad career paths and multiple career ladders for the employee. Broad paths and multiple ladders provide exposure to more areas of the organization and different ways of thinking. This exposure in turn enhances idea generation and problem-solving, and encourages cooperative activities among departments and individuals. Staffing procedures in these organizations are apt to be fairly open. Entrepreneurial individuals are goal- and action-oriented. Thus, employees should not be selected for entrepreneurial tasks simply based on their knowledge and skills, or their past performance on unrelated tasks. Open selection procedures allow for more self-selection into entrepreneurial positions and hence a better match between the entrepreneurial requirements of the organization and the individual's needs.

Training and development practices can promote entrepreneurial behavior to the extent that they are applicable to a broad range of job situations and encourage high employee participation. Changing job demands and the need to keep abreast of the newest technologies suggest a need for continuous, ongoing training, as well as training activities that are less structured or standardized and which focus on individualized knowledge requirements. This type of training approach enables employees to respond in unique ways to new challenges, adapt to dynamic environmental conditions, and feel comfortable with ambiguity. Training on opportunity recognition and resource leveraging is also worthwhile. Training programs should include an attitudinal component as well, where acceptance of change, a willingness to take risks and assume responsibility, and the value of collaborative innovation and shared achievements are central themes. Finally, there is some value in teaching political skills to prospective entrepreneurs, including ways to obtain sponsors, build resource networks, and avoid early publicity of new concepts and ventures.

Organizations communicate performance expectations and reinforce desired employee behaviors through their performance appraisal and reward practices, both of which should be designed around specific criteria. Entrepreneurship is fostered where performance evaluations and discretionary compensation are based on long-term results and a balanced emphasis on individual and group performance. Moreover, given that risk implies failure, appraisal and reward systems should reflect a tolerance of failure and offer some employment security. Because entrepreneurial individuals tend to demonstrate a high need for achievement but are also reward conscious, it is important that they be active participants both in setting high performance standards and in designing customized reward systems.

For their part, appraisals should be conducted at intermittent and irregular time intervals in entrepreneurial organizations, rather than at uniform or fixed intervals. They should be tailored to the life cycle of an entrepreneurial project. This is because entrepreneurial events require time to evolve, with each one encountering unique sets of obstacles and with various projects typically at different stages of development. In addition, entrepreneurial success often depends on the ability of employees to obtain resources from novel sources or in nontraditional ways, and occasionally to violate or ignore standard company policies and procedures. Accordingly, performance appraisals need to emphasize end results or outcomes, rather than the methods employed to achieve those results. The evaluation of employees should include explicit measures of innovativeness and risk assumption, which implies use of qualitative and subjective measures of performance.

With regard to rewards, personal incentives (financial *and* nonfinancial) are necessary to reinforce the risk-taking and persistence required when implementing an entrepreneurial concept. To retain entrepreneurial employees, these incentives must be significant. Individual incentives must be balanced by rewards linked to group performance over longer periods of time, so as to encourage cooperative, interdependent behavior. Taking responsibility for innovation and achieving a longer-term commitment can be furthered by compensation practices that emphasize external pay equity and incentives such as stock options and profit sharing. The customized nature of these reward systems also suggests that responsibility for their design and implementation be decentralized, or delegated to the divisional or departmental level.

Some Evidence to Support the Relationships

This discussion has identified critical HRM practices that are believed to be facilitators of entrepreneurship. However, this list is not intended to be comprehensive. Rather, it captures a set of key probable relationships based on the available evidence, which is quite limited. One of the few studies that attempted to determine if HRM practices actually affect entrepreneurial performance in companies was conducted by Morris and

Jones (1995). They conducted a cross-sectional survey of multiple managers in companies representing a wide range of industries. The study focused on human resource management practices as they were being applied to mid-level operational managers (e.g., purchasing, sales, and R&D managers). A total of 36 practices in the five categories presented in Table 7-2 (i.e., planning and job design, selection and staffing, training and development, appraisal, and compensation) were evaluated. For instance, respondents were asked to characterize the extent to which selection and staffing practices rely primarily on internal versus external sources for job candidates, and are based on implicit versus explicit selection criteria.

Using the median scores produced from the survey, companies were split into two groups, those with a stronger entrepreneurial orientation and those with a weaker entrepreneurial orientation. Statistical analysis was then used to determine whether companies that were more entrepreneurial differed from their less entrepreneurial counterparts with regard to the 36 HRM practices. Of the 36 items investigated, 14 demonstrated significant differences. Table 7-3 summarizes these findings. Aspects of all five of our major HRM areas are represented here, from a reliance on selection and staffing procedures designed around multiple career paths to explicit measurement of innovative and risk-taking behaviors in the appraisal process, and compensation practices that included bonuses and incentives based on long-term performance, an emphasis on job security over high pay, and greater stress on individual rather than group performance.

Further examination of the practices associated with an entrepreneurial orientation suggests that the performance appraisal and training/development areas generated the highest numbers of practices that distinguish more entrepreneurial from less entrepreneurial organizations. Next in order was compensation, followed by selection and staffing, and, lastly, planning and job design.

Entrepreneurial Motivation and the Critical Role of Reward Systems

One of the most visible and influential parts of a company's HRM system is the reward and compensation program. Ultimately, employees come to work each day to achieve rewards. These rewards can take any number of forms. Some people seek financial rewards; others seek power and status; while still others strive for personal development and career enhancement, self-actualization, or social rewards (e.g., friendships, camaraderie). Clearly, rewards represent a very potent tool to influence employee behavior on the job, especially the set of rewards over which management has direct control. To appreciate the role of such rewards, one must first understand

TABLE 7-3

Individual HRM Practices Associated with the Company's Entrepreneurial Orientation

When surveying a large sample of companies from a cross-section of industries, Morris and Jones divided companies into two groups based on whether they had a stronger or weaker entrepreneurial orientation. They then compared the human resource management practices in these two groups of companies. The results suggested a number of significant differences in the practices of the companies. Specifically, the entrepreneurial companies were more likely to engage in the following 14 HRM practices:

1 Designed jobs to enable multiple career paths rather than a single career path for employees.

2 Engaged in extensive socialization efforts with new employees to acclimate them to the values, norms, and work environment of the company.

3 Emphasized high levels of employee involvement in their own appraisal process.

4 Based employee appraisals more on longer-term performance.

5 Put significant emphasis on individual over group performance when rewarding employees.

6 Included an emphasis on employee risk-taking in the appraisal process.

7 Explicitly evaluated employees based on their innovativeness on the job.

8 Designed training programs around active employee involvement.

9 Had a longer-term approach to the training of employees.

10 Conducted training programs that were more group- than individual-oriented.

11 Developed training approaches that reflected individual employee development needs.

12 Approached training as more of an ongoing than an intermittent activity.

13 Designed employee incentives and rewards around a longer-term performance orientation.

14 Placed more emphasis on job security over high pay when designing compensation and reward systems.

SOURCE: Adapted from M. H. Morris and F. Jones, "Relationships among Environmental Turbulence, Human Resource Management, and Corporate Entrepreneurship," *Journal of Business and Entrepreneurship*, 7 (1995): 161–176.

the nature of employee motivation. The question is not whether an employee is generically motivated or not, but whether he or she is motivated toward specific behaviors. In our case, the concern is with entrepreneurial motivation.

A practical approach to explaining how motivated an employee will be to innovate on the job, take calculated risks, and be proactive is called the expectancy model (Porter and Lawler, 1968). Simply stated, this model posits that motivation is

FIGURE 7-2

A Model of Motivation for Entrepreneurial Behavior

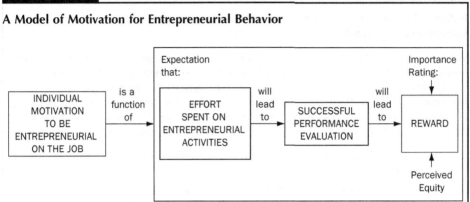

determined by (1) how much a person perceives a direct relationship between the effort he or she puts forth toward some behavior or task and successful performance on the company's employee appraisal or evaluation system, (2) how much that person perceives a direct relationship between a good performance appraisal and achievement of rewards, and (3) whether the company is offering the correct rewards. The expectancy model is illustrated in Figure 7-2.

Let us explore this model in more depth. In a real job situation, some of the specific entrepreneurial tasks toward which the manager desires the employee to expend *effort* could include generating new ideas, doing research or background work to support those ideas, persevering in refining an idea that others have rejected, experimenting with new processes or approaches on the job, and being creative in finding resources to do something new, among others. The *performance evaluation* system refers to management's formal method of evaluating the employee's work output. This might be something as simple as a letter indicating the employee's performance has been excellent, good, average, or poor, or as involved as a multiple-item rating survey subjectively filled out by managers and coworkers that also incorporates the employee's inputs. *Rewards* refer to the benefit or gain the employee receives in return for his or her work efforts. Rewards can be extrinsic or intrinsic, but again, the principal concern is with those rewards managers control or can affect. Examples include regular pay, bonuses, profit share, equity or shares in the company, an expense account, job security, promotions, expanded job responsibilities, autonomy, public or private recognition, free time to work on pet projects, money for research or trips to conferences where the employee can learn more about his or her entrepreneurial concept, and so on.

The diagram presented in Figure 7-2 can be helpful in identifying some of the reasons employees might *not* be motivated to be entrepreneurial on the job. Here, we will identify 15 possible reasons. Keep in mind that the model is all about linkages (or expectancies). The first linkage is between employee effort and management's evaluation of employee performance. Starting with effort, if employees (1) do not understand what management means by "being entrepreneurial on the job," or (2) believe it is not possible to accomplish entrepreneurial behavior in this company no matter how hard one tries, or (3) perceive that they are not personally capable of being entrepreneurial, then they are likely to be unmotivated. Alternatively, employees may believe that it is possible to be entrepreneurial, but see no linkage between doing so and how they are evaluated. This can happen because (4) there is no formal appraisal or assessment of employees, (5) the performance appraisal criteria are unclear, (6) the criteria on which employees are evaluated do not explicitly include innovativeness, risk-taking, and proactive efforts, (7) other non-entrepreneurial criteria receive much more emphasis from managers, (8) the evaluations are done in an arbitrary or unfair fashion, or (9) there are ways to get a good evaluation without actually doing entrepreneurial things (e.g., politicking).

Let's assume that employees know that they can be entrepreneurial in this company, and if they do so, they will receive a better performance appraisal. They still might not be motivated. The second linkage in Figure 7-2 involves identifying reasons employees might not see a relationship between doing well on the performance evaluation system and receiving a reward. Reasons for this could include (10) managers asking for one behavior, but actually rewarding some quite different behavior, or (11) employees believing the reward will be earned regardless of the evaluation (e.g., everyone around here gets the same reward), or (12) employees finding other ways to earn the reward without putting effort toward entrepreneurship (e.g., currying favor with the boss).

Finally, even if employees see a link between effort and performance, and between performance and reward, they may be unmotivated because management is offering the wrong rewards. Examples of problems here could include (13) rewards are being offered that are too small given the effort that is required to push an entrepreneurial initiative through in the face of internal resistance, (14) the type of reward being offered is not one to which an employee currently attaches the most importance, or (15) the reward is considered inequitable or unfair, possibly because of what employees know other people are receiving, especially when they think these other employees are performing to a lower standard.

These instances are but some of the ways that entrepreneurial motivation becomes a problem. The job of the manager is to ensure that the employee sees the desired linkages between the types of entrepreneurial efforts being requested, the manner in which the employee will be evaluated, and the rewards received. Just as important is the need to ensure the right rewards are being offered, a task that requires considerable creativity as well as insight into the nature of one's workers. New employees entering the corporate environment today bring with them a set of expectations and needs that are not likely to be satisfied by conventional salary packages. Further, the needs of individuals change, so a reward that worked well last year may be unsuccessful this year. While it may not be feasible to develop distinctive reward and measurement systems for each employee, it is important to include enough flexibility in these systems to at least partially accommodate individual requirements.

The possibilities are actually unlimited when it comes to creative approaches to rewarding entrepreneurial performance. Table 7-4 provides an illustration of what some

---

TABLE 7-4

Examples of Creative Approaches to Rewarding Employees

Following are some examples of what some companies are doing with rewards and awards to encourage entrepreneurial behaviors among their employees:

- Employees put a percentage of their salary at risk and then can either lose it, double it, or triple it based on team performance.
- Personalized "innovator" jackets, shirts, and leather folders are given to employees who make entrepreneurial contributions.
- When a new idea is accepted by the company, the CEO awards shares of stock to the employee.
- Employees are given $500 to spend on an innovative idea that relates to their job.
- A company rents out a major sports stadium; fills the stands with employees, families, and friends; and then has innovation champions run onto the field as their name and achievement appears on the scoreboard.
- A company sets targets, and then 30 percent of incremental earnings above target is placed into a bonus pool which is paid out based on each employee's performance rating.
- Small cash awards are given to employees who try something new and fail—and the best failure of the quarter receives a larger award.
- Some companies have point systems where employees receive differing amounts of points for different categories of innovation contributions. Points are redeemable for computers, merchandise, free daycare, tuition reimbursement, and other types of rewards.
- Small cash amounts are given for innovative suggestions, and then redeemable points (for more significant cash awards) are earned based on how far the suggestion moves through the process of development, approval, implementation, and impact (cost savings or revenue generation).
- A parking spot is reserved for the "innovator of the month."

(Continued)

TABLE 7-4	(Continued)

Examples of Creative Approaches to Rewarding Employees

- Team members working on a major innovation are awarded shares of zero value at project outset, and as milestones are achieved (on time) predetermined values are added to the shares. Milestones not achieved lead to a decline in share value.
- Another company ties cash awards for employees to a portfolio of innovation activities produced over time, including ideas generated, patents applied for, prototypes developed, and so forth.
- Employees receive recognition for innovation suggestions, and then a drawing is held at the end of the year of all accepted suggestions, with the winner receiving a sizeable financial award.
- One company has a "frequent innovator" program that works like an airline frequent flier program.
- "Hero biographies" are written about an employee, his or her background, and an innovation that he or she has championed; the stories are full of praise and a little humor.
- One company provides gift certificates within a day of an employee idea being implemented, while another takes employees to a "treasure box" where they can choose from among a number of gifts.
- A company gives employees 15 percent of out-of-pocket savings achieved by their ideas in the first two years of use, and, if the idea is for a product, 3 percent of first year sales.
- The top performing team in terms of innovation is sent to a resort for a week.
- A company gives a savings bond to the employee who raises the most challenging question in management meetings.
- One organization has $500 "on-the-spot" awards for anyone showing special initiative.
- Companies have their own Olympics, rodeos, competitions, game shows, hit parades, and murder mysteries in an attempt to recognize initiative and excellence.
- Others have praise and recognition boards, threshold performance clubs, attaperson awards, and some allow innovators to appear in company advertisements.

SOURCE: Adapted from various sources, including B. Nelson, *1001 Ways to Reward Employees*, New York: Workman Press, 2005.

companies are currently doing. The key here is to use examples from other companies to stimulate ideas, but to develop programs that fit the personality of one's own company, the nature and needs of employees, and the competitive circumstances in which the company finds itself. At the same time, financial rewards do not have to be large, and some of the more glamorous efforts such as stock options and profit-sharing are often less impacting than offering recognition, compensatory time, and rewards that effectively empower employees to pursue their ideas within the company.

Just as important as the formal rewards or compensation given to employees is the need for awards and recognition. Entrepreneurial companies find novel ways to say "thank you" to their innovative employees. These companies typically have cultures of celebration, where work might be stopped at any time, and in any part of the company, and a plaque, certificate, pin, bouquet of roses, or any of hundreds of other forms of recognition are given to employees based on their entrepreneurial initiatives. The company has ceremonies or rituals that often might seem strange or superficial or even silly to an outside observer, but that are rich in meaning to the employees. People in these companies take pride in one another's accomplishments. It is not unusual for the most valued form of recognition to come not from senior management, but from the employee's peers.

Effective use of awards requires a clear strategy. Consistent with the expectancy model previously discussed, it is vital that management clearly establish (and communicate) the link between the desired behaviors and a given award. Just as important is the need to be consistent in who gets awards, why, and when. Wilson (2003) has identified some additional guidelines for successful employee recognition programs, and these are summarized in Table 7-5.

Subordinates' View of the Entrepreneurial Manager

HRM practices must also concentrate on the development of entrepreneurial managers. It is one thing to pursue an entrepreneurial initiative as a manager or employee, but a very different thing to manage people, departments, and resources in an entrepreneurial manner. This latter challenge leads us to the question "What is an entrepreneurial manager?" It is our belief that the most valuable perspective on this question may come from the people who work for this manager.

From the vantage point of the subordinate, what attributes are associated with having an entrepreneurial boss? Do employees really want to work for an entrepreneurial manager? In a major study, Pearce et al. (1997) attempted to answer these questions. The research involved 102 managers and over 1,500 subordinates. The findings identified 11 key behaviors that define an entrepreneurial manager:

- Efficiently gets proposed actions through red tape and into practice
- Displays enthusiasm for acquiring skills
- Quickly changes course of action when results are not being achieved
- Encourages others to take the initiative for their own ideas
- Inspires others to think about their work in new and stimulating ways

TABLE 7-5

Principles to Guide the Use of Awards Programs to Encourage Entrepreneurship

Principle 1: Emphasize success but also provide recognition for innovative efforts that fail. Focus on the positive aspects of both success and failure.

Principle 2: Deliver recognition and reward in an open and publicized way. If not made public, recognition loses much of its impact and defeats much of the purpose for which it is provided.

Principle 3: Provide recognition in a personal and honest manner. Avoid providing recognition that is too "slick" or overproduced, but also too cheap or superficial.

Principle 4: Tailor your recognition and reward to the unique needs of the people involved. Having many recognition and reward options will enable management to acknowledge accomplishment in ways appropriate to the particulars of a given situation, selecting from a larger menu of possibilities.

Principle 5: Timing is crucial. Recognize contributions throughout a project. Reward contributions close to the time an achievement is realized.

Principle 6: Avoid the perception that the awards are being given in a manner that is paternalistic, and that seems random and casual.

Principle 7: Strive for a clear, unambiguous, and well-communicated connection between accomplishments and rewards. Be sure people understand why they receive awards and the criteria used to determine awards.

Principle 8: Follow up on the recognition or award. Reinforce it in meetings, in newsletters, at end of the year meetings, and in employee annual reviews.

Principle 9: Recognize recognition. That is, recognize people who recognize others for doing what is best for the company.

SOURCE: Adapted from T. Wilson, *Innovative Reward Systems for the Changing Workplace*, New York: McGraw-Hill Publishers, 2003.

- Devotes time to helping others find ways to improve products and services
- Goes to bat for good ideas of others
- Boldly moves ahead with a promising new approach when others might be more cautious
- Vividly describes how things could be in the future and what is needed to get there
- Gets people to rally together to meet a challenge
- Creates an environment where people get excited about making improvements

Six months after having subordinates evaluate managers on these 11 behaviors, Pearce assessed the satisfaction levels of employees with the managers. Results of the data analysis clearly indicated that managers who are more entrepreneurial in their behavior have a positive impact on their subordinates' satisfaction. The findings demonstrated that, as entrepreneurial behaviors increased, subordinates' satisfaction with supervision increased. Whereas 62 percent of the subordinates of entrepreneurial managers reported high levels of satisfaction, 69 percent of subordinates of more bureaucratic managers reported low levels of satisfaction with their supervisors. Further, 8 of the 11 behaviors cited were able to discriminate significantly between high and low levels of subordinate satisfaction.

It appears that there are payoffs from having a company that is more entrepreneurial in the form of higher financial performance, and also payoffs from having managers who are more entrepreneurial in the form of more satisfied employees.

The Need for a Champions Program

Another valuable human resource management approach to fostering entrepreneurship involves the creation of a formal champions program. Such a program encourages ambitious and talented entrepreneurs from throughout the organization to suggest, develop, champion, and implement new products, services and processes. Champions deeply believe in an idea and badly want senior management's blessing to go after it. The champion's role is to encourage the project during its critical stages, keep key decision-makers and sponsors aware of the project's status, mentor team members, help the team get its resource needs met, and enthusiastically promote the project at the highest levels of the company. Product champions also have to be true believers in the project team.

Ideally, champions are not simply designated by management. Rather, they emerge from all parts of the company. This notion of emerging champions is critical. Where senior managers attempt to "pick the winners" in terms of pre-identification of those individuals they would like to see become champions, or that they believe have the most champion potential, the results are typically disappointing. Thus, the key is to build an internal environment or infrastructure that enables these kinds of individuals to "step up to the plate." The infrastructure must incorporate properly developed rewards and incentives, effective use of performance appraisals, flexibility in terms of resources, open communication, incentives for inter-functional cooperation, and the elimination of red tape.

The champions program must be well conceptualized. Management must establish the nature and scope of a champion's responsibilities, a procedure by which champions bring forth their ideas, a process for approving and empowering champions, and an appraisal and reward structure tailored to champions while they are involved in a project (Greene et al. 1999). The program is augmented by internal communications efforts directed at all employees where elements of the program are explained and employees are made aware of how to get involved, who is currently active, the status of current projects, and success stories. The company should also develop a set of characteristics that the organization looks for in a champion. Examples include passion, self-confidence, calculated risk-taking, demonstrated team and networking skills, and a tendency to be well organized.

THE INNOVATOR'S NOTEBOOK

Innovation through People at 3M

3M's Larry Wendling is the vice president of research, and he has been responsible for reinvigorating the culture of innovation at what has always been revered as a bastion of corporate entrepreneurship.

Wendling discovered that the fragmentation of the 4,000 researchers, engineers, and scientists (9,200 worldwide), a move made by the company to foster innovation, was doing just the opposite. Scientists working on technologies that did not fall within 3M's areas of expertise had no idea what to do to get their new concepts to market. Based on his findings, Wendling set out to strip "technologies of the present," such as adhesives used in Post-it notes and Scotch tape, from R&D's list of top priorities and to reorganize the disparate researchers into one cohesive innovation powerhouse.

Scientists in R&D were freed up to think outside of 3M's existing product lines. To do this, Wendling moved most of the scientists out of the central R&D division into the seven major business units. The remaining scientists were then let loose to research new concepts in markets that were projected to grow by at least 10 percent annually. In order to keep the technologies moving toward commercialization, Wendling brought in eight full-time marketers to focus the researchers on the overarching goal: new products.

The new structure allowed the central R&D researchers to find and partner with the business units that best understand the market for a new product. Wendling found that once scientists were able to get their products from the lab to the market, they get hooked on the process. By getting researchers excited about commercializing their research, Wendling has succeeded in streamlining 3M's R&D.

CEO, George Buckley, also stresses the importance of "incremental innovations." While every scientist and engineer at 3M dreams of finding the newest breakthrough innovation (the next Post-it Note if you will), Buckley realizes the intellectual challenge of finding innovations that cost next to nothing.

Most significant are the seven principles or "pillars" of innovation that have been established at 3M to sustain this innovation resurgence. These pillars are:

1. *Top-down commitment to innovation* that makes innovation the business model.
2. *A culture of individual freedom* allowing the inventor to pursue something not on his daily worksheet.
3. *Access to multiple technologies.* 3M is one of the most technologically diverse companies with 42 technology platforms. The real key is blending those technologies together.
4. *The use of networking.* Informal networking is extraordinarily powerful and there are formal ways to perpetuate that network such as 3M's tech forum—a grass roots organization of 9,200 technical people whose primary objective is to keep talking to each other.
5. *Rewards and recognitions* are very important. 3M's recognition programs are peer nominated and peer driven. What motivates engineers and scientists doing good work is the recognition by their peers.
6. *Measurement and accountability* for innovation efforts, including the percentage of total sales coming from new products over the past four years, and linkages between innovation performance and career progression.
7. *Customer or societal connections* are vital, such that new technologies must address a customer or societal need. The focus should not be on products, but on the technologies that can work for customers.

The results speak for themselves. Product development life cycles have now been reduced from an average of four years to two and a half, operating profits are up 23 percent, and even though 3M's current CEO, George Buckley, trimmed R&D spending by 8 percent, that is to $1.29 billion in 2009, it still remained steady as a percentage of revenue at 5.6 percent.

CEO George Buckley and VP Larry Wendling's new efforts have been well worth it. 3M has been reinvigorated for innovation through its people.

Discussion Questions

1. Describe how the concept of "creative abrasion" may be applied to 3M's pillars of innovation.

2. How does 3M's approach compare to HRM policies as applied to entrepreneurial behavior (Table 7-2)?

3. Relate the "critical role of reward systems" from our chapter to the 3M pillars.

SOURCES Adapted from Daniel Del Re, "Pushing Past Post-Its," *Business 2.0,* Vol. 6 #10, November 1, 2005: 54–56; John Dodge, "A Culture of Innovation at 3M," *Design News,* November 13, 2007; and Dana Mattioli and Kris Maher, "At 3M Innovation Comes in Tweaks and Snips," *Wall Street Journal,* accessed online, April 25, 2010.

Summary and Conclusions

The human resource management function can serve a critical role in supporting the strategic goals and direction of a company. This chapter has argued that management's overall perspective on HRM, as well as the design of particular HRM practices, have an impact on levels of entrepreneurship demonstrated within an organization. A number of relationships between particular HRM practices and entrepreneurial behavior were examined. Further, evidence was provided which supports a number of these relationships in practice.

At the same time, some of the findings from the survey of companies that was summarized in the chapter were surprising. For instance, levels of entrepreneurship were higher in companies where training programs were more group- than individual-oriented, and where compensation/reward practices emphasized job security over high pay. And yet, there may be a logic to these findings as well. While it appears that training should be customized and career-oriented, with high levels of employee participation, training also represents an effective venue for helping employees appreciate the value of cooperative behaviors and cross-functional perspectives. Such an appreciation is emphasized by many who have studied the phenomenon of entrepreneurship in organizations. It seems that training should include some team emphasis, while other HRM variables (e.g., performance assessment) have a more individualistic bent. Alternatively, the finding for compensation/reward practices reflects a desire for some level of security when pursing entrepreneurial events that often fail. Some have argued that financial rewards must be appreciable in order to incentivize the entrepreneurial employee not to leave the company and go it alone (e.g., Pinchot and Pellman, 1999). And yet, the fact that the risks involved with corporate ventures are often more career-related than related to one's personal financial loss and the negative connotation attached to failure in many organizations combine to suggest that entrepreneurship may flourish where employees are given a certain amount of job security.

It is also important that the HRM practices employed by a company demonstrate internal consistency. For instance, encouragement of risk-taking and innovative behaviors would seem consistent with individualized performance assessment and compensation, but also with a longer-term orientation, as entrepreneurial events take time to come to fruition. Moreover, individualized appraisal and reward practices would seem consistent with high levels of employee involvement in the training and appraisal areas.

While the chapter provided direction in terms of where to concentrate efforts when seeking to foster entrepreneurship, the challenge from a managerial standpoint becomes the variable nature of HRM practices and entrepreneurial behavior. Managers must identify desired levels of entrepreneurship, and then determine the corresponding levels of particular HRM practices necessary to achieve the entrepreneurship performance goal. There may be very high levels of entrepreneurship that are dysfunctional from an organizational standpoint, in that the overall risk exposure of the company becomes too great; too many entrepreneurial events are underway to ensure strategic control and/or resources are being so diverted to entrepreneurial ventures that mainstream businesses are undermined.

It is not enough for senior management to simply declare that "entrepreneurship is important in this company and we want a culture of champions and innovation." The chapter discussed the importance of going the next step and creating a formal "champions" program to provide rewards and resources to support innovative efforts. We investigated the valuable role not only of compensation and rewards, but also of awards and recognition, in fostering sustainable entrepreneurial performance. Beyond this, it was emphasized that entrepreneurship in organizations is ultimately about destruction and construction. In this context, the chapter included a discussion of the need for healthy friction or abrasion in an organization. Creative abrasion requires the abandonment of certain assumptions, the rejection of accepted precepts, and the elimination of established methods. It also results in concepts or solutions that can disrupt the work lives of people in companies, making them break out of patterns and comfort zones.

Many questions remain about the ways in which human resources management practices affect entrepreneurship in companies. For example, how important is the relative emphasis on hierarchical versus egalitarian compensation, on high versus low base salaries, on stock options and perquisites? Further, it would seem relevant to examine various "packages" of HRM practices. A combined package of selection, training, and appraisal options might have a differential impact on entrepreneurship than the sum of the impacts of the individual practices. In addition, it may be that the HRM practices that facilitate entrepreneurship differ depending on the level in the company (e.g., top, middle, entry levels). Not only will the manifestations of entrepreneurship vary at these different levels, but so too might the impact of relying on internal versus external sources of job candidates or of internal versus external equity considerations in fixing compensation levels. Finally, the HRM practices of a company will interact with any number of other organizational variables in affecting entrepreneurship. Examples of such variables include company structure, technologies employed, types of budgetary and control systems, culture, and stage of the organizational life cycle.

References

Baden-Fuller, C. 1997. "Strategic Renewal: How Large Complex Organizations Prepare for the Future," *Studies of Management and Organization* (Summer).

Balkin, D. B., and Logan, J. W. 1988. "Reward Policies that Support Entrepreneurship," *Compensation and Benefits Review*, 20: 18–25.

de Chambeau, F., and Shays, E. M. 1984. "Harnessing Entrepreneurial Energy within the Corporation," *Management Review*, 17–20.

Greene, P. G., Brush, C. G., and Hart, M. M. 1999. "The Corporate Venture Champion: A Resource-Based Approach to Role and Process," *Entrepreneurship Theory and Practice* (March): 103–122.

Hamel, G. 2000. *Leading the Revolution* (Boston, MA: Harvard Business School Press).

Hirshberg, J. 1998. *The Creative Priority* (New York: Harper Books).

Hornsby, J. S., and Kuratko, D. F. 2003. "Human Resource Management in U.S. Small Businesses: A Replication & Extension," *Journal of Developmental Entrepreneurship*, 8(1): 73–92.

Hornsby, J. S., and Kuratko, D. F. 2005. *Frontline HR: A Handbook for the Emerging Manager* (Mason, OH: Thomson Publishers).

Jimenez-Jimenez, D., and Sanz-Valle, R. 2008. "Could HRM Support Organizational Innovation?," *International Journal of Human Resource Management*, 19(7): 1208–1223.

Morris, M. H., and Jones, F. F. 1993. "Human Resource Management Practices and Corporate Entrepreneurship: An Empirical Assessment from the USA," *International Journal of Human Resource Management*, 4: 873–896.

Morris, M. H., and Jones, F. F. 1995. "Relationships among Environmental Turbulence, Human Resource Management and Corporate Entrepreneurship," *Journal of Business and Entrepreneurship*, 7: 161–176.

Olian, J. D., and Rynes, S. L. 1984. "Organizational Staffing: Integrating Practice with Strategy," *Industrial Relations*, 23: 170–183.

Pearce, J. A., Kramer, T. R., and Robbins, D. K. 1997. "Effects of Managers' Entrepreneurial Behavior on Subordinates," *Journal of Business Venturing*, 12: 147–160.

Pinchot, G., and Pellman, R. 1999. *Intrapreneuring in Action* (San Francisco: Berrett-Koehler).

Porter, L. W., and Lawler, E. L. III. 1968. *Managerial Attitudes and Performance* (Homewood, IL: Richard D. Irwin).

Sathe, V. 2006. "From Surface to Deep Corporate Entrepreneurship," *Human Resource Management*, 27(4): 389–411.

Schuler, R. S. 1989. "Strategic Human Resource Management and Industrial Relations," *Human Relations*, 22(2): 157–184.

Schuler, R. S. and Jackson, S. 2007. *Strategic Human Resource Management* (Malden, MA: Blackwell Publishing).

Shane, S. 1996. "Renegade and Rational Championing Strategies," *Organization Studies*.

Wilson, T. 2003. *Innovative Reward Systems for the Changing Workplace* (New York: McGraw-Hill Publishers).

CHAPTER 8

CORPORATE STRATEGY AND ENTREPRENEURSHIP

Introduction

Entrepreneurship is more than a course of action one pursues; it is more than a mindset. At the level of the organization, entrepreneurship can provide a theme or direction to a company's entire operation. It can serve as an integral component of a company's strategy and, in some instances, serve as the core or defining component of the strategy. A strategy, at its essence, attempts to capture where the company wants to go and how it plans to get there. When entrepreneurship is introduced to strategy, the possibilities regarding where the company can go, how fast, and how it gets there are greatly enhanced.

Yet many companies ignore entrepreneurship in their strategies. Their strategic focus emphasizes the achievement of efficiencies in operations, market positions they want to occupy, ways in which they plan to differentiate themselves, or some other underlying variable. While entrepreneurship could potentially be part of any of these strategies, it typically is not included either explicitly or implicitly. In fact, the integration of entrepreneurship with strategy can take many forms. This integration implies that innovation and new value creation play a significant part in the company's strategic direction (Amit et al., 2000).

In this chapter, we will investigate the relationship between entrepreneurship and company strategy. Forces creating the need for entrepreneurial strategies will be identified within the context of the new competitive landscape. The concept of dominant logic will be introduced, together with the need for entrepreneurship to serve as the dominant logic in a company. Technological considerations within the context of corporate strategy are reviewed. Key concepts surrounding strategic management as it relates to entrepreneurship will be explored. The major elements of an entrepreneurial strategy will be presented. In addition, the chapter will examine critical mistakes made when formulating entrepreneurial strategies.

The Changing Landscape

Companies find themselves operating in a new competitive landscape. The contemporary business environment can be characterized in terms of increasing risk, decreased ability to forecast, fluid company and industry boundaries, a managerial mindset that must unlearn traditional management principles, and new structural forms that not only allow for change, but also help create it (Hamel, 2000). This new landscape can be described in terms of four powerful forces: *change, complexity, chaos,* and *contradiction* (Bettis and Hitt, 1995; Hitt and Reed, 2000).

No organization is immune to the immense pressure of change. The pressures on today's managers and employees are unprecedented. Many managers' organizational learning took place in an environment much different from the one they face in the decade ahead. In the past, the playing field was level, if not pitched to their advantage. Many of the rules were obvious. Structure was the manager's friend. Hierarchy provided context and orientation. Time helped, and there was enough of it. Uncertainty was to be avoided. But today's corporate environment is nothing like this. It's not that the rules have been tinkered with. The game itself is different!

Complexity is another critical force in the new landscape. Change comes from many different directions, often at the same time. There are new markets, technologies, economic realities, demographic patterns, emotional requirements for managing, and communication networks. Customer groupings are shifting and becoming more differentiated. Competitors come and go. Competition involves not only the traditional head-to-head competition with competitors, but also collaboration with certain companies. Further, change in any one area (e.g., technology) interacts with changes in other areas (e.g., suppliers and customers). The net effect is that there is simply much more to manage than in the past.

Chaos is the third critical force in the new competitive landscape. The common-language meaning of the term *chaos* is *confusion,* and confusion describes the new business landscape. But the scientific use of the term is perhaps even more descriptive. Chaos theory describes systems with outcomes that are governed by nonlinear differential equations. Random events can cause extreme consequences in the business. The principal managerial implication of chaos theory is that small changes or shocks to the system can have a major impact (hence, things are nonlinear). There is sensitive dependence on initial conditions, which means that causality between one business variable and another business variable is difficult to establish or understand. Further, the scale effects of change are largely unpredictable. Stacey (1996, p. 265) describes the phenomenon in the following manner: "Under conditions of nonlinearity and randomness, incremental changes that may themselves seem insignificant can precipitate major discontinuous or qualitative change because of the emergent properties triggered by marginal adjustments."

Finally, the business environment is filled with many contradictions, and dealing with paradox becomes a critical aspect of managing in the new competitive landscape. Collins and Porras (1996) explain: "The tyranny of the '*or*' pushes people to believe

that things must be either A *or* B, but not both" (p. 43). They argue that such exclu-
sionary thinking is wrong-headed. Rather, managers should embrace contradiction by
replacing *or* with *and*. For instance, quality can be higher *and* operating costs can be
lower. Companies can do more for customers *and* charge them less. Companies can
compete with other companies *and* collaborate with them. Products can be standardized *and* customized.

Another way to visualize the changing landscape is from the perspective of what are
called *strategic inflection points* (Grove, 1996). An inflection point occurs when the old
strategic picture dissolves and gives way to the new, allowing the adaptive and proactive business to ascend to new heights. Put another way, a strategic inflection point
is when the balance of forces shifts from the old ways of doing business and the old
ways of competing to the new. Before the strategic inflection point, the industry simply was more like the old. After this point, the industry is profoundly redefined, often
evolving into entirely new structures and value chains. Once the inflection point is
reached, there is no going back. The competitive conditions and rules never return
to the former state. As a result, companies that do not proactively navigate the inflection point tend to peak and then decline. Some examples of strategic inflection points
are illustrated in Table 8-1. The table also summarizes actions taken in response to the
inflection point and results achieved.

TABLE 8-1

Strategic Inflection Points

Example (Category)	*What Changed*	*Actions Taken*	*Results*
Wal-Mart (competition)	Superstores enter small communities	Some stores specialize (e.g., become category killers)	Home Depot and Toys"R"Us thrive; many others perish
PCs (technology)	Price/performance of PCs proved to be far superior	Some companies adapt microcompu- ters as building blocks; others be- come systems integrators	Adaptive compa- nies thrive; others face severe difficulties
Demographic time bomb (customers)	Kids have increased computer affinity	Growth of CD-ROM educational and en- tertainment software aimed at kids	Computers become ubiquitous

(Continued)

TABLE 8-1	(Continued)		
Strategic Inflection Points			
Example (Category)	*What Changed*	*Actions Taken*	*Results*
Travel agencies (suppliers)	Airlines capped commissions; Internet reservation services appear	Travel agents attempt to charge consumers	Travel agency economics turn tougher; many fail
Telecommunications (deregulation)	Competition is introduced and intensifies in equipment and long-distance service	AT&T divests the Bell operating companies, downsizes, restructures, and adapts to a competitive world with consumer marketing	AT&T and the former Bell operating companies' combined valuation is over four times what it was ten years ago

SOURCE: Adapted from A. S. Grove, *Only the Paranoid Survive*, London: Harper Collins Business, 1996: 77.

Since the nature of an inflection point is so unpredictable, how can organizations know when the time is right to make changes? As Grove (1996, p. 35) states, "You don't … but you can't wait until you do know … timing is everything." If management undertakes a process of adapting to the new while the company is still healthy, and the ongoing business forms a protective bubble in which management can experiment with new ways of doing business, it becomes possible to capitalize on and retain the company's strength, keep employees, and maintain the company's strategic position.

Does the Dominant Logic Fit the Competitive Landscape?

How does a company achieve sustainable advantage in the new competitive landscape? Addressing this issue requires that we first examine what has been termed the *dominant logic* of the company (Bettis and Prahalad, 1995). This interesting notion refers to the way in which managers conceptualize the business and make critical resource allocation decisions. Every organization has a dominant logic, even if managers do not recognize or formally acknowledge it. The dominant logic at Microsoft seems to involve a commitment to the Windows standard, and the exploitation of a common architecture. At GE Capital, the logic is defined by the company's competence in risk management and deal structuring. Thus, the dominant logic of a company attempts to capture the prevailing mindset, and it drives the overall focus of the systems and routines in the company. Further, it filters and interprets information from the environment, attenuates complexity, and guides the strategies, systems, and behavior of the organization. In fact, managers will often consider only information and intelligence that is believed to be relevant to the company's prevailing dominant logic.

The dominant logic that is optimal for the company in today's environment may well be inappropriate for the environment that will exist five years hence. Microsoft may find that technological developments surrounding the Internet make the Windows standard less relevant—or at least limit its future potential. Stated differently, the dominant logic tends to capture competitive advantage in the present, and may be oblivious to future possibilities. The implication is that the dominant logic must be periodically unlearned, and openness to such unlearning should be an integral aspect of the corporate culture. Routines and habits that pertain to the existing dominant logic can inhibit the learning of new processes and operating methods. Thus, a relationship exists between the ability to learn and the need to unlearn. Moreover, the longer a dominant logic has been in place within an organization, the harder it is to unlearn. Unfortunately, it often takes a crisis before existing assumptions, routines, and systems are questioned. The new competitive landscape can be counted on to produce the kinds of crises and upheavals that illustrate the pitfalls of a well-entrenched dominant logic.

One means of creating a *dynamic dominant logic* is to make entrepreneurship the basis upon which the organization is conceptualized and resources are allocated. As a dominant logic, entrepreneurship promotes strategic agility, flexibility, creativity, and continuous innovation throughout the company. Further, the overriding focus of the company is opportunity identification, discovery of new sources of value, and product and process innovation that will lead to greater profitability. And finally, an emphasis on entrepreneurial activity is translated into the objectives, strategies, reward systems, control systems, planning approaches, structure, and so forth of the company.

The Role of Strategic Management and Corporate Strategy

Achieving sustainable advantage in the new competitive landscape also requires that managers think and act strategically and that they formulate appropriate strategies. In a sense, dominant logic sets the context for the company's overall direction, while strategy and strategic management more specifically define that direction and determine how well it is accomplished.

Strategic management is a process that guides how the basic work of the organization is approached, ensures the continuous renewal and growth of the company, and, more particularly, provides a context for developing and implementing the strategy that drives the company's operations (Schendel and Hofer, 1978). The formulation of plans for the effective management of external opportunities and threats in light of a company's internal strengths and weaknesses is a major component of strategic management. This planning component includes defining the company's mission, specifying achievable objectives, developing strategies, and setting policy guidelines.

Still, strategic management is more than writing a plan or developing a strategy. It is a way of thinking—one that many managers never really grasp. Strategic thinking requires more of an external than internal focus. It implies a continuous search for new sources of competitive advantage. It involves looking beyond immediate crises and day-to-day demands and envisioning the market and the company's position three, five, and ten years from now. It entails an ability to see the big picture, meaning that the manager envisions all of the resources and core capabilities of the company in terms of how they might be uniquely combined to create new sources of value. Lastly, it implies discipline in identifying a path or position and ensuring that fellow employees stay focused on the target, while also being flexible in the tactical approaches employed. The strategic manager keeps his or her eye on the prize in terms of not being discouraged by serious obstacles, not being distracted by situational opportunities that are inconsistent with the strategic vision, and not giving in to the temptation to take shortcuts.

Coupled with strategic management is the concept of strategy. As noted at the outset of this chapter, a strategy is a statement regarding what the company wants to be and how it plans to get there. Strategy creates a sense of unity, or consistency of action, throughout an organization. In order for people to work toward common objectives, they must know what the objectives are. If employees do not have a strong understanding that innovation is essential to the realization of the company's objectives, then their actions on the job each and every day will not contribute to innovation. As they make choices in their jobs, strategy can provide direction to those choices.

Michael Porter (1996) draws a critical distinction between strategy and operational effectiveness, arguing that managers are increasingly preoccupied with the latter and ignorant of the former. Operational effectiveness is concerned with activities that enable the company to perform similar activities *better* than competitors perform them. Thus, through the use of total quality management principles, self-directed work teams, downsizing, outsourcing, business process reengineering techniques, or other tools, the company attempts to produce current products at lower costs, provide better customer service, offer higher product quality, or otherwise outperform rivals.

Strategy, in Porter's view, is about performing *different* activities than competitors, or performing similar activities in *different* ways. Southwest Airlines provides a vivid example. The company's strategy is built around short-haul routes, frequent flights, travel to mid-sized cities and secondary airports in larger cities, low-cost fares, and no-frills flights. More fundamentally, the strategy depends on truly empowered employees, a different approach to customers and ticketing, and a unique system for managing ground operations. It is a strategy that enables the company to turn flights around in record time, and provide a better on-time arrival record than anyone in the business. In the past few years, virtually every other U.S. airline has attempted to mimic some part of the Southwest strategy—an approach that misses the whole point of strategy.

To stay competitive over the short run, the company must continually improve operational effectiveness. However, there is a point of diminishing returns on this front. And as the company's managers become more preoccupied with operational effectiveness, they gradually forget about strategy. Meanwhile, the competitive landscape is changing. New players emerge that are capable of competing with established players in spite of small size and limited resources, or companies from seemingly unrelated industries are suddenly competing in the company's market space. In either instance, these new competitors offer a totally unique value proposition and/or compete in new and different ways. The company finds it is both unfamiliar and unprepared for these new circumstances, even though its costs may be lower or its quality higher than ever before.

Integrating Entrepreneurship with Strategy

Not only can entrepreneurship serve as the dominant logic of a company, but it also plays an important role in the company's strategy. The integration of entrepreneurship with strategy has two aspects, both of which are critical. We will refer to these two aspects as *entrepreneurial strategy* and a *strategy for entrepreneurship*.

DEVELOPING A CORPORATE STRATEGY THAT IS ENTREPRENEURIAL

The first of these is concerned with applying creativity and entrepreneurial thinking to the development of a core strategy for the company. Ireland et al. (2009, p. 21) define an entrepreneurial strategy as *"a vision-directed, organization-wide reliance on entrepreneurial behavior that purposefully and continuously rejuvenates the organization and shapes the scope of its operations through the recognition and exploitation of entrepreneurial opportunity."* A highly entrepreneurial strategy is not an obvious one. Discovering unique positions in the marketplace is difficult, as is breaking away from established ways of doing things. Such a strategy implies a higher level of risk, especially when first implemented. The Dell Direct Method that lies at the core of Dell Computer's strategy is an example of the application of entrepreneurial thinking to strategy. The same can be said about the strategy at Southwest Airlines previously discussed. Both of these examples capture an aggressive corporate position, and each centers on a unique and proprietary approach to defining and creating value for the market.

At the same time, there are companies that engage in some level of entrepreneurial activity, but do not integrate those activities into their core strategies. Evidence of different corporate approaches can be found in data collected from 15 large corporations in the United States, United Kingdom, and Sweden (Covin and Miles, 2007). This research specifically examined the relationship between corporate venturing activity (a specific form of entrepreneurial activity discussed in Chapter 4) and the company's overall business strategy, discovering the existence of five models or approaches. These models are illustrated in Figure 8-1 and are as follows: corporate venturing and business strategy are weakly linked or unrelated (Model 1), business strategy drives corporate venturing (Model 2), corporate venturing drives business strategy (Model 3), corporate venturing and business strategy are reciprocally interdependent (Model 4), and corporate venturing as the business strategy (Model 5).

FIGURE 8-1

Observed Configurations of the Corporate Venturing Business Strategy Relationship

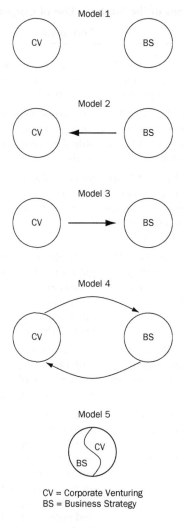

CV = Corporate Venturing
BS = Business Strategy

SOURCE: Adapted from J. G. Covin, and M. P. Miles, "Strategic Use of Corporate Venturing," *Entrepreneurship Theory and Practice*, February 2007. Reprinted with permission of John Wiley and Sons.

An important conclusion of this research is that, while entrepreneurial activity is common in established companies, such activity is not necessarily embraced as an essential element of those companies' strategies. Covin and Miles (2007) hypothesized that companies that embrace entrepreneurship as core to their strategies will out-perform those that do not over the long run. The ways in which the corporations integrated entrepreneurship into their business strategies are summarized in the propositions shown in Table 8-2.

TABLE 8-2

Organizational Manifestations of the Strategic Use of Corporate Venturing (CV)

Proposition	Comment
P1: Companies that strategically use CV are more likely than their non-strategic counterparts to set formal CV objectives.	Formal objectives force executives to consider why they are supporting CV and what they hope to accomplish with CV.
P2: Companies that strategically use CV are more likely than their non-strategic counterparts to recognize the role of CV in the realization of strategic intent.	CV can be used to create a portfolio of strategic options, some of which may enable the company to realize its stretch goals.
P3: Companies that strategically use CV are more likely than their non-strategic counterparts to place a greater weight on "strategic fit" or "strategic logic" than on financial analyses when evaluating CV initiatives.	Strategically important CV projects will often be rejected if evaluated on a strictly financial basis.
P4: Companies that strategically use CV are more likely than their non-strategic counterparts to consciously assess the strategic relevance of CV initiatives.	To facilitate an effective process of strategic renewal, corporate management should consciously assess the strategic relevance of CV initiatives that may have autonomously emerged beyond the boundaries of the corporate strategy.
P5: Companies that strategically use CV are more likely than their non-strategic counterparts to treat CV as a learning tool.	CV can enable companies to explore potentially significant new product, market, and/or technology domains without making major "up-front" commitments.
P6: Companies that strategically use CV are more likely than their non-strategic counterparts to facilitate "strategic conversations" within their organizations.	Open and direct communications between corporate entrepreneurs and top managers can improve the quality of strategic decision making by facilitating a better understanding of corporate strategy among the former parties and a better understanding of markets, technologies, and entrepreneurial opportunities among the latter.

(Continued)

| TABLE 8-2 | (Continued) |

Organizational Manifestations of the Strategic Use of Corporate Venturing (CV)

Proposition	*Comment*
P7: Companies that strategically use CV are more likely than their non-strategic counterparts to make external CV investments as complements to internal R&D investments.	Internal R&D programs that build knowledge relevant to acquired ventures can facilitate knowledge absorption from those ventures and the discovery, evaluation, and exploitation of future entrepreneurial opportunities.
P8: Companies that strategically use CV are more likely than their non-strategic counterparts to engage in CV as means for appropriating greater value from their existing competencies.	CV initiatives can be used to leverage a company's core competencies in novel product, market, and/or technology domains, thereby enhancing the value of those competencies to the company.
P9: Companies that strategically use CV are more likely than their non-strategic counterparts to recognize and exploit the potential of CV initiatives to create new competitive games or new market spaces.	CV can enable companies to explore new business models and ways of competing for the purposes of repositioning or redefining themselves and extending the dominant strategic logics of their industries.

SOURCE: Adapted from J. G. Covin, and M. P. Miles (2007), "Strategic Use of Corporate Venturing," *Entrepreneurship Theory and Practice*, 31(2).

DEVELOPING A STRATEGY FOR ENTREPRENEURSHIP

The second consideration when integrating entrepreneurship and strategy concerns the need to develop a strategy to guide the particular entrepreneurial activities taking place within the company. At its essence, this is a strategy for determining how entrepreneurial the company really strives to be and how it will achieve that level of entrepreneurship. The strategy for entrepreneurship might cover any number of areas. Six of the most salient decision areas are outlined below.

1. Where does the company want to position itself on the entrepreneurial grid (see Chapter 3)? From an overall standpoint, is the company's strategy one of high frequency and low degree of entrepreneurship, high degree and low frequency, or some other combination? What is the company's desired risk profile?

2. To what extent is the entrepreneurial emphasis in the company that of growing new businesses and starting new ventures outside the mainstream of the company versus transforming the existing enterprise and its internal operations into a more entrepreneurial environment?

3. In what areas does the company want to be an innovation leader versus innovation follower vis-à-vis the industry?

4. In what areas of the company is management looking for higher versus lower levels of entrepreneurial activity? Which business units or product areas are expected to innovate the most? Which departments are expected to be the real home for entrepreneurship, setting direction and providing leadership for the rest of the company?

5. What is the relative importance over the next three years of product versus service versus process innovation? What is the relative importance of new versus existing markets?

6. To what extent is innovation expected to come from senior management, middle management, or first-level management? Is there clear direction in terms of the types of innovation expected at each level?

Other issues come into play beyond these six, particularly in the management of innovation. Because of their importance, we will elaborate upon some of these issues in the next section.

If we compare these two aspects of integrating entrepreneurship with strategy (i.e., *entrepreneurial strategy* and *strategy for entrepreneurship*), both address issues that are external and internal to the company. However, the application of entrepreneurial thinking to the company's core strategy is primarily dealing with external questions. Where are unfilled spaces in the marketplace? How can the company differentiate itself on a sustained basis? In what ways can the company lead the customer? Alternatively, the development of a strategy for entrepreneurship is especially concerned with internal questions, including the types of innovative efforts that will receive resources, and from where in the company innovations are expected to come. In a sense, it is about stimulating the internal market, the competitive marketplace inside the company, for ideas and innovation. Clearly, the two aspects are related. For instance, internal process innovation in ground operations was critical for the ability of Southwest Airlines to differentiate itself as a low-cost, on-time airline.

Managing Innovation Strategically: A Portfolio Approach

A core part of a company's strategy for entrepreneurship is the need to approach innovation in a strategic manner. Innovation lies at the heart of entrepreneurship. Yet, while companies will have strategies for increasing sales, cutting costs, financing growth, and improving operations, they frequently will not have a strategy for innovation. All too often, innovation activities can be characterized as piecemeal, tactical, and reactive. Resource commitments, priorities, and deadlines for projects are continually being changed. Projects are begun, but most fail to make it to commercialization.

Accountability for innovation results is vague or limited. The general approach is cautious, with an emphasis on finding sure-bet winners. The result is a company that is both inefficient and ineffective at innovation.

Strategic innovation represents a different path. Here, the company formulates explicit goals and strategies for innovation, executes those strategies, monitors innovation performance, and then makes adjustments based on deviations between the goals and actual performance. Strategic innovation pertaining to product-focused entrepreneurial initiatives has the following seven core components:

1. The company makes a strong commitment to an active policy of finding and developing new products, with top management heavily involved in project initiation and support.

2. Innovation is defined as a company-wide task, not simply the responsibility of an R&D department or new product development department in isolation.

3. Strategies are formulated for the nature of the new products and services to be developed, including the extent to which innovation projects are concentrated around the company's current product line or are more diversified, and the desired levels of innovativeness, quality, and customization.

4. Strategies are formulated for the nature of the technologies to be utilized in new products and processes.

5. Strategies are formulated for the types of markets to be served through the company's innovative efforts, including how new or mature these markets are in general, and the newness of these markets to the company.

6. There is a clear sense of how aggressive or defensive the innovation efforts of the company are intended to be and a clear understanding of the planned levels of resource commitment to innovation as a percentage of company revenues.

7. The company has a planned approach for sourcing new product ideas, and a policy regarding the relative reliance on external (i.e., outsourced or licensed) versus internal product development.

Just as important is the need for companies to move away from a project mentality when managing innovation and to adopt a "portfolio" mentality. An effective risk-management strategy involves the company creating and managing a portfolio of innovations. Hence, at any point in time, a set of projects is underway within the company, some of which might be breakthrough products or services, while others might be incremental improvements to existing products or services. Evidence suggests, for instance, that new-to-the-world products account for about 10 percent of corporate innovation activity, new lines for 20 percent, line extensions for 26 percent, and product revisions for 26 percent.

The key is balance across projects. Management attempts to draw a balance of (a) high-risk, high-return projects against lower-risk, lower-return projects; (b) discontinuous or dynamically continuous innovations against continuous innovations and imitations; (c) projects with shorter development cycles and payoffs against ones with

---

FIGURE 8-2

The Innovation Portfolio: Classifying Innovation by Type and Level of Newness

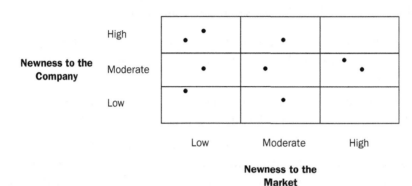

Key: Each dot represents an innovative product or service or process project on which the firm is working.

TABLE 8-3

Characteristics of Different Types of Innovation

Category	Risk	Potential Return	Investment Required	Number of People Involved	Level of Management Approval	Development Cycle
New to the world	High	High	Major	20–35	Director level	3–4 years
New to market	High	High	Major	10–15	Director level	2–4 years
New product line	Moderate	High	Major	10–15	Director level	1–3 years
Extension of existing line	Moderate	Moderate	Moderate	5–6	Business unit level	18 months
Product revision	Low	Moderate	Low	3–5	Product manager	6–12 months
Product support innovation	Low	Low	Low	1–3	Functional manager	3–6 months

longer-term outcomes; (d) products/services intended for markets the company currently serves against ones for markets that are new to the company; and (e) projects utilizing new and emerging technologies against those relying on technologies with which the company is familiar. Figure 8-2 provides a hypothetical example of an innovation portfolio, while Table 8-3 illustrates how the characteristics of different types of innovations reflect these trade-offs.

Thinking in terms of a portfolio also implies a different perspective on failure. Given that the portfolio concept is borrowed from finance, consider for a moment a portfolio of financial investments. The wise investor is most concerned with returns achieved on a total set of stocks, bonds, and other investments. He or she does not overreact to the failure of any stock. Rather, the role of failure is recognized and accepted. The same goes for a portfolio of innovations. It is anticipated that some will be major winners, some will be moderate successes, and some will be losers.

To guide the creation of the innovation portfolio within a company, the reader may find Figure 8-3 to be useful. The axes in Figure 8-3 are the *company's knowledge*

FIGURE 8-3

New Product/Service Opportunity Matrix

Company's Knowledge Pertaining to the New Products'/Service's Targeted Market			
High	Moderate Innovation Success Probability	High Innovation Success Probability	Highest Innovation Success Probability
Medium	Low Innovation Success Probability	Moderate Innovation Success Probability	High Innovation Success Probability
Low	Lowest Innovation Success Probability	Low Innovation Success Probability	Moderate Innovation Success Probability
	Low	Medium	High

**Company's Knowledge
Pertaining to the New
Product's/Service's
Core Technology**

pertaining to the new product's/service's targeted market and the *company's knowledge pertaining to the new product's/service's core technologies.* Individual projects are positioned within the matrix based on where they fall on each axis. In general, product and service innovations tend to be most successful when they are technologically similar to products or services currently offered by the company and targeted toward markets that are well-known to the company. By contrast, as the company ventures into technology and/or market domains that are less related to those of its current operations, the chances for innovation success diminish.

As reported in Chapter 3, most new product introductions succeed. This is largely because most new product introductions involve incremental innovations. When innovation involves venturing into unfamiliar markets with truly new products, which are often based on novel or recently developed technologies, the success rate can drop precipitously. Consider the Campbell et al. (2003) study of corporate venturing as practiced in 95 corporations and eight countries around the world. These researchers found *no* instances of success among the 22 companies that pursued what they called *new legs* ventures, or internal corporate ventures that were founded as major growth initiatives in novel (to the initiating company) product and market domains.

The lesson seems to be obvious: Innovating "close to home" offers the greatest chances of individual innovation success. However, a company's long-run performance will often be limited and major opportunities missed if the company consistently overlooks possible breakthrough innovations with commensurately higher risk in favor of more incremental innovations with commensurately lower risk. The essence of the portfolio approach to innovation is to *selectively* embrace initiatives that occupy varying risk–return positions along the innovation spectrum. Moreover, the overall innovation success rate is less important than limiting losses incurred when entrepreneurial initiatives fail. The adoption of milestone planning (discussed in Chapter 13) can enable companies to limit their losses when high-risk, high-return initiatives don't yield the hoped-for results.

The design of the innovation portfolio also has implications for how a company structures its innovation activities. Considering the categories of innovation shown in Table 8-3, products in the portfolio that are newer to the market and not well understood by the company will tend to require a more centralized new product development team with an emphasis on cross-functional participation and learning. Projects that involve line extensions, product revisions, and product support innovations (not all that new to the market and the company has some experience in the area) often benefit from the existence of small decentralized teams that emphasize efficiency and speed of delivery. Chapter 9 presents a more detailed discussion of the structural forms that facilitate innovation success.

Integrating entrepreneurship and strategy within the corporation requires an understanding of the role of technology as a determinant of organizational success. Technological advancements often create entrepreneurial opportunities and the exploitation of those opportunities can lead to further technological advancements. The following sections address technology management related matters that tend to be of strategic importance to the entrepreneurial corporation.

Technology, Entrepreneurship, and Strategy

We can define technology as the tools, devices, and knowledge that help transform inputs into outputs. Never in history has the pace of technological advance been so fast. Whether it is new polymers, optical data storage, high-tech ceramics, digital electronics, or developments in biochemistry, every facet of business is affected. As a result, just as the contemporary business environment can be characterized as the age of entrepreneurship, so too can it be characterized as the age of technology. In fact, entrepreneurs drive the commercialization of new technologies, and technological developments greatly enhance the level of entrepreneurial activity.

Technology is an important trigger for entrepreneurial activity within corporations, in that it represents both opportunity and threat. For instance, technology is shortening product life cycles, which suggests that companies have a smaller window of opportunity, or time period, in which they can act on an innovative opportunity. Shorter windows also suggest the corporate entrepreneur must have an exit strategy, or harvesting plan, even as the innovation is still in the development stages. Technology is also redefining market segments. Mass markets are disappearing as markets become segmented, fragmented, and niched. This trend creates tremendous new product opportunity in that a single product strategy gives way to customized solutions for different market segments. Markets also become globalized, suggesting distance and size no longer matter, and the playing field between small and large companies is more level. Industry definitions start to become less meaningful as new industries rapidly appear and boundaries blur among existing ones.

As a result, the company finds itself competing in nontraditional markets and facing nontraditional competitors in its existing markets. Under such circumstances, the entrepreneurial company can redefine the rules of the competitive game like Nucor did with steel and Seatrain did with shipping. Other developments driven by technology include organizational restructuring and changing employee relationships. The communications and information revolutions enabled by technology make possible flatter organizations, virtual companies, and companies where people's offices are wherever the people happen to be at a point in time. The need for the company to own or control assets and people is markedly reduced.

We have previously argued for an innovation strategy in companies. The innovation strategy should be complemented by a technology strategy. Technology strategy consists of the overall set of decisions and actions that relate to a company's acquisition and utilization of technology. Some elements of technology strategy include...

- Technology choices—e.g., analogue or digital electronics technology?

- Technology sources—e.g., develop internally or acquire from external sources?

- Competitive timing—e.g., be a technology pioneer or follower?

- Technology investment level—e.g., level of R&D funding?

- Technology policies—e.g., criteria for evaluating R&D project proposals?

- R&D focus—e.g., product development and engineering, applied research, or basic research?

- Model of technological innovation—e.g., is the company product-driven, market-driven, technology-driven?

A company can be thought of as having a technology strategy if (a) its technology-related decisions and actions are planned or (b) its technology-related decisions and actions are mutually supportive and internally consistent regardless of whether this profile of decisions and actions was planned (i.e., it has an emergent technology strategy). Some companies do not fit either of these profiles. While this third type of company may be making technology-related decisions, it should not be regarded as having a technology strategy.

The relationship between technology strategy and business strategy should be thought of and treated as different than the relationship between functional area strategy (like marketing strategy) and business strategy. Whereas functional area strategy should follow from and help to operationalize business strategy, technology strategy exists on the same level and is not subordinate to business strategy. Technological possibilities create strategic opportunities, and the pursuit of such opportunities often gives rise to future technological possibilities. As such, technology planning should be an inherent, inseparable part of the business planning process.

A useful model for conceptualizing how technology-related concerns enter into the business planning process was proposed by Fusfeld (1978). Briefly, Fusfeld proposed a multistep process for identifying areas in which technology investments should be made. An important insight of Fusfeld's model is that, for business planning purposes, generic technologies should be distinguished from the products or services in which they are embedded. Accordingly, the first two steps of Fusfeld's model include (step 1) identify the generic technologies employed by your company and (step 2)

FIGURE 8-4

Product-Technology Matrix

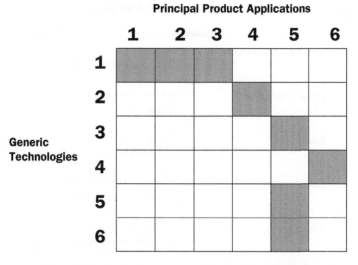

Principal Product Applications

Generic Technologies

Generic Technologies

1. Particle separation
2. Metal fiber formation
3. Molded material formation
4. Noise control
5. Static electricity control
6. Energy conservation

Product Applications

1. Industrial anti-pollution
2. Commercial filtration devices
3. Medical filtration devices
4. Construction products
5. Wall/floor coverings
6. Internal combustion engines

SOURCE: Adapted from A. R. Fusfeld (1978), "How to Put Technology into Corporate Planning," *Technology Review*, 80(6): 51–55. Reprinted by permission of MIT Press.

identify their applications (i.e., products or services in which they can be found). Figure 8-4 is a product-technology matrix that could result from such identification efforts. This matrix portrays a hypothetical company that has both a technology emphasis on particle separation and a product emphasis on wall/floor coverings.

The third step of Fusfeld's model is the consideration of how technology affects various dimensions of product/service acceptability, followed by (step 4) the determination (via market research) of the importance placed by the company's markets on these dimensions. The basic question the company should be trying to answer is "How much will market demand increase given some level of improvement, *attributable to technological advancements*, in the preceding dimensions of product/service acceptability?" The key insight here is that technology can make products and services less

FIGURE 8-5

Profiling a Technology's Benefits by Market Segments

Demand for Product/Service Attribute

Lower ◄─────────────────► Higher

Functional performance	*******************
	####################
Low acquisition cost	****************
	########
Ease of use	******************
	############
Low operating costs	*********************
	#################
Reliability	************************
	################
Serviceability	***************
	#################
Compatibility	*************
	####################

```
****    Market segment 1: Individual consumers
####    Market segment 2: Institutional market
```

SOURCE: Adapted from A. R. Fusfeld (1978), "How to Put Technology into Corporate Planning," *Technology Review*, 80(6): 51–55. Reprinted by permission of MIT Press.

expensive, higher performing, more reliable, easier to use, and so on, and companies need to know how these demand-generating dimensions of product/service acceptability are valued by particular target markets. Figure 8-5 is a hypothetical example of how the value placed on particular dimensions of product/service acceptability might vary in different market segments. The principal lesson of Fusfeld's model is that companies should invest in technologies that have a positive influence on the dimensions of product/service acceptability most valued by their customers.

Technology Limits and Platforms

Companies frequently rely on a number of technologies in providing a product or service to the marketplace, but there are usually one or two core technologies that are the key to the company's ongoing ability to be competitive with that product or service. These technologies have life cycles. As money and effort are invested in a technology, the initial yield from that investment is often low. At some point there is a breakthrough development, and the yield of the technology both in terms of new applications and product/service performance takes off. Eventually, diminishing returns set in, where the additional potential of the technology begins to slow, even with large investments in continued development. Stated differently, every technology has limits.

As a technology begins to reach its limits, the implications for companies dependent on that technology are immense. Foster (1986, p. 32) notes, "Limits determine which technologies, which machines, and which processes are about to become obsolete.... Management's ability to recognize limits is crucial to determining whether they succeed or fail, because limits are the best clue they have for recognizing when they will need to develop a new technology." The impending limits of a given technology become especially significant when there is an emerging technology on the horizon. This new technology has yet to be exploited, but it is clearly not subject to the same limits. At some point, users begin to abandon the current technology and jump to the new one (which has its own life cycle). The eventual takeoff in the new technology's life cycle serves to accelerate the maturation and decline of the old technology.

Further insights can be gained by considering the valuable work of Christensen (1997). He distinguishes between "sustaining" and "disruptive" technologies. Sustaining technologies maintain a rate of improvement, giving customers more or better in the attributes (e.g., quality, speed, size) they already have. Thus, a currently used technology begins to reach its limits in terms of enhancement of the company's product performance on one or two key attributes (i.e., quality cannot get much better, speed much faster, or size much smaller). New (sustaining) technologies are employed that allow the company to continue (or sustain) the trajectory of attribute enhancement.

Disruptive technologies introduce a different set of attributes than ones customers historically value. Consider the microwave oven when first introduced or the use of lasers in correcting myopic eyesight. Disruptive technologies might perform poorly on the attributes that are currently important to customers, but they open up entirely new horizons in terms of capabilities in other areas. Cellular telephones at first did not perform well in terms of reception and reach, but they allowed mobility and communication regardless of time or place. Customers resist using disruptive technologies in applications they know and understand, so these technologies are initially used and valued only in new markets or new applications (typically niche markets). Christensen (1997) recounts the resistance on the part of computer manufacturers as the architecture of disk drives eventually shrank from 14 to 3.5 inches. Companies failed to see that the reduction in storage capacity enabled other attributes such as lighter weight and lower power consumption that led to the successful introduction of PCs and ultimately portable computers.

The threat to mainstream companies is roundabout. The disruptive technology is first employed in entirely new markets, not the mainstream market (again, these new markets are often niche segments ignored by the mainstream companies). Once the disruptive technology has this foothold in the marketplace, sustaining technologies are applied to improve performance on an array of the more traditional attributes. In fact, performance improves at a rapid pace, such that the once-ignored (or underserved) needs of customers in established markets are met as well. Established, mainstream companies who ignored the disruptive technology suddenly find themselves losing market share to entrepreneurial players who saw the future first. Ironically, by focusing on the existing needs of current customers, the established company can eventually lose those customers. And when they do finally embrace the disruptive technology, making up the lost ground is almost impossible. Another irony involves the tendency of the mainstream company to continue using technology to improve performance on accepted attributes such that the company overshoots what the marketplace needs and is willing to pay for in terms of those attributes. The company with the disruptive technology doesn't perform as well on those accepted attributes but eventually performs well enough while also offering a set of new attributes.

The message is that companies cannot afford to ignore either disruptive technologies or the niche markets they initially create. Management must be able to classify technologies as sustaining and disruptive, determine the disruptive technologies that are likely to have a strategic impact on the company's products and markets, and identify the niche markets likely to be created by the new technology. Managers may need to create autonomous structures to facilitate the internal development of disruptive technologies and to ensure the company has a position in emerging markets.

A related concept is that of the "technological platform." Here the company selects the core technology or technologies around which it defines the future. Platforms are underlying technological capabilities in which a company invests in order to generate a range of different products, applications, and improvements (Kuczmarski et al., 2001). Skills and capabilities with the technologies that define a platform become a core competency of the company. For its part, a disruptive technology effectively provides a company with a new platform, redefining not only the limits on the performance possibilities on accepted attributes but also introducing capabilities on new attributes. Thus, mainstream operations in a company might be built around a given platform, but autonomous units might be organized around a new platform.

Technology-Push versus Market-Pull Approaches to Innovation

Many companies have an overall orientation that guides or drives how entrepreneurial activity is manifested in innovation processes. Two of the dominant approaches are called the *technology-push* and *market-pull* innovation processes. With the technology-push approach, employees within the company (usually technically qualified engineers or scientists) see a technical possibility and strive to capitalize on it. They are typically versed in the existing state of the art on the technical side and recognize a means of overcoming an existing technical limitation or obstacle. Alternatively, they see a new way in which a technology might be applied. The tendency with this approach is to be caught up in the technical possibilities, while assuming the marketplace need. Even where a customer need has been clearly identified, many of the substantive issues surrounding whether customers would actually buy the innovation and how competitors are going to react are ignored. Examples of such issues include the level of satisfaction among consumers with whatever they are currently using, their perceived switching costs, the dynamics of their buying process, and the different people who play a role in their buying decisions.

Technology-push approaches also frequently suffer from what is called the *perfection syndrome*. Technical people not only see the technological possibilities in an innovation, but they frequently want to pursue those possibilities as far as they can. They want to perfect the new product or service, adding as many "bells and whistles," or features and functionality, as their research, design, and testing work will allow. In effect, they overengineer the innovation. More often than not, the marketplace wants a new product that is good enough, not the best possible. The additional time and money necessary to make an innovation the best possible drives up prices (and sometimes product complexity) beyond what the customer is willing to pay or results in features the customer is paying for but that he or she does not really want. From the customer's vantage point, a new product or service represents a series of trade-off decisions in terms of what is an acceptable value package.

Conversely, market-pull approaches to innovation start with the customer and are typically driven by marketing people. Market research plays a critical role. Customers are often the source of the new product idea, or at least their input is instrumental in the design and development of the product. While this seems like a safer approach, and is consistent with a customer-driven philosophy, it also suffers from limitations. The foremost limitation is the often mistaken assumption that customers know their needs and can describe them in a way that results in new products. Customers generally know what they like and dislike about what is currently available on the market, and the feedback they provide is usually only with this reference point in mind.

We can relate the technology-push and market-pull approaches to the outcomes of the innovation process. Returning to the types of innovation described in Chapter 3, technology-driven approaches often result in breakthrough products and services, including both discontinuous and dynamically continuous innovations. This is the good news. However, they also produce a lot of failures that can be described as "better mousetraps nobody wanted." These are new products that are technically advanced but for which there is inadequate market demand to justify their introduction. Sometimes they are too far ahead of the market. Alternatively, market-pull approaches frequently result in incremental advances, including both continuous innovation and imitation. While more readily acceptable in the marketplace, such innovations have shorter-term payoffs with less long-run potential. Further, they also produce a common type of failure, the so-called "me-too product hitting a competitive brick wall." In essence, the customer does not see enough uniqueness or difference in the new product and so continues to rely on his or her current solution.

The implication is that neither approach is better. Inter-functional involvement throughout the stages of the new product development process is the key. Innovation management should represent a continuous matching process, where the technical limits and possibilities are explored and matched against an intimate understanding of market segments, underlying customer needs and buying processes, and competitors' capabilities. Just as important is the ability to envision the customer not simply as he or she is now, but as he or she will be.

Key Strategic Concepts: Entrepreneurship as the Driver

The role of entrepreneurship in strategy and the role of strategy in entrepreneurship can be better appreciated by considering some salient concepts that surround the strategy formulation process. These include *strategic advantage*, *strategic positioning*, *strategic flexibility*, and *strategic leverage*.

STRATEGIC ADVANTAGE

Markets are dynamic; no one is standing still. Companies leapfrog one another in terms of product improvements, cost reductions, and enhancements to customer service levels. They find themselves in a never-ending battle to preempt, protect against, and surpass competitors. It is all about competitive advantage, which results from "an enduring value differential between the products or services of one organization and those of its competitors in the minds of customers" (Duncan et al., 1998). For its part, strategy is the set of commitments and actions taken by management to first develop and then exploit a competitive advantage in the marketplace.

Yesterday's competitive advantages can be today's disadvantages. Black & Decker's consolidation into a few global-scale facilities in the 1980s proved a disadvantage in the 1990s. Organizational practices, core competencies, and business models confer advantages because of specific factors present under particular conditions over a particular period of time. Not only do the underlying factors subsequently change, but also "the very existence of competitive advantage sets in motion creative innovations that, as competitors strive to level the playing field, cause the advantage to dissipate" (Christensen, 2001, p. 109).

Innovation is the key to developing and successfully exploiting competitive advantages. Innovation coupled with continuous learning provides the edge. This combination brings something new into being: new products, new internal processes, new business models, and new markets. It can enable companies to bring products more rapidly to the market, to customize those products, and to add new functionality to those products.

The challenge is to develop innovation as a core competence of the company. The company's strategy for entrepreneurship serves to stimulate such innovation. In a global economy, the most successful strategies call for the company to rely on innovations that offer fundamentally superior value to existing buyers or to create new markets through a quantum leap in buyer value. Companies able to exploit the competitive advantages they own today, while simultaneously using innovation to shape the advantages they intend to own and use tomorrow, increase the probability of long-term survival, growth, and financial success.

STRATEGIC POSITIONING

Strategic positioning is concerned with how the company wants to be perceived in the marketplace. Positions can be defined on many bases, including attributes or benefits offered, price/quality levels, capabilities relative to competitors, or customers and applications that the company specializes in. Entrepreneurial strategy is all about positioning. It is a process of perceiving new positions that attract customers from established ones or draw new customers into the market.

Underlying strategic positioning is a distinct set of attributes that a company does differently and better than others. These activities represent the linkage both to strategy and to entrepreneurship. Finding and implementing a strategic position that holds meaningful potential for the company—meaning one that not only represents a unique value proposition but is also meaningfully different from those of competitors—is fundamentally an entrepreneurial challenge. FedEx provides an example. When a package or letter absolutely has to be somewhere and absolutely has to be there quickly, customers rely on this company more than any other. The company's ability to provide fast and highly reliable delivery to virtually anywhere at a reasonable price is tied to the management of their novel hub-and-spoke operating model, an innovative logistics system on the ground, a unique organizational structure, and creative approaches to human resource management activities.

Entrepreneurial thinking can be applied not only to the identification of the strategic position the company seeks to occupy but also to the way the company manages each of the underlying activities that make it possible to occupy that position. Further, many trade-offs can come into play among these activities, and entrepreneurial approaches are often needed to ensure activities are combined in ways that do not compromise the value proposition. Activities must fit with and reinforce one another. As Porter (1996, p. 70) notes, "Fit (among key organizational activities) locks out imitators by creating a chain that is as strong as its strongest link." Innovation that enhances value or lowers cost from one activity area can serve to lower costs or increase the value customers receive from a complementary activity area.

Effective strategic positioning is critical for competitive advantage. As with competitive advantage, the appropriateness of the company's positioning can change both as a function of marketplace developments and developments affecting the internal value chain of the company. For example, other companies crowd into similar positions, new customer groups or purchase occasions arise, new needs emerge as societies evolve, new distribution channels appear, new technologies are developed, or new machinery or information systems become available. Companies also become complacent, assuming they "own" a given position, and they stop looking for innovative ways to enhance the position, develop it further, or take it in new but consistent directions. As an exception to the rule, FedEx has extended its effective positioning with creative applications of technology to various internal activities. However, they have also capitalized on and extended their position to a family of related companies, including FedEx Ground, FedEx Freight Custom, FedEx Custom Critical, and FedEx Trade Networking.

STRATEGIC FLEXIBILITY AND ADAPTATION

Companies require appropriate strategic direction to traverse the new competitive landscape successfully, but this direction should be coupled with flexibility. Strategic flexibility involves a willingness to rethink continuously and make adjustments to the company's strategies, action plans, and resource allocations as well as to the company structure, culture, and managerial systems. How quickly and adroitly can managers adapt to changes in the competitive set or in competitor strategies, to a shift in the power or change in the structure within the value chain, or to changes in the availability or cost of components and raw materials? These adjustments allow for the fact that management knows where the company wants to go and how it wants to be positioned but that there are different ways to get there. Flexibility demands keen insights into the organization's resources, capabilities, and competencies.

Hitt and colleagues (1998) have proposed a model for building strategic flexibility into organizations. As illustrated in Figure 8-6, their model starts with strategic leadership at the top of the organization, which means senior executives who are visionary, entrepreneurial, and transformational (and willing to pay the price of transformation and persevere long enough to see their entrepreneurial visions realized). Assuming this kind of leadership is in place, the following five factors contribute to building strategic leadership: (1) a unique set of dynamic core competencies (i.e., competencies that are continually improved and enhanced), (2) creative approaches to human capital (e.g., the use of contract labor, outsourcing, and employee sharing in non-core areas of the company), (3) effective incorporation of new and emerging technologies (i.e., technologies that enable the company to recognize changing market needs or conditions quickly, customize products, and serve different markets in different

FIGURE 8-6

Building Strategic Flexibility and Competitive Advantage

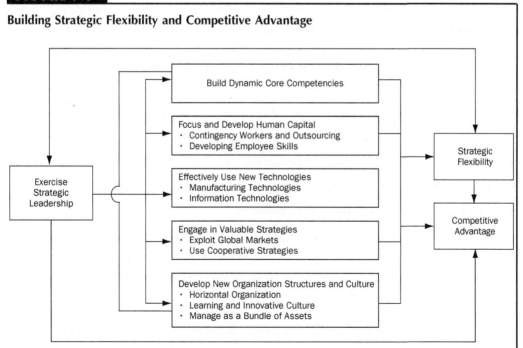

SOURCE: Adapted from Hitt, Keats, and DeMarie (1998), *Academy of Management Executive: The Thinking Manager's Source.* Copyright © 1998 by Academy of Management (NY). Reproduced with permission of Academy of Management (NY) in the format Textbook via Copyright Clearance Center.

ways), (4) strategic alliances and a global market presence (i.e., a diversified approach to markets and cooperative approach to penetrating those markets), and (5) company structures that are flattened and cultures that stress learning and accountability for innovation (i.e., structures and cultures that enable the company to recognize patterns and trends, make quick adjustments, and continuously experiment in the marketplace).

STRATEGIC LEVERAGE

One vehicle for achieving flexibility is called leveraging. At its most basic level, leveraging refers to doing more with less. Consider the base word *lever*. Acting as a lever, a metal rod or wooden pole enables an individual to dislodge or move an object he or she would be unable to move on his or her own. In a similar vein, corporate entrepreneurs and entrepreneurial companies are brilliant leveragers of resources. As Hamel and Prahalad (1994, p. 128) note, "Getting to the future first is more a function of resourcefulness than resources ... Resourcefulness stems not from an elegantly structured strategic architecture, but from a deeply felt sense of purpose, a broadly shared dream, a truly seductive view of tomorrow's opportunity." In highly entrepreneurial companies, ambition forever outpaces resources.

The implication is that corporate entrepreneurs are not constrained by the resources they currently control or have at their disposal. They are able to leverage resources in a number of creative ways. Stated differently, the concept of resource leveraging has a number of dimensions:

- Stretching resources much further than others have done in the past
- Getting uses out of resources that others are unable to realize
- Using other people's (or company's) resources to accomplish one's own purpose
- Complementing one resource with another to create higher combined value
- Using certain resources to obtain other resources

Leveraging is not something one simply decides to do. It is not a mechanical process—it is a creative process. Companies and managers within companies develop a capacity for resource leveraging. Some are more creative; others are less so. The ability to recognize a resource that is not being used completely, to see how the resource could be used in a nonconventional way, and to convince those that control the resource to let you use it requires insight, experience, and skill. The same can be said for the ability to get team members to work extra hours; convince departments to perform activities they normally do not perform; or put together unique sets of resources that, when blended, are synergistic.

Of all the types of leveraging approaches mentioned, one of the most powerful concerns the ability to use other people's resources to accomplish the entrepreneur's purpose. Examples of the ways in which this is done include bartering, borrowing, renting, leasing, sharing, recycling, contracting, and outsourcing. These efforts can be directed at other departments and units within the company or at suppliers, distributors, customers, and other external organizations. They frequently entail both informal initiatives, such as the exchange of favors and the use of networks, and formal initiatives, such as strategic alliances and joint ventures.

Discussions of resource productivity can also be misconstrued, at least in some companies. The leveraging philosophy is not about cutting resources, or squeezing them as much as possible in an attempt to increase productivity. Managers seeking to create the lean and mean enterprise often find the end result is more mean than lean. The long-term outcome is frequently less productivity and more inefficiency. Rather, leveraging is about finding and using resources more intelligently, more creatively, and in a more focused manner.

Entrepreneurial Strategy: Some Contributing Factors

Strategy does not exist in a vacuum. As suggested earlier, strategy and strategic management go hand in hand. Even the most entrepreneurial of strategies will fail unless coupled with management practices that support and reinforce the strategy. Let us consider some of the key ingredients that go hand in hand with a well-conceptualized entrepreneurial strategy.

DEVELOPING AN ENTREPRENEURIAL VISION

Great organizations are driven by clear visions. It is important that senior management conceptualize and communicate a vision of organization-wide entrepreneurship. Vision comes from the top, while entrepreneurial behavior comes from throughout the organization. This shared vision requires identification of a company-specific concept of entrepreneurship, as well as what have been termed "big hairy audacious goals" (or BHAGs, for short) that spell out a bold, daunting challenge—one that stretches every member of the company (Collins and Porras, 1996).

INCREASING THE PERCEPTION OF OPPORTUNITY

Entrepreneurial behavior is opportunity-seeking behavior. Entrepreneurial strategy represents a quest to find and exploit untapped opportunities—opportunities that arise from areas of uncertainty both inside and outside the organization. If every employee is to be considered a potential entrepreneur, then the ability to recognize opportunity becomes paramount. Employees are unable to see opportunity because they are surrounded by constraints on the one hand and crises on the other. Ironically, the very act of pursuing an opportunity tends to subsequently make people more opportunity-aware. The challenge is getting employees to take that first step.

A useful concept is the opportunity horizon, which represents the outer limit on management's vision regarding the opportunities open to the company. For many companies, the opportunity horizon is quite constrained. Managers are unable to escape the past, and so future possibilities are little more than extensions of what the company is doing now and where it has been historically. For instance, the needs and demands of current customers might so overwhelm management thinking that the company is unable to imagine unusual ways to create value for new markets or new customer segments. Figure 8-7 represents a framework for use in assessing the company's (or a given unit's) approach to opportunity.

INSTITUTIONALIZING CHANGE

Change is good. It enriches people, adding to their experiences and deepening their insights. It represents new opportunities for employees. Strategies can sometimes serve to preserve the status quo; in some instances unintentionally. In entrepreneurial companies, strategy should be conceived as a vehicle for change. In fact, in the new competitive landscape, strategy provides focus and direction for change both within the company and in the marketplace. The opposite of accepting the status quo is to continually challenge every aspect of a business, looking for better ways, processes that can be done differently, and things that can be eliminated.

INSTILLING THE DESIRE TO BE INNOVATIVE

Innovation takes many forms in companies. A strategy that encourages innovation will be effective only if company leaders make clear what types of innovation the company seeks and from where in the company these innovations are expected to come. The concept of an innovation portfolio was introduced earlier in this chapter. The innovation portfolio emphasizes the need to pursue, at the same time, innovations that are higher and lower in risk, discontinuous and continuous, product-focused and process-focused, and that have differing market potentials. The portfolio perspective suggests that innovations can originate from throughout the organization. Not every employee necessarily has to initiate or champion an innovation. But every employee should have some role in one or more innovative initiatives at a given point in time. When 3M created its 15 percent rule, mandating that managers dedicate time to innovation that is not part of their normal job, they were saying that innovation is expected of people who do not necessarily see themselves as innovators. The desire

FIGURE 8-7

Opportunity Assessment and Internal Value Creation

Exploiting External Opportunities

Source / Current Efforts	New technology applications	Untapped or underserved customers/markets	Further penetration of current markets	Supply chain management	Outsourcing	Competitor vulnerabilities	Strategic alliances	Financial leveraging	Social patterns and developments	Regulatory changes	Other
Aggressively pursued											
Partially tapped											
Untapped											

Finding New Internal Sources of Value

Source / Current Efforts	Marketing and sales approaches	Human resource management	Operations and production methods	Information resources	Equipment and facilities	Patents and intellectual property	Financial resources	R&D resources	Logistical management	Administration	Other
Aggressively pursued											
Partially tapped											
Untapped											

to be innovative stems from a sense of involvement in, ownership of, and responsibility for innovative projects.

INVESTING IN PEOPLE'S IDEAS

Ideas, together with an individual's personal commitment to them, represent the single greatest asset in a company. Unfortunately, companies tend to treat ideas like targets in a shooting gallery, and they come up with the most inventive means of shooting them down. Or their concept of idea support begins and ends with a suggestion box. Fostering idea generation requires that management continually plow and fertilize the fields. Investments are needed in intelligence-gathering activities of all types. Infrastructure is needed to support information storage, reporting, and sharing. This must be reinforced by the norms and values of the company. Forums are needed for airing ideas. Pools of capital are required for investing in ideas. Managers at all levels must define their jobs in terms of listening to, productively challenging, endorsing, feeding, sponsoring, and investing in the ideas of employees. The two most precious words in the organization should be "what if?" Approached in this manner, the internal environment of the company becomes a marketplace of ideas and strategic management becomes a set of activities devoted to making this marketplace work efficiently.

SHARING RISKS AND REWARDS WITH EMPLOYEES

Entrepreneurship is about risk and reward. The relationship is direct but nonlinear. This is a fundamental precept of entrepreneurial behavior and investor behavior. Ignoring the risk–reward relationship when striving to develop entrepreneurial strategies within companies misses the whole point of entrepreneurship. It is not that employees must have the potential to become multimillionaires as a function of entrepreneurial behavior. In fact, the absolute size of rewards is a secondary consideration. However, sustainable entrepreneurship requires that employees experience some of the risk and meaningfully participate in the rewards. The implication is that individuals and teams lose in terms of salary, bonuses, freedom, research support, or other resources if projects fail or under-perform, and they do quite well when projects are highly successful.

RECOGNIZING THE CRITICAL IMPORTANCE OF FAILURE

Failure is a sign of experience, learning, and progress. Not only can overall projects fail, but the likelihood of project demise is a function of how the champion deals with lots of small failures along the way. Doing something entrepreneurial means experimenting, and experimentation is all about trying something and, when it does not work out, trying something else. Importantly, the experimenter never loses sight of the quest. He or she becomes fairly thick-skinned in dealing with rejection and failure but open-minded about ways to adapt and new avenues to attempt. Many attempts are needed before success is achieved.

Learning from failure, as opposed to expecting punishment for it, is promoted in entrepreneurial companies. By encouraging plenty of experimentation and risk-taking, there are more chances for a new product hit. As an example, one of the early founders of 3M, Francis G. Oakie, had an idea to replace razor blades with sandpaper (Von Hipple et al., 1999). He believed that men could rub sandpaper on their face rather than use a sharp razor. He was wrong and the idea failed. But his idea continued until he developed a waterproof sandpaper for the auto industry—a blockbuster success! In the process, 3M's philosophy of innovation was born. Innovation is often a numbers game; the more ideas a company has, the better the chances for a successful innovation. Further, one of the underlying principles that guide the strategic management of the company is never kill an idea, no matter how different or unrealistic the idea appears. This philosophy has paid off for 3M. Antistatic videotape, translucent dental braces, synthetic ligaments for knee surgery, heavy-duty reflective sheeting for construction signs, and, of course, Post-it notes, are just some of the great innovations developed by the company. Overall, the company has a catalogue of 60,000 products that generate almost $11 billion in sales. We will further examine the matter of how to view failure in Chapter 10 where we introduce some different conceptualizations of failure from a cultural perspective.

Implementation Issues: Fatal Visions

Strategy formulation is half the battle—implementation is the other half. The actual execution of a strategy is as important as the strategy itself. Many organizations make unintentional errors while applying a specific strategy to their particular context. Porter (1991) has noted five fatal mistakes to which organizations continually fall prey in their attempts to implement a strategy. These are especially relevant for entrepreneurial strategies:

Flaw 1: Misunderstanding industry attractiveness: There is a tendency to associate attractiveness with those industries that are growing the most rapidly, appear to be glamorous, or use the fanciest technology. Attractiveness has much more to do with high barriers to entry, the ability to differentiate, the existence of few effective substitutes, and the ability to influence suppliers and customers. The more high tech or high glamour a business is, the more likely that many new competitors will enter it and make it unprofitable.

Flaw 2: No real competitive advantage: Merely copying, imitating, or slightly improving upon the strategy of competitors is not entrepreneurial. It may seem easier, and it may seem less risky, but it means the venture has no real competitive advantage. To succeed, new ventures must develop unique ways to compete.

Flaw 3: Pursuing an unsustainable competitive position: Companies try to be customer service leaders when customer service innovations are easy to mimic; they attempt to be technology leaders when they do not have the necessary internal capacity to continually produce desirable technical innovations. Alternatively, they pursue strategies that place conflicting demands on different parts of the company.

Flaw 4: Compromising strategy for growth: A careful balance must exist between growth and the competitive strategy that makes a business successful. Pressures exist for companies to maximize sales growth, which often means capitalizing on short-term opportunities that are inconsistent with or distract management from the core strategy. Although fast growth can be tempting in certain industries, it is imperative to maintain and grow strategic advantage as well.

Flaw 5: Failure to explicitly communicate strategy internally: It is essential to clearly communicate the company's strategy to every employee. The assumption that employees know the strategy and understand its implications for how they deal with particular issues or decisions is a dangerous one. Management must be explicit not only regarding the strategy itself but also in what it means for marketing, human resource management, production, and other areas of the company.

The more a company's strategy is matched to core competencies and a well-integrated chain of internal activities, the easier the implementation will be. However, implementation of strategy is also where flexibility and adaptation are most vital. Implementation involves an iterative process. Action programs are executed, results are assessed, adjustments are made, conditions change, more adjustments are made, certain tactics are abandoned and others added, results are assessed, additional adjustments are made, and so forth. In many instances, one or more of the creative adjustments prove to be the factor that makes a strategy successful over time.

THE INNOVATOR'S NOTEBOOK

Reigning in Innovation at Google

Marissa Mayer is Google's vice president for Search Products & User Experience. She leads the company's product management efforts on search products—Web search, images, news, books, products, maps, Google Earth, Google Toolbar, Google Desktop, Google Health, Google Labs, and more.

She joined Google in 1999 as Google's first female engineer and led the user interface and Web server teams at that time. Her efforts have included designing and developing Google's search interface, internationalizing the site to more than 100 languages, defining Google News, Gmail, and Orkut, and launching more than 100 features and products on Google.com. Several patents have been filed on her work in artificial intelligence and interface design. She has been involved in virtually every aspect of the development of Google's Web pages, from the layout of the site to new software that allows users to search their computers' hard drives. The company's mission to "organize the world's information" is no small feat and has led to such initiatives as digitizing the world's libraries, offering free voice calls, providing satellite images of the world, and giving away wireless broadband service.

Google's founders, Larry Page and Sergey Brin encourage idea generation at all levels of the organization. Facilitating this process is an ideas mailing list that is open to anyone in the company and allows people to post idea proposals. Part of Mayer's role is to sort through the list and promote the good ideas for additional scrutiny from upper management. With the company's revenues nearing $24 billion and nearly 19,000 employees worldwide, her job is becoming increasingly complicated.

As the idea gatekeeper, it is easy to imagine animosity developing between Mayer and those employees who have had their ideas dismissed. Insiders cite Mayer's ability to effectively communicate with both the MBAs and the PhDs as being critical to her ability to manage the idea flow. Determining when pet projects are ready to be promoted to the top is a process that Mayer conducts through an established process, which includes discussing ideas during open office hours and brainstorming sessions; however, it is Mayer's willingness to put protocol aside in order to speak with programmers informally that ensures that ideas are brought to light.

One example of her affable nature leading to innovation is evident in the development of Google's popular desktop search. In 2003, during a casual chat with a worker, Mayer learned about a project being worked on by an Australian engineer, Steve Lawrence. He was developing software that would allow him to search the contents of his computer, which was running on the Linux operating system. Mayer contacted Lawrence, got him to commit to developing a version of the software that could run on any PC, and then provided a team to assist him. The end result was that the desktop search was brought to market in October 2004, beating Microsoft by two months.

Typically Mayer is exposed to ideas through her three-times a week office hours. Groups get about five minutes to make their case. The goal is to gain Mayer's approval so that a proposed idea can be taken forward. Some ideas that have recently come across her desk are to provide the Google site in additional languages, to provide a link from the Google home page to the site for Hurricane Katrina victims, and to offer new software that would get Google closer to providing personalized search engines, which track users' preferences and then provide tailored information to improve results. Of the three, the only idea that made it through her rigorous screening process was the personalized search engine. After questioning the proposed product name and pressing the team on the product's features, Mayer approved the project for Larry Page's review.

In order to keep her idea review process as efficient as possible, Mayer has to remain objective when it comes to evaluating the procedures that she has set in place. For instance, Mayer maintained Google's Top 100 priorities list for years in order to rank projects based on their level of importance. In its inception, the list was effective in allowing Mayer to keep track and prioritize Google's various initiatives; however, as the company grew, the list grew with it, eventually reaching 270 projects. Realizing that the list had run its course, Google's execs retired it. Given the breakneck speed of innovation, Mayer must not only keep ideas from inundating the company but she must also ensure that she does not become the bottleneck preventing commercially viable ideas from getting to market.

From an outsider's perspective, Mayer at times appears to be the matriarch of Google, keeping all of the employees in line. In some respects, Mayer is responsible for keeping the "family" happy. Google's culture of "geek machismo," which regularly leads to intellectual sparring, can get out of control. Mayer's job is to keep the company on course while maintaining the company's culture of fearlessness. No wonder she was selected the youngest woman ever to be included on *Fortune's* Most Powerful Women list. Her ability to remain accessible to Google's employees and their ideas will be vital to the company beating its competitors in the future.

Discussion Questions

1. Relate the chapter definition of a "corporate entrepreneurial strategy" to the role that Marissa Mayer must fulfill at Google.

2. Would Google's approach to ideas be an "entrepreneurial strategy" or a "strategy for entrepreneurship"? Be specific in your distinction.

3. In developing an entrepreneurial strategy, what factors are evident in the Google approach?

SOURCES: Adapted from Ben Elgin, "Managing Google's Idea Factory," *BusinessWeek Online*, October 3, 2005; and company Web site accessed April 17, 2010.

Summary and Conclusions

The pervasive dynamism and uncertainty in the new competitive landscape requires companies to develop entrepreneurial capacity. Entrepreneurial actions are any newly fashioned behavior through which companies exploit opportunities others have not noticed or exploited. Novelty, in terms of new resources, new customers, new markets, or a new combination of resources, customers, and markets is the defining characteristic of entrepreneurial actions. When the actions taken in a large company to form competitive advantages and to exploit them through a strategy are grounded in entrepreneurial actions, the company is employing an *entrepreneurial strategy*. Further, when establishing direction and priorities for the product, service and process innovation efforts of the company, the company is formulating its *strategy for entrepreneurship*.

This chapter has explored the concept of entrepreneurship as the new dominant logic of a company. In this regard, three factors become evident. First, as a dominant logic, entrepreneurial strategy promotes strategic agility, flexibility, creativity, and continuous innovation throughout the company. Second, the overriding focus of the company is opportunity identification, discovery of new sources of value, and product and process innovation that will lead to greater profitability. And third, this strategy is translated into the objectives, reward systems, control systems, planning approaches, structure, and human resource management practices of the company. It is reinforced by the company culture. Moreover, sustainable advantage in the new competitive landscape requires a dominant logic that is dynamic. Entrepreneurship captures such dynamism, with its emphasis on continued innovation of all degrees and types.

Technology represents an especially potent tool for the corporate entrepreneur. Its effects both as an opportunity and threat frequently serve as the triggering event for product and process innovation. In a sense, technology liberates the corporate entrepreneur, freeing him or her from established ways of doing things and from current limitations and structures. The challenge is to properly interpret the technology horizon, which necessitates that the company "escape the tyranny of the currently served market" (Hamel and Prahalad, 1994). The ability to distinguish sustaining from disruptive technologies and to recognize the corresponding implications for where the marketplace is likely to go become the basis for entrepreneurial action and leadership in the corporation.

References

Amit, R. H., Brigham, K., and Markman, G. D. 2000. "Entrepreneurial Management as Strategy," in Meyer, G. D., and Heppard, K. A. (eds.) *Entrepreneurship as Strategy* (Thousands Oaks, CA: Sage Publications): 83–99.

Bettis, R. A., and Prahalad, C. K. 1995. "The Dominant Logic: Retrospective and Extension," *Strategic Management Journal*, 16(1): 5–14.

Bettis, R. A., and Hitt, M. A. 1995. "The New Competitive Landscape," *Strategic Management Journal*, 16(Summer Special Issue): 7–19.

Campbell, A., Birkinshaw, J., Morrison, A., and van Basten Batenburg, R. 2003. "The Future of Corporate Venturing," *MIT Sloan Management Review*, 45(1): 30–37.

Christensen, C. 1997. *The Innovator's Dilemma* (Cambridge, MA: Harvard Business School Press).

Christensen, C. 2001. "The Past and Future of Competitive Advantage," *Sloan Management Review*, 42(2): 105–110.

Collins, J. C., and Porras, J. I. 1996. "Building Your Company's Vision," *Harvard Business Review*, 74(5): 65–77.

Covin, J. G., and Miles, M. P. 2007. "Strategic Use of Corporate Venturing," *Entrepreneurship Theory and Practice*, 31(2): 183–208.

Duncan, W. J., Ginter, P., and Swayne, L. 1998. "Competitive Advantage and Internal Organizational Assessment," *Academy of Management Executive*, 12(3): 6–16.

Foster, R. 1986. *The Attacker's Advantage* (New York: Summit Books).

Fusfeld, A. R. 1978. "How to Put Technology into Corporate Planning," *Technology Review*, 80(6): 51–55.

Grove, A. S. 1996. *Only the Paranoid Survive* (London, England: Harper Collins Publishers).

Hamel, G. 2000. *Leading the Revolution* (Boston, MA: Harvard Business School Press).

Hamel, G., and Prahalad, C. K. 1994. *Competing for the Future* (Boston, MA: Harvard Business School Press).

Hitt, M. A., and Reed, T. S. 2000. "Entrepreneurship in the New Competitive Landscape," in Meyer, G. D., and Heppard, K. A. (eds.), *Entrepreneurship as Strategy* (Thousand Oaks, CA: Sage Publications): 23–47.

Ireland, R. D., Covin, J. G., and Kuratko, D. F. 2009. "Conceptualizing Corporate Entrepreneurship Strategy," *Entrepreneurship Theory and Practice*, 33(1): 19–46.

Kuczmarski, T., Middlebrooks, A., and Swaddling, J. 2001. *Innovating the Corporation* (Chicago: NTC Publishing Group).

Porter, M. E. 1991. "Knowing Your Place—How to Assess the Attractiveness of Your Industry and Your Company's Position in It," *Inc.* (Sept.): 90–94.

Porter, M. E. 1996. "What is Strategy?", *Harvard Business Review*, 74(6): 61–78.

Schendel, D., and Hofer, C. 1978. *Strategic Management: A New View of Business Policy and Planning* (Boston: Little Brown and Company).

Stacey, R. D. 1996. *Complexity and Creativity in Organizations* (San Francisco: Berrett-Koehler).

Von Hipple, E., Thomke, S., and Sonnack, M. 1999. "Creating Breakthroughs at 3M," *Harvard Business Review*, 77(5): 47–57.

CHAPTER 9

STRUCTURING THE COMPANY
FOR ENTREPRENEURSHIP

Introduction

The design of an organization has many elements, but three overarching ones are the company structure, communication flows, and control system. This chapter will explore issues surrounding structure and internal communication, while control will be the focus of Chapter 14. Structure refers to the formal pattern of how people and jobs are grouped and how the activities of different people or functions are connected. We typically think of structure in terms of some sort of organizational chart filled with boxes, lines, and arrows, suggesting a hierarchical set of relationships regarding who reports to whom. As we shall see, structure is much more than this and has important implications for entrepreneurship.

Structures are created to bring order and logic to company operations. Start-up ventures often begin with very little structure. They operate in a fairly loose and informal manner, and this means they are quite nimble. In fact, the speed and flexibility this provides is one of the major assets of small companies. However, as we saw in Chapter 1, companies evolve through life cycle stages, and the challenges of ongoing growth and increasing size make it impossible to operate efficiently or effectively without creating more formal structures. Once formalized, the structure is not static. It is continually changed as management struggles with the need to balance differentiation of activities and people against integration of activities and people. Unfortunately, structures tend to become increasingly bureaucratic as they evolve, and entrepreneurship suffers (Block and MacMillan, 1993).

In this chapter, we will examine the types of structures that develop in companies, and the ways in which they discourage entrepreneurial behavior. Alternative approaches to key structural variables will be presented, and examples of companies that have tried radical new approaches to structuring will be highlighted. Let us begin, though, with a look at the key elements that go into the structure of a company.

The Components of Structure

At the most basic level, managers attempting to design a company structure are dealing with issues of *differentiation* and *integration*. Differentiation refers to the ways decision-making authority is distributed, tasks are grouped, and people are assigned to tasks.

Integration refers to the ways in which people and functions are coordinated. The actual way in which these issues are addressed entails a whole host of decisions. Stated differently, the design of a structure includes a highly interdependent set of components. Some key questions include:

- How many levels should there be in the organization?

- What should be the targeted span of control?

- How centralized or decentralized should operations be?

- How formal or informal should structural relations be?

- Should the structure emphasize functional specialization or cross-functional interaction?

- How much of a sense of bigness versus smallness should the structure convey?

- To what extent should the structure emphasize control versus autonomy?

- How rigid versus flexible should the structure be?

- To what extent should decision making and communication be more top-down versus bottom-up?

Galbraith (1995) argues that these questions come down to four major policy areas: specialization, shape, distribution of power, and departmentalization. Specialization is concerned with the number and types of specialties to be used in performing the work of the company. More specialization means specific tasks might be performed better, but integration of these tasks into a total outcome is more difficult. If we relate this policy area to innovation, environments that produce discontinuous or dynamically continuous innovation typically require more specialization compared to those producing more continuous innovation or imitation.

Shape has to do with the number of people forming departments or areas at each hierarchical level. If there are more people per department, then fewer levels are required. More people implies a broader span of control, or number of people reporting to a given manager, while fewer levels means the organization is flatter. Flatter structures typically result in better communication and faster decision making, and are consistent with greater delegation of responsibility. Alternatively, structures that are more hierarchical tend to rely on power to settle issues rather than multilevel dialogue and debate.

Distribution of power occurs both vertically (up and down the different levels of the company structure) and horizontally (across a given level within the structure). Vertically, power can be concentrated in the higher levels of the organization, suggesting a more centralized structure, or it can be pushed down in the organization so that people at lower levels are empowered to make decisions and have discretion over how resources are used. Such decentralized structures are consistent with the encouragement of individual initiative, experimentation, and innovation. The greater the decentralization, the more the challenge becomes one of ensuring these individual efforts are consistent with the strategic direction of the company, are integrated with other initiatives and activities within the company, and are representative of more than incremental or marginally profitable advances.

Departmentalization, or the forming of people into departments, groups, or areas, occurs once an organization reaches a certain threshold size in terms of employment. People can be organized in a variety of ways, the most common of which are functions (e.g., accounting, marketing), product lines (e.g., widgets, gadgets), markets or customer segments (e.g., consumer, industrial, government), geographic regions (e.g., northern Europe, southeastern United States), or work flow processes (e.g., new product development processes, customer acquisition and maintenance processes, order processing and fulfillment processes). It is also common to use combinations of the above, such as where processes are organized around products, or where functional structures exist within geographic regions. The appropriate structure depends on the competitive circumstances (including product and market diversity), strategy, and resources of the company.

How Structures Evolve

If we look at a company when it is first started, and chart the ways in which the structure changes as the company evolves, no single pattern will exist even between two companies operating under the exact same circumstances. Nonetheless, there are some general directions that one might expect a structure to take as a company grows.

Griener (1972), in his classic work on the organizational life cycle, talks about companies evolving through stages of evolution and revolution (see Chapter 1). Structure is one of the variables that change over these stages. He suggests the initial structure is highly informal, often without formal titles or any kind of organizational chart. Subsequently, a functional structure is put in place with centralized control. Next comes a decentralized and geographically organized structure built around profit centers. This is followed by a movement toward merged product groups or strategic business units together with centralization of administrative and staff functions at head office. Then the company adopts matrix structures, cross-functional team approaches, the reassignment of head office staff to consultative teams, and process integration. Griener emphasizes a dynamic in which new structures are introduced that enable the company to effectively address emerging conditions at one point in time, but that produce side effects which ultimately require a new structural solution.

A similar picture of structural evolution is painted by Mintzberg (1979). In his schema, most organizations start with entrepreneurial structures, although a minority begin with craft structures. The craft structure is very task focused and is organized around skills; although skills are relatively standardized. There is a very limited administrative component and little supervision required, such as with a pottery studio or gasoline station. An entrepreneurial structure involves a vertical division of labor, with the entrepreneur making all the important decisions and providing direct supervision of other employees. Even so, it is a fairly informal and organic structure, with limited administrative infrastructure and no middle management. As they grow in age and size, companies implement an administrative structure (Mintzberg refers to it as bureaucratic). Intermediate levels of supervision are put in place, and the hierarchy of authority is made more elaborate. Meanwhile, a technostructure is developed in which efforts to plan and coordinate work are standardized. Thus, a distinction is drawn between designing work and supervising it. So long as the company concentrates on a few fairly related product lines, they retain the administrative structure. However, as products and markets become more diversified, the administrative structure is replaced by a divisional structure. Divisions are created as distinct entities that serve their own markets, with a head office that coordinates their activities through an impersonal performance control system. Subsequently, organizations adopt various types of matrix structure. Here, managers operate with dual or multiple reporting relationships. They may have product responsibility in a geographic region or may work both in marketing and on a major innovative project.

The evolution of structure is not as deterministic as it sounds, and many variants are possible in a given stage of a company's evolution. The transformations that occur as a company ages, grows, and diversifies include both major redesigns and ongoing adjustments. That is, structural transitions take place that represent changes in kind as well as degree. Levels are added and deleted, control is centralized and decentralized, flexibility is decreased and increased, and so forth.

The company finds that it must continually adjust the structure to reflect both external pressures (e.g., changing competitive conditions, new market structures, technological developments) and internal priorities (e.g., the need to achieve efficiencies, achieve greater coordination, improve responsiveness to the market). A company operates effectively based on a well-coordinated set of relations between structural design, company age and size, the technology of the company, and the conditions of the industry in which it operates. A move to a new stage of development typically requires the structure be redesigned, and a new set of relationships among these variables be established.

The substantive reorganizations that occur over time affect everyone in the organization. They also have important implications for entrepreneurship. The relative emphasis on entrepreneurship in a company will likely differ depending upon the structure and so will the emphasis on frequency of entrepreneurship (number of events) versus degree of entrepreneurship (level of innovativeness, risk taking, and proactiveness). Unfortunately, entrepreneurship is usually not an overriding consideration in restructuring efforts and so tends to be systematically undermined as the company evolves. Let us explore these relationships in greater detail.

Types of Structures: Links to an Entrepreneurial Strategy

A lot of attention has been paid by researchers to the fit between the external environment, the strategy of a company, and the company structure. While any number of different structures can be found in companies, some general structure types have been identified and linked to both strategy and the environment. It is generally argued that the structure of a company follows from the strategy, although examples exist of structures that, once in place, affect new strategic directions taken by the company (Chandler, 1962; Harris and Ruefli, 2000). If entrepreneurship and innovation are integral parts of the company's strategy, then inconsistencies with certain general types of structure can be problematic. For example, research indicates that organic structures, as described below, facilitate the ability of entrepreneurial strategies to enhance a company's financial performance, while mechanistic structures do not (Covin and Slevin, 1988).

Miller (1983, 1986, 1996) attempts to synthesize contemporary thinking on the strategy–structure linkage. He suggests the structure of a company can be categorized as one of the following:

- Simple Structure—Highly informal with coordination of tasks accomplished by direct supervision, and all strategies determined at the top. Little specialization of tasks exists, and there is very limited formalization in terms of programs, rules, or regulations. There is a low degree of bureaucracy, and information systems are unsophisticated. Little need exists for integrating mechanisms, and power is concentrated at the top.

- Machine Bureaucracy—A mechanistic and rigid structure in which coordination of tasks is achieved through standardization of work. The structure is hierarchical and very bureaucratic. The need to follow formal guidelines and plans is stressed. A large technostructure exists in the company to design and plan operations. Technology is somewhat automated and integrated into operations. Well-developed information systems exist, but they focus on internal reporting and output tracking rather than on market developments. Power is concentrated among top executives and those who design workflow processes, with little disseminated to middle- or lower-level management.

- Organic—Limited hierarchy and highly flexible structure. Groups of trained specialists from different work areas collaborate to design and produce complex and rapidly changing products. Emphasis is on extensive personal interaction and face-to-face communication, frequent meetings, use of committees, and other liaison devices to ensure collaboration. Power is decentralized and authority is linked to expertise. Few bureaucratic rules or standard procedures exist. Sensitive information-gathering systems are in place for anticipating and monitoring the external environment.

- Divisional—Self-contained profit centers exist for producing and marketing different product lines or groups. Divisions can differ significantly from one another in terms of their structures, with some being more organic and others more bureaucratic. There is overall pressure for divisions to conform, and for formalization and standardization of procedures and methods. While divisions tend to become more bureaucratic with time, they operate somewhat independently, with a fair amount of decision-making authority delegated to divisional managers. Control is facilitated by sophisticated management information systems. Coordination across divisions is achieved via interunit committees and a staff infrastructure at the head office.

Different types of structures are good for accomplishing particular outcomes under particular circumstances. For instance, simple structures work well in small, rapid-growth ventures operating in fragmented industries where competition is intense. Machine bureaucracies work well in stable, predicable environments and are good for producing high volumes of products and achieving efficiencies in production and distribution. Table 9-1 takes this discussion much further, specifically relating each of these

TABLE 9-1

Four General Types of Structures

Type Characteristics	Simple Structure	Machine Bureaucracy	Organic	Divisionalized
Power centralization	All at the top	CEO and designers of workflow	Scientists, technocrats, and middle managers	Divisional executives
Bureaucratization	Low, informal	Many formal rules, policies, and procedures	Organic	Bureaucratic
Specialization	Low	Extensive	Extensive	Extensive
Differentiation	Minimal	Moderate	Very high	High
Integration and coordination of effort	By CEO via direct supervision	By technocrats via formal procedures	By integrating personnel and task forces via mutual adjustment	By formal committees via plan and budgets

(Continued)

Information systems	Crude, informal	Cost controls and budgets	Informal scanning, open communication	Management information systems and profit centers
Technology	Simple, custom	Mass production, large batch/line	Sophisticated product, automated or custom	Varies
Competition	Extreme	High	Moderate	Varies
Dynamism/ uncertainty	Moderate	Very low	Very high	Varies
Growth	Varies	Slow	Rapid	Varies
Concentration ratio	Very low	High	Varies	Varies
Barriers to entry	None	Scales barriers	Knowledge barriers	Varies

	Business-Level Strategies		**Corporate-Level Strategies**	
Favored Strategy	***Niche Differentiation***	***Cost Leadership***	***Innovative Differentiation***	***Conglomeration***
Marketing emphasis	Quality, service, convenience	Low price	New products, high quality	Image
Production emphasis	Economy	Efficiency	Flexibility	Vertical integration
Asset management	Parsimony	Intensity	Parsimony	Varies
Innovation and R&D	Little	Almost none	Very high	Low to moderate
Product-market scope	Very narrow	Average	Average	Very broad

SOURCE: Adapted from D. Miller, "Configurations of Strategy and Structure: Towards a Synthesis," *Strategic Management Journal*, 7(3), 1986: 233–249. © John Wiley & Sons Limited. Reproduced with permission.

prototypes of structure to the type of environmental conditions under which the structure is most productive, and to the types of corporate strategies that tend to be most appropriate. While the table demonstrates logical linkages, it is not intended as an exhaustive summary of the possible sets of relationships that can work effectively.

The configuration of structure, strategy, and environmental conditions should be guided by a theme. Such a theme can capture the vision of senior management, unique organizational competencies, a competitive advantage, or core elements of the company culture. Clearly, entrepreneurship represents a potential theme. Miller (1996, p. 507) notes, "The aspirations of a CEO intent on technological leadership may, for example, produce a strategy of focused R&D, a think-tank culture, and an organic culture."

Let us further explore the role structure plays in accommodating, or inhibiting, innovative behavior. Innovation requires creative thinking and collaboration. A personal sense of empowerment and room to maneuver are important. Innovation necessitates a level of flexibility in terms of resource utilization and time horizons. Quick decisions are often required during the innovative process, and decision making is both rational and instinctual. Champions and team members must be able to span boundaries within the organization. Innovation is also a communication-intensive activity, including both extensive lateral and vertical communication, much of which is informal and unplanned. Other requirements include ongoing experimentation and adaptation of the concept or idea.

Not surprisingly, then, major innovation is most likely under structures that most closely mimic the organic structure. Both high degree and frequency of entrepreneurship are consistent with this type of structure. Conversely, the lowest levels of entrepreneurial intensity are likely with machine bureaucracies, or mechanistic structures. Extensive hierarchy and bureaucracy are inconsistent with unstructured problem solving. People are more compartmentalized, which limits communication and encourages resistance to change. Ideas that do not emerge from formal processes and with proper documentation are often ignored. Pursuing multiple and alternative paths to the realization of an entrepreneurial concept is discouraged. Such structures demand fixed over flexible goals and well-defined over fluid processes.

Between these two endpoints lie the simple and the divisional structures. The simple structure allows for speed and flexibility. Incremental or continuous innovation is likely if the CEO drives it. At the same time, it is too primitive, undifferentiated, and centralized to support complex innovation. The reliance on simple technologies further limits the likelihood of discontinuous and even dynamically continuous innovation. These characteristics suggest that the degree of entrepreneurship will be low under such structures, and the frequency of entrepreneurship will be low to moderate. Where divisional structures are employed, corporate strategies tend to be the least focused, and the implications for innovative activity are least apparent. As divisions themselves can differ in the extent to which their individual structures are organic or mechanistic, levels of entrepreneurship are likely to vary among different divisions. For this reason, it is important to track levels of entrepreneurial intensity over time, and compare these levels among divisions (see Chapter 13). If the divisional structures tend to become more mechanistic over time, especially where the head office emphasizes measures for standardization and conformity among divisions, degree and frequency of entrepreneurship will suffer. Further, because divisions tend to be built around product lines, markets, and/or geographic regions, they are more likely to produce incremental improvements rather than new-product break-throughs. They tend to be preoccupied with improving and extending current product lines and with better satisfying the expressed needs and wants of the current customer base. Bold moves that redefine the market and reinvent the industry are generally incom-patible with the performance objectives and reward systems of established divisions. The head office, which coordinates the various divisions, may be focused on diversification moves, but it is often diversification through acquisition. The implication is that fre-quency of entrepreneurship will vary considerably among divisions, and degree of entre-preneurship will be low to moderate.

When a company has a divisional structure (and especially if the company is orga-nized as a machine bureaucracy), significant innovation may require separate structures (separate from mainstream divisions) such as the New Ventures Division at Procter & Gamble or the Xerox New Enterprises unit. A subsequent problem arises, however, in that innovations that come out of these separate units are often resisted or given luke-warm support by mainstream divisions. The "not invented here" mindset prevails, with the mainstream division feeling it is inheriting an unwanted offspring. Success rates are greater if mainstream divisions endorse and take ownership of projects in the separate venture units at inception.

Innovation also affects structure itself, with a number of new and untested structural designs appearing in contemporary organizations (Pettigrew and Fenton, 2000). These new company designs are especially conducive to entrepreneurship. Examples include network, cellular, and virtual structures. Let us consider network structures, which are a logical outgrowth of the growing reliance on outsourcing, subcontracting, strategic alli-ances, and joint ventures (each of which is, parenthetically, a vehicle for achieving inno-vation). Network structures facilitate new knowledge development and allow companies to leverage their market presence. They can also produce efficiencies in terms of asset uti-lization. Network approaches entail high degrees of integration across formal boundaries between organizations and units. Pettigrew and Fenton (2000) describe the case of Ove Arup, a large global engineering and consultancy firm. The company was formerly orga-nized around 50 independent units reporting to a main board. As pictured in Figure 9-1, the corporate board has been redefined as a policy board, with five operating boards be-neath it, and with business operations carried out by groups reporting to one of the oper-ating boards. The groups are organized according to technical, business, or geographic interests and are aligned into networks. In fact, two kinds of networks run horizontally across groups, skill networks and market networks. They link specialists throughout the company. Strategy and functional committees exist to provide horizontal links at the

FIGURE 9-1

The Network Structure at Ove Arup

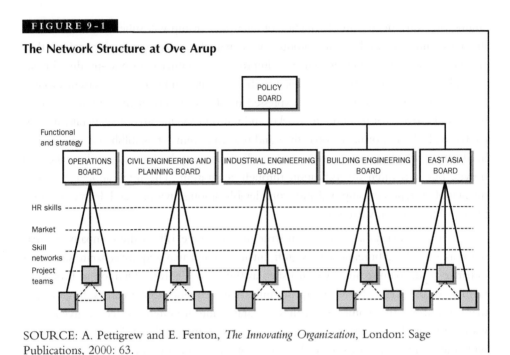

SOURCE: A. Pettigrew and E. Fenton, *The Innovating Organization*, London: Sage Publications, 2000: 63.

board level. Staff are assigned to particular project teams at a central level by networking through the group leaders. A specific objective in moving to this type of structure was to achieve company-wide innovation.

Another example of experimentation with structure can be found at Saab Training Systems, a unit within Saab that provides computer-aided training equipment for military purposes (Mullern, 2000). Saab adopted a team-based structure after formerly relying on a hierarchical, functional structure. The objective was flexibility. Over 40 teams were created, with each reporting to the managing director and management team (a total of two hierarchical levels). When teams exceed a size of eight or so, they split into two teams. The team-based approach is designed around basic business processes, with five different types of teams (see Figure 9-2). For instance, business teams are responsible for one or more products and one or more geographic areas. They have overall responsibility for each customer contract. Delivery teams handle logistics for each order, and product teams take care of design and production activities in a project. The mix of teams involved in an order is dissolved once the final project is delivered to the customer. While there is a sequential nature to some of the team activities, the reality is that the teams are highly interdependent. Yet the desire is to have teams operating almost as individual companies with a high degree of operational freedom and responsibility for innovative product and process development.

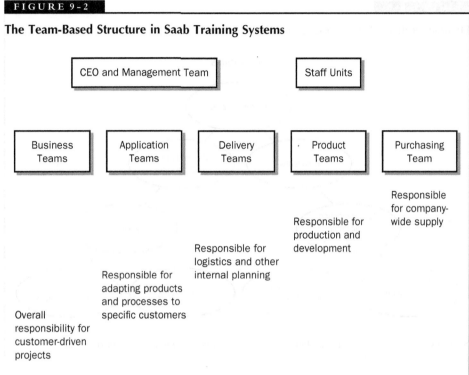

FIGURE 9-2

The Team-Based Structure in Saab Training Systems

SOURCE: T. Mullern, "Integrating the Team-Based Structure in the Business Process: The Case of Saab Training Systems," in A. Pettigrew and E. Fenton, eds., *The Innovating Organization*, London: Sage Publications, 2000: 248.

An increasingly popular term is the *boundaryless* organization. General Electric has emphasized this notion (Amernic et al., 2007). Eliminating boundaries is actually a component of most of the innovative approaches to structuring discussed earlier. The idea is to take people out of boxes and eliminate artificial barriers that slow things down and create pockets of resistance to change. Boundaries are eliminated both within the organization and between the organization and key outside players. The major external boundary-related changes in companies include: the outsourcing of key functions; greater use of strategic alliances with suppliers, distributors, and other companies; and reductions in how diversified companies are (Pettigrew and Fenton, 2000). Boundaries are eliminated in many ways, ranging from collaborative R&D efforts to the linking of two organizations via an Internet-based electronic data interchange. Some companies are going much further with such linkages, such as PPG Industries, which has moved from selling paint to General Motors to running the customer's entire painting operation.

FIGURE 9-3

Elements Reflected in New Organizational Forms

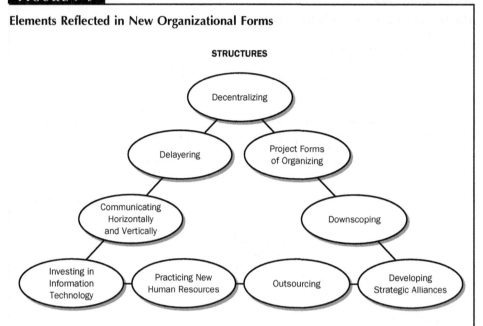

SOURCE: A. Pettigrew and E. Fenton, *The Innovating Organization*, London: Sage Publications, 2000: 38.

Experimentation with different organizational designs is increasingly the norm in larger companies. Pettigrew and Fenton (2000) see companies experimenting not only with their structures, but also in two closely related areas: processes and boundaries. Figure 9-3 captures many of the principal variables receiving managerial attention. Structural changes such as delayering (removing layers of hierarchy) and decentralization (removing central control) are accompanied by process changes, including the ways horizontal units communicate and interact, the integration of new information technology capabilities, and reliance on new types of human resource management practices (in such areas as job design, use of contract labor, and so forth). Changing boundaries occur as the company relies on outsourcing, strategic alliances, and other methods for linking internal operations to external organizations.

Perhaps the overriding consideration as companies struggle to find the right structure is the level of turbulence in the external environment. That is, regardless of the type of structure currently in place, as environments become more dynamic, threatening, and complex, organizations find that competitive survival forces them to become more entrepreneurial. This, in turn, means they must find ways to move the company toward more organic structures.

An Entrepreneurial Structure and the Concept of Cycling

So what is a truly entrepreneurial structure? The answer will vary depending on the size, age, products, markets, processes, and technologies of a company. This reality suggests that a company's structure must be subject to continual experimentation and change. Further, there is an art to designing an entrepreneurial structure, as many of the conventional rules of organizational design must be abandoned (see Table 9-2) for

---

TABLE 9-2

Twenty Structure-Related Suggestions for Innovation

1. Insist on a maximum of two levels of management between the bottom and top in any division-size unit.

2. Most business can be done in independent operating units of 250 or fewer people (with their own boards of directors, including outsiders): Reorganize accordingly within the next 18 months.

3. Within the next nine months, eliminate ALL first-line supervisors.

4. Within the next year, transfer one-third of all staffers at the division level or above to customer-focused operating units (of 250 or fewer people—see No. 2) and then transfer another one-third the following year.

5. Within four years, reduce corporate staff to a maximum of ten people per billion dollars in revenue (and no squirreling away "temporary assignees" stolen from divisions).

6. Require remaining members of all "central" (corporate, division) staffs to sell their services to line units at market rates; allow those line units, in turn, to buy any and all services from anybody, anywhere.

7. Destroy all organization charts. Now.

8. All top division/corporate managers: Pledge two days per month to customer visits and two days per month to supplier and distributor visits. Visit, in depth, at least three "neat" companies per year (*outside your industry*).

9. Aim for one-third employee ownership of the corporation within five years.

10. Chief executive officers and division general managers: Within the next 12 months, promote to a position of significant responsibility at least one rabble rouser who doesn't like you or agree with you (on much of anything).

11. Insist that no one serves on a strategic planning staff for more than 24 months. (Twenty-five percent of all strategy staff members should have worked for a customer or competitor.)

12. Make sure all work teams are largely self-contained, encompassing almost all functional skills within their confines.

13. Allow the CEO to sit on a maximum of one outside board.

14. Vacate all facilities more than three stories high.

15. Within 24 months, end all physical segregation of functional departments.

(Continued)

TABLE 9-2	(Continued)

Twenty Structure-Related Suggestions for Innovation

16. At all off-site meetings, make sure that at least 25 percent of all attendees are "outsiders" (customers, vendors, etc.).

17. In companies with at least $250 million in revenue, create corporate vice president positions for the following: knowledge management, perceived quality and brand-equity management, innovation, industrial design, horizontal systems integration, cycle-time management. (Incumbents will each be supported by a one-person professional staff max.)

18. Within four years, at least one-third of division-level chiefs should be 32 or younger.

19. Within 24 months, make sure you have at least one non-U.S. board member (companies of $50 million to $1 billion). Companies over $1 billion should have 25 percent non-U.S. board members within four years.

20. Let no senior manager have an office of more than 225 square feet.

SOURCE: From *The Circle of Innovation* by Tom Peters, Copyright © 1997 by Excel/ A California Partnership. Used by permission of Alfred A. Knopf, a division of Random House, Inc.

examples of unconventional approaches). Galbraith (1995, p. 6) explains, "Organizational designs that facilitate variety, change, and speed are sources of competitive advantage. These designs are difficult to execute and copy because they are intricate blends of many different design policies." However, if we return to the earlier set of questions that must be addressed when designing a structure (i.e., number of levels, span of control, etc.), there are some basic principles to guide the design process.

We believe entrepreneurship flourishes where there are fewer layers or levels in the structure of a company. Further, spans of control are broader. The general orientation is toward a more horizontal and less vertical design. Decentralization and empowerment are the watchwords in terms of operations, while clear vision and strategic direction come from the top. At the same time, the dominant direction in terms of the flow of ideas is bottom-up, not top-down. The structure also emphasizes simplicity and smallness within a large enterprise by employing such devices as pseudo-autonomous units, companies within companies, or empowered teams. Cross-functional interaction and cooperation are priorities, but the clash of ideas from inter-functional interaction is also encouraged. Vehicles are put in place to facilitate extensive and rapid communication among parties at all levels and in all functions. There is less formalization of roles and positions within the structure. Empowerment efforts are not token or random, but are designed to be systematic and consistent. Staff functions are kept lean.

Slevin and Covin (1990) propose some additional elements (see also Table 9-3). They argue that a company's entrepreneurial behavior correlates positively with company performance when the organizational structure has the following:

1. Managers allowed to freely vary their operating styles

2. Authority that is assigned based on the expertise of the individual

TABLE 9-3

Other Elements of Mechanistic versus Organic Organizational Structure

Organic Structure	*Mechanistic Structure*
1. Channels of Communication Open with free flow of information throughout the organization	**1. Channels of Communication** Highly structured, restricted information flow
2. Operating Styles Allowed to vary freely	**2. Operating Styles** Must be uniform and restricted
3. Authority for Decisions Based on expertise of the individual	**3. Authority for Decisions** Based on formal line management position
4. Free Adaptation By the organization to changing circumstances	**4. Reluctant Adaptation** With insistence on holding fast to tried-and-true management principles despite changes in business conditions
5. Emphasis on Getting Things Done Unconstrained by formally laid out procedures	**5. Emphasis on Formally Laid Down Procedures** Reliance on tried-and-true management principles
6. Loose, Informal Control With emphasis on norm of cooperation	**6. Tight Control** Through sophisticated control systems
7. Flexible On-Job Behavior Permitted to be shaped by the requirements of the situation and personality of the individual doing the job	**7. Constrained On-Job Behavior** Required to conform to job descriptions
8. Participation and Group Consensus Used Frequently	**8. Superiors Make Decisions with Minimum Consultation and Involvement of Subordinates**

SOURCE: Reprinted from D. P. Slevin and J. G. Covin, "Juggling Entrepreneurial Style and Organizational Structure—How to Get Your Act Together," *MIT Sloan Management Review*, 31(2), 1990: p. 44, by permission of the publisher. Copyright © 1990, by Massachusetts Institute of Technology. All rights reserved.

3. Free adaptation of the organization to changing circumstances

4. An emphasis on results rather than processes or procedures

5. Loose, informal controls with an emphasis on a norm of cooperation

6. Flexible on-the-job behavior, shaped by requirements of situation and personality of the employee

7. Frequent use of participation and group consensus

8. Open channels of communication with free flow of information.

The proper blend of decision variables will not guarantee entrepreneurship will occur, nor will an inappropriate blend ensure it does not. However, the appropriate structural design can go a long way toward influencing the types of innovations that are produced and the frequency with which they are produced on a consistent basis over time. Further, and building upon the earlier discussion, the following linkages should be kept in mind:

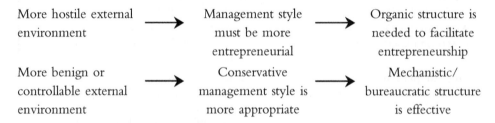

The work of Slevin and Covin (1990) also helps explain patterns that occur in companies over time. As illustrated in Figure 9-4, there is a need to achieve fit between management style (the relative emphasis on entrepreneurship) and organization structure (more organic versus mechanistic). Thus, a good fit exists with an organic structure and an emphasis on entrepreneurial management, producing an effective entrepreneurial company (Cell 1 of Figure 9-4). Similarly, a good fit exists between conservative managerial orientation and a mechanistic structure, resulting in an efficient bureaucratic organization (Cell 3). Organizations are much more problematic when the structure and management style are inconsistent, as in Cells 2 and 4.

An especially intriguing notion is the concept of *cycling*. Here, the successful company is able to move back and forth, or cycle, between Cells 1 and 3 of Figure 9-4. The inference is that companies move through periods of stability and conservatism and periods of innovation and change. Thus, the company may start out as a highly entrepreneurial organization, but growth may create a need for controls, formalization of procedures, and the addition of hierarchy, indicating a move from Cell 1 to Cell 3. Over time, the Cell 3 company builds more bureaucracy and can become stagnant. A need arises to reinvigorate the company with new ideas, research insights, and

Entrepreneurial Leadership, Structure, and the Concept of Cycling

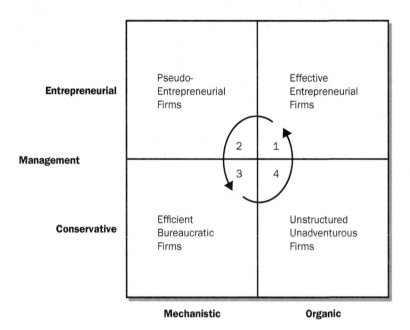

SOURCE: Reprinted from D. P. Slevin and J. G. Covin, "Juggling Entrepreneurial Style and Organizational Structure—How to Get Your Act Together," *MIT Sloan Management Review*, 31(2), 1990, p. 44, by permission of the publisher. Copyright © 1990, by Massachusetts Institute of Technology. All rights reserved.

innovation, suggesting a need to shift back to Cell 1. And the cycle continues. Obviously, some companies cannot make such transitions without severe disruption. Some get caught in Cells 2 and 4, where external forces might have created a determination among managers to be entrepreneurial, but without the necessary changes being made to the structure of the company, so that it remains fundamentally mechanistic. The result can be a dysfunctional company. Changes, if they are to be successful, must occur on both dimensions simultaneously.

Significantly, the phenomenon of cycling recognizes that organic structures and mechanistic structures can each facilitate the accomplishment of certain tasks required for successful innovation. In particular, organic structures are well suited to the recognition and initial pursuit of innovative opportunities, whereas mechanistic structures are better suited to the execution of established innovative projects (Duncan, 1976). Thus, through cycling, the company is able to align its structural form with the phase-related requirements of the innovation process. This is not to suggest that cycling is always an optimal approach to the management of innovation. For example, cycling may be better suited to the management of innovation among companies operating in environments characterized by large and infrequent product-market or technological changes than among firms operating in environments characterized by continuous and incremental product-market or technological changes (Ahuja et al., 2008). This is because, for example, companies may suffer from de-emphasizing entrepreneurial initiatives and escalating their commitment to efficiency-seeking in environments calling for continuous innovation. Additionally, structural change can be difficult and painful to execute on a regular basis, so the need to frequently redesign structure such that the firm can keep up with the pace of innovation in a constantly changing environment will be an unpalatable option for companies operating in such environments.

A different take on organizing for innovation might find management attempting to create parallel structures and management styles within the organization. Consistent with the concept of the "ambidextrous organization" (see Chapter 12), the efficient and conservative manager and a mechanistic style may be appropriate for certain key parts of the business (e.g., processing insurance claims in a large insurance company), while organic structures with entrepreneurial management are applied in units charged with new product and market development.

It should also be remembered that structures are usually designed and modified in reaction to some strategic need in the company. Management sees a need to reduce costs, eliminate duplication of effort, achieve greater coordination, or bring more speed to core aspects of operations. Unless the encouragement of entrepreneurial behavior is an explicit objective when redesigning the structure, the probability is great that entrepreneurship will actually suffer under whatever structure is implemented.

Structures to Support New Product/Service Development Projects

A different structural question concerns how companies organize people around the new product or service development process. This requires a structure that not only gets the right inputs into the process at the right time, but also facilitates both creative abrasion and cross-functional collaboration. The goal is also to get employees to take ownership of a project, getting as many people as possible believing that they invented the product or service. Empirical studies of the new product development process reveal that five individual- and organization-related factors are consistently related to new product success: (1) a cross-functional new product development team; (2) a strong and responsible project leader; (3) a new product development team with responsibility for the entire project; (4) the commitment of the project leader and the team members to the new product development project; and (5) intensive communication among team members during the course of the new product development process (Ernst, 2002, p. 14).

A host of structural challenges surround new product development. Who should be involved in which projects, at what stages or points in the projects, in what capacity, accountable for what deliverables, and evaluated on what criteria? Who will play the role of champion for a given project, and how can different champions be identified, motivated, and compensated? How does the company achieve trust, openness, communication, cooperation, and team spirit among departments and among key managers in so far as innovation activities are concerned?

Many structural options are available for addressing these challenges. Table 9-4 provides a synopsis of 10 different structural approaches used by companies to produce

TABLE 9-4

Structures for Product/Service Development

Type of Organizational Structure	Description	Advantage(s)	Disadvantage(s)
New product division	Large and self-sufficient division	Centralized coordination and control	Coordination with other divisions
		Top management attention assured	Inflexibility due to size
		Resources adequate Long-term commitment	Opportunity for vested interests
New product department	Department within division	Specialization Integration of efforts	Few resources Less authority
New product manager	One manager who is responsible for a new product	Simplicity	Can overwhelm one manager Cooperation from others difficult

(Continued)

| TABLE 9-4 | (Continued) |

Structures for Product/Service Development

Type of Organizational Structure	Description	Advantage(s)	Disadvantage(s)
Product or brand manager	New product responsibility added to normal duties	Best for line extensions or modifications	Not suited to truly innovative products Manger torn between regular and new product duties
New product committee	Standing committee with diverse representation	Several functional areas involved	Dilutes responsibility across members
Cross-functional project team	New product group set up for the duration of a project	Flexible, fluid, involves diverse perspectives	Often hard to get functional department support
Task force or ad hoc committee	Temporary matrix approach	Tap specialized managers on full-time or part-time basis	Multiple demands placed on group members
Venture team	Internal as well as external personnel used	Brings in outsiders' expertise	May garner resources greater than the worth of the project
Outside suppliers	Contract with another company to develop product	Utilizes specialists for independent work	Can be costly Coordination and control problems
Multiple organization forms	Use of hybrid forms depending on nature of project	Form designed to fit needs of the project	Difficulties in managing, coordinating, and evaluating the efforts of several unique structural forms

new products and services. When deciding which of these to use, management is effectively deciding the extent to which the structure is more:

- Simple versus Complex

- Centralized versus Decentralized

- Formal versus Informal

- Autonomous versus Integrated
- Highly Specialized versus More Generalist
- Full-time versus Part-time

Thus, as one moves from the traditional R&D department to a new product committee to a cross-functional team, the structure becomes more complex, authority becomes more decentralized, and rules and processes become more informal. At the same time, unit autonomy becomes greater, and the group of people working on the project is more specialized. It is also likely, as one moves across these three structural alternatives, that decision making and conflict resolution become less hierarchical and more participative. Information will flow more vertically than horizontally, and information sharing is likely to increase.

Companies today are experimenting with new structures essentially on a trial-and-error basis. Much remains to be learned about what works and why. It appears that the effectiveness of a given approach depends upon the type of innovation activity undertaken. For instance, venture teams are more likely to produce disruptive innovations and to do so on a fairly timely basis. Product managers can be expected to come up with line extensions or minor modifications of existing products. The greatest trend appears to be toward the use of multiple structural forms. Page (1993) reported that, while multidisciplinary teams are by far the most widely used organizing structures for new product development efforts, better than half of the companies he surveyed were using multiple forms, such as a cross-functional team and a new products department or new products manager. Other evidence suggests that the degree of fit between the innovative team or venture and the mainstream organization affects the success of innovations. That is, regardless of the particular structural form, success is more likely where there are high levels of awareness, commitment, and connection between the venture unit and the corporate parent (Thornhill and Amit, 2001).

Entrepreneurial Projects: Structures within Structures

As previously suggested, entrepreneurial projects require structures themselves. A key issue concerns how project structures fit within the overall organizational structure. Table 9-4 summarizes some of the popular ways that companies organize units or teams to manage innovation projects. However, there is another consideration. Much happens along the way as an entrepreneurial concept goes from a loose idea to a formal project with an assigned team and budget. The company needs a mechanism that reflects the evolutionary nature of entrepreneurial events inside the organization.

We recommend that companies adopt an approach wherein innovation opportunities are produced through three different internal channels or structural mechanisms.

TABLE 9-5

The Entrepreneurial Project Development Framework

Characteristic	"Ray of Light" ⟶ Projects	"Emerging Potential" ⟶ Projects	"Mainstream Development" ⟶ Projects
Project financing	No budget	Seed capital	Formal budget
Management approval	Not approved	Approved by Opportunity Review Board	Approved by senior management/ directors
Supportive research	Exploratory research	Formal market research	Extensive industry, competitive, and customer intelligence
Process followed	Early conceptualizing	Concept refinement/ prototype testing	Formal New Product Development process
Initiator/leader	Driven by initiator/anyone in company	Champion-assigned (20%–30% of his/her time)	Driven by new products manager and integrated team
Degree of project risk	Low to medium	Medium	Medium to high
Period of development	Short	Medium	Medium to high
Innovativeness	Low to medium	Medium to high	Medium to high
Outcomes	Produces short (3–5 pages) concept plan	Produces formal business plan	Results in launch or gets canned

Each of these is described in Table 9-5, in what we have labeled the Entrepreneurial Project Development Framework.

Under this framework, opportunities can be pursued as either "ray of light" projects, "emerging potential" projects, or "mainstream development" projects. Ray of light projects are bootstrapped, meaning resources are obtained in clever, creative, and informal ways. An employee (any employee) has an idea and is encouraged to pursue it. He or she begs or borrows resources, pursues the idea in his or her free time, and is concerned with formulating the concept or core value proposition and with demonstrating the existence and size of a market for the idea. The end product is a short business concept plan that can be sold to management. Management then decides whether to defer, or pass, on the ray of light project, approve it as an emerging potential project, or make it a mainstream development project.

Emerging potential projects (which might have begun as either ray of light or emerging potential projects) involve concepts that are brought to some type of review committee, which we shall call the Opportunities Review Board. The makeup of this board might include a mix of levels of management and functional expertise, with members regularly rotating off and on. Special expertise might be added to deal with certain projects. The board members review and approve proposals from employees and are able to allocate seed capital to projects up to some fixed amount. They can also endorse the employee as champion (or assign someone else) and free up 20 to 30 percent of the champion's work time for his or her pursuit of that project. The seed capital is used for research, staff assistance, and related expenses. The end product is a formal business plan that is submitted to the directors. If approved, the emerging potential project becomes a mainstream development project.

Mainstream development projects are where the new product, service, and process efforts that have been prioritized by senior management are developed. A formal budget is allocated, and some sort of structure is in place (e.g., a cross-functional new product team is assigned to the project, or a venture team is put together). A systematic process is followed with key performance benchmarks monitored after each major stage. Extensive intelligence is gathered. The end product is typically a major product launch, although it is anticipated that some of these projects may still be terminated or dropped along the way.

The benefits of having three mechanisms for generating innovation are many. First, much more innovation is likely to result. This approach is consistent with the goal of facilitating innovation of all types on an ongoing basis throughout the organization. It encourages a portfolio of innovation projects, helping the company balance full-scale development activities by having both high-risk, high-return and low-risk, moderate-return projects. Second, innovation is clearly being defined as a corporate-wide task, not R&D in isolation. Third, the likelihood of inter-functional involvement and coordination is much greater. Fourth, employees are more likely to take responsibility for innovation, champions are more likely to emerge, and accountability will not just be for design but also for implementation. Finally, ray of light and emerging potential approaches bring more flexibility and speed to the innovation process and will most likely cost less money than relying solely on a mainstream development for every new product.

An important consideration regarding the existence of project structures within organization structures is the question of how much planning autonomy should be granted by corporate-level managers to project leaders. Specifically, should corporate- or project-level managers be responsible for tasks such as setting the innovation project's goals, establishing a timetable for the achievement of those goals, choosing the formal criteria used to measure the project's performance, identifying the event milestones used to assess the project's progress, and formulating the project's commercialization or business strategy? Recent research by Garrett and Covin (2009), in which the projects of interest were internal corporate ventures, revealed that planning autonomy—that is, placing planning-related responsibility in the hands of project-level managers—is positively associated with project performance. However, such autonomy was more positively related to the performance of internal corporate ventures when those ventures offered products dissimilar to those of the corporate parent's other businesses. As such, autonomy appears to be most helpful to project performance when higher-level corporate managers do not possess pertinent product-related knowledge that might facilitate project success.

Structuring Relationships between Entrepreneurial Initiatives and the Corporation: Some Organization Design Alternatives

The question of how companies can be structured to support entrepreneurship should also consider more fundamental issues. Two key issues include determining (a) whether a given entrepreneurial initiative should be part of an organization's internal structure (or developed externally) and (b) if it is part of the internal structure, which type(s) of structural design to employ. Burgelman (1984) proposed a useful framework for determining how the relationships between entrepreneurial initiatives and their corporate contexts should be structured. Burgelman's thesis is that appropriate designs for entrepreneurial initiatives should be chosen in consideration of those initiatives' strategic importance to the corporation and their operational relatedness to the core capabilities of the corporation. In assessing *strategic importance*, managers should focus on questions such as the following:

- Is the initiative consistent with the corporation's existing scope of business operations?

- Can the initiative be employed to transition the corporation to new and more attractive business domains?

- Does the initiative create options for the corporation to move in new strategic directions where the attractiveness of these new directions is currently unknown?

- Will the initiative potentially enhance the corporation's competitiveness in its chosen product-market domains or favorably reposition the corporation within those domains?

Operational relatedness is assessed by asking questions such as the following:

- To what extent does the initiative's success likely require the acquisition of product-, technology-, or market-related knowledge not currently possessed by the corporation?

- Are the functional area activities (e.g., marketing, production) to be performed within the initiative complementary and closely linked to those of one or more of the corporation's existing businesses?

- Do the corporation's core competencies provide a basis for strategic advantage in the industry arena targeted by the initiative?

- Can the corporation transfer strategically relevant resources and capabilities from current operations to the initiative?

According to Burgelman (1984), an initiative's strategic importance has implications for the degree to which corporate management needs to maintain greater control over development of the entrepreneurial initiative. An initiative's operational relatedness has implications for the degree of efficiency attainable when managing both current operations and the entrepreneurial initiative.

The result of the preceding assessments is the ability to classify any entrepreneurial project into one of three categories of strategic importance—very important, uncertain, and not important—and into one of three categories of operational relatedness—strongly related, partly related, and unrelated. The initiative is then positioned within the organization design alternatives grid, shown in Figure 9-5, based on these assessments.

FIGURE 9-5

Organization Designs for Corporate Entrepreneurship

Operational Relatedness		Very Important	Uncertain	Not Important
	Unrelated	Special Business Units	Independent Business Units	Complete Spin Off
	Partly Related	New Product/Business Department	New Venture Division	Contracting
	Strongly Related	Direct Integration	Micro New Ventures Department	Nurturing and Contracting

Strategic Importance

SOURCE: Adapted from R. A. Burgelman, "Designs for Corporate Entrepreneurship in Established Firms," *California Management Review*, 46(3), 1984: 154–166. Copyright © 1984, by the Regents of the University of California. Reprinted from the *California Management Review*, Vol. 26, No. 3. By permission of The Regents.

Nine distinct design possibilities are suggested. A corporation is not limited to the use of one of these designs. Rather, the company could employ as many of them as is warranted by the diversity of their entrepreneurial initiatives. The possible organization designs or structures include:

- *Direct integration* (high strategic importance, strong operational relatedness): The entrepreneurial initiative is pursued within the mainstream operations of the corporation.

- *New product/business department* (high strategic importance, partial operational relatedness): A separate department for the entrepreneurial initiative is created in that part of the corporation (division or group) where significant potential exists for sharing capabilities and skills.

- *Separate business units* (high strategic importance, low operational relatedness): A specially dedicated and operationally distinct unit is created inside the corporate structure to house the entrepreneurial initiative.

- *Micro new ventures department* (uncertain strategic importance, strong operational relatedness): An organizational unit is created where autonomously emerging entrepreneurial initiatives are pursued without the constraint of currently having to fit with the corporation's strategy.

- *New venture division* (uncertain strategic importance, partial operational relatedness): An organizational division is designed to house a wide range of potentially interesting entrepreneurial initiatives that are of ambiguous fit with the corporation.

- *Independent business units* (uncertain strategic importance, low operational relatedness): A specially dedicated and operationally distinct unit is created outside the corporate structure to house the entrepreneurial initiative.

- *Nurturing plus contracting* (low strategic importance, strong operational relatedness): The corporation's knowledge and competencies are leveraged in entrepreneurial initiatives that are moved outside the corporate structure (e.g., outsourcing some part of the entrepreneurial project) and in which that knowledge or those competencies constitute strategic assets for the initiative.

- *Contracting* (low strategic importance, partial operational relatedness): The corporation's knowledge and competencies are leveraged in entrepreneurial initiatives that are moved outside the corporate structure (by contracting to some outside organization) and in which that knowledge or those competencies add some value to the initiative's operations.

- *Complete spin off* (low strategic importance, low operational relatedness): The total separation of the entrepreneurial initiative from the corporation.

Thus, a key premise of Burgelman's (1984) design alternatives framework is that not all entrepreneurial initiatives are the same, and this fact must be reflected in the specific attributes of the structures employed to house those initiatives. A one–size–fits–all mentality with respect to structuring for entrepreneurship won't work.

THE INNOVATOR'S NOTEBOOK

The Signode V-Team Structure

Venture teams offer corporations the opportunity to capitalize on individual talents together with collective wisdom and energy. A classic example from some years back was Signode, a $750-million-a-year manufacturer of plastic and steel strapping for packaging and materials handling, located in Glenview, Illinois. The company's leaders wanted to chart new directions to become a $1-billion-plus company. In pursuit of this goal, Signode devised an aggressive strategy for growth by developing new "legs" for the company. It formed a corporate development group to pursue markets outside the company's core business but within the framework of its corporate strengths. It also formed venture teams, but before launching the first of these, top management identified the company's global business strengths and broad areas with potential for new product lines: warehousing/shipping; packaging; plastics for non-packaging, fastening, and joining systems; and product identification and control systems.

Each new business opportunity suggested by a venture team was to have the potential to generate $50 million in business within five years. In addition, each opportunity had to build on one of Signode's strengths: industrial customer base and marketing expertise, systems sales and service capabilities, containment and reinforcement technology, steel and plastic process technology, machine and design capabilities, and production and distribution know-how. The assessment criteria were based on selling to business-to-business markets. The basic technology to be employed in the new business had to already exist, and there had to be a strong likelihood of attaining a major market share within a niche. Finally, the initial investment in the new opportunity had to be $30 million or less.

Based on these criteria, Signode began to build its V-Team (venture team) approach to entrepreneurship. It took three months to select the first team members, and initial teams had three common traits: high risk-taking ability, creativity, and the ability to deal with ambiguity. All participants were multidisciplinary volunteers who would work full-time on developing new consumer product packaging businesses. The team members came from diverse back-grounds: design engineering, marketing, sales, and product development. They set up shop in rented office space five miles from the company's headquarters. Not all six teams were able to develop highly successful new ventures. However, the efforts did pay off for Signode as one venture team developed a business plan to manufacture plastic trays for frozen entrees that could be used in either regular or microwave ovens, which did indeed turn out to be a $50-million-a-year business within five years. The V-Team experience rekindled enthusiasm and affected moral throughout the organization. Most importantly, the V-Team approach became Signode's strategy to invent its own future rather than waiting for things to happen.

Discussion Questions

1. How does Signode's structure compare to the general types of structures presented in Table 9-1?

2. What is the essence of the V-Team concept that makes it a component of the structures outlined in Table 9-4?

3. Compare Signode's approach to venture development with the organiza-tional design alternatives presented at the end of the chapter.

SOURCE: Adapted from Donald F. Kuratko, Entrepreneurship: Theory, Process, Practice (Mason, OH: Cengage/Southwestern, 2009); Mark Forhman and Perry Pascarella, "Achieving Purpose-Driven Innovation," *Industry Week March 19, 1990: 20–26, and personal interview, 2006.*

Summary and Conclusions

We use the term *structure* to describe the formal ways in which a company organizes people and tasks. Entrepreneurship requires structure, but is often a victim of the types of structural arrangements created in companies. Companies create structures to man-age the existing demands of the business. Entrepreneurship is about creating new things and moving in new directions. As a result, entrepreneurial efforts almost always chal-lenge and often conflict with the structure currently in place.

In this chapter, we have explored the underlying elements that go into the structure of a company as well as some of the more prevalent types of structures that can be found in modern organizations. We have looked at ways in which structures evolve and how entrepreneurship is systematically constrained as the structure evolves. In general, we have argued that entrepreneurship is facilitated under structures that are more organic in nature. A number of guiding principles were proposed to help make the structure more consistent with continuous entrepreneurship.

It was also emphasized that the structure of a company must be continually recreated. In essence, the structure that works today is likely to demonstrate significant inadequacies 18 months from now. A complex mix of variables determines the appropriate structure for a company, and those variables are subject to ongoing change. This brings us to an important caveat: structure is a matter of balance (Hamel and Prahalad, 1994). Empowerment without direction results in anarchy. Having a hundred independent businesses within one large organization can result in lots of wasted resources and missed opportunities unless the linkages among these units are exploited. Similarly, organizations must balance lean and flexible aspects of the organization against the need for administrative controls and some level of bureaucracy in other areas of the company. They must balance a customer focus against a technological focus.

Structure can be an important facilitator of entrepreneurship because it can give employees a sense that they have room to maneuver and innovate while also allowing their interaction with others in the organization. It can help accommodate a larger volume of entrepreneurial initiatives and also facilitate the speed at which such initiatives move from inception to implementation. Yet structure does not work in isolation. Its ability to contribute to a more entrepreneurship-friendly environment is a function of interactions between structural elements and other organizational variables. One of the most important of these other variables is the company control system, a subject that we discuss in Chapter 14.

References

Ahuja, G., Lampert, C. M., and Tandon, V. 2008. "Moving Beyond Schumpeter: Management Research on the Determinants of Technological Innovation," *The Academy of Management Annals*, 2(1): 1–98.

Amernic, J., Craig, R., and Tourish, D. 2007. "The Transformational Leader as Pedagogue, Physician, Architect, Commander and Saint: Five Root Metaphors in Jack Welch's Letters to Stockholders of General Electric," *Human Relations*, 60(12): 1839–1872.

Block, Z., and MacMillan, I. 1993. *Corporate Venturing* (Boston: Harvard Business School Press).

Burgelman, R. A. 1984. "Designs for Corporate Entrepreneurship in Established Firms," *California Management Review*, 46(3): 154–166.

Chandler, A. 1962. *Strategy and Structure* (Cambridge, MA: MIT Press).

Covin, J. G., and Slevin, D. P. 1988. "The Influence of Organization Structure on the Utility of an Entrepreneurial Top Management Style," *Journal of Management Studies*, 25(3): 217–234.

Duncan, R. 1976. "The Ambidextrous Organization: Designing Dual Structures for Innovation," in Kilman, R., and Pondy, L. (eds.) *The Management of Organizational Design* (New York: North Holland): 167–188.

Ernst, H. 2002. "Success Factors of New Product Development: A Review of the Empirical Literature," *International Journal of Management Reviews*, 4(1): 1–40.

Galbraith, J. 1995. *Designing Organizations* (San Francisco: Jossey-Bass).

Garrett, R. P., Jr., and Covin, J. G. 2009. "Parent Corporation Resource Provision and Managerial Oversight as Determinants of Internal Corporate Venture Performance." Paper presented at the Academy of Management Meetings, Chicago, IL.

Griener, L. 1972. "Revolution and Evolution as Organizations Grow," *Harvard Business Review*, 50(4): 37–46.

Hamel, G., and Prahalad, C. K. 1994. *Competing for the Future* (Boston: Harvard Business School Press).

Harris, I. C., and Ruefli, T. 2000. "The Strategy/Structure Debate: An Examination of the Performance Implications," *Journal of Management Studies*, 37(4): 587–603.

Miller, D. 1983. "The Correlates of Entrepreneurship in Three Types of Firms," *Management Science*, 29(7): 770–791.

Miller, D. 1986. "Configurations of Strategy and Structure: Towards a Synthesis," *Strategic Management Journal*, 7(3): 233–239.

Miller, D. 1996. "Configurations Revisited," *Strategic Management Journal*, 7(7): 505–512.

Mintzberg, H. 1979. *The Structuring of Organizations* (Englewood Cliffs, NJ: Prentice-Hall).

Mullern, T. 2000. "Integrating the Team-Based Structure in the Business Process: The Case of Saab Training Systems," in Pettigrew, A., and Fenton, E. (eds.) *The Innovating Organization*, (London: Sage Publications).

Page, A. L. 1993. "Assessing New Product Development Practices and Performance: Establishing Crucial Norms," *Journal of Product Innovation Management*, 10(2): 273–290.

Pettigrew, A., and Fenton, E. 2000. *The Innovating Organization* (London: Sage Publications).

Slevin, D. P., and Covin, J. G. 1990. "Judging Entrepreneurial Style and Organizational Structure—How to Get Your Act Together," *Sloan Management Review*, 31(2): 43–53.

Thornhill, S., and Amit, R. 2001. "A Dynamic Perspective of Internal Fit in Corporate Venturing," *Journal of Business Venturing*, 16(1): 25–50.

CHAPTER 10

DEVELOPING AN ENTREPRENEURIAL CULTURE

Introduction

How do we get to the fabric of a company, to its essence? What is the stuff the organization is really made of? To answer such questions, we must consider the culture of a company. Like so many other organizational concepts, there is a tendency to think of culture as a metaphor. But culture is very real. It is a word that describes something intangible and imprecise, but also something that is real and transcends every aspect of an organization. A simple way to think about culture is that it captures the personality of the company and what it stands for.

Entrepreneurship is not only affected by the culture in a company, in truly entrepreneurial organizations it is a core element of the culture. The ongoing process of entrepreneurship becomes rooted in the company personality (Leavy, 2005). A culture that is risk averse, or very process driven, is almost by definition discouraging employees from acting in an entrepreneurial manner. At the same time, culture itself is complex and not easily changeable. A non-innovative company could bring in an extremely entrepreneurial CEO, and it could take seven to ten years (or more) for that individual to substantively change the organization's culture.

In this chapter, we will examine the nature of culture and the role it plays in sustaining the entrepreneurial spirit within a company. The values and norms associated with an entrepreneurial culture will be explored, together with the ways in which such a culture is manifested. A number of suggestions will be made for affecting an organization's culture. Attention will also be devoted to the concept of failure as an aspect of culture, why it is so critical for entrepreneurial success, and new approaches for thinking about and managing failure.

The Nature of Culture in Organizations

Culture can be defined as an organization's basic beliefs and assumptions about what the company is about, how its members should behave, and how it defines itself in relation to its external environment. Cultures have certain characteristics, regardless of the organization (Trice and Beyer, 1993). They are collective, meaning that their components are shared by most, if not all, of the people in a company. They have an emotional aspect, in that employees define and identify with the culture on an emotional level. While they are historically based, cultures are also dynamic. Thus, a culture reflects the unique history of a group of people interacting over time, but it also is subject to continuous change as people come and go and based on developments in the external environment. Cultures are also inherently symbolic. Things such as the way people dress or the types of recognition ceremonies that take place are actually reflections of other things, such as individualism or pride of accomplishment. Finally, cultures are fuzzy. They include elements that may seem contradictory or paradoxical. There are often ambiguities in the various symbols, rites, or values found within the company.

Every company has a culture, but these cultures tend to differ along some key dimensions. For instance, it is possible to talk about "positive" versus "negative" cultures. A culture is positive the more that its elements are in line with an organization's vision, mission, and strategies. Positive also implies there is a fit between the culture and the competitive environment in which the company finds itself. Thus, in a more turbulent environment, a more positive culture is going to be one built around entrepreneurship. Alternatively, a culture can be described as "strong" or "weak" depending on how deeply held and thoroughly permeating are the core values and assumptions of the company. Service to the customer may be a shared value, but the level of commitment and internalization of that value among employees might be lukewarm. In addition, the culture can be thought of as "homogeneous" if it is shared generally by all employees, or "heterogeneous" if there are multiple cultures or subcultures shared by different groups within the organization (e.g., those in R&D compared to those in marketing and sales). Lastly, a culture is more "inconsistent" than "consistent" if its elements conflict, such as where a company does things to reinforce conservatism and avoidance of failure, while also pushing symbols of innovation and the embracing of change.

Understanding characteristics such as these helps to explain why culture is not something that is easily managed. Unlike the decision to develop a new product, or change the company structure, the amorphous nature of culture makes it impossible to make precise changes to it at specific points in time. Rather, the leadership of the company attempts to shape, form, or mold culture with a systematic set of initiatives and forms of reinforcement that are implemented over an extended time period. Stated differently, changing a culture is analogous to trying to turn a large ocean liner around in the ocean. To appreciate how this is done, we must consider the major elements of a culture.

The Pieces and Parts of Culture

The culture of a company touches and influences everything that people do. It is manifested in hundreds of different ways, some planned and many unplanned, some controllable and some that don't readily lend themselves to management control. One way to classify the many components of culture involves distinguishing among the following six elements:

- **Values**—the things that employees think are worth having or doing, or are intrinsically desirable; values express preferences for certain behaviors and outcomes; entrepreneurial values might include creativity, integrity, perseverance, individualism, achievement, accountability, ownership, and change, among others.

- **Rules of Conduct**—accepted norms and rules in the company; the behaviors that represent accepted ways to attain outcomes; the general understanding regarding everything from ethical behavior to how one dresses, who one speaks to about or how much one questions a particular issue, and appropriate behavior styles in a meeting.

- **Vocabulary**—the language, acronyms, jargon, slang, signs, slogans, metaphors, gestures, gossip, and even songs that are commonly used in the company; can include proverbs such as 3M's "never kill a product idea."

- **Methodology**—the perception of how things actually get accomplished in the company, such as the reliance on rational processes, politicking, or rule-bending. For instance, having a sponsor and preparing a business plan with certain key ingredients might be part of the methodology for innovating in a company.

- **Rituals**—rites, ceremonies, and taboos, including random recognition ceremonies, annual off-site conferences, Christmas parties, as well as how employees are welcomed, let go, and retire. The awarding of a pink Cadillac at Mary Kay Cosmetics is a ritual.

- **Myths and Stories**—the histories, sagas, mythologies, and legends of an organization; includes a sense of "who are the heroes in this company." Entrepreneurial companies not only have legends and ways to continually retell stories of how past heroes did unusual things, but they create new heroes and role models all the time.

If we consider these elements in more basic terms, cultures consist of *substance* and *forms* (Trice and Beyer, 1993). Substance refers to shared systems of values, beliefs, and norms. Forms are the concrete ways in which the substance is manifested in the organization. They are observable, and include everything from vocabulary, myths, rituals and ceremonies, ways of dressing, and office décor. The forms are the means by which the substance of the culture is expressed, affirmed, and communicated.

In Figure 10-1, this distinction is taken a step further. Culture is pictured as existing at three different levels: assumptions, values, and artifacts. Tying this to the preceding discussion, the first two levels are more about substance while the third is concerned more with forms. The first level includes invisible aspects that people are not

FIGURE 10-1

The Levels of Culture

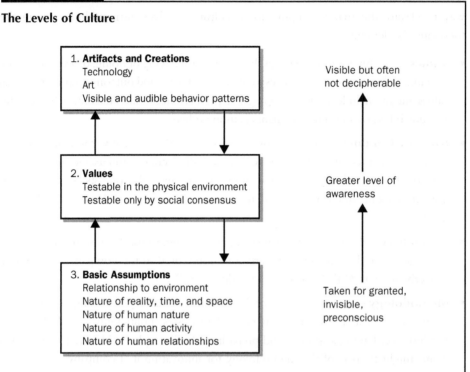

SOURCE: Schein, E. H. (1999), *The Corporate Culture Survival Guide*, San Francisco: Jossey-Bass. Reprinted with permission of John Wiley & Sons, Inc.

necessarily conscious of or that they simply take for granted. At this level one finds basic assumptions about people, what it takes to be successful in the marketplace, and a host of other aspects of work and the external environment. Employees are likely to make assumptions about the importance (or unimportance) of entrepreneurship for company success, the motivations and innate entrepreneurial potential of the people in the company, what it takes to accomplish entrepreneurship within the organization, and so forth. It can be quite difficult to determine the assumptions held by employees of a company, but they play a critical role in determining behavior.

The second level is one at which people are more conscious or generally aware. Here we find the commonly held values within the organization. Although not really visible or tangible, values have clear meaning to employees. Examples of important values in an entrepreneurial context were previously cited, and will be explored in more detail later in this chapter.

At the third level are the artifacts and creations that symbolize company culture. Artifacts are highly visible or observable manifestations of the culture. They include rituals, rules of conduct, methodology, myths, and vocabulary. Although visible, the meaning or interpretation of an artifact is not always clear. For example, management could design the physical layout of company offices to encourage openness, quick communication, information sharing, and innovation partnerships among employees. For their part, employees might interpret the artifact differently. They could conclude that it conveys a desire to encourage collectivism over individualism, or reflects distrust and an attempt to check up on them, or is a reflection of tight spending and efficiency. The ultimate meaning of the artifact or creation is arrived at over time, based on how it is managed, the kinds of messages that are consistently reinforced, and the interplay of the artifact with other components of the culture.

The inference is that, if the goal is to create work environments that support entrepreneurship, culture underlies all the other components of the workplace (i.e., reward systems, organizational structures, control systems, the strategic direction of the company, etc.). As Leavy (2005, p. 42) notes in his assessment of the amazing record of innovation at 3M, "The mistake that many companies have tended to make in looking at 3M is to focus too much on specific innovation practices and policies, and not enough on the philosophy and values underpinning them." In fact, rewards, controls, and other aspects of the workplace can themselves capture and reinforce elements of the culture. The entrepreneurial potential of a positive, strong, and consistent culture is significant, leading one team of researchers to conclude: "Organizational cultures can enhance and inspirit us. They can remove us from the boxes and traps in which we exist, making our lives richer and giving meaning to our daily tasks. (This) is the goal of cultural management" (Tropman and Morningstar, 1989, p. 120).

Core Ideology and the Envisioned Future

Entrepreneurial companies are guided by a vision. They have a sense of what they are and what they want to become. They also understand the things about their organizations that are subject to change, and those that should never change. Collins and Porras (1994) argue that a great vision starts with a "core ideology." By using the term *core* they capture elements of an organization that should not change as products mature, markets evolve, technologies emerge, or the leadership of the company comes and goes. Thus, the core ideology includes core values, or what the company stands for, as well as core purpose, or the reason the company exists.

Core values are the essential and enduring principles and tenets of an organization. Meaningful levels of entrepreneurship cannot be sustained over time unless entrepreneurship is reflected in the core values of the company. For instance, Google, the world's leading search engine, nurtures a culture of continuous creativity and innovative ideas. A position of chief culture officer (CCO) was created to ensure an environment of individual ideas and creativity. At the Walt Disney Company, creativity, dreams, and imagination form some of the core values. Complementing these values is the core purpose, which is a source of guidance and inspiration to the organization. Again, entrepreneurship should be implicit in the company's core purpose. The reason for being at 3M is to solve unsolved problems innovatively, while the purpose at Mary Kay Cosmetics is to give unlimited opportunity to women. Cisco Systems, a leader in the information technology space, aims to be the industry leader in game-changing technologies (i.e., innovations that change the direction or focus of an entire industry). Each of these purposes goes well beyond suggesting that entrepreneurship might be important—they allow for bold initiatives in accomplishing a purpose that transcends the current products and processes of the company.

The other part of a vision concerns what the organization aspires to become, which Collins and Porras (1994) refer to as the "envisioned future." While the core purpose can be a never-ending quest, the envisioned future is about setting clear and compelling goals that the company commits to achieve over the next 10 or 20 years. It is coupled with a vivid description of what it will take to get there. General Electric set the goal of being #1 or #2 in every market they serve, while Nike sought to crush Adidas, and Sam Walton set revenue goals that seemed completely unrealistic to people outside Wal-Mart. These are ambitious goals that take on a life of their own and stimulate ongoing progress in an organization. They require extraordinary effort and there is a real chance of failure. They motivate people and evoke passion and conviction. Once they are achieved, the company sets new ones.

Generic Culture Types

One of the great debates among those who study culture concerns whether there are general properties of cultures that can be found in many different organizations, or, alternatively, whether each culture is unique unto itself. With the latter view, researchers have proposed a number of typologies or classifications of culture types. The idea is that most companies will tend to fit into one of the categories contained within a given typology. Table 10-1 outlines some examples of these typologies. They differ considerably, reflecting different underlying variables. Some are based on levels of control exercised, others on the extent to which the company is more people-oriented or task-oriented, and still others on psychological traits.

Prominent among the perspectives presented in Table 10-1 is the work of Deal and Kennedy (2000). They argue that distinct types of cultures evolve within companies, and that these types have a direct and measurable impact on strategy and performance.

TABLE 10-1

Examples of Types of Organizational Culture

Types of Organizational Cultures	Dominant Ideologies	Authors
Type A	Hierarchical control, high specialization, short-term employment, individual responsibility, individual decision making	Ouchi, 1981
Type J	Clan control, low specialization, lifetime employment, collective responsibility, collective decision making	
Type Z	Clan control, moderate specialization, long-term employment, individual responsibility, consensual decision making	
Process	Low risk, "cover your tail" mentality, tight hierarchy	Deal and Kennedy, 2000
Tough guy–Macho	High risk, quick feedback, fluctuating structure	
Work hard–Play hard	Moderately low risk, race to the quick, flexible structure	
Bet-your-company	Very high risk, slow feedback, clear-cut hierarchy	
Sensation-thinking	Impersonal, abstract, certainty, specificity, authoritarian	Mitroff and Kilmann, 1975
Intuition-thinking	Flexible, adaptive, global notions, goal-driven	
Intuition-feeling	Caring, decentralized, flexible, no explicit rules or regulations	
Sensation-feeling	Personal, homelike, relationship-driven, nonbureaucratic	
Apathetic	Demoralizing and cynical orientation	Sethia and Von Glinow, 1985
Caring	High concern for employees, no high-performance expectations	
Exacting	Performance and success really count	
Integrative	High concern for employees with high concern for performance	
Paranoid	Fear, distrust, suspicion	Kets de Vries and Miller, 1984

(Continued)

TABLE 10-1 (Continued)		
Examples of Types of Organizational Culture		
Types of Organizational Cultures	*Dominant Ideologies*	*Authors*
Avoidant	Lack of self-confidence, powerlessness, inaction	
Charismatic	Drama, power, success, abject followership	
Bureaucratic	Compulsive, detailed, depersonalized, rigid	
Schizoid	Politicized, social isolation	

SOURCE: Trice, Harrison M., Beyer, Janice M., *Cultures of Work Organizations*, © 1993, p. 17. Reprinted with permission of Pearson Education, Inc., Upper Saddle River, NJ.

Companies are social environments, with tribal habits, well-defined cultural roles for individuals, and various strategies for determining inclusion, reinforcing identity, and adapting to change. Moreover, their cultures will generally be related to one of four prototypes:

- **The Process Culture**—a world of little or no feedback where employees find it hard to measure what they do. Instead, they concentrate on how it is done. The hierarchy is tight and employees are cautious "fence sitters." Avoidance of failure is important. Processes themselves can stifle the company and become quite bureaucratic.

- **The Tough Guy/Macho Culture**—a world of competitive individualists who regularly take high personal risks and get quick feedback on whether their actions were right or wrong. The structure fluctuates. Financial stakes of not succeeding can be high, as can rewards from succeeding. Orientation is more short term, and employee turnover can be high.

- **The Work Hard/Play Hard Culture**—fun and action is the rule here, and employees take few risks, all with quick feedback. To succeed, the culture encourages employees to maintain a high level of relatively low-risk activity. Much gets done in this culture, as it is very action-oriented. Orientation here is also fairly short term. Often a strong customer focus and sales orientation.

- **The Bet-the-Company Culture**—an environment of big-stakes decisions, where considerable time passes before employees know whether decisions have paid off. It is a high-risk, slow-feedback environment with a clear-cut hierarchy. Decisions are deliberate because of the risk. Pressure is ongoing. They often produce major technological breakthroughs and high-quality inventions.

While a number of variables are considered in this taxonomy, especially prominent are risk and the speed with which the company receives feedback on the appropriateness of their decisions. Both of these factors are associated with entrepreneurship. The degree of risk associated with the company's activities (risk avoidance or low risk, calculated or managed risk, high risk) says something about the amount and types of entrepreneurial initiatives that will be pursued. Cultures that have a stronger process orientation are likely to discourage entrepreneurial behavior, where the bet-the-company culture will likely pursue entrepreneurship that is high on degree but low on frequency (see Chapter 3). Similarly, limited market feedback or accountability, such as where a company enjoys captive demand or monopoly market conditions, does not foster entrepreneurial behavior, while rapid feedback encourages a higher frequency but lower degree of entrepreneurial activity.

Even where the executive is able to properly decipher and characterize the company's culture, and where that culture is relatively strong, Deal and Kennedy (2000) raise a fundamental and troubling concern. Might strategic moves that appear necessary given contemporary market realities actually harm the culture and have long-term adverse implications for the company? In recent years companies have actively pursued a number of strategic initiatives that could serve to undermine the basic culture of the organization. As managers aggressively pursue such strategies as outsourcing, downsizing, reengineering, mergers, and leveraged buy-outs, they often fail to consider the implications of these initiatives for the culture and its role in the company.

Elements of an Entrepreneurial Culture

We have discussed how types of culture might affect levels of entrepreneurship in a company. We now turn to a more fundamental question: What is an entrepreneurial culture? Exceptional organizations such as DSM, the highly successful Dutch specialty metals company, or Koch Industries, one of the largest privately held companies in America, understand that entrepreneurship is not an activity; it is a culture (Kirschbaum, 2005). It infuses the values, symbols, vocabulary, myths, rules of conduct, and methodology of the company.

As we have seen, a culture has many elements. The challenge lies in determining the ones that are most conducive to entrepreneurship. A look at the perspectives presented in Table 10-2 may shed some light. The table presents a synopsis of work done by different writers on the cultural elements that foster innovation and entrepreneurship. While it may appear that a variety of elements come into play, there is a certain commonality to the things being emphasized. If we synthesize these perspectives, the entrepreneurial culture would seem to have the following elements:

- focus on people and empowerment
- value creation through innovation and change
- rewards for innovations

TABLE 10-2

Components of an Entrepreneurial Culture: Three Perspectives

Timmons and Spinelli (2009)	*Kuratko (2009)*
Clarity, being well-organized	Top management support
High standards, pressure for excellence	Autonomy/work discretion
Commitment	Rewards/reinforcement
Responsibility	Time availability
Recognition	Open organizational boundaries
Esprit de corps	Empowerment
	Value creation
Peters (1997)	Attention to detail
Listening	
Embracing change	
Customer focus	
Total integrity	
Excellence	
Involve everyone in everything	
Experimentation	
Fast-paced innovation	
Small starts and fast failure	
Visible management	
Measurement/accountability	

- learning from failure
- collaboration and teamwork
- freedom to grow and to fail
- commitment and personal responsibility
- emphasis on the future and a sense of urgency

These core values are richly embedded in the DNA of entrepreneurial companies. Consider the cultures of 3M, Nokia, IDEO, and DSM. At 3M, the cornerstone value shaping the culture is an unshakeable belief in the power of ideas and individual initiative; Nokia emphasizes a sense of community where you can trust your colleagues and peers so that it is possible to take fairly significant risks; IDEO nurtures a culture of openness, where people have room to grow, experimentation is a way of life, and learning comes from trying (Leavy, 2005). In their work with entrepreneurial companies in Germany, Kriegesmann et al. (2005) observe among individual managers a consistent willingness to alter their own skill profiles proactively.

It must also be kept in mind that most large organizations are quite complex. Their internal environments are filled with competing demands, a multiplicity of tasks and commitments, and people operating under differing time horizons. As a result, organizations are confronted with a number of conflicting value choices. The creation of an entrepreneurial culture is not simply a matter of identifying a value to be emphasized, but choosing between values that both conflict with one another and coexist in an organization. That is, management must strike a balance among certain values.

Tropman and Morningstar (1989) examine what they term "primary values" and draw implications for entrepreneurship. As illustrated in Figure 10-2, value choices must be made in ten areas. Each set of values is pictured as a continuum, and the points that have been placed along each continuum indicate the type of balance an entrepreneurial company might try to strike. For instance, most companies have multiple purposes (often pursued by various subcultures in the company), but the entrepreneurial company has strong focus on one overriding purpose. The point becomes to achieve a balance while having a dominant emphasis. The same goes for the relative emphasis on excellence versus satisfactory performance and comfort. Entrepreneurial companies set priorities in terms of the areas where they are truly superlative and driven in terms of performance, while in other areas they may simply be "good enough." Organizations can also contain considerable diversity, and conflicts arise among different interest groups (e.g., technical versus non-technical employees, minorities versus majorities, and union members versus management). The balance here involves respecting differences while finding areas of commonality or similarity between class or group interests and overall organizational interests or purpose. It is just as important to capitalize on the friction between various interests in a positive way, as we saw in our discussion of creative abrasion in Chapter 6. Similar conclusions apply to the personal goals of individuals within the company compared to overall organizational goals.

The need for entrepreneurial companies to empower employees might seem to indicate a consensus form of decision making. Yet, a balance is required in that entrepreneurial companies must move quickly, and building consensus on every decision is unrealistic. A major issue is the relative reliance on quantitative or fact-based and numbers-driven decision making versus a more qualitative approach. Consider the earlier discussion of calculated risk-taking, which implies a systematic attempt to identify and quantify key risk factors. At the same time, innovating and venturing into the unknown do not always lend themselves to hard numbers. Judgment, instinct, and subjective assessments play a vital role in entrepreneurship. With regard to integrity versus expediency,

FIGURE 10-2

Core Cultural Values and Entrepreneurship

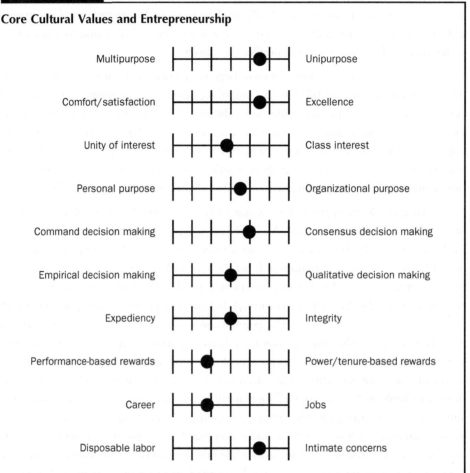

SOURCE: *Entrepreneurial Systems for the 1990s*, "Core Cultural Values and Entrepreneurship," J. E. Tropman and G. Morningstar. Copyright © 1989 by Greenwood Publishing Group. Reproduced with permission of Greenwood Publishing Group, Inc., Westport, CT.

the placement along the continuum is not meant to suggest a company should not demonstrate the highest integrity at all times. Rather, it must do so while also stressing the need to get things done. Too often, the entrepreneurial company becomes overzealous in terms of its action-orientation, and integrity suffers. The high pressure and strong work ethic of the entrepreneurial manager are not always shared by other employees and team members. There is a need for sensitivity to those who view it as a job. They may put in an honest day's work, but are not willing to give the daily 15-hour effort an entrepreneur gives. Entrepreneurial behavior clearly must be incentivized, and is most consistent with performance-based rewards. Yet for entrepreneurship to exist in those corporations where power and tenure-based rewards are the expected norm, again some balance is required. Finally, entrepreneurship is quite people-based, and so the balance on that continuum is much closer to the "intimate concerns" side. One can go too far here, though, moving beyond people's professional needs and concerns into their personal lives.

There is one more element to consider when thinking about the architecture of the company culture. We use the term "healthy discontent" to describe an emphasis on constant improvement. Employees in entrepreneurial companies are not complacent, even after a major achievement. They always want to "raise the bar." They look at daily processes and think "we can do this better." They are always critiquing, raising positive criticisms, and challenging the way things have been or are (Hamel, 2000). Managers at all levels get their hands dirty, spend time out in the field, visit customers, ride along on delivery routes, and so forth. Healthy discontent always requires a balancing act, as it can easily become negative and give rise to defensiveness and political gamesmanship.

Entrepreneurial Development through Culture: Eli Lilly & Co.

Culture is rich in entrepreneurial companies. An excellent case in point is Eli Lilly & Co., one of the world's leading pharmaceutical companies with annual revenue exceeding $20 billion. The company has manufacturing plants in 13 countries, clinical research conducted in more than 50 countries, and employs over 42,000 people. In order to compete with pharmaceutical giants Pfizer, GlaxoSmithKline, and Roche, Lilly has created the Center of Excellence (COE) initiative. This is a new operating model that fundamentally reorganizes the company into five business units: cancer, diabetes, established markets, emerging markets, and animal health.

This new initiative aims to drive innovative discoveries and establish a more innovative culture at Lilly. The pharmaceutical industry must rely on innovation to survive, and Eli Lilly believes that four major elements directly inspire innovation in their culture: (1) an innovative environment in which all stakeholders are rewarded for their innovations; (2) continuous investment in R&D; (3) encouraging talented people with their ideas; and (4) world-class facilities to facilitate the innovation process. So we see environment, people, rewards, and structure leading the way as critical elements.

Exploring a Key Value: Individualism

Entrepreneurship does not happen without individuals. Someone must champion a concept, persevere in the face of resistance and rejection, make adaptations, and keep the idea alive. But it also does not happen without teams. A motivated, coordinated group of individuals, each having their own skills and contribution to make, are critical for moving an entrepreneurial event through what can be a lengthy process filled with obstacles. This brings us to a value that exists in most companies, even if management is unaware of it: individualism versus collectivism.

Individualism refers to a self-orientation, an emphasis on self-sufficiency and control, the pursuit of individual goals that may or may not be consistent with those of one's colleagues, and a value system where people derive pride from their own accomplishments. A group or collective orientation involves the subordination of personal interests to the goals of the larger work group, an emphasis on sharing, a concern with group welfare, and antipathy toward those outside the group.

In a work context, there are positive and negative aspects to both individualism and a group or collective orientation. Table 10-3 provides a summary of these pros and cons. In essence, an individualistic ethic may foster development of an individual's self-confidence, lead to a greater sense of personal responsibility, create more of a competitive spirit, and produce higher-risk, breakthrough innovations. It can also produce selfishness, higher levels of stress, and interpersonal conflict. A collectivist orientation offers the advantages of more harmonious relationships between individuals, greater synergies, more social support, and can result in a steady stream of incremental improvements and moderate innovations. On the downside, this group focus can entail the loss of individual identity, greater emotional dependency, a tendency to "free ride" on the efforts of others, compromises rather than optimizing behavior, and "group think," where individuals get locked into a singular, shared way of viewing or approaching a problem.

The ability to achieve and sustain entrepreneurship in a company is dependent upon a balance between the need for individual initiative and the spirit of cooperation and group ownership of innovation (Morris et al., 1993). Too much individualism can harm entrepreneurship, as can too much collectivism. This balance is shown in Figure 10-3. As the entrepreneurial process unfolds, the individual champion requires not just specialist expertise, but teams of people, some of whom can fill multiple roles. Members of these teams are able to collaborate in meeting tight timelines, identifying and overcoming unanticipated obstacles, and finding angles and opportunities that often redefine the original concept, putting it on a more successful path. Sometimes it is the entrepreneur who keeps the team on track, and other times it is the team that is the voice of reason and consistency.

A Culture with a Different View of Failure

Managers struggle with the concept of failure, not only with their own decisions that result in outcomes well below expectations, but also the failings of employees for whom they are directly responsible (especially when they perceive that these failings

TABLE 10-3

Merits of Individualism vs. Collectivism

Positive Aspects

Individualism	Collectivism
• Employee develops stronger self-concept, more self-confidence	• Greater synergies from combined efforts of people with differing skills
• Consistent with achievement motivation	• Ability to incorporate diverse perspectives and achieve comprehensive view
• Competition among individuals encourages greater number of novel concepts and ideas, breakthrough innovations	• Individuals treated as equals
• Stronger sense of personal responsibility for performance outcomes	• Relationships more personalized, synchronized, harmonious, while interpersonal conflicts are discouraged
• Linkage between personal effort and rewards create greater sense of equity	• Greater concern for welfare of others, network of social support available
	• More consensus regarding direction and priorities
	• Credit for failures and successes equally shared
	• Teamwork produces steady, incremental progress on projects

Negative Aspects

Individualism	Collectivism
• Emphasis on personal gain at the expense of others, selfishness, materialism	• Loss of personal and professional self to group/collective
• Individuals have less commitment/loyalty, are more "up for sale"	• Greater emotional dependence of individuals on the group or organization
• Differences among individuals are emphasized	• Less personal responsibility for outcomes
• Interpersonal conflicts are encouraged	• Individuals "free ride" on efforts of others, rewards not commensurate with effort
• Greater levels of personal stress, pressure from individual performance	• Tendency toward "group think"
• Insecurity can result from over dependence on one's self	• Outcomes can represent compromises among diverse interests, reflecting need to get along more than need for performance
• Greater feelings of loneliness, alienation, and anomie	• Collectives can take more time to reach consensus, may miss opportunities
• Stronger incentive for unethical behavior, expediency	
• Onus of failure falls on the individual	

FIGURE 10-3

The Relationship between Entrepreneurship and an Emphasis on the Individual versus the Group or Collective

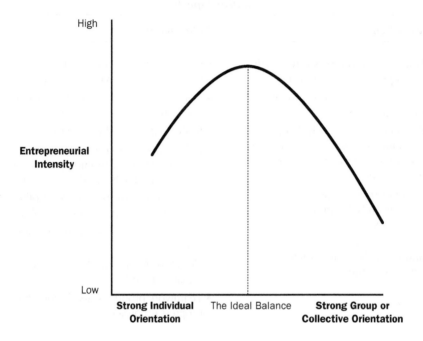

SOURCE: Morris, M. H., Allen, J. A., and Avila, A. (1993), "Individualism and the Modern Corporation: Implications for Innovation and Entrepreneurship," *Journal of Management*, Vol. 19, p. 3.

reflect back on them). Kriegesmann et al. (2005) have noted a tendency within companies to develop "zero error cultures" as companies strive to meet ever-higher performance standards in a hypercompetitive marketplace. Managers mistakenly believe that zero errors are proof of high performance standards. When a dogma of zero errors is coupled with traditional reward systems that reinforce short-term positive contributions, the result tends to be a strong emphasis on predictable tried-and-tested behavior patterns.

Kriegesmann et al. (2005) find that many organizations hope that personnel will think more creatively and take risks, but they are actually being rewarded for well-proven, trusted methods and fault-free work. They further note that there is a fundamental contradiction between the rhetoric of innovation and a culture of fear and unease when dealing with change. It is not uncommon for companies to create cultures of imitation and plagiarism. In effect, they promote safe actions and there is an antipathy toward making errors. The result is innovation incompetence, where bold initiatives are avoided and initiatives are pursued only when there is an apparent guarantee of outcomes. These authors argue that such cultures encourage reproduction of past patterns, while being closed to change and avoiding critical analysis.

The culture of the entrepreneurial company celebrates failure. Consider the example of Nokia, where the culture includes a pervasive sense that "this is a place where you are allowed to have a bit of fun, to think unlike the norm, where you are allowed to make a mistake" (Leavy, 2005, p. 39). Another case in point can be found at BMW, where one of their most entrepreneurial factories gives out a "flop of the month" award to honor employees who champion innovative ideas that fail during implementation. The award is given by the senior executive, and the initiatives are called "successful failures" (Kriegesmann et al., 2005). In these types of companies, it is recognized that failure goes hand in hand with innovating and with learning. In fact, if one is not failing now and again, one is probably not trying anything new. Yet failure on the job is something employees often avoid at all costs, instead opting for the safer middle route. Fear of failure is a certain recipe for mediocrity.

The beginning point in dealing with employee fear of failure is recognizing that the sanctions and likely outcomes of failure are perceived, and perceptions can differ significantly from reality. This distinction explains much of the problem in organizations. Employees attach certain costs to failing. They do not want to have the onus of failure attached to their names. It is these perceived costs that should be the focus of management.

Consider a very different situation, bankruptcy, which is clearly a type of failure. Bankruptcy laws in the United States are extremely liberal. While one can debate the pluses and minuses of such liberal laws, there is one major benefit. Liberal bankruptcy laws serve to reduce the perceived cost of failure associated with entrepreneurial start-ups. They are an incentive for innovation.

Now consider a large corporation. The manager should ask a simple question: How can I reduce the perceived cost of failure associated with innovation or entrepreneurial behavior in this company? Answering this question implies the manager has a clear sense regarding the specific costs associated with failure. Is it job loss, a smaller pay raise, a missed promotion, a blemished record, loss of autonomy, personal embarrassment, loss of stature, or something else? An interesting exercise is to ask people in organizations to cite people they know who have attempted something entrepreneurial, then failed, and then paid a clear price in terms of job loss or some of these other significant costs. They are often hard-pressed to come up with any specific examples. This reality further reinforces the perceptual nature of failure. It may be that much of the perceived cost of failure is psychological. But these costs can be reduced by openly recognizing failures in a positive way, while continually reinforcing the valuable learning that results from failure. At one major company, for example, managers pride themselves on the fact that even failures that might end up on the front page of a major newspaper do not destroy careers. Similarly, a favorite maxim among managers at Johnson & Johnson is the recognition that "failure is our most important product."

Conceptualizing Failure

Companies also should distinguish among the different types of failure. *Moral failure*, which occurs when there is a breach of ethics or an employee acts in an immoral fashion, should be addressed aggressively with a zero tolerance policy. *Personal failure* is related to inadequacies in one's skills, understanding of an assignment or task, attention to detail, motivation levels, willingness to learn, and so forth. It is dealt with personal counseling, coaching, and training. *Uncontrollable failures* are those that occur due in part to events or forces beyond the control of the individual employee. This is where much of the failure associated with entrepreneurship comes into play. These failures should be celebrated and should be the subject of systematic documentation and learning efforts.

The real problem, however, has to do with how we conceptualize failure. As shown at the top of Figure 10-4, people tend to view failure and success as opposites. Success is a continuum along which one moves, where movement in one direction produces increments of success, and movement in the other direction results in increments of failure. The problem here is that if one is succeeding more, then he or she assumes they are failing less. Entrepreneurial companies take an alternative view, as shown at the bottom of Figure 10-4. Both success and failure can be occurring at the same time, such that a company can have any number of successful initiatives and any number of failures. Something that is not all that successful is not viewed as being somewhat a failure. Importantly, avoiding failure in no way ensures success. Failures can be steps toward ultimate success. Hence, experiencing failures can enhance the likelihood of success, but only if learning is taking place.

Learning from Entrepreneurial Failure

As corporate innovative activity increases in organizations, it can be expected that entrepreneurial projects created to pursue new opportunities will experience increases in failure and "die" for a variety of reasons (Shepherd and Kuratko, 2009). Despite the very best commitment by those inside an organization, projects can still fail. Project

FIGURE 10-4

Alternative Views of Failure

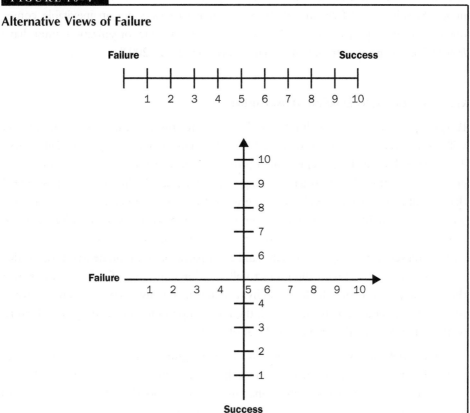

failure can be described as the "termination of a project due to the realization of unacceptably low performance as operationally defined by the key resource providers" (Shepherd et al., 2009, p. 589). How the organizational environment is set up to deal with project failure can be a critical factor in the "learning" that employees are supposed to gain from the failure.

Although the goal of innovative projects is to successfully pursue an entrepreneurial opportunity and failure means that goal has not been met, failure can still be an important source for learning. Indeed, conventional wisdom extols the benefits of learning from failure, suggesting that we learn more from our failures than our successes. This failure-to-success sequence has been observed in cases of, for example, new product development (Maidique and Zirger, 1985), internal corporate venturing (McGrath, 1995), and joint venturing (Peng and Shenkar, 2002). Learning from failure is an important aspect of the entrepreneurial process, but is not automatic or instantaneous (Shepherd and Cardon, 2009). Subsequent success is not an inevitable consequence of prior project failure. For success to occur, the organization must have *learned* from its prior entrepreneurial failures (Green et al., 2003)

GRIEF AS A BLOCK TO LEARNING FROM FAILURE

Regardless of the reasons behind a project's failure, those committed to the project will likely feel they have lost something important when the project fails (dies). Thus, the failure of the entrepreneurial project (project death) can generate a negative emotional reaction that obstructs learning—namely, grief. It should be acknowledged that not all project failures will generate grief. Rather, there are certain project circumstances and individual predispositions under which project failure is most likely to result in a felt sense of grief. We don't always feel the same level of emotion for each entrepreneurial project that fails. And for a particular entrepreneurial project, different people involved with the project will feel differently. Grief will be greater over the loss of projects for which the individual has made sustained emotional "investments" (Jacobs et al., 2000). In general, the more importance attached by an individual to the failed project, the greater the level of grief.

While grief can also trigger a process of meaningful reconstruction, the process of recovering from grief to learn from the failure experience will be influenced by the individual's grief orientation, emotional intelligence, and the organization's norms and routines used for helping its members deal with their emotions.

The traditional process of recovering from grief involves focusing on the particular loss to construct an account that explains why the loss occurred. As a plausible account for the failure is constructed, individuals are able to begin to break the emotional bonds to the failed project. However, empirical research has found that this "loss orientation" toward grief recovery can sometimes exacerbate the negative emotional reaction (Nolen-Hoeksema et al., 1997; Davis and Nolen-Hoeksema, 2001).

A "restoration orientation" is an alternate approach and is based on both distracting oneself from thinking about the failure event and being proactive toward secondary causes of stress. Distraction takes the individual's thoughts away from the source of his or her negative emotions and addressing secondary causes of stress brought on by the failure (such as emotional feelings of depression or physical repercussions like loss of sleep) can diminish the primary stressor—the entrepreneurial failure. However, avoiding negative emotions is unlikely to be successful in the long-run—suppressing emotions can lead to further physical and psychological problems and these suppressed emotions are likely to reemerge and do so at an inopportune time (Archer, 1999).

Shepherd (2009) proposed a dual process model of recovering from the grief over entrepreneurial failure. Based on this dual process model, an innovator recovers more quickly from a failure if he or she oscillates between a loss and a restoration orientation. This oscillation means that the innovator can gain the benefits of both orientations while minimizing the costs of maintaining either for an extended period. By oscillating (switching back and forth) between these orientations innovators can learn more from their failure experiences.

The organizations in which people work affect their thoughts, feelings, and actions in the workplace (Brief and Weiss, 2002). Therefore, rather than normalize failure, an organization can develop support mechanisms to help its members regulate their grief in a way consistent with the dual process model. Although emotions are still generated by a project failure, they can be managed to minimize interference to learning and maintain high levels of commitment to subsequent projects. An organization can help build its members' coping self-efficacy (the belief in one's capabilities to mobilize the motivation, cognitive resources, and courses of action needed to recover from major setbacks arising from the organization's entrepreneurial activities) (Shepherd and Cardon, 2009).

One way that an organization can assist in the grief-recovery process is through self-help support groups for dealing with the emotions generated by project failure. Self-help groups are the most common form of social support group (also known as peer or mutual support groups), partly because of their low cost and the perception by participants of a low-threat environment. Therefore, while coping self-efficacy is an individual's belief in one's ability to cope, organized support from within the company can provide avenues for employees to support each other and, in doing so, play a role in developing a member's coping self-efficacy (Benight and Bandura, 2003). To the extent that social support efforts can help employees build their efficacy for recovering from grief generated by project failure, they are effective in helping individuals learn from project failure and remain committed to subsequent projects.

Organizations can also use rituals as a mechanism for assisting in grief recovery. Rituals represent "standardized, detailed sets of techniques and behaviors that the culture prescribes to manage anxieties and express common identities" (Trice and Beyer, 1993, p. 80). For example, the benefits of funeral rituals may extend beyond the loss of a loved one in a community to the loss of something important within an organizational context. Harris and Sutton (1986) analyzed parties, picnics, and dinners that occurred in six organizations going out of business ("dying organizations"). They proposed that parting ceremonies for displaced workers caused by organizational death serve the purposes of providing emotional support for the workers. As organizations die, employees are likely to 1) have a negative emotional response to that loss and mourn and 2) benefit from the emotional support provided by the rituals of parting ceremonies. In particular, these rituals enhance individuals' self-efficacy for coping with loss. A similar process could be used by organizations when an entrepreneurial project fails—that is, offer some form of parting or funeral ritual. In fact, many companies have used rituals to address failure. For example, a subsidiary of H.J. Heinz shot off a cannon in celebration of a "perfect failure" (Peters and Waterman, 1982) while Eli Lilly threw "perfect failure" parties for excellent scientific work that, nevertheless, resulted in failure (Burton, 2004).

In short, the inevitability of entrepreneurial project failure encourages the adoption of social support mechanisms as means for developing failure-related coping skills. When innovation is the mission of a particular organizational unit, grief will be a predictable consequence of project failures; and the need for social support mechanisms that enable corporate innovators to cope with failure-related grief will be imperative.

Cultures within Cultures

While we tend to think in terms of a dominant culture that pervades throughout an organization, the reality is that companies also develop subcultures. That is, within the overall culture, a number of subcultures evolve, coexist, and occasionally clash with one another. Where companies have multiple divisions or operating units that are geographically dispersed, unique cultures can emerge over time in some of these units. Similarly, different functional areas can develop unique cultures, such as the company sales organization, or the research and development department. It is not unusual in companies to find that levels of entrepreneurship differ among divisions, strategic business units, and functional area departments. These differences are frequently rooted in the subcultures that are found within these units or departments.

One might expect that areas that are more affected by developments in the company's external environment, and especially departments that interact more with key components of the external environment (e.g., customers, competitors), will develop unique cultures that are somewhat removed from the dominant culture of the company. They will adopt values and norms that are more in line with the demands of these external constituencies relative to the demands of company management. Where the external environment is highly turbulent, one would expect these units to adopt a more entrepreneurial orientation.

Subcultures can impact the ways in which entrepreneurship is manifested within a company. For instance, a strong entrepreneurial culture within the marketing area might be expected to result in considerably more emphasis on new products and services that are customer-originated. Where the production or operations group is more entrepreneurially oriented, one might expect a strong emphasis on innovative new processes for making products or delivering services. At the same time, it is not unusual for a highly entrepreneurial subculture in one area to conflict with other parts of the organization that are much less entrepreneurial. This abrasion can produce negative or positive outcomes. While it sometimes results in overt or subversive attempts to undermine the more entrepreneurial unit, these conflicts can often force those with entrepreneurial ideas to adapt or refine their innovative concepts in ways that make them stronger. Outcomes of such conflicts ultimately depend on the strategic leadership from the top of the organization, and the extent to which leaders espouse an entrepreneurial vision.

Leadership and Culture

A difference exists between entrepreneurial leadership and an entrepreneurial culture. An organization can have one or more people at the top who drive innovative performance. But if those people leave, innovative performance will go as well, unless it has been embedded in the culture. Kotter (1996, p. 156) notes, "Culture changes only after you have successfully altered people's actions, after the new behavior produces some group benefit for a period of time, and after people see the connection between the new actions and the performance improvement." So, management does not change the culture and then entrepreneurship happens. Rather, the organization moves to an entrepreneurial culture through a process of transformation that includes ongoing innovation, continuous reinforcement, results, extensive internal communication, and working through coalitions of employees. This transformation is a slow process involving focused changes to artifacts, steady redefinition and prioritization of values, and the eventual permeation of the underlying assumptions that define why the company exists and how things get done.

The movement toward an entrepreneurial culture is well summarized in Timmons and Spinelli's (2009) "Chain of Greatness," which is illustrated in Figure 10-5. Vision coupled with learning produces an entrepreneurial mindset throughout the organization. Accountability and responsibility for innovative initiatives is assigned and assumed, as employees take ownership of these initiatives and of the organization itself. The end result is a strong, positive, and consistent culture that is achievement-driven, pride inducing, and personally fulfilling for employees. The chain of greatness becomes both reinforcing and perpetuating.

FIGURE 10-5

Timmons' Chain of Greatness

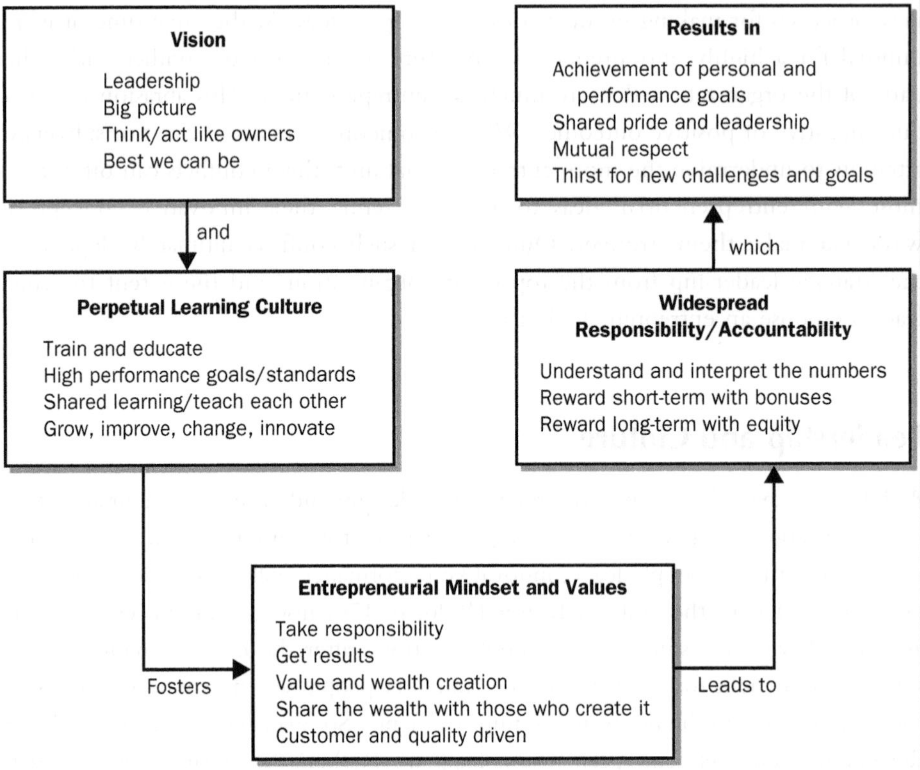

Vision

Leadership
Big picture
Think/act like owners
Best we can be

and

Perpetual Learning Culture

Train and educate
High performance goals/standards
Shared learning/teach each other
Grow, improve, change, innovate

Fosters

Entrepreneurial Mindset and Values

Take responsibility
Get results
Value and wealth creation
Share the wealth with those who create it
Customer and quality driven

Leads to

Widespread Responsibility/Accountability

Understand and interpret the numbers
Reward short-term with bonuses
Reward long-term with equity

which

Results in

Achievement of personal and
  performance goals
Shared pride and leadership
Mutual respect
Thirst for new challenges and goals

SOURCE: *New Venture Creation,* 5e, Jeffry Timmons, copyright © 1999, The McGraw-Hill Companies. Reproduced with permission of the McGraw-Hill Companies.

THE INNOVATOR'S NOTEBOOK

Why Intuit Welcomes Failure

Intuit Inc. is a leading provider of financial management, tax and online banking solutions for consumers, small and mid-sized businesses, accountants, and financial institutions. Best known for its accounting software QuickBooks, Intuit has learned since its start in 1983 that failure is nothing to be feared. Scott Cook, Intuit's cofounder, has developed a systematic process of innovation that includes regular free-association sessions, customer interviews, and "follow me home," visits to customers. The goal is to identify customers' "pain points" and resolve them by making adjustments to Intuit's product offerings. Each division uses this process to arrive at a product that people will pay for, use, and enjoy.

One problem with striving to have customers enjoy your product when you are selling financial software is that for most people finance is inherently not enjoyable. Despite Intuit controlling 79 percent of the retail software market for tax preparation, there are approximately 20 million people who continue to prepare their taxes without the use of tax software or a professional tax preparer. To continue its growth Intuit must understand the needs of these consumers and find products that will fit their needs. So, it would seem that Intuit's biggest competitor is the consumers themselves.

In order to become more receptive to customers' needs, the company had to become more tolerant of failure as employees began making what would have at one time been considered outlandish suggestions (such as a tax-preparation product that would adjust to the user's emotional state) in an attempt to innovate. No one endorsed this movement more than Scott Cook. The defining moment of Cook's philosophy came when Quicken, a product for assisting individuals manage their personal finances, was starting to take off. Market research revealed that customers were using Quicken to manage their business finances, but Cook wrote the discovery off as an anomaly. After a follow-up survey revealed an increasing number of business Quicken users, Cook realized the market potential for an accounting software product aimed at small businesses.

Rather than dismissing his initial mistake of ignoring what the market was trying to tell him, Cook recognized where he went wrong and began to teach his employees to "savor the surprises." He instilled the notion that employees should not only be open to signs in the market but also actively seek them out. This lesson has translated into the company dispatching employees to visit customers. Those initiatives led to annual revenues for QuickBooks amounting to over $700 million.

What makes Intuit's management philosophy unique? The focus on new ideas for growth. A few years back Cook had concluded that the

(Continued)

size of the company, nearly $1 billion with 4,000 employees along with the management's lack of operational experience, had led to the failure of several of Intuit's initiatives. Cook believed in his ability to develop new ideas, but wanted the new executives to bring into the company the much needed discipline required for successful execution. Thus the company embarked on a strategy of disciplined innovation in the search for new ideas.

Here is one example of the search for good ideas. Based on research conducted by employees meeting with customers, Intuit found that more than half of American small business owners who have computers continue to use simple spreadsheets or pencil and paper to manage their finances. In response, Intuit formed a ten-person team to explore why these people were not using QuickBooks. The team discovered that the small businesses with which they spoke did not make the association between accounting and good financial management. The next step for the team was to simplify QuickBooks by stripping out features. The group took the prototype to their potential customers to get feedback. Again they were told that the product was too complicated. Customers wanted to be able to track the money coming in and the money going out. The team realized that some customers were getting hung up on the accounting terminology, so they relabeled inputs like "accounts payable" as "money out." The first prototype had reduced the number of QuickBooks setup screens to 125, but by the end of the new product's development, the team had reduced that number to 3. The process involved six cycles of customer interviews and led to QuickBooks: Simple Start Edition. The product was launched in September 2004 and outsold all accounting software in the United States except for QuickBooks.

Over the last few years the strategy has worked with 2009 revenues of $3.2 billion and growing to 7,800 employees. By encouraging employees to try new things, Intuit has been able to keep the entrepreneurial spirit alive and well. Visible gestures, such as awards for 'The Failure We Learned the Most From," have kept the culture that Cook instilled firmly rooted.

Discussion Questions

1. What specific pieces or parts of culture are apparent in the Intuit story?

2. How would you categorize the culture at Intuit according to Table 10-1 in our chapter?

3. Compare the elements of failure described in the chapter to the perspective Intuit takes with new ideas. How would you recommend Intuit handle failures?

SOURCE: Adapted from David Kirkpatrick, "Throw It at the Wall and See if It Sticks," *Fortune,* December 12, 2005: 142–150; and company Web sites accessed April 17, 2010.

Summary and Conclusions

In this chapter we have examined the need to embed entrepreneurship into the culture of an organization. The nature of culture has been explored and, while a complex and time-consuming undertaking, it was argued that culture can be managed. Culture exists at different levels, and manifests itself through a variety of symbols. There also may be different types of cultures, each of which has implications for the frequency and degree of entrepreneurship in the organization. In addition, key elements of an entrepreneurial culture were presented.

Entrepreneurial cultures involve big visions for what can be achieved, encouragement of healthy dissatisfaction, an ongoing sense of urgency, and acceptance of change as a norm. We also explored the role of individualism versus collectivism in companies. While significant emphasis is placed these days on teams and groups, managers must not forget the vital role played by individuals in affecting entrepreneurship. The design of jobs, company structures, performance appraisals, and rewards should balance incentives for individual initiative and risk-taking against reinforcements for teamwork and group outputs.

Lastly, we took a look at the value of failure. Entrepreneurial companies accept the reality that failure goes with the territory. It is a sign of progress, and its absence is an indication that nothing new is being attempted. Of course, employees tend to be skeptical when the boss says it is okay to make mistakes. Also we explored the notion of learning from failure and the role that grief can play in obstructing the learning process. The need is for a culture that embraces the systematic management of failure, where a philosophy of failure is widely communicated, grief recovery methods are employed, rewards and awards are given for entrepreneurial initiatives that do not work out, and efforts are formally organized to document and derive learning lessons from failed efforts.

References

Archer, J. 1999. *The Nature of Grief: The Evolution and Psychology of Reactions to Loss* (New York: Routledge).

Brief, A. P., and Weiss, H. M. 2002. "Organizational Behavior: Affect in the Workplace," *Annual Review of Psychology*, 53(1): 279–307.

Benight, C. C., and Bandura, A. 2003. "Social Cognitive Theory of Traumatic Recovery: The Role of Perceived Self-Efficacy," *Behaviour Research and Therapy*, 42: 1129–1148.

Burton, T. M. 2004. "Flop Factor: By Learning from Failures, Lilly Keeps Drug Pipeline Full," *Wall Street Journal* (Eastern Edition) A1.

Collins, J. C., and Porras, J. I. 1994. *Built to Last* (New York: HarperBusiness).

Davis, C. G., and Nolen-Hoeksema, S. 2001. "How Do People Make Sense of Loss?" *American Behavioral Scientist*, 44(5): 726–741.

Deal, T., and Kennedy, A. 2000. *Corporate Cultures* (Reading, MA: Perseus Publishing).

Green, S. G., Welsh, M. A., and Dehler, G. E. 2003. "Advocacy, Performance, and Threshold Influences on Decisions to Terminate New Product Development," *Academy of Management Journal*, 46: 419–434.

Hamel, G. 2000. *Leading the Revolution* (Boston: Harvard Business School Press).

Harris, S. G., and Sutton, R. I. 1986. "Functions of Parting Ceremonies in Dying Organizations," *Academy of Management Journal*, 29: 5–30.

Jacobs, S., Mazure, C., and Prigerson, H. 2000. "Diagnostic Criteria for Traumatic Grief," *Death Studies*, 24(3): 185–199.

Kets de Vries, M., and Miller, D. 1984. *The Neurotic Organization* (San Francisco: Jossey-Bass).

Kirschbaum, R. 2005. "Open Innovation in Practice," *Research & Technology Management*, 48(4): 24–28.

Kotter, J. 1996. *Leading Change* (Boston: Harvard Business School Press).

Kriegesmann, B., Kley, T., and Schwering, M. 2005. "Creative Errors and Heroic Failures: Capturing Their Innovative Potential," *Journal of Business Strategy*, 26(3): 57–64.

Kuratko, D. F. 2009, *Entrepreneurship: Theory, Process, & Practice*, 8th edition (Mason, OH: Cengage/South-Western Publishing).

Leavy, B. 2005. "A Leader's Guide to Creating an Innovation Culture," *Strategy & Leadership*, 33(4): 38–45.

Maidique, M. A., and Zirger, B. J. 1985. "The New Product Learning Cycle," *Research Policy*, 14: 299–313.

McGrath, R. G. 1995. "Advantage from Adversity: Learning from Disappointment in Internal Corporate Ventures," *Journal of Business Venturing*, 10: 121–142.

Mitroff, I., and Kilmann, R. 1975. "Stories Managers Tell: A New Tool for Organizational Problem-Solving," *Management Review*, July: 18–28.

Morris, M. H., Allen, J. A., and Avila, A. 1993. "Individualism and the Modern Corporation: Implications for Innovation and Entrepreneurship," *Journal of Management*, 19(3): 595–612.

Nolen-Hoeksema, S., McBride, A., and Larson, J. 1997. "Rumination and Psychological Distress among Bereaved Partners," *Journal of Personality and Social Psychology*, 72: 855–862.

Ouchi, W. 1981. *Theory Z: How American Business Can Meet the Japanese Challenge* (Reading, MA: Addison-Wesley).

Peng, M. W., and Shenkar, O. 2002. "Joint Venture Dissolution as Corporate Divorce," *Academy of Management Executive*, 16(2): 92–105.

Peters, T. J., and Waterman, R. H. 1982. *In Search of Excellence* (New York: Harper Collins).

Peters, T. 1997. *The Circle of Innovation* (New York: Alfred A. Knopf).

Sethia, N., and Von Glinow, M. A. 1985. "Arriving at Four Cultures by Managing the Reward System," in R. Kilmann et al. (eds.), *Gaining Control of the Corporate Culture* (San Francisco: Jossey-Bass): 400–420.

Shepherd, D. A. 2009. *Lemons to Lemonade: Squeezing Every Last Drop of Success out of Your Mistakes* (Wharton School Publishing: Philadelphia: PA).

Shepherd, D. A., and Cardon, M. 2009. "Negative Emotional Reactions to Project Failure and the Self-Compassion to Learn from the Experience," *Journal of Management Studies*, 46(6): 923–949.

Shepherd, D. A., and Kuratko, D. F. 2009. "The Death of an Innovative Project: How Grief Recovery Enhances Learning," *Business Horizons*, 52(5): 451–458.

Shepherd, D. A., Covin, J. G., and Kuratko, D. F. 2009. "Corporate Failure from Entrepreneurship: Managing the Grief Process," *Journal of Business Venturing*, 24(6): 588–600.

Timmons, J., and Spinelli, S. 2009. *New Venture Creation* (Burr Ridge, IL: Irwin McGraw-Hill).

Trice, H., and Beyer, J., 1993. *The Cultures of Work Organizations* (Englewood Cliffs, NJ: Prentice-Hall).

Tropman, J., and Morningstar, G. 1989. *Entrepreneurial Systems for the 1990s* (Westport, CT: Quorum).

3

ACHIEVING AND SUSTAINING ENTREPRENEURIAL PERFORMANCE

"*The greatest difficulty in the world is not for people to accept new ideas, but to make them forget about old ideas.*"

—JOHN MAYNARD KEYNES, ECONOMIST

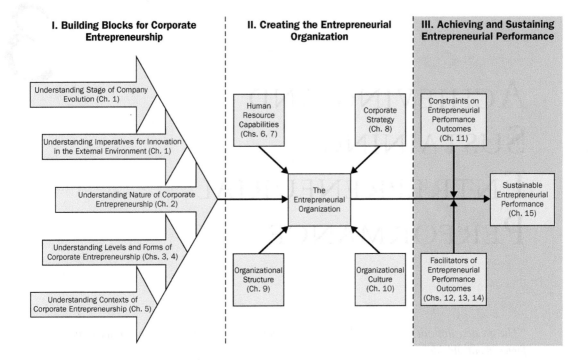

Section Introduction

This final section of the book outlines practical methods for achieving and sustaining high levels of entrepreneurial performance within organizations. Each of these five chapters is designed to examine a particular facet of entrepreneurial performance. These facets include the major constraints that entrepreneurial employees must regularly overcome, the roles that leaders must play when initiating and implementing entrepreneurial activity, the methods to assess entrepreneurial activity over time, critical ways in which organizational controls can hinder or facilitate entrepreneurial behavior, and finally, the concluding thoughts on sustaining entrepreneurial efforts in the future.

Chapter 11

Constraints on Entrepreneurial Performance

Introduction

Company survival depends on continuous growth and an ability to defend against the ongoing moves of competitors. The quests for survival and sustainable advantage are the reasons many companies have come to recognize the critical importance of entrepreneurial activity. One survey of executives found that the leading reasons for emphasizing entrepreneurship inside their companies were strategic necessity (to remain competitive) and the maturing of existing businesses (Block and MacMillan, 1993). The problem today concerns *how* to make it happen and, assuming the company can do so, *how much* to let it happen.

The pursuit of entrepreneurship within a company creates a new and potentially complex set of challenges on both a theoretical and practical level. On a theoretical level, company-wide entrepreneurship is not included in, or accommodated by, most of the theories, models, or frameworks that have been developed to guide managerial practice. Progress is being made in these areas, yet the field is still emerging. As a result, we are still learning about what kind of entrepreneurship is likely under various types of company structures, control systems, reward approaches, cultures, and other managerial variables. Limited progress in theory building hinders our ability to predict, explain, and shape the environment in which corporate entrepreneurship flourishes.

On a practical level, managers typically find themselves in uncharted territory when it comes to entrepreneurship. They lack guidelines regarding how to formulate entrepreneurial strategies, manage entrepreneurial employees, or redirect resources towards entrepreneurial initiatives. Traditional management practices often do not apply when trying to foster entrepreneurship (see Table 11-1). Further, most of the infrastructure within a company (systems, structures, policies and procedures, etc.) has been put in place for reasons other than to accommodate entrepreneurship. Companies tend to develop in ways that enable them to efficiently manage the present. This means they are not organized in ways that allow them to create the future. As a result, entrepreneurship usually clashes with the mainstream operations of the company. More fundamentally, entrepreneurship can be extremely threatening to the people who do the everyday work of the organization because it can be disruptive, uncomfortable, irritating, and distracting.

TABLE 11-1	
Obstacles and Effects of Traditional Practices	
Traditional Management Practices	*Adverse Effects*
Enforce standard procedures to avoid mistakes	Innovative solutions blocked, funds misspent
Manage resources for efficiency and ROI	Competitive lead is lost, low market penetration
Control against plan	Facts that should replace assumptions are ignored
Plan long-term	Nonviable goals locked in, high failure costs
Manage functionally	Entrepreneur failure and/or venture failure
Avoid moves that risk the base business	Missed opportunities
Protect the company's base business at all possible cost	Venturing dumped when base business threatened
Judge new steps from prior experience	Wrong decisions about competition and markets
Compensate uniformly	Low motivation and inefficient operations
Promote compatible individuals	Loss of innovators

SOURCE: Adapted from H. B. Sykes, and Z. Block, "Corporate Venturing Obstacles: Sources and Solutions," *Journal of Business Venturing*, 4(3) 1989: 161. Elsevier Science Publishing Co., Inc. Reprinted by permission.

Not surprisingly, there are many in companies who will go out of their way to not only resist an entrepreneurial idea but also actually kill it.

In this chapter, we examine the barriers and obstacles within companies that constrain the ongoing entrepreneurial process. A framework for categorizing these obstacles is presented. In addition, some of the most consequential challenges are discussed including the ethical dilemmas that surround entrepreneurial behavior. Insights are provided regarding where to begin in efforts to remove the barriers and overcome the obstacles.

A Framework for Understanding the Obstacles

There are, in reality, hundreds of factors within the typical company that constrain entrepreneurship. In fact, there can be so many obstacles as to make entrepreneurship seem like a hopeless pipedream. Yet we find entrepreneurship happening even in the most stifling and bureaucratic of organizations. The key is to first identify the relevant obstacles, the ones that represent the greatest threat to a new concept or idea. The corporate entrepreneur must examine obstacles with an eye towards determining:

- Which constraints can be ignored?

- Which can be worked around?

- Which can be eliminated?

- Which can be converted into facilitators of entrepreneurship?

- Which must be accepted even if they limit the scope or scale of what the corporate entrepreneur can accomplish?

Given the large number of potential constraints, it is helpful to identify general categories into which they can be grouped. A useful framework for capturing virtually all the obstacles breaks them down into six groups: *systems, structure, strategic direction, policies, people,* and *culture* (Morris, 1998). These categories are based on an extensive review of the literature on corporate innovation and entrepreneurship, surveys of hundreds of medium-sized and large industrial organizations, and in-depth assessments of three Fortune 500 companies.

Examples of the specific constraints found within each category are provided in Table 11-2. This set of items is not an exhaustive list but instead includes some of the more pervasive problem areas. Let us examine each of the categories in more detail.

SYSTEMS

Maturing organizations are typically dependent upon a number of formal managerial systems that have evolved over the years. These systems exist to provide stability, order, and coordination to an increasingly complex internal corporate environment. The trade-off, however, is a strong disincentive for entrepreneurship.

For example, employee reward and measurement systems often encourage safe, conservative behaviors that produce short-term payoffs. Other times, they are vague, inconsistent, or perceived as inequitable. Kerr (1975) explains that many managers are guilty of the "folly of rewarding A, while hoping for B." They tend to ask for or expect innovative behavior, but actually measure and reward non-innovative behaviors. Control systems encourage managers to micromanage the expenditure of every dollar and to establish quantifiable performance benchmarks in as many activity areas as possible. These benchmarks become ends in themselves. They also convey a lack of trust in employee discretion. Budgeting systems provide no flexibility for the funding of bootleg or unofficial projects and tend to reward the politically powerful. There is no money for experimenting on the job. Costing systems are frequently based on arbitrary allocation schemes, where any product or project can be made to look

TABLE 11–2

Categories of Organizational Constraints on Corporate Entrepreneurship

Systems	Structures	Strategic Direction	Policies and Procedures	People	Culture
• Misdirected reward and evaluation systems • Oppressive control systems • Inflexible budgeting systems • Arbitrary cost allocation systems • Overly rigid, formal planning systems	• Too many hierarchical levels • Overly narrow span of control • Responsibility without authority • Top-down management • Restricted communication channels • Lack of accountability for innovation and change	• Absence of innovation goals • No formal strategy for entrepreneurship • No vision from the top • Lack of commitment from senior executives • No entrepreneurial role models at the top	• Long, complex approval cycles • Extensive red-tape and documentation requirements • Over-reliance on established rules of thumb • Unrealistic performance criteria	• Fear of failure • Resistance to change • Parochial bias • "Turf" protection • Complacency • Short-term orientation • Inappropriate skills and talents for managing entrepreneurial change	• Ill-defined values • Lack of consensus over value and norm priorities • Lack of fit of values with current competitive context • Values that conflict with innovativeness, risk-taking, and proactiveness

SOURCE: Adapted from M. M. Morris, *Entrepreneurial Intensity*, Westport, CT: Quorum Books, 1998: 97.

untenable simply as a function of the overhead or indirect fixed costs that are assigned to it and must be recovered.

Planning, although critical for successful entrepreneurship, often serves as an obstacle. It becomes formulaic. The problem occurs because of an overemphasis on superfluous analysis, on form instead of content, on the planning document instead of the planning process, and on having professional planners write the plan (instead of relying on those charged with actually implementing it). The result is an overly rigid process that is incapable of quickly responding to new opportunities.

STRUCTURES

As a company designs more hierarchical levels into the organizational structure, the ability to identify market opportunities, achieve management commitment, reallocate resources, take risks, or implement effective marketplace moves becomes problematic. Entrepreneurship suffers the farther away decision making becomes from everyday operations, everyday interactions with customers and competitors, and everyday work on new technologies and products. Moreover, hierarchies tend to be accompanied by two other entrepreneurial barriers, top-down (rather than bottom-up) management and restrictive (rather than open) channels of communication. The result is frequently intransigence, which leads to a lack of commitment to innovation and change at all levels of the organization.

There is also a tendency to continually narrow the span of control of managers over subordinates, in effect compartmentalizing operations as companies mature. The result is over-supervised employees with little room to be creative or improvise. Furthermore, as employees become more segmented and compartmentalized, frames of reference become quite narrow. The ability to integrate perspectives and methods across boundaries is stifled. Meanwhile, accountability for effective change efforts is sufficiently diffused such that no one has a positive stake in ensuring that change occurs.

Structures that assign responsibility for entrepreneurial activities to managers without delegating adequate amounts of authority represent an additional constraint. Lacking the authority to try new methods or approaches for addressing obstacles or expending required resources, the manager is likely to become frustrated and perhaps cynical.

STRATEGIC DIRECTION

While the desire may be to achieve entrepreneurship throughout the company, little can be accomplished without meaningful direction from the top. Established companies frequently have sophisticated planning systems that produce comprehensive strategies for marketing, production, and corporate finance but ignore the subject of entrepreneurship and innovation altogether. In the absence of specific goals for product and process innovation and a strategy for accomplishing such goals, entrepreneurship will only result haphazardly or by chance.

More fundamental, however, is the lack of commitment from senior executives to the principle of institutionalized entrepreneurship. This requires leaders who are visionaries, seeing the company and its people for what they can be, not what they have been. It requires leaders who are engaged in entrepreneurial processes as they occur throughout the enterprise. Instead, senior management is more typically cautious, suspicious, or completely unaware of efforts to break with tradition and capitalize on opportunity. Middle- and lower-level employees are strongly influenced by the role models found at the top of the organization. What they often find are politicians and technocrats who are well versed in the art of corporate survival.

POLICIES AND PROCEDURES

Those involved in entrepreneurial endeavors are, by definition, addressing the unknown. Their efforts are often undermined by organizational policies and procedures that were established to bring order and consistency to the everyday operations of the company. These procedural requirements tend to be relatively well-known. Operating guidelines are established based on the rules of experience, with a premium placed on conservatism. The corporate entrepreneur comes to view these policies and procedures as burdensome red tape, and many find success to be unattainable unless rules are bent or broken.

Two of the most costly side-effects of detailed operating policies are complex approval cycles for new ventures and elaborate documentation requirements. These obstacles not only consume an inordinate amount of the corporate entrepreneur's time and energy but also frequently serve as well-designed mechanisms for incrementally dismantling an innovative concept. A related problem is the tendency for existing policies and procedures to impose unrealistic timetables and performance benchmarks on entrepreneurial programs. Deadlines and performance standards that reflect everyday operations often create an incentive to compromise on truly novel ideas. The corporate entrepreneur finds it necessary to tailor innovations to performance criteria that reflect the present and the past rather than the competitive requirements of the future.

PEOPLE

Practical experience tells us that people represent the greatest obstacle to entrepreneurship. The number one priority in any attempt to increase the entrepreneurial intensity of an organization must be to change people's attitudes and perceptions and, specifically, to get them to be accepting of change and tolerant of failure in their work. Entrepreneurship is concerned with change and the management of change efforts. There is, however, a natural tendency for people to resist change. Given the opportunity, employees become comfortable with established ways of doing things. They value predictability and stability and are frequently skeptical of the need for change. Change is viewed as threatening and is met with a defensive, parochial attitude. This is especially the case where employees have no role in the change program.

Furthermore, employees demonstrate a tendency to be preoccupied with the demands of the present, not the future. Correspondingly, it may be unrealistic to expect them to adopt a long-term perspective or to recognize the need for continual adaptation. In addition, the entrepreneurial spirit is stifled by a pervading fear of failure that is prevalent in most companies. People come to believe it is better to avoid failure than to risk success. They apparently perceive there is more to lose than to gain. We are not suggesting that failure should be congratulated but rather to understand that failure is an important medium for learning; it should be embraced as such. It is a sign of progress. The reality is that a majority of highly novel ventures (whether companies, products, services, or processes) fail, suggesting the need for a realistic appraisal of the outcome of any entrepreneurial effort.

Motivating people is also a problem, especially for those driven by a need for power and status. Such individuals approach questions of innovation from the standpoint of "turf protection." They hoard resources, especially information. They resist open communication and are suspicious of collaborative efforts.

One additional people-related issue concerns a general lack of skills and talents in the entrepreneurial area. While there is ample creative potential in every employee of the company, many have never learned to develop or channel their creative energies. Some convince themselves that they are incapable of creative thinking. Others refuse to look beyond their current field of reference for ideas and solutions. Still others, on finding a creative solution, lack the skills necessary to bend the rules, build the coalitions, and work through or around the system to achieve successful implementation. Such problems are compounded by the apparent inability of many of those in supervisory positions to motivate and manage creative individuals.

Management may be able to fix the structure and remove bureaucratic rules and procedures, but the challenges involved in getting employees to embrace entrepreneurship, change the way they do things, collaborate on projects involving untested (and seemingly crazy) ideas, and give up resources to support entrepreneurial initiatives can be especially vexing. While entrepreneurship represents tremendous opportunity to the company at large, it threatens the individuals inside the organization. For many employees, entrepreneurship means that current products will be eliminated, budgets will be reallocated, processes will be modified, and someone other than themselves will be a star. As a result, the pathways of most new ideas are blocked by:

- Discomfort—Formal and informal resistance to change
- A Blind Eye—Making premature and uninformed judgments

- Neophobia—the dread of anything new or novel, fear of the unknown; a sense of embarrassment or humiliation that accompanies the admission that existing products or procedures are inferior to new proposals

- Caution—it's safer to have the "me too—later" attitude

- Order—entrepreneurship is a threat to the predictability and continuity on which all businesses are based—a new idea frequently represents a potential or real disruption of this continuity; the unwritten principle in business requires that disruptions be strictly controlled or held to a minimum, no matter what they are

- Inconvenience—Anticipation of the extra trouble in handling and implementing new ideas: "We have enough work as it is"

- Politics—new ideas frequently pose a threat to the organizational stature and vested interests of managers who are anxious to maintain the existing hierarchical structure.

The dilemma of a large institution trying to nurture a people-focused entrepreneurial atmosphere, while maintaining corporate controls, can be addressed if disciplined reporting systems are balanced with an environment built around mutual trust and open communication (Sathe, 1989). Risk-taking by individuals is strongly related to support, structure, and resources. Management has to act on two fronts simultaneously. One side of the battle involves offering incentives for entrepreneurial efforts and making resources accessible. This can be thought of as the "upside". The other side concerns reducing the perceived costs associated with failure, helping employees get comfortable with trying things that have a good chance of not working out. It also requires an overt effort to protect entrepreneurial individuals in terms of their career development. We can label this "management of the downside."

CULTURE

As we demonstrated in Chapter 10, companies noted as successful innovators tend to foster a strong organizational culture. This culture is built around a central set of values that pervades every aspect of company operations. Employees are continually reinforced to internalize these values, and those who do not internalize them rarely last. These values are the lifeblood of the company, creating the standards and providing the direction for growth and development.

Where companies fail to clearly define what they stand for, or do not achieve a consensus over value priorities (e.g., customer needs, quality, efficiency, service, and reliability), entrepreneurship will have no focus. Even when priorities exist, values can be inconsistent with current competitive requirements. For instance, the company that stresses reliability or efficiency may find the marketplace puts a much higher premium on flexibility and value for the dollar.

Furthermore, entrepreneurship must itself become part of the organizational value system. This means company-wide commitment to innovation, calculated risk-taking, and proactiveness. Such a commitment becomes impossible when the pervading emphasis is on imitation of competitors, conservation, and self-aggrandizement.

Coming Up Short: Limitations of the Corporate Entrepreneur

In addition to these major sets of obstacles, entrepreneurial initiatives can be held back or derailed because of a number of shortcomings of the corporate entrepreneur. These are limitations that, in spite of a desire to pursue entrepreneurial ideas, often lead the manager or employee to fail.

LACK OF POLITICAL SAVVY: LEARNING TO WORK THE SYSTEM

Unpopular as it may be, politics is a reality in the work environment. All organizations are inherently political. They are made up of individuals acting in their own interests. To implement corporate entrepreneurship, an innovative corporate entrepreneur must attempt to influence other people, particularly the key stakeholders on whom the concept depends. Failure to identify those stakeholders and to anticipate and influence their behavior can drastically slow the corporate entrepreneur's progress, if not stifle him or her completely. There are numerous types of "political" problems that present critical roadblocks to the corporate entrepreneurial process. Many of the obstacles that follow have political undertones or political ramifications associated with them.

LACK OF TIME: CRISIS MANAGEMENT

Employees have jobs to perform. If anything, intensified competition and the information age have resulted in employees having less free time on the job. Many people stay busy simply trying to keep up with the wealth of information that inundates them on the job each day, and the continuous changes in technology that affect how they do their jobs. Further, they continually face crises that require all of their energies. There just isn't a lot of time during the workday to experiment and try new things. A few companies, 3M for example, formally encourage their employees to spend a portion of their time on individual "pet projects."

LACK OF INCENTIVE TO INNOVATE: BEYOND TOKENISM

Traditionally, corporations do not sufficiently reward (financially or otherwise) employees for being innovative. Many companies have recently implemented reward systems for cost-saving suggestions or ideas presented through structured suggestion programs, but these efforts often represent token gestures. With few exceptions, rewards for innovative thinking and behavior are not systematically built into corporate performance systems.

Corporate entrepreneurs are motivated by all kinds of rewards (e.g., bonuses, free time, profit share, pool of capital to use on future projects, stock options). They should also be ready to share some of the downside risks associated with their concepts or ideas. As in the case of any independent entrepreneurial venture, corporate entrepreneurs should realize the rewards associated with venture success as well as the risks associated with venture failure.

Lack of Financial Credibility: Inability to Project Believable Numbers

New concepts require financing, and financing requires good financial justification. For this reason, successful corporate entrepreneurs must either be adept at financial projections and calculations, or recruit a member of their team who has this knowledge and is willing and able to develop this portion of the venture plan.

The reason for this is quite simple. Boards of directors, presidents and vice presidents, and intracapital (money inside the company that is available for entrepreneurial projects) evaluation committees are not going to invest money in a new venture unless the entrepreneur or champion can demonstrate the potential for a return on the investment equal to or greater than the profit margins the company needs to make. Any entrepreneurial venture must cover its own opportunity costs—the foregone returns the company could have made if the allocated resources had been used in some other way. Often, corporate entrepreneurs are so in love with their venture idea that they approach these decision makers unprepared, are denied the initial capital to develop an idea, get frustrated, and give up.

The problem, of course, is that the entrepreneur is creating the new. A market may be created where it did not exist before. A need may be addressed that was never met before. When dealing with the unknown, hard numbers based on realistic assumptions are not easy to generate. And when they are generated, such numbers are easy targets for those who are skeptical about a given project and want to see it eliminated.

Yet the reality is that even in large organizations, funds are limited, and support for products and services is determined by extensive market research, detailed financial projections, and contingency plans in case the sales projections are overestimated. One corporate entrepreneur at 3M asked for $20 million to continue the research and development on what became laser disks. In his meeting with the board of directors, his biggest obstacle was criticism of his financial projections and profit margins. Whether the corporate entrepreneur is asking for $20,000 or $20 million, even from a company as large and innovative as 3M, careful planning and clear projections are a must.

LACK OF PEOPLE DEVELOPMENT SKILLS: AUTOCRACY RULES

Too many of today's corporate leaders still adhere to Douglas MacGregor's top-down, "do as I say" style of management. Managers with an autocratic, or Theory X, style are not prone to allow people to make mistakes. They question the motives and intentions of their employees, assuming they are driven only by financial rewards and security. Consequently, it is difficult for them to understand or encourage the excitement a subordinate might have about a new venture idea. It is also difficult for them to empower employees or trust the intentions of a potential corporate entrepreneur.

Many of these managers suffer from what has been termed the "that's not my idea" syndrome. It is hard for them to imagine that one of their subordinates is capable of having and developing a viable innovative product or service. And if the employee does come up with a worthwhile idea, these top-down, controlling type managers often try to take the credit. Frequently, they will want to create a task force or ad hoc committee to look into the idea, effectively taking control away from the corporate entrepreneur.

LACK OF LEGITIMACY: UNTESTED CONCEPT AND UNTESTED ENTREPRENEUR

Achieving credibility or legitimacy for an entrepreneurial idea is usually difficult. Since the concept has no real track record—customers, suppliers, etc.—the corporate entrepreneur encounters internal skepticism. At best, there will be reluctant and lukewarm supporters. At worst, there will be individuals determined to undermine the concept. Building confidence and credibility can be a slow, painstaking process; however, it is critical to the survival of the entrepreneurial idea.

Even more important is the legitimacy of the corporate entrepreneur. Companies are apt to invest in an untested concept if the corporate entrepreneur is tested. They may invest in a fairly certain or tested idea even if the corporate entrepreneur is untested. But the likelihood of investing in an untested idea and an untested entrepreneur is slim. Corporate entrepreneurs must find ways to get experience on innovative projects, volunteering to help with the initiatives of others, trying to take leadership roles in teams, and succeeding on their own small initiatives before pushing for big ones.

LACK OF "SEED" CAPITAL: THE PROBLEM OF EARLY RESOURCES

In the initial stages, any new idea requires an adequate supply of resources, including people, materials, and often access to capacity in the organization's production and service systems. Yet the corporate entrepreneur generally faces severe constraints in the amount of resources available for the new concept. When the idea is new, it is most vulnerable and most in need of refinement and adaptation—and yet it is least likely to receive financial support at this stage. Further, the corporate entrepreneur, more often than not, is seen as an internal competitor attempting to take resources from someone or something else. This means that even if the corporate entrepreneur could succeed in securing the needed resources, those resources may end up being conceded with reluctance and lingering resentment.

Lack of Open Ownership: Protecting Turf

When Joline Godfrey of Polaroid was trying to create a service business in a manufacturing company (the development of a photo treasure hunt for vacationers called "Odysseum"), the marketing department claimed her idea fell into their domain and argued that it was time for them to take over (Kuratko and Hodgetts, 2007). This is a common occurrence in large organizations. Often, departments are more concerned with protecting their turf than they are with developing new ideas that will benefit the organization. Frequently, the corporate entrepreneur will run into "power plays" and battles for control over decision making occurring between vice presidents and/or their respective areas of responsibility. Successful corporate entrepreneurs need to make themselves aware of these power plays and, if at all possible, stay out of them. Either that, or they must ensure they are aligned with the vice president or department that wins the battle.

Lack of a Sponsor: Someone to Watch Over You

To help them in their assessment of the political realities, corporate entrepreneurs need a supporter who oversees the progress of the corporate venture from higher in the organization. Sponsors act as coaches for entrepreneurs. They also act as buffers, guarding innovators against unnecessary organizational bureaucratic interference, and allow the corporate entrepreneur to concentrate on his or her venture. Sponsors can also help the champion create alliances needed to build venture teams by introducing the entrepreneur to the right people in the organization. They help keep threatening projects undercover for as long as possible. Sponsors are most effective if they have personally championed an idea earlier in their career. When this is the case, they also serve as role models who can offer empathy and optimism through a critical but trusting attitude.

Lack of Energy and Shared Enthusiasm: The Inertia Problem

Inertia represents one of the most serious problems confronting corporate entrepreneurs. It refers to a lack of movement or support, a lack of energy, and resistance insofar as some new concept or idea is concerned. Block and MacMillan (1993) found five specific causes of the dangerous but very real problem of inertia:

- *Indifference:* The new concept's initial small size renders key parts of the organization indifferent to providing the cooperation required to get the project launched. Although support may be required from engineering, marketing, or the sales force, it may receive very little attention simply because the idea is considered insignificant compared to the ongoing business. This can also happen in external relations, with suppliers, customers, and distributors simply ignoring the concept because it is so small.

- *Distraction:* The people responsible for conducting the company's major ongoing business may simply be too distracted by day-to-day pressures. If the concept needed the support of the manufacturing facility, for example, this project becomes, at best, a distraction from the principal business and, at worst, a disruptive irritation.

- *Competition:* Competitors can mobilize their clout with distributors and suppliers to deny support to the fledgling venture.

- *Disaffection:* Resistance to the corporate entrepreneur's progress and even attempts to subvert him or her can be initiated by people in the organization who either do not believe in corporate entrepreneurship, are envious, or feel that the corporate entrepreneur is disturbing their comfort zones. In particular, people in staff functions whose mission is to ensure homogeneity in the organization may attempt to stifle the corporate entrepreneur with procedures, rules, and policies. Anything that is new and requires different treatment will tend to disrupt and threaten their systems. This attitude can extend beyond the boundaries of the company—to agencies, unions, or any other entity that has a vested interest in preserving the status quo.

- *Direct threat:* Determined opponents of the corporate entrepreneur who see his or her idea as an attack on their position or a direct threat to their part of the organization. Once again, this type of resistance can extend beyond the organization's boundaries.

LACK OF PERSONAL RENEWAL: THE ISSUE OF REINFORCED DENIAL

Andy Grove (1996) former CEO of Intel has discussed the problems of past success leading individuals to be overconfident in current projects to continually avoid or resist anything new. Senior managers become successful by having been good at what they do. Over time they learn to lead with their strengths. So it's not surprising that they will keep implementing the same strategic and tactical moves that worked for them during the course of their careers. This can be referred to as "reinforced denial."

When the environment changes in such a way as to render the old skills and strengths less relevant, many managers almost instinctively cling to their past. They refuse to acknowledge changes around them. They are willing to work harder at the traditional tasks or skills, in the hope that their hard work will overcome the change. The new is denied through reinforced belief in past success.

LACK OF URGENCY: FEAR AS GOOD AND BAD

Based on his experiences at Intel, Grove (1996) concludes, "The most important role of managers is to create an environment in which people are passionately dedicated to winning in the marketplace. Fear plays a major role in creating and maintaining such passion. Fear of competition, fear of bankruptcy, fear of being wrong and fear of losing can all be powerful motivators." Thus, such fears may be a positive force in the sense that they create an ongoing sense of urgency that catapults people into action. And, the constant reminders of these fears can be a sustaining factor.

However, if the fear becomes a negative force, such as the fear of punishment or retribution by a superior, then it is a major obstacle to corporate entrepreneurship. It takes many years of consistent behavior to eliminate fear of punishment as an inhibitor of entrepreneurship. It takes only one incident to introduce it. News of this incident will spread through the organization like wildfire and discourage everyone from introducing new ideas. Once an environment of fear takes over, it will lead to paralysis throughout the organization and severely constrain entrepreneurial behavior.

LACK OF APPROPRIATE TIMING: THE RESOURCE SHIFT DILEMMA

The lack of resources to support innovation was discussed earlier; however, the actual timing of resource allocations is also critical. Assume the corporate entrepreneur is able to convince senior management to move resources to a new initiative. The timing of the transfer of resources from its current use to the new has to be done with crucial balance in mind. If resources are moved from the old business, the old task, or the old product too early it can be costly. With a little more effort, significant unrealized potential might have been achieved. On the other hand, if management hangs on to the old business too long it could cause opportunities to be missed. The company misses a chance to grab a new business opportunity, add momentum to a new product area, or get aligned with the new order of things. Most typically, managers act too slowly and too late in their movement of resources, causing the entrepreneurial project to stall.

Corporate Innovators or Rogue Managers: An Ethical Dilemma

Some of the most visible entrepreneurial stories emerging from the corporate world over the past two decades have resulted in bankruptcy or complete dissolution of the companies involved—often due to highly questionable and clearly unethical behaviors. The corporate misdeeds of Enron, Global Crossing, Andersen, and WorldCom as well as the huge financial failures on Wall Street including the complete demise of Lehman Brothers and Merrill Lynch are even more disturbing to the extent that these companies were the more visible symbols of a far deeper and disturbing pattern in corporate actions.

The popular business press has, at times, created the impression that entrepreneurial actions inside the corporation are unethical in and of themselves. Such impressions can be quite misleading, as entrepreneurial actions are not inherently unethical *or* ethical. That is, the degree to which behavior is ethical is a separate dimension from the degree to which it is entrepreneurial. Unfortunately, high-profile cases in which exhibited behavior is unethical while seemingly entrepreneurial (e.g., Enron) can lead casual observers to falsely equate these two behavioral dimensions, giving entrepreneurship a black eye in the process.

Ethical dilemmas represent a formidable constraint in the development of corporate entrepreneurship. How far should employees be encouraged to "disrupt" or "subvert" established standards? Hamel (2000) calls for employees to become "revolutionaries" in order to move organizations into the new competitive landscape. Yet to what extent do managers act in a "revolutionary" manner in the name of innovation before ethical standards are compromised? Without an organization providing the proper entrepreneurial environment and ethical guidance, some managers may display rogue behavior in attaining their goals. In other words, they cross the line of good judgment and commit unethical acts with the initial intention of being entrepreneurial. Hence, companies must be wary of the "rogue manager" acting under the guise of the corporate entrepreneur.

There are various explanations as to why managers involved in entrepreneurial activity might act in an unethical manner. Unethical behavior could result from a cultural condition of extreme, degenerative individualism that sociologist Charles Derber explains as "wilding": "Wilding includes a vast spectrum of self-centered and self-aggrandizing behavior that harms others . . . instrumental wilding is wilding for money, career advancement or other calculable personal gain" (Derber, 1996, pp. 6–7).

While lack of proper ethics may be rooted in the company culture, it is also important to examine the individual manager. Some individuals are simply unethical to begin with. Others develop excessive drive over time and set overly ambitious personal career goals. Corporate entrepreneurs—often described as those managers or employees who do not follow the status quo of their coworkers—are often depicted as visionaries who dream of taking the company in new directions. In practice, though, when attempting to overcome internal obstacles to their professional goals, they can often walk a fine line between clever resourcefulness and outright immoral behavior. This dilemma has only recently begun to receive attention from researchers (Kuratko and Goldsby, 2004; Morris et al., 2002).

Yet another reason managers may behave unethically is not because of greed or ill will, but because they do not clearly grasp their professional responsibilities (Donaldson, 1989). This holds especially true for the managers pursuing entrepreneurial initiatives. There are many aspects of organizational life that can make entrepreneurial activity seem completely unattainable. Yet we find entrepreneurial activity happening even in the most stifling and bureaucratic of organizations (Kuratko et al., 2001). The key for managers is to identify and examine the factors that represent the greatest threat to new concepts or ideas, and then conscientiously examine ways to overcome them. However, it is at this point that the entrepreneurial manager must carefully distinguish creative problem solving from immoral behavior.

Entrepreneurial managers are typically highly motivated individuals who will put extraordinary thought and effort into achieving things previously not done in the organization. However, the previously presented framework of obstacles included systems, structures, and policies and procedures—operational factors that clearly frustrate innovative managers, causing them to deviate from the parameters of the formal organizational structure. A feeling of ambivalence can occur, as the manager feels like he or she is being pulled in two directions. The manager must meet organizational expectations to retain his or her job while pursuing entrepreneurial goals quietly and discreetly. Eventually, the ongoing pursuit of entrepreneurial ideas in a bureaucratic structure may lead managers to develop a set of counternorms under which they start operating (Jansen and Von Glinow, 1985). At this point, managers may put in place new initiatives that will make them look good in the present without concern for the long-term implications on the organization. If managers withhold information and fear a backlash for projects that do not perform quite as grandly as originally presented, or have unanticipated consequences, they can simply move on to another organization, or, if they are lucky, they may have already moved into an executive position in the original company and will order their replacement to take care of the mess. The manager obsessed with his or her career becomes a gamesman (Goodpaster, 1989). As Macoby (1976, p. 101) observes, "Obsessed with winning, the gamesman views all of his actions in terms of whether they will help him succeed in his career. The individual's sense of identity, integrity, and self-determination is lost as he treats himself as an object whose worth is determined by its fluctuating market value. Careerism demands [emotional] detachment."

The other issues represented in the framework presented earlier in the chapter—strategic direction, people, and culture—are reflected in the management approaches of an organization. Carroll (2000) provides three models of management approaches to business ethics: *Moral, Immoral, and Amoral.* Managers following the *Moral Management Model* respect ethical considerations and hold the organization to the highest moral standards and demonstrate a strong ethical leadership to all stakeholders. This, of course, is the ideal model for managers to adopt.

At the other extreme is the *Immoral Management Model*, which is based on the premise that economic opportunities are to be exploited whenever and however possible. The law and socially accepted ethical principles are seen as obstacles to immoral managers, and are maneuvered around in meeting personal and organizational goals. This is the extreme model that most corporate entrepreneurs would not intentionally fall into. This model illustrates managers with deliberate intent to act unethically.

Finally, in the *Amoral Management Model*, managers, while not necessarily acting with malicious intent, believe that the rules of business are different from those of the greater society. These intentionally amoral managers separate their personal ethics from the practice of business, and feel justified by the belief that everyone else does the same. When the corporate entrepreneur is operating within this specific model they believe that operating outside the rules is sanctioned. As a result, the corporate entrepreneur may be pushing the limits of ethical behavior.

Indeed, corporate entrepreneurship is a process that can motivate managers to act beyond the limits of normal rules and procedures in a company. As we have seen in this chapter, there are numerous constraints that confront corporate entrepreneurs. Top-level managers must be committed to innovation, yet they must be committed to ethical behaviors as well.

Ethical corporate entrepreneurship is a process that can prevent the company from becoming stagnant and eroding from the inside. If executives put in place incentives to encourage organizational members to pursue entrepreneurial activities that benefit outside stakeholders as well as themselves, the company can become a community of ongoing excellence.

Chau and Siu (2000) have argued that entrepreneurial organizations by nature will create *higher* cognitive moral development in their members when compared to other organizations. That is, entrepreneurial companies frequently set a higher bar in terms of what is acceptable versus unacceptable behavior. While hostile, unpredictable competitive environments may induce unethical decision making, the participative management style and open-minded attitudes inside entrepreneurial organizations can offset the external pressures. However, if a company does not institute and continually reinforce ethical standards and moral principles, the entrepreneur's work to overcome many of the organizational obstacles may intensify the tenuous balance between corporate entrepreneur and "rogue manager" (Kuratko and Goldsby, 2004).

Overcoming the Obstacles and Constraints

All of the constraints we have discussed share a common element—namely, they represent situations in which, to meet the needs of a new project, the corporate entrepreneur must attempt to convince someone or some unit to change current behavior patterns from what the person or unit might otherwise prefer to do. Therefore, it is important for the entrepreneur to develop an understanding of methods that can be used to gain influence and shape behavior.

Building Social Capital

Corporate entrepreneurs must rely on their ingenuity and persistence to build influence. They need to build "social capital," which is defined as an inventory of trust, gratitude, or obligations that can be "cashed in" when the new project is in demand (Blau, 1964). Building this capital can be accomplished in a number of ways, including: sharing information; creating opportunities for people to demonstrate their skills and competence; and building and using influence networks.

Gaining Legitimacy

The basic strategy for gaining legitimacy is to use personal influence or influence networks to somehow secure endorsements that will convince the necessary supporters of the corporate entrepreneur's viability and credibility. Entrepreneurs also gain legitimacy through experience in various new initiatives started by others, and by first achieving small successes with their own original ideas.

Political Tactics

Corporate entrepreneurs find themselves in a wide range of situations where political skills are critical. The tactics relied upon to achieve legitimacy, garner resources, and overcome inertia and resistance are many and varied. In reality, an unlimited number of political tactics are available to the corporate entrepreneur. One perspective in terms of how to organize these possibilities is presented in Table 11-3. Here, another department is blocking the entrepreneur's team by making unreasonable demands. Examples of tactics the corporate entrepreneur might employ are organized into rule-oriented, rule-evading, personal-political, educational, and organizational-interactional.

The corporate entrepreneur may apply rule-oriented or rule-evading tactics when specifically dealing with the unreasonable requests or demands from different departments in the organization. Personal-political tactics can be applied to adverse situations. They relate to the previous discussion on building social capital. Educational tactics such as persuasion, explanation, and clarification may be useful for unreasonable points of view. Finally, the organizational-interactional tactic of gaining greater autonomy or developing a cross-departmental team may prove valuable when confronting bureaucratic constraints and micromanagement from superiors.

Securing endorsements is particularly important for corporate entrepreneurs. If they can rapidly acquire legitimacy their new project may gain the significant additional

TABLE 11-3

Examples of Political Tactics

Corporate entrepreneurs find themselves in a range of different situations where political skills are critical. The tactics relied upon to achieve legitimacy, garner resources, and overcome inertia and resistance to change are many and varied. Following are examples of five different categories of tactics available to the entrepreneur. In this case, resources are being withheld by some other department, and the department is making an unreasonable request of the entrepreneur's team in an attempt to undermine the concept or project.

1. Rule-oriented tactics
   a. Appeal to some common authority to direct that this request be revised or withdrawn.
   b. Refer to some rule (assuming one exists) that suggests meeting such a request is not necessary.
   c. Require the other department to state in writing why it is making this demand.
   d. Require the other department to consent to having its budget charged with the extra costs involved in meeting its request.

2. Rule-evading tactics
   a. Go through the motions of complying with the request, but with no expectation of actually completing it.
   b. Exceed formal authority and ignore the request altogether.

3. Personal-political tactics
   a. Rely on friendships to induce the other department to modify its request.
   b. Rely on favors, past and future, to accomplish the same result.
   c. Work through political allies in other departments.
   d. Obtain endorsements from senior managers the other department must work with.

4. Educational tactics
   a. Use direct persuasion; that is, try to persuade the other department that its request is unreasonable.
   b. Use what might be called indirect persuasion to help the other department see the problem from the entrepreneur's point of view (ask representative from the other department to sit in on work sessions and observe the difficulty in meeting the request).

5. Organizational-interactional tactics
   a. Seek to change the interaction pattern; for example, require the other department to get executive board approval before making such a request.
   b. Have representatives from the other department assigned to the entrepreneur's team.
   c. Seek to have the team take over other responsibilities or be given more autonomy so that the entrepreneur is not dependent on the other department's support.

SOURCE: Developed based on work by G. Straus in his classic work "Tactics of Lateral Relationships," *Administrative Science Quarterly*, 7 (September), 1962: 166.

benefits of earlier customer acceptance; earlier distributor acceptance; or earlier revenue streams.

RESOURCE ACQUISITION

Block and MacMillan (1993) note, "When it comes to securing resources, accounts of entrepreneurial activity in established corporations are replete with tales of resourceful politicking. Venture managers hijack materials and equipment, appropriate production capacity and personnel time, conceal development activities, and cash in personal favors to secure the resources needed for their new business." The major method of securing the necessary resources is through co-optation, or leveraging, of the resources currently underutilized by the company. Starr and MacMillan (1990) identified four distinct strategies for co-optation:

- *Borrowing:* Borrowing strategies are employed to temporarily or periodically secure the use of assets or other resources, on the premise that they will eventually be returned.

- *Begging:* Begging strategies are employed to secure resources by appealing to the owner's goodwill. In this way, venture managers gain the use of the resources without needing to return them, despite the fact that the owner recognizes the value of the assets. In her research, Kanter (1983) identifies many cases of "tincupping," in which venture managers begged or scrounged resources from the rest of the company.

- *Scavenging:* Scavenging strategies extract usage from goods that others do not intend to use or that they might actually welcome an appropriate opportunity to divest themselves of. This approach involves learning about unused or underused resources (e.g., obsolete inventory, idle equipment, or underutilized personnel).

- *Amplifying:* Amplification is the capacity to lever far more value out of an asset than is perceived by the original owner of the asset.

Morris et al. (2010) examined the rate at which entrepreneurs grow their resource base in a venture's early stages. The study defines "resource acceleration" as the leveraging of available resources to assist the entrepreneur in the early stages of growth. The findings suggest that resource acceleration has a positive effect on company performance by increasing an entrepreneur's awareness of resource options. Thus the corporate entrepreneur's ability to leverage and accelerate the options of resources available may in fact help overcome the resource starvation that is so evident in the early stages of most projects or ventures.

These four strategies allow the corporate entrepreneur to secure resources that would otherwise have to be secured by economic exchange at a much greater cost.

There are three critical benefits of relying on these methods of resource acquisition: by appropriating underutilized resources entrepreneurs reduce the *cost* of implementing something new, they reduce the *risk* of the new project by dramatically bringing down the initial investment, and they increase the *return* on assets of the project or venture.

AN ETHICAL COMPONENT IN TRAINING CORPORATE ENTREPRENEURS

For the ethics challenge to be confronted and to be given the same prominence as innovation in entrepreneurial organizations, a holistic approach is suggested. As Giaco-lone and Knouse (1997, p. 49) propose, "Instead of focusing on one-shot training and moralistic absolutes about what is right and wrong, managers should integrate ethical procedures into the very fabric of the organization." Since the holistic approach em-braces changing the organizational culture, it will have similar steps as the implemen-tation of corporate entrepreneurship. Specific training in ethical actions needs to be tailored to address issues where the company is lacking ethical fortitude or possesses moral ambiguity. An ethics program can be completed with "ethics committees charged with developing ethics policies, evaluating company or employee actions, and/or investigating and adjudicating policy violations . . . ethics officers or ombud-spersons (that are) charged with coordinating policies, providing ethics education, or investigating allegations" (Weaver et al., 1999). Therefore, by instituting compliance and values components into state-of-the-art corporate entrepreneurship programs, a more complete approach to entrepreneurship will make for a better future for both the organization and its members and prevent future ethical dilemmas that confront managers.

Focusing on the Right Obstacles at the Right Time

It is important for corporate entrepreneurs to think in terms of both the immediate and long-term goals of their new projects. They can then isolate the key obstacles to accomplishing these goals at differing time periods, and prioritize where efforts should be focused. Once the obstacles are prioritized, the critical opponents and supporters can be identified. It is these supporters that should be the focus of an inertia-to-action strategy.

Since corporate entrepreneurs want to reach agreements that their supporters will be enthusiastic about implementing, they should attempt to structure "win-win" agreements (agreements that will benefit both parties). Entrepreneurs should seek to reach explicit agreements on the actions that both parties will take to move the project forward. It is especially important to agree on what each party will do to ensure that the next milestone is achieved. The particular issues that entrepreneurs and their supporters must address include the following:

- Who will take what specific actions against which opponent?
- What key implementation steps must be taken, and how should those steps be timed?
- How can we tell if things are not going as planned?
- What major contingency plans are needed, and what events will trigger those plans?

When agreement has been reached with these supporters, there remains little to be done but launch the strategy, focusing the most effort on those activities that will move the project to the next major milestone.

THE INNOVATOR'S NOTEBOOK

Is Apple Its Own Obstacle?

Innovation is one thing, but when a company has innovation with no strategy to define a market, take the lead in that market, and profit from that position, it will most likely find that competition has arisen to seize the opportunity. This scenario has played out for Apple throughout its existence, starting with the Apple II in 1977. The Apple II introduced concepts that were novel at the time, such as a graphical user interface, a mouse, a laser printer, and a color monitor; yet today it has captured only 2 percent of the $180 billion worldwide market for PCs. Most consumers consider Apple's products as being easier to use, more powerful, and more elegant than their rivals. Despite this acknowledgement, Apple's competitors have been able to mimic Apple's innovative features while realizing the profits and scale that Apple has been unable to reach.

So the question is obvious: "If Apple is so great in respect to new product development, why do consumers keep going elsewhere?" Analysts point to Apple's decision to not license its operating system in the 1970s as the root of Apple's decline in the home PC market; however, the same analysts argue that the company could have righted itself by capitalizing on its early lead in the $12 billion education market for PCs, which might have allowed Apple back into consumers' homes. Due to its failure to develop an aggressive sales force, the company slowly ceded its position, resulting in Apple owning only 10 percent of the market today. Another example of Apple's failure to seize a market can be found with the Newton, the first mobile pen-based computer. Although the product was far from perfect, conventional logic would suggest that Apple's position as first-to-market should have translated into it becoming the dominant player in the $3.3 billion market for personal digital assistants (PDAs), but the company has not even managed to capture a substantial stake.

With Apple being arguably the most innovative company in its industry, if not the world, conventional wisdom would argue that it would also be the most successful. So, it would seem that there is more to building a successful company than innovation alone. One critical component to a company's success is turning innovation into commercially viable products, and doing so more profitably than your competitors can. This step seems to be overlooked by Apple time and time again. Apple has been devoted to innovation since its inception, but such single-mindedness can often lead to neglect in other areas. For instance, iTunes was voted the "Coolest Invention of 2003" by *Time* magazine, and by the end of its first year on the market, 20 million songs had been purchased and downloaded from Apple's site; however, Apple generated only $6.2 billion—three-quarters of it from the sale of PCs—during the fiscal year ending September 27, 2003.

Despite PCs representing such a large percentage of its sales, Apple has since fallen to fifth in PC sales in 2009, behind Dell, Hewlett-Packard, Acer, and Toshiba. Apple was once one of the most profitable companies in the PC market, but its operating margins have declined from 20 percent in 1981 to a mere 0.4 percent today, which pales in comparison to the industry average of 2 percent. Notable exceptions are Apple's i-Pod, i-Phone, and i-Pad, the latest innovative developments in the mobile market, where Apple is commanding the world lead with Nokia. These new innovations have vaulted Apple to the top of this emerging market. Only time will tell if they can sustain their lead in this market.

However, Apple's past has skeptics questioning whether the pursuit of innovation is causing companies to lose sight of the risks. In the end, creation for the sake of creation is short-sighted. Innovation will only benefit a company if it generates cash to cover the costs of the innovation and to reward shareholders for the inherent risks. Additionally, consistency and follow-through are necessary; otherwise companies can become obsessed with generating new products rather than profiting from their commercialization. In the case of Apple, this obsession led Apple's founders to develop everything in house, regardless of cost, while competitors such as Microsoft were moving toward specialization by outsourcing functions like manufacturing.

Apple's primary focus has been on developing "cool," while its competitors have focused on generating profit. The problem, as seen by industry observers, is that by the time Apple gets a new product to market, they are ready to work on the next big thing, leaving the monotony of sales and strategic partnerships to its competitors. The issue is that this strategy also means Apple is losing revenue from burgeoning markets that it helped to create. The greatest obstacle for Apple in respect to its drive for innovation has been and continues to be its lack of interest in realizing profits from what it creates. As long as the company continues to be infatuated with creation alone, it will continue to be merely an R&D boutique for its competitors.

Discussion Questions

1. Using Table 11-1, what specific constraints on corporate entrepreneurship would you identify for Apple?

2. What other potential limitations on corporate innovation could Apple experience and why?

3. Discuss the ethical dilemma of "rouge middle managers" as it could apply to Apple.

SOURCE: Adapted from Carleen Hawn, "If He's So Smart . . . Steve Jobs, Apple, and the Limits of Innovation," *Fast Company,* January 2004, vol. 78: 68. Updated March 27, 2010, http://arstechnica.com/hardware/news/2010/01/while-pc-market-rebounds-apple-slips-into-5th-place-in-us.ars

Summary and Conclusions

The good news is that companies are discovering the importance of entrepreneurship as a force for positive internal change and for achieving advantage in the marketplace. The bad news is that most companies have developed in ways that discourage entrepreneurial behavior and penalize the corporate entrepreneur. As a result, executives have little guidance in terms of theory or established managerial practice regarding how to make entrepreneurship happen in their companies.

In this chapter, we have attempted to systematically identify the constraints to sustainable entrepreneurial activity in established companies. A framework was introduced for classifying obstacles based on whether they were more related to systems, structures, strategic direction, policies and procedures, people, or culture. Virtually any of the potentially hundreds of obstacles found in companies will fall into one of these categories. Of course, the categories overlap and are highly interrelated. For instance, control systems include lots of policies and procedures, and they interact with the structure of the company. Reward systems reflect the values that define the culture of the company. Importantly, the framework of obstacles can actually serve as a blueprint for achieving entrepreneurship. Using this same framework, but turning each of the items on its head, managers can begin to redirect the entire organization.

Related to the obstacles are a number of specific constraints that affect the success or failure of the corporate entrepreneur. Included in the chapter were such things as poor political skills, legitimacy, reinforced denial, inertia, turf protection, and the inability to find a sponsor. The question of "rogue managers" versus corporate entrepreneurs is a challenging dilemma that organizations must recognize, especially in light of the highly visible corporate transgressions in recent years. We introduced some of the critical ethical issues that come into play when attempting to work around the constraints presented in this chapter.

A number of strategies were introduced to address overcoming these limitations. Yet when dealing with barriers and obstacles, there is also a danger in overcomplicating things. Corporate entrepreneurs should exercise appropriate caution in moving forward, without losing sight of the most important objective—to ensure that the project continues to make progress. The essence of overcoming barriers, then, is to keep things simple—identify the few key obstacles, understand them, and plan actions that will solve the most critical problems.

References

Blau, P. 1964. *Exchange and Power in Social Life* (New York: John Wiley & Sons).

Block, Z., and MacMillan, I. 1993. *Corporate Venturing* (Boston, MA: Harvard Business School Press).

Carroll, A. B. 2000. "Models of Management Morality for the New Millennium," *Business Ethics Quarterly*, April 11(2): 365–371.

Chau, L. L. F., and Siu, W. S. 2000. "Ethical Decision-Making in Corporate Entrepreneurial Organizations," *Journal of Business Ethics*, 23: 365–375.

Derber, C. 1996. *The Wilding of America* (New York: St. Martin's Press).

Donaldson, T. 1989. *The Ethics of International Business* (New York: Oxford University Press).

Giacolone, R. A., and Knouse, S. B. 1997. "A Holistic Approach to Business Ethics," *Business and Society Review*, 98: 46–49.

Goodpaster, K. E. 1989. "Ethical Imperative and Corporate Leadership," in Kenneth R. Andrews. (ed.) *Ethics in Practice: Managing the Moral Corporation* (Boston: Harvard Business School Press).

Grove, A. S. 1996. *Only the Paranoid Survive* (London, England: Harper Collins Publishers).

Hamel, G. 2000. *Leading the Revolution* (Boston: Harvard Business School Press).

Jansen, E., and Von Glinow, M. 1985. "Ethical Ambivalence and Organizational Reward Systems," *Academy of Management Review*, 10(4): 814–822.

Kanter, R. 1983. *The Change Masters* (New York: Simon & Schuster).

Kerr, S. 1975. "On the Folly of Rewarding A, While Hoping for B," *Academy of Management Journal*, 18 (December): 769–783.

Kuratko, D. F., and Goldsby, M. G. 2004. "Corporate Entrepreneurs or Rogue Middle Managers: A Framework for Ethical Corporate Entrepreneurship," *Journal of Business Ethics*, 55(1): 13–30.

Kuratko, D. F., and Hodgetts, R. M. 2007. *Entrepreneurship: Theory, Process, & Practice*, 7th ed. (Mason, OH: Thomson/South-Western Publishing).

Kuratko, D. F., Ireland, R. D., and Hornsby, J. S. 2001. "The Power of Entrepreneurial Actions: Insights from Acordia, Inc.," *Academy of Management Executive*, 15(4): 60–71.

Macoby, M. 1976. "The Corporate Climber Has to Find His Heart," *Fortune*, December, 101.

Morris, M. H. 1998. *Entrepreneurial Intensity* (Westport, CT: Quorum Books).

Morris, M. H., Kuratko, D. F., Ireland, R. D., Allen, J., and Schindehutte, M. 2010. "Resource Acceleration: Extending Resource-Based Theory in Entrepreneurial Ventures," *Journal of Applied Management and Entrepreneurship*, 15(2): 4–25.

Morris, M. H., Schindehutte, M., Walton, J., and Allen, J. 2002. "The Ethical Context of Entrepreneurship: Proposing and Testing a Developmental Framework," *Journal of Business Ethics*, 40(4): 331–362.

Sathe, V. 1989. "Fostering Entrepreneurship in Large Diversified Firm," *Organizational Dynamics*, 18: 20–32.

Starr, J. A., and MacMillan, I. C. 1990. "Resource Co-Optation via Social Contracting: Resource Acquisition Strategies for New Ventures," *Strategic Management Journal*, 11(Summer): 79–92.

Weaver, G. R., Trevino, L. K., and Cochran, P. L. 1999. "Corporate Ethics Programs as Control Systems: Influences of Executive Commitment and Environmental Factors," *Academy of Management Journal*, 42(1): 41–57.

CHAPTER 12

LEADING THE ENTREPRENEURIAL ORGANIZATION

Introduction

While entrepreneurial initiatives are driven by individuals, the practice of corporate entrepreneurship (CE) is a collective responsibility. In entrepreneurial companies, personnel at all levels actively participate in the process of recognizing and exploiting innovative opportunities. A company cannot sustain high levels of entrepreneurial performance unless people know their particular roles—and how these roles link to entrepreneurial practices and processes occurring throughout the organization.

A beginning point is the role of leaders. Although it is possible in any company to find employees pursuing innovative ideas, the ability to continually produce highly entrepreneurial initiatives that (1) are consistent with the company's overall strategic direction, (2) are actually implemented, and (3) produce tangible results requires strong managerial commitment. Stated differently, entrepreneurship does not happen without leadership. While reality can be more complex, it is common to distinguish three levels of management in organizations: top-level, middle-level, and first-level or front-line managers. At each level, it is critical that managers speak the language of entrepreneurship, reflect the values of entrepreneurship, continually reinforce those who behave entrepreneurially, and actively participate in entrepreneurial projects.

This chapter will focus on the particular roles, responsibilities, and activities of managers at different levels within the entrepreneurial organization. Further, we will explore some of the outcomes of entrepreneurial behavior, and distinguish personal from organizational outcomes. The chapter will specifically examine each of the three levels of management. Important research findings regarding leadership roles and effective managerial practices are reviewed. Finally, the chapter's Innovator's Notebook describes how a Fortune 500 company is able to achieve high levels of entrepreneurship throughout the company.

Top-Level Managers in the Entrepreneurial Organization

People at all levels of a company play critical roles in successful entrepreneurship efforts, regardless of the form the entrepreneurial initiative takes. But senior-level managers are especially critical. Those at the top must fulfill particular roles in the entrepreneurial process. The beginning point involves recognizing that entrepreneurial leadership represents a significant departure from traditional management practices.

TABLE 12-1

Traditional General Management vs. Entrepreneurial Leadership: A Comparison of Beliefs and Philosophies

Attitude toward...	*Traditional General Management*	*Strategic Entrepreneurial Leadership*
Organizational resources and capabilities	Resources and capabilities should be protected	Resources and capabilities should be valued but challenged
The company's "business" and "purpose"	Definitions of "business" and "purpose" are relatively enduring	Definitions of "business" and "purpose" should be periodically re-examined
Business strategy	Play the game better than competitors	Play the game better than competitors *or* play your own game
Organizational architecture	Designed to optimize implementation of the strategy	Designed to allow for strategic flexibility
Meeting customer needs	Stay "close to the customer"	Stay "close to the customer," but also invest in promising innovations that don't currently meet expressed needs
Entrepreneurial activity within the organization	Entrepreneurial activity should follow from strategy	Entrepreneurial activity should lead to as well as follow from strategy
Organizational learning	Institutionalize knowledge to avoid having to relearn business lessons	Institutionalize a questioning attitude such that learning and unlearning can coexist

SOURCE: J. G. Covin, and D. P. Slevin, "The Entrepreneurial Imperatives of Strategic Leadership," in M. A. Hitt, R. D. Ireland, S. M. Camp, and D. L. Sexton, eds., *Strategic Entrepreneurship: Creating a New Mindset*, Oxford, U.K.: Blackwell Publisher, 2002: 309–327. Reprinted with permission of Blackwell Publishing.

Table 12-1 summarizes some of the key differences between these two alternative perspectives on how a company should be led.

Senior managers are ultimately responsible for providing a vision regarding what the company can be and how it can get there. In this vein, it has been argued that "the entrepreneurial message must flow from the top" (Higdon, 2000, p. 16), that top-level managers must be "purveyors of the entrepreneurial vision" (Heller, 1999), and that they must "shape the corporate purpose" (Bartlett and Ghoshal, 1997). Developing and communicating a clear entrepreneurial vision is not easy. Senior executives must put into words, symbols, and actions a unique concept of entrepreneurship for their companies. Such a strategic vision is the mechanism through which those at the top paint the picture of the type of organization they hope to lead in the future—an organization that is opportunity-focused, innovative, and self-renewing.

Top-level managers are also responsible for putting into place "pro-entrepreneurship" organizational architectures. We use the word *architecture* here to describe how the workplace is designed. A pro-entrepreneurship architecture is one where the workplace exhibits structural, cultural, resource, and system attributes that encourage entrepreneurial behavior, both individually and collectively. Earlier chapters described the types of structures, cultures, and systems that support entrepreneurial behavior. In the absence of an entrepreneurial strategic vision, these types of architectures are unlikely to take shape because there will be no overriding philosophical justification or perspective, endorsed by top management, that encourages entrepreneurial thought and action throughout the organization. Alternatively, in the presence of such a vision, the company structure, culture, resources, and systems can sustain increasingly higher levels of entrepreneurial performance.

In addition to the presence of a compelling vision and well-designed company architecture, a third critical ingredient is the existence of the "right" personnel. There is a need for creative, risk-accepting, energetic employees who recognize and pursue opportunities and are tenacious in overcoming resistance to innovative ideas. A discussion of these types of employees was provided in Chapter 6. Miles et al. (2000) talk about the importance of having a "human resource investment philosophy" as a prerequisite to the emergence of widespread and autonomous entrepreneurial behavior throughout the organization. Likewise, in a major survey of innovation practices, the findings indicated that the effective management of innovation depends upon "the environment you create," "the measures and rewards you use," and "the people you have" (Boston Consulting Group, 2005).

Thus, a key role of senior management is to ensure the company employs people with a penchant for entrepreneurship. The leaders of highly entrepreneurial companies understand that the human resource management (HRM) function is central to their success. They invest significantly in "picking and developing people" and elevate the importance of the HRM department. Consistent with this point, Jack Welch, former CEO of General Electric (one of the world's most innovative companies), spent the last years of his tenure actively developing practices, policies, and systems that would enable GE to (1) select and retain entrepreneurially inclined individuals and (2) broadly unleash the entrepreneurial potential that existed in the company's employees.

Beyond these three core responsibilities, our ability to grasp senior management's role in the CE process requires that we consider (1) the entrepreneurial imperatives for which senior management must take ownership, and (2) the need for top managers to balance concerns involving the company's current operations ("mainstream" activity) with concerns involving the company's possible future operations ("newstream" activity). Let us explore each of these two areas.

The Entrepreneurial Imperatives of Strategic Leadership

Entrepreneurial imperatives are those aspects of strategic leadership that are inherently entrepreneurial in that they relate to the recognition and/or exploitation of opportunity. A company's top-level executives are tasked with six entrepreneurial imperatives, summarized as follows and listed in Table 12-2 (see Covin and Slevin, 2002).

NOURISH AN ENTREPRENEURIAL CAPABILITY

Top-level managers are responsible for ensuring that their organizations develop a general capacity for entrepreneurship. To develop such a capacity, executives must

TABLE 12-2

The Entrepreneurial Imperatives of Top-Level Executives

Nourish an Entrepreneurial Capability	Invest in the development of an institutionalized organizational capacity for innovation and entrepreneurship.
Protect Disruptive Innovations	Selectively protect the innovations that seem disruptive or threatening to the organization's mainstream operations by "cocooning" them in their infancy.
Make Opportunities Make Sense	Expand the opportunity "radar screen" such that personnel can recognize and appreciate the hidden opportunities associated with their jobs.
Question the Dominant Logic	Challenge conventional strategic practices, norms, and mindsets such that innovation is not hampered by tradition or other social or psychological constraints.
Revisit the "Deceptively Simple Questions"	Identify growth opportunities through re-asking basic questions such as "What business are we in?" and "What do our customers value?"
Link Entrepreneurship and Strategy	Integrate the entrepreneurial and strategic processes of the organization to facilitate the recognition and exploitation of strategically significant opportunities for innovation.

SOURCE: J. G. Covin, and D. P. Slevin, "The Entrepreneurial Imperatives of Strategic Leadership," in M. A. Hitt, R. D. Ireland, S. M. Camp, and D. L. Sexton, eds., *Strategic Entrepreneurship: Creating a New Mindset*, Oxford, U.K.: Blackwell Publisher, 2002: 309–327.

understand and manipulate the drivers of innovative activity, including the three considerations (i.e., vision, organizational architecture, and human resources) discussed in the
preceding section. Top-level managers should not equate capacity for entrepreneurship
with traditional, planned innovative activity, such as that which takes place within the
research and development (R&D) function. The capability needed is one that allows
innovative ideas to emerge from multiple and diverse locations throughout the organization, and results in autonomous innovations, not simply those that are planned.

Protect Innovations that Threaten the Current Business Model

Organizations tend to ignore, passively discount, actively discredit, or aggressively destroy
innovative ideas whose success might undermine the competitiveness or profitability of
current business operations. Top-level managers need to selectively protect these "disruptive innovations" since they will often evolve into engines that drive future sales growth.
Such protection frequently involves "cocooning" or protecting innovative projects during their infancy, a time at which they are generally most vulnerable to negative interven-
tion from those inside and outside the company who are threatened by the innovation.

Make Opportunities Make Sense for the Organization

The entrepreneurial opportunities recognized by employees will be constrained by
how those individuals think about their company's mission and purpose and their
individual roles within the organization. Top-level managers should actively seek to
expand the "radar screen" used by organizational personnel to define the company's
entrepreneurial opportunities. This might be accomplished by (1) communicating a
broadened definition of the company's "business," (2) challenging employees to define
the company's opportunities from the perspective of an innovation model other than
that which is dominant for their company (e.g., a market-driven innovation model
versus a technology-driven innovation model), and (3) openly and regularly articulat-
ing alternative and plausible future scenarios for their company.

Question the Dominant Logic

As discussed in Chapter 8, dominant logic refers to ways in which managers conceptualize the business and make critical resource-allocation decisions. A company's dominant
logic can subtly and artificially limit individuals' perceptions and actions to those that
conform to conventional and accepted business rules. However, the "rules" of business
are often nothing more than historical assumptions that have never been challenged. By
questioning the dominant logic, top-level managers frequently identify new products,
markets, businesses, business models, and strategies. The various forms entrepreneurship
takes (e.g., strategic renewal, organizational rejuvenation, domain redefinition, business

model reconstruction, as discussed in Chapter 4) emerge when executives deliberately surface and question their company's prevailing dominant logic.

REVISIT THE "DECEPTIVELY SIMPLE QUESTIONS"

The deceptively simple questions are those whose answers define the company and its operations in a very fundamental sense. They include questions like: "What business are we in?", "What is our reason for existence?", "What do our customers value?", "How should we measure 'success'?" Top-level managers typically answer these questions, either consciously or unconsciously, and then move on. However, these are not questions for which there are single, correct, and enduring answers over the course of a company's existence. Entrepreneurial executives regularly revisit such questions in an effort to identify opportunities for future growth.

LINK ENTREPRENEURSHIP AND BUSINESS STRATEGY

Too often, entrepreneurial processes and outcomes are regarded as beyond the scope of strategic management, so entrepreneurship occurs randomly, haphazardly, and often inexplicably. The truth is that companies can and must address matters pertaining to entrepreneurship within their strategic management processes. Building new businesses within the corporation "should be viewed as an integrated and continuous part of the company's strategy-making process, rather than as an insurance policy whose appeal varies according to the prospects of the company's mainstream business" (Burgelman and Valikangas, 2005, pp. 31–32). Similarly, a major study of the 1,000 publicly held companies from around the world that spent the most money on R&D in 2004 concluded that the most successful innovators explicitly and deliberately align their innovation strategies with their corporate strategies (Jaruzelski et al., 2005). Specific means by which entrepreneurial and strategic processes are sometimes linked in organizations were reviewed in Chapter 8.

In short, top-level managers are better able to fulfill their entrepreneurial responsibilities when they heed the preceding entrepreneurial imperatives. Managing in accordance with these imperatives can enable companies to compete successfully in the future. However, companies must take care of their current obligations, performing well in existing domains of business activity, or else the future becomes a moot point. This is the challenge of ambidextrous management, a subject to which we now turn.

Managing Ambidextrously: Balancing the Old and the New

The concept of the ambidextrous organization has been proposed as a model of how successful entrepreneurial organizations operate (see, for example, Birkinshaw and Gibson, 2004; O'Reilly and Tushman, 2004). To be ambidextrous is to be versatile,

TABLE 12-3

Entrepreneurial Leadership and Ambidextrous Management: Balancing Competing Demands

"Mainstream" Exploitation	*"Newstream" Exploration*
Pressures to generate revenue from current business operations	Pressures to search for innovations that will provide revenues in the future
Pressures to serve current customers	Pressures to create new markets
Pressures to respond to current competitors	Pressures to anticipate future competitors
Pressures to efficiently utilize current resources	Pressures to identify resources that will be relevant in five years
Pressures to refine current employee skills and capabilities	Pressures to develop entirely new skill sets
Pressures to improve current products and services	Pressures to invent entirely new products and services
Pressures to invest in advancing current technologies	Pressures to explore new, emerging technologies

or able to use both hands equally well. As summarized in Table 12-3, ambidextrous organizations are those that effectively balance the appropriation of value from current business activity and the search for new value as realized through innovation.

The fundamental drivers of ambidexterity include the need to meet the needs for current performance—that is, doing a good job of serving current customers and addressing current competitive threats—while also ensuring the company is well positioned to generate future profits, find and serve future customers, and fend off future competitive threats. Kanter (1989, p. 45) notes: "Pressures to innovate confront businesses with a demanding balancing act: keeping up with activities already committed to, to reap the benefits of the involvement in them, while at the same time starting new activities that will be of benefit in the future. While caught up in the mainstream, they must also generate 'newstreams.'" The balancing of "mainstream" operations and "newstream" innovations has been referred to as "coordinating *exploitation* activities and *exploration* activities" (Levinthal and March, 1993), "competing on the entrepreneurial edge" (Eisenhardt et al., 2000), and "resolving the paradox of change and preservation" (Baden-Fuller and Volberda, 1997). By whatever name, balancing the old and the new is principally a top-level management responsibility.

The creation of organizational ambidexterity requires that top managers make innovation a core (versus peripheral) activity for their organizations. In doing so, the company's leaders must decide if they should house mainstream and newstream activities in physically separate units within the organization or if major innovative activity should be periodically performed within mainstream units. The former option has been referred to as the "spatial separation approach" to the management of innovation and the latter option as the "temporal separation approach" (Baden-Fuller and Volberda, 1997). The major factors top managers should consider when determining how to address this locus-of-innovation issue are the strategic importance of the innovative initiative and how operationally related the initiative is to current organizational processes and competencies, as discussed in Chapter 9.

Organizational ambidexterity is encouraged when top-level managers assume direct responsibility for both mainstream operations and newstream initiatives. In most organizations, top managers oversee the core of the company's operations. That is, they concern themselves with the pursuit of superior performance within their organization's mainstream businesses. Top-level managers must also give significant, personal attention to their company's newstreams. They do this, in part, by creating direct, unmediated reporting relationships between themselves and those individuals and groups engaged in exploratory, innovation-producing initiatives. By placing themselves in roles where they directly interact with both the exploitation-focused and exploration-focused sides of their organizations, top managers can more effectively balance the resource commitments needed to achieve current *and* future competitiveness.

Finally, top managers help create ambidextrous organizations by setting explicit goals for innovative outcomes. For example, 3M, one of the world's most innovative companies, embraces the objective of having a large percentage of its annual sales revenue (at least 25 percent) generated from products introduced over the preceding five years. When goals such as this are set, innovation is essentially transformed from a discretionary or peripheral activity to a core activity within organizations.

Middle-Level Managers: Linchpins in the Entrepreneurial Organization

The role of middle-level managers is to effectively serve as a conduit between those at the top and those at the operating level or front line. To fulfill this role, middle-level managers interactively synthesize information, disseminate that information to both top- and operating-level managers as appropriate, and champion projects that are intended to create newness (e.g., a product, service, or business unit). In slightly different words, once a commitment is made at the top to pursue a certain set of actions, middle-level managers' responsibilities find them facilitating information and resource flows in ways that support project development and implementation efforts.

Middle-level managers are enablers of individual entrepreneurial actions such as those taken to create new ventures or engage in strategic renewal. As facilitators of information and resource flows, middle-level managers help shape entrepreneurial actions. King et al. (2001, p. 95) see it this way: "Because middle managers must reconcile top-level perspectives and lower-level implementation issues, they help determine the use of competencies that, in turn, affect company performance." The major conclusion, then, is that middle managers play a critical role both as champions and as intermediaries in corporate entrepreneurship. Their central position in the organization allows them to gather and absorb innovative ideas from inside and outside the company. By interacting with first- and top-level managers, those operating in the middle influence and shape entrepreneurial actions as they parcel and integrate knowledge to proactively pursue something new.

The distinction between top-level and middle-level managers is often that of determining strategic actions versus implementing those actions. Thus, middle-level management is where entrepreneurial activities are most likely to experience actual implementation. It is within this context that we focus specifically on the proactive behaviors of middle-level managers in the CE process.

A useful model for capturing entrepreneurial behavior at a middle management level can be found in Figure 12-1. The model focuses on the actions that middle-level managers must take for entrepreneurship to meaningfully contribute to organizational success.

The process of entrepreneurship is often depicted as the interaction of three factors: an entrepreneur, an opportunity, and resources that are acquired and deployed in pursuit of that opportunity (e.g., Ronstadt, 1984). Considering the middle manager in the context of these three factors, a relevant question is, "What do middle-level managers do with respect to resources and opportunities that might be understood as essential types or dimensions of their entrepreneurial behavior?" This question can be answered as follows: Middle-level managers *endorse, refine, and shepherd entrepreneurial opportunities* and *identify, acquire, and deploy resources needed to pursue those opportunities* (Kuratko et al., 2005). Each of these responsibilities is summarized in Table 12-4 and elaborated upon next.

Regarding the *endorsement* of entrepreneurial opportunities, middle-level managers often find themselves responsible for evaluating entrepreneurial initiatives emerging from lower levels in the organization. The evaluative role involves both the decision to lend political support or not as well as the decision of how much support to offer. At the same time, middle-level managers effectively endorse innovative perspectives coming from top-level executives and "sell" their value-creating potential to the primary implementers—first-level managers and their direct reports. Thus, middle-level

FIGURE 12-1

A Model of Middle-Level Managers' Entrepreneurial Behavior

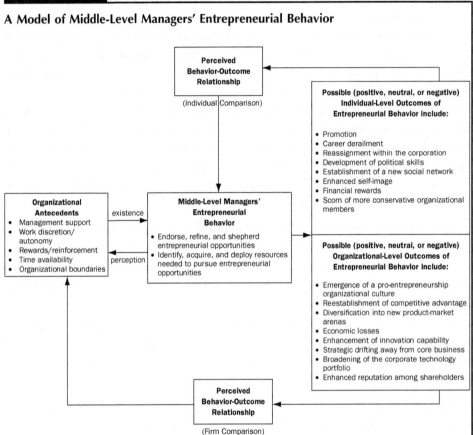

SOURCE: D. F. Kuratko, R. D. Ireland, J. G. Covin, and J. S. Hornsby, 2005. "A Model of Middle-level Managers' Entrepreneurial Behavior," *Entrepreneurship Theory and Practice,* 29(6): 701.

managers are in a position to endorse (or withhold endorsement to) entrepreneurial initiatives originating at various locations throughout the organization.

Entrepreneurial initiatives are inherently experiments that evolve from rudimentary business concepts to more fully defined business models. Middle-level managers have much to do with how entrepreneurial initiatives take shape. They also influence the "shape" of those initiatives per se. In short, middle-level managers serve in an entrepreneurial opportunity *refinement* capacity. Their refinement behaviors characteristically involve molding the entrepreneurial opportunity into one that makes sense for the organization, given the organization's strategy, resources, and political structure.

TABLE 12-4

The Middle-Level Manager's Entrepreneurial Activities

Endorse   Endorse the entrepreneurial initiative by advocating its pursuit to important resource providers and other stakeholders.

Refine   Refine the entrepreneurial initiative to fit the organization's strategy, structure, and resources.

Shepherd   Shepherd the entrepreneurial initiative through the provision of developmental direction and sustained support.

Identify   Identify the resources needed to pursue the entrepreneurial initiative.

Acquire   Acquire the resources needed to pursue the entrepreneurial initiative.

Deploy   Deploy the acquired resources to make the innovative idea a reality.

SOURCE: Adapted from D. F. Kuratko, R. D. Ireland, J. G. Covin, and J. S. Hornsby, "A Model of Middle-Level Managers' Entrepreneurial Behavior," *Entrepreneurship Theory and Practice*, 29(6), 2005: 699–716.

It is characteristically the job of middle-level managers to convert malleable entrepreneurial opportunities into initiatives that fit the organization.

Through the *shepherding* function, middle-level managers champion, protect, nurture, and guide the entrepreneurial initiative. These actions ensure that entrepreneurial initiatives originating at lower organizational levels are not "orphaned" once their continued development requires support beyond that which can be furnished by individuals at those lower levels.

The pursuit of opportunities necessitates the *identification* of resources needed to convert the novel idea or concept into a business reality. Middle-level managers tend to be positioned to best know which resources will be needed as new initiatives gain organizational traction. This is so because, while entrepreneurial initiatives will not necessarily have their impetus within the middle management domain, they will tend to operate and grow under the purview of middle-level managers. Hence, these managers tend to best appreciate what it will take, from a resource standpoint, to sustain the initiative on its growth path.

The *acquisition* of resources essential to the pursuit of entrepreneurial opportunity often requires a broad array of skills and points of leverage on the part of those leading the initiative. Middle-level managers are tasked with obtaining essential resources from top executives as needed to support the more speculative business operations of the organization. This often requires skills of persuasion and negotiation. Middle-level managers also access resources from below, choosing, for example, specific individuals to work on entrepreneurial initiatives and obtaining other existing or possibly new knowledge- and property-based resources needed to implement the envisioned opportunity. Thus, while the resource identification function relates to middle-level managers knowing what resources are needed to pursue the entrepreneurial opportunity, the resource acquisition function relates to them knowing where and how to get those resources.

In an operational sense, resource *deployment* can mean many things including, for example, how amassed resources are configured to enact the initiative, how current resources are mobilized or otherwise leveraged in support of the initiative, the timing of the resource allocation process, and the level and type of resources allocated in pursuit of the opportunity. Middle-level managers are often most responsible for redirecting resources away from existing operations and toward entrepreneurial initiatives appearing to have greater strategic value for the company (Burgelman, 1994). In short, it might be argued that the middle management level is where entrepreneurial opportunities are given the best chance to flourish based on the resources likely to be deployed in their pursuit.

First-Level Managers and Nonmanagerial Personnel: Entrepreneurship at the Grassroots Level

First-level managers, as well as nonmanagerial personnel who work on the front lines, engage in entrepreneurial behaviors that are principally framed for them through interactions with others, both inside and outside the company. When behaving entrepreneurially, these "grassroots-level" personnel operate both as *order takers*, implementing entrepreneurial initiatives endorsed at higher organizational levels, and as *autonomous actors*, pursuing recognized entrepreneurial opportunities that have not been specifically induced from above. In successful entrepreneurial organizations, this latter role of the autonomous actor is not simply tolerated, it's expected. The pursuit of entrepreneurial opportunities is recognized as a collective responsibility, so frontline personnel are encouraged and empowered to act on entrepreneurial opportunities. Importantly, these personnel are often in unique positions to recognize entrepreneurial opportunities because they frequently (1) work at positions within the organization where much of the core transformational activity (e.g., production, marketing, customer service) of the company is performed and (2) have boundary-spanning responsibilities—or important linkages to key external stakeholders—associated with their jobs.

Significant potential to recognize and pursue entrepreneurial opportunities can be found as these individuals go through their daily work routines. Those on the front lines are often in the best position to recognize better structures, processes, and operational tactics that might productively renew the organization or parts of it as well as promising new value propositions or newstream activities that the company might pursue. The centrality of frontline personnel to the key work of the organization enables important learning to take place regarding how the organization might better perform its current business operations or perform new business operations that deliver additional, novel value. By empowering and expecting frontline personnel to act as entrepreneurs, the organization can leverage this learning to its long-term benefit.

In their boundary-spanning roles, first-level managers and operating-level personnel interact with key external stakeholders on the input and output sides of their daily work process. Regarding the former, the linkages that frontline personnel have with supplier organizations, as just one example, can be important conduits through which entrepreneurial opportunities are recognized. That is, based on their interactions with a supplier, a frontline employee might recognize novel resources (of which others in the company are unaware) that might lead to a new business opportunity for the company. This is exactly what happened when a supplier of commodity chemicals was recently able to help one of its customers, a hair care products company, develop a new and successful shampoo product based on information exchanged about the unique warming properties of one of the supplier's chemical offerings. In this instance, the entrepreneurial opportunity was recognized by the frontline employees of the hair care products company who had direct materials procurement responsibilities.

Frontline employees who work closely with customers in a sales, marketing, or distribution capacity are also often well positioned as output-side boundary spanners to recognize and champion entrepreneurial opportunities. In fact, research suggests that successful new product and business ideas often come directly from individuals who interact regularly and closely with a company's customers. It should be kept in mind that over-reliance on first-level managers and nonmanagerial personnel for the generation of entrepreneurial ideas can lead to an emphasis on incremental innovations over more radical innovations. Similarly, a principal reliance on current customers as a source of entrepreneurial ideas can lead to the pursuit of minor or sustaining innovations over major or disruptive innovations. Nonetheless, successful entrepreneurial organizations tend to actively involve frontline employees in the innovation process because of their direct, unmediated access to customers. Through this boundary-spanning linkage, the entrepreneurial company is able to adjust its product/service offerings and associated value propositions such that they remain relevant and desirable to targeted markets.

Guidelines for Entrepreneurial Leadership at Any Organizational Level

Up to this point in our discussion of the entrepreneurship-related roles of personnel throughout the organizational hierarchy, the focus has been on those tasks and responsibilities principally associated with certain levels of management. However, as argued by Cohen (2002), there are also actions and perspectives that can be employed or adopted by personnel at any organizational level in the pursuit of entrepreneurial opportunities. These entrepreneurship-facilitating mechanisms are not constrained to a particular class or level of organizational personnel but, rather, can be thought of as more generic guidelines for the successful practice of corporate entrepreneurship. The specific factors suggested by Cohen (2002) as conducive to successful entrepreneurial leadership at any organizational level include the following:

An obsession with finding new business opportunities. Opportunities can be recognized and pursued by any organizational member. Thus, corporate entrepreneurship can be (and, among the most innovative companies, is) a collective responsibility for which any individual may play a leadership role. A commonality among those who recognize and champion entrepreneurial initiatives is an ever-present obsession with identifying opportunities for value-creating innovation. To be obsessed with opportunity implies that the prospective corporate entrepreneur both actively scans his or her work environment in search of entrepreneurial opportunities as well as considers how current or potentially available resources might be used in the exploitation of those opportunities.

The construction of a "plan" that clearly defines the entrepreneurial opportunity and specifies a strategy for its exploitation. The word "plan" is used loosely here to convey the need for prospective corporate entrepreneurs to clearly and consistently explain their entrepreneurial concept and how it will be pursued. As a matter of protocol, the preparation of a formal business case will often be required to solicit the support needed to pursue a business opportunity. However, even when no such document is required, corporate entrepreneurs must be able to precisely define the targeted entrepreneurial opportunity, describe its value proposition—that is, its basis of appeal to the targeted markets, and articulate in broad terms what resources and actions are needed in order for the opportunity to be pursued. Of course, entrepreneurial initiatives are inherently experiments, so many of the assumptions on which proposed entrepreneurial initiatives are based may be proven incorrect, in which case strategic adjustments will likely be necessary. Nonetheless, prospective entrepreneurs at any organizational level must be able to link a well-defined entrepreneurial opportunity with a clear business concept, then specify a business model through which that business concept will be enacted.

An ability to identify and gain the support of key stakeholders to the entrepreneurial effort. Corporate entrepreneurs at all organizational levels must understand how their initiatives will affect and be affected by stakeholders of the entrepreneurial effort. These stakeholders could be, for example, personnel whose jobs are potentially disrupted by the initiative's pursuit, personnel who control financial, technical, or other resources needed to launch the entrepreneurial initiative, and individuals or collectives outside the corporation whose needs will be addressed by the entrepreneurial initiative. Corporate entrepreneurial initiatives cannot be successfully launched without the political and resource support of key stakeholders. According to Cohen (2002) two mechanisms can be useful in garnering the support of the various stakeholders affected by the entrepreneurial effort. First, entrepreneurial leaders at all levels must be adept at the use of "exchanges" and reciprocity. In other words, corporate entrepreneurs must recognize that the pursuit of entrepreneurial initiatives requires a lot of "give and take" between the corporate entrepreneur (or entrepreneurial team) and key stakeholders. A keen understanding of what stakeholders may want from the corporate entrepreneur or the entrepreneurial initiative in exchange for their support is imperative. Second, entrepreneurial leaders at all levels must be adept at forming alliances with powerful and supportive allies to the entrepreneurial effort. Entrepreneurial initiatives are subject to liabilities of newness and smallness and are, thus, typically vulnerable to adverse political forces whose interests may be threatened by or otherwise do not include the growth of the entrepreneurial venture. In such instances, finding "air cover" in the form of powerful political allies can be essential to sustaining the entrepreneurial initiative's viability.

Variations in Managerial Roles across the Forms of Strategic Entrepreneurship

The preceding discussion related the practice of corporate entrepreneurship—in particular, the corporate venturing form of corporate entrepreneurship in which the focal entrepreneurial initiatives are new businesses—to common and productive actions that can be taken by employees in the pursuit of entrepreneurial success. However, as detailed in Chapter 4, corporate entrepreneurship may occur in forms other than new business creation. Some other forms of strategic entrepreneurship are as follows:

- Strategic renewal—involves the adoption of a new strategy;

- Sustained regeneration—involves the introduction of a new product into a preexisting product category or introduction of an existing product into a new (to the company) but preexisting market;

- Domain redefinition—involves the creation of new or reconfiguration of existing product categories or market space;

- Organizational rejuvenation—involves the enactment of a major internally-focused innovation aimed at improving strategy implementation; and

- Business model reconstruction—involves the design of a new or redesign of an existing business model.

Dess et al. (2003) have examined how some of these forms of entrepreneurship align with the typical roles played by different levels of management. Their insights are consistent with the work of Floyd and Lane (2000, p. 159), who outline particular roles based on level of management:

Top Management Roles

- Ratifying—that is, articulate strategic intent, monitor, endorse and support

- Recognizing—that is, recognize strategic potential, set strategic direction, empower and enable

- Directing—that is, plan, deploy resources, command

Middle Management Roles

- Championing—that is, nurture and advocate, champion, present alternatives to top management

- Synthesizing—that is, categorize issues, sell issues to top management, blend strategic and hands-on information, synthesize

- Facilitating—that is, nourish adaptability and shelter activity, share information, guide adaptation, facilitate learning

- Implementing—that is, implement, revise and adjust, motivate and inspire, coach

Operating Management Roles

- Experimenting—that is, learn and improve, link technical ability and need, initiate autonomous initiatives, experiment and take risks

- Adjusting—that is, respond to the challenge

- Conforming—that is, be a good soldier, follow the system

Table 12-5 depicts the top-level, middle-level, and operating-level (or first-level) management roles associated by Dess et al. (2003) with the strategic renewal, sustained regeneration, domain redefinition, and organizational rejuvenation forms of strategic entrepreneurship. The various managerial roles likely associated with the business model reconstruction form of strategic entrepreneurship are also identified. Our prior discussion of the roles of various levels of management within the entrepreneurial process was aimed at conveying generally observed patterns of effective managerial behavior regardless of the form of corporate entrepreneurship being considered. By contrast, Table 12-5 identifies differences in how various levels of management contribute to the entrepreneurial process among companies pursuing particular forms of strategic entrepreneurship.

TABLE 12-5

Managerial Roles Associated with the Five Strategic Entrepreneurship Forms

Level of Management	Strategic Renewal	Sustained Regeneration	Domain Redefinition	Organizational Rejuvenation	Business Model Reconstruction
Top-level Management	Directing and Ratifying	Directing and Recognizing	Directing and Ratifying	Directing and Recognizing	Directing and Recognizing
Middle-level Management	Championing and Implementing	Synthesizing, Facilitating, and Implementing	Championing and Implementing	Synthesizing, Facilitating, and Implementing	Synthesizing, Facilitating, and Implementing
Operating/ First-level Management	Experimenting and Conforming	Adjusting and Conforming	Experimenting and Conforming	Adjusting and Conforming	Adjusting and Conforming

SOURCE: Adapted from Dess, G. G., Ireland, R. D., Zahra, S. A., Floyd, S. W., Janney, J. J., and Lane, P. J. 2003. "Emerging Issues in Corporate Entrepreneurship," *Journal of Management*, 29(3): 351–378.

Several conclusions can be inferred from Table 12-5. First, regardless of the form of strategic entrepreneurship under consideration, the entrepreneurial processes involved are dependent upon all levels of management for their successful conduct. Again, the successful pursuit of corporate entrepreneurship is a collective responsibility. Second, the specific roles played by particular levels of management in the entrepreneurial process are dependent upon the form of entrepreneurship in question. As such, it is essential that managers (at all levels) exhibit proficiency in the appropriate roles. Finally, entrepreneurial initiatives can develop through "top-down" processes (in which senior executives are the instigators), "bottom-up" processes (in which operating- or first-level managers are the instigators), or what might be referred to as "middle-out" processes (in which middle managers are the instigators, with actions and responsibilities being implied for both higher and lower levels of management). Thus, managers at any level can take a proactive or a reactive role in the entrepreneurial process, but no level of management will or should have a neutral role. Indeed, given the inherent interdependencies between the managerial levels, neutrality or indifference toward the entrepreneurial initiative at any level of management within the entrepreneurial process will likely jeopardize the initiative's success.

Entrepreneurial Outcomes

When managers engage in entrepreneurial behavior, a number of unique, interrelated outcomes occur both at the level of the individual and the organization. Figure 12-1 identified some of the principal individual- and organizational-level outcomes associated with middle-level managers' entrepreneurial behavior. However, these can be extended to the outcomes possible for all managers.

From an individual and organizational standpoint, these outcomes can be positive, neutral, or negative. Both individuals and organizations will compare the outcomes achieved from engaging in entrepreneurial behavior to the incurred costs, including the opportunity costs. Based on these evaluations, companies make decisions about investing in and supporting entrepreneurship, while individuals decide whether it is worth it to continue acting in an entrepreneurial fashion. For the company, the focus is on evaluating the degree to which entrepreneurial actions are enhancing current and future performance. At the level of the individual manager or employee, the concern is whether the personal and career-related benefits are worth the career-related risks, the stress, the emotional commitment, and the extensive time involved in doing something entrepreneurial.

INDIVIDUAL-LEVEL OUTCOMES AND CONSEQUENCES

At the level of the individual manager or employee, outcomes can be either intrinsic (i.e., psychological) or extrinsic (i.e., tangible) in nature. Financial rewards are an example of extrinsic outcomes, while personal reinforcement and a sense of self-achievement are intrinsic outcomes. The various types of incentives will have different effects on employee motivation, including the motivation to take risks and pursue entrepreneurial initiatives.

In general, intrinsic rewards center on the satisfaction individuals receive as a result of developing their own ideas, from being more in control of their destiny, and from having ultimate responsibility for the success of projects in which they are involved. Research addressing the effects of intrinsic rewards on entrepreneurial behavior has produced some interesting findings. Block and MacMillan (1993), for example, found that the following incentives were effective in eliciting entrepreneurial behavior: (1) equity (i.e., shares of stock) and equity equivalents, (2) bonuses, (3) salary increases and promotions, and (4) recognition systems and rewards. Separately, Block and Ornati (1987) found that more than 30 percent of the companies they surveyed compensated venture managers differently than other managers; over half of the respondents believed that variable bonuses based on ROI should be used; and internal fairness was the major obstacle in companies without formalized incentive programs, while determining a venture's goals was the most significant obstacle for organizations with formalized incentive programs.

One implication is that managers will choose to engage in entrepreneurial behavior if they believe that the outcomes resulting from their actions, including various types of rewards, will meet or exceed their expectations. It is generally recognized that the relationship between an individual's efforts and the performance that results from those efforts is moderated by the person's skills, abilities, and role perceptions, while the relationship between performance and outcomes affects whether or not the individual is likely to repeat the behavior (Porter and Lawler, 1968). Further, the individual's satisfaction with the outcome will often be dependent on a perception of equity or fairness. That is, people tend to compare the relationship between their own performance and the rewards they receive with the performance and rewards of some reference person or group (e.g., a coworker or employee in another organization performing similar work).

The issue of perceived equity has important implications for entrepreneurial behavior. Those who are equity sensitive strongly believe that everyone should be rewarded fairly based on invested inputs. When managers who choose to act entrepreneurially are equity sensitive, which is quite typical, they will compare the outcomes received for their entrepreneurial actions to the outcomes realized by those who choose not to act entrepreneurially. Future entrepreneurial behaviors will be more prevalent if past entrepreneurial behaviors are perceived as having been equitably rewarded.

ORGANIZATIONAL-LEVEL OUTCOMES AND CONSEQUENCES

Entrepreneurial actions are often deemed successful or not based on financial considerations, such as the sales or profitability level associated with the entrepreneurial initiative. However, it is also important to consider other types of outcomes. Significant and valuable organizational learning can result from a given entrepreneurial initiative, regardless of whether that initiative succeeds or fails in a financial sense. In addition, by participating in entrepreneurial projects, managers can enhance their entrepreneurial skill levels associated with the opportunity recognition and exploitation processes, better preparing them for future projects. Entrepreneurial initiatives can also positively impact general employee morale and reduce employee turnover.

The relationship between entrepreneurial behavior within the company and performance outcomes is not always easy to decipher. Yet it is important that individuals perceive that there is a relationship, and that it is positive. In order to justify their continuing support, senior managers, for example, must believe that entrepreneurial actions will lead to specific, desired organizational-level outcomes, such as the company's presence in attractive product-market arenas or the pursuit of novel strategic recipes that enhance the company's industry competitiveness. In general, the stronger the perceived association between entrepreneurial actions and favorable organizational outcomes, the greater the likelihood that entrepreneurship will be sustained as a core, defining process of the organization.

As an example, Hornsby et al. (2009) investigated the relationship between various antecedents of entrepreneurial behavior and organizational outcomes. Specifically, they examined five antecedent conditions: management support, work discretion and auton-omy, rewards and reinforcement, time availability, and organizational boundaries. At issue was how much these factors influence outcome variables, such as the number of new ideas suggested by employees, number of new ideas implemented, number of times people were recognized for new ideas, method of recognition, time spent thinking about new ideas, and job satisfaction. Based on data obtained from 530 managers, signif-icant support was found for a relationship between these antecedents and outcomes:

- Management support was related to total satisfaction, as well as recognition for new ideas and use of bonuses.

- Work discretion was related to total satisfaction as well as the number of unofficial improvements that were implemented in the company.

- Rewards/reinforcement was related to total satisfaction, as well as the use of pay raises and recognition for new ideas.

- Time availability was related to total satisfaction as well as the use of "other" methods of compensation.

- Organizational boundaries were related to total satisfaction, as well as the times recognized for job improvement and the use of bonuses.

Perhaps the most important finding in this study is that total job satisfaction was highly related to the existence of a work environment that supports entrepreneurial behavior. This study demonstrated the importance of the perception of an entre-preneurial environment and of sustained entrepreneurial behavior at all levels of management.

THE INNOVATOR'S NOTEBOOK

The Acordia Companies: A Product of Entrepreneurial Leadership

A classic corporate entrepreneurship strategy from a managerial point of view is best illustrated with an example of Anthem Blue Cross and Blue Shield. Under the vision and direction of L. Ben Lytle, chairman and CEO of Anthem Blue Cross and Blue Shield at that time, a startling restructuring plan was put into effect in 1986 to facilitate the entrepreneurial process. In 1983 the com-pany was operating as Blue Cross/Blue Shield of Indiana and was literally bogged down in its own bureaucracy. As a result it was losing ground in a fast-paced, changing insurance industry. However, in 1986, after initiating a corporate entrepreneurship training program, Lytle renamed the company The

Associated Group and divided the company legally, emotionally, physically, geographically, and culturally into operating companies named "Acordia Companies", ranging in size from 42 to 200 employees.

The opportunities for entrepreneurial managers within the organization began to expand with the development of these mini-corporations, which were designed to capture market niches and innovatively develop new ones. Each separate Acordia company had an individual CEO, vice president, and outside board of directors that delegated full authority to run the business. In 1986, The Associated Group was one large corporation with 2,800 employees serving only the state of Indiana, and with all revenue generated from health insurance. By the end of 1991, a five-year strategic plan to restructure and infuse entrepreneurial thinking into the organization was completed. The results had the company employing 7,000 people in 50 different companies, serving 49 states and generating over 25 percent of its $2 billion in revenue in lines of business outside health insurance. It provides an example of the effectiveness that corporate entrepreneurship can have in capturing the imagination of the entire company. It uncovers "builder-types" in the company seeking challenge and accountability of their ideas and innovative abilities.

By 1996 there were 32 Acordia Companies where corporate clients could obtain all types of insurance-related services, including commercial property and casualty coverage, group life and health insurance, third-party claims administration for self-insured benefit plans, and employee benefits consulting. In order to institute self-perpetuating change in the Acordia network, the mini-corporation CEOs were encouraged (and rewarded through stock options) to expand business and then spin off certain parts of the business either geographically or by specialty when there were 200 employees, else there would be too many management layers. In addition, the CEOs were evaluated on their ability to identify and nurture additional potential CEOs within their own organization.

Acordia's experience with entrepreneurial actions as the foundation of its corporate entrepreneurship strategy offers several insights that inform managerial practice. Entrepreneurial actions and the corporate entrepreneurship strategy for which they are a foundation result from intentional decisions. Analysis of the Acordia, Inc., experience suggests that forming an entrepreneurial vision, using new-venture teams, and relying on a compensation system that encourages and supports creative and innovative behaviors are products of careful and deliberate planning.

Upper-level managers must support the importance of entrepreneurial actions, through both words and deeds. Watching managers behave entrepreneurially, including actions taken to deal with the consequences of those behaviors, demonstrates that all parties will work together to cope with the disruption to existing work patterns that novel behaviors create (Kuratko et al., 2001).

The corporate entrepreneurship strategy of Acordia, Inc., was a success, with entrepreneurial actions being used throughout the Acordia companies. Innovative processes helped to streamline company operations. The company became more diversified in its products and markets, in that new products were introduced into multiple markets, while new markets with specific customer needs were regularly identified. The commitment to serve new, highly focused markets led to additional Acordia companies. Using its original competitive advantages as well as innovation, a new advantage was formed in many of the individual companies. Acordia's entrepreneurial journey proved to be the foundation for The Associated Group's success in the early 1990s.

Impressive financial results were recorded during implementation of the corporate entrepreneurship strategy. At the end of 1991, The Associated Group (TAG), the parent organization for all Acordia companies, was earning more than one-fourth of its $2 billion sales revenue from business lines outside Blue Cross/Blue Shield of Indiana's original core product—health insurance. In early 1992, Acordia, Inc., completed a successful IPO. Subsequently, the company's stock traded on the NYSE. In June of the same year, *Business Insurance* ranked Acordia, Inc., as the 10th largest insurance broker in the United States and 14th largest in the world. A remarkable success accomplished through the entrepreneurial leadership exhibited by the then CEO, L. Ben Lytle.

Discussion Questions

1. Explain how Ben Lytle exemplified putting in place a "pro-entrepreneurship organizational architecture" described as a role for top management in the chapter.

2. Relate the key entrepreneurial imperatives of top level executives (Table 12-2) to the efforts exhibited by the top level executives in the Acordia story. Be specific.

3. Using Table 12-3, discuss how Ben Lytle appears to be "managing ambidextrously."

SOURCE: Adapted from D. F. Kuratko, R. D. Ireland, and J. S. Hornsby, "Improving Firm Performance through Entrepreneurial Actions: Acordia's Corporate Entrepreneurship Strategy," *Academy of Management Executive,* 15(4), 2001: 60–71.

Summary and Conclusions

This chapter has explored the entrepreneurial roles and responsibilities of managers and nonmanagerial personnel operating at various levels within the company. Top-level managers must heed the entrepreneurial imperatives of strategic leadership and should recognize that entrepreneurial strategic leadership is fundamentally different than traditional general management. Managers at this level must also concern themselves with balancing the needs of current business with the needs of future business—what is known as the challenge of ambidextrous management. At the middle management level, involvement in the entrepreneurial process pertains to endorsing, refining, and shepherding entrepreneurial opportunities and identifying, acquiring, and deploying resources required to pursue those recognized opportunities. Finally, first-level managers and operating-level, nonmanagerial personnel can be both order-takers and autonomous innovators within the entrepreneurial process. These individuals are critical to the ongoing recognition and exploitation of entrepreneurial opportunity based on their central roles in the transformational work of the organization. They also serve as boundary spanners whose roles link them to key external stakeholders.

The exhibition of entrepreneurial behavior by managers and nonmanagerial employees at all company levels is a function of the value those individuals place on the outcomes of entrepreneurial actions as well as their perceptions of the extent to which the organizational context is conducive to such action. What motivates employees depends on a complex set of needs and wants that is weighted differently across individuals. The enactment of corporate entrepreneurship portends the possibility of highly favorable outcomes for both organizations and their individual members. Critical to such outcomes is the involvement of all levels of managers in the entrepreneurial process. Therefore, identifying and understanding those factors that encourage managers to exhibit a sustained pattern of entrepreneurial behavior is of paramount importance to a company's long-term competitiveness.

References

Baden-Fuller, C., and Volberda, H. W. 1997. "Strategic Renewal: How Large Complex Organizations Prepare for the Future," *International Studies of Management & Organization*, 27(2): 95–120.

Bartlett, C. A., and Ghoshal, S. 1997. "The Myth of the General Manager: New Personal Competencies for New Management Roles," *California Management Review*, 40(1): 92–116.

Birkinshaw, J., and Gibson, C. 2004. "Building Ambidexterity into an Organization," *MIT Sloan Management Review*, 45(4): 47–55.

Block, Z., and MacMillan, I. 1993. *Corporate Venturing* (Boston, MA: Harvard Business School Press).

Block, Z., and Ornati, O. A. 1987. "Compensating Corporate Venture Managers," *Journal of Business Venturing*, 2: 41–51.

Boston Consulting Group. 2005. *Innovation 2005* (Boston, MA: The Boston Consulting Group, Inc.).

Burgelman, R. A. 1994. "Fading Memories: A Process Theory of Strategic Business Exit in Dynamic Environments," *Administrative Science Quarterly*, 39: 24–57.

Burgelman, R. A., and Valikangas, L. 2005. "Managing Internal Corporate Venturing Cycles," *MIT Sloan Management Review*, 46(4): 26–34.

Cohen, A. R. 2002. "Mainstreaming Corporate Entrepreneurship: Leadership at Every Level of Organizations," *Babson Entrepreneurial Review*, October: 5–15

Covin, J. G., and Slevin, D. P. 2002. "The Entrepreneurial Imperatives of Strategic Leadership," in Hitt, M. A., Ireland, R. D., Camp, S. M, and Sexton, D. L. (eds.), *Strategic Entrepreneurship: Creating a New Mindset* (Oxford, U.K.: Blackwell Publishers): 309–327.

Dess, G. G., Ireland, R. D., Zahra, S. A., Floyd, S. W., Janney, J. J., and Lane, P. J. 2003. "Emerging Issues in Corporate Entrepreneurship," *Journal of Management*, 29(3): 351–378.

Eisenhardt, K. M., Brown, S. L., and Neck, H. M. 2000. "Competing on the Entrepreneurial Edge," in Meyer, G. D., and Heppard, K. A. (eds.), *Entrepreneurship as Strategy* (Thousand Oaks, CA: Sage Publications): 49–62.

Floyd, S. W., and Lane, P. J. 2000. "Strategizing throughout the Organization: Managing Role Conflict in Strategic Renewal," *Academy of Management Review*, 25(1): 154–177.

Heller, T. 1999. "Loosely Coupled Systems for Corporate Entrepreneurship: Imagining and Managing the Innovation Project/ Host Organization Interface," *Entrepreneurship Theory and Practice*, 24(2): 25–31.

Higdon, L. I., Jr. 2000. "Leading Innovation," *Executive Excellence*, 17(8): 15–16.

Hornsby, J. S., Kuratko, D. F., Shepherd, D. A., and Bott, J. P., 2009. "Managers' Corporate Entrepreneurial Actions: Examining Perception and Position," *Journal of Business Venturing*, 24(3): 236–247.

Jaruzelski, B., Dehoff, K., and Bordia, R. 2005. "The Booz Allen Hamilton Global Innovation 1000: Money Isn't Everything," *Strategy+Business*, 41(Winter): reprint no. 05406.

Kanter, R. M. 1989. "Swimming in Newstreams: Mastering Innovation Dilemmas," *California Management Review*, 31(4): 45–69.

King, A. W., Fowler, S. W., and Zeithaml, C. P. 2001. "Managing Organizational Competencies for Competitive Advantage: The Middle-Management Edge," *Academy of Management Executive*, 15(2): 95–106.

Kuratko, D. F., Ireland, R. D., and Hornsby, J. S. 2001. "Improving Firm Performance through Entrepreneurial Actions: Acordia's Corporate Entrepreneurship Strategy," *Academy of Management Executive*, 15(4): 60–71.

Kuratko, D. F., Ireland, R. D., Covin, J. G., and Hornsby, J. S. 2005. "A Model of Middle-Level Managers' Entrepreneurial Behavior," *Entrepreneurship Theory and Practice*, 29(6): 699–716.

Levinthal, D. A., and March, J. G. 1993. "The Myopia of Learning," *Strategic Management Journal*, 14: 95–112.

Miles, G., Heppard, K. A., Miles, R. E., and Snow, C. C. 2000. "Entrepreneurial Strategies: The Critical Role of Top Management," in Meyer, G. D., and Heppard, K. A. (eds.), *Entrepreneurship as Strategy* (Thousand Oaks, CA: Sage Publications): 101–114.

O'Reilly, C. A., III, and Tushman, M. L. 2004. "The Ambidextrous Organization," *Harvard Business Review*, 82(4): 74–81.

Porter, L. W., and Lawler, E. L. III. 1968. *Managerial Attitudes and Performance* (Homewood, IL: Richard D. Irwin, Inc.).

Ronstadt, R. C. 1984. *Entrepreneurship* (Dover, MA: Lord Publishing).

CHAPTER 13

ASSESSING CORPORATE ENTREPRENEURIAL PERFORMANCE

Introduction

As the entrepreneurial organization aggressively pursues the future, managers must continually assess the actual levels of entrepreneurial activity occurring within the company. They also must track outcomes of this activity, and particularly outcomes related to innovation, competitive position, and financial performance. Entrepreneurship involves significant uncertainty, ambiguity, and risk. It is easy for projects to be initiated that have little chance of success, or that are unrelated to the competencies and overall strategies of the company. It is also not uncommon for projects to be started but never completed. And even when desired levels and types of entrepreneurship are achieved, it can be quite difficult to maintain that level over time. Given these realities, the sustainable benefits of corporate entrepreneurship can be realized only when management institutes and uses a performance tracking system.

Companies that approach corporate entrepreneurship as an "experimental program" tend to achieve relatively little in the way of results. Senior executives in such companies become frustrated with the lack of performance and move on to the next hot management trend. Alternatively, companies that institute corporate entrepreneurship as a "process" that infiltrates and permeates the entire organization tend to achieve dramatic results over time. They eventually see improved internal efficiencies, higher employee morale, and major improvements in financial performance. This notion of implementing a process that imbues the culture, structure, and systems of a company implies that it takes considerable time to create a truly entrepreneurial company, making it all the more vital that ongoing progress be assessed on a regular and systematic basis.

In this chapter we examine the methods currently available for assessing entrepreneurial performance in companies. Attention is devoted to evaluating the organization as a whole as well as individual innovation projects. An integrative framework called the Entrepreneurial Health Audit is introduced as a logical structure to guide the assessment process. In addition, an approach is provided to facilitate the company's ongoing planning efforts for entrepreneurial projects. The critical role of innovation goals is explored, with examples provided of the types of goals that can drive a company's entrepreneurial performance.

Assessing Entrepreneurial Activity in Companies

Assessment involves the measuring of processes and outcomes. Thus, assessment requires attention not only to various kinds of results but also to the experiences that lead to those outcomes. Assessment is most likely to lead to improvement when it is part of a larger set of conditions that promote change. In many respects, this notion of assessment as a process of continuous change and improvement echoes the Japanese outlook on improvement known as *kaizen*—a philosophy of continuous improvement with a 200-year view of the future. Although it is probably not necessary—or possible—to view assessment over centuries, it is possible and important to take a perspective that incorporates the possibility of assessing changes and improvements over the next 10 or so years.

Unfortunately, assessment and organizational improvement are often perceived as exercises to be implemented in order to meet an urgent need—shareholder pressure, stakeholder opinions, market demands, image, and so forth. In great companies, effective assessment programs become embedded in the organizational culture. They are acknowledged, discussed, deliberated, reviewed, and refined. Effective assessment is perceived as an integral part of the overall mission, and it focuses, very simply, on learning. Specifically, assessment is one of the driving forces in creating what Peter Senge (2006) calls "'learning organizations,' organizations in which people continually expand their capacity to create the results they truly desire, where new and expansive patterns of thinking are nurtured, collective aspiration is set free, and people are continually learning how to learn together" (p. 1). Assessment at its best is all of these things—and more.

The ability to assess progress or performance is especially complex when it comes to entrepreneurship. We are dealing with an activity that is inherently messy, hard to control, and fairly uncertain. Further, it is an activity that gives rise to resistance from fellow employees and other stakeholders, and entails numerous obstacles that must be overcome. Those who are expected to be entrepreneurial are also expected to meet the demands of their everyday jobs, and many struggle with the need to balance administrative skills against entrepreneurial skills. Further, it is often easy to lose sight of the need to discover new opportunities and develop innovative solutions when one is caught up in the politics, deadlines, and immediate crises that characterize normal organizational life.

It should be remembered that entrepreneurship is both a way of thinking (cognition) and a way of acting (behavior). The two elements have implications for the way in which assessments or performance evaluations are designed and managed. For example, Jelinek and Litterer (1995) found difficulties in analyzing entrepreneurial companies using traditional management theories. They argue for the importance of measuring the shared cognitions (or ways of thinking) among those in the company. They posit that this approach would capture the constant innovation that results from entrepreneurial activity, which they call "systemic flexibility." The authors conclude that *shared* management and measurement processes are necessary for facilitating a corporate culture and strategy that sustains entrepreneurial activity. At the operational level, measurement systems are key for recognizing anomalies (signals for mindful alertness) that can become inputs for coordinated decision making that produces results (exploiting opportunities).

So in some ways, the purpose of measurement in highly entrepreneurial companies appears to differ from what it is in non-entrepreneurial companies. Management and measurement systems in entrepreneurial companies have much to do with the company's propensity for "ambiguity absorption." The managerial systems in entrepreneurial companies are adept at dealing with high levels of ambiguity and uncertainty, which contributes to organizational flexibility. Ambiguity absorption is captured with measurement approaches that focus both on cognitions, or how employees think, and on specific behaviors. For instance, Covin et al. (2006) emphasize the need to measure the frequency as well as the nature of product, service, and process innovation (both failures and successes). The authors make it clear that flexible measurement systems must be designed to identify emerging opportunities that arise while managers are busy tracking developments in existing products and markets as they evolve through their life cycles.

Beyond the need to measure cognitions and behaviors is the importance of assessing performance outcomes that result from entrepreneurial actions within a company. Consider the relationship between levels of entrepreneurship and company performance. This relationship has been approached differently across time. During the 1980s, for example, some argued that it was difficult if not almost impossible for people to act entrepreneurially in what often had become highly bureaucratic organizational structures (Morse, 1986). At the same time, however, others were suggesting that for companies of any size (in terms of sales volume and number of employees, among other dimensions), entrepreneurial actions were possible, should be encouraged, and could be expected to enhance company performance (Burgelman, 1984; Kanter, 1986).

Witnessed throughout the 1990s was a virtual revolution with respect to the perceived value of entrepreneurial actions as a contributor to organizational success (Covin and Slevin, 1991). This significant change paralleled the rapid emergence of profound adjustments in how companies defined their business, utilized their human resources, and competed in the global economy. Speaking to this matter, Zahra et al.

(1999) point out that "Some of the world's best-known companies had to endure painful transformation to become more entrepreneurial. These companies had to endure years of reorganization, downsizing, and restructuring. These changes altered the identity or culture of these companies, infusing a new entrepreneurial spirit throughout their operations... change, innovation, and entrepreneurship became highly regarded words that describe what successful companies must do to survive."

Extending this position to the current day, the twenty-first century is a time when corporate entrepreneurship is intimately tied to the ability of companies to establish sustainable competitive advantage and maintain profitable growth (Hornsby et al., 2009; Kuratko et al., 2001; Kuratko et al., 2005). Moreover, some argue rather convincingly that a lack of entrepreneurial actions in the fast-paced and complex global economy can be a sure recipe for failure (Kuratko, 2009a).

Specifically, there is extensive evidence of strong, statistically significant relationships between levels of entrepreneurship within a company and a number of indicators of company performance (Dess et al., 2003; Garvin and Levesque, 2006; Hill and Birkinshaw, 2008; Vanhaverbeke and Peeters, 2005). Examples of such indicators include profits, the income-to-sales ratio, the rate of growth in revenue, the rate of growth in assets, the rate of growth in employment, and composite measures of financial and nonfinancial criteria. This linkage between entrepreneurship and performance appears to be especially strong for companies that operate in increasingly turbulent environments.

A Systematic Approach: The Entrepreneurial Health Audit

It is impossible to know if a goal or performance standard has been reached without some sort of measurement process. Or, more simply, to get where the company wants to go, management must know where the company is at present. Before a strategy for entrepreneurship can be formulated or the internal environment can be properly designed, senior executives must have an accurate understanding of the company's current level of entrepreneurial intensity. Just as important is the ability to diagnose factors contributing to the overall entrepreneurial health of the organization.

Measurement at the level of the individual can be useful in helping managers and others examine and refine their own leadership styles, as well as in characterizing employee behavior over time. At the organizational level, measures can be used to benchmark and track company-wide entrepreneurial performance, establish norms and draw industry comparisons, formulate entrepreneurship goals, develop strategies, and assess relationships between entrepreneurial actions and company performance variables over time.

How do we measure entrepreneurship in a company? It is our recommendation that a systematic approach be adopted that involves three steps or stages. Together, these steps form what can be called the *Entrepreneurial Health Audit* (Ireland et al., 2006).

Step I: Assessing the Company's Entrepreneurial Intensity (EI)   The entrepreneurial performance of a company at a given point in time is reflected in its entrepreneurial intensity score. As noted in Chapter 3, EI is concerned with the degree and frequency of entrepreneurship.

To assess degree of entrepreneurship, measures are needed of company innovativeness, risk-taking, and proactiveness. Innovativeness refers to the seeking of creative, unusual, or novel solutions to problems and needs. These solutions take the form of new technologies and processes, as well as new products and services. Risk-taking involves the willingness to commit significant resources to opportunities having a reasonable chance of costly failure. These risks are typically manageable and calculated. Proactiveness is concerned with pursuing initiatives in advance of rivals' actions, and with doing what is necessary to anticipate and act upon an entrepreneurial opportunity. Such pioneering behavior usually entails considerable perseverance, adaptability, and tolerance of failure. Assessment of frequency of entrepreneurship involves measuring the number of new products, services, and process innovations introduced over some defined time period.

Table 13-1 includes a proven measurement instrument for assessing EI within a company (Miller and Friesen, 1982; Morris and Sexton, 1996). Degree of entrepreneurship is assessed with the first 12 questions, while the remaining items focus on frequency. Weights of .7 and .3 are placed, respectively, on scores for degree and frequency. To obtain a score for the overall company, the instrument is typically applied to a large number of managers representing different functional areas within the company. Annual measurements allow the company to first benchmark itself and then track progress over time. The instrument can also be applied at the divisional, functional, or unit level within the company, so that units can be benchmarked and compared.

In interpreting EI scores, it is important to keep in mind that norms for entrepreneurial intensity will differ among industries. As we have noted, EI tends to be associated with higher levels of company performance, and this relationship appears to be most marked when operating in highly turbulent environments. However, we are not suggesting that higher levels of EI are always better. Rather, the issue is one of achieving high levels of EI relative to one's industry, as opposed to some absolute standard.

TABLE 13-1

Measuring the Firm's Entrepreneurial Intensity (EI)*

(Please note that questions 4, 6, 7, and 11 are reverse scaled)

I. Company Orientation

For the following statements, please circle the number that best corresponds to your level of agreement with each statement.

Our company is characterized by:	Strongly Agree				Strongly Disagree
1. A high rate of new product/service introductions, compared to our competitors (including new features and improvements)	1	2	3	4	5
2. An emphasis on continuous improvement in methods of production and/or service delivery	1	2	3	4	5
3. Risk-taking by key executives in seizing and exploring chancy growth opportunities	1	2	3	4	5
4. A "live and let live" philosophy in dealing with competitors	1	2	3	4	5
5. Seeking of unusual, novel solutions by senior executives to problems via the use of "idea people," Brainstorming, etc	1	2	3	4	5
6. A top management philosophy that emphasizes proven products and services, and the avoidance of heavy new product development costs	1	2	3	4	5

In our company, top-level decision making is characterized by:

	Strongly Agree				Strongly Disagree
7. Cautious, pragmatic, step-at-a-time adjustments to problems	1	2	3	4	5
8. Active search for big opportunities	1	2	3	4	5
9. Rapid growth as the dominant goal	1	2	3	4	5
10. Large, bold decisions despite uncertainties of the outcomes	1	2	3	4	5
11. Compromises among the conflicting demands of owners, government, management, customers, employees, suppliers, etc.	1	2	3	4	5
12. Steady growth and stability as primary concerns	1	2	3	4	5

(Continued)

II. New Product Introduction

1. What is the number of new products your company introduced during the past two years? _____

	Significantly Less		Same		Significantly More
2. How many product improvements or revisions did you introduce during the past two years?	1	2	3	4	5
3. How does the number of new product introductions at your organization compare with those of your major competitors?	1	2	3	4	5

	Not at all				To a great extent
4. To what degree did these new product introductions include products that did not previously exist in your markets ("new to the market")?	1	2	3	4	5

III. New Service Introduction (for those who sell services)

1. What is the number of new services your company introduced during the past two years? _____

	Significantly Less		Same		Significantly More
2. How many existing services did you significantly revise or improve during the past two years?	1	2	3	4	5
3. How does the number of new service introductions your company made compare with those of the competitors?	1	2	3	4	5

	Not at all				To a great extent
4. To what degree did these new service introductions include services that did not previously exist in your markets?	1	2	3	4	5

IV. New Process Introduction

1. Please estimate the number of significant new methods or operational processes your organization implemented during the past two years. Examples of process innovations include new systems for managing customer service or inventories, an improved process for collecting receivables, a major new sales or distribution approach, etc. _____

*EI Questionnaire adapted from D. Miller, "The Correlates of Entrepreneurship in Three Types of Firms," *Management Science,* 29(3), 1983: 770–791; and M. H. Morris, and D. F. Kuratko, *Corporate Entrepreneurship,* Dallas, TX: Harcourt Press, 2002.

Measurement of EI also provides numerous opportunities for developing a richer understanding of how entrepreneurship works in a particular company. For example, the relative importance of degree and frequency when measuring entrepreneurial actions may vary depending on certain strategic factors, such as the pace of technological change in an industry, the levels of competitive intensity, or the heterogeneity of market demand. Also, the conditions under which degree or frequency is the strongest contributor to performance can be assessed. It has been speculated that frequency and degree may contribute fairly equally to short-term results, whereas a greater degree of entrepreneurship has a stronger long-term impact. Such a possibility is implicit in the work of Hamel and Prahalad (1991). Using a baseball analogy of hitting many singles versus attempting to hit a home run, they emphasize the value of companies pursuing multiple smaller projects at a time as opposed to pursuing a potentially breakthrough project. A risk–reward trade-off is involved in which the former are thought to generate short- and intermediate-term profits, whereas the latter significantly impact long-term profitability. In any event, the EI measure is a powerful assessment tool for capturing the degree and frequency of entrepreneurship at the organizational level.

Step II: Diagnosing the Climate for Corporate Entrepreneurship   While the assessment of EI captures how entrepreneurial the company is, a need also exists to determine the underlying reasons *why* a given level of EI is being achieved. In a sense, management must determine the entrepreneurial health of the organization. The Corporate Entrepreneurship Climate Instrument (CECI) is a diagnostic tool for assessing, evaluating, and managing the internal environment of the company in a manner that supports entrepreneurship. By taking inventory of the company's current situation, executives can identify organizational systems and structures that are inconsistent with, or represent obstacles to, higher levels of EI.

Originally developed by Kuratko et al. (1990), and further refined in more recent research studies (Hornsby et al., 2002; Hornsby et al., 2008; Hornsby et al., 2009;) as the CEAI (Corporate Entrepreneurship Assessment Instrument), the CECI is designed around five key antecedents to the creation of sustainable entrepreneurship within a company. These antecedents include (1) *management support* (the willingness of top-level managers to facilitate and promote entrepreneurial behavior, including the championing of innovative ideas and providing the resources people require to take entrepreneurial actions), (2) *work discretion/autonomy* (top-level managers' commitment to tolerate failure, provide decision-making latitude and freedom from excessive oversight, and delegate authority and responsibility to managers), (3) *reinforcement* (developing and using systems that reinforce entrepreneurial behavior, highlight significant achievements, and encourage pursuit of challenging work), (4) *time availability* (evaluating workloads to ensure that individuals and groups have the time needed to pursue innovations and that their jobs are structured in ways that support efforts to achieve short- and long-term organizational goals), and (5) *organizational boundaries* (precise explanations of outcomes expected from organizational work and development of mechanisms for evaluating, selecting, and using innovations). In addition, the instrument reflects the key dimensions of company climate discussed earlier.

The full CECI survey can be found in Table 13-2. It consists of 78 Likert-style questions. The instrument has been shown to be psychometrically sound as a viable means for assessing areas requiring attention and improvement in order to achieve intended results through use of a corporate entrereneurship (CE) strategy. The instrument can be used to develop a profile of a company across the dimensions and climate variables previously described. Low scores in an area suggest the need for training and development activities to enhance the company's readiness for entrepreneurial behavior and implementation of a CE strategy.

TABLE 13-2

The Corporate Entrepreneurship Climate Instrument* (CECI)

We are interested in learning about how you perceive your workplace and organization. Please read the following items. Using the scale below please indicate how much you agree or disagree with each of the statements. If you strongly agree, write "5." If you strongly disagree write "1." There are no right or wrong answers to these questions so please be as honest and thoughtful as possible in your responses. All responses will be kept strictly confidential. Thank you for your cooperation!

Strongly Disagree	Disagree	Not Sure	Agree	Strongly Agree
1	2	3	4	5

Section 1: Management Support for Corporate Entrepreneurship

_____ 1. My organization is quick to use improved work methods.

_____ 2. My organization is quick to use improved work methods that are developed by workers.

_____ 3. In my organization, developing one's own ideas is encouraged for the improvement of the corporation.

_____ 4. Upper management is aware and very receptive to my ideas and suggestions.

_____ 5. A promotion usually follows from the development of new and innovative ideas.

_____ 6. Those employees who come up with innovative ideas on their own often receive management encouragement for their activities.

_____ 7. The "doers on projects" are allowed to make decisions without going through elaborate justification and approval procedures.

(Continued)

| TABLE 13-2 | (Continued) |

The Corporate Entrepreneurship Climate Instrument* (CECI)

_____ 8. Senior managers encourage innovators to bend rules and rigid procedures in order to keep promising ideas on track.

_____ 9. Many top managers have been known for their experience with the innovation process.

_____ 10. Money is often available to get new project ideas off the ground.

_____ 11. Individuals with successful innovative projects receive additional rewards and compensation beyond the standard reward system for their ideas and efforts.

_____ 12. There are several options within the organization for individuals to get financial support for their innovative projects and ideas.

_____ 13. People are often encouraged to take calculated risks with ideas around here.

_____ 14. Individual risk takers are often recognized for their willingness to champion new projects, whether eventually successful or not.

_____ 15. The term "risk taker" is considered a positive attribute for people in my work area.

_____ 16. This organization supports many small and experimental projects, realizing that some will undoubtedly fail.

_____ 17. An employee with a good idea is often given free time to develop that idea.

_____ 18. There is considerable desire among people in the organization for generating new ideas without regard for crossing departmental or functional boundaries.

_____ 19. People are encouraged to talk to employees in other departments of this organization about ideas for new projects.

Strongly Disagree	Disagree	Not Sure	Agree	Strongly Agree
1	2	3	4	5

Section 2: Work Discretion

_____ 20. I feel that I am my own boss and do not have to double check all of my decisions with someone else.

_____ 21. Harsh criticism and punishment result from mistakes made on the job.

_____ 22. This organization provides the chance to be creative and try my own methods of doing the job.

_____ 23. This organization provides the freedom to use my own judgment.

_____ 24. This organization provides the chance to do something that makes use of my abilities.

_____ 25. I have the freedom to decide what I do on my job.

_____ 26. It is basically my own responsibility to decide how my job gets done.

(_Continued_)

_____ 27. I almost always get to decide what I do on my job.

_____ 28. I have much autonomy on my job and am left on my own to do my own work.

_____ 29. I seldom have to follow the same work methods or steps for doing my major tasks from day to day.

Section 3: Rewards/Reinforcement

_____ 30. My manager helps me get my work done by removing obstacles and roadblocks.

_____ 31. The rewards I receive are dependent upon my innovation on the job.

_____ 32. My supervisor will increase my job responsibilities if I am performing well in my job.

_____ 33. My supervisor will give me special recognition if my work performance is especially good.

_____ 34. My manager would tell his/her boss if my work was outstanding.

_____ 35. There is a lot of challenge in my job.

Section 4: Time Availability

_____ 36. During the past three months, my work load kept me from spending time on developing new ideas.

_____ 37. I always seem to have plenty of time to get everything done.

_____ 38. I have just the right amount of time and work load to do everything well.

_____ 39. My job is structured so that I have very little time to think about wider organizational problems.

_____ 40. I feel that I am always working with time constraints on my job.

_____ 41. My coworkers and I always find time for long-term problem solving.

Strongly Disagree	_Disagree_	_Not Sure_	_Agree_	_Strongly Agree_
1	**2**	**3**	**4**	**5**

Section 5: Organizational Boundaries

_____ 42. In the past three months, I have always followed standard operating procedures or practices to do my major tasks.

_____ 43. There are many written rules and procedures that exist for doing my major tasks.

_____ 44. On my job I have no doubt of what is expected of me.

_____ 45. There is little uncertainty in my job.

_____ 46. During the past year, my immediate supervisor discussed my work performance with me frequently.

_____ 47. My job description clearly specifies the standards of performance on which my job is evaluated.

(Continued)

TABLE 13-2	(Continued)

The Corporate Entrepreneurship Climate Instrument* (CECI)

_____ 48. I clearly know what level of work performance is expected from me in terms of amount, quality, and timelines of output.

Section 6: Specific Climate Variables

_____ 49. This company definitely rewards employees who take calculated risks and innovate.

_____ 50. Jobs in this company tend to be broadly defined with considerable discretion in how tasks are performed.

_____ 51. In this company, employees can pursue multiple career paths.

_____ 52. This company tries hard to develop the creative potential of employees.

_____ 53. Annual performance appraisals in this company include an evaluation of employee innovativeness.

_____ 54. Around here, it seems like there is more concern with process than with performance.

_____ 55. This company does a good job of balancing incentives for individual initiative with incentives for team collaboration.

_____ 56. If you are not innovating on the job, you cannot get ahead in this company.

_____ 57. An overly bureaucratic structure takes away from our ability to be entrepreneurial in this company.

_____ 58. Our company is organized in a way that encourages managers to "micromanage" employees and projects.

_____ 59. We have too many levels of management in this company.

_____ 60. I would characterize the company structure as being highly flexible.

_____ 61. A rigid chain of command limits our ability to experiment with new ideas.

_____ 62. Red tape and slow approval cycles are problems in this company.

_____ 63. Managers in this company strongly believe in delegating decision-making responsibility.

_____ 64. Controls are very tight in this company; we tend to count every dollar and every hour.

_____ 65. Senior management focuses on eliminating any slack within budgets.

_____ 66. Once budgets are finalized and accepted, they are difficult to revise.

_____ 67. The lines of command clearly allocate authority and responsibility to each business unit/department.

_____ 68. The organizational structure is very clearly defined and delineated.

Strongly Disagree	Disagree	Not Sure	Agree	Strongly Agree
1	2	3	4	5

_____ 69. In this company, employees have a lot of say in how things are done.

(*Continued*)

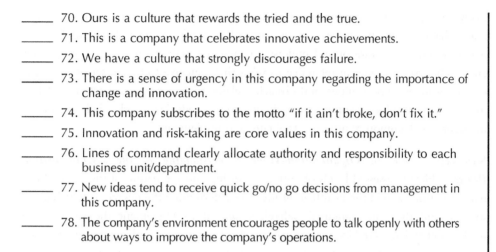

_____ 70. Ours is a culture that rewards the tried and the true.

_____ 71. This is a company that celebrates innovative achievements.

_____ 72. We have a culture that strongly discourages failure.

_____ 73. There is a sense of urgency in this company regarding the importance of change and innovation.

_____ 74. This company subscribes to the motto "if it ain't broke, don't fix it."

_____ 75. Innovation and risk-taking are core values in this company.

_____ 76. Lines of command clearly allocate authority and responsibility to each business unit/department.

_____ 77. New ideas tend to receive quick go/no go decisions from management in this company.

_____ 78. The company's environment encourages people to talk openly with others about ways to improve the company's operations.

*CECI is adapted from original work done by D. F. Kuratko, R. M. Montagno, and J. S. Hornsby, 1990. "Developing an Entrepreneurial Assessment Instrument for an Effective Corporate Entrepreneurial Environment," *Strategic Management Journal*, 11: 49–58; and J. S. Hornsby, D. F. Kuratko, and S. A. Zahra, 2002. "Middle Managers' Perception of the Internal Environment for Corporate Entrepreneurship: Assessing a Measurement Scale," *Journal of Business Venturing*, 17: 49–63.

Essentially concerned with a company's "entrepreneurial health," the instrument can significantly benefit organizations and would be of interest to both managers and researchers. For managers, the instrument provides an indication of a company's likelihood of being able to successfully implement a CE strategy. It highlights areas of the work environment that should be the focus of ongoing design and development efforts. Further, the CECI can be used as an assessment tool for evaluating corporate training needs in the areas of entrepreneurship and innovation. Determining these training needs can set the stage for improving managers' skills and increasing their sensitivity to the challenges of prioritizing and supporting corporate entrepreneurial activity. Beyond this, the instrument can be combined with other measures to explore a host of questions surrounding entrepreneurial behavior in established organizations. For instance, CECI provides a basis for determining ways in which controllable factors within the work environment influence employee actions, together with insights regarding the relative importance of various contextual factors in different industry, market, and company contexts.

The tacit knowledge of managers at the executive, middle, and operating levels regarding the role of entrepreneurship within the company and what the company is explicitly doing to reinforce entrepreneurial behavior, is critical. Managers are most likely to engage in entrepreneurial behavior when the organizational antecedents to that behavior (e.g., incentive systems, control systems) are well designed. Further, managers must be aware of and understand these antecedents. Individuals assess their entrepreneurial capacities in reference to what they perceive to be is a set of organizational resources, opportunities, and obstacles related to entrepreneurial activity. Determining that the value of entrepreneurial behavior exceeds that of other behaviors leads managers to champion, synthesize, facilitate, and implement.

Step III: Create an Organization-Wide Understanding of the CE/Innovation Process Having assessed levels of entrepreneurship and the nature of the internal climate, the third step in the health audit involves determining the degree to which a CE strategy and the entrepreneurial behaviors needed to implement the strategy are understood and accepted by affected parties. A CE strategy is implemented successfully only when all actors are committed to it. Hence, individuals must be aware of the intent and mission surrounding a CE strategy. Key decision makers must find ways to explain their intent and mission to those from whom entrepreneurial efforts are expected. In addition, the readiness of each actor to display entrepreneurial behavior should be realistically assessed. Actions to enhance entrepreneurial skills of employees should then be set into motion. These commitments and processes help to shape a common vision around the importance of a CE strategy and entrepreneurial behavior as the cornerstones to an effective strategic adaptation process.

As a way for organizations to develop a sound program for understanding entrepreneurial activity, a CE employee development program should be established. Following are some suggested elements for such a program (Kuratko, 2009b).

The Entrepreneurial Experience—Review managerial and organizational behavior concepts, review definitions of corporate entrepreneurship and related concepts, examine the entrepreneurial process as it applies to established companies, and review several entrepreneurial cases.

Entrepreneurial Breakthroughs—Present an overview of entrepreneurial breakthroughs in the company and in other companies. Best practices in terms of highly entrepreneurial initiatives can be reviewed. This challenges participants to think innovatively and emphasizes the need for "breaking out of the box" in today's organizations. Importantly, employees must be given a reference point in terms of the types of entrepreneurial activities that are expected of them.

Innovative Thinking—The process of thinking creatively is foreign to most bureaucratic organizations. Misconceptions about thinking creatively should be reviewed and a discussion of the most common creativity inhibitors presented. After completing a creativity inventory, participants engage in several exercises designed to facilitate their own creative thinking.

Idea Acceleration Process—Participants should generate a set of specific ideas on which they would like to work. Issues of strategic fit can be examined, together with a review of the types of criteria used by the organization when evaluating new concepts. Additionally, participants can determine needed resources to accomplish their projects.

Barriers, Facilitators, and Triggers to Entrepreneurial Thinking—Climate factors from the CECI are reviewed. The most common barriers to innovative behavior should be examined and discussed. The process includes examining a number of aspects of the corporation including structural barriers and facilitators. Specific types of internal and external triggers for different forms of entrepreneurship can be explored. Participants can complete exercises that will help them deal with barriers in the workplace. In addition, video case histories are shown that depict actual corporate entrepreneurs who have been successful in dealing with corporate barriers. Time in this module, or in a distinct module, might be devoted to strategies for soliciting sponsors and leveraging internal corporate resources.

Sustaining Innovation Teams—The concept of forming Innovation Teams to focus on specific innovations is examined. Managers work together to form teams based on the ideas that have been circulating among the entire group. Team dynamics is reviewed for each group to understand.

The Corporate Venture Plan—After participants examine the facilitators and barriers to behaving innovatively in their organization, groups are asked to begin the process of completing a plan. The plan includes setting goals, establishing a work team, assessing current conditions, developing a step-by-step timetable for project completion, and project evaluation.

Finally, it is important to note that training must reinforce entrepreneurship as more than a one-time or occasional activity. The more widespread the understanding of corporate entrepreneurship, the more likely it is that real culture changes will occur in the organization.

Assessing Individual Entrepreneurial Projects

Highly entrepreneurial companies have any number of innovative projects underway at a given point in time. The projects in this innovation portfolio must also be subject to periodic evaluation. Thus, in addition to overall levels of entrepreneurship at an organization, division, or department level, individual projects must be evaluated.

The beginning point is solid analysis and critique of project feasibility, followed by detailed evaluations of progress as a project evolves through key stage gates. Corporate entrepreneurs must put their ideas through this analysis to discover if they contain any fatal flaws.

UNDERSTANDING HOW PROJECTS EVOLVE

The new product or service development process usually does not evolve in a neat, orderly fashion. In fact, there is certain level of chaos to be found in the most successful of projects. Nonetheless, there are some key steps that generally must be accomplished to produce a commercially viable new product, service, or process. These are outlined in Figure 13-1.

Ideas for innovations come from a variety of sources, both inside and outside the company. Effective innovators have a system for regularly generating and cataloging ideas, and this includes both active (e.g., patent searches, attending research conferences

FIGURE 13-1

Innovation as a Linear Process

SOURCE: "The Levels of Culture" from E. H. Schein, *The Corporate Culture Survival Guide*, Copyright © 1999, Jossey-Bass. Reprinted with permission of John Wiley & Sons, Inc.

and trade shows, conducting market research, internal brainstorming sessions) and passive (informal conversations at work, ideas that come to an employee while doing some other task) search efforts. The largest number of ideas is discarded during the screening stage. The company applies a set of evaluative criteria to the ideas and rates them. Of key concern are fit with the company (e.g., skills, capabilities, strategic direction) and fit with the market (e.g., clearly identified need, competitive opening, growth potential). The remaining ideas are then subjected to a concept testing phase, where a hypothetical product is explained to relevant audiences, including customers, to get their reactions. Potential benefit segments are identified. Focus groups, interviews, and surveys are often used. Often business cases are prepared for the most promising surviving concepts.

These concepts, now fairly well defined around some core benefit, must then be transformed into a physical product (or service delivery model) and undergo performance testing. Technical feasibility analysis involves establishing the exact technical requirements for designing and producing the product, ensuring these requirements can be met on a reasonable time and cost schedule. A physical product or service model is engineered and unit production costs are estimated. Design engineers may conceive different versions of the product (or service delivery system) based on the many trade-off decisions that must be made among product attributes. Next comes technical product or service testing, which subjects the innovation to a rigorous examination of tolerances and performance capabilities under differing circumstances. Products are often placed in customer locations (or beta test sites) and their use is monitored.

Profitability analysis is then performed to determine breakeven points in terms of the initial investment as well as rates of return that will be realized based on projected cash flows. To confirm initial sales projections and finalize decisions regarding price, packaging, promotion, and distribution, test marketing is then performed using a representative subset of the intended market. Market launch efforts have become fairly complex and sophisticated undertakings that are often initiated a year or more before a product or service hits the market. The company is attempting to successfully penetrate the innovators and early adopters, while laying the ground for penetration of the more general market.

Although a logical evolution of necessary activities, the innovation process is rarely so linear or smooth. It normally involves considerable feedback, and requires multiple iterations in accomplishing a given activity. These iterations might involve progress in one area or by one team that then necessitates adjustments in another area, and subsequent progress in the second area then requires new work in the first area. Extensive information must be shared back and forth across the various individuals and units

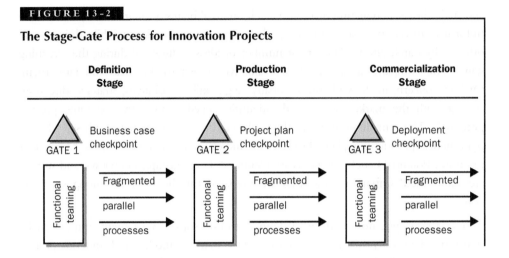

FIGURE 13-2

The Stage-Gate Process for Innovation Projects

involved in the process. Given these characteristics, many companies have found the "stage-gate system" to be an effective approach to the innovation process.

With the stage-gate system, creative activities that move the project forward are separated from evaluation activities (see Figure 13-2). The stages consist of a number of the activities contained in the linear process previously described, but many of these activities are done in parallel, or extensively overlap one another. Parallel processing demands concurrent problem solving instead of sequential steps, which will result in less recycling and reworking. Thus, in the first stage, idea generation and concept testing may occur in tandem. This stage would then be followed by a gate in which concepts are eliminated and a decision is made to further invest in certain of them, allowing them to move into the next stage. Now, technical work and initial financial analysis may be done, and a prototype produced. Then comes an evaluative gate, and so forth. Thus, rather than a single major "go/no go" decision early in the process, such decisions are made at each gate, meaning a project can be killed right up to the point of launch. The stage-gate system is closer to what companies do in practice, with a typical reliance on 4 to 6 stages, multiple activities in a stage, and a go/no go decision after each stage.

Measuring Innovation Performance in Projects

It is difficult to ensure systematic achievement of management intentions without clearly formulated objectives to guide and motivate activities. Moreover, the manager is unable to assess how the company is doing in a particular area if he or she does not know what the company was trying to accomplish in the first place. As a case in point, assume that management has voiced general criticism regarding a lack of innovation in the company over the past five years. However, because objectives for numbers of products/services, development cycle times, and a host of related performance indicators are absent, one is making judgments simply based on perceptions of what competitors did over a similar period, or some general notion of what the market required.

Consistent with a portfolio approach to new product development activity, there is a need to establish multiple performance targets. Table 13-3 provides an example of the set of objectives a company or division might specify for the coming three years. Here, objectives have been established in seven areas ranging from numbers and types of innovation projects underway to the average development cycle for new products.

A goal that is receiving much attention in companies concerns the percentage of company revenues that will come from new products and services introduced over the next three to five years. For instance, Page (1993) reported a norm among innovating companies of 38 percent, meaning that five years from now these companies expect 38 percent of their sales will come from products the company is currently not selling. By setting and widely publicizing this type of goal, management makes clear that innovation is a normal and expected activity.

Closely tied to the establishment of objectives is the need to hold individuals, teams, and departments accountable for innovation performance. The ability to do so is dependent upon the identification of specific performance measures that can be tracked over time. Unfortunately, most companies do not measure their innovation efforts, in part because accounting and control systems do not deal effectively with innovation. However, where objectives have been quantified, they effectively provide measures that management can track. Thus, each of the objectives specified in Table 13-3 lend themselves to fairly straightforward tracking.

An interesting perspective on performance monitoring is provided by Kuczmarski (1996). He proposes a set of ten indices that can be readily calculated on an annual basis (see Table 13-4). These include outcome measures that are both financial (e.g., success or hit rate, innovation revenue per employee) and nonfinancial (e.g., innovation portfolio mix), as well as process measures (e.g., process pipeline flow, R&D innovation emphasis ratio). The intent is not to overwhelm the company with too many metrics. In fact, the more typical problem is too few performance measures. Management needs to focus on identifying those measures that best fit the company's competitive situation, its resources, and the amount and type of innovation being emphasized.

Another tool for evaluating new innovative projects is the *Yellow Light Variables Approach* developed by Balachandra (1984). Here, the focus is on simple yet clear

TABLE 13-3

Example of a Format for Setting Innovation Objectives

A. Projects in development at any one point in time	10
i. New products	
• New to the market	1
• New to company/new product lines	1
• New products in existing lines	2
ii. Product revisions	
• Product improvements/new features	2
• Products in new markets/market segments	1
• Product repositionings	1
iii. Product support	
• New selling approaches	0
• New distribution approaches	1
• New marketing approaches	1
• New administrative approaches	1
B. New product launches	4 per year
C. Average development cycle time*	
• New products	18 months
• Product revisions	6 months
* Defined as period that lapses from format allocation of resources to the project until commercial delivery of new product on widespread basis	
D. Average development cost	
• New products	$2 mil
• Product revisions	$1.1 mil
• Product support	$240,000
E. Percentage of total company revenue in three years' time that is to come from products not currently on the market	35%
F. Percentage of each manager's time spent on innovative activity	10%
G. Average ROI on new product development projects	30%

warning signs that should be recognized as managers evaluate "go/no go" decisions as a project unfolds. After studying over 100 new product development projects for which the actual decisions were known, 14 variables were identified that were critical in all of the "go/no go" decisions. The following list includes all of these decision variables from the study.

TABLE 13-4

Measures for Assessing Innovation Performance

1. Survival rate
   (3 years)

Number of commercialized new products
still on the market
+
Total number of new products commercialized

2. Success/hit
   rate (3 years)

Number of new products exceeding three-year
original revenue forecasts
+
Total number of new products commercialized

3. R&D innovation
   effectiveness ratio

Cumulative three-year gross profits from
commercialized new products
+
Cumulative three-year R&D expenditures allocated
solely to new products

4. R&D innovation
   emphasis ratio

Cumulative three-year R&D expenditures allocated
solely to new products
+
Cumulative three-year R&D expenditures

5. Innovation sales ratio

Cumulative three-year annual revenues generated
from commercialized new products
+
Total annual revenues

6. Newness
   investment ratio

Cumulative three-year expenditures allocated to
new-to-world or new-to-country products
+
Cumulative three-year new product total expenditures

7. Innovation
   portfolio mix

Percentage of new products (by number and revenues)
commercialized by type
- new-to-the-world
- line extension
- repositioning
- new-to-the-company
- product line
- improvements

8. Process
   pipeline flow

Number of new product concepts in each stage
of the development process at year end

9. Innovation revenues
   per employee

Total annual revenues from commercialized new products
+
Total number of full-time equivalent employees devoted
solely to innovation initiatives

(Continued)

TABLE 13-4   (Continued)

Measures for Assessing Innovation Performance

10. Return on innovation   Cumulative three-year net profits from
                                   commercialized new products
                                          +
                                   Cumulative three-year new product total expenditures
                                   (for all commercialized, failed, or killed new products)

SOURCE: Adapted from T. Kuczmarski, *Innovation: Leadership Strategies for the Competitive Edge* (Chicago: NTC Publishing Group), 1996: 182.

---

1. Number of projects in portfolio

2. Profitability of company

3. Time of anticipated completion

4. Smoothness of technological route

5. Pressure on project leader

6. Probability of commercial success

7. Number of end users

8. Top management support

9. Project workers' commitment

10. Occurrence of a chance event with positive impact

11. Product in infancy stage in life cycle

12. Favorable internal competition

13. Emergence of product champion

14. Research manager is product champion

However, the significant value of this research was the development of *red light* and *yellow light* variables that become indicators for termination of a project or at least for cautious progress. The "red light" variables that would indicate termination of the project include probability of technical success, availability of raw materials, sustainability of the market, and problematic government regulations. If any of these demonstrate extreme negative results then the project should be reviewed for termination. The "yellow light" variables may be the most intriguing and helpful since they demonstrate warning signs for the project to be adjusted or certainly for the managers to proceed with caution. The "yellow light" variables include subjective probability of commercial success, support and commitment of personnel, smoothness of technological route, number of end users, presence of project champion, number of projects in R&D portfolio, anticipated competition, and profitability of the company. Each of these individually may not be devastating; however, taken in tandem with others they may indicate severe problems ahead.

A reality of most innovative projects is that some of the most critical data will be hard to identify. To address this challenge, Table 13-5 provides a question format that can be used in identifying the "yellow light" variables. Here the number of "yes" answers could indicate a potential "go" decision in moving the project forward, while an increasing number of "no" answers could signal the need for a thorough review before any further

---

TABLE 13-5

Question Format for the *"Yellow Light"* Variables

1. Has the technological route for the project been smooth?

2. Has the probability of commercial success increased or remained the same?

3. Has the number of end users remained the same or decreased?

4. Is the new product out of the infancy stage in its life cycle?

5. Did an external chance event with a positive impact on the project occur since the last review?

6. Is it likely that a competing company is bringing out a similar product in the near future (around the time this product is planned to be introduced)?

7. Does a complementary project whose outcome may be beneficial to this project exist within the company?

8. Has the pressure on the project leader from top management and R&D management remained the same or decreased?

9. Has top management support increased or remained the same?

10. Has project workers' commitment increased or remained the same?

11. Is there a project champion?

12. Is the R&D manager the project champion?

13. Has the profitability of the company increased or remained the same?

14. Has the number of projects in the development portfolio decreased or remained the same?

SOURCE: R. Balachandra, "Critical Signals for Making Go/No Go Decisions in New Product Development," *Journal of Product Innovation Management*, 2, 1984: 98. Reprinted by permission of John Wiley and Sons.

decision to proceed is made. The research has shown that, in general, projects receiving less than 11 "yes" answers are candidates for a very thorough review. Such a review could disclose whether a project should be terminated and the resources released for other projects demonstrating stronger potential, or investigated for which signals demonstrated unfavorably and whether more resource allocations would enhance the evaluation of those signals, allowing the project to continue.

The purpose of this evaluative tool is to create a stronger awareness of the critical variables that lie behind a project's deterioration, while providing a clear indication of the direction a project is actually taking. When managers use this tool as an indicator of potential trouble, "go/no go" decisions can be made on a more timely basis.

ASKING THE RIGHT QUESTIONS FOR A NEW PROJECT

Many important evaluation-related questions should be asked. Ten sets of preliminary questions that can be used to screen an innovative idea are presented here:

1. Is it a new product, service, or process idea? Is it proprietary? Can it be patented or copyrighted? Is it unique enough to get a significant head start on the competition? Or can it be easily copied?

2. Has a prototype or model been tested by independent testers who try to blow up the system or rip the product to shreds? What are its weak points? Will it stand up? What level of research and development should it receive over the next five years? If a service, has it been tested on customers? Will customers pay their hard-earned money for it?

3. Has it been taken to trade shows? If so, what reactions did it receive? Were any sales made? Has it been taken to distributors? Have they placed any orders?

4. Is the product or service easily understood by customers, distributors, bankers, venture capitalists, accountants, lawyers, and insurance agents? Is the process easily understood by internal users?

5. What is the overall market? What are the market segments? Can the product penetrate these segments? Are there special niches that can be exploited?

6. Has market research been conducted? Who else is considered part of the market? How big is the market? How fast is it growing? What are the trends? How strong are customer loyalties and how high are their switching costs? What is the projected life cycle of the product or service? What degree of penetration can be achieved? Are there any testimonials from customers and purchasing agents? What type of advertising and promotion plans will be used?

7. What distribution and sales methods will be used—jobbers, independent sales representatives, company sales force, direct mail, door-to-door sales, supermarkets, service

stations, company-owned stores? How will the product be transported—company-owned trucks, common carriers, postal service, or air freight?

8. How will the product be made? How much will it cost? For example, will it be produced in-house or by others? Will production be by job shop or continuous process? What is the present capacity of company facilities? What is the breakeven point?

9. Will the business concept be developed and licensed to others, or developed and sold off?

10. Can the company get, or has it already lined up, the necessary skills to manage the new concept or venture? Who are the workers? Are they dependable and competent? How much capital will be needed now? How much more in the future? Have major stages in financing been developed?

A single strategic variable seldom determines the ultimate success or failure of a new corporate venture. Instead, in most situations, a combination of variables influences the outcome. Thus it is important to identify and investigate these variables before the new idea is put into practice. The results of a "feasibility criteria approach" enable the corporate entrepreneur to judge the idea's business potential. The "feasibility criteria approach," developed as a criteria selection list, allows insights into the viability of a venture and is based on the following questions:

- *Is it proprietary?* The product does not have to be patented, but it should be sufficiently proprietary to permit a long head start against competitors and a period of extraordinary profits early in the venture to offset start-up costs.

- *Are the initial production costs realistic?* Most estimates are too low. A careful, detailed analysis should be made so that no large unexpected expenses crop up.

- *Are the initial marketing costs realistic?* Answering this question requires the entrepreneur to identify target markets, market channels, and promotion strategy.

- *Does the product have potential for very high margins?* This potential is almost a necessity for a fledgling company. The financial community understands gross margins and, without the promise of high margins, obtaining funding can be difficult.

- *Is the time required to get to market and to reach the breakeven point realistic?* In most cases faster is better. In all cases the venture plan is tied to this answer, and an error here can spell trouble later on.

- *Is the potential market large?* In determining the potential market, one must look three to five years into the future because some markets take that long to emerge.

- *Is the product or service the first of a growing family?* If it is, the venture will be more attractive to investors. After all, if a large return is not made on the first product, it might be realized on the second, third, or fourth product.

- *Is there an initial customer?* Financial backers are impressed when a venture can list its first ten customers by name. This pent-up demand also means that the first quarter's results are likely to be good and the focus of attention can be directed to later quarters.

- *Are development costs and calendar times realistic?* Preferably, they should be zero. A ready-to-go product gives the venture a major advantage over competitors. If there are costs, they should be complete and detailed and tied to a month-by-month schedule.

- *Is this a growing industry?* Industry growth is not absolutely essential if profits and company growth are evident, but there is less room for mistakes. In a growing industry, good companies do even better.

- *Are the product and the need for it understood by the financial community?* If financiers can grasp the concept and its value, chances for funding will increase. For example, a portable heart-monitoring system for post-coronary patient monitoring is a product that many will understand. Undoubtedly, some of those hearing the presentation for the product will have already had coronaries or heart problems of some sort.

The methods and questions described here are designed to offer managers in entrepreneurial companies the ability to monitor the progress of innovative projects. No one method is the absolute answer and each company must find the best approach for its projects. It is important to establish a system of thorough planning for any new innovative project. We now examine a few planning devices that could assist corporate entrepreneurs in the development of their venture.

Discovery-Driven Planning

Although one can never perfectly predict the future, planning is a process that allows ventures to stay on track through preparation, expectation, and dedication to the objective. One method of planning that offers a systematic way to challenge the underlying assumptions upon which many new projects are based was developed by McGrath and MacMillan (1995). It imposes a strict discipline that is captured in four essential documents: a *reverse income statement,* pro forma operations specs, a *key assumptions checklist,* and a *milestone planning chart.* Let's explain each of these briefly for a better understanding of this procedure.

For the *reverse income statement,* the revenue and expense estimates are developed from the bottom-up as opposed to the traditional top-down approach. When working up the income statement you determine how much revenue it will take to deliver the level of profits required and how much cost can be allowed. The underlying philosophy is to create the desired profitability right up front and then impose discipline to the revenue and cost figures. This required profitability should then equal necessary revenue minus allowable costs. The *pro forma operation specs* simply lay out all of the activities needed to produce, sell, service, and deliver the product or service to the potential customer. In total, those activities comprise the allowable costs for this project to be completed. The *assumption checklist* is an outline of the major assumptions used in determining the project steps. This checklist is valuable in ensuring that each assumption is carefully researched and checked as each step of the project unfolds. Finally, the *milestone planning chart* is put into place to track the actual stage of each accomplishment according to the plan. The value here is that the organization can postpone resource commitments to the proposed project until evidence from the previous milestone indicates that the risk of taking the next step is justified.

As a planning and evaluation tool, discovery-driven planning outlines the "make or break" uncertainties indicative of most new innovative projects and assists managers in evaluating them at the lowest possible cost.

Developing a Comprehensive Corporate Venture Plan

When it is time to establish the complete picture of a proposed venture, corporate entrepreneurs must be ready to prepare a formal venture plan. A comprehensive venture plan, which should be the result of debate and reflections upon the entire direction of the new project or venture, is the major tool used today in conveying the essential components, market feasibility, financial capability, and contingent directions that all interested resource persons wish to see. Thus, in today's corporate world, the corporate venture plan (business plan) has become the minimum that is expected for any innovative project. We offer a few reminders about what a corporate venture plan should do. An effective corporate venture plan venture will:

- Describe every aspect of a particular venture
- Include the marketing research
- Clarify and outline financial needs
- Identify potential obstacles and alternative solutions
- Establish milestones for continuous and timely evaluations
- Serve as a communication tool for all assessments purposes

However, it is important to recognize the important elements in the plan. Table 13-6 offers some helpful hints that offer insights into developing each segment of a plan.

TABLE 13-6

Helpful Hints for Developing the Corporate Venture Plan

I. Executive Summary

- No more than two pages. This is the most crucial part of your plan because you must capture the reader's interest.
- What, how, and why, etc. must be summarized for initial impact.
- Describe the "fit" with the current corporate strategy for innovation.

II. Venture Description Segment

- Articulate the concept clearly.
- A short description of the industry should be covered here.
- The potential impact of the new venture should be described clearly.
- Any uniqueness or distinctive features of this venture should be clearly described.

III. Marketing Segment

- Convince executives that sales projections and competition can be met.
- Use and disclose market studies.
- Identify target market, market position, and market share.
- Evaluate all competition and specifically cover why and how you will be better than your competitors.
- Identify all market sources and assistance used for this segment.
- Demonstrate pricing strategy since your price must penetrate and maintain a market share to produce profits. Thus the lowest price is not necessarily the best price.

IV. Operations Segment

- Identify clearly the mode of this corporate venture:
- – internal corporate venturing (created and owned by the corporation)
- – cooperative corporate venturing (joint venture)
- – external corporate venturing (acquisition or investment)
- Describe the potential operating needs in terms of facilities (plant, storage, office space) and equipment (machinery, computers, furnishings, supplies).
- Describe the general operations of this venture.
- Provide estimates of operating costs—be careful, too many corporate entrepreneurs underestimate their costs.

V. Management Segment

- Supply resumes of all key people in the management of your venture.
- Cover the added assistance (if any) of advisers, consultants, and directors.
- Give information on how and how much everyone is to be compensated.

(Continued)

VI. Financial Segment

- Create stages of financing for purposes of allowing evaluation by the company at various points.
- Describe the needed sources for your funds and the uses you intend for the money.
- Develop and present a budget.
- Provide actual estimated statements.

VII. Critical Risks Segment

- Discuss potential risks before executives point them out, e.g.,
- – Any potentially unfavorable industry-wide trends.
- – Sales projections not achieved.
- – Greater than expected innovation and development costs.
- Provide some alternative courses of action

VIII. Harvest Strategy Segment

- Outline a plan for the orderly transfer of company assets (ownership).
- Describe the plan for transition of leadership.
- Mention the preparations needed for continuity of the business.

IX. Milestone Schedule Segment

- Develop a timetable or chart to demonstrate when each phase of the venture is to be completed. This shows the relationship of events and provides a deadline for accomplishment.

SOURCE: D. F. Kurakto, R. V. Monatgno, and F. J. Sabatine, *The Entrepreneurial Decision*, Muncie, IN: The Midwest Entrepreneurial Education Center, College of Business, Ball State University, 2002.

The corporate venture plan is a major tool used in guiding the direction of a proposed venture or new concept, as well as the primary document in managing it. But it is also more than the mechanical activity of writing up sections based on a checklist or outline. A great plan is a living and breathing document where the parts are internally consistent and reinforce one another, and where ongoing changes can be made. And when made, such changes ripple through the entire document, resulting in many other changes, adjustments, and improvements. The process starts when corporate entrepreneurs begin to gather information and conduct analysis, and then continues as projections are made, decisions are formulated and implemented, and modifications are made both to the projections and the decisions based on the measurement of results. It represents a continuous way of thinking and operating. The clearer the plan, the more powerful it becomes for continuous evaluation. Table 13-7 illustrates a comprehensive assessment tool for each component of the venture plan.

Sustainable Entrepreneurship: A Dual Focus

These planning and assessment activities ultimately serve a single purpose: sustainable entrepreneurship. Sustainability implies some level of consistency in the levels of innovativeness, risk-taking, and proactiveness that a company is able to achieve over a number of years. This consistency is not an easy undertaking for any company. It is much like the challenge, week to week and year to year, of sustaining a customer obsession, or a total quality orientation. To be sustainable, entrepreneurship requires tremendous vigilance, discipline, and emotional commitment.

Ironically, consistency in levels of entrepreneurship involves a paradox—companies must move both incrementally and boldly at the same time. While one might tend to associate sustainability with continuous improvement, a concept associated with total quality management (Juran, 1989; Hodgetts et al., 1999), this is a mistake. We believe the key to sustainability is the ability of a company to move on two parallel paths: continuous improvement and radical innovation. Continuous improvement is incremental and additive. It is characterized more by "rapid inching." New product features, enhanced company capabilities, increases in customer service levels, and improved efficiencies are achieved on an ongoing basis. It is reflected in a philosophy of moving the company 12 inches each day rather than remain in one place for an indefinite period of time while waiting to make a giant leap forward. Alternatively, radical innovation implies explosive and market-defining advances. The concern is with dramatic, revolutionary progress.

Too many companies demonstrate a strong bias towards the incremental, and antipathy towards revolution. Radical innovation is underemphasized because it is risky, highly unpredictable, and involves too many unknowns. Instead, companies go to great lengths to reinforce step-by-step advances. Table 13-8 provides a comparison of these two perspectives and helps illustrate why so much time and attention is given to the former. In the final analysis, sustainable entrepreneurship demands that companies operate in two worlds: anticipating the needs of current markets over the next few years, while finding ways to create entirely new markets and entirely new value propositions through radical leaps.

This dual focus must be kept in mind as companies attempt to assess entrepreneurial performance. Incremental innovation requires shorter time frames, smaller investments, and typically produces results that are fairly easy to measure. Assessing progress with these efforts is relatively straightforward. Radical innovation involves different metrics. Realistic time frames for project completion are harder to estimate, financial returns are achieved over many years, and both failure rates and required rates of return are considerably higher. Also, much more adaptation occurs in radical projects as they

TABLE 13-7

The Components of a Comprehensive Corporate Venture Plan

There are ten suggested components of a corporate venture plan. As you develop your plan, you should assess each component. Be honest in your assessment since the main purpose is to improve your venture plan and increase your chances of success. For instance, if your goal is to obtain internal company financing, you will be asked to submit a complete plan for your venture. The venture plan will help company executives to more adequately evaluate your business idea. This assessment tool can help you and your venture team self-evaluate the venture plan before it is submitted to senior executives.

The Venture Assessment Tool

Directions: **The brief description of each component will help you write that section of your plan. After completing your plan, use the scale provided to assess each component.**

5	4	3	2	1
Outstanding	Very Good	Good	Fair	Poor
Thorough and complete in all areas	Most areas covered but could use improvement in detail	Some areas covered in detail but other areas missing	A few areas covered but very little detail	No written parts

The Ten Components of a Corporate Venture Plan

1. Executive Summary—This is the most important section because it has to convince the reader that the venture concept can succeed. In no more than two pages, you should summarize the highlights of the plan. This means that the key elements of the following components should be mentioned.

The executive summary must be able to stand on its own. It is not simply an introduction to the rest of the venture plan. This section should articulate the new venture concept clearly, describe its uniqueness, formulate the "fit" with the corporate innovation strategy, and demonstrate the future growth potential. Because this section summarizes the plan, it is often best to write this section last.

Rate this component:

5	4	3	2	1
Outstanding	*Very Good*	*Good*	*Fair*	*Poor*

2. Venture Description Segment—This section should provide background information about your industry, a general description of your innovative concept, and the specific mission that you are trying to achieve. Your product or service should be described in terms of its unique qualities and value to the customer. Specific short-term and long-term objectives must be defined. You should clearly state what sales, market share, and profitability objectives you want your business to achieve.

(Continued)

TABLE 13-7   (Continued)

The Components of a Comprehensive Corporate Venture Plan

Key Elements	Have you covered this in the plan?	Is the answer clear? (yes or no)	Is the answer complete? (yes or no)
a. What is your innovative concept?			
b. What products or services does it entail?			
c. Why does it promise to be successful?			
d. What is the growth potential?			
e. How is it unique?			

Rate this component:

5	4	3	2	1
Outstanding	Very Good	Good	Fair	Poor

3. Marketing Segment—There are two major parts to the marketing segment. The first is *research and analysis.* You should identify the target market. Measure your market size and trends, and estimate the market share you expect. Be sure to include support for your sales projections. For example, if your figures are based on published marketing research data, be sure to cite the source. Do your best to make realistic and credible projections. Describe your competition in considerable detail, identifying their strengths and weaknesses. Finally, explain how you will be better than your competitors.

The second part is the *marketing plan.* This critical section should include your market strategy, sales and distribution, pricing, advertising, promotion, and public awareness. Demonstrate how your pricing strategy will result in a profit based on the type of corporate venture you are proposing. Make sure to validate your innovation's "fit" with the company's strategy for innovation.

Key Elements	Have you covered this in the plan?	Is the answer clear? (yes or no)	Is the answer complete? (yes or no)
a. Who will be your customers? (Target Market)			
b. How big is the market? (Number of Customers)			
c. Who will be your competitors?			
d. How are their businesses prospering?			
e. How will you promote sales?			
f. What market share can be achieved?			
g. Do you have a pricing strategy?			
h. What advertising and/or promotional strategy are you suggesting?			

(Continued)

Rate this component:

5	4	3	2	1
Outstanding	Very Good	Good	Fair	Poor

4. Operations Segment—In this segment it is important to describe the mode of this corporate venture concept (internal, external, or cooperative) and outline its advantages. Operating needs, projected operating costs, and general plans for operations should all be considered in this section.

Key Elements	Have you covered this in the plan?	Is the answer clear? (yes or no)	Is the answer complete? (yes or no)
a. What is the mode of this corporate venture? (internal corporate venture; cooperative corporate venture; external corporate venture)			
b. Have you outlined the advantages of this mode of venturing for the company?			
c. Any operational needs in terms of facilities (plant, storage offices) or equipment (machinery, computers, furnishings)?			
d. What estimates do you have for operating costs?			
e. Have you described the general operations of this new venture for the company?			

Rate this component:

5	4	3	2	1
Outstanding	Very Good	Good	Fair	Poor

5. Management Segment—Start by describing the management team, their unique qualifications, and how you compensate them (including salaries, employment agreements, stock purchase plans, levels of ownership, and other considerations). Discuss how your venture would be structured and consider including a diagram illustrating who reports to whom. Finally, include a discussion of the potential contribution of the board of directors, advisers, or consultants.

(Continued)

TABLE 13-7   (Continued)

The Components of a Comprehensive Corporate Venture Plan

Key Elements	Have you covered this in the plan?	Is the answer clear? (yes or no)	Is the answer complete? (yes or no)
a. Who will manage the venture?			
b. What qualifications does the team possess?			
c. How many employees are expected?			
d. How much will you pay your employees and what type of benefits will you offer them?			
e. What consultants or specialists will you use?			

Rate this component:

5	4	3	2	1
Outstanding	*Very Good*	*Good*	*Fair*	*Poor*

6. Financial Segment–Determine the stages where your venture will require financing and identify the expected financing sources (internal venture fund or outside equity sources). Also, clearly show what return on investment these sources will achieve by investing in your business. It is good to develop a budget for the venture. If the work is done well, pro forma financial statements could then be prepared to represent the projected financial achievements expected from your venture plan. They also provide a standard by which to measure the actual results of operating your venture. They are a valuable tool to help you manage and control your business. Two key financial statements must be presented: an income statement (profit and loss), and a cash flow statement (cash inflows and outflows). These statements typically cover a one-year period. Be sure you state any assumptions and projections you made when calculating the figures.

Key Elements	Have you covered this in the plan?	Is the answer clear? (yes or no)	Is the answer complete? (yes or no)
a. Have you staged the funding needs so that sources can gauge the venture's progression and expected needs?			
b. What is your total expected income for the first year? Quarterly for the next two years? (*Forecast*)			
c. What is your expected monthly cash flow during the first year?			
d. What sales volume will you need in order to make a profit during the three years?			
e. What will be the breakeven point?			
f. What are your total financial needs?			
g. What are your funding sources?			

(*Continued*)

Rate this component:

5	4	3	2	1
Outstanding	*Very Good*	*Good*	*Fair*	*Poor*

7. *Critical Risks Segment*—Discuss potential risks before they happen. Here are some examples: potentially unfavorable industry-wide trends, unexpected innovation or development costs that could exceed estimates, sales projections that are not achieved. The idea is to recognize risks and identify alternative courses of action. Your main objective is to show that you can anticipate and control (to a reasonable degree) the company's risks.

Key Elements	*Have you covered this in the plan?*	*Is the answer clear? (yes or no)*	*Is the answer complete? (yes or no)*
a. What potential problems have you identified?			
b. Have you calculated the risks?			
c. What alternative courses of action are there?			

Rate this component:

5	4	3	2	1
Outstanding	*Very Good*	*Good*	*Fair*	*Poor*

8. *Harvest Strategy Segment*—Ensuring the survival of an internal venture is hard work. An innovation team's protective feelings for an idea built from scratch make it tough to grapple with such issues as management succession and harvest strategies. With foresight, however, corporate entrepreneurs can keep their dream alive, ensure the vitality of their ventures, and usually strengthen their venture and the company in the process. Thus identifying issues involved with harvesting of the venture as well as management transitions are essential in the early stages (even if they are to change later on in the development of the venture).

Key Elements	*Have you covered this in the plan?*	*Is the answer clear? (yes or no)*	*Is the answer complete? (yes or no)*
a. Have you planned for the orderly transfer of the venture assets if ownership is passed to this corporation?			
b. Is there a continuity of strategy for an orderly transition of management?			

(Continued)

| **TABLE 13-7** | (Continued) |

The Components of a Comprehensive Corporate Venture Plan

Rate this component:

5	4	3	2	1
Outstanding	*Very Good*	*Good*	*Fair*	*Poor*

9. Milestone Schedule Segment—This is an important segment of the venture plan because it requires you to determine what tasks you need to accomplish in order to achieve your objectives. Milestones and deadlines should be established and monitored on an ongoing basis. Each milestone is related to all the others, and together they comprise a timely representation of how your objective is to be accomplished.

Key Elements	*Have you covered this in the plan?*	*Is the answer clear? (yes or no)*	*Is the answer complete? (yes or no)*
a. How have you set your objectives?			
b. Have you set deadlines for each stage of your growth?			

Rate this component:

5	4	3	2	1
Outstanding	*Very Good*	*Good*	*Fair*	*Poor*

10. Appendix—This section includes important background information that was not included in the other sections. This is where you would put such items as resumes of the management team, names of references and advisers, drawings, documents, licenses, agreements, and any materials that support the plan. You may also wish to add a bibliography of the sources from which you drew information.

Key Elements	*Have you covered this in the plan?*	*Is the answer clear? (yes or no)*	*Is the answer complete? (yes or no)*
a. Have you included any documents, drawings, agreements, or other materials needed to support the plan?			
b. Are there any names of references, advisers, or technical sources you should include?			
c. Are there any other supporting documents?			

Rate this component:

5	4	3	2	1
Outstanding	*Very Good*	*Good*	*Fair*	*Poor*

(Continued)

Summary: Your Self-Evaluation of the Corporate Venture Plan

Directions: For each of the corporate venture plan sections that you assessed in the components sections, circle the assigned points on this review sheet and then total the circled points.

Components Points

1. Executive Summary	5	4	3	2	1
2. Venture Description	5	4	3	2	1
3. Marketing	5	4	3	2	1
4. Operations	5	4	3	2	1
5. Management	5	4	3	2	1
6. Financial	5	4	3	2	1
7. Critical Risks	5	4	3	2	1
8. Harvest Strategy	5	4	3	2	1
9. Milestone Schedule	5	4	3	2	1
10. Appendix	5	4	3	2	1

Total Points: —

Scoring:

50 pts.—Outstanding! The ideal corporate venture plan. Solid!

45–49 pts.—Very Good. Most components covered adequately.

40–44 pts.—Good. The plan is sound with a few areas that need to be polished.

35–39 pts.—Above Average. The plan has some good areas but needs improvement before presentation to the company.

30–34 pts.—Average. Some areas are covered in detail yet certain areas show weakness.

20–29 pts.—Below Average. Most areas need greater detail and improvement.

Below 20 pts.—Poor. Plan needs to be thought through with better research and substantiation for this venture concept.

SOURCE: Adapted from: Donald F. Kuratko, *Developing an Effective Entrepreneurial Business Plan*, (Kelley School of Business, Indiana University, 2010); Gary Getz and Edward G. Tuttle, "A Comprehensive Approach to Corporate Venturing," *Handbook of Business Strategy* (New York: Thomson Financial Media, 2000); and Julian Birkinshaw, Rob van Batenburg, and Gordan Murray, "Venturing to Succeed," *Business Strategy Review*, 2002: 13(4): 10–17.

evolve over time. This means fundamental changes are taking place in team structure, resource requirements, types of products or services that are created, target markets, business models, and planned exit strategies. As such, the assessment challenge is much greater. Just as difficult is the ability of a company to ensure it is achieving an appropriate balance between the incremental and the radical.

TABLE 13-8

A Comparison of Constant Improvement and Innovation

	Constant Incremental Improvement	Radical Innovation
1. Effect	Long-term and long-lasting but not dramatic	Short-term but dramatic
2. Pace	Small steps	Big steps
3. Time Frame	Continuous and incremental	Intermittent and non-incremental
4. Change	Gradual and constant	Abrupt and volatile
5. Involvement	Everybody	A select few "champions"
6. Approach	Collectivism, group efforts, systems approach	Rugged individualism, individual ideas and efforts
7. Mode	Maintenance and improvement	Scrap and rebuild
8. Spark	Conventional know-how and state of the art	Technological breakthroughs, new inventions, new theories
9. Practical Requirements	Little investigation, great effort to maintain improvement	Large investigation, little effort to maintain improvement
10. Effort Orientation	People	Technology
11. Evaluation Criteria	Process and efforts for better results	Results for profit
12. Advantage	Works well in slow-growth economy	Better suited to fast-growth economy

SOURCE: Adapted from R. M. Hodgetts, D. F. Kuratko, and J. S. Hornsby, "Quality Implementation in Small Business: "Perspectives from the Baldridge Award Winners," *SAM Advanced Management Journal*, 64(1), 1999: 37–47.

THE INNOVATOR'S NOTEBOOK

Measuring Innovation at Samsung

At the core of Samsung's continued success is the magnitude of its technical research. Samsung spends more on R&D than Intel, Microsoft, and Sony with approximately $5 billion annually going to the development of new products. By investing in its future, Samsung has been able to take the lead in the markets for LCD TVs, multimedia mobile phones, and memory chips. In addition, Samsung provides components for other companies' products, which have been commercially successful, to put it mildly. Some of these include Apple iPods, Dell computers, Microsoft Xboxes, Nokia phones, and Sony Playstation Portables.

So, how has Samsung been able to keep its entrepreneurial drive as it has continued to grow? For one thing, the company has provided the necessary resources to allow the momentum of its R&D prowess to remain strong. Of its 160,000 employees, 40,000 are researchers spread across 18 research centers around the world. Samsung's R&D vision is to simply "Create New Space" through New Technologies; New Markets; New Businesses; and New Lifestyles. While it sounds rather esoteric, Samsung applies what they refer to as a 3-P Strategy to implement this vision. The 3-P strategy entails:

- Product Innovation: open innovation; strong patent power; and implementation of next generation technologies
- People Innovation: enhance innovation capability; develop into a networked organization; and build strong teamwork.
- Process Innovation: do it the Six Sigma Way; robust and efficient project management processes; and IT infrastructure enhancement

Even though the 3-P strategy is in place, how does Samsung measure its innovative accomplishments? Certainly global awards from your peers can be a significant assessment. In 2010 Samsung won the International CES (Consumer Electronics Show) Innovations Awards for 23 different products, including three best of innovation awards. Samsung has won more than 100 CES Innovation Awards in three years, for multiple product categories like; TVs, home theater, digital audio, cameras, home appliances, and mobile phones.

The International CES is produced by the Consumer Electronics Association (CEA), the preeminent trade association promoting growth in the consumer technology industry. CEA represents more than 2,000 corporate members involved in the design, development, manufacturing, distribution, and integration of consumer electronics products.

As a widely renowned consumer technology awards program that began in 1976, the prestigious Innovations Design and Engineering Awards recognize achievements in product design and engineering sponsored by the Consumer Electronics Association. The Innovation entries are judged based on the following criteria: engineering qualities, based on technical specs and materials used; aesthetic and design qualities, using photos provided; the product's intended use/function and user value; and unique/novel features that consumers would find attractive.

Samsung's products that won "Best of Innovations 2010" Awards include: two LED HDTVs, one plasma TV, two Blu-ray players, two digital audio players, two digital cameras, one refrigerator, six mobile phones, and one LCD monitor. The "Eco-Design and Sustainable Technology" Award winners include; FTQ307NWGX—a 30″ free-standing induction range, with fast & efficient cooking, precise controls, cool-to-the-touch features and easy clean. Reclaim™ (SPH-m560)—The first phone in the U.S. constructed from eco-friendly bio-plastics, and the only one honored in its category in 2010. The 700Z—Samsung's first OLED digital photo frame with a 7-inch screen, Blue-tooth, and Wi-Fi.

These awards are clear indicators that Samsung is living up to its innovative vision as measured by the best in the consumer electronics industry.

Discussion Questions:

1. Do you think Samsung is assessing its corporate innovative activities? Explain based on our chapter material.

2. Using Table 13-1, how would you assess the EI (Entrepreneurial Intensity) at Samsung?

3. Which measurement tool from the chapter would you recommend that Samsung utilize and why?

SOURCE: Adapted from: Peter Lewis, "A Perpetual Crisis Machine," Fortune, Tuesday, September 6, 2005; Samsung company Web sites accessed April 21, 2010; and Consumer Electronics Association Web site accessed April 21, 2010.

Summary and Conclusions

This chapter has emphasized the vital role that assessment and evaluation efforts play in achieving sustainable entrepreneurship within companies. We have argued that management must continually assess the levels of entrepreneurial activity being achieved within the company, and the types of results being produced. Rather than becoming merely a "program" for a company to institute, corporate entrepreneurship must be a "process" that infiltrates and permeates the entire organization. Central to this notion of an integrated process is the logic of ongoing assessment, and the ability to continually improve based on performance feedback.

Assessments are first needed at an overall company level, as well as at the divisional, unit, and departmental levels. The chapter explored some of the challenges in assessing company-wide entrepreneurship. The entrepreneurial health audit was introduced as a three-stage framework for determining not only levels of entrepreneurship being achieved in the organization, but also the extent to which the corporate environment is conducive to supporting high levels of entrepreneurship. The health audit enables the diagnosis of problem areas and the establishment of priorities for enhancing levels of entrepreneurship throughout the organization.

We then examined assessments at the level of individual entrepreneurial projects. The nature of how new product and service projects tend to evolve was reviewed. Emphasis was placed on the need to establish goals for the types and amount of innovative efforts the company will pursue, create and manage a portfolio of innovative projects, have an organized process for managing innovation, and identify appropriate measures for the assessment of each project. A number of examples of innovation goals and innovation performance measures were provided.

It was also argued that planning is essential to the success of any entrepreneurial undertaking. Carefully prepared plans are simply the formulation of goals, objectives, and directions for the future of any new product, service, or process. The absence of a plan could mean failure before even starting, while the presence of a good plan will help identify ideas that have only limited potential before too much is invested in them. A logical approach to planning entrepreneurial initiatives was presented, together with a number of helpful hints that can enhance, and common errors that can undermine, the planning process. A systematic method for evaluating the quality of company plans and planning efforts was also introduced.

The chapter closed with a discussion of sustainable entrepreneurship, and the implications of sustainability for the assessment of entrepreneurial performance over time. It was suggested that sustainability requires a dual focus, with the company striving to maintain incremental innovation while at the same time achieving radical breakthroughs. Fundamental differences were noted in how a company measures and evaluates efforts in these two distinct arenas.

References

Balachandra, R. 1984. "Critical Signals for Making Go/No Go Decisions in New Product Development," *Journal of Product Innovation Management*, 2: 92–100.

Birkinshaw, J., van Batenburg, R., and Murray, G., 2002. "Venturing to Succeed," *Business Strategy Review*, 13(4): 10–17.

Burgelman, R. A. 1984. "Designs for Corporate Entrepreneurship," *California Management Review*, 26: 154–166.

Covin, J. G., Green, K. M, and Slevin, D. P. 2006. "Strategic Process Effects on the Entrepreneurial Orientation-Sales Growth Rate Relationship," *Entrepreneurship Theory and Practice*. 30(1): 57–81.

Covin, J. G., and Slevin, D. P. 1991. "A Conceptual Model of Entrepreneurship as Firm Behavior," *Entrepreneurship Theory and Practice*, 16(1): 7–25.

Dess, G. G., Ireland, R. D., Zahra, S. A., Floyd, S. W., Janney, J. J., and Lane, P. J., 2003. "Emerging Issues in Corporate Entrepreneurship," *Journal of Management*, 29(3), 351–378.

Garvin, D. A., and Levesque, L. C., 2006. "Meeting the Challenge of Corporate Entrepreneurship," *Harvard Business Review* 84, 102–112.

Gee, R. F. 1994. Finding and Commercializing New Businesses, *Research Technology Management* 37(1): 49–56.

Getz, G., and Tuttle, E. G. 2000. "A Comprehensive Approach to Corporate Venturing," *Handbook of Business Strategy* (New York: Thomson Financial Media).

Hamel, G., and Prahalad, C. E. 1991. "Corporate Imagination and Expeditionary Marketing," *Harvard Business Review* (July–Aug.), 69(4): 31–93.

Hill, S. A., and Birkinshaw, J., 2008. "Strategy—Organization Configurations in Corporate Venturing Units: Impact on Performance and Survival," *Journal of Business Venturing*, 23(4): 423–444.

Hodgetts, R. M., Kuratko, D. F., and Hornsby, J. S. 1999. "Quality Implementation in Small Business: Perspectives from the Baldrige Award Winners," *SAM Advanced Management Journal* (Winter): 37–47.

Hornsby, J. S., Kuratko, D. F., and Zahra, S. A. 2002. "Middle Managers' Perception of the Internal Environment for Corporate Entrepreneurship: Assessing a Measurement Scale," *Journal of Business Venturing*, 17: 49–63.

Hornsby, J. S., Holt, D. T., and Kuratko, D. F., 2008. "The Dynamic Nature of Corporate Entrepreneurship Constructs: An Assessment of the Corporate Entrepreneurship Assessment Instrument (CEAI)," In *Best Paper Proceedings: Academy of Management*, Anaheim, CA, August.

Hornsby, Jeffrey S., Kuratko, Donald F., Shepherd, Dean A., and Bott, Jennifer P., 2009. "Managers' Corporate Entrepreneurial Actions: Examining Perception and Position," *Journal of Business Venturing* 24(3), 236–247.

Ireland, R. D., Kuratko, D. F., and Morris, M. H. 2006. "The Entrepreneurial Health Audit: Is Your Firm Ready for Corporate Entrepreneurship?" *Journal of Business Strategy*, March/April, 27(1): 10–17.

Jelinek, M., and Litterer, J. A. 1995. "Toward Entrepreneurial Organizations: Meeting Ambiguity with Engagement," *Entrepreneurship: Theory and Practice*, 19(3): 137–168.

Juran, J. M. 1989. *Juran on Leadership for Quality* (New York: Free Press).

Kanter, R. M. 1986. "Supporting Innovation and Venture Development in Established Companies," *Journal of Business Venturing*, 1: 47–60.

Kuratko, D. F. 2009a. "The Entrepreneurial Imperative of the 21st Century," *Business Horizons*, 52(5), 421–428.

Kuratko, D. F., 2009b. *Entrepreneurship: Theory, Process, & Practice*, 8th ed. (Mason: OH, Thomson/South-Western).

Kuratko, D. F., and Hodgetts, R. M. 2007. *Entrepreneurship: Theory, Process, & Practice*, 7th ed. (Mason: OH, Thomson/South-Western).

Kuratko, D. F., Ireland, R. D., Covin, J. G., and Hornsby, J. S., 2005. "A Model of Middle Level Managers' Entrepreneurial Behavior." *Entrepreneurship Theory and Practice*, 29(6): 699–716.

Kuratko, D. F, Ireland, R. D., and Hornsby, J. S. 2001. "Improving Firm Performance through Entrepreneurial Actions: Acordia's Corporate Entrepreneurship Strategy," *Academy of Management Executive*, 15(4), 60–71.

Kuratko, D. F., Montagno, R. V., and Hornsby, J. S. 1990. "Developing an Entrepreneurial Assessment Instrument for an Effective Corporate Entrepreneurial Environment," *Strategic Management Journal*, 11 (Special Issue): 49–58.

Kuczmarski, T. 1996. *Innovation: Leadership Strategies for the Competitive Edge* (Chicago: NTC Publishing Group).

McGrath, R. G., and MacMillan, I. C. 1995. "Discovery-Driven Planning," *Harvard Business Review*, 73(4): 4–12.

Miller, D. and Friesen, P. H. 1982. "Innovation in Conservative and Entrepreneurial Firms: Two Models of Strategic Momentum," *Strategic Management Journal*, 3(1): 1–25.

Morris, M. H., and Kuratko, D. F. 2002. *Corporate Entrepreneurship* (Dallas, TX: Harcourt Press).

Morris, M. H., and Sexton, D. L. 1996. "The Concept of Entrepreneurial Intensity: Implications for Company Performance," *Journal of Business Research*, 36(1): 5–13.

Morse, C. W. 1986. "The Delusion of Intrapreneurship," *Long Range Planning*, 19: 92–95.

Page, A. L. 1993. "Assessing New Product Development Practices and Performance: Establishing Crucial Norms," *Journal of Product Innovation Management*, 10: 273–290.

Senge, P. M. 2006. *The Fifth Discipline: The Art & Practice of the Learning Organization* (New York: Broadway Business).

Vanhaverbeke, W., and Peeters, N., 2005. "Embracing Innovation as Strategy: Corporate Venturing, Competence Building, and Corporate Strategy Making." *Creativity and Innovation Management*, 14(3): 246–257.

Zahra, S. A., Kuratko, D. F., and Jennings, D. F. 1999. "Entrepreneurship and the Acquisition of Dynamic Organizational Capabilities," *Entrepreneurship: Theory and Practice*, 23(3): 5–10.

CHAPTER 14

CONTROL AND ENTREPRENEURIAL ACTIVITY

Introduction

Control sounds like an oppressive word. It evokes images of restraint, dominance, regulation, rigidity, and conformity. Yet organizations would be reduced to chaos without meaningful control mechanisms. Policies, procedures, and rules are needed to ensure order, achieve coordination, and maintain efficiency. Without them, quality is inconsistent, order schedules are missed, customers are improperly billed, money is spent where it should not be spent, and employees take inappropriate shortcuts. Controls come in many forms, but they ultimately create a sense of accountability and help ensure the company assets are being efficiently employed.

Control systems in companies tend to start out simple. Over time, they steadily evolve, becoming more sophisticated and complex. Herein lies the problem. As more procedures, systems, and documentation requirements are added, managers are increasingly encouraged to micromanage each and every expenditure, and to establish quantifiable performance benchmarks in as many activity areas as possible. These benchmarks can become ends in themselves, while conveying a lack of trust in employees. And then there is the issue of efficiency versus effectiveness. Efficiency is concerned with minimizing the amount of expenditures or resources needed to accomplish a task. Effectiveness is a concern with ensuring that the correct tasks are being accomplished. Control systems have historically placed a heavy emphasis on efficiency, sometimes ignoring or even undermining effectiveness issues.

The development of control systems also has implications for the level of entrepreneurship exhibited in a company. Control systems that attempt to influence the way in which resources are being used (e.g., employee time, facilities and equipment, marketing programs), in addition to monitoring how efficiently they are being used, can at the same time undermine employee motivation and creativity (Morris et al., 2006). Control measures provide structure to tasks and operations within the enterprise, in effect providing criteria on which a given task is evaluated. However, they can become bureaucratic, slowing down the organization, stifling the employee, and encouraging almost mechanical performance to ensure one looks good in terms of the control measures (again, becoming an end in themselves rather than a means to an end). Thus, Pinchot (2000) observes "many centralized companies with highly sophisticated control systems are, in fact, out of control." Yet, in spite of these dangers, the evidence suggests that, when used in the proper balance, certain control processes may in fact be beneficial to innovative activity in organizations (Goodale, et al., 2011).

In this chapter, we examine the relationship between control and entrepreneurship. Types of control measures will be reviewed, together with underlying dimensions of a control system. Approaches to control that encourage entrepreneurial behavior will be explored, and the need to achieve a balance between the looseness and tightness of controls will be emphasized. Attention will also be devoted to control over a company's financials and the role of open book accounting in supporting entrepreneurship. Finally, the concept of the profit pool will be introduced as a vehicle for discovering new opportunities within the current operations of a company.

The Nature of Control in Organizations

A control system can be defined as those formal and informal mechanisms that help managers ensure that resources are obtained and used effectively and efficiently in the accomplishment of the organization's objectives (Anthony and Govindarajan, 2001). A broader perspective suggests that it includes any process in which a person, group, or organization determines or intentionally affects how another person, group, or organization will act (Tannebaum, 1988). Controls are intended to guard against the possibility that people will do something the organization doesn't want them to do, or fail to do something they should do. They prescribe a set of activities for dealing with situations as they arise.

We should also expand on the question "control over what?" An easy way to address such a question is to conceptualize the application of controls to inputs, processes (or behaviors), and outputs. Controls over inputs coming into the company could include such things as hiring practices and purchasing policies. Behavior control focuses on regulating the activities of organizational members through operating procedures and personal evaluations. Output controls involve setting targets for and measuring achievement. The chief output-related concerns are performance goals, performance tracking, and the resolution of performance variances.

The term *control system* implies a carefully constructed and well-integrated set of items. In actuality, the system of controls in an organization is an agglomeration of hundreds and even thousands of documents, policies, procedures, processes, rules, objectives, guidelines, pieces of information, technologies, and equipment. Some of the elements are formal, others are informal. That is, control practices arise from conscious managerial efforts and from informal mechanisms that emerge through the spontaneous interactions of workers over time. Further, pieces and parts are continually added, modified, and deleted.

We can conclude that a company does not really design a comprehensive control system and implement it in one fell swoop, nor does it throw out an existing control system and put a new one in place. Rather, the set of control mechanisms evolves, with components subject to change. Changes are typically incremental, such as the elimination of a procedure or the addition of a new form to be filled out. Occasionally, bolder initiatives are pursued, such as a mandate from senior management to cut paperwork requirements or approval processes by 50 percent.

Table 14-1 provides examples of some of the many elements that might comprise an organization's control system. The list barely scratches the surface, but illustrates the diverse set of ways in which behavior in companies is governed, monitored, and evaluated. When put together, these elements can have a pervasive impact on employee attitudes, motivation, perceptions, and outlooks. Further, they heavily interact with the structure of the company (see Chapter 9), and they both reflect and influence the culture of the company (see Chapter 10).

The various control measures and mechanisms can be grouped into four general categories: simple control, technological control, bureaucratic/administrative control,

---

TABLE 14-1

A Sample of 30 Elements in an Organization's Control System

Budgets	Travel policies
Production testing and monitoring equipment	Performance reviews
	Strategic and operational plans
Time clocks	Timetables
Objectives	Rules governing internal communications
Purchasing policies	Procedure manuals
Hiring rules	Financial and resource audits
Annual employee, department, division reports	Sales activity reports
Production schedules	Schedules
Customer satisfaction surveys	Financial statements
Job descriptions and job analysis	Employee tests
Sales quotas	Spending approval processes
Cameras in the workplace	Security systems and ID cards
Efficiency measures	Sexual harassment policies
Expense reimbursement procedures	Complaint-handling procedures
Hierarchical sign-offs on expense requests	

and cultural/concertive control (Bisbe and Otley, 2004; Cirka, 1997). Simple control is the direct personal supervision exercised by the manager over his or her subordinates. Technological control deals with the technology-based techniques used in production and service delivery processes. Bureaucratic and administrative control covers the formal rules, procedures, and policies used in established organizations. Concertive or cultural control deals with the control brought about by shared values, norms, and the conformance to the beliefs of those within the organization.

Organizations out of Control: A Story of Unintended Consequences

Control is vital in organizations. Without controls, it would be impossible to know what is going on, distinguish high from low performers, satisfy customers on a consistent basis, be cost competitive, or find ways to continually improve. As companies grow in size and operations become more diverse, controls become more complex. The problem is that control can feed on itself, continually growing and ultimately strangling an organization. At some point in the evolution of an organization, control tends to beget control.

A natural tendency when someone is either not doing something they are supposed to do, or doing something they are not supposed to do, is to put a rule or mandated procedure in place. Next, one needs paperwork or some other means of monitoring compliance with the rule or procedure. Following this, one needs to hire people who will oversee this monitoring process and produce reports. Then, these people start to enhance the monitoring process, adding more procedures and paperwork. Perhaps additional help is needed to handle these new additions to the control system. Eventually, the controllers themselves require control, and a new hierarchy of controls is put in place so that they can be monitored. And so it goes.

Control initiatives are almost always well intentioned. Yet they frequently have unintended consequences. They become problematic for at least four reasons. Let's start with the "trust problem." Most employees desire a certain sense of order in their work lives, and control mechanisms help provide order and accountability. However, as the control measures evolve, they intrude further and further into the way in which an employee performs his or her job. At some point, the employee asks "what is this company trying to tell me?" when he or she is required to fill out some superfluous form, get approval before taking some ridiculously routine action, or follow an unnecessarily detailed procedure. All too often, the conclusion is "they think I'm stupid," "they think I don't have better things to do with my time," or "they just don't trust me." It is this last conclusion that most undermines the willingness of employees to tap their creative energies, come up with innovative ideas, fight for those ideas, and persevere in getting them implemented.

The next unintended consequence of controls is the "slowness problem." Well-conceptualized controls can eliminate mistakes and wastage, reducing the need to redo some task, while ensuring better coordination of resources. The end result can be enhanced speed, where tasks are accomplished on a timely basis, and customers are more quickly satisfied. Again, though, controls tend to evolve to the point where they actually slow the organization down. Where no flexibility exists in how things are done, or there are extremely detailed documentation requirements, or elaborate steps must be followed by the employee to complete a task, not only will things take much more time, but people are actually being disincentivized to move quickly.

Another unintended result of the control system can be referred to as the "means–end problem." Control systems are meant to be a means towards an end, where the end is the achievement of some desired organizational outcome, such as less wastage or fewer mistakes. Consider a rather bizarre example that happened at a major university. Concerned about excessive student drinking and the resultant inappropriate behaviors, the university created an elaborate set of rules and restrictions for parties in fraternity houses. One of the more interesting efforts was something called the "potato chip rule." On the assumption that potato chips were the most popular food item at parties, and that consuming more potato chips encouraged party-goers to stay longer and drink more, a rule was put in place limiting the amount of potato chips that could be present at a party. Obviously, this meant that the group hosting the party had to take time to take inventory of the stock of potato chips, monitor anyone bringing extra chips to the party, and do whatever it took to stay under the mandated limited. So, the fraternity may feel it has to create the position of "potato chip enforcer". Further, some university employee would have to go around and make sure each and every party was in compliance with the rule. Of course, documents would be needed to track potato chip compliance, and a procedure would have to be put in place for dealing with those in violation. Now, all of this seems ludicrous, but it is not as far removed as one might imagine from what happens with over-control in companies. Managers get so caught up in trying to create and enforce control mechanisms that they lose sight of what the controls were ultimately meant to accomplish. In the previous example, one can be sure that the fraternities closely adhered to the potato chip rule (or found inventive ways to get around it). That is, they made sure they *looked good in terms of the control measure.* But the real goal, responsible drinking, was completely lost in the shuffle. From the standpoint of the fraternity members, or the employees in a company, the control system becomes an end in itself, rather than a means to an end.

Then there is the "efficiency–effectiveness problem." It is perhaps the most profoundly disturbing of all the unintended consequences, and is directly related to the means–end problem. In simple terms, efficiency is about doing things right, while effectiveness is about doing the right things (Drucker, 2008). Again, we can illustrate the problem with an example. A company was concerned about the rapidly growing cost of office supplies. The cost per employee for supplies (an efficiency measure) was up 30 percent from what was thought to be normal. Management was unsure whether employees were simply being wasteful, taking supplies home for personal use, or if there was some other explanation (maybe people were just working harder). Regardless, they put a new rule in place. One of the cost increases involved spending for legal pads. Up to this point, when employees needed supplies, they simply went to a supply room and took what was needed. Under the new rule, whenever employees wanted a new legal pad, they had to turn in the cardboard backing from the old pad. The rule apparently worked, as the result was a reduction in expenditures for legal pads. There was an improvement in the *efficiency* measure, and management was happy. However, the actual effect of the rule is not so simple. Not only did it undermine trust, but the restriction led people to simply do without pads, especially if they didn't think to hold on to the backing of the ones they had used up. For some, it was just not worth the hassle. Others bought their own pads. Lending pads to one another was certainly discouraged. Taking pads home was not eliminated, as one just had to remember to bring the backing in to work. *Effectiveness*, which in this case would be the extent to which employees are better able to do their jobs well because they have the necessary office supplies, was either ignored or undermined.

Putting these problems together, it becomes apparent that the company with a highly developed and complex control system may actually be controlling the wrong things, or nothing at all. This conclusion is especially likely given the creativity of people and their abilities to find ways around things in which they do not believe or see as necessary. In fact, the considerable time that is wasted finding inventive ways around rules and procedures takes away from the time that might have been spent inventing new and better products, services, and processes.

Dimensions of Control and Entrepreneurship

As management attempts to grapple with the myriad elements of a control system, it is worth stepping back and assessing overall characteristics of the controls that are in place. A control system can be characterized based on a number of key attributes. Examples include the: degree of formality and prescriptiveness, desire for conformance and compliance, degree of rigidity, desire for consistency, use of coercive power, distribution of authority and responsibility, desire for individual initiative, level of freedom and discretion, degree of horizontal interaction and communication, and level of detail. Figure 14-1 attempts to summarize these attributes in terms of seven underlying dimensions.

In theory, control systems are designed around attributes such as these in a manner that accomplishes effective outcomes. The principal outcomes sought through control efforts include *risk reduction, elimination of uncertainty, highly efficient operations, goal conformance,* and *specific role definitions.* Unfortunately, outcomes such as these tend to be inconsistent with entrepreneurship. Yet it is our view that control systems can actually facilitate entrepreneurial behavior in companies, as reflected on the right-hand side of Figure 14-1.

Entrepreneurship appears to be more consistent with *risk tolerance,* where there is less rigidity in the organizational structure with a greater degree of empowerment and autonomy, areas of responsibility are less clearly delineated, conduct is less prescribed, and administrative consistency is expected. Further, entrepreneurship seems more likely where the control system allows for *management of uncertainty,* and there is less formality and rigidness in the approach to planning for the future, budget mechanisms are more flexible in accommodating new opportunities as they emerge, and organizational goals are more focused on achieving ends rather than prescribing means (Morris, 1998).

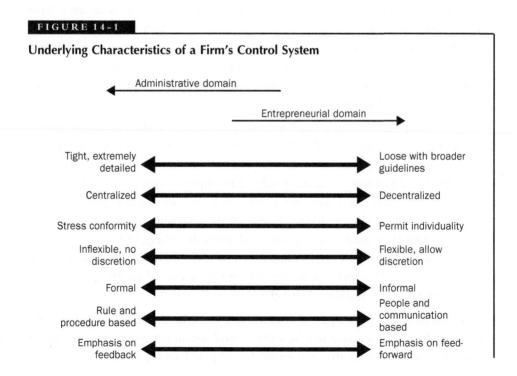

FIGURE 14-1

Underlying Characteristics of a Firm's Control System

Administrative domain

Entrepreneurial domain

Tight, extremely detailed	Loose with broader guidelines
Centralized	Decentralized
Stress conformity	Permit individuality
Inflexible, no discretion	Flexible, allow discretion
Formal	Informal
Rule and procedure based	People and communication based
Emphasis on feedback	Emphasis on feedforward

In addition, the likelihood of entrepreneurial behavior seems greater where there is *enlightened efficiency*, where a level of discretion or slack is deliberately designed into cost controls and budgeting, budget deviations are more tolerated, performance is not measured at fixed intervals, and success measures include both financial and nonfinancial indicators. Also, an internal environment that supports entrepreneurship will most likely focus on *goal congruence*. With the greater degree of freedom and autonomy that might be expected in a more entrepreneurial company, it is expected that self-control and social control will play a larger role than procedural control in aligning the goals of the individual with that of the organization. The control system might be expected to include incentives tied to organizational success factors. Finally, the facilitation of entrepreneurship appears to be more consistent with *role flexibility*, where employees are empowered to exercise discretion and personal initiative in performing their jobs, and the control system focuses more on the outer boundaries for activities and behaviors.

THE ENTREPRENEURIAL PHILOSOPHY OF CONTROL

Managers must periodically ask a simple question: What is our concept of control in this company? If we consider all of the ingredients that go into the complex system of formal and informal controls in a an organization, is there a guiding philosophy? Stevenson and Jarillo-Mossi (1989) argue that two general philosophies dominate, although clearly many degrees lie between the two. The first is what they term *command and control*. The term has a military connotation, which is appropriate. Control is tight, with orders coming from above and with the expectation that they will be executed exactly as they are given. Decisions are made as if superiors are present. Extensive control measures are used to track whether commands are executed and to provide detailed feedback to management.

The second philosophy of control is more consistent with the creation of an entrepreneurial environment (see also Table 14-2). It is called *no surprises*. The concern is with a control system that generates adequate information on a timely basis for all who really "need to know." No one is subject to surprises because of a lack of information. The principal link is between control and company performance, such that performance levels are close enough to targets for the company to maintain credibility, achieve coordination among key groups, and properly anticipate resource requirements. Control mechanisms produce indicators or early warning signals of problems before they occur. This approach is very different from one where the purpose is to check up on people or mandate their behaviors on the job.

An entrepreneurial philosophy of control has some related aspects. Consistent with our earlier discussion, it is one in which the control system conveys a sense of trust. If the organization mandates that employees be subjected to electronic time cards to

TABLE 14-2

The Critical Elements of an Entrepreneurial Philosophy of Control

- Control based on "no surprises"
- Looser but effective control elements
- A mindset of giving up control to gain control
- Empowerment and discretion that is built into the job
- Mutual trust
- Emphasis on self-control
- Organizational slack in terms of resource availability
- Pools of internal venture capital
- Varying levels of control based on the types of entrepreneurial behavior being sought
- Open and shared control information
- Simultaneous loose-tight properties

document when they begin and end their work, or provide detailed justifications for every expense when they travel, then there is an implicit (and perhaps explicit) statement being made: We don't trust you to simply do the work you are paid to do without close monitoring, and we don't trust you to spend money wisely when traveling for the company. Now, there are those who will argue that such mechanisms are critical for figuring out where money is being spent and where profits are being made in the business, and that it has nothing to do with trust. Employees are likely to see it differently. More importantly, practices such as these do not reinforce trust, or produce an enhanced feeling of empowerment. Trust is an important beginning point in getting employees to move down the path towards trying new things, relying on unconventional approaches for overcoming obstacles, and being willing to experience failure along the way.

Another core principle in the entrepreneurial philosophy of control is to *give up control to gain control*. It is a simple but powerful notion. When a manager gives up control over some activity or area of responsibility, and instead allows the employee to handle it, control is being given up. And yet, if the empowered employee responds by being more conscientious, more creative, or harder working, then control is actually being gained. The control is not over the intermediate actions of the employee, but over the employee's performance or final output. Control is also gained over the employee's sense of accomplishment and job satisfaction.

Consider the supervisor who lets employees set their own work schedules, or determine their own pay rates. By giving up control over these decisions, the manager wants more than to make the employees feel empowered and trusted. The real objective is to get employees to take ownership, realize the implications of their behavior for the company, fellow workers, and themselves, and produce an outcome that is better than if the supervisor had simply mandated the decision or performed the activity. Thus, employees may be more willing to work a less-desirable shift or put in extra hours, and set a reasonable wage rate about which they do not complain.

The ability to obtain better results from employees than one would get by exercising complete control over these decisions requires that the manager have a clear strategy that includes answers to the following questions:

- Over what specific activity, responsibility, or requirement is management giving up control?

- Do the employees have or can they obtain the proper information to exercise control over the activity or behavior?

- Is it clear that this is a real and permanent relinquishment of control, with no second-guessing?

- What specific impact on behavior is management attempting to have?

- Over what variables is control actually being gained, and how is it manifested?

If control is, in part, about accountability, then giving up control is about greater accountability. Where there is an elaborate system of control measures, employees can be secure in the knowledge that if they complied with the control system, then their accountability is absolved; they have fulfilled their responsibility. They need not take any further responsibility for outcomes or the implications of their behavior for company performance. However, by giving up control to the employees, there is a much deeper sense of responsibility not just for accomplishing a task or behaving in a certain manner, but for the quality of task performance and the impact it has on the organization.

As previously noted, to give up control is to empower. Mintzberg (1996, p. 63) explains that "Empowerment really means stopping the disempowerment of people—but this just brings us back to hierarchy—for empowerment (typically) reinforces hierarchy." He argues that true empowerment goes beyond tokenism or the delegation of some task or authority as if one were granting a gift to the employee from on high. Instead, people get power when it is logically and intrinsically designed into their jobs. This distinction is reflected in the following two scenarios:

Scenario A: The vice president of purchasing invites the purchasing agent to attend a decision meeting from which she is normally excluded, or empowers the purchasing agent to make a particular vendor selection decision when the VP usually makes them all.

Scenario B: The vice president of purchasing sets up a team of purchasing agents to make vendor selection decisions, and tells them to come only to him when they are deadlocked on a choice.

It is the latter scenario that not only empowers, but encourages people to apply themselves and to demonstrate initiative. Empowerment means authority is delegated. The employee has a degree of discretion and some level of autonomy. He or she is accountable for a decision or action and the corresponding outcome.

To complete our entrepreneurial philosophy of control, two final points are in order. First, the relationship between entrepreneurship and control is not one of simply getting more entrepreneurship when there is less control. Control is vital for sustained entrepreneurship. The real issue is the nature and intent of the controls and how they are used. However, there comes a point beyond which more control has deleterious effects on entrepreneurial activity.

Secondly, control levels can also be expected to vary with the type of entrepreneurship the company seeks. Incremental innovation can occur in more tightly controlled environments, while discontinuous innovation requires extensive autonomy. One can also link control to the type of structure producing the innovation. Figure 14-2 illustrates how various innovation structures imply different degrees of control. Levels of control are higher with entrepreneurial projects that are sanctioned within a mainstream functional area such as production or marketing. The resultant innovation is apt to be

FIGURE 14-2

Relating Types of Innovation Initiatives to Control

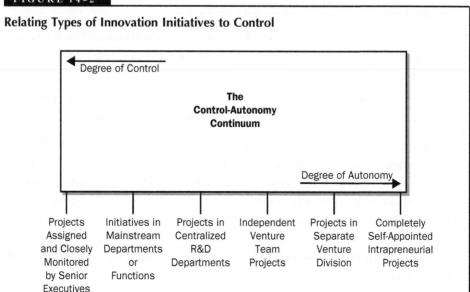

continuous or incremental. Tight control is replaced with greater autonomy when separate new venture divisions are created. These separate divisions are more likely to demonstrate higher levels of entrepreneurial intensity. The implication is that the concept of control in an organization must be flexible in terms of different types of decisions. At a minimum, controls designed for everyday operations must be different from those designed to encourage significant innovation activities.

A Paradox: Simultaneous Looseness and Tightness

Entrepreneurship poses a unique dilemma for control efforts in companies. In theory, companies should design control systems in a manner that facilitates effective company outcomes (e.g., efficiency, risk reduction, conformity). As we have noted, entrepreneurship is more consistent with an environment that encourages the management of uncertainty, risk tolerance, experimentation, and empowerment. A paradox results, in that contemporary organizations risk failure if employees operate with few constraints, but they also risk stagnation and ultimate demise if they don't free up the creative talents of their employees. It would seem that this paradox creates a need for a balanced approach to control.

To illustrate the concept of balance, let us elaborate on three of the earlier-mentioned characteristics of the company's control system:

- *Administrative formality/informality:* The extent to which the organization relies upon explicit, stated, and/or documented mechanisms (e.g., rules, procedures, policies) in guiding resource allocation and employee behavior.

- *Managerial flexibility/inflexibility:* The degree to which discretion and/or freedom is given to junior managers to interpret or ignore rules and procedures in performing their jobs.

- *Budgetary tightness/looseness:* The extent to which budgets impose strict restrictions on how resources are allocated and how performance is evaluated.

It may not be so much a question of whether controls are less formal, allow for more discretion, or are fiscally looser as it is the ability of the organization to strike a balance on each of these dimensions. Such a balance would seem consistent with the notion of simultaneous *loose–tight properties* identified by Peters and Waterman in their study of excellence (1982), the "freedom within a framework" noted by Collins (2001) in his study of "good to great" companies, and Marginson's (2002) discussion of a control system that encourages individual initiative within the context of overall corporate direction.

How formal should administrative controls be? Administrative formality would seem vital in operations of large size and scope, especially given the ongoing demands of growth. Otherwise, operations will be plagued with inefficiencies, errors, waste, and a degree of chaos. Yet the concept of balance suggests that self-control (by employees over themselves) and social control (by fellow employees over a given employee) play a larger role than formal procedures in aligning the goals of the individual with those of the organization. The need for informal mechanisms seems especially pertinent in complex settings where goals tied to entrepreneurial behavior must coexist with goals related to operational performance and competitive efficiencies. Thus, we argue for moderate or intermediate levels of formality, as this will encourage risk tolerance. Less rigidity in organizational systems permits employees to try new approaches. Areas of responsibility are less narrowly delineated, and conduct is less prescribed, while administrative consistency is still expected.

Turning to levels of discretion that managers are permitted, process and product innovation involve the unknown, and imply change. The ability to bridge the unknown and overcome resistance to change appears to be more consistent with role flexibility, where employees are empowered to exercise discretion and personal initiative in performing their jobs (Barringer and Bluedorn, 1999). For its part, the control system focuses more on the outer boundaries for activities and behaviors. Yet exploration by employees of new and different things can also lead to unrealistic concepts, projects that are inconsistent with the strategic direction of the company, and initiatives having resource requirements that exceed potential returns. Again, the implication is that companies must strike a balance, where discretion is subject to parameters, and employee autonomy is earned (Sathe, 2003).

With budgetary or resource control, entrepreneurship would seem to require financial discipline, but with budget mechanisms that are flexible in accommodating new opportunities as they emerge, and organizational goals that are focused on achieving ends rather than prescribing means (Shih and Yong, 2001). The likelihood of entrepreneurial behavior is greater when enlightened efficiency is emphasized. Thus, the organization institutes clear and specific financial accountability. Otherwise, significant money is wasted on ill-conceived or inappropriate initiatives. However, rather than strictly imposing detailed line-item budgets, broader expenditure categories are emphasized, a level of *slack* is deliberately designed into cost controls and budgeting (see below), budgetary deviations within broader categories are tolerated, performance measurement does not have to occur at fixed intervals, and success measures include financial and nonfinancial indicators. The budgetary system may include incentives tied to organizational success factors and goal congruence (Simons, 1995). The dual needs for fiscal accountability and individual experimentation suggest an emphasis on intermediate levels of budgetary control, as opposed to very loose or very tight controls.

The limited research on control and entrepreneurship tends to approach the relationship as linear, where more control means less entrepreneurship (Bisbe and Otley, 2004). However, a consideration of the diverse ways in which people and tasks are affected by and respond to control mechanisms suggests things are a bit more complex. It would seem the relationship between various dimensions of control and entrepreneurship should be curvilinear (actually, an inverted U) (Morris et al, 2006). We believe that entrepreneurship will be highest at intermediate levels of administrative formality, managerial discretion, and resource and budgetary tightness. Further, levels of entrepreneurship will be lower when things are too informal or highly formal, when there is total discretion or virtually no discretion, and where budgets are extremely loose but also when they are highly detailed and rigidly imposed.

Approaching Control and Entrepreneurship as Complementary

There might be a tendency among some to regard control processes as antithetical to the interests of corporate entrepreneurship. However, the manner in which operational control is manifested in organizations has been shown to have great significance for the success of innovative behaviors and initiatives. Covin and Slevin (2002) refer to what they call the "hardware" side of organizations, which includes company strategy, structure, systems, and procedures. These elements provide the context from which employees take their cues on how to behave on the job. Control systems exist as part of this hardware and, therefore, can be of great consequence to how individuals behave, including their entrepreneurial behaviors. For organizations to productively support entrepreneurial activity, they need the alignment of control factors with other variables that influence corporate entrepreneurship (e.g., company structure, incentive systems). In fact, the evidence suggests that control systems can positively contribute to the successful introduction of new products and technologies (e.g., Das and Joshi, 2007; Khazanchi et al., 2007; Naveh, 2007). In one study of 133 new product development projects, Poskela and Martinsuo (2009) explored relationships between seven management control variables and the extent to which a new product concept created new product or market development opportunities—what they termed "strategic renewal." Their research indicated that several of the management control variables studied were positively associated with strategic renewal among early-development-stage product innovation projects.

Goodale et al. (2011) explored relationships among the antecedents to corporate entrepreneurship, operational control mechanisms, and innovation performance. Their research of 177 companies found that control mechanisms are not inherently antithetical to the interests of corporate entrepreneurship. Rather, factors that create entrepreneurship in established companies actually operate in concert with control mechanisms to promote innovation performance. These findings have three important implications for managing entrepreneurial activity. First, managers should design and develop innovation-facilitating and control-facilitating mechanisms that complement one another such that the entrepreneurial potential that resides within the organization is leveraged for the highest and best organizational purposes. Second, managers should understand innovation as a process that's amenable to the application of structured, disciplined oversight. The successful pursuit of innovation demands that managers approach new opportunities with the understanding that the means for generating potentially desirable innovation outcomes can be understood and deliberately constructed. There are rules, methods, and general process knowledge that can serve as resources in facilitating successful innovation. Finally, successful innovation is a product of organizational systems in which control elements and entrepreneurship elements operate in concert. Thus, managers should adopt a systems perspective recognizing the interfaces and interdependencies that exist between forces that foster the innovation process and forces that control it.

Expanding on the Concept of Slack

A company's control efforts are especially concerned with people and money. Management tries to ensure that employees are earning their pay, the company is not paying more than it has to for everything from raw materials to travel, items are not purchased that are not really needed, people are not misappropriating funds, and so forth. Moreover, any company, no matter the size, has limited resources. As a rule, different departments, units, and projects compete for these resources. Recognizing the importance of the above, entrepreneurial companies still find ways to make excess resources available for informal experimentation, unsanctioned trials, and research on brand new, untested ideas.

This brings us to a key feature of entrepreneurial control systems: *organizational slack*. The concept of slack implies a degree of looseness in resource availability. Employees are able to tap into resources without going through a formal approval process. They can "borrow" expertise, research, money, materials, equipment, and other resources as they develop, test, and refine original concepts. No slack exists when the company is so busy counting everything that can be counted, forcing strict accountability for each penny of a given department's budget, and tracking every minute of an employee's time on the job. Without slack, there is little room to try anything new or different. Experimentation becomes almost impossible.

Managing slack involves a fine balancing act. If money is hanging on trees, such that virtually anyone can easily get funding for any new idea, huge amounts will be wasted. Further, there will be little organizational benefit from the subsequent failures that occur. It is important that entrepreneurial champions have to fight for their ideas. Their concepts can only benefit when they are challenged and encounter resistance. But where controls on resources are too tight, the incentive to innovate disappears. The time and effort one must invest to obtain formal resource support, and the high probability that requests will ultimately be rejected, lead the employee to conclude that the costs of personal innovation far outweigh any potential benefits. New ideas almost always require initial work to refine, revise, and adapt them into a form that makes sense for the organization. They also require extensive internal selling, and selling is a lot easier when the innovator has data and other evidence to support his or her innovation. But in the absence of slack, it is hard to develop ideas and concepts to the point where they can be sold, and it is difficult to generate supporting evidence. In effect, slack supports the creation of an underground economy of percolating ideas within the organization.

Slack is very much tied to the budgeting processes in companies. A tight control system mandates that budgets be prepared for units, departments, functional activities, and projects before money can be spent. It prescribes the format for budgets. Limits are established for the time period covered by the budget. Detailed line-item breakdowns are required. Types of expenditures that are permitted in the budget are specified, and "miscellaneous" or "other" categories are not allowed. Approval of budgets entails meetings at multiple levels in the organization. Alternatively, a budgeting process that allows for slack is more flexible. Time periods covered by different budgets can vary. Expense categories are more broadly defined. In a sense, the budget consists of a number of buckets instead of detailed line items, and the resources in the bucket can be applied creatively to accomplish the basic purpose of the bucket.

The question is also not simply whether there is a limited or high amount of slack resources, but the types of resources in question, as well as how much slack there is relative to the demand for those resources. Resources differ in how much discretion a manager or employee has in terms of what they can do with the resource. For instance, financial resources imply high degrees of discretion, while slack in terms of excess machine time would not lend itself to as much discretion over what can be done with it. There tends to be a stronger relationship between allowing for more slack and company performance with high-discretion resources (George, 2005). Separately, the relevant question may not be how much slack a company has relative to other companies, but rather, how much slack exists relative to internal demands for those slack resources. Having slack resources but also having lots of internal competition for those resources appears to be a good thing (George, 2005).

Internal Venture Capital Pools

While slack applies to operational budgets, it is important that entrepreneurial initiatives not undermine operational needs. Thus, simply having slack is not enough. There is a need to provide financial support for entrepreneurial initiatives through special seed and venture capital (VC) funds that are separate from operational budgets. In Chapter 4, we introduced corporate venture capital as a form of entrepreneurial activity in companies. In that discussion, the focus was on large, often multimillion dollar, investments in major new technologies developed as potential new businesses both inside and outside the company. However, the VC model can also be pursued on a more modest scale within mainstream operations.

Brandt (1986, p. 93) explains, "Creating budget detours is the philosophy and ... experimentation is the key." These mainstream funds should be available from multiple sources within the organization. In companies that have experimented in this area, successful financing schemes are often administered by councils or boards consisting of employees at or near the same level in the organization as those employees want to apply for funding (notably, not senior executives). Consider an example. A company creates opportunity review boards in strategically selected parts of the company. Each board has permanent members who rotate on and off every two years, together with special ad hoc members who have expertise related to particular proposals that are submitted. The membership is drawn principally from middle- or lower-level management. Any employee in the unit can apply to the fund, and their innovative ideas can be fairly rough. A business plan of five pages or less is enough to call a board meeting. The board is empowered to provide staged investments, from fairly easy to get seed money for initial research to increasingly larger amounts that are tied to the achievement of specific development targets. The board might also be given authority to free up an increasing percentage of the employee's work time to focus on the innovative project.

The key is to try more than one approach. Different funding pools might be created depending on the scope, scale, and innovativeness of projects. There will usually be limits to the size of an internal venture capital fund, and to the amount that can be invested in a project, but both of these might vary considerably depending on the purpose of the fund. Funds might include a deal structure where the employee gets an equity stake in the concept once it develops past a certain point, or otherwise shares in the returns. Another option would be to have the employee share in the downside risk, should the concept fail. Pinchot and Pellman (1999) suggest the concept of *intracapital*, which is a resource bank account awarded to employees who successfully pursue entrepreneurship within the company. The bank account consists of a budget the champion is allowed to spend on his or her next idea without asking anyone for permission. It can be used for research, travel, equipment, self-improvement, or any other expenditure that can be reasonably tied to new project development.

While considering issues surrounding budgetary support for entrepreneurship, it is also worthwhile to question the kinds of initiatives that tend to receive funding in companies. While the evidence is extremely limited, one study examined 49 innovative projects (of which 29 received funding) from a sample of large companies (Koen, 2000). The most important funding criterion was the strategic fit of the project with the company. Factors differentiating funded from unfunded projects included carefully choosing and developing a good working relationship with an executive sponsor, requesting low initial start-up funding, and marketplace competitiveness. If a project was funded, factors that affected the level of funding included the credibility of the team and market attractiveness.

Control and Costs: The Open Book Revolution

The entrepreneurial philosophy of control extends to the financial records and books of the company. If there is one thing senior executives seem intent on controlling, it is access to the numbers. The prevalent belief seems to be that employees must never see what the company is spending in various areas, how much people are earning, the margins on products, or the profits of individual business units and the overall company. The reasons for such a belief are many, ranging from "it's none of their business" and "it will undermine their motivation" to "they will somehow use it against us" and "competitors will find out." But such thinking is out of step with the contemporary environment and the nature of today's workforce.

An alternative operating model is called *open book management* (Case, 1998). It is an approach that attempts to change the link between the employee and the company. Rather than motivating employees to pay attention to quality, efficiency, good customer service, or some other operational concern, open book management gets them to focus on the bottom line—the success of the business over time. Whereas much managerial time is spent on telling employees *what* the company wants to achieve (goals, performance levels) and *what* employees are expected to do to achieve these goals and levels, with open book management, the emphasis is on *why* things are happening and *why* improved performance is needed in certain areas. Based on a better understanding of these *whys*, the employee is in a stronger position to discover innovative approaches to *how* goals and levels can be achieved. Table 14-3 summarizes the key ingredients constituting the open book approach.

Open book management strives to get all employees to think and act differently—to think like owners. The company's books, financials, and numbers are shared with

---

TABLE 14-3

Open Book Management and Entrepreneurship: The Ingredients

Open book management is a way of running a company that gets everyone to focus on helping the business make money. It is an approach to business built around the following six principles:

- Every employee has access to the company's financials and all the other numbers that are critical to tracking the company's performance.
- There is an overt and ongoing attempt to get the information in front of employees.
- The company teaches the basics of the business (what the numbers mean) to everyone.
- Employees learn that, whatever else they do, part of their job is to move the numbers in the right direction.
- People are empowered to make decisions in their jobs based on what they know.
- Employees have a stake in the company's success, and share in the risk of failure.

SOURCE: Adapted from Davis, T.R.V. 1997. "Open-book management: Its promise and pitfalls," *Organizational Dynamics*, 25(3): 7–20.

---

everyone, so that people see the relationships between what they do and how the company or their unit performs. Employees are given training in how to interpret these numbers, and how these numbers are impacted by decisions and performance levels in various parts of the company. Courses in business fundamentals are taught to everyone regardless of job description. Scorecards are prepared in which key numbers are regularly communicated to the workforce. Employees see corporate scorecards, business unit scorecards, and department scorecards. If a business unit or department sets a goal in some area, progress is tracked and linked to the numbers on the financial statements. All employees get involved in goal setting, and they see the linkages between the performance goals for their area and overall company performance.

The key to the open book approach is that people take joint responsibility for moving the numbers in the right direction. Employees are encouraged to experiment with creative ways to affect performance. A critical aspect is that employees share directly in rewards when targets are met. In fact, both risks and rewards are tied to the numbers. That is, the rewards are linked to numbers that people regularly see, understand, and can affect. However, when performance comes up short, employees receive less. Compensation plans might vary from gain sharing and stock options to bonuses and salary increases.

For hesitant managers, Case (1995, p. 29) explains, "Open book management comes with a built-in self-regulator that ought to still the hearts of owners who fear letting go. The most important checks and balances—the numbers—are part of the system. If somebody makes a bad decision, its effects on the bottom line are right up where everybody can see them—and react accordingly."

The open book approach is clearly about trust and enlightened control. It is also consistent with the creation of a more entrepreneurial environment. Not only is this approach built around the concept of taking ownership, it encourages employees to look at the relationships between what they do and company performance. More than product innovation, it facilitates ongoing process innovation, as people come to understand how to affect the numbers, and they look for unique ways to accomplish their jobs. Product innovation is also encouraged, as employees can better appreciate the limits to revenue growth from current offerings. As new products and services are added, they get a vivid picture of the ways in which the numbers are affected.

The Concept of Profit Pools

Numbers can tell another story about entrepreneurial opportunity, this one on the profit side of the equation. The concept of a "profit pool" has been proposed by Gadiesh and Gilbert (1998), both of Bain and Company. Simply put, a profit pool is the total profits earned in an industry at all points along the industry's value chain. All the product or service segments in the value chain are identified and each is assessed in terms of its current and potential profits. Note the focus is not on revenues, as the areas accounting for the most sales are frequently not the most profitable. Figure 14-3 provides an illustration of the profit pool for the U.S. automobile industry. In this example, manufacturing (auto makers) and selling cars (dealers) are responsible for most of the revenues, but auto leasing is the most profitable, followed by insurance.

Profitability can be expected to differ significantly across the segments in the profit pool. Further, each segment can be broken down into individual products (e.g., in the auto example, different auto insurance products), customer groups (e.g., students, fleet buyers), geographic markets (e.g., western Canada, cities in New England with population less than 50,000), and distribution channels (e.g., auto insurance sold through independent agents versus company reps versus the Internet). Profitability measures are generated for each of these subcomponents (or subsegments), and again significant differences are likely to appear.

The profit measure itself should be some form of contribution margin. Thus, rather than distort figures by allocating overhead in arbitrary ways, the analyst is concentrating on revenue minus the variable and direct fixed costs for each segment and subsegment.

By examining where and how money is being made, management can determine where to concentrate entrepreneurial efforts, including the development of new

FIGURE 14-3

The Profit Pool in the Auto Industry

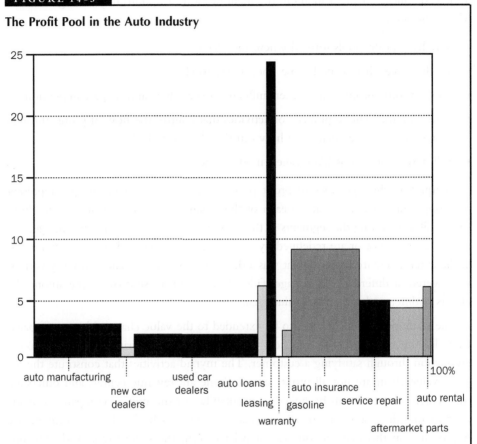

SOURCE: Reprinted by permission of Harvard Business Review. [75/76]. From "Profit Pools: A Fresh Look at Strategy" by Gadiesh, O. and Gilbert, J., 05/1998 & 03/1998. Copyright © 1998 by the Harvard Business School Publishing Corporation; all rights reserved.

products and markets. A vivid example can be found with U-Haul. The company managed to redefine the entire consumer truck rental business by examining the profit pool and recognizing the potential in accessories (boxes, tape, insurance, carts), even as truck rentals continued to dominate revenues. Once identified, strategies were formulated to maximize control of the profit pool segment.

Profit pool structures can be quite complex. Creative insights are needed to recognize and quantify all of the current and potential components. Signs of untapped profit potential might include the existence of higher barriers to competitive entry in a segment, a product or service that is not well differentiated (but could be), or a sub-segment that is being ignored, among others. Gadiesh and Gilbert (1998) suggest some basic questions that can aid in the identification of opportunity through the lens of a profit pool:

- Why have profit pools formed where they have?

- Are the forces that created those pools likely to change?

- How do some profit sources exert influence over others and shape competition?

- Where are the "choke points," or activities that control the flow of profits through the rest of the value chain, and how can they be controlled?

- Will new, more profitable business models emerge?

Interpreting the dynamics of profit pools is difficult. Ongoing changes represent both opportunities and threats to each of the organizations in the value chain. Profit levels will shift among the segments in the pool over time. New segments emerge, and others cease to exist or are redefined by technological change and other developments in the external environment. What was a deep pool becomes shallow as entry barriers are lowered or differential advantages fade. Power tends to shift over time among the players at different levels in the value chain.

The profit pool concept can also be extended to the value chain within a company. Consider the chain of value creation that occurs from acquiring resources through production through satisfying a customer. The myriad activities that constitute the internal value chain are not all profit centers. Some are revenue centers and others are cost centers. But each can be linked to profitability of the unit or company, as made clear in our discussion of open book management. Each also has subcomponents. Approached in this manner, one can step back from the company and identify untapped or underexploited sources of profit contribution or customer value creation. Anheuser-Busch was able to do this with packaging, while American Airlines transformed its Sabre reservation service into a profit center called Travelocity. Open book management facilitates this kind of thinking, in that the open and detailed sharing of the numbers helps in the identification of untapped profit pool segments in the company's operations.

The profit pool concept is an important part of the corporate entrepreneur's toolkit. When approached creatively, new sources of profit within the industry can be identified, priorities can be established for acquisitions and expansion, insights can be produced for targeting new customer groups and distribution channels, and internal operations can be refocused. Ultimately, the business model of the company can be redefined.

Sony's Aggressive Controls in a Dampened Economy

Sony Corporation, headquartered in Tokyo, Japan, is one of the world's largest media conglomerates with over 171,000 employees and revenue exceeding $79.5 billion in 2009. Sony is one of the leading manufacturers of electronics, video, communications, video game consoles, and information technology products for the consumer and professional markets. Sony Corporation is the electronics business unit and the parent company of the Sony Group, which is engaged in business through its five operating segments—electronics, games, entertainment (motion pictures and music), financial services, and other. These make Sony one of the most comprehensive entertainment companies in the world. Sony's principal business operations include Sony Corporation (Sony Electronics in the U.S.), Sony Pictures Entertainment, Sony Computer Entertainment, Sony Music Entertainment, Sony Ericsson, and Sony Financial. As a semiconductor maker, Sony is among the Worldwide Top 20 Semiconductor Sales Leaders. The company's current slogan is *"Make. Believe."*

Yet the economic collapse of 2008 reverberated through the organization and challenged the very essence of the company slogan. CEO, Howard Stringer set out a restructuring process to reign in some of the costs. The first steps taken in response to the global economic crisis in 2008 were to quickly adjust production levels and to engage in immediate restructuring and cost-cutting initiatives. Below are some of the initiatives and the progress that Sony has made so far.

- Cost reductions throughout the Sony Group of more than $300 billion in fiscal year 2009 compared to fiscal year 2008 through restructuring and other initiatives.

- Reducing 57 manufacturing sites by approximately 10 percent and furthering the shift to manufacturing in low-cost areas and with OEM/ODM partners. Sony closed eight manufacturing sites.

- Streamlining the workforce by reducing headcount in the electronics business by approximately 8,000 and reducing the temporary workforce by more than 8,000.

- Sony's Electronics and Game businesses are now merged and reconfigured as two strong new groups: the Consumer Products & Devices Group and the Networked Products & Services Group. The first group represents the traditional and vital hardware; the second will provide new network differentiation.

According to Mr. Springer's letter to the shareholders in 2009, "we have adjusted production, lowered inventory levels, reduced marketing and other operational expenses, and curtailed or delayed portions of our investment plans. We will continue these and other efforts to improve efficiency and will wage a continuous battle to make this company leaner, quicker and stronger and, therefore, better able to *innovate,* lead and flexibly navigate in these increasingly competitive times."

Going further, Mr. Springer discussed the company's goals as a leading global provider of networked consumer electronics, entertainment, and services. He stated, "we must strengthen each of the pillars of our core businesses and be coordinated in our efforts to innovate for further growth. Innovation has always been one of Sony's celebrated strengths, and it is through innovation that we will continue to develop the unique products, content and services that deliver rich user experiences and inspiration to our customers. This innovation is what has driven Sony's success in the past, and this in turn has driven our brand—one of the strongest weapons in our arsenal—to what it is today. To let this innovation drive Sony to new heights, we need to challenge our engineers, designers and producers to enhance our exciting hardware with a new focus on the software and content that will help establish our differentiation going forward, nurture an "Asset Light" corporate structure (*minimizing our fixed assets in order to maximize business flexibility, while maintaining our differentiating technology through continued research and development*) and efficiently use our capital so that it will generate sufficient returns on our investments...... We are all firmly committed to leading Sony with the innovative spirit that is embedded in its DNA."

Discussion Questions

1. Could the concept of "unintended consequences" discussed in the chapter be applied to the actions of Sony's CEO?

2. Discuss the "entrepreneurial philosophy of control" (Table 14-2) in relation to the restructuring efforts at Sony.

3. How does the concept of "balancing looseness and tightness" apply to Sony and the approach they have taken?

SOURCE: Adapted from: various Web sites discussing Sony Corp., Sony Global Headquarters Web site, investor relations site, and letter to shareholders. Accessed April 24, 2010.

Summary and Conclusions

This chapter has looked at control systems in companies and their implications for entrepreneurship. A control system is a combination of measures, tools, and information that act together to maintain actual performance close to desired performance. The specific measures and tools are intended to either induce desired behavior or limit dysfunctional behavior.

Control systems can represent a significant obstacle to entrepreneurship, especially when they focus on efficiency to the exception of effectiveness, encourage micromanagement of resources, and become ends instead of means in terms of their impact on employee behavior. Overreliance on formalization and procedural control can end up promoting minimally acceptable behavior. Moreover, controls that enforce rigid and conformist behavior are incompatible with innovation and the ability to compete in a rapidly changing environment. At the same time, recent research has shown that certain characteristics of control can actually serve to facilitate entrepreneurship and innovation in companies. The issue is one of balance, where entrepreneurial companies demonstrate simultaneous "loose–tight" properties.

The question is not one of less control versus more control. The challenge for managers is to redefine the organization's concept of control. A distinction was drawn between a "command and control" approach versus an "early warning" approach, and it was argued that the latter is needed in companies striving to be entrepreneurial. Entrepreneurship is facilitated by a looser, more flexible "early warning" approach, where mutual trust, discretion, and organizational slack are guiding principles. Other elements of an entrepreneurial philosophy of control were presented, including the concepts of "giving up control to gain control" and "open book management." Flexible control can preempt impending problems, but also serve as an active force for effective innovation. Specifically, the control system becomes a vehicle for managing uncertainty, promoting risk tolerance, encouraging focused experimentation, and empowering employees.

Dynamic environments necessitate internal adaptation, and adaptation requires a movement to less formal control and more horizontal communication. Similarly, as organizations move away from hierarchies to flatter structures, the need for managers and management control lessens. While these may be the general patterns in many companies, the actual levels and types of control should reflect the degree and frequency of entrepreneurship sought by management. If the desire is for infrequent or incremental innovation, controls can be somewhat more formal, rigid, and centralized. Breakthrough innovation demands significantly greater autonomy and flexibility. Another issue is the overall level of innovation in the company. Companies that are consistently more innovative than others over time come to rely on lower levels of formalized control.

In the final analysis, the impact of control systems transcends the controls themselves. Because of their central role in affecting all members of an organization, and all facets of operations, the control system is closely linked to structure, planning systems, goal-setting processes, reward systems, and other key components of the organization. Thus, entrepreneurship will be the result of interactive effects among a combination of variables.

References

Anthony, A. N., and Govindarajan, V. 2001. *Management Control Systems* (Chicago, IL: Irwin).

Barringer, B. R., and Bluedorn, A. 1999. "The Relationship between Corporate Entrepreneurship and Strategic Management," *Strategic Management Journal*, 20(3): 421–444.

Bisbe, J. and Otley, D. 2004. "The Effects of the Interactive Use of Management Control Systems on Product Innovation," *Accounting, Organizations and Society*, 29(8): 709–737.

Brandt, S. 1986. *Entrepreneuring in Established Companies* (Homewood, IL: Dow-Jones Irwin).

Case, J. 1995. "The Open Book Revolution," *INC.*, 17 (June): 26–43.

Case, J. 1998. *The Open-book Experience: Lessons from Over 100 Companies Who Successfully Transformed Themselves* (New York: Basic Books).

Collins, J. 2001. *Good to Great* (New York, NY: Harper Collins).

Cirka, C. 1997. *A Piece of the Puzzle: Employee Responses to Control Practices and Effects on Firm Control Strategy* (Philadelphia: Temple University).

Covin, J. G. and Slevin, D. P. 2002. "The Entrepreneurial Imperatives of Strategic Leadership," in Hitt, M., Ireland, R. D., Camp, M., and Sexton, D. (eds.), *Strategic Entrepreneurship: Creating a New Mindset* (Oxford, UK: Blackwell Publishers).

Das, S. R. and Joshi, M. P. 2007. "Process Innovativeness in Technology Services Organizations: Roles of Differentiation Strategy, Operational Autonomy and Risk-Taking Propensity," *Journal of Operations Management*, 25(3): 643–660.

Drucker, P. 2008. *The Essential Drucker: The Best of Sixty Years of Peter Drucker's Essential Writings on Management* (New York: Harper Collins).

Gadiesh, O., and Gilbert, J. 1998. "Profit Pools: A Fresh Look at Strategy," *Harvard Business Review*, 76 (May–June): 139–147.

George, G. (2005). "Slack Resources and the Performance of Privately Held Firms," *Academy of Management Journal*, 48(4): 661–676.

Goodale, J. C., Kuratko, D. F., Hornsby, J. S., and Covin, J. G. 2011. "Operations Management and Corporate Entrepreneurship: The Moderating Effect of Operations Control on the Antecedents of Corporate Entrepreneurial Activity in Relation to Innovation Performance," *Journal of Operations Management*, 29(2): in-press.

Khazanchi, S., Lewis, M. W., and Boyer, K. K. 2007. "Innovation-Supportive Culture: The Impact of Organizational Values on Process Innovation," *Journal of Operations Management*, 25(4): 871–884.

Koen, P. 2000. "Developing Corporate Intrapreneurs," *Engineering Management Journal*, 12(2) (June): 3–7.

Mintzberg, H. 1996. "Musings on Management," *Harvard Business Review*, 74 (July–Aug.): 61–67.

Marginson, D. E. 2002. "Management Control Systems and Their Effects on Strategy Formulation at Middle Management Levels: Evidence for a U.K. Organization," *Strategic Management Journal*, 23(11): 1019–1031.

Morris, M. H., Schindehutte, M., and Allen, J. 2006. "Balanced Management Control Systems as a Mechanism for Achieving Corporate Entrepreneurship," *Journal of Managerial Issues*, 18(4): 468–495.

Morris, M. H. 1998. *Entrepreneurial Intensity* (Westport, CT: Quorum).

Naveh, E. 2007. "Formality and Discretion in Successful R&D Projects," *Journal of Operations Management*, 25(1), 110–125.

Peters, T., and Waterman, R. 1982. *In Search of Excellence: Lessons from America's Best-Run Companies* (New York, NY: Warner Books).

Pinchot, G., III. 2000. *Intrapreneuring* (San Francisco: Berrett-Koehler).

Pinchot, G., III, and Pellman, R. 1999. *Intrapreneuring in Action* (San Francisco: Berrett-Koehler).

Poskela, J., and Martinsuo, M. 2009. "Management Control and Strategic Renewal in the Front End of Innovation," *Journal of Product Innovation Management*, 26(5), 671–684.

Sathe, V. 2003. *Corporate Entrepreneurship* (Cambridge, UK: Cambridge University Press).

Shih, M. S., and Yong, L. C. 2001. "Relationship of Planning and Control Systems with Strategic Choices: A Closer Look," *Asia Pacific Journal of Management*, 18(4): 481–494.

Simons, R. 1995. "Control in an Age of Empowerment," *Harvard Business Review*, 63(2): 80–88.

Stevenson, H. H., and Jarillo-Mossi, J. 1989. "Preserving Entrepreneurship as Companies Grow," in R. Kuhn, (ed.) *Creativity and Strategy in Mid-Sized Firms* (Englewood Cliffs, NJ: Prentice-Hall): 134–155.

Tannebaum, A. S. 1988. "Control in Organizations," in T. Lowe and T. J. Machin, (eds.) *New Perspectives in Management Control* (London, UK: The Macmillan Press).

CHAPTER 15

SUSTAINING ENTREPRENEURIAL PERFORMANCE IN THE TWENTY-FIRST CENTURY

Introduction

Entrepreneurship is a phenomenon that has captivated the interest of executives in many corporate boardrooms. There is a danger, though, as managers can get too caught up in the excitement of a particular innovation or inspiring stories of individual entrepreneurs. While it is easy to become enamored with the idea of entrepreneurship, such infatuation misses the real point. The true value of entrepreneurship as a corporate concept lies in the extent to which it helps organizations create *sustainable* competitive advantage. The challenge is not simply one of being more competitive today, but delivering superior value and leading the markets in which you compete over the next ten years.

The focus of the preceding chapters has been on achieving high levels of entrepreneurial performance in organizations. We have seen that entrepreneurship is a thread that can be woven through many facets of a company. It can serve as the dominant logic, a measurable objective, a part of corporate strategy, an element in the company culture, a performance criterion for use in employee appraisals and compensation programs, and more. There are entrepreneurial approaches to managerial tasks (i.e., entrepreneurial strategies, methods of resource acquisition, structures), and there are entrepreneurial outcomes from managerial efforts (i.e., new ventures, products, processes, technologies, and markets). Companies, units within companies, and employees within units can all be characterized in terms of their levels of entrepreneurial intensity.

But it must be remembered that levels of entrepreneurship within organizations are never constant. They not only vary across departments and units, but they vary considerably over time. Even the most entrepreneurial of companies goes through cycles, with ebbs and flows in terms of the frequency and degree of entrepreneurial activity. While some companies struggle to muster even a minimal amount of entrepreneurial activity, all companies battle mightily to *sustain* entrepreneurial performance over time.

In this final chapter, we examine the issue of *sustainable entrepreneurial activity*. We begin with the need for individuals to develop a personal strategy or approach to entrepreneurial endeavors—one they can use on an ongoing basis. Following this, the concept of triggers is introduced, together with an identification of the leading types of events that trigger entrepreneurial behavior in companies. The need to manage triggers, while creating an ongoing sense of urgency in the organization, is discussed. Other vehicles for sustaining entrepreneurship, such as enlightened experimentation and organizational learning, are also explored. Finally, we take a look at how paradoxes and portfolios will transform the entrepreneurial organization of the twenty-first century into a dynamic incubator.

A Personal Approach to the Entrepreneurial Process

There are innumerable ways in which a given entrepreneurial project might be successfully initiated and completed in a company. The effectiveness of any one approach depends on the scope and scale of the project, the team members involved, the nature of the organization, and conditions in the external environment (Covin et al., 2000). And yet, there are certain principles to which the individual corporate entrepreneur or *champion* may always want to adhere. Stated differently, corporate entrepreneurs should develop a personal style or approach that they bring to any entrepreneurial opportunity. And, while the approach should be tailored to the individual's skills and talents, it should reflect a few basic considerations. The following eight principles represent a foundation around which the corporate entrepreneur can design his or her personal model:

- Solidify a relationship with a sponsor
- Build a flexible team structure
- Insulate the project and keep it quiet as long as possible
- Become a guerrilla
- Promise less but deliver more
- Experiment and produce early wins
- Manage project momentum
- Attempt to set the parameters

The champion begins with a strategy for getting a *sponsor*, an activity that is much more involved than simply obtaining the endorsement for one's project from someone at a higher level in the organization (see the following section on the *importance of a sponsor*). Sponsor selection must be approached systematically, as the entrepreneur is looking for someone with relevant credibility, someone who will be around when needed, and someone with whom he or she has a personal fit. A relationship must be established and then carefully nurtured. It is a two-way relationship predicated on trust and mutual investments. The willingness of a sponsor to protect the champion and the project, to provide advice and contacts, and to be associated with a project represents a significant investment. Defending a champion when he or she steps out of line, or steps on someone's toes, is a lot to expect from a sponsor. Motivating the champion when he or she wants to give up is another, often unexpected, role of the sponsor. The corporate entrepreneur must have a well-planned approach for reciprocating this investment. Communication styles, as well as the medium and frequency of communication, are important. Honesty, especially regarding setbacks, budgetary problems, and an inability to meet targets, is vital. So, too, is the need to stick to an agreed upon path, produce evidence of progress, and provide the sponsor with research and other ammunition for dealing with critics. Knowing when and when not to use the sponsor and ensuring one does not embarrass the sponsor are also part of the approach.

The social skills necessary for managing the sponsor relationship are also needed for building a team. Corporate entrepreneurs look for two things when constructing a team: skill sets that complement their own skills, and people who believe in the concept or vision. Teams will have formal and informal members, and relationships with both must be cultivated. Champions develop a sense of the type of team structure that works best for them. They ensure that individual roles are well communicated and agreed to, and that a consistent and mutually acceptable decision-making style is employed. The corporate entrepreneur's approach includes techniques for motivating the team, reinforcing members, sharing achievements, and accepting responsibility for all that goes wrong (Burgelman, 1984; Kanter, 1985).

Entrepreneurial projects are most vulnerable in their infancy. Flaws exist, elements have not been completely thought through, and aspects of the project look extremely threatening to one or more stakeholders in the organization. The corporate entrepreneur must develop a strategy to protect a project from early mortality. The goal is to insulate projects from detailed scrutiny by senior managers, departments not involved in the project, or other potential critics. Such insulation can be achieved in various ways. Endorsement by the sponsor and other senior managers, creation of an unofficial advisory group, and involving key departments in some tangible way can be sources of insulation. However, these activities create visibility, and must be balanced against a strategy of working underground and keeping publicity to a minimum. Many entrepreneurial successes come about because the team "bootlegged" their time (after hours, lunches, dinners, etc.), kept the project under cover in the formative period, and built credibility for the project before unveiling it. Also, the less one can appear to be openly competing for someone else's resources, the better. Insulation can also be achieved by placing a project outside the mainstream of the company structure, and by "buying" a window of time for project development before there will be any formal review.

The heart and soul of the corporate entrepreneur's approach concerns how he or she deals with lack of resources, bureaucratic obstacles, and rejection of critical requests. Champions must be guerrillas, with a personal style for gaining access to resources they do not control, circumventing obstacles, and keeping ideas alive that have been killed. Individuals differ in terms of their salesmanship abilities, political skills, tenacity, and skills at the creative employment or manipulation of resources. These differences suggest the style one employs will be, by definition, highly individualistic. It is a style that must reflect the champion's strengths and compensate for his or her weaknesses (Busenitz and Barney, 1997).

Another aspect of the corporate entrepreneur's model or approach to projects concerns the management of expectations. The rule here is simple: under-promise and over-deliver. If the project's potential is overemphasized from the outset (or is exaggerated by those not involved in the project), expectations can be so high that there will never be satisfaction with whatever the team produces. Again, a balance is involved, as the corporate entrepreneur wants to get key people excited about a project and its possibilities. The entrepreneur conveys a vision of what can be, but is conservative in terms of specific performance levels that will be achieved at specific points in time. Subsequently, he or she never fails to exceed these performance levels, initially by small amounts and eventually by significant amounts. Conservatism is especially critical with regard to the expectations of those who are not involved as sponsors, endorsers, contributors, or participants in the project.

The earlier the champion can show progress, the better. This can be difficult, as some projects demand a significant level of preliminary research and development activity before anything tangible can be produced. The champion requires a strategy for producing deliverables, or some kind of evidence that a project is moving forward, things are being accomplished, and benchmarks are being met. These deliverables might include favorable market research findings (e.g., surveys, focus groups, test markets), technical test results, simulations, drawings, prototypes, feedback from beta test sites, endorsements from key accounts, or any number of other signs of progress. This kind of action-orientation should be coupled with a sense that a consistent stream of small victories are occurring, where the champion has set a series of targets that reflect the logical evolution of a project.

The preceding two principles can be taken a step further. The champion should have in mind an overall time horizon over which a project will unfold. Expectations are managed across this time horizon, and are steadily raised. Similarly, small wins evolve into more significant accomplishments. The point becomes that a project has momentum, and the momentum builds over time. As momentum builds, the champion is able to achieve buy-in with key individuals and departments on a logical and sequential basis. Momentum that peaks too early can find attention subsequently shifting to other projects and priorities. At the same time, the lack of a sense that things are building in the early and middle stages of a project will often result in defections by key people and loss of key resources.

Finally, the corporate entrepreneur must have an approach for influencing the rules of the game. The more a champion must make a project work within the context of someone else's rules, the harder it is to succeed. Further, those rules are subject to change in midstream. Champions should look for ways to set or negotiate the parameters under which the venture team operates. Examples of areas over which the corporate entrepreneur should seek agreement at the outset of a project include the establishment of performance benchmarks that make sense given the type of project being pursued, acceptable processes for obtaining approvals for expenditures, decisions over which the champion has discretion, an overall project timeframe and timeframes for individual project stages, reporting responsibilities, and the amount of control the champion has over various resources (including people).

As the corporate entrepreneur develops a personal model or process for managing entrepreneurial initiatives, he or she may find it helpful to refer regularly to the so-called Corporate Innovator's Commandments (see Table 15-1). Many of the principles previously cited capture the essence of these commandments.

We can see these principles and commandments in action by considering the case of 3M's now famous Post-it notes. An adhesives engineer at 3M was able to secure a sponsor (one of his managers), gather a few excited engineers to help on the project, and certainly kept this "unsticky" adhesive underground until a practical use for it could be found. Breaking some of the traditional rules, and realizing they would ask for forgiveness later, the team left samples of the adhesive pads on the desks of all the clerical personnel at the Minneapolis headquarters. They used a similar approach (and some CEO letterhead) to get the product (which was not yet in production) on the desks of executive secretaries of Fortune 500 CEOs. Watching the subsequent applications of this new idea allowed this project to rise up from under-promising to over-delivering. Today, Post-it notes account for almost one-third of all 3M's revenues.

The Importance of Sponsors

In many companies, the introduction of new ideas triggers the "impatience clock." Corporate entrepreneurs need to be shielded from impatient executives who are driven by results. A results orientation can sometimes destroy the innovation before it

TABLE 15-1

The Corporate Innovator's Commandments

1. Come to work each day *willing* to give up your job for the innovation.
2. Circumvent any bureaucratic orders aimed at stopping your innovation.
3. Ignore your job description—do any job needed to make your innovation work.
4. Build a spirited innovation team that has the "fire" to make it happen.
5. Keep your innovation "underground" until it is prepared for demonstration to the corporate management.
6. Find a key upper-level manager who believes in you and your ideas and who will serve as a sponsor to your innovation.
7. Permission is rarely granted in organizations; thus, always seek forgiveness for the "ignorance" of the rules that you will display.
8. Always be realistic about the ways to achieve the innovation goals.
9. Share the glory of the accomplishments with everyone on the team.
10. Convey the innovation's vision through a strong venture plan.

SOURCE: Donald F. Kuratko, *Entrepreneurship: Theory, Process, Practice* (Mason, OH: Cengage/Southwestern, 2009), p. 69.

ever gets off the ground. Therefore, *sponsors* are corporate managers at the higher levels willing to protect entrepreneurial individuals by building environments of safety around them. While we briefly mentioned sponsors back in Chapter 6, it is important to emphasize the need for these people in the corporate entrepreneurship process. Sponsors aid corporate entrepreneurs in gaining access to resources and information and have a sincere belief in the corporate entrepreneurs' vision and capabilities. They also assist in keeping the entrepreneurial project "under the radar screen," where it has less visibility and is not as likely to become a target for elimination. Most important, the sponsors protect the entrepreneurs from being fired if certain corporate rules are violated.

Following are some of the questions to ask when attempting to identify a sponsor in your organization (Pinchot, 1985):

- Has this person been challenged and yet proceeded anyway? Is the person willing to handle controversy?
- Does the person have a deep personal commitment to innovation and innovative people?
- Can you gain the respect of this person?

- How (un)important is another step up the corporate ladder to this person?

- Does this person know when to fight, when to give up gracefully, and when it really does not matter?

- Does the person understand clearly the corporate decision-making structure?

- Does this person have the respect of other key corporate decision makers and have access to them?

Establishing mutual trust with a sponsor may be the most important aspect of working within a corporate environment. The selection of a sponsor should not only reflect the personality and position of the champion, but also the nature of the innovative project. It is worthwhile for the champion to consider three aspects of the project itself before deciding the level, functional background, and particular identity of the sponsor to be approached:

Nonfinancial resources—time, facilities, equipment, advice, and personnel needed by the champion to successfully complete the innovative project.

Investment—venture money needed to keep the project moving along and avoid needless delays.

Critics—the extent of political opposition likely to be encountered by the champion; the sponsor must be willing and able to defend the corporate entrepreneur and deter the critics.

It is also important to recognize the potential for retirements, promotions, and transfers to alter the sponsor–corporate entrepreneur relationship. Loss of the sponsor, or organizational changes that make the sponsor less able to influence the progress of a particular project, can lead to the demise of a project. It is therefore critical to establish a formal network as soon as possible.

Beware of the "Dark Side" of Entrepreneurship

The rewards, successes, and achievements of entrepreneurs have been extolled by many observers. However, a "dark side" of entrepreneurship also exists. That is, a potentially destructive element resides within the energetic drive of successful entrepreneurs. In exploring this dual-edge perspective, Kets de Vries (1985) notes specific negative factors that can permeate the personality of entrepreneurs and dominate their behavior. Although each of these factors possesses a positive aspect, it is important for entrepreneurs to understand the potentially destructive aspects. While this "dark side" is descriptive of start-up entrepreneurs, it can also be manifested in corporate entrepreneurship.

THE CONFRONTATION WITH RISK

Entrepreneurial activity entails risk. While they are rarely directly proportional, higher rewards usually mean higher risk. Similarly, concepts that are more innovative, or involve bolder breaks with current practice, typically represent higher risk and also higher reward. This is why entrepreneurs tend to evaluate risk very carefully. The manner in which they confront risk is a potential dark side for entrepreneurs. Entrepreneurs face a number of different types of risk. These can be grouped into four basic areas.

Financial Risk. In most start-up ventures the individual puts a significant portion of his or her savings or other resources at stake. This money or these resources will, in all likelihood, be lost if the venture fails. With corporate entrepreneurship, the company is assuming the financial risk. But the individual carries the weight of knowing he or she is responsible for losing the company's money.

Career Risk. A question frequently raised by would-be entrepreneurs is the effect of pursuing an entrepreneurial concept on their career, job advancement, vertical and lateral mobility, job rewards, and general marketability. This is a major concern to managers who have a secure organizational job with a high salary and a good benefits package.

Family and Social Risk. Doing something entrepreneurial requires a tremendous amount of the individual's energy and time, especially with a regular job to perform. Consequently, his or her other commitments may suffer. Entrepreneurs who are married, and especially those with children, expose their families to the risks of an incomplete family experience and the possibility of permanent emotional scars. In addition, old friends may vanish slowly because of missed interaction.

Psychic Risk. The greatest risk may be to the well-being of the entrepreneur. Job loss can be replaced; lost time can be attributed to learning or laying the groundwork for a future entrepreneurial pursuit; financial losses can be recovered; spouse, children, and friends can usually adapt. But some entrepreneurs who have suffered catastrophes have been unable to bounce back, at least not immediately. The psychological impact has proven to be too severe for them.

Entrepreneurs can also fail to appreciate the fact that risks such as these are shared with other people, and/or that other people are affected by the downside when things do not work out.

ENTREPRENEURIAL STRESS

In addition, risk is related to stress. The hazardous potential of entrepreneurial stress has been the focus of a number of research studies (Akande, 1992; Buttner, 1992). In general, stress can be viewed as a function of discrepancies between a person's expectations and ability to meet demands, as well as discrepancies between the individual's expectations and personality. If a person is unable to fulfill role demands, then stress occurs.

Given the struggle for resources and support, entrepreneurs must bear the responsibility for their mistakes while playing a multitude of roles, such as salesperson, recruiter, spokesperson, and negotiator. These simultaneous demands can lead to role overload. Being entrepreneurial requires a large commitment of time and energy, frequently at the expense of family and social activities. Finally, entrepreneurs are often working alone or with a small number of employees, even when operating in a large company.

Some of the most common entrepreneurial goals are achievement, independence, wealth, and work satisfaction. Research studies indicate that those who achieve these goals often pay a high price. A majority of entrepreneurs surveyed had back problems, indigestion, insomnia, or headaches. To achieve their goals, however, these entrepreneurs were willing to tolerate stress and its side-effects. The rewards justified the costs.

The Entrepreneurial Ego

In addition to the challenges of risk and stress, the entrepreneur also may experience the negative effects of an inflated ego. In other words, certain characteristics that usually propel entrepreneurs into success also can be exhibited to their extreme. We examine four of these characteristics that may hold destructive implications for corporate entrepreneurs.

An Overbearing Need for Control. Entrepreneurs are driven by a strong sense that they can affect change in their environments. They desire to control both their venture and their destiny. Their internal locus of control can spill over into a preoccupation with controlling everything. An obsession for autonomy and control may cause entrepreneurs to work in structured situations *only* when they have created the structure on *their* terms. This has serious implications for networking in an entrepreneurial team, since entrepreneurs can visualize the external control by others as a threat of subjugation or infringement on their will. It also has potentially detrimental implications for working in a corporate context, where collaboration is critical and control is exerted by other people, as well as by procedures and systems over which the entrepreneur has little influence.

A Sense of Distrust. To remain alert to competition, customers, and government regulations, entrepreneurs are continually scanning the environment. Not only are they on the watch for developments that could undermine their ventures, but they try to anticipate and act on developments before others have had the chance. They also tend to distrust the motives of others, thinking they are trying to either kill or steal the entrepreneur's idea. This distrustful state can result in their focusing on trivial things, causing them to lose sight of reality, distort reasoning and logic, and take destructive actions.

An Overriding Desire for Success. The overwhelming desire to succeed is often tied to a person's ego. The individual is driven to succeed and takes pride in demonstrating that success. Although entrepreneurs frequently find (or perceive) that the odds are stacked against them, and that problems without clear solutions never seem to stop coming, they also have faith that they will ultimately prevail. Thus, they can develop a certain sense of defiance, while denying any feelings of insignificance. Their belief in themselves evolves into a conviction that they are indispensable, that without them the project either will fail or it will be much less than it could be. The person and his or her ego become more important than the needs of the project. The likelihood of this happening is even greater in a corporate context, where the entrepreneur is required to play politics, share credit, swallow pride, and invest precious time in activities that have little to do with moving a project forward. The loss of perspective can alienate others and ensure the demise of a project.

Unrealistic Optimism. The ceaseless optimism that emanates from entrepreneurs (even in the bleakest times of a project or venture) is a key factor in the drive toward success. Entrepreneurs maintain a high enthusiasm level that gives others a sense of faith and conviction when a concept seems unworkable or the obstacles seem overwhelming. However, when taken to an extreme, this optimistic attitude can lead to a fantasy approach that undermines the credibility of the venture and the entrepreneur. A self-deceptive state may arise in which entrepreneurs ignore trends, facts, and reports and delude themselves into thinking everything will turn out fine. This type of behavior can lead to an inability to handle the reality of project setbacks and needs.

These examples do not imply that *all* corporate entrepreneurs fall prey to the negative side, or that each of the characteristics presented always gives way to dysfunctional behaviors. Yet companies that wish to encourage entrepreneurial behavior on the part of their employees should recognize both the upside and downside. The corporate environment represents a counterbalance to some of these negative behaviors, such as unrealistic optimism—but the work environment must also be somewhat tolerant of the idiosyncrasies of the entrepreneurial personality.

Recognizing and Managing the Triggering Events

What are the factors that lead individuals within an established company to develop and implement something new? It would seem that the decision to act entrepreneurially occurs as a result of interactions among organizational characteristics, individual characteristics, and some kind of precipitating event. We will call this precipitating event a "trigger." The trigger provides the impetus to behave entrepreneurially when other conditions are conducive to such behavior. While it is generally recognized that entrepreneurship involves a process, the ability to manage and facilitate that process on an ongoing basis requires that managers understand what gets things going in the first place.

Based on the research that has been conducted, one might be tempted to conclude that entrepreneurship in established companies is primarily externally driven. For example, it appears that the positive relationship between the entrepreneurial orientation of a company and bottom-line performance is especially strong when companies must cope with a dynamic, threatening, and complex external environment (Davis et al., 1991; Zahra, 1993; Zahra et al., 1999). Kuratko (2009a) indicates a stronger need for entrepreneurial management when companies face diminishing opportunity streams, rapid changes in the external environment, and shortened decision windows. The implications would appear to be that the principal triggers for corporate entrepreneurship are aggressive competitor moves, changes in industry or market structure, regulatory threats, and related external factors. Others point out that the factors in the external environment and considerations within the organization interact, challenging managers to respond creatively and act in innovative ways (Zahra and O'Neil, 1998).

Yet people in established companies pursue ideas that come to them simply because the ideas intrigue them, they believe in them, or they take exception to the fact that others have rejected their ideas. Also, some companies have planned programs for innovation regardless of what is happening in the external environment at a given point in time, or they have cultures in which initiation of innovation is simply expected. Examples include Google, Procter & Gamble, 3M, Ideo, Intel, and Merck. Thus, various internal triggers seem to be relevant, such as senior management directives, targeted employee rewards, resource availability, and problems in controlling costs.

Table 15-2 summarizes the more prevalent triggers for entrepreneurial activity in corporations. Some of these are more specific than others (e.g., a particular customer complaint), and some can be broken down in more detail (e.g., employee initiative, inventory problems). In addition, there is potential overlap among some of the items (e.g., declining profits and rising costs). Nonetheless, they tend to capture the range of triggering events that commonly influence innovative behavior in established organizations.

Just as important is the need to identify relevant ways in which triggers can be grouped or categorized. Five key ways for grouping triggering events include:

- Is the entrepreneurial event triggered by internal or external developments?

- Is entrepreneurship a response to an opportunity or a threat?

TABLE 15-2	

Triggering Events for Corporate Entrepreneurship

Specific customer request	Senior management initiative
Competitor threat or action	Personal initiative on the part of one or more employees
Changes in people's lifestyles/expectations	Ongoing innovation program in the company
New sales targets	Strategic growth target
Public relations/image	New marketing initiative
Substitute product or service	Diversification
Declining market share	Availability of new equipment
Declining profits	Availability of new resources
Declining sales	Availability of new distribution channel or method
Improved quality control	New management
Poor quality of an existing product or service	Perception of increasing risk
Rising costs	Vertical integration
Problem with existing logistical performance	Geographical expansion
Specific customer complaint	Internal opportunities
Supplier request	Inventory problems
Availability of new IT or online systems	Staff training
Regulatory requirement	Horizontal integration
Decreasing size of the market	New investment by a supplier
New investment by a buyer	Change in accounting practices
Supplier complaint	

SOURCE: From M. Schindehutte, M. H. Morris, and D. F. Kuratko, "Triggering Events, Corporate Entrepreneurship and the Marketing Function," *Journal of Marketing Theory and Practice* 8(2), (Spring 2000). Copyright © 2000 by M. E. Sharpe, Inc. Reprinted with permission of M. E. Sharpe, Inc.

- Is the entrepreneurial event pushed by technology or pulled by the market?

- Is the entrepreneurial event driven by top management directives (top-down) or did it originate from lower-level employees (bottom-up)?

- Did the entrepreneurial event occur based on a systematic or deliberate search process or more by chance or opportunism?

While there are other ways in which these initiating factors could be classified, each has potential strategic relevance. For instance, it may be that resource requirements differ markedly for entrepreneurial projects triggered by internal developments as opposed to those initiated principally by external developments, and for technology-driven projects versus market-driven projects. Triggers from outside the company, such as technological change, may tend to produce entrepreneurial projects that are more innovative or that represent bigger departures from the status quo than triggers from inside the company. Triggers related to the actions of competitors might lead to more imitation, while those related to a threat from a substitute product might produce more innovative solutions. Managerial support may be more easily obtainable for entrepreneurial projects triggered by threats (e.g., an impending government regulation) as opposed to opportunities (e.g., an untapped market niche). The same may be true for those where the source of the trigger is more top-down as opposed to bottom-up. Further, in terms of outcomes, if the trigger is some successful action by a competitor, then the entrepreneurial project may represent a reactive response that comes too late to have any marketplace impact. Similarly, it may be that entrepreneurial events that are in response to a particular supplier or customer request are associated with higher levels of success.

In one exploratory survey directed at a sample of 20 large companies, Morris et al. (2000) attempted to discern the relative reliance on the triggers identified in Table 15-2. Senior executives were asked to identify up to five entrepreneurial initiatives that had been pursued within their companies in the past three years. A total of 82 entrepreneurial initiatives were identified. Internal factors were surprisingly prevalent among the most frequently mentioned triggers, including "employee initiative," "strategic program," "new growth target," "new marketing initiative," and "public relations/image." The principal external triggers were "a specific customer request," "a competitor threat," and "a change in people's lifestyles or expectations."

The study also drew a distinction between planned and unplanned triggers, those that were internal versus external to the company, and those that were more controllable versus uncontrollable by management. The largest proportion of the triggers tended to be planned, internal, and controllable. The entrepreneurial initiatives were more likely to be driven by perception of opportunity as opposed to threat. Further, a large majority of respondents indicated the effort to discover the idea or concept was planned/deliberate/conscious as opposed to random/accidental/coincidence. In about a quarter of the cases, the idea or concept was a fairly unexpected development. Over two-thirds of the initiatives were driven by an awareness of demand in the marketplace (market-pull) as opposed to being novel innovations for which the company is trying to create a market. Projects tended to be pursued to attract new customers as opposed to retaining existing customers.

It is also noteworthy that all of the projects had an internal champion, and this person tended to initiate the project. The champion's primary motivation tended to be growth of revenues or profits, personal satisfaction, and job requirements. The single biggest overall factor motivating entrepreneurial behavior included profit opportunity, managerial leadership, and the passion and drive of individual employees.

A number of implications can be drawn from this discussion for the concept of sustainable entrepreneurship. The ability to encourage entrepreneurship on an ongoing basis requires that managers first identify the types of triggers that are prevalent in the company, and determine if any key triggers are not occurring for particular reasons. There is a need to systematically review both successful and unsuccessful products, services, and processes that have been pursued by the company over the past five years. Further, managers should apply the groupings or categories previously given, and then look for associations between types of triggers and types of entrepreneurial projects, and between types of triggers and the outcomes of entrepreneurial endeavors.

Companies must also develop an understanding of the needs and motives of potential champions, as certain types of individuals may respond more to particular triggers. In addition, companies may find that the composition of venture teams is associated with the type of trigger that drives a particular project. For instance, teams dominated by R&D or technical personnel may be driven more by internal and planned triggers, while those teams that have a strong marketing emphasis may be driven more by external and unplanned triggers. Finally, it is likely that certain types of triggers will be more salient under particular industry and market conditions.

By studying the triggering process in their organizations, managers can gain insights regarding the triggers to be emphasized under a given set of circumstances, how resources and incentives should be allocated to facilitate certain triggers, and ways in which the organization should be structured so as to take maximal advantage of particular types of triggers. In the final analysis, planning and the strategic management of the triggering process become vital for sustainable entrepreneurship.

Building an Adaptive Organization

When a company is confronted with dynamic, threatening, and complex change in the external environment, it is forced to adapt. Adaptation typically involves various forms of innovation. For their part, adaptation and innovation are dependent on the ability to learn, and learning requires timely and relevant information. Accordingly, much emphasis is placed today on the "learning organization" and the "learning manager."

Senge (1990) refers to a learning organization as one that continually improves through its capacity to learn from its experiences. Learning in this context refers to the acquisition of new knowledge by employees who are able and willing to apply the knowledge in making decisions or influencing others in the organization. It also includes the unlearning of old routines as a parallel activity to the learning of new routines. Unlearning is especially important in an entrepreneurial context, as long-held assumptions and past experiences that hold little relevance for the contemporary environment frequently act as blocks to an entrepreneurial project.

Underlying the learning process is the organization's ability to find or generate information, organize or code it, process it, store it, generate reports from it, interpret it, share it, and act on it. Our concern is with the company's ability to learn in ways that facilitate entrepreneurship, and this is a notable area of weakness in companies. Most companies do not have systematic methods to ensure learning. In one study, Block and MacMillan (1993) found that, among companies that tend to engage in more entrepreneurial activity, few conducted any systematic study or review of completed or abandoned projects. They reported a number of reasons including:

- Key people involved with the project may have left the company.

- The champion responsible for the project may have been reassigned to a distant location.

- A number of individuals may have participated, with each having been involved with a different aspect of the experience at a different time.

- Few records may have been kept.

- Accounting figures are not always consolidated and readily accessible.

Furthermore, many entrepreneurship-related experiences may not have been positive, and there may be a certain reluctance to unearth these skeletons. For these reasons and more, each effort at corporate entrepreneurship unfortunately starts off as an entirely new process and evolves in its own way. As Block and MacMillan (1993, p. 312) aptly conclude, "Managers are often very curious about what *other* companies have done and how their ventures have performed, but overlook the most relevant learning of all—the learning that can be extracted from their own venturing experience. Such experience has been achieved at great expense to the organization, and to ignore or discard it is to squander an irreplaceable asset."

Organizations must be prepared to track each entrepreneurial project or effort to identify underlying reasons for success or failure. By constructing project histories, management can extract maximal "learning" from the entrepreneurial experience. If organizations are to learn, and use what is learned to improve future performance, they must make a systematic effort to get the facts, examine them carefully, and draw conclusions about what to do and what to avoid in the future. The objective should always be to discover what errors occurred at any stage of the entrepreneurial project, why those errors occurred, and, most significantly, how they can be avoided in future projects. Ten critical areas that should be the focus of learning efforts within a given company include:

- Styles of champions that work and do not work

- Venture team structures that are most effective for certain types of innovation projects

- Models of successful projects in terms of key steps or stages, and the identification of the models that best fit different types of projects

- Approaches to goal setting and monitoring that keep projects on track

- Methods of opportunity identification that are especially productive given the nature of the company, industry, and market

- Ways of achieving the appropriate balance between autonomy and control on innovation projects

- Venture funding approaches that encourage successful projects

- Human resource management policies that encourage individual initiative and group collaboration around innovation projects

- Techniques for optimally managing the timing and allocation of resources (funds, functional specialists, staff people, facilities, and equipment) across the stages of a project

- Effective means of getting mainstream units in the company to adopt or assume ownership of projects developed by venture teams

Each entrepreneurial effort represents an experiment. Learning is critical not only to enable management to redirect the individual employee more effectively but also to enable management to gather cumulative information on the entrepreneurial experiences that will help encourage and nurture activity more effectively in the future. Table 15-3 identifies some ways in which companies can maximize learning.

Learning occurs not only at an organizational level across different entrepreneurial projects, but within the projects themselves. That is, for a project to evolve from point A to point B to point C, learning must take place. The more innovative the project, the more it breaks new ground, the more learning is required in order to move the project forward. Existing knowledge in the company proves inadequate, and more exploration is necessary. McGrath (2001) has provided evidence that, with highly innovative projects requiring high levels of exploration, learning effectiveness is greater when teams are given more autonomy both in setting goals and in conducting operations. Alternatively, when working on less innovative projects, or ones where the

---

TABLE 15-3

Maximizing Learning from Corporate Entrepreneurial Projects

There are three levels of learning effort that organizations can implement to gain the most benefit from each entrepreneurial project.

Level 1: The project champion writes a report about the experience, including a statement of the most important things learned and recommendations for the future designed to help the company's overall entrepreneurial effort. A useful question for the champion to address is: "If you could do this project over again, what would you do differently?" This first level of learning effort represents the simplest and easiest approach. It will yield information that is useful but far from complete.

Level 2: Key project and senior management people hold one or more meetings to discuss the progress of the project. Reports should be written that present conclusions and recommendations for future actions. The company should hold separate meetings dedicated to assessing the project experience, or it can perform this assessment as part of the agenda of other meetings held in connection with the entrepreneurial activity. If it decides to hold separate meetings, they can be conducted either periodically or at the time a project changes its status in some way (e.g., by being terminated, combined with an existing unit, or established as an ongoing business unit).

Level 3: The company conducts a full-fledged, in-depth study of the entrepreneurial experience, which will probably require the participation of people from outside the organization to obtain objectivity as well as expertise. The third level involves a significant research project—one that is time-consuming and may be quite difficult to accomplish. An undertaking of this magnitude should probably be reserved for major projects involving amounts of money that are highly significant to the company.

SOURCE: Adapted from Zenas Block and Ian MacMillan, *Corporate Venturing*, Boston, MA: Harvard Business School Publishing, 1993.

---

existing knowledge base of the company is more adequate, learning effectiveness is enhanced when goals are clearly specified and there is less operational autonomy.

An *adaptive company* increases opportunity for its employees, initiates change, and instills a desire to be innovative. Entrepreneurial managers can build an adaptive company in several ways. The following are not inflexible rules, but they do enhance a venture's chance of remaining adaptive and innovative both through and beyond the growth stage (Kuratko, 2009a).

SHARE THE ENTREPRENEURIAL VISION

The entrepreneurial vision must be permeated throughout the organization in order for employees to understand the company's direction and share in the responsibility for its growth. The senior-level managers can communicate the vision directly to the employees through meetings, conversations, or seminars. It also can be shared through symbolic events or activities such as social gatherings, recognition events, and displays. Whatever the format, having a shared vision allows the organization's personnel to catch the dream and become an integral part of creating the future (Hanks and McCarrey, 1993).

INCREASE THE PERCEPTION OF OPPORTUNITY

This can be accomplished with careful job design. The work should have defined objectives for which people will be responsible. Each level of the hierarchy should be kept informed of its role in producing the final output (i.e., a new process, service, product, business model, market). Top management must regularly review the company's opportunity horizon, attempt to stretch that horizon, and reinforce a focus throughout the organization on opportunity recognition. Another way to increase the perception of opportunity is through a careful coordination and integration of the functional areas. This allows employees in different functional areas to work together and recognize new possibilities through one another's eyes.

INSTITUTIONALIZE CHANGE AS THE ORGANIZATION'S GOAL

This entails a preference for innovation and change rather than preservation of the status quo. If opportunity is to be perceived, the environment of the enterprise must not only encourage it but also establish it as a goal. Within this context, a desire for opportunity can exist if resources are made available and departmental barriers are reduced.

INSTILL THE DESIRE TO BE INNOVATIVE

The desire of personnel to pursue opportunity must be carefully nurtured. Words alone will not create the innovative climate. Specific steps such as the following should be taken.

A Reward System. Explicit forms of recognition should be given to individuals who pursue innovative opportunities. For example, bonuses, awards, salary advances, and promotions should be tied directly to the innovative attempts of personnel.

An Environment that Allows for Failure. The fear of failure must be minimized by the general recognition that often many attempts are needed before a success is achieved. This does not imply that failure is sought or desired. However, learning from failure, as opposed to expecting punishment for it, is promoted. When this type of environment exists, people become willing to accept the challenge of change and innovation.

Flexible Operations. Flexibility creates the possibility of change taking place and having a positive effect. If a venture remains too rigidly tied to plans or strategies, it will not be responsive to new technologies, customer changes, or environmental shifts. Innovation will not take place because it will not "fit in."

Development of I-Teams. In order for the environment to foster innovation, *I-Teams* (Innovation Teams) with performance goals need to be established. These must be not just work groups but visionary, committed teams that have the authority to create new directions, set new standards, and challenge the status quo (Dingee et al., 2001).

Create a Sense of Urgency

For most companies, making innovation happen has become either the #1 priority or is very high on the priority list (Kuratko, 2009b). Corporate leaders have come to appreciate the critical need for innovation in response to the new competitive landscape. But they also are coming to recognize that their organizations are not inherently good at innovating. The problem is not whether companies can focus attention and resources in such a manner as to develop and launch one new product or service at a particular point in time (although many do struggle with this, and making an innovation happen inside the company is not the same thing as making it successful in the marketplace). The problem is sustainable innovation—making innovation happen on an ongoing basis and throughout the company.

The great challenge for any company wishing to achieve sustainable entrepreneurship involves creating an ongoing sense of urgency throughout the organization. When there is a crisis, employees feel the urgency, but when the crisis is surmounted, complacency eventually sets in. Management must create an environment where urgency is felt all the time. Koch Industries represents an excellent case in point. A sense of urgency is built into the core values of the company. Urgency in this context refers to a compelling sense that organizational survival depends on change. It is an imperative that suggests one either innovates or falls behind—there is no middle ground. It is a permanent mandate for trying to make the company's products and processes obsolete. Urgency is a call for immediate action, a pressing need to do things differently, a belief that time is running out.

Earlier we discussed triggers for corporate entrepreneurship. Many of these triggers involve threatening conditions, such as a competitor's preemptive moves, loss of key accounts, or costs that undermine company profitability. The message seems to be that companies seek entrepreneurial behaviors from their employees when they are in trouble, and the sense of crisis motivates employees to make innovation happen. The reality is that employees are always capable of entrepreneurial behavior, but most of the time they and their bosses do not perceive the need for innovation and change. Such complacency has a number of causes, ranging from strong financial performance of the company (at least for the moment) and a preoccupation with the demands and crises of day-to-day operations, to a tendency to underestimate the extent to which things are changing in the external environment. Further, innovation is disruptive. And, managers have a natural tendency to exalt in the past accomplishments and reputation of the company, even when those accomplishments have little to do with current marketplace conditions and that reputation may no longer be deserved.

Entrepreneurial companies instill in their employees a burning desire to make things better. People demonstrate a combination of paranoia (someone is out there right now figuring a superior way to do this), competitiveness (we can out-innovate anyone), pride (with our people and passion, magic is possible) and obsession (we are focused and will not quit before we reach the top of the mountain).

A beginning point in creating urgency is to rethink the fundamental assumptions that underlie the business. Six key assumptions management may wish to adopt include:

- Our best employees, and even our good employees, have professional options that do not involve our company.
- Customer loyalties are fleeting; creating a "wow" experience for customers is impossible if we are not continually finding new and better approaches.
- The gap between us and the competition is smaller than we think in those situations where we are ahead, and is larger in those situations where we are behind.
- The latest, greatest technology has problems, but we cannot afford to ignore it.
- Our business model is working, and yet it needs to be fixed.
- The company could be out of business in 24 months.

Coupled with the need for different assumptions are some caveats. Creating a sense of urgency is different than creating a sense of crisis. Urgency is a call to action, but it is not about short-sightedness, expediency, or change for the sake of change. The imperative for innovation and change does not preclude the need for strategy and planning. Further, a sense of urgency does not lessen the need to build operations around sound business fundamentals. In fact, such fundamentals as a customer focus, a quality emphasis, value for money, and investing in one's employees should be the focal point of the concern for urgency. There becomes an urgent need to find new ways of delighting customers, to achieve even higher levels of quality, and so forth.

TABLE 15-4

Does the Company Have a Sense of Urgency?

Urgency is something that pervades the entrepreneurial company, and is reflected in many facets of daily operations. Following are ten questions that can be used to gauge the extent to which management has created a sense of urgency within an organization.

1. How big is the comfort zone surrounding managers at each level in the organization? Are managers regularly expected to challenge one another's comfort zones?

2. Does the company measure itself against the best, but even more so against itself?

3. If a customer complains or is not satisfied, does the company measure how quickly the situation is rectified, and has that time been reduced by at least 10 percent in the past year?

4. Do managers in the company want to change the world?

5. Which of the following is most emphasized in the company: (a) thorough and well-formulated analysis, (b) properly managed consensus-building, (c) sensitivity to process and procedure, or (d) a willingness to take action and make something happen?

6. If timetables are not met, are the perceived costs or penalties significant?

7. How much of this year's sales must come from products that did not exist three years ago?

8. To what extent can decision making be characterized as a compromise to satisfy multiple constituencies?

9. When managers talk about "the future" are they referring to a time that is twenty, ten, five, or two years from now?

10. How much of a sense of regret do managers feel for missed opportunities and missed targets?

One means for taking stock of the relative level of urgency versus complacency in an organization is for managers to periodically assess their operations using the ten questions presented in Table 15-4. Indicators of a strong sense of urgency include managers having relatively small comfort zones, pressure for a meaningful percentage of sales from new products, a sense that the future is now, a primacy placed on action over analysis or compromise, and a greater concern with "missing the boat" rather than "sinking the boat" when it comes to the pursuit of new opportunities. Moreover, the pressure for improvement is not simply because of what someone else is doing—the company benchmarks itself against itself. There is an expectation that no matter how well the company performs in a given area, we must raise the bar for ourselves and everyone else.

The New Strategic Imperative: Embrace Paradoxes

Not all corporate entrepreneurs produce dramatic breakthroughs. Ironically, those that attempt to overthrow the establishment frequently find that the returns they achieve can be less than those received by less ambitious entrepreneurs. This is an example of the fundamental paradoxes confronting corporate entrepreneurship. The entrepreneurial organization of tomorrow will be one filled with paradoxes, and will require managers who are adept at managing them. Nadler and Tushman (1999) argue for the new organizational imperatives to be focused around increasing speed, portfolio businesses models, abbreviated life cycles, "go to market" flexibility, competitive innovation, and intra-enterprise cannibalism. Table 15-5 outlines these imperatives as a challenge for twenty-first century organizations to embrace. In that vein we present some of the more vexing paradoxes that surround the entrepreneurial efforts of companies in the twenty-first century.

THE PARADOX OF SIZE AND SCOPE

Smaller companies are quick and flexible. They can innovate on the fly. The technological revolution has empowered them to operate globally, while creative leveraging strategies enable them to compete on the same playing field with much bigger organizations. As a result, many large companies are transforming themselves into confederations of small, fairly independent companies. And yet, being larger offers important benefits of scale and scope. The ability of bigger companies to achieve economies, leverage the value chain, capitalize on strategic partnerships, and exploit opportunities in distribution is unsurpassed.

THE PARADOX OF RISK AND RETURN

The relationship between what the corporate entrepreneur does and the outcomes or returns achieved is not a simple one. It is often assumed that major breakthroughs, or higher risk ventures, generate higher returns. But this is not always the case, as returns are influenced by timing, managerial competence, market conditions, and a host of environmental factors. Even if one controls for all of these factors, doing something that is highly entrepreneurial only raises the possible ceiling on returns if one is successful. Actual returns are unique to the venture.

The general level of risk facing any corporate entrepreneur will increase in the coming years simply because more entrepreneurial activity will be occurring. Within this broader context, the probability of failure will be higher for those individuals and organizations who pursue both very low and very high levels of entrepreneurial activity. The highest returns will come to those who can sustain a balance of degree and frequency of entrepreneurial activity over time.

TABLE 15-5

The New Strategic Imperatives

1. Increase Strategic Clock Speed

Speed involves an organizational capacity to understand, anticipate, and respond appropriately to those external changes that fundamentally alter the rules of engagement and the sources of value in a given industry. Timing is everything. During periods of radical, discontinuous change, the first movers enjoy significant advantages.

2. Focus Portfolios with Various Business Models

Companies are reshaping their portfolios in the pursuit of strategic focus, concentrating on those businesses where they can create sustainable value by applying their core competencies to provide competitive advantage. In effect, companies are breaking up and reassembling the traditional value chain.

3. Abbreviated Strategic Life Cycles

The pace of change in the environment will require the organization of the future to significantly change its underlying strategy on a regular basis of between 18 months and 5 years, depending upon the industry. Indeed, it is not uncommon to hear executives, as they talk about strategic cycles, talk in terms of "Web years," signifying a compressed timeframe of 3 months rather than 12.

4. Create "Go-to-Market" Flexibility

Various market segments offer widely divergent demands for the same core product or service in terms of pricing options, sales and service support, speed of delivery, customization, and so forth.

5. Enhance Competitive Innovation

Innovation has traditionally focused on products and processes. The successful organization of the future will also develop exceptional skills to innovate in two other areas: strategy development and organizational design.

6. Manage Intra-Enterprise Cannibalism

In the successful organization of the future, the idea of cannibalism will become routine, an accepted part of each company's strategy. The pace of innovation and the abbreviated strategic cycles will force companies to place multiple bets on an ongoing basis, acknowledging that a new product may be well on its way to obsolescence by the time it reaches the market.

SOURCE: Reprinted from *Organizational Dynamics*, 28(1), David A. Nadler and Michael L. Tushman, "The Organization of the Future: Strategic Imperatives and Core Competencies for the 21st Century," pp. 45–60, Copyright © 1999, with permission from Elsevier.

THE PARADOX OF THE INDIVIDUAL AND THE TEAM

Corporate entrepreneurship requires a visionary champion with drive and commitment. However, a dedicated team of specialists and generalists is also needed. The problem becomes one of emphasizing both individualism and collective teamwork at the same time. Unfortunately, a policy or procedure that incentivizes an individual's actions can serve as a disincentive for collective action. Similarly, a preoccupation with teams can come at the expense of entrepreneurial initiative.

Nonetheless, in an age of multiple careers and lessened organizational loyalty, the corporate entrepreneur will have to be less of a team dictator and more of a team collaborator. He or she will have to share ownership and control with team members. The objective will be to build a project based on core competencies and to focus on the continued development of knowledge assets that can deliver these competencies. Thus, the internal team itself becomes fluid or subject to change.

The Paradox of Flexibility and Control

Large corporations have downsized, restructured, and reengineered in a quest to become faster and more flexible. The question becomes one of maintaining flexibility while also being able to exert sufficient control over resources and operations. In the years ahead, entrepreneurial companies will focus less on accumulating assets and achieving control through ownership and more on building a fluid, adaptable organization which is highly leveraged. That is, they will be able to achieve market penetration through external alliances and networks, not by an increase in their physical asset base. They will effectively gain control by giving up control.

The Paradox of Constructive and Destructive Behavior

Corporate entrepreneurship requires both stability and turbulence. Where there is an established infrastructure, corporate entrepreneurship is facilitated. Yet turbulence creates opportunities for proactive entrepreneurs. There is a related paradox in that entrepreneurship is both constructive and destructive. Entrepreneurial individuals create the new, and in doing so, they peremptorily make existing products, services, and processes obsolete. Within companies, entrepreneurs make what have heretofore been well-functioning operations unnecessary. In the future, this creative destruction will accelerate, as corporate entrepreneurs find they must continually make their own products obsolete. Along the way, whole new entrepreneurial opportunities will be created for recycling, retrofitting, and identifying alternative distribution channels (reaching new markets) for the products being displaced.

The Paradox of Success and Failure

While it is normal to think in terms of winners and losers in business, sustained entrepreneurship is not that simple. Entrepreneurs are often competitive, with a need to win. They are replacing conventional managers who have a need to avoid failure. Yet many entrepreneurs fail multiple times. They can frequently describe an entire portfolio of successes and failures, where one solid hit is followed by a strike out and two ground outs, and then a home run.

Within failure are the seeds for success. Corporate entrepreneurs must increasingly believe in the successful failure, where lessons from unsuccessful efforts are used to adapt one's concepts and ideas into something that will work. This is important on two levels. A general increase in new product and service introductions by definition means a higher failure rate. Similarly, as individuals find themselves doing more entrepreneurial activity, they will also begin to fail more often. Success will increasingly be a function of one's ability to overcome the psychological fear or avoidance of failure that is ingrained in virtually all of us.

The Entrepreneurial Mindset

Even the most entrepreneurial of managers can lose the entrepreneurial edge. The pressures of the day-to-day administrative demands of organizational policies and procedures, and the need for more systematic approaches as an innovative concept grows into a large internal enterprise, force the corporate entrepreneur to become more administratively oriented. Figure 15-1 provides a clear and simple illustration of the danger of entrepreneurs evolving into bureaucrats who in turn stifle innovation. The classic bureaucrat believes in the status quo while blocking all capabilities for change. The entrepreneur believes in change as the future goal and perceives the capabilities exist for achieving change. Thus the entrepreneurial mindset is one of belief in change and innovation while recognizing and developing the capabilities to achieve such changes. Table 15-6 provides an outline of the key characteristics of this mindset.

FIGURE 15-1

The Entrepreneurial Mindset Framework

		FUTURE GOALS	
		Change/Innovation	**Status Quo**
	Possible	Entrepreneur	Satisfied manager
PERCEIVED CAPABILITY TO ACHIEVE			
	Blocked	Frustrated manager	Classic bureaucrat

TABLE 15-6

Characteristics of the Entrepreneurial Mindset

1. They passionately seek new opportunities. Habitual entrepreneurs stay alert, always looking for the chance to profit from change and disruption in the way business is done. Their greatest impact occurs when they create entirely new business models. New business models revolutionize how revenues are made, costs are incurred, or operations are conducted, sometimes throughout an entire industry. One reason that the emergence of the Internet as a new medium of business has been accompanied by dizzyingly high company valuations is that investors perceive its potential to profitably transform virtually every aspect of economic life.

2. They pursue opportunities with enormous discipline. Habitual entrepreneurs not only are alert enough to spot opportunities, but make sure that they act on them. Most maintain some form of inventory, or register, of unexploited opportunities. They make sure that they revisit their inventory of ideas often but they take action only when it is required. They make investments only if the competitive arena is attractive and the opportunity is ripe.

3. They pursue only the very best opportunities and avoid exhausting themselves and their organizations by chasing after every option. Even though many habitual entrepreneurs are wealthy, the most successful remain ruthlessly disciplined about limiting the number of projects they pursue. They go after a tightly controlled portfolio of opportunities in different stages of development. They tightly link their strategy with their choice of projects, rather than diluting their efforts too broadly.

4. They focus on execution—specifically, adaptive execution. Both words are important. People with an entrepreneurial mindset execute—that is, they get on with it instead of analyzing new ideas to death. Yet they are also adaptive—able to change directions as the real opportunity, and the best way to exploit it, evolve.

5. They engage the energies of everyone in their domain. Habitual entrepreneurs involve many people—both inside and outside the organization—in their pursuit of an opportunity. They create and sustain networks of relationships rather than going it alone, making the most of the intellectual and other resources people have to offer and helping those people to achieve their goals as well.

In order to maintain this "entrepreneurial mindset," the manager must assume certain ongoing responsibilities (McGrath and MacMillan, 2000). The first responsibility involves *framing the challenge*. In other words, there needs to be a clear definition of the specified challenges that everyone involved with innovative projects should address.

It is important to think in terms of, and regularly reiterate, the challenge. Second, leaders have the responsibility to *absorb the uncertainty* that is perceived by team members. Entrepreneurial leaders make uncertainty less daunting. The idea is to create the self-confidence that lets others act on opportunities without seeking managerial permission. Employees must not be overwhelmed by the complexity inherent in many innovative situations. A third responsibility is to *define gravity*—that is, what must be accepted and what cannot be accepted. The term *gravity* is used to capture limiting conditions. For example, there is gravity on Earth, but that does not mean it must limit our lives. If freed from the psychological cage of believing that gravity makes flying impossible, creativity can permit us to invent an airplane or spaceship. This is what the entrepreneurial mindset is all about—seeing opportunities where others see barriers and limits. A fourth responsibility of entrepreneurial leadership involves *clearing obstacles* that arise as a result of internal competition for resources. This can be a problem especially when the entrepreneurial innovation is beginning to undergo significant growth. A growing venture will often find itself pitted squarely against other (often established) aspects of the company in a fierce internal competition for funds and staff (remember Chapter 11 on constraints). Creative tactics, political skills, and an ability to regroup, reorganize, and attack from another angle become invaluable. A final responsibility for entrepreneurial leaders is to keep their finger on the pulse of the project. This involves constructive monitoring and control of the developing opportunity.

In the contemporary organization, all managers must be entrepreneurs. Accordingly, responsibilities such as those described here must become a core part of how every manager's job is defined. Doing so will help limit the extent to which individual champions begin that inexorable transition from corporate entrepreneur to corporate bureaucrat.

The Twenty-First Century Entrepreneurial Company: A Dynamic Incubator

In addition to managing paradox, the dynamic entrepreneurial organizations of the twenty-first century will be ones that are capable of merging strategic action with entrepreneurial action on an ongoing basis. Strategic management focuses on achieving competitive advantage within a particular industry and market context. Entrepreneurship seeks to exploit opportunities others have missed or ones that have not been completely exploited. Thus, strategic actions provide the context within which entrepreneurial actions are pursued (Ireland et al., 2001). Figure 15-2 illustrates the interface between the strategic actions (advantage-seeking behavior) and the entrepreneurial actions (opportunity-seeking behavior) of a company.

FIGURE 15-2

Entrepreneurial and Strategic Actions

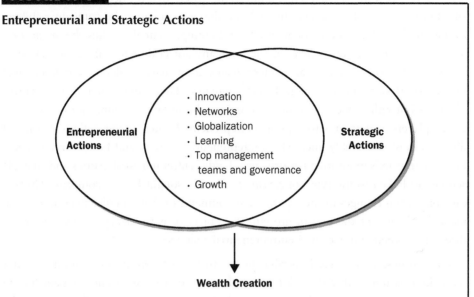

- Innovation
- Networks
- Globalization
- Learning
- Top management teams and governance
- Growth

Entrepreneurial Actions

Strategic Actions

Wealth Creation

SOURCE: *Academy of Management Executive: The Thinking Manager's Source* by Hitt, Keats, DeMarie. Copyright © 2001 by Academy of Management (NY). Reproduced with permission of Academy of Management (NY) in the format Textbook via Copyright Clearance Center.

To create wealth, companies will need to establish linkages between entrepreneurial actions and strategic actions within six dominant "domains" (Ireland et al., 2001). First, the competitive mindset of managers must be based on *innovation*, and innovation efforts of the company must be managed strategically. Innovations that are well timed, consistent with marketplace realities, difficult to imitate, and that fit well with the company's core competencies represent the strategic objective. Further, entrepreneurial and strategic actions are used to create and exploit *networks* of relationships between the organization and other organizations and individuals. Such networks provide the company with access to competitively valuable information, enable faster market penetration, allow for risk sharing, and enhance the company's innovation capabilities.

In addition, entrepreneurial and strategic actions must combine to facilitate *internationalization*, or the exploitation of global opportunities. Tapping global markets requires product innovations, innovations in management systems and structures, and innovative use of networks and alliances, all of which must be managed strategically. Another key domain is *organizational learning*, where companies make a strategic commitment to learning and to rapid transfer of knowledge throughout their organization.

As we saw earlier in this chapter, learning is intimately tied to successful entrepreneurial activity. A key task of organizational leadership is to enhance the company's abilities to use intellectual assets both strategically and entrepreneurially. Thus the *top management team and governance structures* in the company are critical to enhancing entrepreneurial performance. Top management teams must have a shared entrepreneurial vision that they translate into goals and strategies. Their role is not that of passive observers but rather one where they are intimately involved in innovation, and serve as key players in networks to support entrepreneurial and strategic actions. Boards of directors must also visibly encourage entrepreneurial activity and be held accountable for the company's innovative performance. Lastly, entrepreneurial actions and strategic actions are linked to the types of *growth opportunities* sought by the company. Growth can come from changes in the external environment, or from inefficiencies in existing markets. No matter the rate of growth, the objective is to manage growth properly through designed and executed entrepreneurial strategies.

One purpose of strategic leadership in companies is to ensure innovation does not occur in a vacuum—that the spirit and enthusiasm that go with entrepreneurship do not lead managers to forget the fundamentals. Consider the findings of a recent study. Researchers examined 1,435 companies that had been listed among the 500 largest in the world any time since 1965 (Collins, 2000). They sought to identify companies that were able to make a shift from good to great performance (defined as having generated cumulative shareholder returns greater than three times the market average over 15 years). Only 11 of the 1,435 companies showed a sustained and verifiable shift from good to great. This stunning finding led to the following conclusion:

> "The truth is, there's nothing new about being in a New Economy. Yes, the Internet is a big deal, but electricity was bigger. And in each evolution of the economy over the past 150 years, the best executives have adhered to the same basic principles, with rigor and discipline. I can't tell you exactly what a corporation will look like 50 or 100 years from now. But I can promise this: If you toss out all the time-proven fundamentals, you'll have no chance whatsoever of building an enduring, great company." (Collins, 2000, p. 208)

The entrepreneurial organization in the twenty-first century will be conceptualized as a collection of portfolios. Portfolio thinking is about strategic balance, where the company balances a mix of objectives, such as risk versus return, income versus growth, and short-term versus long-term performance. Entrepreneurial organizations will be built around four major portfolios:

Portfolio of competencies—the set of skills and capabilities that capture what the organization does best. The strategic direction of the company will be built around these competencies, while outside providers will be relied upon for most of the activities not reflected in these competencies. In the leading entrepreneurial companies, core competencies will include the ability to innovate, adapt, and manage change. Management will recognize the need to invest in both exploitative (of current resources and markets) competencies and exploratory (of new frontiers) competencies. These companies will alternate between exploiting a given innovation or technology platform (while experimenting with others) and ultimately moving to new platforms (Covin et al., 2003).

Portfolio of resources—the set of financial, physical, human, organizational, relational, and intellectual resources that are innovation enabling. Although organizations are repositories of all kinds of resources, the leaders recognize that certain resources are instrumental for innovation, and also define the limits on the innovation capacity of the company. The portfolio is managed in a way that these resources complement one another. Within the resource portfolio might also be found a portfolio of different kinds of entrepreneurs within the company, and a portfolio of partners and alliances (Morris et al., 2010).

Portfolio of innovations—a balanced mix of new product, service, and process projects. The leaders will be those companies that pursue multiple innovations at a given time, including new to the world or new to the market innovations, new lines, lines extensions, and incremental improvements. Projects will routinely benefit one another through systematic experimentation and learning. The organization of tomorrow will be one that continuously cycles through periods of rapid evolution and periodic revolution, alternating between periods of high entrepreneurial intensity and lower entrepreneurial intensity (Leifer et al., 2000; Morris and Sexton, 1996).

Portfolio of ventures—the devolution of the company into a confederation of smaller ventures that have autonomy but whose contributions can be seamlessly coordinated and integrated. Individual ventures will vary in terms of their levels of entrepreneurial intensity and position in the organizational life cycle (Kuratko et al., 2001).

From a portfolio perspective, the organization becomes a *dynamic incubator*. Ideas, concepts, products, and ventures are regularly spawned in this incubator. The organization creates environments that support the growth and development of ideas into concepts, then into products or processes, then into ventures (or into additions to existing ventures). Further, products and ventures mature and are harvested for a complete cycle of venture development.

What Does the Future Hold for the BlackBerry?

Innovation knows no boundaries or borders. This is the opening statement on the home Web page of the Canadian company Research in Motion (RIM). This is the company responsible for developing the popular mobile device known as the BlackBerry. Originally a mobile device used to access e-mail, the company has helped to turn wireless e-mail into a must-have for people on the go achieving cultural status by being incorporated into its users' lexicon: "blackberrying" now means to e-mail from a mobile phone. The ubiquity of these BlackBerry devices in the corporate environment and the compulsive use of its ability to quickly send and receive e-mail earned it the nickname "Crackberry" in a reference to users feeling they cannot live without it. RIM announced in February 2009 that they were expanding their global operations by opening an office and training facility in Australia increasing their total workforce to 12,000 worldwide. The BlackBerry product line celebrated its 10th anniversary, while RIM celebrated 25 years as a company. In 10 years RIM has sold over 50 million wireless handset units worldwide, making it the second best-selling smartphone in the world. In 2009, Fortune Magazine named RIM as the fastest growing company in the world with a growth of 84 percent in profits over three years despite the recession.

In spite of all this success, the ever changing technological market leaves even the very best companies behind the innovation curve quickly. The company that popularized the smartphone (BlackBerry) as the must have tool for the twenty-first-century worker is now quickly losing ground to Apple's iPhone, and a slew of devices based on Google's Android mobile operating system. Unless it can find new ways to innovate their own brand, RIM could end up on a list of "former dominant tech companies" such as Palm or Motorola that are struggling today to survive. Even more disturbing is a recent study by a marketing research company which found that nearly 40 percent of BlackBerry users would switch to Apple's iPhone as their next smartphone purchase, and 33 percent of them would switch to an Android phone if given the option. Not exactly a loyal customer base.

To make matters worse, it seems that Apple's iPhone will be offered by the nation's No. 1 wireless carrier Verizon. And it has been reported that Apple now controls a majority of mobile developer's mindshare with the latest 3,000 mobile app projects registering 67 percent for iPhones and 22 percent for iPads. As Apple has shown an application ecosystem for devices is equally important, especially one that can bridge work and play. That type of ecosystem barely exists for BlackBerry today so their innovations must take that into account. Somehow, RIM in its focus on enterprise customers missed that it was the consumer driving the smartphone market.

Meanwhile the Co-CEO of RIM Jim Balsillie has promised that RIM has plenty of new innovative devices yet to be unveiled. It now becomes a question of speed to the market since Apple with the iPad, (reportedly Google is soon to follow) is extending beyond just phones into other places such as a car, a TV, etc. Can RIM innovate fast enough to keep a hold on the market share they had built up so fast in ten years? Even though their website opens with, *"Innovation knows no boundaries or borders,"* RIM has found that sustaining innovative leadership is a continuous challenge in today's world.

Discussion Questions:

1. Discuss managing the "triggering events" (Table 15-2) as it applies to Research in Motion.

2. What elements from "building an adaptive organization" discussed in the chapter, would be relevant for the maker of the BlackBerry?

3. Using the paradoxes described in the chapter, outline a strategy for RIM as it tries to sustain its innovative leadership.

SOURCE: Adapted from: Michael V. Copeland, "BlackBerry's Corporate Problem," *Fortune Magazine,* April 6, 2010; Philip Elmer-DeWitt, Apple Now Controls 89 percent of Mobile Developers' Mindshare," CNN Money, April 2, 2010; Research in Motion corporate Web site, and other articles related to the BlackBerry, accessed April 24, 2010.

Summary and Conclusions

In this final chapter, we examined the issue of *sustainable entrepreneurial activity*. We explored the need for individuals to develop a personal strategy or approach to entrepreneurial endeavors—one they can use on an ongoing basis. Following this, we examined the concept of triggers, together with an identification of the leading types of events that trigger entrepreneurial behavior in companies. The need to manage triggers, while creating an ongoing sense of urgency in the organization, was presented. We also delved into the "dark side" of entrepreneurship in order to make corporate entrepreneurs aware of the hidden pitfalls within entrepreneurial activity. The dimensions for building an adaptive company were explored with critical elements such as enlightened experimentation, organizational learning, sharing the vision, increasing the perception of opportunity, instilling a desire to be innovative, and creating a sense of urgency, as keys for sustaining an entrepreneurial company. Finally, we presented the need to embrace paradoxes and portfolios as transformational vehicles for the entrepreneurial organization of the twenty-first century to become a dynamic incubator.

As the rules of the competitive game keep changing, companies have begun to realize that sustainable competitive advantage is fleeting. And yet, in the midst of this turmoil, successful companies have made the fundamental discovery that innovation drives success (McGregor, 2008). The ability to continually innovate (to engage in an ongoing process of entrepreneurial actions) has become the source of competitive advantage.

A Final Epilogue

While entrepreneurial actions are a phenomenon that have captivated the interest of executives in many corporate boardrooms, there is a danger that managers can get too caught up in the excitement of a particular innovation or inspiring stories of individual corporate entrepreneurs. It is easy to become enamored with the idea of innovation, but the true value of innovation lies in the extent to which it becomes a corporate strategy to create sustainable competitive advantage (Vanhaverbeke and Peeters, 2005).

In the new competitive landscape, the opportunities and threats are revolutionary in nature—that is, they happen swiftly and are relentless in their frequency, affecting virtually all parts of an organization simultaneously. The business environment is filled with ambiguity and discontinuity, and the rules of the game are subject to constant revision. The job of management effectively becomes one of continual experimentation—experimenting with new structures, new reward systems, new technologies, new methods, new products, new markets, and much more. The quest remains the same: sustainable competitive advantage. The fundamentals remain the same: great products, creating real value for customers, highly motivated employees, and providing products when and where the customer chooses. But the path is less clear. It is our belief that entrepreneurship represents the guiding light, the roadmap, and the motivating force for companies as they attempt to find their way down this path.

Achieving an entrepreneurial organization is not something that management can simply decide to do. Corporate entrepreneurship is not a fad, and it does not produce instant success. It requires considerable time and investment, and there must be continual reinforcement. By their nature, organizations impose constraints on entrepreneurial behavior. To be sustainable, the entrepreneurial spirit must be integrated into the mission, goals, strategies, structure, processes, and values of the organization. Flexibility, speed, innovation, and entrepreneurial leadership are the cornerstones. The managerial mindset must become an opportunity-driven mindset, where actions are never constrained by resources currently controlled.

A sustainable entrepreneurial orientation will drive organizations to new heights in the twenty-first century. As Baumol (2004) states,

> "The outlook is, indeed, that there will be no break in the acceleration of innovation, and that the innovations in prospect will be as difficult for us to comprehend as those now thoroughly familiar to us would have been to our ancestors.... And the record shows that both independent entrepreneurs and large companies have provided astonishingly substantial additions to the economy's cornucopia of outputs. The one dreams up and inaugurates the breakthroughs while the other contributes crucial improvements to performance. The innovative process is indeed implicitly a partnership between the small entity and the large, between David and Goliath, and in this case, both emerge victorious, and the economy gains a victory as well."

This new millennium has been characterized as an age of instant information, ever-increasing development and application of technology, experimental change, revolutionary processes, and global competition. It is now an age filled with turbulence and paradox. As Kuratko (2009b) points out, the words used to describe the new innovation regime of the twenty-first century are: *Dream, Create, Explore, Invent, Pioneer,* and *Imagine*! Twenty years ago these words could only be found at Disney World, while today they exist as a mantra for every innovative-minded organization. We believe this is a point in time when the gap between what can be imagined and what can be accomplished has never been smaller. It is a time requiring innovative vision, courage, calculated risk-taking, and strong leadership. In essence it is *the entrepreneurial imperative of the twenty-first century* organization.

The challenge of sustaining entrepreneurial excellence can be accomplished only if those who manage companies are willing to:

Expect more than others think is *practical*,

Dare more than others think is *wise*,

Risk more than others think is *safe*, and

Dream more than others think is *possible*.

The future belongs to those who imagine, believe in, and create entrepreneurial excellence!

References

Akande, A. 1992. "Coping with Entrepreneurial Stress," *Leadership & Organization Development Journal*, 13(2): 27–32.

Baumol, W. J. 2004. "Entrepreneurial Cultures and Subcultures," *Academy of Management Learning & Education*, 3(3): 316–326.

Block, Z., and MacMillan, I. 1993. *Corporate Venturing* (Boston, MA: Harvard Business School Publishing).

Burgelman, R. 1984. "Managing the Corporate Venturing Process," *Sloan Management Review*, 25(2) (Winter): 33–48.

Busenitz, L., and Barney, J. 1997. "Differences between Entrepreneurs and Managers in Large Organizations: Biases and Heuristics in Strategic Decision-Making," *Journal of Business Venturing*, 12(1): 9–30.

Buttner, E. H. 1992. "Entrepreneurial Stress: Is It Hazardous to Your Health?" *Journal of Managerial Issues* (Summer): 223–240.

Collins, J. 2000. "Don't Rewrite the Rules of the Road," *Business Week* (August 28): 206–208.

Covin, J. G., Slevin, D. P., and Heeley, M. B. 2000. "Pioneers and Followers: Competitive Tactics, Environment, and Firm Growth," *Journal of Business Venturing*, 15: 175–210.

Covin, J. G., Ireland, R. D., and Kuratko, D. F. 2003. "Exploration and Exploitation Functions of Corporate Venturing," *Proceedings: National Academy of Management*, August (CD Rom): 7.

Davis, D., Morris, M., and Allen, J. 1991. "Perceived Environmental Turbulence and Its Effect on Selected Entrepreneurship, Marketing, and Organizational Characteristics in Industrial Firms," *Journal of Marketing Science*, 19 (Spring): 43–51.

Dingee, A. M., Haslett, B., and Smollen, L. E. 2001. "Characteristics of a Successful Entrepreneurial Management Team," *Annual Editions 00/01* (Guilford, CT: Dushkin/McGraw Hill): 71–75.

Hanks, S. H., and McCarrey, L. R. 1993. "Beyond Survival: Reshaping Entrepreneurial Vision in Successful Growing Ventures," *Journal of Small Business Strategy* (Spring): 1–12.

Ireland, R. D., Hitt, M., Camp, S. M., and Sexton, D. L. 2001. "Integrating Entrepreneurship and Strategic Management Actions to Create Firm Wealth," *Academy of Management Executive*, 15(1): 49–63.

Kanter, R. 1985. "Supporting Innovation and Venture Development in Established Companies," *Journal of Business Venturing*, 1(1): 47–60.

Kets de Vries, M. F. R. 1985. "The Dark Side of Entrepreneurship," *Harvard Business Review* (Nov./Dec.): 160–167.

Kuratko, D. F. 2009a. *Entrepreneurship: Theory, Process, & Practice* (Mason, OH: South-Western Publishing).

Kuratko, D. F. 2009b. "The Entrepreneurial Imperative of the 21st Century," *Business Horizons*, 52(5): 421–428.

Kuratko, D. F., Ireland, R. D., and Hornsby, J. S. 2001. "The Power of Entrepreneurial Outcomes: Insights from Acordia, Inc.," *Academy of Management Executive*, 15(4): 60–71.

Leifer, R., McDermott, C., O'Connor, G., Peters, L., Rice, M., and Veryzer, R. 2000. *Radical Innovation* (Boston, MA: Harvard Business School Press).

McGrath, R. 2001. "Exploratory Learning, Innovative Capacity, and Managerial Oversight," *Academy of Management Journal*, 44(1) (Feb.): 118–133.

McGrath, R. G., and MacMillan, I. 2000. *The Entrepreneurial Mindset* (Boston, MA: Harvard Business Press).

McGregor, J. 2008. The World's Most Innovative Companies. *Business Week* online: Retrieved April 23, 2010.

Morris, M. H., and Sexton, D. L. 1996. "The Concept of Entrepreneurial Intensity," *Journal of Business Research*, 36(1): 5–14.

Morris, M. H., Kuratko, D. F., and Schindehutte, M. 2000. "Triggering Events, Corporate Entrepreneurship and the Marketing Function," *Journal of Marketing Theory and Practice*, 8(2) (Spring): 18–30.

Morris, M. H., Kuratko, D. F., Allen, J., Ireland, R. D., and Schindehutte, M. 2010. "Resource Acceleration: Extending Resource Based Theory in Entrepreneurial Ventures," *Journal of Applied Management & Entrepreneurship*, 15(2): 4–25.

Nadler, D. A., and Tushman, M. L. 1999. "The Organization of the Future: Strategic Imperatives and Core Competencies for the 21st Century," *Organizational Dynamics*, 28(1): 45–60.

Pinchot, III, G. 1985. *Intrapreneuring* (New York: Harper & Row).

Senge, p. 1990. *The Fifth Discipline* (New York: Doubleday Currency).

Vanhaverbeke, W., and Peeters, N., 2005. "Embracing Innovation as Strategy: Corporate Venturing, Competence Building, and Corporate Strategy Making," *Creativity and Innovation Management*, 14(3): 246–257.

Zahra, S. A. 1993. "Environment, Corporate Entrepreneurship, and Financial Performance: A Taxonomic Approach," *Journal of Business Venturing*, 8: 319–340.

Zahra, S. A., and O'Neil, H. M. 1998. "Charting the Landscape of Global Competition: Reflections on Emerging Organizational Challenges and Their Implications for Senior Executives," *The Academy of Management Executive*, 12: 13–21.

Zahra, S. A., Kuratko, D. F., and Jennings, D. F. 1999. "Corporate Entrepreneurship and the Acquisition of Dynamic Organizational Capabilities," *Entrepreneurship Theory and Practice*, 23(3): 5–10.

INDEX